TEST CRICKET
RECORDS
—— FROM 1877 ——

Compiled by James Gibb
Introduced by John Arlott

COLLINS
Glasgow · London · Sydney

Author's Note

All Test matches traditionally considered official and included in such works as Roy Webber's *Playfair Book of Test Cricket* and Arthur Wrigley's *Book of Test Cricket* have been retained. Exclusion of the early South African Tests would have caused confusion. However, the England *v* Rest of the World matches in 1970 have been excluded.

Official scorebooks have been consulted (where available) to correct the figures for batsmen and bowlers. Players initials have also been altered in the light of fresh information, e.g. A. C. Russell and E. Tyldesley of England are now C. A. G. Russell and G. E. Tyldesley while A. D. Nourse (sen.) of South Africa is A. W. Nourse (he was christened Arthur William) and added 'Dave' later. To avoid confusion his son, Dudley, is A. D. Nourse.

Finally I should like to acknowledge the help and encouragement of the following given by: Gordon J. Tratalos, Robert Brooke, Geoffrey Saulez, Tony Dobbs, Geoff Wilde, Ken Latham and Brian Hunt.

First published 1979
© Copyright James Gibb 1979
Set in 8 point Plantin and printed in Great Britain by
William Collins Sons & Company Limited
Glasgow, London and Sydney

ISBN 0 00 411690 9 (paperback)
ISBN 0 00 411691 7 (hardback)

Contents

Introduction

The pace and intensity of Test cricket are now so high that its record books are out of date almost before they can be printed. Yet there was never a time when the ordinary cricket follower was more in need of assistance in order to follow such a headlong run of international play. That is why this statistical survey of James Gibb is so timely and, in being so hard on the heels of events, so valuable.

Consider, in the 37 years between the first Test (in 1877) and the outbreak of the First World War, the then three Test-playing countries – England, Australia and South Africa – played 134 games. Between the two wars – 1919 to 1939 – with the accession to Test status of West Indies, India and New Zealand, the number was another 140 in 20 years; an overall 274 in 62 years. From the restart in 1946 to the end of the English summer of 1978, though, with the entry of Pakistan balanced by the withdrawal of South Africa, the five senior members of the International Cricket Conference reached the figure of 830 – another 556 in 32 years. Fifteen more were played in the subsequent winter. By comparison with the pre-1914 era, that represents an increase in frequency from four, to over seventeen Tests a calendar year. Thus, this is not simply a book of statistics, but a history couched in figures.

The generation of today accepts Test cricket as the highest level of the game. It was not always so. Before the First World War even such authoritative voices as *Wisden* used constantly to lament that international matches were adversely affecting the fair course of the County Championship. That was, in the eyes of the average English cricket follower of that time, the major competition. Indeed, the feeling among the players themselves is indicated by the fact that two of the leading amateurs of the day, both of them England captains – F. S. Jackson and A. E. Stoddart – refused invitations to play in Test matches against Australia in order to take part in a Championship game between their two counties.

Now, of course, under the regulations of the Test and County Cricket Board, they would not be allowed to withdraw. The current importance of Test cricket is not, though, simply a matter of official prejudice. It is the brutal but sad truth that three-day county cricket – accepted by the players themselves as the most satisfactory and satisfying form of the game – is incapable of paying its way, to such an extent that only sponsorship, the one-day competitions, radio and television rights now keep it solvent. So Test cricket has emerged as the first-class game's major internal money earner, not only in England, but in Australia as well. In India, Pakistan and West Indies, domestic competitions still attract fair attendances; but the main revenue comes from Tests.

That is why the Packer organization, in its move to compete with the official game, has launched solely international – and not state or regional – matches.

Even when Roy Webber attempted it, up to 1939, complete scores demanded a dauntingly weighty volume. Mr Gibb has held a balance between the exhaustive and bulky complete record and the near-pocket reference of this book of all Test results. Although he does not give detailed scores, he gives the total of every innings and includes, in each match, the score of every batsman who made 50 runs or over; and the figures of every bowler who took four or more wickets. Thus he affords a fair view of both team and individual performance.

Forty or so years ago, the frequency of Tests was such that England might pass a season without a visiting Test-playing team; or a year without sending away a major representative side. So the ordinary follower of the game retained a fair memory of which teams visited when; who took which sides to Australia or South Africa. How many current followers of the game, though – or for that matter, even professional reporters – could recite the Test series played between 1974 and 1978? Without consulting this book, see how many you – or the friends with you – can recall, in sequence and with their outcomes. As a simple, basic guide, the number is twenty-seven.

Page by page this is a history of growth. When, in March 1877, the Melbourne Club challenged James Lillywhite's team of English professionals in the – successful – attempt to prove that eleven Australians could compete with eleven Englishmen on even terms, no one had any idea that they were inaugurating international cricket. Yet so it was to prove. The English team was simply a party of mercenaries, touring for profit; and far from the strongest the country could have put out; while the leading Victorian players refused to turn out for Australia. For some years English teams to Australia were purely commercial ventures. Indeed, on one occasion, two English teams toured there and still left a number of the best players behind. Even at home, the English teams used to be selected by the committee of the county on whose ground the match was to be played. It was not until 1899 that MCC undertook responsibility for choosing teams for home Tests and only in 1903 that they assumed responsibility for overseas touring sides.

The first thirty Tests were played between England and Australia; South Africa first met England in 1889; the first South Africa-Australia Test took place in 1902. West Indies in 1928 in England; New Zealand at home in 1930; India in 1932 and Pakistan in 1954 at Lord's were the subsequent entrants. Gradually these countries played series between themselves, except South Africa, who never met West Indies, India or Pakistan, withdrew from the International Cricket Council on becoming a republic in 1961, and ceased to play official Test matches after 1970.

Until 1939 England often sent less than full-strength sides to play overseas, even in West Indies where, in fact, they never won a series – though they first went there in 1929-30 – until 1959-60. Even as late as 1954, too, England put out an 'experimental' team against Pakistan – and lost. Meanwhile Australia, in rather haughty fashion, never played a Test – and then only one – against New Zealand until 1945-46; and then not another until 1973-74. Relations strained to the point of warfare, too, put an end to matches between India and Pakistan from 1960-61 until the winter of 1978-79.

Meanwhile, the Kerry Packer operation has affected national strengths; England significantly; Australia – to a considerable degree – Pakistan and West Indies, at times, have been weakened by defections to W.S.C. Nothing, though, has yet checked the strong flow of Test cricket recorded here.

Valuably, and unequivocally, Mr. Gibb gives the full Test career figures of everyone who ever played in a Test match. To look through them is to light upon some killing quiz questions: for instance, who did the following play for – H. I. Young, N. C. Tufnell, T. U. Groube, H. M. Thirlow, D. B. M. Smith, G. A. Hearne, G. P. D. Hartigan, W. F. E. Marx, C. K. Singh, J. M. Neblett? Beware traps.

Many will come to this book to verify a fact, only to stay reading on, through much surprisingly fresh information. For instance, it is intriguing to discover that on the six occasions when the Nawab of Pataudi (junior) won the toss and put his opponents in to bat, his team never won; while Richie Benaud sent in Australia's opponents three times and won every time.

Consider Sir Donald Bradman's 6996 runs for Australia at 99.94; surely he would have scored another 4 to make it 7000 at 100 if he had realized it would give him two round figures – or is it better as it is? Less well known is the fact that Albert Trott had a batting average of 102.50 for Australia when, inexplicably left out of the Australian touring team of 1896, he came here, joined Middlesex and retains that remarkable Test career average.

So do the facts intrigue and beguile, as well as inform.

Hampshire   *John Arlott*
November 1978

Abbreviated scores of all Test Matches from 1876-77

Individual performances limited to an innings of 50 or over or 4 or more wickets.

1876–77: Australia v England (Played 2, Aus won 1, Eng won 1)
First Test at Melbourne, Mar. 15–19. Aus won by 45 runs.
```
      AUS:  245   (C. Bannerman retired hurt 165)
        &   104   (A. Shaw 5 for 38, G. Ulyett 4 for 39)
      ENG:  196   (H. Jupp 63; W. E. Midwinter 5 for 78)
        &   108   (T. Kendall 7 for 55)
```
Second Test at Melbourne, Mar. 31–April 4. Eng won by 4 wickets.
```
      AUS:  122   (A. Hill 4 for 27)
        &   259   (J. Southerton 4 for 46, James Lillywhite 4 for 70)
      ENG:  261   (G. Ulyett 52; T. Kendall 4 for 82)
        &   122–6 (G. Ulyett 63)
```

1878–79: Australia v England (Played 1, Aus won 1)
Test at Melbourne, Jan. 2–4. Aus won by 10 wickets.
```
      ENG:  113   (C. A. Absolom 52; F. R. Spofforth 6 for 48)
        &   160   (F. R. Spofforth 7 for 62)
      AUS:  256   (A. C. Bannerman 73; T. Emmett 7 for 68)
        &    19–0
```

1880: England v Australia (Played 1, Eng won 1)
Test at The Oval, Sept. 6–8. Eng won by 5 wickets.
```
      ENG:  420   (W. G. Grace 152, A. P. Lucas 55, Lord Harris 52)
        &    57–5
      AUS:  149   (F. Morley 5 for 56)
        &   327   (W. L. Murdoch 153*)
```

1881–82: Australia v England (Played 4, Aus won 2, Eng won 0, Drawn 2)
First Test at Melbourne, Dec. 31–Jan. 4. Match Drawn.
```
      ENG:  294   (G. Ulyett 87, W. Bates 58, J. Selby 55)
        &   308   (J. Selby 70, W. H. Scotton 50*; W. H. Cooper 6 for 120)
      AUS:  320   (T. P. Horan 124)
        &   127–3
```
Second Test at Sydney, Feb. 17–21. Aus won by 5 wickets.
```
      ENG:  133   (G. E. Palmer 7 for 68)
        &   232   (G. Ulyett 67, R. G. Barlow 62; T. W. Garrett 4 for 62, G. E.
                   Palmer 4 for 97)
      AUS:  197   (W. Bates 4 for 52)
        &   169–5
```
Third Test at Sydney, Mar. 3–7. Aus won by 6 wickets.
```
      ENG:  188   (A. Shrewsbury 82; G. E. Palmer 5 for 46)
        &   134   (T. W. Garrett 6 for 78, G. E. Palmer 4 for 44)
      AUS:  260   (P. S. McDonnell 147, A. C. Bannerman 70; E. Peate 5 for 43)
        &    66–4
```
Fourth Test at Melbourne, Mar. 10–14. Match Drawn.
```
      ENG:  309   (G. Ulyett 149; T. W. Garrett 5 for 80)
        &   234–2 (G. Ulyett 64, R. G. Barlow 56, W. Bates 52*)
      AUS:  300   (W. L. Murdoch 85, P. S. McDonnell 52; W. E. Midwinter 4 for 81)
```

1882: England v Australia (Played 1, Aus won 1)
Test at The Oval, Aug. 28–29. Aus won by 7 runs.
```
      AUS:   63   (R. G. Barlow 5 for 19, E. Peate 4 for 31)
        &   122   (H. H. Massie 55; E. Peate 4 for 40)
      ENG:  101   (F. R. Spofforth 7 for 46)
        &    77   (F. R. Spofforth 7 for 44)
```

1882–83: Australia v England (Played 4, Eng won 2, Aus won 2)
First Test at Melbourne, Dec. 30–Jan. 2. Aus won by 9 wickets.
    AUS: 291   (G. J. Bonnor 85)
       &   58–1
    ENG: 177   (G. E. Palmer 7 for 65)
       &   169   (G. Giffen 4 for 38)
Second Test at Melbourne, Jan. 19–22. Eng won by an innings and 27 runs.
    ENG: 294   (W. W. Read 75, W. Bates 55, C. F. H. Leslie 54; G. E. Palmer
                       5 for 103, G. Giffen 4 for 89)
    AUS: 114   (W. Bates 7 for 28)
       &   153   (W. Bates 7 for 74)
Third Test at Sydney, Jan. 26–30. Eng won by 69 runs.
    ENG: 247   (W. W. Read 66, E. F. S. Tylcote 66; F. R. Spofforth 4 for 73)
       &   123   (F. R. Spofforth 7 for 44)
    AUS: 218   (A. C. Bannerman 94; F. Morley 4 for 47)
       &   83   (R. G. Barlow 7 for 40)
Fourth Test at Sydney, Feb. 17–21. Aus won by 4 wickets.
    ENG: 263   (A. G. Steel 135)
       &   197
    AUS: 262   (G. J. Bonnor 87, J. M. Blackham 57)
       & 199–6 (A. C. Bannerman 63, J. M. Blackham 58*)

1884: England v Australia (Played 3, Eng won 1, Aus won 0, Drawn 2)
First Test at Old Trafford, July 10–12. Match Drawn.
    ENG: 95   (H. F. Boyle 6 for 42, F. R. Spofforth 4 for 42)
       & 180–9 (G. E. Palmer 4 for 47)
    AUS: 182
Second Test at Lord's, July 21–23. Eng won by an innings and 5 runs.
    AUS: 229   (H. J. H. Scott 75, G. Giffen 63; E. Peate 6 for 85)
       &   145   (G. Ulyett 7 for 36)
    ENG: 379   (A. G. Steel 148; G. E. Palmer 6 for 111)
Third Test at The Oval, Aug. 11–13. Match Drawn.
    AUS: 551   (W. L. Murdoch 211, P. S. McDonnell 103, H. J. H. Scott 102;
                       Hon. A. Lyttelton 4 for 19)
    ENG: 346   (W. W. Read 117, W. H. Scotton 90; G. E. Palmer 4 for 90)
       &   85–2

1884–85: Australia v England (Played 5, Eng won 3, Aus won 2, Drawn 0)
First Test at Adelaide, Dec. 12–16. Eng won by 8 wickets.
    AUS: 243   (P. S. McDonnell 124, J. M. Blackham 66; W. Bates 5 for 31)
       &   191   (P. S. McDonnell 83; R. Peel 5 for 51)
    ENG: 369   (W. Barnes 134, W. H. Scotton 82, G. Ulyett 68; G. E. Palmer
                       5 for 81)
       &   67–2
Second Test at Melbourne, Jan. 1–5. Eng won by 10 wickets.
    ENG: 401   (J. Briggs 121, A. Shrewsbury 72, W. Barnes 58; S. P. Jones
                       4 for 47)
       &   7–0
    AUS: 279   (A. H. Jarvis 82, T. P. Horan 63, J. W. Trumble 59)
       &   126   (W. Barnes 6 for 31)
Third Test at Sydney, Feb. 20–24. Aus won by 6 runs.
    AUS: 181   (T. W. Garrett 51*; W. Flowers 5 for 46, W. Attewell 4 for 53)
       &   165   (W. Bates 5 for 24)
    ENG: 133   (T. P. Horan 6 for 40, F. R. Spofforth 4 for 54)
       &   207   (W. Flowers 56, J. M. Read 56; F. R. Spofforth 6 for 90)
Fourth Test at Sydney, Mar. 14–17. Aus won by 8 wickets.
    ENG: 269   (W. Bates 64, W. Barnes 50; G. Giffen 7 for 117)
       &   77   (F. R. Spofforth 5 for 30, G. E. Palmer 4 for 32)
    AUS: 309   (G. J. Bonnor 128, A. C. Bannerman 51; W. Barnes 4 for 61)
       &   40–2
Fifth Test at Melbourne, Mar. 21–25. Eng won by an innings and 98 runs.
    AUS: 163   (F. R. Spofforth 50; G. Ulyett 4 for 52)
       &   125
    ENG: 386   (A. Shrewsbury 105*, W. Barnes 74, W. Bates 61)

1886: England v Australia (Played 3, Eng won 3, Aus won 0)
First Test at Old Trafford, July 5–7. Eng won by 4 wickets.
  AUS: 205 (S. P. Jones 87; G. Ulyett 4 for 46)
   & 123 (R. G. Barlow 7 for 44)
  ENG: 223 (W. W. Read 51; F. R. Spofforth 4 for 82)
   & 107–6
Second Test at Lord's, July 19–21. Eng won by an innings and 106 runs.
  ENG: 353 (A. Shrewsbury 164, W. Barnes 58; F. R. Spofforth 4 for 73)
  AUS: 121 (J. Briggs 5 for 29)
   & 126 (J. Briggs 6 for 45)
Third Test at The Oval, Aug. 12–14. Eng won by an innings and 217 runs.
  ENG: 434 (W. G. Grace 170, W. W. Read 94, J. Briggs 53; F. R. Spofforth
       4 for 65)
  AUS: 68 (G. A. Lohmann 7 for 36)
   & 149 (G. A. Lohmann 5 for 68)

1886–87: Australia v England (Played 2, Eng won 2, Aus won 0)
First Test at Sydney, Jan. 28–31. Eng won by 13 runs.
  ENG: 45 (C. T. B. Turner 6 for 15, J. J. Ferris 4 for 27)
   & 184 (J. J. Ferris 5 for 76)
  AUS: 119
   & 97 (W. Barnes 6 for 28)
Second Test at Sydney, Feb. 25–Mar. 1. Eng won by 71 runs.
  ENG: 151 (C. T. B. Turner 5 for 41, J. J. Ferris 5 for 71)
   & 154 (C. T. B. Turner 4 for 52, J. J. Ferris 4 for 69)
  AUS: 84 (G. A. Lohmann 8 for 35)
   & 150 (W. Bates 4 for 26)

1887–88: Australia v England (Played 1, Eng won 1)
Test at Sydney, Feb. 10–15. Eng won by 126 runs.
  ENG: 113 (C. T. B. Turner 5 for 44, J. J. Ferris 4 for 60)
   & 137 (C. T. B. Turner 7 for 43)
  AUS: 42 (G. A. Lohmann 5 for 17, R. Peel 5 for 18)
   & 82 (R. Peel 5 for 40, G. A. Lohmann 4 for 35)

1888: England v Australia (Played 3, Eng won 2, Aus won 1)
First Test at Lord's, July 16–17. Aus won by 61 runs.
  AUS: 116 (R. Peel 4 for 36)
   & 60 (R. Peel 4 for 14, G. A. Lohmann 4 for 33)
  ENG: 53 (C. T. B. Turner 5 for 27)
   & 62 (J. J. Ferris 5 for 26, C. T. B. Turner 5 for 36)
Second Test at The Oval, Aug. 13–14. Eng won by an innings and 137 runs.
  AUS: 80 (J. Briggs 5 for 25)
   & 100 (W. Barnes 5 for 32, R. Peel 4 for 49)
  ENG: 317 (R. Abel 70, W. Barnes 62, G. A. Lohmann 62*; C. T. B. Turner
       6 for 112)
Third Test at Old Trafford, Aug. 30–31. Eng won by an innings and 21 runs.
  ENG: 172 (C. T. B. Turner 5 for 86)
  AUS: 81 (R. Peel 7 for 31)
   & 70 (R. Peel 4 for 37)

1888–89: South Africa v England (Played 2, Eng won 2, SA won 0)
First Test at Port Elizabeth, Mar. 12–13. Eng won by 8 wickets.
  SA: 84 (C. A. Smith 5 for 19, J. Briggs 4 for 39)
   & 129 (A. J. Fothergill 4 for 19)
  ENG: 148 (A. R. Innes 5 for 43)
   & 67–2
Second Test at Cape Town, Mar. 25–26. Eng won by an innings and 202 runs.
  ENG: 292 (R. Abel 120, H. Wood 59; W. H. Ashley 7 for 95)
  SA: 47 (J. Briggs 7 for 17)
   & 43 (J. Briggs 8 for 11)

1890: England v Australia (Played 2, Eng won 2, Aus won 0)
First Test at Lord's, July 21–23. Eng won by 7 wickets.
  AUS: 132 (J. J. Lyons 55; W. Attewell 4 for 42)
   & 176 (J. E. Barrett 67*)

ENG: 173   (G. Ulyett 74; J. J. Lyons 5 for 30)
    & 137–3 (W. G. Grace 75*)
Second Test at The Oval, Aug. 11–12. Eng won by 2 wickets.
AUS: 92   (F. Martin 6 for 50)
    & 102   (F. Martin 6 for 52)
ENG: 100   (J. J. Ferris 4 for 25)
     & 95–8 (J. J. Ferris 5 for 49)

1891–92: Australia v England (Played 3, Aus won 2, Eng won 1)
First Test at Melbourne, Jan. 1–6. Aus won by 54 runs.
AUS: 240   (W. Bruce 57; J. W. Sharpe 6 for 84)
    & 236   (J. J. Lyons 51)
ENG: 264   (G. Bean 50, W. G. Grace 50; R. W. McLeod 5 for 55)
    & 158   (C. T. B. Turner 5 for 51)
Second Test at Sydney, Jan. 29–Feb. 3. Aus won by 72 runs.
AUS: 145   (G. A. Lohmann 8 for 58)
    & 391   (J. J. Lyons 134, A. C. Bannerman 91, W. Bruce 72; J. Briggs
              4 for 69)
ENG: 307   (R. Abel 132*; G. Giffen 4 for 88)
    & 157   (A. E. Stoddart 69; G. Giffen 6 for 72, C. T. B. Turner 4 for 46)
Third Test at Adelaide, Mar. 24–28. Eng won by an innings and 230 runs.
ENG: 499   (A. E. Stoddart 134, R. Peel 83, W. G. Grace 58, J. M. Read 57)
AUS: 100   (J. Briggs 6 for 49)
    & 169   (J. Briggs 6 for 87)

1891–92: South Africa v England (Played 1, Eng won 1, SA won 0)
Test at Cape Town, Mar. 19–22. Eng won by an innings and 189 runs.
SA: 97   (J. J. Ferris 6 for 54)
    &   83   (J. J. Ferris 7 for 37)
ENG: 369   (H. Wood 134*)

1893: England v Australia (Played 3, Eng won 1, Aus won 0, Drawn 2)
First Test at Lord's, July 17–19. Match Drawn.
ENG: 334   (A. Shrewsbury 106, F. S. Jackson 91; C. T. B. Turner 6 for 67)
    & 234–8 dec. (A. Shrewsbury 81, W. Gunn 77; G. Giffen 5 for 43)
AUS: 269   (H. Graham 107, S. E. Gregory 57; W. H. Lockwood 6 for 101)
Second Test at The Oval, Aug. 14–16. Eng won by an innings and 43 runs.
ENG: 483   (F. S. Jackson 103, A. E. Stoddart 83, W. G. Grace 68, A. Shrews-
              bury 66, A. Ward 55, W. W. Read 52; G. Giffen 7 for 128)
AUS: 91   (J. Briggs 5 for 34, W. H. Lockwood 4 for 37)
    & 349   (G. H. S. Trott 92, A. C. Bannerman 55, G. Giffen 53; J. Briggs
              5 for 114, W. H. Lockwood 4 for 96)
Third Test at Old Trafford, Aug. 24–26. Match Drawn.
AUS: 204   (W. Bruce 68; T. Richardson 5 for 49, J. Briggs 4 for 81)
    & 236   (A. C. Bannerman 60; T. Richardson 5 for 107)
ENG: 243   (W. Gunn 102*, G. Giffen 4 for 113)
    & 118–4

1894–95: Australia v England (Played 5, Eng won 3, Aus won 2)
First Test at Sydney, Dec. 14–20. Eng won by 10 runs.
AUS: 586   (S. E. Gregory 201, G. Giffen 161, F. A. Iredale 81, J. M. Blackham
              74; T. Richardson 5 for 181)
    & 166   (J. Darling 53; R. Peel 6 for 67)
ENG: 325   (A. Ward 75, J. Briggs 57; G. Giffen 4 for 75)
    & 437   (A. Ward 117, J. T. Brown 53; G. Giffen 4 for 164)
Second Test at Melbourne, Dec. 29–Jan. 3. Eng won by 94 runs.
ENG: 75   (C. T. B. Turner 5 for 32)
    & 475   (A. E. Stoddart 173, R. Peel 53; G. Giffen 6 for 155)
AUS: 123   (T. Richardson 5 for 57)
    & 333   (G. H. S. Trott 95, F. A. Iredale 68, W. Bruce 54; R. Peel 4 for 77)
Third Test at Adelaide, Jan. 11–15. Aus won by 382 runs.
AUS: 238   (G. Giffen 58; T. Richardson 5 for 75)
    & 411   (F. A. Iredale 140, W. Bruce 80, A. E. Trott 72*; R. Peel 4 for 96)
ENG: 124   (S. T. Callaway 5 for 37, G. Giffen 5 for 76)
    & 143   (A. E. Trott 8 for 43)

Fourth Test at Sydney, Feb. 1–4. Aus won by an innings and 147 runs.

AUS: 284   (H. Graham 105, A. E. Trott 85*; J. Briggs 4 for 65)
ENG: 65
&   72   (G. Giffen 5 for 26, C. T. B. Turner 4 for 33)

Fifth Test at Melbourne, Mar. 1–6. Eng won by 6 wickets.

AUS: 414   (J. Darling 74, S. E. Gregory 70, G. Giffen 57, J. J. Lyons 55; R. Peel 4 for 114)
&   267   (G. Giffen 51, J. Darling 50; T. Richardson 6 for 104)
ENG: 385   (A. C. MacLaren 120, R. Peel 73, A. E. Stoddart 68; G. H. S. Trott 4 for 71, G. Giffen 4 for 130)
&   298–4 (J. T. Brown 140, A. Ward 93)

1895–96: South Africa v England (Played 3, Eng won 3, SA won 0)
First Test at Port Elizabeth, Feb. 13–14. Eng won by 288 runs.

ENG: 185   (J. Middleton 5 for 64)
&   226   (S. M. J. Woods 53; J. Middleton 4 for 66)
SA: 93   (G. A. Lohmann 7 for 38)
&   30   (G. A. Lohmann 8 for 7)

Second Test at Johannesburg, Mar. 2–4. Eng won by an innings and 197 runs.

ENG: 482   (T. Hayward 122, H. R. Bromley-Davenport 84, C. W. Wright 71, A. J. L. Hill 65, C. B. Fry 64; G. A. Rowe 5 for 115, J. H. Sinclair 4 for 118)
SA: 151   (G. A. Lohmann 9 for 28)
&   134   (C. Heseltine 5 for 38)

Third Test at Cape Town, Mar. 21–23. Eng won by an innings and 33 runs.

SA: 115   (G. A. Lohmann 7 for 42)
&   117   (A. J. L. Hill 4 for 8)
ENG: 265   (A. J. L. Hill 124)

1896: England v Australia (Played 3, Eng won 2, Aus won 1)
First Test at Lord's, June 22–24. Eng won by 6 wickets.

AUS: 53   (T. Richardson 6 for 39)
&   347   (G. H. S. Trott 143, S. E. Gregory 103; J. T. Hearne 5 for 76, T. Richardson 5 for 134)
ENG: 292   (R. Abel 94, W. G. Grace 66)
&   111–4

Second Test at Old Trafford, July 16–18. Aus won by 3 wickets.

AUS: 412   (F. A. Iredale 108, G. Giffen 80, G. H. S. Trott 53; T. Richardson 7 for 168)
&   125–7 (T. Richardson 6 for 76)
ENG: 231   (A. F. A. Lilley 65*, K. S. Ranjitsinhji 62)
&   305   (K. S. Ranjitsinhji 154*)

Third Test at The Oval, Aug. 10–12. Eng won by 66 runs.

ENG: 145   (H. Trumble 6 for 59)
&   84   (H. Trumble 6 for 30)
AUS: 119   (J. T. Hearne 6 for 41)
&   44   (R. Peel 6 for 23, J. T. Hearne 4 for 19)

1897–98: Australia v England (Played 5, Aus won 4, Eng won 1)
First Test at Sydney, Dec. 13–17. Eng won by 9 wickets.

ENG: 551   (K. S. Ranjitsinhji 175, A. C. MacLaren 109, T. Hayward 72, G. H. Hirst 62)
&   96–1 (A. C. MacLaren 50*)
AUS: 237   (H. Trumble 70, C. E. McLeod 50*; J. T. Hearne 5 for 42)
&   408   (J. Darling 101, C. Hill 96; J. T. Hearne 4 for 99)

Second Test at Melbourne, Jan. 1–5. Aus won by an innings and 55 runs.

AUS: 520   (C. E. McLeod 112, F. A. Iredale 89, G. H. S. Trott 79, S. E. Gregory 71, C. Hill 58)
ENG: 315   (K. S. Ranjitsinhji 71, W. Storer 51; H. Trumble 4 for 54)
&   150   (M. A. Noble 6 for 49, H. Trumble 4 for 53)

Third Test at Adelaide, Jan. 14–19. Aus won by an innings and 13 runs.

AUS: 573   (J. Darling 178, F. A. Iredale 84, C. Hill 81, S. E. Gregory 52; T. Richardson 4 for 164)
ENG: 278   (G. H. Hirst 85, T. Hayward 70; W. P. Howell 4 for 70)

    &   282   (A. C. MacLaren 124, K. S. Ranjitsinhji 77; C. E. McLeod 5 for 65,
                 M. A. Noble 5 for 84)
Fourth Test at Melbourne, Jan. 29–Feb. 2. Aus won by 8 wickets.
    AUS: 323   (C. Hill 188; J. T. Hearne 6 for 98)
       &   115–2 (C. E. McLeod 64*)
    ENG: 174   (E. Jones 4 for 56)
       &   263   (K. S. Ranjitsinhji 55)
Fifth Test at Sydney, Feb. 26–Mar. 2. Aus won by 6 wickets.
    ENG: 335   (A. C. MacLaren 65, N. F. Druce 64; E. Jones 6 for 82)
       &   178   (H. Trumble 4 for 37)
    AUS: 239   (C. E. McLeod 64; T. Richardson 8 for 94)
       &   276–4 (J. Darling 160, J. Worrall 62)

1898–99: South Africa v England (Played 2, Eng won 2, SA won 0)
First Test at Johannesburg, Feb. 14–16. Eng won by 32 runs.
    ENG: 145
       &   237   (P. F. Warner 132*; J. Middleton 5 for 51)
    SA: 251   (J. H. Sinclair 86; A. E. Trott 4 for 61)
       &   99   (A. E. Trott 5 for 49)
Second Test at Cape Town, April 1–4. Eng won by 210 runs.
    ENG: 92   (J. H. Sinclair 6 for 26, J. Middleton 4 for 18)
       &   330   (J. T. Tyldesley 112)
    SA: 177   (J. H. Sinclair 106; A. E. Trott 4 for 69)
       &   35   (S. Haigh 6 for 11, A. E. Trott 4 for 19)

1899: England v Australia (Played 5, Aus won 1, Eng won 0, Drawn 4)
First Test at Trent Bridge, June 1–3. Match Drawn.
    AUS: 252   (C. Hill 52; W. Rhodes 4 for 58, J. T. Hearne 4 for 71)
       &   230–8 dec. (C. Hill 80)
    ENG: 193   (C. B. Fry 50; E. Jones 5 for 88)
       &   155–7 (K. S. Ranjitsinhji 93*)
Second Test at Lord's, June 15–17. Aus won by 10 wickets.
    ENG: 206   (F. S. Jackson 73, G. L. Jessop 51; E. Jones 7 for 88)
       &   240   (A. C. MacLaren 88*, T. Hayward 77)
    AUS: 421   (C. Hill 135, V. T. Trumper 135*, M. A. Noble 54)
       &   28–0
Third Test at Headingley, June 29–July 1. Match Drawn.
    AUS: 172   (J. Worrall 76; H. I. Young 4 for 30)
       &   224   (H. Trumble 56; J. T. Hearne 4 for 50)
    ENG: 220   (A. F. A. Lilley 55; H. Trumble 5 for 60)
       &   19–0
Fourth Test at Old Trafford, July 17–19. Match Drawn.
    ENG: 372   (T. Hayward 130, A. F. A. Lilley 58)
       &   94–3
    AUS: 196   (M. A. Noble 60*; W. M. Bradley 5 for 67, H. I. Young 4 for 79)
       &   346–7 dec. (M. A. Noble 89, V. T. Trumper 63, J. Worrall 53)
Fifth Test at The Oval, Aug. 14–16. Match Drawn.
    ENG: 576   (T. Hayward 137, F. S. Jackson 118, C. B. Fry 60, K. S. Ranjitsinhji
                 54; E. Jones 4 for 164)
    AUS: 352   (S. E. Gregory 117, J. Darling 71, J. Worrall 55; W. H. Lockwood
                 7 for 71)
       &   254–5 (J. Worrall 75, C. E. McLeod 77, M. A. Noble 69*)

1901–02: Australia v England (Played 5, Aus won 4, Eng won 1)
First Test at Sydney, Dec. 13–16. Eng won by an innings and 124 runs.
    ENG: 464   (A. C. MacLaren 116, A. F. A. Lilley 84, T. Hayward 69, L. C.
                 Braund 58; C. E. McLeod 4 for 84)
    AUS: 168   (S. F. Barnes 5 for 65)
       &   172   (L. C. Braund 5 for 61, C. Blythe 4 for 30)
Second Test at Melbourne, Jan. 1–4. Aus won by 229 runs.
    AUS: 112   (S. F. Barnes 6 for 42, C. Blythe 4 for 64)
       &   353   (R. A. Duff 104, C. Hill 99; S. F. Barnes 7 for 121)
    ENG: 61   (M. A. Noble 7 for 17)
       &   175   (J. T. Tyldesley 66; M. A. Noble 6 for 60, H. Trumble 4 for 49)

Third Test at Adelaide, Jan. 17–23. Aus won by 4 wickets.
ENG: 388   (L. C. Braund 103*, T. Hayward 90, W. G. Quaife 68, A. C. MacLaren 67)
  &   247   (H. Trumble 6 for 74)
AUS: 321   (C. Hill 98, V. T. Trumper 65, S. E. Gregory 55; J. Gunn 5 for 76)
  &   315–6   (C. Hill 97, J. Darling 69, H. Trumble 62*)
Fourth Test at Sydney, Feb. 14–18. Aus won by 7 wickets.
ENG: 317   (A. C. MacLaren 92, J. T. Tyldesley 79; J. V. Saunders 4 for 119)
  &   99   (J. V. Saunders 5 for 43, M. A. Noble 5 for 54)
AUS: 299   (M. A. Noble 56, W. W. Armstrong 55; G. L. Jessop 4 for 68, L. C. Braund 4 for 118)
  &   121–3   (R. A. Duff 51*)
Fifth Test at Melbourne, Feb. 28–Mar. 4. Aus won by 32 runs.
AUS: 144   (T. Hayward 4 for 22, J. Gunn 4 for 38)
  &   255   (C. Hill 87; L. C. Braund 5 for 95)
ENG: 189   (H. Trumble 5 for 62)
  &   178   (M. A. Noble 6 for 98)

1902: England v Australia (Played 5, Aus won 2, Eng won 1, Drawn 2)
First Test at Edgbaston, May 29–31. Match Drawn.
ENG: 376   (J. T. Tyldesley 138, Hon. F. S. Jackson 53, W. H. Lockwood 52*)
AUS: 36   (W. Rhodes 7 for 17)
  &   46–2
Second Test at Lord's, June 12–14. Match Drawn.
ENG: 102–2   (Hon. F. S. Jackson 55*)
Third Test at Bramall Lane, Sheffield, July 3–5. Aus won by 143 runs.
AUS: 194   (S. F. Barnes 6 for 49)
  &   289   (C. Hill 119, V. T. Trumper 62; W. Rhodes 5 for 63)
ENG: 145   (J. V. Saunders 5 for 50, M. A. Noble 5 for 51)
  &   195   (A. C. MacLaren 63, G. L. Jessop 55; M. A. Noble 6 for 52, H. Trumble 4 for 49)
Fourth Test at Old Trafford, July 24–26. Aus won by 3 runs.
AUS: 299   (V. T. Trumper 104, C. Hill 65, R. A. Duff 54, J. Darling 51; W. H. Lockwood 6 for 48, W. Rhodes 4 for 104)
  &   86   (W. H. Lockwood 5 for 28)
ENG: 262   (Hon. F. S. Jackson 128, L. C. Braund 65; H. Trumble 4 for 75)
  &   120   (H. Trumble 6 for 53, J. V. Saunders 4 for 52)
Fifth Test at The Oval, Aug. 11–13. Eng won by 1 wicket.
AUS: 324   (H. Trumble 64*, M. A. Noble 52; G. H. Hirst 5 for 77)
  &   121   (W. H. Lockwood 5 for 45)
ENG: 183   (H. Trumble 8 for 65)
  &   263–9   (G. L. Jessop 104, G. H. Hirst 58*; J. V. Saunders 4 for 105, H. Trumble 4 for 108)

1902–03: South Africa v Australia (Played 3, Aus won 2, SA won 0, Drawn 1)
First Test at Johannesburg, Oct. 11–14. Match Drawn.
SA: 454   (L. J. Tancred 97, C. B. Llewellyn 90, A. W. Nourse 72, E. A. Halliwell 57)
  &   101–4
AUS: 296   (R. A. Duff 82*, C. Hill 76, V. T. Trumper 63; C. B. Llewellyn 6 for 92, J. H. Sinclair 4 for 129)
  &   372–7 dec. (C. Hill 142, W. W. Armstrong 59, M. A. Noble 53*)
Second Test at Johannesburg, Oct. 18–21. Aus won by 159 runs.
AUS: 175   (C. B. Llewellyn 5 for 43)
  &   309   (W. W. Armstrong 159*; C. B. Llewellyn 5 for 73)
SA: 240   (J. H. Sinclair 101)
  &   85   (J. V. Saunders 7 for 34)
Third Test at Cape Town, Nov. 8–11. Aus won by 10 wickets.
AUS: 252   (C. Hill 91*, V. T. Trumper 70; C. B. Llewellyn 6 for 97)
  &   59–0
SA: 85   (W. P. Howell 4 for 18, J. V. Saunders 4 for 37)
  &   225   (J. H. Sinclair 104; W. P. Howell 5 for 81)

1903–04: Australia v England (Played 5, Eng won 3, Aus won 2)
First Test at Sydney, Dec. 11–17. Eng won by 5 wickets.

```
AUS:   285   (M. A. Noble 133; E. G. Arnold 4 for 76)
  &    485   (V. T. Trumper 185*, R. A. Duff 84, C. Hill 51; W. Rhodes 5 for 94)
ENG:   577   (R. E. Foster 287, L. C. Braund 102, J. T. Tyldesley 53)
  &    194-5 (T. Hayward 91, G. H. Hirst 60*)
```
Second Test at Melbourne, Jan. 1–5. Eng won by 185 runs.
```
ENG:   315   (J. T. Tyldesley 97, P. F. Warner 68, T. Hayward 58; W. P. Howell
              4 for 43, H. Trumble 4 for 107)
  &    103   (J. T. Tyldesley 62; H. Trumble 5 for 34)
AUS:   122   (V. T. Trumper 74; W. Rhodes 7 for 56)
  &    111   (W. Rhodes 8 for 68)
```
Third Test at Adelaide, Jan. 15–20. Aus won by 216 runs.
```
AUS:   388   (V. T. Trumper 113, C. Hill 88, R. A. Duff 79, M. A. Noble 59)
  &    351   (S. E. Gregory 112, M. A. Noble 65, V. T. Trumper 59; B. J. T.
              Bosanquet 4 for 73)
ENG:   245   (G. H. Hirst 58)
  &    278   (P. F. Warner 79, T. Hayward 67; A. J. Hopkins 4 for 81)
```
Fourth Test at Sydney, Feb. 26–Mar. 3. Eng won by 157 runs.
```
ENG:   249   (A. E. Knight 70*; M. A. Noble 7 for 100)
  &    210   (T. Hayward 52)
AUS:   131   (E. G. Arnold 4 for 28, W. Rhodes 4 for 33)
  &    171   (M. A. Noble 53*; B. J. T. Bosanquet 6 for 51)
```
Fifth Test at Melbourne, Mar. 5–8. Aus won by 218 runs.
```
AUS:   247   (V. T. Trumper 88; L. C. Braund 8 for 81)
  &    133   (G. H. Hirst 5 for 48)
ENG:    61   (A. Cotter 6 for 40, M. A. Noble 4 for 19)
  &    101   (H. Trumble 7 for 28)
```

1905: England v Australia (Played 5, Eng won 2, Aus won 0, Drawn 3)
First Test at Trent Bridge, May 29–31. Eng won by 213 runs.
```
ENG:   196   (J. T. Tyldesley 56; F. Laver 7 for 64)
  & 426-5 dec. (A. C. MacLaren 140, Hon. F. S. Jackson 82*, J. T. Tyldesley 61)
AUS:   221   (C. Hill 54, M. A. Noble 50; Hon. F. S. Jackson 5 for 52)
  &    188   (S. E. Gregory 51; B. J. T. Bosanquet 8 for 107)
```
Second Test at Lord's, June 15–17. Match Drawn.
```
ENG:   282   (C. B. Fry 73, A. C. MacLaren 56)
  &    151-5 (A. C. MacLaren 79)
AUS:   181   (Hon. F. S. Jackson 4 for 50)
```
Third Test at Headingley, July 3–5. Match Drawn.
```
ENG:   301   (Hon. F. S. Jackson 144*)
  &    295-5 dec. (J. T. Tyldesley 100, T. Hayward 60; W. W. Armstrong
                    5 for 122)
AUS:   195   (W. W. Armstrong 66; A. Warren 5 for 57)
  &    224-7 (M. A. Noble 62)
```
Fourth Test at Old Trafford, July 24–26. Eng won by an innings and 80 runs.
```
ENG:   446   (Hon. F. S. Jackson 113, T. Hayward 82, R. H. Spooner 52; C. E.
              McLeod 5 for 125)
AUS:   197   (J. Darling 73; W. Brearley 4 for 72)
  &    169   (R. A. Duff 60; W. Brearley 4 for 54)
```
Fifth Test at The Oval, Aug. 14–16. Match Drawn.
```
ENG:   430   (C. B. Fry 144, Hon. F. S. Jackson 76, T. Hayward 59; A. Cotter
              7 for 148)
  &    261-6 dec. (J. T. Tyldesley 112*, R. H. Spooner 79)
AUS:   363   (R. A. Duff 146, J. Darling 57; W. Brearley 5 for 110)
  &    124-4
```

1905–06 South Africa v England (Played 5, SA won 4, Eng won 1)
First Test at Johannesburg, Jan. 2–4. SA won by 1 wicket.
```
ENG:   184
  &    190   (P. F. Warner 51; G. A. Faulkner 4 for 26)
SA:     91   (W. S. Lees 5 for 34)
  &    287-9 (A. W. Nourse 93*, G. C. White 81)
```
Second Test at Johannesburg, Mar. 6–8. SA won by 9 wickets.
```
ENG:   148
```

      & 160   (F. L. Fane 65, R. O. Schwarz 4 for 30)
SA: 277   (J. H. Sinclair 66; S. Haigh 4 for 64)
      & 33–1
Third Test at Johannesburg, Mar. 10–14. SA won by 243 runs.
SA: 385   (C. M. H. Hathorn 102, A. W. Nourse 61; W. S. Lees 6 for 78)
      & 349–5 dec. (G. C. White 147, L. J. Tancred 73, A. W. Nourse 55)
ENG: 295   (F. L. Fane 143; S. J. Snooke 4 for 57, R. O. Schwarz 4 for 67)
      & 196   (D. Denton 61; S. J. Snooke 8 for 70)
Fourth Test at Cape Town, Mar. 24–27. Eng won by 4 wickets.
SA: 218   (C. Blythe 6 for 68)
      & 138   (G. C. White 73; C. Blythe 5 for 50, W. S. Lees 4 for 27)
ENG: 198   (J. H. Sinclair 4 for 41, G. A. Faulkner 4 for 49)
      & 160–6 (F. L. Fane 66*)
Fifth Test at Cape Town, Mar. 30–April 2. SA won by an innings and 16 runs.
ENG: 187   (J. N. Crawford 74; J. H. Sinclair 4 for 45)
      & 130   (A. W. Nourse 4 for 25)
SA: 333   (A. E. E. Vogler 62*, S. J. Snooke 60)

1907: England v South Africa (Played 3, Eng won 1, SA won 0, Drawn 2)

First Test at Lord's, July 1–3. Match Drawn.
ENG: 428   (L. C. Braund 104, G. L. Jessop 93, J. T. Tyldesley 52; A. E. E
            Vogler 7 for 128)
SA: 140   (A. W. Nourse 62; E. G. Arnold 5 for 37)
      & 185–3 (P. W. Sherwell 115)
Second Test at Headingley, July 29–31. Eng won by 53 runs.
ENG: 76   (G. A. Faulkner 6 for 17)
      & 162   (C. B. Fry 54; G. C. White 4 for 47)
SA: 110   (C. Blythe 8 for 59)
      & 75   (C. Blythe 7 for 40)
Third Test at The Oval, Aug. 19–21. Match Drawn.
ENG: 295   (C. B. Fry 129, R. E. Foster 51)
      & 138   (A. E. E. Vogler 4 for 49)
SA: 178   (S. J. Snooke 63; C. Blythe 5 for 61)
      & 159–5

1907–08: Australia v England (Played 5, Aus won 4, Eng won 1, Drawn 0)

First Test at Sydney, Dec. 13–19. Aus won by 2 wickets.
ENG: 273   (G. Gunn 119; A. Cotter 6 for 101)
      & 300   (G. Gunn 74, J. Hardstaff 63; J. V. Saunders 4 for 68)
AUS: 300   (C. Hill 87; A. Fielder 6 for 82)
      & 275–8 (H. Carter 61)
Second Test at Melbourne, Jan. 1–7. Eng won by 1 wicket.
AUS: 266   (M. A. Noble 61; J. N. Crawford 5 for 79)
      & 397   (W. W. Armstrong 77, M. A. Noble 64, V. T. Trumper 63, C. G.
            Macartney 54, H. Carter 53; S. F. Barnes 5 for 72)
ENG: 382   (K. L. Hutchings 126, J. B. Hobbs 83; A. Cotter 5 for 142)
      & 282–9 (F. L. Fane 50)
Third Test at Adelaide, Jan. 10–16. Aus won by 245 runs.
AUS: 285   (C. G. Macartney 75; A. Fielder 4 for 80)
      & 506   (C. Hill 160, R. J. Hartigan 116, M. A. Noble 65)
ENG: 363   (G. Gunn 65, J. N. Crawford 62, J. Hardstaff 61)
      & 183   (J. Hardstaff 72; J. A. O'Connor 5 for 40, J. V. Saunders 5 for 65)
Fourth Test at Melbourne, Feb. 7–11. Aus won by 308 runs.
AUS: 214   (V. S. Ransford 51; J. N. Crawford 5 for 48, A. Fielder 4 for 54)
      & 385   (W. W. Armstrong 133*, H. Carter 66, V. S. Ransford 54; A.
            Fielder 4 for 91)
ENG: 105   (J. B. Hobbs 57; J. V. Saunders 5 for 28)
      & 186   (J. V. Saunders 4 for 76)
Fifth Test at Sydney, Feb. 21–27. Aus won by 49 runs.
AUS: 137   (S. F. Barnes 7 for 60)
      & 422   (V. T. Trumper 166, S. E. Gregory 56; J. N. Crawford 5 for 141,
            W. Rhodes 4 for 102)
ENG: 281   (G. Gunn 122*, J. B. Hobbs 72)
      & 229   (W. Rhodes 69; J. V. Saunders 5 for 82)

1909: England v Australia (Played 5, Aus won 2, Eng won 1, Drawn 2)
First Test at Edgbaston, May 27–29. Eng won by 10 wickets.
    AUS: 74   (C. Blythe 6 for 44, G. H. Hirst 4 for 28)
        &   151   (C. Blythe 5 for 58, G. H. Hirst 5 for 58)
    ENG: 121   (W. W. Armstrong 5 for 27)
        &   105–0   (J. B. Hobbs 62*)
Second Test at Lord's, June 14–16. Aus won by 9 wickets.
    ENG: 269   (J. H. King 60; A. Cotter 4 for 80)
        &   121   (W. W. Armstrong 6 for 35)
    AUS: 350   (V. S. Ransford 143*; A. E. Relf 5 for 85)
        &   41–1
Third Test at Headingley, July 1–3. Aus won by 126 runs.
    AUS: 188   (W. Rhodes 4 for 38)
        &   207   (S. F. Barnes 6 for 63)
    ENG: 182   (J. Sharp 61, J. T. Tyldesley 55; C. G. Macartney 7 for 58)
        &   87   (A. Cotter 5 for 38, C. G. Macartney 4 for 27)
Fourth Test at Old Trafford, July 26–28. Match Drawn.
    AUS: 147   (S. F. Barnes 5 for 56, C. Blythe 5 for 63)
        &   279–9 dec. (V. S. Ransford 54*, C. G. Macartney 51; W. Rhodes 5 for 83)
    ENG: 119   (F. Laver 8 for 31)
        &   108–3   (R. H. Spooner 58)
Fifth Test at The Oval, Aug. 9–11. Match Drawn.
    AUS: 325   (W. Bardsley 136, V. T. Trumper 73, C. G. Macartney 50; D. W. Carr 5 for 146)
        &   339–5 dec. (W. Bardsley 130, S. E. Gregory 74, M. A. Noble 55)
    ENG: 352   (J. Sharp 105, W. Rhodes 66, C. B. Fry 62, K. L. Hutchings 59; A. Cotter 6 for 95)
        &   104–3   (W. Rhodes 54)

1909–10: South Africa v England (Played 5, SA won 3, Eng won 2)
First Test at Johannesburg, Jan. 1–5. SA won by 19 runs.
    SA: 208   (G. A. Faulkner 78, A. W. Nourse 53; G. H. T. Simpson-Hayward 6 for 43)
        &   345   (G. A. Faulkner 123; C. P. Buckenham 4 for 110)
    ENG: 310   (J. B. Hobbs 89, W. Rhodes 66; A. E. E. Vogler 5 for 87, G. A. Faulkner 5 for 120)
        &   224   (G. J. Thompson 63; A. E. E. Vogler 7 for 94)
Second Test at Durban, Jan. 21–26. SA won by 95 runs.
    SA: 199   (G. H. T. Simpson-Hayward 4 for 42)
        &   347   (G. C. White 118, A. W. Nourse 69, S. J. Snooke 53)
    ENG: 199   (J. B. Hobbs 53; A. E. E. Vogler 5 for 83)
        &   252   (J. B. Hobbs 70; G. A. Faulkner 6 for 87)
Third Test at Johannesburg, Feb. 26–Mar. 3. Eng won by 3 wickets.
    SA: 305   (G. A. Faulkner 76, G. C. White 72, A. E. E. Vogler 65; C. P. Buckenham 5 for 115)
        &   237   (S. J. Snooke 52; G. H. T. Simpson-Hayward 5 for 69)
    ENG: 322   (D. Denton 104, F. E. Woolley 58*; G. A. Faulkner 4 for 89, A. E. E. Vogler 4 for 98)
        &   221–7   (J. B. Hobbs 93*; A. E. E. Vogler 4 for 109)
Fourth Test at Cape Town, Mar. 7–9. SA won by 4 wickets.
    ENG: 203   (F. E. Woolley 69, M. C. Bird 57)
        &   178   (F. E. Woolley 64; A. E. E. Vogler 5 for 72)
    SA: 207   (G. J. Thompson 4 for 50)
        &   175–6
Fifth Test at Cape Town, Mar. 11–14. Eng won by 9 wickets.
    ENG: 417   (J. B. Hobbs 187, W. Rhodes 77, G. J. Thompson 51; N. O. Norton 4 for 47)
        &   16–1
    SA: 103   (C. Blythe 7 for 46)
        &   327   (G. A. Faulkner 99)

1910–11: Australia v South Africa (Played 5, Aus won 4, SA won 1)
First Test at Sydney, Dec. 9–14. Aus won by an innings and 114 runs.
    AUS: 528   (C. Hill 191, W. Bardsley 132, D. R. A. Gehrs 67; R. O. Schwarz 5 for 102)

SA: 174 (G. A. Faulkner 62, R. O. Schwarz 61; A. Cotter 6 for 69, W. J. Whitty 4 for 33)
& 240 (A. W. Nourse 64*, P. W. Sherwell 60; W. J. Whitty 4 for 75)
Second Test at Melbourne, Dec. 31–Jan. 4. Aus won by 89 runs.
AUS: 348 (W. Bardsley 85, W. W. Armstrong 75, V. S. Ransford 58)
& 327 (V. T. Trumper 159; R. O. Schwarz 4 for 76, C. B. Llewellyn 4 for 81)
SA: 506 (G. A. Faulkner 204, S. J. Snooke 77, J. H. Sinclair 58*; W. W. Armstrong 4 for 134)
& 80 (W. J. Whitty 6 for 17, A. Cotter 4 for 47)
Third Test at Adelaide, Jan. 7–13. SA won by 38 runs.
SA: 482 (J. W. Zulch 105, S. J. Snooke 103, G. A. Faulkner 56; W. W. Armstrong 4 for 103)
& 360 (G. A. Faulkner 115, C. B. Llewellyn 80; W. J. Whitty 6 for 104)
AUS: 465 (V. T. Trumper 214*, W. Bardsley 54, V. S. Ransford 50; C. B. Llewellyn 4 for 107)
& 339 (C. Kelleway 65, W. Bardsley 58, C. Hill 55; R. O. Schwarz 4 for 48)
Fourth Test at Melbourne, Feb. 17–21. Aus won by 530 runs.
AUS: 328 (W. Bardsley 82, V. S. Ransford 75, C. Kelleway 59)
& 578 (W. W. Armstrong 132, C. Hill 100, V. S. Ransford 95, V. T. Trumper 87, D. R. A. Gehrs 58)
SA: 205 (A. W. Nourse 92*; W. J. Whitty 4 for 78)
& 171 (G. A. Faulkner 80; H. V. Hordern 5 for 66)
Fifth Test at Sydney, Mar. 3–7. Aus won by 7 wickets.
AUS: 364 (C. G. Macartney 137, W. Bardsley 94, H. V. Hordern 50; R. O. Schwarz 6 for 47)
& 198–3 (V. T. Trumper 74*, C. G. Macartney 56)
SA: 160 (G. A. Faulkner 52; H. V. Hordern 4 for 73)
& 401 (J. W. Zulch 150, G. A. Faulkner 92; W. J. Whitty 4 for 66)

1911–12: Australia v England (Played 5, Eng won 4, Aus won 1)
First Test at Sydney, Dec. 15–21. Aus won by 146 runs.
AUS: 447 (V. T. Trumper 113, R. B. Minnett 90, W. W. Armstrong 60)
& 308 (C. Kelleway 70, C. Hill 65; F. R. Foster 5 for 92, J. W. H. T. Douglas 4 for 50)
ENG: 318 (J. W. Hearne 76, J. B. Hobbs 63, F. R. Foster 56; H. V. Hordern 5 for 85)
& 291 (G. Gunn 62; H. V. Hordern 7 for 90)
Second Test at Melbourne, Dec. 30–Jan. 3. Eng won by 8 wickets.
AUS: 184 (S. F. Barnes 5 for 44)
& 299 (W. W. Armstrong 90; F. R. Foster 6 for 91)
ENG: 265 (J. W. Hearne 114, W. Rhodes 61; H. V. Hordern 4 for 66, A. Cotter 4 for 73)
& 219–2 (J. B. Hobbs 126*)
Third Test at Adelaide, Jan. 12–17. Eng won by 7 wickets.
AUS: 133 (F. R. Foster 5 for 36)
& 476 (C. Hill 98, H. Carter 72, W. Bardsley 63, T. J. Matthews 53; S. F. Barnes 5 for 105)
ENG: 501 (J. B. Hobbs 187, F. R. Foster 71, W. Rhodes 59; A. Cotter 4 for 125)
& 112–3 (W. Rhodes 57*)
Fourth Test at Melbourne, Feb. 9–13. Eng won by an innings and 225 runs.
AUS: 191 (R. B. Minnett 56; S. F. Barnes 5 for 74, F. R. Foster 4 for 77)
& 173 (J. W. H. T. Douglas 5 for 46)
ENG: 589 (W. Rhodes 179, J. B. Hobbs 178, G. Gunn 75, F. E. Woolley 56, F. R. Foster 50)
Fifth Test at Sydney, Feb. 23–Mar. 1. Eng won by 70 runs.
ENG: 324 (F. E. Woolley 133*, G. Gunn 52; H. V. Hordern 5 for 95)
& 214 (G. Gunn 61; H. V. Hordern 5 for 66)
AUS: 176
& 292 (R. B. Minnett 61, V. T. Trumper 50; F. R. Foster 4 for 43, S. F. Barnes 4 for 106)

1912: Tournament in England between England, Australia and South Africa
Australia v South Africa (Played 3, Aus won 2, SA won 0, Drawn 1)
First Test at Old Trafford, May 27–28. Aus won by an innings and 88 runs.
    AUS: 448   (W. Bardsley 121, C. Kelleway 114; S. J. Pegler 6 for 105)
    SA: 265   (G. A. Faulkner 122*; W. J. Whitty 5 for 55)
    &   95   (C. Kelleway 5 for 33)
Second Test at Lord's, July 15–17. Aus won by 10 wickets.
    SA: 263   (H. W. Taylor 93; W. J. Whitty 4 for 68)
    &   173   (C. B. Llewellyn 59; T. J. Matthews 4 for 29)
    AUS: 390   (W. Bardsley 164, C. Kelleway 102; S. J. Pegler 4 for 79)
    &   48–0
Third Test at Trent Bridge, Aug. 5–7. Match Drawn.
    SA: 329   (A. W. Nourse 64, G. C. White 59*)
    AUS: 219   (W. Bardsley 56; S. J. Pegler 4 for 80)

England v South Africa (Played 3, Eng won 3, SA won 0)
First Test at Lord's, June 10–12. Eng won by an innings and 62 runs.
    SA: 58   (F. R. Foster 5 for 16, S. F. Barnes 5 for 25)
    &   217   (C. B. Llewellyn 75; S. F. Barnes 6 for 85)
    ENG: 337   (R. H. Spooner 119, F. E. Woolley 73; S. J. Pegler 7 for 65)
Second Test at Headingley, July 8–10. Eng won by 174 runs.
    ENG: 242   (F. E. Woolley 57; A. W. Nourse 4 for 52)
    &   238   (R. H. Spooner 82, J. B. Hobbs 55; G. A. Faulkner 4 for 50)
    SA: 147   (S. F. Barnes 6 for 52)
    &   159   (S. F. Barnes 4 for 63)
Third Test at The Oval, Aug. 12–13. Eng won by 10 wickets.
    SA: 95   (S. F. Barnes 5 for 28, F. E. Woolley 5 for 41)
    &   93   (S. F. Barnes 8 for 29)
    ENG: 176   (J. B. Hobbs 68; G. A. Faulkner 7 for 84)
    &   14–0

England v Australia (Played 3, Eng won 1, Aus won 0, Drawn 2)
First Test at Lord's, June 24–26. Match Drawn.
    ENG: 310–7 dec. (J. B. Hobbs 107, W. Rhodes 59)
    AUS: 282–7 (C. G. Macartney 99, C. Kelleway 61)
Second Test at Old Trafford, July 29–31. Match Drawn.
    ENG: 203   (W. Rhodes 92; W. J. Whitty 4 for 43, G. R. Hazlitt 4 for 77)
    AUS: 14–0
Third Test at The Oval, Aug. 19–22. Eng won by 244 runs.
    ENG: 245   (J. B. Hobbs 66, F. E. Woolley 62; R. B. Minnett 4 for 34, W. J. Whitty 4 for 69)
    &   175   (C. B. Fry 79; G. R. Hazlitt 7 for 25)
    AUS: 111   (F. E. Woolley 5 for 29, S. F. Barnes 5 for 30)
    &   65   (F. E. Woolley 5 for 20, H. Dean 4 for 19)

1913–14: South Africa v England (Played 5, Eng won 4, SA won 0, Drawn 1)
First Test at Durban, Dec. 13–17. Eng won by an innings and 157 runs.
    SA: 182   (H. W. Taylor 109; S. F. Barnes 5 for 57)
    &   111   (S. F. Barnes 5 for 48)
    ENG: 450   (J. W. H. T. Douglas 119, J. B. Hobbs 82, M. C. Bird 61, Hon. L. H. Tennyson 52)
Second Test at Johannesburg, Dec. 26–30. Eng won by an innings and 12 runs.
    SA: 160   (G. P. D. Hartigan 51; S. F. Barnes 8 for 56)
    &   231   (A. W. Nourse 56; S. F. Barnes 9 for 103)
    ENG: 403   (W. Rhodes 152, C. P. Mead 102, A. E. Relf 63; J. M. Blanckenberg 5 for 83)
Third Test at Johannesburg, Jan. 1–5. Eng won by 91 runs.
    ENG: 238   (J. B. Hobbs 92)
    &   308   (C. P. Mead 86, J. W. H. T. Douglas 77; C. Newberry 4 for 72)
    SA: 151   (J. W. Hearne 5 for 49)
    &   304   (J. W. Zulch 82, H. W. Taylor 70, J. M. Blanckenberg 59; S. F. Barnes 5 for 102)
Fourth Test at Durban, Feb. 14–18. Match Drawn.
    SA: 170   (P. A. M. Hands 51; S. F. Barnes 7 for 56)

                &   305–9 dec. (H. W. Taylor 93; S. F. Barnes 7 for 88)
     ENG: 163   (J. B. Hobbs 64; C. P. Carter 6 for 50)
            &   154–5 (J. B. Hobbs 97)
Fifth Test at Port Elizabeth, Feb. 27–Mar. 3. Eng won by 10 wickets.
     SA: 193   (P. A. M. Hands 83; J. W. H. T. Douglas 4 for 14)
            &   228   (H. W. Taylor 87, J. W. Zulch 60; M. W. Booth 4 for 49)
     ENG: 411   (C. P. Mead 117, F. E. Woolley 54; E. B. Lundie 4 for 101)
            &   11–0

1920–21: Australia v England (Played 5, Aus won 5, Eng won 0)
First Test at Sydney, Dec. 17–22. Aus won by 377 runs.
     AUS: 267   (H. L. Collins 70)
            &   581   (W. W. Armstrong 158, H. L. Collins 104, C. Kelleway 78, C. G.
                         Macartney 69, W. Bardsley 57, J. M. Taylor 51)
     ENG: 190   (F. E. Woolley 52)
            &   281   (J. B. Hobbs 59, J. W. Hearne 57, E. H. Hendren 56)
Second Test at Melbourne, Dec. 31–Jan. 4. Aus won by an innings and 91 runs.
     AUS: 499   (C. E. Pellew 116, J. M. Gregory 100, J. M. Taylor 68, H. L.
                         Collins 64, W. Bardsley 51)
     ENG: 251   (J. B. Hobbs 122, E. H. Hendren 67; J. M. Gregory 7 for 69)
            &   157   (F. E. Woolley 50; W. W. Armstrong 4 for 26)
Third Test at Adelaide, Jan. 14–20. Aus won by 119 runs.
     AUS: 354   (H. L. Collins 162, W. A. S. Oldfield 50; C. H. Parkin 5 for 60)
            &   582   (C. Kelleway 147, W. W. Armstrong 121, C. E. Pellew 104, J. M.
                         Gregory 78*; H. Howell 4 for 115)
     ENG: 447   (C. A. G. Russell 135*, F. E. Woolley 79, J. W. H. Makepeace 60,
                         J. W. H. T. Douglas 60; A. A. Mailey 5 for 160)
            &   370   (J. B. Hobbs 123, C. A. G. Russell 59, E. H. Hendren 51; A. A.
                         Mailey 5 for 142)
Fourth Test at Melbourne, Feb. 11–16. Aus won by 8 wickets.
     ENG: 284   (J. W. H. Makepeace 117, J. W. H. T. Douglas 50; A. A. Mailey
                         4 for 115)
            &   315   (W. Rhodes 73, J. W. H. T. Douglas 60, P. G. H. Fender 59,
                         J. W. H. Makepeace 54; A. A. Mailey 9 for 121)
     AUS: 389   (W. W. Armstrong 123*, J. M. Gregory 77, H. L. Collins 59, W.
                         Bardsley 56; P. G. H. Fender 5 for 122)
            &   211–2 (J. M. Gregory 76*, J. Ryder 52*)
Fifth Test at Sydney, Feb. 25–Mar. 1. Aus won by 9 wickets.
     ENG: 204   (F. E. Woolley 53; C. Kelleway 4 for 27)
            &   280   (J. W. H. T. Douglas 68; A. A. Mailey 5 for 119)
     AUS: 392   (C. G. Macartney 170, J. M. Gregory 93; P. G. H. Fender 5 for 90)
            &   93–1 (W. Bardsley 50*)

1921: England v Australia (Played 5, Aus won 3, Eng won 0, Drawn 2)
First Test at Trent Bridge, May 28–30. Aus won by 10 wickets.
     ENG: 112   (J. M. Gregory 6 for 58)
            &   147   (E. A. McDonald 5 for 32)
     AUS: 232   (W. Bardsley 66)
            &   30–0
Second Test at Lord's, June 11–14. Aus won by 8 wickets.
     ENG: 187   (F. E. Woolley 95; A. A. Mailey 4 for 55, E. A. McDonald 4 for 58)
            &   283   (F. E. Woolley 93, Hon. L. H. Tennyson 74*; J. M. Gregory
                         4 for 76, E. A. McDonald 4 for 89)
     AUS: 342   (W. Bardsley 88, J. M. Gregory 52; F. J. Durston 4 for 102)
            &   131–2 (W. Bardsley 63*)
Third Test at Headingley, July 2–5. Aus won by 219 runs.
     AUS: 407   (C. G. Macartney 115, W. W. Armstrong 77, C. E. Pellew 52,
                         J. M. Taylor 50; C. H. Parkin 4 for 106)
            &   273–7 dec. (T. J. E. Andrews 92)
     ENG: 259   (J. W. H. T. Douglas 75, Hon. L. H. Tennyson 63, G. Brown 57;
                         E. A. McDonald 4 for 105)
            &   202
Fourth Test at Old Trafford, July 23–26. Match Drawn.
     ENG: 362–4 dec. (C. A. G. Russell 101, G. E. Tyldesley 78*)
            &   44–1

AUS: 175   (C. H. Parkin 5 for 38)
Fifth Test at The Oval, Aug. 13–16. Match Drawn.
ENG: 403–8 dec. (C. P. Mead 182*, Hon. L. H. Tennyson 51; E. A. McDonald
    5 for 143)
  &   244–2 (C. A. G. Russell 102*, G. Brown 84, J. W. Hitch 51*)
AUS: 389   (T. J. E. Andrews 94, J. M. Taylor 75, C. G. Macartney 61)

1921–22: South Africa v Australia (Played 3, Aus won 1, SA won 0, Drawn 2)
First Test at Durban, Nov. 5–9. Match Drawn.
AUS: 299   (J. Ryder 78*, C. G. Macartney 59, J. M. Gregory 51; J. M.
    Blanckenberg 5 for 78)
  &   324–7 dec. (C. G. Macartney 116, J. Ryder 58)
SA: 232   (J. W. Zulch 80; J. M. Gregory 6 for 77)
  &   184–7
Second Test at Johannesburg, Nov. 12–16. Match Drawn.
AUS: 450   (H. L. Collins 203, J. M. Gregory 119, J. Ryder 56; C. P. Carter
    6 for 91)
  &   7–0
SA: 243   (A. W. Nourse 64; J. M. Gregory 4 for 71)
  &   472–8 dec. (C. N. Frank 152, A. W. Nourse 111, H. W. Taylor 80)
Third Test at Cape Town, Nov. 26–29. Aus won by 10 wickets.
SA: 180   (J. W. Zulch 50; A. A. Mailey 4 for 40)
  &   216   (C. G. Macartney 5 for 44)
AUS: 396   (J. Ryder 142, H. L. Collins 54; J. M. Blanckenberg 4 for 82)
  &   1–0

1922–23: South Africa v England (Played 5, Eng won 2, SA won 1, Drawn 2)
First Test at Johannesburg, Dec. 23–28. SA won by 168 runs.
SA: 148   (A. S. Kennedy 4 for 37, V. W. C. Jupp 4 for 59)
  &   420   (H. W. Taylor 176, W. H. Brann 50; A. S. Kennedy 4 for 132)
ENG: 182   (J. M. Blanckenberg 6 for 76)
  &   218   (E. P. Nupen 5 for 53)
Second Test at Cape Town, Jan. 1–4. Eng won by 1 wicket.
SA: 113   (P. G. H. Fender 4 for 29)
  &   242   (R. H. Catterall 76, H. W. Taylor 68; G. G. Macaulay 5 for 64, A. S.
    Kennedy 4 for 58)
ENG: 183   (J. M. Blanckenberg 5 for 61, A. E. Hall 4 for 49)
  &   173–9 (A. E. Hall 7 for 63)
Third Test at Durban, Jan. 18–22. Match Drawn.
ENG: 428   (C. P. Mead 181, F. T. Mann 84, P. G. H. Fender 60; A. E. Hall
    4 for 105)
  &   11–1
SA: 368   (H. W. Taylor 91, C. M. Francois 72, R. H. Catterall 52, A. W.
    Nourse 52; A. S. Kennedy 5 for 88)
Fourth Test at Johannesburg, Feb. 9–13. Match Drawn.
ENG: 244   (A. W. Carr 63; A. E. Hall 6 for 82)
  &   376–6 dec. (F. E. Woolley 115*, C. A. G. Russell 96, F. T. Mann 59, A.
    Sandham 58)
SA: 295   (T. A. Ward 64, A. W. Nourse 51, L. E. Tapscott 50*)
  &   247–4 (H. W. Taylor 101, A. W. Nourse 63)
Fifth Test at Durban, Feb. 16–22. Eng won by 109 runs.
ENG: 281   (C. A. G. Russell 140, C. P. Mead 66)
  &   241   (C. A. G. Russell 111)
SA: 179
  &   234   (H. W. Taylor 102; A. S. Kennedy 5 for 76)

1924: England v South Africa (Played 5, Eng won 3, SA won 0, Drawn 2)
First Test at Edgbaston, June 14–17. Eng won by an innings and 18 runs.
ENG: 438   (J. B. Hobbs 76, E. H. Hendren 74, H. Sutcliffe 64, F. E. Woolley
    64, R. Kilner 59; G. M. Parker 6 for 152)
SA: 30   (A. E. R. Gilligan 6 for 7, M. W. Tate 4 for 12)
  &   390   (R. H. Catterall 120, J. M. Blanckenberg 56, M. J. Susskind 51;
    A. E. R. Gilligan 5 for 83, M. W. Tate 4 for 103)
Second Test at Lord's, June 28–July 1. Eng won by an innings and 18 runs.
SA: 273   (R. H. Catterall 120, M. J. Susskind 64)

         &   240   (M. J. Susskind 53)
ENG: 531–2 dec. (J. B. Hobbs 211, F. E. Woolley 134*, H. Sutcliffe 122, E. H.
                Hendren 50*)
Third Test at Headingley, July 12–15. Eng won by 9 wickets.
ENG: 396   (E. H. Hendren 132, H. Sutcliffe 83; S. J. Pegler 4 for 116)
         &   60–1
SA: 132   (H. W. Taylor 59*; M. W. Tate 6 for 42)
         &   323   (R. H. Catterall 56, H. W. Taylor 56)
Fourth Test at Old Trafford, July 26–29. Match Drawn.
SA: 116–4 (T. A. Ward 50)
Fifth Test at The Oval, Aug. 16–19. Match Drawn.
SA: 342   (R. H. Catterall 95, M. J. Susskind 65)
ENG: 421–8 (E. H. Hendren 142, F. E. Woolley 51, M. W. Tate 50)

1924–25: Australia v England (Played 5, Aus won 4, Eng won 1)
First Test at Sydney, Dec. 19–27. Aus won by 193 runs.
AUS: 450   (H. L. Collins 114, W. H. Ponsford 110; M. W. Tate 6 for 130)
         &   452   (J. M. Taylor 108, A. J. Richardson 98, H. L. Collins 60; M. W.
                Tate 5 for 98)
ENG: 298   (J. B. Hobbs 115, E. H. Hendren 74*, H. Sutcliffe 59; J. M. Gregory
                5 for 111, A. A. Mailey 4 for 129)
         &   411   (F. E. Woolley 123, H. Sutcliffe 115, J. B. Hobbs 57, A. P. Freeman
                50*)
Second Test at Melbourne, Jan. 1–8. Aus won by 81 runs.
AUS: 600   (V. Y. Richardson 138, W. H. Ponsford 128, A. E. V. Hartkopf 80,
                J. M. Taylor 72)
         &   250   (J. M. Taylor 90; M. W. Tate 6 for 99, J. W. Hearne 4 for 84)
ENG: 479   (H. Sutcliffe 176, J. B. Hobbs 154)
         &   290   (H. Sutcliffe 127, F. E. Woolley 50; A. A. Mailey 5 for 92, J. M.
                Gregory 4 for 87)
Third Test at Adelaide, Jan. 16–23. Aus won by 11 runs.
AUS: 489   (J. Ryder 201*, T. J. E. Andrews 72, A. J. Richardson 69; R. Kilner
                4 for 127)
         &   250   (J. Ryder 88; R. Kilner 4 for 51, F. E. Woolley 4 for 77)
ENG: 365   (J. B. Hobbs 119, E. H. Hendren 92)
         &   363   (W. W. Whysall 75, H. Sutcliffe 59, A. P. F. Chapman 58)
Fourth Test at Melbourne, Feb. 13–18. Eng won by an innings and 29 runs.
ENG: 548   (H. Sutcliffe 143, W. W. Whysall 76, R. Kilner 74, J. B. Hobbs 66,
                E. H. Hendren 65; A. A. Mailey 4 for 186)
AUS: 269   (J. M. Taylor 86)
         &   250   (J. M. Taylor 68; M. W. Tate 5 for 75)
Fifth Test at Sydney, Feb. 27–Mar. 4. Aus won by 307 runs.
AUS: 295   (W. H. Ponsford 80; M. W. Tate 4 for 92, R. Kilner 4 for 97)
         &   325   (T. J. E. Andrews 80, C. Kelleway 73, W. A. S. Oldfield 65*; M. W.
                Tate 5 for 115)
ENG: 167   (C. V. Grimmett 5 for 45)
         &   146   (C. V. Grimmett 6 for 37)

1926: England v Australia (Played 5, Eng won 1, Aus won 0, Drawn 4)
First Test at Trent Bridge, June 12–15. Match Drawn.
ENG: 32–0
Second Test at Lord's, June 26–29. Match Drawn.
AUS: 383   (W. Bardsley 193*; R. Kilner 4 for 70)
         &   194–5 (C. G. Macartney 133*)
ENG: 475–3 dec. (E. H. Hendren 127*, J. B. Hobbs 119, F. E. Woolley 87, H.
                Sutcliffe 82, A. P. F. Chapman 50*)
Third Test at Headingley, July 10–13. Match Drawn.
AUS: 494   (C. G. Macartney 151, W. M. Woodfull 141, A. J. Richardson 100;
                M. W. Tate 4 for 99)
ENG: 294   (G. G. Macaulay 76; C. V. Grimmett 5 for 88)
         &   254–3 (H. Sutcliffe 94, J. B. Hobbs 88)
Fourth Test at Old Trafford, July 24–27. Match Drawn.
AUS: 335   (W. M. Woodfull 117, C. G. Macartney 109; C. F. Root 4 for 84)
ENG: 305–5 (G. E. Tyldesley 81, J. B. Hobbs 74, F. E. Woolley 58)

Fifth Test at The Oval, Aug. 14–18. Eng won by 289 runs.
```
ENG:   280   (H. Sutcliffe 76; A. A. Mailey 6 for 138)
  &    436   (H. Sutcliffe 161, J. B. Hobbs 100)
AUS:   302   (J. M. Gregory 73, H. L. Collins 61)
  &    125   (W. Rhodes 4 for 44)
```

1927–28: South Africa v England (Played 5, Eng won 2, SA won 2, Drawn 1)
First Test at Johannesburg, Dec. 24–27. Eng won by 10 wickets.
```
SA:    196   (R. H. Catterall 86; G. Geary 7 for 70)
  &    170   (C. L. Vincent 53; W. R. Hammond 5 for 36, G. Geary 5 for 60)
ENG:   313   (G. E. Tyldesley 122, H. Sutcliffe 102, W. R. Hammond 51; H. L.
             E. Promnitz 5 for 58)
  &     57–0
```
Second Test at Cape Town, Dec. 31–Jan. 4. Eng won by 87 runs.
```
ENG:   133   (G. F. Bissett 5 for 37, C. L. Vincent 4 for 22)
  &    428   (H. Sutcliffe 99, R. E. S. Wyatt 91, P. Holmes 88, G. E. Tyldesley 87)
SA:    250   (H. W. Taylor 68; A. P. Freeman 4 for 58)
  &    224   (H. W. Taylor 71)
```
Third Test at Durban, Jan. 21–25. Match Drawn.
```
SA:    246   (H. G. Deane 77, E. P. Nupen 51)
  &    464–8 dec. (J. F. W. Nicolson 78, R. H. Catterall 76, H. G. Deane 73,
             E. P. Nupen 69, H. W. Taylor 60)
ENG:   430   (W. R. Hammond 90, G. E. Tyldesley 78, P. Holmes 70, G. T. S.
             Stevens 69; C. L. Vincent 6 for 131, E. P. Nupen 4 for 94)
  &    132–2 (G. E. Tyldesley 62*, P. Holmes 56)
```
Fourth Test at Johannesburg, Jan. 28–Feb. 1. SA won by 4 wickets.
```
ENG:   265   (R. E. S. Wyatt 58; A. E. Hall 6 for 100, G. F. Bissett 4 for 43)
  &    215   (P. Holmes 63; G. F. Bissett 4 for 70)
SA:    328   (H. W. Taylor 101, H. B. Cameron 64)
  &    156–6
```
Fifth Test at Durban, Feb. 4–8. SA won by 8 wickets.
```
ENG:   282   (G. E. Tyldesley 100, W. R. Hammond 66, H. Sutcliffe 51; E. P.
             Nupen 5 for 83)
  &    118   (G. F. Bissett 7 for 29)
SA:    332–7 dec. (R. H. Catterall 119, H. B. Cameron 53)
  &     69–2
```

1928: England v West Indies (Played 3, Eng won 3, WI won 0)
First Test at Lord's, June 23–26. Eng won by an innings and 58 runs.
```
ENG:   401   (G. E. Tyldesley 122, A. P. F. Chapman 50; L. N. Constantine
             4 for 82)
WI:    177   (V. W. C. Jupp 4 for 37)
  &    166   (J. A. Small 52; A. P. Freeman 4 for 37)
```
Second Test at Old Trafford, July 21–24. Eng won by an innings and 30 runs.
```
WI:    206   (C. A. Roach 50; A. P. Freeman 5 for 54)
  &    115   (A. P. Freeman 5 for 39)
ENG:   351   (D. R. Jardine 83, W. R. Hammond 63, H. Sutcliffe 54, J. B. Hobbs
             53)
```
Third Test at The Oval, Aug. 11–14. Eng won by an innings and 71 runs.
```
WI:    238   (C. A. Roach 53; M. W. Tate 4 for 59)
  &    129   (A. P. Freeman 4 for 47)
ENG:   438   (J. B. Hobbs 159, G. E. Tyldesley 73, H. Sutcliffe 63, M. W. Tate
             54; H. C. Griffith 6 for 103, G. N. Francis 4 for 112)
```

1928–29: Australia v England (Played 5, Eng won 4, Aus won 1)
First Test at Brisbane, Nov. 30–Dec. 5. Eng won by 675 runs.
```
ENG:   521   (E. H. Hendren 169, H. Larwood 70, A. P. F. Chapman 50)
  &    342–8 dec. (C. P. Mead 73, D. R. Jardine 65*; C. V. Grimmett 6 for 131)
AUS:   122   (H. Larwood 6 for 32)
  &     66   (J. C. White 4 for 7)
```
Second Test at Sydney, Dec. 14–20. Eng won by 8 wickets.
```
AUS:   253   (W. M. Woodfull 68; G. Geary 5 for 35)
  &    397   (H. S. T. L. Hendry 112, W. M. Woodfull 111, J. Ryder 79; M. W.
             Tate 4 for 99)
```

ENG: 636　(W. R. Hammond 251, E. H. Hendren 74, G. Geary 66; D. D. J. Blackie 4 for 148)
&　16–2

Third Test at Melbourne, Dec. 29–Jan. 5. Eng won by 3 wickets.
AUS: 397　(J. Ryder 112, A. F. Kippax 100, D. G. Bradman 79)
&　351　(D. G. Bradman 112, W. M. Woodfull 107; J. C. White 5 for 107)
ENG: 417　(W. R. Hammond 200, D. R. Jardine 62, H. Sutcliffe 58; D. D. J. Blackie 6 for 94)
&　332–7　(H. Sutcliffe 135)

Fourth Test at Adelaide, Feb. 1–8. Eng won by 12 runs.
ENG: 334　(W. R. Hammond 119*, J. B. Hobbs 74, H. Sutcliffe 64; C. V. Grimmett 5 for 102)
&　383　(W. R. Hammond 177, D. R. Jardine 98; R. K. Oxenham 4 for 67)
AUS: 369　(A. A. Jackson 164, J. Ryder 63; J. C. White 5 for 130, M. W. Tate 4 for 77)
&　336　(J. Ryder 87, D. G. Bradman 58, A. F. Kippax 51; J. C. White 8 for 126)

Fifth Test at Melbourne, Mar. 8–16. Aus won by 5 wickets.
ENG: 519　(J. B. Hobbs 142, M. Leyland 137, E. H. Hendren 95)
&　257　(J. B. Hobbs 65, M. W. Tate 54, M. Leyland 53*; T. W. Wall 5 for 66)
AUS: 491　(D. G. Bradman 123, W. M. Woodfull 102, A. G. Fairfax 65; G. Geary 5 for 105)
&　287–5　(J. Ryder 57*)

1929: England v South Africa (Played 5, Eng won 2, SA won 0, Drawn 3)
First Test at Edgbaston, June 15–18. Match Drawn.
ENG: 245　(E. H. Hendren 70; A. L. Ochse 4 for 79)
&　308–4 dec. (W. R. Hammond 138*, H. Sutcliffe 114)
SA: 250　(B. Mitchell 88, R. H. Catterall 67; H. Larwood 5 for 57)
&　171–1　(R. H. Catterall 98, B. Mitchell 61*)

Second Test at Lord's, June 29–July 2. Match Drawn.
ENG: 302　(H. Sutcliffe 100, M. Leyland 73; A. J. Bell 6 for 99, D. P. B. Morkel 4 for 93)
&　312–8 dec. (M. Leyland 102, M. W. Tate 100*; A. L. Ochse 4 for 99)
SA: 322　(D. P. B. Morkel 88, J. A. J. Christy 70, H. G. Owen-Smith 52*)
&　90–5

Third Test at Headingley, July 13–16. Eng won by 5 wickets.
SA: 236　(R. H. Catterall 74, C. L. Vincent 60; A. P. Freeman 7 for 115)
&　275　(H. G. Owen-Smith 129)
ENG: 328　(F. E. Woolley 83, W. R. Hammond 65; N. A. Quinn 6 for 92)
&　186–5　(F. E. Woolley 95*)

Fourth Test at Old Trafford, July 27–30. Eng won by an innings and 32 runs.
ENG: 427–7 dec. (F. E. Woolley 154, R. E. S. Wyatt 113, M. Leyland 55)
SA: 130　(D. P. B. Morkel 63; A. P. Freeman 7 for 71)
&　265　(H. B. Cameron 83, H. W. Taylor 70; A. P. Freeman 5 for 100)

Fifth Test at The Oval, Aug. 17–20. Match Drawn.
ENG: 258　(H. Sutcliffe 104; C. L. Vincent 5 for 105)
&　264–1　(H. Sutcliffe 109*, W. R. Hammond 101*, J. B. Hobbs 52)
SA: 492–8 dec. (H. W. Taylor 121, H. G. Deane 93, D. P. B. Morkel 81, H.B. Cameron 62, Q. McMillan 50*)

1929–30: New Zealand v England (Played 4, Eng won 1, NZ won 0, Drawn 3)
First Test at Christchurch, Jan. 10–13. Eng won by 8 wickets.
NZ: 112　(M. J. C. Allom 5 for 38, M. S. Nichols 4 for 28)
&　131
ENG: 181
&　66–2

Second Test at Wellington, Jan. 24–27. Match Drawn.
NZ: 440　(C. S. Dempster 136, J. E. Mills 117, M. L. Page 67; F. E. Woolley 7 for 76)
&　164–4 dec. (C. S. Dempster 80*)
ENG: 320　(M. S. Nichols 78*; F. T. Badcock 4 for 80)
&　107–4　(K. S. Duleepsinhji 56*)

Third Test at Auckland, Feb. 14–17. Match Drawn.
ENG: 330–4 dec. (K. S. Duleepsinhji 117, E. H. Bowley 109, F. E. Woolley 59)
NZ: 96–1 (C. S. Dempster 62*)
Fourth Test at Auckland, Feb. 21–24. Match Drawn.
ENG: 540 (G. B. Legge 196, M. S. Nichols 75, K. S. Duleepsinhji 63, E. W. Dawson 55)
& 22–3
NZ: 387 (T. C. Lowry 80, G. L. Weir 63, H. M. McGirr 51; M. J. C. Allom 4 for 42)

1929–30: West Indies v England (Played 4, West Indies won 1, Eng won 1, Drawn 2)
First Test at Bridgetown, Jan. 11–16. Match Drawn.
WI: 369 (C. A. Roach 122, F. I. de Caires 80, J. E. D. Sealey 58; G. T. S. Stevens 5 for 105)
& 384 (G. A. Headley 176, C. A. Roach 77, F. I. de Caires 70; G. T. S. Stevens 5 for 90)
ENG: 467 (A. Sandham 152, E. H. Hendren 80)
& 167–3 (A. Sandham 51)
Second Test at Port of Spain, Feb. 1–6. Eng won by 167 runs.
ENG: 208 (E. H. Hendren 77; H. C. Griffith 5 for 63)
& 425–8 dec. (E. H. Hendren 205*, L. E. G. Ames 105; L. N. Constantine 4 for 165)
WI: 254 (E. A. C. Hunte 58, L. N. Constantine 52; W. E. Astill 4 for 58, W. Voce 4 for 79)
& 212 (W. Voce 7 for 70)
Third Test at Georgetown, Feb. 21–26. WI won by 289 runs.
WI: 471 (C. A. Roach 209, G. A. Headley 114, E. A. C. Hunte 53)
& 290 (G. A. Headley 112, C. R. Browne 70*; W. E. Astill 4 for 70)
ENG: 145 (E. H. Hendren 56; L. N. Constantine 4 for 35, G. N. Francis 4 for 40)
& 327 (E. H. Hendren 123; L. N. Constantine 5 for 87)
Fourth Test at Kingston, April 3–12. Match Drawn.
ENG: 849 (A. Sandham 325, L. E. G. Ames 149, G. Gunn 85, E. H. Hendren 61, J. O'Connor 51, R. E. S. Wyatt 58; O. C. Scott 5 for 266)
& 272–9 dec. (E. H. Hendren 55, A. Sandham 50; O. C. Scott 4 for 108)
WI: 286 (R. K. Nunes 66)
& 408–5 (G. A. Headley 223, R. K. Nunes 92)

1930: England v Australia (Played 5, Aus won 2, Eng won 1, Drawn 2)
First Test at Trent Bridge, June 13–17. Eng won by 93 runs.
ENG: 270 (J. B. Hobbs 78, A. P. F. Chapman 52, R. W. V. Robins 50*; C. V. Grimmett 5 for 107)
& 302 (J. B. Hobbs 74, E. H. Hendren 72, H. Sutcliffe 58 retired hurt; C. V. Grimmett 5 for 94)
AUS: 144 (A. F. Kippax 64*; R. W. V. Robins 4 for 51)
& 335 (D. G. Bradman 131)
Second Test at Lord's, June 27–July 1. Aus won by 7 wickets.
ENG: 425 (K. S. Duleepsinhji 173, M. W. Tate 54; A. G. Fairfax 4 for 101)
& 375 (A. P. F. Chapman 121, G. O. B. Allen 57; C. V. Grimmett 6 for 167)
AUS: 729–6 dec. (D. G. Bradman 254, W. M. Woodfull 155, A. F. Kippax 83, W. H. Ponsford 81)
& 72–3
Third Test at Headingley, July 11–15. Match Drawn.
AUS: 566 (D. G. Bradman 334, A. F. Kippax 77, W. M. Woodfull 50; M. W. Tate 5 for 124)
ENG: 391 (W. R. Hammond 113, C. V. Grimmett 5 for 135)
& 95–3
Fourth Test at Old Trafford, July 25–29. Match Drawn.
AUS: 345 (W. H. Ponsford 83, W. M. Woodfull 54, A. F. Kippax 51, C. V. Grimmett 50)
ENG: 251–8 (H. Sutcliffe 74, K. S. Duleepsinhji 54; S. J. McCabe 4 for 41)
Fifth Test at The Oval, Aug. 16–22. Aus won by an innings and 39 runs.
ENG: 405 (H. Sutcliffe 161, R. E. S. Wyatt 64, K. S. Duleepsinhji 50; C. V.

          Grimmett 4 for 135)
          &   251   (W. R. Hammond 60, H. Sutcliffe 54; P. M. Hornibrook 7 for 92)
  AUS: 695   (D. G. Bradman 232, W. H. Ponsford 110, A. A. Jackson 73, W. M.
                    Woodfull 54, S. J. McCabe 54, A. G. Fairfax 53*; I. A. R. Peebles
                    6 for 204)

1930-31: Australia v West Indies (Played 5, Aus won 4, WI won 1)
First Test at Adelaide, Dec. 12–16. Aus won by 10 wickets.
    WI: 296   (E. L. Bartlett 84, C. A. Roach 56, G. C. Grant 53*; C. V. Grim-
                mett 7 for 87)
      &   249   (G. C. Grant 71*, L. S. Birkett 64; A. Hurwood 4 for 86, C. V.
                Grimmett 4 for 96)
  AUS: 376   (A. F. Kippax 146, S. J. McCabe 90; O. C. Scott 4 for 83)
      &   172–0   (W. H. Ponsford 92*, A. Jackson 70*)
Second Test at Sydney, Jan. 1–5. Aus won by an innings and 172 runs.
  AUS: 369   (W. H. Ponsford 183, W. M. Woodfull 58; O. C. Scott 4 for 66)
    WI: 107   (C. V. Grimmett 4 for 54)
      &   90   (A. Hurwood 4 for 22)
Third Test at Brisbane, Jan. 16–20. Aus won by an innings and 217 runs.
  AUS: 558   (D. G. Bradman 223, W. H. Ponsford 109, A. F. Kippax 84; H. C.
                Griffith 4 for 133)
    WI: 193   (G. A. Headley 102*; R. K. Oxenham 4 for 39, C. V. Grimmett
                4 for 95)
      &   148   (C. V. Grimmett 5 for 49)
Fourth Test at Melbourne, Feb. 13–14. Aus won by an innings and 122 runs.
    WI: 99   (H. Ironmonger 7 for 23)
      &   107   (A. G. Fairfax 4 for 31, H. Ironmonger 4 for 56)
  AUS: 328–8 dec. (D. G. Bradman 152, W. M. Woodfull 83)
Fifth Test at Sydney, Feb. 27–Mar. 4. WI won by 30 runs.
    WI: 350–6 dec. (F. R. Martin 123*, G. A. Headley 105, G. C. Grant 62)
      &   124–5 dec.
  AUS: 224   (A. G. Fairfax 54; G. N. Francis 4 for 48)
      &   220   (A. G. Fairfax 60*; H. C. Griffith 4 for 50)

1930-31: South Africa v England (Played 5, SA won 1, Eng won 0, Drawn 4)
First Test at Johannesburg, Dec. 24–27. SA won by 28 runs.
    SA: 126   (I. A. R. Peebles 4 for 43, W. Voce 4 for 45)
      &   306   (B. Mitchell 72, R. H. Catterall 54, H. B. Cameron 51; W. Voce
                4 for 59, W. R. Hammond 4 for 63)
  ENG: 193   (E. P. Nupen 5 for 63)
      &   211   (W. R. Hammond 63, M. J. Turnbull 61; E. P. Nupen 6 for 87)
Second Test at Cape Town, Jan. 1–5. Match Drawn.
    SA: 513–8 dec. (I. J. Siedle 141, B. Mitchell 123, H. W. Taylor 117, R. H.
                Catterall 56)
  ENG: 350   (E. H. Hendren 93, W. R. Hammond 57, M. Leyland 52)
      &   252   (E. H. Hendren 86, W. R. Hammond 65)
Third Test at Durban, Jan. 16–20. Match Drawn.
    SA: 177   (W. Voce 5 for 58)
      &   145–8 (H. W. Taylor 64*)
  ENG: 223–1 dec. (W. R. Hammond 136*, R. E. S. Wyatt 54)
Fourth Test at Johannesburg, Feb. 13–17. Match Drawn.
  ENG: 442   (M. Leyland 91, W. R. Hammond 75, E. H. Hendren 64; A. E. Hal
                4 for 105)
      &   169–9 dec. (E. P. Nupen 6 for 46)
    SA: 295   (H. W. Taylor 72, B. Mitchell 68, I. J. Siedle 62; I. A. R. Peebles
                6 for 63)
      &   280–7 (B. Mitchell 74, H. B. Cameron 69*; W. Voce 4 for 87)
Fifth Test at Durban, Feb. 21–25. Match Drawn.
    SA: 252   (B. Mitchell 73, I. J. Siedle 57; I. A. R. Peebles 4 for 67)
      &   219–7 dec.
  ENG: 230   (M. W. Tate 50; C. L. Vincent 6 for 51)
      &   72–4

1931: England v New Zealand (Played 3, Eng won 1, NZ won 0, Drawn 2)
First Test at Lord's, June 27–30. Match Drawn.

NZ: 224   (C. S. Dempster 53; I. A. R. Peebles 5 for 77)
  &   469–9 dec. (C. S. Dempster 120, M. L. Page 104, R. C. Blunt 96; I. A. R.
      Peebles 4 for 150)
ENG: 454   (L. E. G. Ames 137, G. O. B. Allen 122, F. E. Woolley 80; W. E.
      Merritt 4 for 104)
  &   146–5
Second Test at The Oval, July 29–31. Eng won by an innings and 26 runs.
ENG: 416–4 dec. (H. Sutcliffe 117, K. S. Duleepsinhji 109, W. R. Hammond
      100*)
NZ: 193   (T. C. Lowry 62; G. O. B. Allen 5 for 14)
  &   197   (H. G. Vivian 51; I. A. R. Peebles 4 for 63)
Third Test at Old Trafford, Aug. 15–18. Match Drawn.
ENG: 224–3 (H. Sutcliffe 109*, K. S. Duleepsinhji 63)

1931–32: Australia v South Africa (Played 5, Aus won 5, SA won 0)
First Test at Brisbane, Nov. 27–Dec. 3. Aus won by an innings and 163 runs.
AUS: 450   (D. G. Bradman 226, W. M. Woodfull 76, W. A. S. Oldfield 56*;
      A. J. Bell 4 for 120)
SA: 170   (B. Mitchell 58; H. Ironmonger 5 for 42)
  &   117   (T. W. Wall 5 for 14, H. Ironmonger 4 for 44)
Second Test at Sydney, Dec. 18–21. Aus won by an innings and 155 runs.
SA: 153   (S. J. McCabe 4 for 13, C. V. Grimmett 4 for 28)
  &   161   (C. V. Grimmett 4 for 44)
AUS: 469   (K. E. Rigg 127, D. G. Bradman 112, S. J. McCabe 79, W. M.
      Woodfull 58; A. J. Bell 5 for 140)
Third Test at Melbourne, Dec. 31–Jan. 6. Aus won by 169 runs.
AUS: 198   (K. E. Rigg 68, A. F. Kippax 52; A. J. Bell 5 for 69, N. A. Quinn
      4 for 42)
  &   554   (D. G. Bradman 167, W. M. Woodfull 161, S. J. McCabe 71, A. F.
      Kippax 67; Q. McMillan 4 for 150, C. L. Vincent 4 for 154)
SA: 358   (K. G. Viljoen 111)
  &   225   (J. A. J. Christy 63; C. V. Grimmett 6 for 92, H. Ironmonger
      4 for 54)
Fourth Test at Adelaide, Jan. 29–Feb. 2. Aus won by 10 wickets.
SA: 308   (H. W. Taylor 78, B. Mitchell 75, H. B. Cameron 52; C. V. Grim-
      mett 7 for 116)
  &   274   (B. Mitchell 95, H. W. Taylor 84, J. A. J. Christy 51; C. V. Grim-
      mett 7 for 83)
AUS: 513   (D. G. Bradman 299*, W. M. Woodfull 82; A. J. Bell 5 for 142)
  &   73–0
Fifth Test at Melbourne, Feb. 12–15. Aus won by an innings and 72 runs.
SA: 36   (H. Ironmonger 5 for 6, L. J. Nash 4 for 18)
  &   45   (H. Ironmonger 6 for 18)
AUS: 153

1931–32: New Zealand v South Africa (Played 2, SA won 2, NZ won 0)
First Test at Christchurch, Feb. 27–Mar. 1. SA won by an innings and 12 runs
NZ: 293   (F. T. Badcock 64, A. W. Roberts 54; Q. McMillan 4 for 61)
  &   146   (G. L. Weir 74*; Q. McMillan 5 for 66)
SA: 451   (B. Mitchell 113, J. A. J. Christy 103, E. L. Dalton 82, D. P. B.
      Morkel 51)
Second Test at Wellington, Mar. 4–7. SA won by 8 wickets.
NZ: 364   (H. G. Vivian 100, C. S. Dempster 64, F. T. Badcock 53, I. B.
      Cromb 51*; Q. McMillan 5 for 125)
  &   193   (H. G. Vivian 73; N. A. Quinn 4 for 37)
SA: 410   (X. C. Balaskas 122*, K. G. Viljoen 81, J. A. J. Christy 62; H. G.
      Vivian 4 for 58)
  &   150–2 (B. Mitchell 53, J. A. J. Christy 53)

1932: England v India (Played 1, Eng won 1)
Test at Lord's, June 25–28. Eng won by 158 runs.
ENG: 259   (D. R. Jardine 79, L. E. G. Ames 65; M. Nissar 5 for 93)
  &   275–8 dec. (D. R. Jardine 85*, E. Paynter 54; M. Jahangir Khan 4 for 60)
IND: 189   (W. E. Bowes 4 for 49)
  &   187   (L. Amar Singh 51)

1932–33: Australia v England (Played 5, Eng won 4, Aus won 1)
First Test at Sydney, Dec. 2–7. Eng won by 10 wickets.
    AUS: 360   (S. J. McCabe 187*; H. Larwood 5 for 96, W. Voce 4 for 110)
        &   164   (H. Larwood 5 for 28)
    ENG: 524   (H. Sutcliffe 194, W. R. Hammond 112, Nawab of Pataudi 102)
        &   1–0
Second Test at Melbourne, Dec. 30–Jan. 3. Aus won by 111 runs.
    AUS: 228   (J. H. Fingleton 83)
        &   191   (D. G. Bradman 103*)
    ENG: 169   (H. Sutcliffe 52; W. J. O'Reilly 5 for 63, T. W. Wall 4 for 52)
        &   139   (W. J. O'Reilly 5 for 66, H. Ironmonger 4 for 26)
Third Test at Adelaide, Jan. 13–19. Eng won by 338 runs.
    ENG: 341   (M. Leyland 83, R. E. S. Wyatt 78, E. Paynter 77; T. W. Wall
               5 for 72)
        &   412   (W. R. Hammond 85, L. E. G. Ames 69, D. R. Jardine 56; W. J.
               O'Reilly 4 for 79)
    AUS: 222   (W. H. Ponsford 85; G. O. B. Allen 4 for 71)
        &   193   (W. M. Woodfull 73*, D. G. Bradman 66; G. O. B. Allen 4 for 50,
               H. Larwood 4 for 71)
Fourth Test at Brisbane, Feb. 10–16. Eng won by 6 wickets.
    AUS: 340   (V. Y. Richardson 83, D. G. Bradman 76, W. M. Woodfull 67;
               H. Larwood 4 for 101)
        &   175
    ENG: 356   (H. Sutcliffe 86, E. Paynter 83; W. J. O'Reilly 4 for 120)
        & 162–4 (M. Leyland 86)
Fifth Test at Sydney, Feb. 23–28. Eng won by 8 wickets.
    AUS: 435   (L. S. Darling 85, S. J. McCabe 73, L. P. J. O'Brien 61, W. A. S.
               Oldfield 52; H. Larwood 4 for 98)
        &   182   (D. G. Bradman 71, W. M. Woodfull 67; H. Verity 5 for 33)
    ENG: 454   (W. R. Hammond 101, H. Larwood 98, H. Sutcliffe 56, R. E. S.
               Wyatt 51; P. K. Lee 4 for 111)
        & 168–2 (W. R. Hammond 75*, R. E. S. Wyatt 61*)

1932–33: New Zealand v England (Played 2, NZ won 0, Eng won 0, Drawn 2)
First Test at Christchurch, Mar. 24–27. Match Drawn.
    ENG: 560–8 dec. (W. R. Hammond 227, L. E. G. Ames 103, F. R. Brown 74,
               W. Voce 66)
    NZ: 223   (G. L. Weir 66, J. L. Kerr 59)
        &   35–0
Second Test at Auckland, Mar. 31–April 3. Match Drawn.
    NZ: 158   (C. S. Dempster 83*; W. E. Bowes 6 for 34)
        &   16–0
    ENG: 548–7 dec. (W. R. Hammond 336*, R. E. S. Wyatt 60)

1933: England v West Indies (Played 3, Eng won 2, WI won 0, Drawn 1)
First Test at Lord's, June 24–27. Eng won by an innings and 27 runs.
    ENG: 296   (L. E. G. Ames 83*, C. F. Walters 51; E. A. Martindale 4 for 85)
    WI: 97   (R. W. V. Robins 6 for 32)
        &   172   (G. A. Headley 50; H. Verity 4 for 45, G. G. Macaulay 4 for 57)
Second Test at Old Trafford, July 22–25. Match Drawn.
    WI: 375   (G. A. Headley 169*, I. Barrow 105; E. W. Clark 4 for 99)
        &   225   (C. A. Roach 64, L. N. Constantine 64; James Langridge 7 for 56)
    ENG: 374   (D. R. Jardine 127, R. W. V. Robins 55; E. A. Martindale 5 for 73)
Third Test at The Oval, Aug. 12–15. Eng won by an innings and 17 runs.
    ENG: 312   (A. H. Bakewell 107, C. J. Barnett 52; E. A. Martindale 5 for 93)
    WI: 100   (C. S. Marriott 5 for 37)
        &   195   (C. A. Roach 56; C. S. Marriott 6 for 59)

1933–34: India v England (Played 3, Eng won 2, India won 0, Drawn 1)
First Test at Bombay, Dec. 15–18. Eng won by 9 wickets.
    IND: 219
        &   258   (L. Amarnath 118, C. K. Nayudu 67; M. S. Nichols 5 for 55)
    ENG: 438   (B. H. Valentine 136, C. F. Walters 78, D. R. Jardine 60; M. Nissar
               5 for 90)
        &   40–1

Second Test at Calcutta, Jan. 5–8. Match Drawn.
ENG: 403   (James Langridge 70, D. R. Jardine 61, H. Verity 55*, L. Amar
                    Singh 4 for 106)
         &   7–2
IND: 247   (Dilawar Hussain 59, V. M. Merchant 54; H. Verity 4 for 64)
         & 237   (Dilawar Hussain 57; H. Verity 4 for 76)

Third Test at Madras, Feb. 10–13. Eng won by 202 runs.
ENG: 335   (A. H. Bakewell 85, D. R. Jardine 65, C. F. Walters 59; L. Amar
                    Singh 7 for 86)
         & 261–7 dec. (C. F. Walters 102; S. Nazir Ali 4 for 83)
IND: 145   (H. Verity 7 for 49)
         & 249   (Yuvraj of Patiala 60; James Langridge 5 for 63, H. Verity 4 for 104)

1934: England v Australia (Played 5, Aus won 2, Eng won 1, Drawn 2)
First Test at Trent Bridge, June 8–12. Aus won by 238 runs.
AUS: 374   (A. G. Chipperfield 99, S. J. McCabe 65, W. H. Ponsford 53; K.
                    Farnes 5 for 102)
         & 273–8 dec. (S. J. McCabe 88, W. A. Brown 73; K. Farnes 5 for 77)
ENG: 268   (E. H. Hendren 79, H. Sutcliffe 62, G. Geary 53; C. V. Grimmett
                    5 for 81, W. J. O'Reilly 4 for 75)
         & 141   (W. J. O'Reilly 7 for 54)

Second Test at Lord's, June 22–25. Eng won by an innings and 38 runs.
ENG: 440   (L. E. G. Ames 120, M. Leyland 109, C. F. Walters 82; T. W. Wall
                    4 for 108)
AUS: 284   (W. A. Brown 105; H. Verity 7 for 61)
         & 118   (H. Verity 8 for 43)

Third Test at Old Trafford, July 6–10. Match Drawn.
ENG: 627–9 dec. (M. Leyland 153, E. H. Hendren 132, L. E. G. Ames 72, H.
                    Sutcliffe 63, G. O. B. Allen 61, H. Verity 60*, C. F. Walters 52;
                    W. J. O'Reilly 7 for 189)
         & 123–0 dec. (H. Sutcliffe 69*, C. F. Walters 50*)
AUS: 491   (S. J. McCabe 137, W. M. Woodfull 73, W. A. Brown 72; H.
                    Verity 4 for 78)
         &   66–1

Fourth Test at Headingley, July 20–24. Match Drawn.
ENG: 200   (C. V. Grimmett 4 for 57)
         & 229–6
AUS: 584   (D. G. Bradman 304, W. H. Ponsford 181; W. E. Bowes 6 for 142)

Fifth Test at The Oval, Aug. 18–22. Aus won by 562 runs.
AUS: 701   (W. H. Ponsford 266, D. G. Bradman 244; W. E. Bowes 4 for 164,
                    G. O. B. Allen 4 for 170)
         & 327   (D. G. Bradman 77, S. J. McCabe 70; W. E. Bowes 5 for 55, E. W.
                    Clark 5 for 98)
ENG: 321   (M. Leyland 110, C. F. Walters 64)
         & 145   (C. V. Grimmett 5 for 64)

1934–35: West Indies v England (Played 4, WI won 2, Eng won 1, Drawn 1)
First Test at Bridgetown, Jan. 8–10. Eng won by 4 wickets.
WI: 102   (K. Farnes 4 for 40)
         & 51–6 dec. (C. I. J. Smith 5 for 16)
ENG: 81–7 dec.
         & 75–6 (E. A. Martindale 5 for 22)

Second Test at Port of Spain, Jan. 24–28. WI won by 217 runs.
WI: 302   (J. E. D. Sealy 92, L. N. Constantine 90; C. I. J. Smith 4 for 100)
         & 280–6 dec. (G. A. Headley 93)
ENG: 258   (E. R. T. Holmes 85*, J. Iddon 73)
         & 107

Third Test at Georgetown, Feb. 14–18. Match Drawn.
ENG: 226   (L. G. Hylton 4 for 27)
         & 160–6 dec. (R. E. S. Wyatt 71)
WI: 184   (G. A. Headley 53, K. L. Wishart 52; W. E. Hollies 7 for 50)
         & 104–5

Fourth Test at Kingston, Mar. 14–18. WI won by an innings and 161 runs.
WI: 535–7 dec. (G. A. Headley 270*, J. E. D. Sealy 91, R. S. Grant 77; G. A. E.

Paine 5 for 168)
ENG: 271   (L. E. G. Ames 126, J. Iddon 54)
  & 103   (E. A. Martindale 4 for 28)

1935: England v South Africa (Played 5, SA won 1, Eng won 0, Drawn 4)
First Test at Trent Bridge, June 15–18. Match Drawn.
ENG: 384–7 dec. (R. E. S. Wyatt 149, M. Leyland 69, H. Sutcliffe 61)
SA: 220   (I. J. Siedle 59, H. B. Cameron 52; M. S. Nichols 6 for 35)
  &   17–1
Second Test at Lord's, June 29–July 2. SA won by 157 runs.
SA: 228   (H. B. Cameron 90)
  & 278–7 dec. (B. Mitchell 164*)
ENG: 198   (R. E. S. Wyatt 53; X. C. Balaskas 5 for 49)
  & 151   (A. B. C. Langton 4 for 31, X. C. Balaskas 4 for 54)
Third Test at Headingley, July 13–16. Match Drawn.
ENG: 216   (W. R. Hammond 63, A. Mitchell 58; C. L. Vincent 4 for 45,
          A. B. C. Langton 4 for 59)
  & 294–7 dec. (W. R. Hammond 87*, A. Mitchell 72, D. Smith 57; C. L.
          Vincent 4 for 104)
SA: 171   (E. A. B. Rowan 62)
  & 194–5 (B. Mitchell 58)
Fourth Test at Old Trafford, July 27–30. Match Drawn.
ENG: 357   (R. W. V. Robins 108, A. H. Bakewell 63, M. Leyland 53; R. J.
          Crisp 5 for 99)
  & 231–6 dec. (W. R. Hammond 63*, A. H. Bakewell 54; C. L. Vincent
          4 for 78)
SA: 318   (K. G. Viljoen 124, H. B. Cameron 53; W. E. Bowes 5 for 100)
  & 169–2 (A. D. Nourse 53*)
Fifth Test at The Oval, Aug. 17–20. Match Drawn.
SA: 476   (B. Mitchell 128, E. L. Dalton 117, A. B. C. Langton 73*, K. G.
          Viljoen 60; H. D. Read 4 for 136)
  & 287–6 (E. L. Dalton 57*)
ENG: 534–6 dec. (M. Leyland 161, L. E. G. Ames 148*, W. R. Hammond 65)

1935–36: South Africa v Australia (Played 5, Aus won 4, SA won 0, Drawn 1)
First Test at Durban, Dec. 14–18. Aus won by 9 wickets.
SA: 248   (E. A. B. Rowan 66; L. O'B. Fleetwood-Smith 4 for 64)
  & 282   (A. D. Nourse 91, I. J. Siedle 59; W. J. O'Reilly 5 for 49)
AUS: 429   (S. J. McCabe 149, A. G. Chipperfield 109, W. A. Brown 66, L. S.
          Darling 60; A. B. C. Langton 4 for 113)
  & 102–1 (W. A. Brown 55)
Second Test at Johannesburg, Dec. 24–28. Match Drawn.
SA: 157   (W. J. O'Reilly 4 for 54)
  & 491   (A. D. Nourse 231)
AUS: 250   (J. H. Fingleton 62, W. A. Brown 51; B. Mitchell 4 for 26, A. B. C.
          Langton 4 for 85)
  & 274–2 (S. J. McCabe 189*)
Third Test at Cape Town, Jan. 1–4. Aus won by an innings and 78 runs.
AUS: 362–8 dec. (W. A. Brown 121, J. H. Fingleton 112; X. C. Balaskas
          4 for 126)
SA: 102   (C. V. Grimmett 5 for 32)
  & 182   (I. J. Siedle 59; C. V. Grimmett 5 for 56, W. J. O'Reilly 4 for 35)
Fourth Test at Johannesburg, Feb. 15–17. Aus won by an innings and 184 runs.
SA: 157   (W. J. O'Reilly 5 for 20)
  &   98   (C. V. Grimmett 7 for 40)
AUS: 439   (J. H. Fingleton 108, L. P. J. O'Brien 59, W. J. O'Reilly 56*; E. Q.
          Davies 4 for 75, X. C. Balaskas 4 for 165)
Fifth Test at Durban, Feb. 28–Mar. 3. Aus won by an innings and 6 runs.
SA: 222   (K. G. Viljoen 56, A. D. Nourse 50; C. V. Grimmett 7 for 100)
  & 227   (B. Mitchell 72; C. V. Grimmett 6 for 73, W. J. O'Reilly 4 for 47)
AUS: 455   (J. H. Fingleton 118, W. A. Brown 84, L. S. Darling 62; B. Mitchell
          5 for 87)

1936: England v India (Played 3, Eng won 2, India won 0, Drawn 1)
First Test at Lord's, June 27–30. Eng won by 9 wickets.

IND: 147   (G. O. B. Allen 5 for 35)
    & 93   (G. O. B. Allen 5 for 43, H. Verity 4 for 17)
ENG: 134   (M. Leyland 60; L. Amar Singh 6 for 35)
    & 108–1 (H. Gimblett 67*)
Second Test at Old Trafford, July 25–28. Match Drawn.
IND: 203   (H. Verity 4 for 41)
    & 390–5 (V. M. Merchant 114, S. Mushtaq Ali 112, C. Ramaswami 60)
ENG: 571–8 dec. (W. R. Hammond 167, J. Hardstaff jr. 94, T. S. Worthington
                87, R. W. V. Robins 76, H. Verity 66*)
Third Test at The Oval, Aug. 15–18. Eng won by 9 wickets.
ENG: 471–8 dec. (W. R. Hammond 217, T. S. Worthington 128; M. Nissar
                5 for 120)
    & 64–1
IND: 222   (V. M. Merchant 52, S. Mushtaq Ali 52; J. M. Sims 5 for 73)
    & 312   (C. K. Nayudu 81, Dilawar Hussain 54; G. O. B. Allen 7 for 80)

1936–37: Australia v England (Played 5, Aus won 3, Eng won 2)
First Test at Brisbane, Dec. 4–9. Eng won by 322 runs.
ENG: 358   (M. Leyland 126, C. J. Barnett 69; W. J. O'Reilly 5 for 102)
    & 256   (G. O. B. Allen 68; F. A. Ward 6 for 102)
AUS: 234   (J. H. Fingleton 100, S. J. McCabe 51; W. Voce 6 for 41)
    & 58   (G. O. B. Allen 5 for 36, W. Voce 4 for 16)
Second Test at Sydney, Dec. 18–22. Eng won by an innings and 22 runs.
ENG: 426–6 dec. (W. R. Hammond 231*, C. J. Barnett 57)
AUS: 80   (W. Voce 4 for 10)
    & 324   (S. J. McCabe 93, D. G. Bradman 82, J. H. Fingleton 73)
Third Test at Melbourne, Jan. 1–7. Aus won by 365 runs.
AUS: 200–9 dec. (S. J. McCabe 63)
    & 564   (D. G. Bradman 270, J. H. Fingleton 136)
 ENG: 76–9 dec. (M. W. S. Sievers 5 for 21)
    & 323   (M. Leyland 111*, R. W. V. Robins 61, W. R. Hammond 51;
                L. O'B. Fleetwood-Smith 5 for 124)
Fourth Test at Adelaide, Jan. 29–Feb. 4. Aus won by 148 runs.
AUS: 288   (S. J. McCabe 88, A. G. Chipperfield 57*)
    & 433   (D. G. Bradman 212, S. J. McCabe 55, R. G. Gregory 50; W. R.
                Hammond 5 for 57)
ENG: 330   (C. J. Barnett 129, L. E. G. Ames 52; W. J. O'Reilly 4 for 51,
                L. O'B. Fleetwood-Smith 4 for 129)
    & 243   (R. E. S. Wyatt 50; L. O'B. Fleetwood-Smith 6 for 110)
Fifth Test at Melbourne, Feb. 26–Mar. 3. Aus won by an innings and 200 runs.
AUS: 604   (D. G. Bradman 169, C. L. Badcock 118, S. J. McCabe 112, R. G.
                Gregory 80; K. Farnes 6 for 96)
ENG: 239   (J. Hardstaff jr. 83; W. J. O'Reilly 5 for 51, L. J. Nash 4 for 70)
    & 165   (W. R. Hammond 56)

1937: England v New Zealand (Played 3, Eng won 1, NZ won 0, Drawn 2)
First Test at Lord's, June 26–29. Match Drawn.
ENG: 424   (W. R. Hammond 140, J. Hardstaff jr 114, E. Paynter 74; A. W.
                Roberts 4 for 101, J. Cowie 4 for 118)
    & 226–4 dec. (C. J. Barnett 83*, J. Hardstaff jr. 64)
NZ: 295   (A. W. Roberts 66*, D. A. R. Moloney 64, W. M. Wallace 52)
    & 175–8 (W. M. Wallace 56)
Second Test at Old Trafford, July 24–27. Eng won by 130 runs.
ENG: 358–9 dec. (L. Hutton 100, C. J. Barnett 62, J. Hardstaff jr. 58; J. Cowie
                4 for 73)
    & 187   (F. R. Brown 57; J. Cowie 6 for 67)
NZ: 281   (W. A. Hadlee 93, H. G. Vivian 58; A. W. Wellard 4 for 81)
    & 134   (H. G. Vivian 50; T. W. J. Goddard 6 for 29)
Third Test at The Oval, Aug. 14–17. Match Drawn.
NZ: 249   (M. P. Donnelly 58, M. L. Page 53, A. W. Roberts 50; R. W. V.
                Robins 4 for 40)
    & 187   (H. G. Vivian 57)
ENG: 254–7 dec. (J. Hardstaff jr. 103, D. C. S. Compton 65)
    & 31–1

1938: England v Australia (Played 4, Eng won 1, Aus won 1, Drawn 2)
First Test at Trent Bridge, June 10–14. Match Drawn.
ENG: 658–8 dec. (E. Paynter 216*, C. J. Barnett 126, D. C. S. Compton 102, L. Hutton 100; L. O'B. Fleetwood-Smith 4 for 153)
AUS: 411   (S. J. McCabe 232, D. G. Bradman 51; K. Farnes 4 for 106, D. V. P. Wright 4 for 153)
& 427–6   (D. G. Bradman 144*, W. A. Brown 133)
Second Test at Lord's, June 24–28. Match Drawn.
ENG: 494   (W. R. Hammond 240, E. Paynter 99, L. E. G. Ames 83; W. J. O'Reilly 4 for 93, E. L. McCormick 4 for 101)
& 242–8 dec. (D. C. S. Compton 76*)
AUS: 422   (W. A. Brown 206*, A. L. Hassett 56; H. Verity 4 for 103)
& 204–6   (D. G. Bradman 102*)
Third Test at Headingley, July 22–25. Aus won by 5 wickets.
ENG: 223   (W. R. Hammond 76; W. J. O'Reilly 5 for 66)
& 123   (W. J. O'Reilly 5 for 56, L. O'B. Fleetwood-Smith 4 for 34)
AUS: 242   (D. G. Bradman 103, B. A. Barnett 57; K. Farnes 4 for 77)
& 107–5
Fourth Test at The Oval, Aug. 20–24. Eng won by an innings and 579 runs.
ENG: 903–7 dec. (L. Hutton 364, M. Leyland 187, J. Hardstaff jr. 169*, W. R Hammond 59, A. Wood 53)
AUS: 201   (W. A. Brown 69; W. E. Bowes 5 for 49)
& 123   (K. Farnes 4 for 63)
1938–39: South Africa v England (Played 5, Eng won 1, SA won 0, Drawn 4)
First Test at Johannesburg, Dec. 24–28. Match Drawn.
ENG: 422   (E. Paynter 117, P. A. Gibb 93, B. H. Valentine 97; N. Gordon 5 for 103)
& 291–4 dec. (P. A. Gibb 106, E. Paynter 100, W. R. Hammond 58)
SA: 390   (E. L. Dalton 102, B. Mitchell 73, A. D. Nourse 73, A. B. C. Langton 64*, K. G. Viljoen 50; H. Verity 4 for 61)
& 108–1
Second Test at Cape Town, Dec. 31–Jan. 4. Match Drawn.
ENG: 559–9 dec. (W. R. Hammond 181, L. E. G. Ames 115, B. H. Valentine 112, P. A. Gibb 58; N. Gordon 5 for 157)
SA: 286   (A. D. Nourse 120; H. Verity 5 for 70)
& 201–2   (E. A. B. Rowan 89*; P. G. V. van der Bijl 87)
Third Test at Durban, Jan. 20–23. Eng won by an innings and 13 runs.
ENG: 469–4 dec. (E. Paynter 243, W. R. Hammond 120)
SA: 103   (K. Farnes 4 for 29)
& 353   (B. Mitchell 109, E. A. B. Rowan 67, K. G. Viljoen 61)
Fourth Test at Johannesburg, Feb. 18–22. Match Drawn.
ENG: 215   (L. Hutton 92; A. B. C. Langton 5 for 58)
& 203–4 (W. R. Hammond 61*)
SA: 349–8 dec. (E. A. B. Rowan 85, A. Melville 67, B. Mitchell 63)
Fifth Test at Durban, Mar. 3–14. Match Drawn.
SA: 530   (P. G. V. van der Bijl 125, A. D. Nourse 103, A. Melville 78, R. E. Grieveson 75, E. L. Dalton 57; R. T. D. Perks 5 for 100)
& 481   (A. Melville 103, P. G. V. van der Bijl 97, B. Mitchell 89, K. G. Viljoen 74; K. Farnes 4 for 74)
ENG: 316   (L. E. G. Ames 84, E. Paynter 62; E. L. Dalton 4 for 59)
& 654–5   (W. J. Edrich 219, W. R. Hammond 140, P. A. Gibb 120, E. Paynter 75, L. Hutton 55)
1939: England v West Indies (Played 3, Eng won 1, WI won 0, Drawn 2)
First Test at Lord's, June 24–27. Eng won by 8 wickets.
WI: 277   (G. A. Headley 106, J. B. Stollmeyer 59; W. H. Copson 5 for 85)
& 225   (G. A Headley 107; W. H. Copson 4 for 67)
ENG: 404–5 dec. (L. Hutton 196, D. C. S. Compton 120)
& 100–2
Second Test at Old Trafford, July 22–25. Match Drawn.
ENG: 164–7 dec. (J. Hardstaff jr. 76)
& 128–6 dec. (L. N. Constantine 4 for 42)
WI: 133   (G. A. Headley 51; W. E. Bowes 6 for 33)
& 43–4

Third Test at The Oval, Aug. 19–22. Match Drawn.
ENG:　352　(J. Hardstaff jr. 94, N. Oldfield 80, L. Hutton 73; L. N. Constantine 5 for 75)
　&　366–3　(L. Hutton 165*, W. R. Hammond 138)
WI:　498　(K. H. Weekes 137, V. H. Stollmeyer 96, L. N. Constantine 79, G. A. Headley 65, J. B. Stollmeyer 59; R. T. D. Perks 5 for 156)

1945–46: New Zealand v Australia (Played 1, Aus won 1)
Test at Wellington, Mar. 29–30. Aus won by an innings and 103 runs.
NZ:　42　(W. J. O'Reilly 5 for 14, E. R. H. Toshack 4 for 12)
　&　54
AUS:　199–8 dec. (W. A. Brown 67, S. G. Barnes 54; J. Cowie 6 for 40)

1946: England v India (Played 3, Eng won 1, India won 0, Drawn 2)
First Test at Lord's, June 22–25. Eng won by 10 wickets.
IND:　200　(R. S. Modi 57*; A. V. Bedser 7 for 49)
　&　275　(V. M. Mankad 63, L. Amarnath 50; A. V. Bedser 4 for 96)
ENG:　428　(J. Hardstaff jr. 205*, P. A. Gibb 60; L. Amarnath 5 for 118)
　&　48–0
Second Test at Old Trafford, July 20–23. Match Drawn.
ENG:　294　(W. R. Hammond 69, L. Hutton 67, C. Washbrook 52, D. C. S. Compton 51; L. Amarnath 5 for 96, V. M. Mankad 5 for 101)
　&　153–5 dec. (D. C. S. Compton 71*)
IND:　170　(V. M. Merchant 78; R. Pollard 5 for 24, A. V. Bedser 4 for 41)
　&　152–9　(A. V. Bedser 7 for 52)
Third Test at The Oval, Aug. 17–20. Match Drawn.
IND:　331　(V. M. Merchant 128, S. Mustaq Ali 59; W. J. Edrich 4 for 68)
ENG:　95–3

1946–47: Australia v England (Played 5, Aus won 3, Eng won 0, Drawn 2)
First Test at Brisbane, Nov. 29–Dec. 4. Aus won by an innings and 332 runs.
AUS:　645　(D. G. Bradman 187, A. L. Hassett 128, C. L. McCool 95, K. R. Miller 79; D. V. P. Wright 5 for 167)
ENG:　141　(K. R. Miller 7 for 60)
　&　172　(E. R. H. Toshack 6 for 82)
Second Test at Sydney, Dec. 13–19. Aus won by an innings and 33 runs.
ENG:　255　(W. J. Edrich 71, J. T. Ikin 60; I. W. Johnson 6 for 42)
　&　371　(W. J. Edrich 119, D. C. S. Compton 54; C. L. McCool 5 for 109)
AUS:　659–8 dec. (S. G. Barnes 234, D. G. Bradman 234)
Third Test at Melbourne, Jan. 1–7. Match Drawn.
AUS:　365　(C. L. McCool 104*, D. G. Bradman 79)
　&　536　(A. R. Morris 155, R. R. Lindwall 100, D. Tallon 92)
ENG:　351　(W. J. Edrich 89, C. Washbrook 62, N. W. D. Yardley 61; B. Dooland 4 for 69)
　&　310–7　(C. Washbrook 112, N. W. D. Yardley 53*)
Fourth Test at Adelaide, Jan. 31–Feb. 6. Match Drawn.
ENG:　460　(D. C. S. Compton 147, L. Hutton 94, J. Hardstaff jr. 67, C. Washbrook 65; R. R. Lindwall 4 for 52)
　&　340–8 dec. (D. C. S. Compton 103*, L. Hutton 76; E. R. H. Toshack 4 for 76)
AUS:　487　(K. R. Miller 141*, A. R. Morris 122, A. L. Hassett 78, I. W. Johnson 52)
　&　215–1　(A. R. Morris 124*, D. G. Bradman 56*)
Fifth Test at Sydney, Feb. 28–Mar. 5. Aus won by 5 wickets.
ENG:　280　(L. Hutton retired ill 122, W. J. Edrich 60; R. R. Lindwall 7 for 63)
　&　186　(D. C. S. Compton 76; C. L. McCool 5 for 44)
AUS:　253　(S. G. Barnes 71, A. R. Morris 57; D. V. P. Wright 7 for 105)
　&　214–5　(D. G. Bradman 63)

1946–47: New Zealand v England (Played 1, Drawn 1)
Test at Christchurch, Mar. 21–25. Match Drawn.
NZ:　345–9 dec. (W. A. Hadlee 116, B. Sutcliffe 58; A. V. Bedser 4 for 95)
ENG:　265–7 dec. (W. R. Hammond 79; J. Cowie 6 for 83)

1947: England v South Africa (Played 5, Eng won 3, SA won 0, Drawn 2)
First Test at Trent Bridge, June 7–11. Match Drawn.

SA: 533 (A. Melville 189, A. D. Nourse 149, T. A. Harris 60; W. E. Hollies 5 for 123)
& 166–1 (A. Melville 104*, K. G. Viljoen 51*)
ENG: 208 (D. C. S. Compton 65, W. J. Edrich 57; L. Tuckett 5 for 68)
& 551 (D. C. S. Compton 163, N. W. D. Yardley 99, T G. Evans 74, C. Washbrook 59, W. J. Edrich 50; V. I. Smith 4 for 143)
Second Test at Lord's, June 21–25. Eng won by 10 wickets.
ENG: 554–8 dec. (D. C. S. Compton 208, W. J. Edrich 189, C. Washbrook 65; L. Tuckett 5 for 115)
& 26–0
SA: 327 (A. Melville 117, A. D. Nourse 61; D. V. P. Wright 5 for 95)
& 252 (B. Mitchell 80, A. D. Nourse 58; D. V. P. Wright 5 for 80)
Third Test at Old Trafford, July 5–9. Eng won by 7 wickets.
SA: 339 (K. G. Viljoen 93, B. Mitchell 80, D. V. Dyer 62; W. J. Edrich 4 for 95)
& 267 (A. D. Nourse 115, A. Melville 59; W. J. Edrich 4 for 77)
ENG: 478 (W. J. Edrich 191, D. C. S. Compton 115; L. Tuckett 4 for 148)
& 130–3
Fourth Test at Headingley, July 26–29. Eng won by 10 wickets.
SA: 175 (B. Mitchell 53, A. D. Nourse 51; H. J. Butler 4 for 34)
& 184 (A. D. Nourse 57; K. Cranston 4 for 12)
ENG: 317–7 dec. (L. Hutton 100, C. Washbrook 75; N. B. F. Mann 4 for 68)
& 47–0
Fifth Test at The Oval, Aug. 16–20. Match Drawn.
ENG: 427 (L. Hutton 83, N. W. D. Yardley 59, D. C. S. Compton 53, C. Gladwin 51*; N. B F. Mann 4 for 93)
& 325–6 dec. (D. C. S. Compton 113)
SA: 302 (B. Mitchell 120 O. C. Dawson 55)
& 423–7 (B. Mitchell 189*, A. D. Nourse 97)

1947–48: Australia v India (Played 5, Aus won 4, India won 0, Drawn 1)
First Test at Brisbane, Nov. 28–Dec. 4. Aus won by an innings and 226 runs.
AUS: 382–8 dec. (D. G. Bradman 185, K. R. Miller 58; L. Amarnath 4 for 84)
IND: 58 (E. R. H. Toshack 5 for 2)
& 98 (E. R. H. Toshack 6 for 29)
Second Test at Sydney, Dec. 12–18. Match Drawn.
IND: 188 (D. G. Phadkar 51)
& 61–7
AUS: 107 (V. S. Hazare 4 for 29)
Third Test at Melbourne, Jan. 1–5. Aus won by 233 runs.
AUS: 394 (D. G. Bradman 132, A. L. Hassett 80; L. Amarnath 4 for 78, V. M. Mankad 4 for 135)
& 255–4 dec. (D. G. Bradman 127*, A. R. Morris 100*)
IND: 291–9 dec. (V. M. Mankad 116, D. G. Phadkar 55*; I. W. Johnson 4 for 59)
& 125 (I. W. Johnson 4 for 35, W. A. Johnston 4 for 44)
Fourth Test at Adelaide, Jan. 23–28. Aus won by an innings and 16 runs.
AUS: 674 (D. G. Bradman 201, A. L. Hassett 198*, S. G. Barnes 112, K. R. Miller 67; C. R. Rangachari 4 for 141)
IND: 381 (V. S. Hazare 116, D. G. Phadkar 123; I. W. Johnson 4 for 64)
& 277 (V. S. Hazare 145, H. R. Adhikari 51; R. R. Lindwall 7 for 38)
Fifth Test at Melbourne, Feb. 6–10. Aus won by an innings and 177 runs.
AUS: 575–8 dec. (R. N. Harvey 153, W. A. Brown 99, S. J. E. Loxton 80, D. G. Bradman retired hurt 57)
IND: 331 (V. M. Mankad 111, V. S. Hazare 74, D. G. Phadkar 56*)
& 67

1947–48: West Indies v England (Played 4, WI won 2, Eng won 0, Drawn 2)
First Test at Bridgetown, Jan. 21–26. Match Drawn.
WI: 296 (G. E. Gomez 86, J. B. Stollmeyer 78; J. C. Laker 7 for 103)
& 351–9 dec. (R. J. Christiani 99, E. A. V. Williams 72, W. Ferguson 56*; R. Howorth 6 for 124)
ENG: 253 (J. Hardstaff jr. 98, J. D. Robertson 80; P. E. Jones 4 for 54)
& 86–4 (J. D. Robertson 51*)

Second Test at Port of Spain, Feb. 11–16. Match Drawn.

ENG: 362 (S. C. Griffith 140, J. C. Laker 55; W. Ferguson 5 for 137)
& 275 (J. D. Robertson 133; W. Ferguson 6 for 92)
WI: 497 (A. G. Ganteaume 112, G. M. Carew 107, F. M. M. Worrell 97, G. E. Gomez 62)
& 72–3

Third Test at Georgetown, Mar. 3–6. WI won by 7 wickets.

WI: 297–8 dec. (F. M. M. Worrell 131*, R. J. Christiani 51; K. Cranston 4 for 78)
& 78–3
ENG: 111 (J. D. C. Goddard 5 for 31)
& 263 (J. Hardstaff jr. 63; W. Ferguson 5 for 116)

Fourth Test at Kingston, Mar. 27–April 1. WI won by 10 wickets.

ENG: 227 (J. D. Robertson 64, L. Hutton 56; H. H. H. Johnson 5 for 41)
& 336 (W. Place 107, J. Hardstaff jr. 64, L. Hutton 60; H. H. H. Johnson 5 for 55)
WI: 490 (E. D. Weekes 141, W. Ferguson 75, K. R. Rickards 67)
& 76–0

1948: England v Australia (Played 5, Aus won 4, Eng won 0, Drawn 1)

First Test at Trent Bridge, June 10–15. Aus won by eight wickets.

ENG: 165 (J. C. Laker 63; W. A. Johnston 5 for 36)
& 441 (D. C. S. Compton 184, L. Hutton 74, T. G. Evans 50; K. R. Miller 4 for 125, W. A. Johnston 4 for 147)
AUS: 509 (D. G. Bradman 138, A. L. Hassett 137, S. G. Barnes 62; J. C. Laker 4 for 138)
& 98–2 (S. G. Barnes 64*)

Second Test at Lord's, June 24–29. Aus won by 409 runs.

AUS: 350 (A. R. Morris 105, D. Tallon 53; A. V. Bedser 4 for 100)
& 460–7 dec. (S. G. Barnes 141, D. G. Bradman 89, K. R. Miller 74, A. R. Morris 62)
ENG: 215 (D. C. S. Compton 53; R. R. Lindwall 5 for 70)
& 186 (E. R. H. Toshack 5 for 40)

Third Test at Old Trafford, July 8–13. Match Drawn.

ENG: 363 (D. C. S. Compton 145*; R. R. Lindwall 4 for 99)
& 174–3 dec. (C. Washbrook 85*, W. J. Edrich 53)
AUS: 221 (A. R. Morris 51; A. V. Bedser 4 for 81)
& 92–1 (A. R. Morris 54*)

Fourth Test at Headingley, July 22–27. Aus won by 7 wickets.

ENG: 496 (C. Washbrook 143, W. J. Edrich 111, L. Hutton 81, A. V. Bedser 79)
& 365–8 dec. (D. C. S. Compton 66, C. Washbrook 65, L. Hutton 57, W. J. Edrich 54; W. A. Johnston 4 for 95)
AUS: 458 (R. N. Harvey 112, S. J. E. Loxton 93, R. R. Lindwall 77, K. R. Miller 58)
& 404–3 (A. R. Morris 182, D. G. Bradman 173*)

Fifth Test at The Oval, Aug. 14–18. Aus won by an innings and 149 runs.

ENG: 52 (R. R. Lindwall 6 for 20)
& 188 (L. Hutton 64; W. A. Johnston 4 for 40)
AUS: 389 (A. R. Morris 196, S. G. Barnes 61; W. E. Hollies 5 for 131)

1948–49: India v West Indies (Played 5, WI won 1, India won 0, Drawn 4)

First Test at New Delhi, Nov. 10–14. Match Drawn.

WI: 631 (C. L. Walcott 152, E. D. Weekes 128, R. J. Christiani 107, G. E. Gomez 101; C. R. Rangachari 5 for 107)
IND: 454 (H. R. Adhikari 114*, K. C. Ibrahim 85, R. S. Modi 63, L. Amarnath 62)
& 220–6

Second Test at Bombay, Dec. 9–13. Match Drawn.

WI: 629–6 dec. (E. D. Weekes 194, A. F. Rae 104, F. J. Cameron 75*, R. J. Christiani 74, C. L. Walcott 68, J. B. Stollmeyer 66)
IND: 273 (D. G. Phadkar 74; W. Ferguson 4 for 126)
& 333–3 (V. S. Hazare 134*, R. S. Modi 112, L. Amarnath 58*)

Third Test at Calcutta, Dec. 31–Jan. 4. Match Drawn.

WI: 366   (E. D. Weekes 162, C. L. Walcott 54; Ghulam Ahmed 4 for 94,
            S. A. Banerjee 4 for 120)
  &   336–9 dec. (C. L. Walcott 108, E. D. Weekes 101)
IND: 272   (R. S. Modi 80, V. S. Hazare 59, S. Mushtaq Ali 54)
  &   325–3 (S. Mushtaq Ali 106, R. S. Modi 87, V. S. Hazare 58*)
Fourth Test at Madras, Jan. 27–31. WI won by an innings and 193 runs.
WI: 582   (J. B. Stollmeyer 160, A. F. Rae 109, E. D. Weekes 90, G. E.
            Gomez 50; D. G. Phadkar 7 for 159)
IND: 245   (R. S. Modi 56; J. Trim 4 for 48)
  &   144   (V. S. Hazare 52; P. E. Jones 4 for 30)
Fifth Test at Bombay, Feb. 4–8. Match Drawn.
WI: 286   (J. B. Stollmeyer 85, E. D. Weekes 56; D. G. Phadkar 4 for 74)
  &   267   (A. F. Rae 97; S. N. Banerjee 4 for 54)
IND: 193
  &   355–8 (V. S. Hazare 122, R. S. Modi 86; P. E. Jones 5 for 85)

1948–49: South Africa v England (Played 5, Eng won 2, SA won 0, Drawn 3)
First Test at Durban, Dec. 16–20. Eng won by 2 wickets.
SA: 161   (A. V. Bedser 4 for 39)
  &   219   (W. W. Wade 63; D. V. P. Wright 4 for 72)
ENG: 253   (L. Hutton 83, D. C. S. Compton 72; N. B. F. Mann 6 for 59,
            A. M. B. Rowan 4 for 108)
  &   128–8 (C. N. McCarthy 6 for 43)
Second Test at Johannesburg, Dec. 27–30. Match Drawn.
ENG: 608   (C. Washbrook 195, L. Hutton 158, D. C. S. Compton 114, J. F.
            Crapp 56)
SA: 315   (B. Mitchell 86, W. W. Wade 85)
  &   270–2 (E. A. B. Rowan 156*, A. D. Nourse 56*)
Third Test at Cape Town, Jan. 1–5. Match Drawn.
ENG: 308   (C. Washbrook 74; A. M. B. Rowan 5 for 80)
  &   276–3 dec. (L. Hutton 87, A. J. Watkins 64*. J. F. Crapp 54, D. C. S.
            Compton 51*)
SA: 356   (B. Mitchell 120, A. D. Nourse 112, O. E. Wynne 50; D. C. S.
            Compton 5 for 70)
  &   142–4 (R. O. Jenkins 4 for 48)
Fourth Test at Johannesburg, Feb. 12–16. Match Drawn.
ENG: 379   (A. J. Watkins 111 C. Washbrook 97. J. F. Crapp 51; C. N.
            McCarthy 5 for 114)
  &   253–7 dec. (L. Hutton 123; A. M. B. Rowan 4 for 69)
SA: 257–9 dec. (A. D. Nourse 129* W. W. Wade 54)
  &   194–4 (E. A. B. Rowan 86*, K. G. Viljoen 63)
Fifth Test at Port Elizabeth, Mar. 5–9. Eng won by 3 wickets.
SA: 379   (W. W. Wade 125, B. Mitchell 99, A. D. Nourse 73; A. V. Bedser
            4 for 61)
  &   187–3 dec. (B. Mitchell 56)
ENG: 395   (F. G. Mann 136*; A. M. B. Rowan 5 for 167)
  &   174–7 (N. B. F. Mann 4 for 65)

1949: England v New Zealand (Played 4, Eng won 0, NZ won 0, Drawn 4)
First Test at Headingley, June 11–14. Match Drawn.
ENG: 372   (D. C. S. Compton 114, L. Hutton 101; T. B. Burtt 5 for 97, J.
            Cowie 5 for 127)
  &   267–4 dec. (C. Washbrook 103*, W. J. Edrich 70)
NZ: 341   (F. B. Smith 96, M. P. Donnelly 64; T. E. Bailey 6 for 118)
  &   195–2 (B. Sutcliffe 82, F. B. Smith 54*)
Second Test at Lord's, June 25–28. Match Drawn.
ENG: 313–9 dec. (D. C. S. Compton 116. T. E. Bailey 93; T. B. Burtt 4 for 102)
  &   306–5 (J. D. Robertson 121, L. Hutton 66)
NZ: 484   (M. P. Donnelly 206, B. Sutcliffe 57; W. E. Hollies 5 for 133)
Third Test at Old Trafford, July 23–26. Match Drawn.
NZ: 293   (M. P. Donnelly 75, J. R. Reid 50; T. E. Bailey 6 for 84)
  &   348–7 (B. Sutcliffe 101, M. P. Donnelly 80)
ENG: 440–9 dec. (R. T. Simpson 103, W. J. Edrich 78, L. Hutton 73, T. E.
            Bailey 72*; T. B. Burtt 6 for 162)

Fourth Test at The Ova., Aug. 13–16. Match Drawn.

NZ: 345   (B. Sutcliffe 88, V. J. Scott 60, W. M. Wallace 55; A. V. Bedser 4 for 74)

   &   308–9 dec. (J. R. Reid 93, W. M. Wallace 58, B. Sutcliffe 54; J. C. Laker 4 for 78)

ENG: 482   (L. Hutton 206, W. J. Edrich 100, R. T. Simpson 68; G. F. Cresswell 6 for 168. J. Cowie 4 for 123)

1949–50: South Africa v Australia (Played 5. Aus won 4, SA won 0, Drawn 1)

First Test at Johannesburg, Dec. 24–28. Aus won by an innings and 85 runs.

AUS: 413   (A. L. Hassett 112, S. J. E. Loxton 101. I. W. Johnson 66)

SA: 137   (E. A. B. Rowan 60; K. R. Miller 5 for 40)

   &   191   (W. A. Johnston 6 for 44)

Second Test at Cape Town, Dec. 31–Jan. 4. Aus won by 8 wickets.

AUS: 526–7 dec. (R. N. Harvey 178, J. R. Moroney 87, K. R. Miller 58, A. L. Hassett 57; N. B. F. Mann 4 for 105)

   &   87–2

SA: 278   (E. A. B. Rowan 67, A. D. Nourse 65; C. L. McCool 5 for 41)

   &   333   (A. D. Nourse 114, H. J. Tayfield 75; R. R. Lindwall 5 for 32)

Third Test at Durban, Jan. 20–24. Aus won by 5 wickets.

SA: 311   (E. A. B. Rowan 143, A. D. Nourse 66; W. A. Johnston 4 for 75)

   &   99   (I. W Johnson 5 for 34, W. A. Johnston 4 for 39)

AUS: 75   (H. J. Tayfield 7 for 23)

   &   336–5 (R. N. Harvey 151* S. J. E. Loxton 54)

Fourth Test at Johannesburg, Feb. 10–14. Match Drawn.

AUS: 465–8 dec. (J. R. Moroney 118 A. R. Morris 111, K. R. Miller 84, R. N. Harvey 56*. A. L. Hassett 53; M. G. Melle 5 for 113)

   &   259–2 (J. R. Moroney 101* R. N. Harvey 100)

SA: 352   (G. M. Fullerton 88. E. A. B. Rowan 55. N. B. F. Mann 52)

Fifth Test at Port Elizabeth, Mar. 3–6. Aus won by an innings and 259 runs.

AUS: 549–7 dec. (A. L. Hassett 167. A. R. Morris 157, R. N. Harvey 116)

SA: 158   (K R. Miller 4 for 42)

   &   132   (A. D. Nourse 55)

1950: England v West Indies (Played 4, WI won 3, Eng won 1)

First Test at Old Trafford, June 8–12. Eng won by 202 runs.

ENG: 312   (T. G. Evans 104. T. E. Bailey 82*; A. L. Valentine 8 for 104)

   &   288   (W. J. Edrich 71)

WI: 215   (E. D. Weekes 52; R. Berry 5 for 63)

   &   183   (J. B. Stollmeyer 78; W. E. Hollies 5 for 63, R. Berry 4 for 53)

Second Test at Lord's, June 24–29. WI won by 326 runs.

WI: 326   (A. F. Rae 106. E. D. Weekes 63, F. M. M. Worrell 52; R. O. Jenkins 5 for 116)

   &   425–6 dec (C. L Walcott 168*, G. E. Gomez 70, E. D. Weekes 63; R. O. Jenkins 4 for 174)

ENG: 151   (S. Ramadhin 5 for 66. A. L. Valentine 4 for 48)

   &   274   (C Washbrook 114; S. Ramadhin 6 for 86)

Third Test at Trent Bridge, July 20–25. WI won by 10 wickets.

ENG: 223

   &   436   (C. Washbrook 102, R. T. Simpson 94 W. G. A. Parkhouse 69. J. G. Dewes 67. T. G. Evans 67; S. Ramadhin 5 for 135)

WI: 558   (F. M. M. Worrell 261, E. D. Weekes 129. A. F. Rae 68; A. V. Bedser 5 for 127)

   &   103–0 (J. B. Stollmeyer 52*)

Fourth Test at the Oval, Aug. 12–16. WI won by an innings and 56 runs.

WI: 503   (F. M. M. Worrell 138, A. F. Rae 109, G. E. Gomez 74, J. D. C. Goddard 58*; D. V. P. Wright 5 for 141)

ENG: 344   (L. Hutton 202*; J. D. C. Goddard 4 for 25, A. L. Valentine 4 for 121)

   &   103   (A. L. Valentine 6 for 39)

1950–51: Australia v England (Played 5, Aus won 4, Eng won 1)

First Test at Brisbane, Dec. 1–5. Aus won by 70 runs.

AUS: 228   (R. N. Harvey 74; A. V. Bedser 4 for 45)

   &   32–7 dec. (T. E. Bailey 4 for 22)

ENG: 68–7 dec. (W. A. Johnston 5 for 35)
   & 122   (L. Hutton 62*; J. B. Iverson 4 for 43)
Second Test at Melbourne, Dec. 22–27. Aus won by 28 runs.
AUS: 194   (A. L. Hassett 52; A. V. Bedser 4 for 37, T. E. Bailey 4 for 40)
   & 181   (F. R. Brown 4 for 26)
ENG: 197   (F. R. Brown 62; J. B. Iverson 4 for 37)
   & 150   (W. A. Johnston 4 for 26)
Third Test at Sydney, Jan. 5–9. Aus won by an innings and 13 runs.
ENG: 290   (F. R. Brown 79, L. Hutton 62; K. R. Miller 4 for 37)
   & 123   (J. B. Iverson 6 for 27)
AUS: 426   (K. R. Miller 145*, I. W. Johnson 77, A. L. Hassett 70; A. V.
            Bedser 4 for 107, F. R. Brown 4 for 153)
Fourth Test at Adelaide, Feb. 2–8. Aus won by 274 runs.
AUS: 371   (A. R. Morris 206; D. V. P. Wright 4 for 99)
   & 403–8 dec. (J. W. Burke 101*, K. R. Miller 99, R. N. Harvey 68)
ENG: 272   (L. Hutton 156*)
   & 228   (R. T. Simpson 61; W. A. Johnston 4 for 73)
Fifth Test at Melbourne, Feb. 23–28. Eng won by 8 wickets.
AUS: 217   (A. L. Hassett 92, A. R. Morris 50; A. V. Bedser 5 for 46, F. R.
            Brown 5 for 49)
   & 197   (G. B. Hole 63, R. N. Harvey 52; A. V. Bedser 5 for 59)
ENG: 320   (R. T. Simpson 156*, L. Hutton 79; K. R. Miller 4 for 76)
   & 95–2 (L. Hutton 60*)

1950–51: New Zealand v England (Played 2, Eng won 1, NZ won 0, Drawn 1)
First Test at Christchurch, Mar. 17–21. Match Drawn.
NZ: 417–8 dec. (B. Sutcliffe 116, W. M. Wallace 66, J. R. Reid 50, W. A.
            Hadlee 50)
   & 46–3
ENG: 550   (T. E. Bailey 134*, R. T. Simpson 81, D. C. S. Compton 79, F. R.
            Brown 62, C. Washbrook 58; A. M. Moir 6 for 155)
Second Test at Wellington, Mar. 24–28. Eng won by 6 wickets.
NZ: 125   (D. V. P. Wright 5 for 48)
   & 189   (V. J. Scott 60; R. Tattersall 6 for 44)
ENG: 227   (L. Hutton 57)
   & 91–4

1951: England v South Africa (Played 5, Eng won 3, SA won 1, Drawn 1)
First Test at Trent Bridge, June 7–12. SA won by 71 runs.
SA: 483–9 dec. (A. D. Nourse 208, J. H. B. Waite 76, G. M. Fullerton 54)
   & 121   (A. V. Bedser 6 for 37)
ENG: 419–9 dec. (R. T. Simpson 137, D. C. S. Compton 112, L. Hutton 63, W.
            Watson 57; C. N. McCarthy 4 for 104, G. W. A. Chubb 4 for 146)
   & 114   (A. M. B. Rowan 5 for 68, N. B. F. Mann 4 for 24)
Second Test at Lord's, June 21–23. Eng won by 10 wickets.
ENG: 311   (D. C. S. Compton 79, W. Watson 79, J. T. Ikin 51; G. W. A.
            Chubb 5 for 77, C. N. McCarthy 4 for 76)
   & 16–0
SA: 115   (R. Tattersall 7 for 52)
   & 211   (G. M. Fullerton 60, J. E. Cheetham 54; R. Tattersall 5 for 49)
Third Test at Old Trafford, July 5–10. Eng won by 9 wickets.
SA: 158   (A. V. Bedser 7 for 58)
   & 191   (E. A. B. Rowan 57; A. V. Bedser 5 for 54)
ENG: 211   (G. W. A. Chubb 6 for 51)
   & 142–1 (L. Hutton 98*)
Fourth Test at Headingley, July 26–31. Match Drawn.
SA: 538   (E. A. B. Rowan 236, P. N. F. Mansell 90, C. B. van Ryneveld 83,
            R. A. McLean 67)
   & 87–0 (E. A. B. Rowan 60*)
ENG: 505   (P. B. H. May 138, L. Hutton 100, T. E. Bailey 95, F. A. Lawson
            58; A. M. B. Rowan 5 for 174)
Fifth Test at the Oval, Aug. 16–18. Eng won by 4 wickets.
SA: 202   (E. A. B. Rowan 55; J. C. Laker 4 for 64)
   & 154   (J. C. Laker 6 for 55)

ENG: 194   (D. C. S. Compton 73; M. G. Melle 4 for 9)
& 164–6

1951–52: India v England (Played 5, India won 1, Eng won 1, Drawn 3)
First Test at New Delhi, Nov 2–7. Match Drawn.
ENG: 203   (J. D. Robertson 50; S. G. Shinde 6 for 91)
& 368–6 (A. J. Watkins 138*, D. B. Carr 76, F. A. Lowson 68; V. M. Mankad 4 for 58)
IND: 418–6 dec. (V. S. Hazare 164*, V. M. Merchant 154)
Second Test at Bombay, Dec. 14–19. Match Drawn.
IND: 485–9 dec. (V. S. Hazare 155, P. Roy 140, C. D. Gopinath 50*; J. B. Statham 4 for 96)
& 208
ENG: 456   (T. W. Graveney 175, A. J. Watkins 80; V. M. Mankad 4 for 91)
&   55–2
Third Test at Calcutta, Dec. 30–Jan. 4. Match Drawn.
ENG: 342   (R. T. Spooner 71, A. J. Watkins 68, C. J. Poole 55; V. M. Mankad 4 for 89)
& 252–5 dec. (R. T. Spooner 92, C. J. Poole 69*)
IND: 344   (D. G. Phadkar 115, V. M. Mankad 59; F. Ridgway 4 for 83, R. Tattersall 4 for 104)
& 103–0 (V. M. Mankad 71*)
Fourth Test at Kanpur, Jan. 12–14. Eng won by 8 wickets.
IND: 121   (R. Tattersall 6 for 48, M. J. Hilton 4 for 32)
& 157   (H. R. Adhikari 60; M. J. Hilton 5 for 61)
ENG: 203   (A. J. Watkins 66; Ghulam Ahmed 5 for 70, V. M. Mankad 4 for 54)
&   76–2
Fifth Test at Madras, Feb. 6–10. India won by an innings and 8 runs.
ENG: 266   (J. D. Robertson 77, R. T. Spooner 66; V. M. Mankad 8 for 55)
& 183   (J. D. Robertson 56; V. M. Mankad 4 for 53, Ghulam Ahmed 4 for 77)
IND: 457–9 dec. (P. R. Umrigar 130, P. Roy 111, D. G. Phadkar 61)

1951–52 Australia v West Indies (Played 5, Aus won 4, WI won 1)
First Test at Brisbane, Nov. 9–13. Aus won by 3 wickets.
WI: 216   (R. R. Lindwall 4 for 62)
& 245   (E. D. Weekes 70, G. E. Gomez 55; D. T. Ring 6 for 80)
AUS: 226   (R. R. Lindwall 61; A. L. Valentine 5 for 99)
& 236–7 (S. Ramadhin 5 for 90)
Second Test at Sydney, Nov. 30–Dec. 5. Aus won by 7 wickets.
WI: 362   (R. J. Christiani 76, F. M. M. Worrell 64, C. L. Walcott 60, G. E. Gomez 54, R. R. Lindwall 4 for 66)
& 290   (J. D. C. Goddard 57*, E. D. Weekes 56)
AUS: 517   (A. L. Hassett 132, K. R. Miller 129, D. T. Ring 65; A. L. Valentine 4 for 111)
& 137–3
Third Test at Adelaide, Dec. 22–25. WI won by 6 wickets.
AUS: 82   (F. M. M. Worrell 6 for 38)
& 255   (D. T. Ring 67; A. L. Valentine 6 for 102)
WI: 105   (W. A. Johnston 6 for 62)
& 233–4
Fourth Test at Melbourne, Dec. 31–Jan. 3. Aus won by 1 wicket.
WI: 272   (F. M. M. Worrell 108; K. R. Miller 5 for 60)
& 203   (J. B. Stollmeyer 54, G. E. Gomez 52)
AUS: 216   (R. N. Harvey 83; J. Trim 5 for 34)
& 260–9 (A. L. Hassett 102; A. L. Valentine 5 for 88)
Fifth Test at Sydney, Jan. 25–29. Aus won by 202 runs.
AUS: 116   (G. E. Gomez 7 for 55)
& 377   (K. R. Miller 69, A. L. Hassett 64, C. C. McDonald 62, G. B. Hole 62; F. M. M. Worrell 4 for 95)
WI: 78   (K. R. Miller 5 for 26)
& 213   (J. B. Stollmeyer 104; R. R. Lindwall 5 for 52)

1951–52: New Zealand v West Indies (Played 2, WI won 1, NZ won 0, Drawn 1)
First Test at Christchurch, Feb. 8–12. WI won by 5 wickets.
    NZ: 236   (S. Ramadhin 5 for 86)
    &   189   (S. Ramadhin 4 for 39)
    WI: 287   (F. M. M. Worrell 71, C. L. Walcott 65, S. C. Guillen 54; T. B.
                   Burtt 5 for 69)
    & 142–5 (F. M. M. Worrell 62*)
Second Test at Auckland, Feb. 15–19. Match Drawn.
    WI: 546–6 dec. (C. L. Walcott 115, J. B. Stollmeyer 152, F. M. M. Worrell
                   100, A. F. Rae 99, E. D. Weekes 51)
    NZ: 160   (V. J. Scott 84)
    &   17–1

1952: England v India (Played 4, Eng won 3, Ind won 0, Drawn 1)
First Test at Headingley, June 5–9. Eng won by 7 wickets.
    IND: 293   (V. L. Manjrekar 133, V. S. Hazare 89; J. C. Laker 4 for 39)
    & 165   (D. G. Phadkar 64, V. S. Hazare 56; F. S. Trueman 4 for 27, R. O.
                   Jenkins 4 for 50)
    ENG: 334   (T. W. Graveney 71, T. G. Evans 66; Ghulam Ahmed 5 for 100)
    & 128–3 (R. T. Simpson 51)
Second Test at Lord's, June 19–24. Eng won by 8 wickets.
    IND: 235   (V. M. Mankad 72, V. S. Hazare 69*; F. S. Trueman 4 for 72)
    & 378   (V. M. Mankad 184; J. C. Laker 4 for 102, F. S. Trueman
                   4 for 110)
    ENG: 537   (L. Hutton 150, T. G. Evans 104, P. B. H. May 74, T. W. Graveney
                   73, R. T. Simpson 53; V. M. Mankad 5 for 196)
    &   79–2
Third Test at Old Trafford, July 17–19. Eng won by an innings and 207 runs.
    ENG: 347–9 dec. (L. Hutton 104, T. G. Evans 71, P. B. H. May 69)
    IND: 58   (F. S. Trueman 8 for 31)
    &   82   (A. V. Bedser 5 for 27, G. A. R. Lock 4 for 36)
Fourth Test at The Oval, Aug. 14–19. Match Drawn.
    ENG: 326–6 dec. (D. S. Sheppard 119, J. T. Ikin 53, L. Hutton 86)
    IND: 98   (A. V. Bedser 5 for 41, F. S. Trueman 5 for 48)

1952–53: India v Pakistan (Played 5, India won 2, Pak won 1, Drawn 2)
First Test at New Delhi, Oct. 16–18. India won by an innings and 70 runs.
    IND: 372   (H. R. Adhikari 81*, V. S. Hazare 76, Ghulam Ahmed 50; Amir
                   Elahi 4 for 134)
    PAK: 150   (Hanif Mohammad 51; V. M. Mankad 8 for 52)
    & 152   (V. M. Mankad 5 for 79, Ghulam Ahmed 4 for 35)
Second Test at Lucknow, Oct. 23–26. Pak won by an innings and 43 runs.
    IND: 106   (Fazal Mahmood 5 for 52)
    & 182   (L. Amarnath 61*; Fazal Mahmood 7 for 42)
    PAK: 331   (Nazar Mohammad 124*)
Third Test at Bombay, Nov. 13–16. Ind won by 10 wickets.
    PAK: 186   (Waqar Hassan 81; L. Amarnath 4 for 40)
    & 242   (Hanif Mohammad 96, Waqar Hassan 65; V. M. Mankad 5 for 72)
    IND: 387–4 dec. (V. S. Hazare 146*, P. R. Umrigar 102)
    &   45–0
Fourth Test at Madras, Nov. 28–Dec. 1. Match Drawn.
    PAK: 344   (A. H. Kardar 79, Zulfiqar Ahmed 63*)
    IND: 175–6 (P. R. Umrigar 62)
Fifth Test at Calcutta, Dec. 12–15. Match Drawn.
    PAK: 257   (Imtiaz Ahmed 57, Hanif Mohammad 56, Nazar Mohammad 55;
                   D. G. Phadkar 5 for 72)
    & 236–7 dec. (Waqar Hassan 97)
    IND: 397   (R. H. Shodhan 110, D. G. Phadkar 57; Fazal Mahmood 4 for 141)
    &   28–0

1952–53: Australia v South Africa (Played 5, Aus won 2, SA won 2, Drawn 1)
First Test at Brisbane, Dec. 5–10. Aus won by 96 runs.
    AUS: 280   (R. N. Harvey 109, A. L. Hassett 55; M. G. Melle 6 for 71, J. C.
                   Watkins 4 for 41)
    & 277   (A. R. Morris 58, R. N. Harvey 52; H. J. Tayfield 4 for 116)

```
         SA:  221   (D. T. Ring 6 for 72)
          &   240   (D. J. McGlew 69, K. J. Funston 65; R. R. Lindwall 5 for 60)
Second Test at Melbourne, Dec. 24-30. SA won by 82 runs.
         SA:  227   (A. R. A. Murray 51; K. R. Miller 4 for 62)
          &   388   (W. R. Endean 162*. J. H. B. Waite 62)
        AUS:  243   (C. C. McDonald 82. K. R. Miller 52; H. J. Tayfield 6 for 84)
          &   290   (R. N. Harvey 60. D. T. Ring 53; H. J. Tayfield 7 for 81)
Third Test at Sydney, Jan. 9-13. Aus won by an innings and 38 runs.
         SA:  173   (K. J. Funston 56; R. R. Lindwall 4 for 40)
          &   232   (W. R. Endean 71, R. A. McLean 65; R. R. Lindwall 4 for 72)
        AUS:  443   (R. N. Harvey 190. C. C. McDonald 67, D. T. Ring 58, K. R.
                     Miller 55; A. R. A. Murray 4 for 169)
Fourth Test at Adelaide, Jan. 24-29. Match Drawn
        AUS:  530   (A. L. Hassett 163, C. C. McDonald 154, R. N. Harvey 84, G. B.
                     Hole 59; H. J. Tayfield 4 for 142)
          &  233-3 dec. (R. N. Harvey 116, A. R. Morris 77)
         SA:  387   (K. J. Funston 92. J. C. Watkins 76, W. R. Endean 56; W. A.
                     Johnston 5 for 110 R. Benaud 4 for 118)
          &  177-6  (D. J. McGlew 54)
Fifth Test at Melbourne, Feb. 6-12. SA won by 6 wickets.
        AUS:  520   (R. N. Harvey 205, A. R. Morris 99, I. D. Craig 53)
          &   209   (E. R. H. Fuller 5 for 66)
         SA:  435   (J. C. Watkins 92, R. A. McLean 81, J. E. Cheetham 66, J. H. B.
                     Waite 64, P. N. F. Mansell 52; W. A. Johnston 6 for 152)
          &  297-4  (R. A. McLean 76*. W. R. Endean 70, J. C. Watkins 50)
```

1952-53: West Indies v India (Played 5, WI won 1, India won 0, Drawn 4)
First Test at Port of Spain, Jan. 21-28. Match Drawn.

```
        IND:  417   (P. R. Umrigar 130, M. L. Apte 64, G. S. Ramchand 61)
          &   294   (P. R. Umrigar 69, D. G. Phadkar 65  M. L. Apte 52)
         WI:  438   (E. D. Weekes 207, B. H. Pairaudeau 115; S. P. Gupte 7 for 162)
          &  142-0  (J. B. Stollmeyer 76*, A. F. Rae 63*)
Second Test at Bridgetown, Feb. 7-12. WI won by 142 runs.
         WI:  296   (C. L. Walcott 98)
          &   228   (J. B. Stollmeyer 54; D. G. Phadkar 5 for 64)
        IND:  253   (M. L. Apte 64, V. S. Hazare 63, P. R. Umrigar 56; A. L. Valentine
                     4 for 58)
          &   129   (S. Ramadhin 5 for 26)
Third Test at Port of Spain, Feb. 19-25. Match Drawn.
        IND:  279   (G. S. Ramchand 62. P. R. Umrigar 61; F. M. King 5 for 74)
          &  362-7 dec. (M. L. Apte 163*, V. M. Mankad 96, P. R. Umrigar 67)
         WI:  315   (E. D. Weekes 161; S. P. Gupte 5 for 107)
          &  192-2  (J. B. Stollmeyer 104*. E. D. Weekes 55*)
Fourth Test at Georgetown, Mar. 11-17. Match Drawn.
        IND:  262   (V. M. Mankad 66, C. V. Gadkari 50*; A. L. Valentine 5 for 127)
          &  190-5
         WI:  364   (C. L. Walcott 125. E. D. Weekes 86, F. M. M. Worrell 56; S. P.
                     Gupte 4 for 122)
Fifth Test at Kingston, Mar. 28-April 4. Match Drawn.
        IND:  312   (P. R. Umrigar 117. P. Roy 85; A. L. Valentine 5 for 64)
          &   444   (P. Roy 150, V. L. Manjrekar 118; G. E. Gomez 4 for 72, A. L.
                     Valentine 4 for 149)
         WI:  576   (F. M. M. Worrell 237, C. L. Walcott 118, E. D. Weekes 109, B. H.
                     Pairaudeau 58; S. P. Gupte 5 for 180, V. M. Mankad 5 for 228)
          &   92-4
```

1952-53: New Zealand v South Africa (Played 2, SA won 1, NZ won 0, Drawn 1)
First Test at Wellington, Mar. 6-10. SA won by an innings and 180 runs.

```
         SA:  524-8 dec. (D. J. McGlew 255*, A. R. A. Murray 109; R. W. Blair
                     4 for 98)
         NZ:  172   (B. Sutcliffe 62)
          &   172   (J. C. Watkins 4 for 22)
Second Test at Auckland, Mar. 13-17. Match Drawn.
         SA:  377   (W. R. Endean 116, J. H. B. Waite 72, J. E. Cheetham 54)
          &  200-5 dec. (D. J. McGlew 50)
```

NZ: 245   (H. J. Tayfield 5 for 62)
&   31–2

1953: England v Australia (Played 5, Eng won 1, Aus won 0, Drawn 4)
First Test at Trent Bridge, June 11–16. Match Drawn.
AUS: 249   (A. L. Hassett 115, A. R. Morris 67, K. R. Miller 55; A. V. Bedser
               7 for 55)
&   123   (A. R. Morris 60; A. V. Bedser 7 for 44)
ENG: 144   (R. R. Lindwall 5 for 57)
&   120–1 (L. Hutton 60*)
Second Test at Lord's, June 25–30. Match Drawn.
AUS: 346   (A. L. Hassett 104, A. K. Davidson 76, R. N. Harvey 59; A. V.
               Bedser 5 for 105, J. H. Wardle 4 for 77)
&   368   (K. R. Miller 109, A. R. Morris 89, R. R. Lindwall 50; F. R. Brown
               4 for 82)
ENG: 372   (L. Hutton 145, T. W. Graveney 78, D. C. S. Compton 57; R. R.
               Lindwall 5 for 66)
&   282–7 (W. Watson 109, T. E. Bailey 71)
Third Test at Old Trafford, July 9–14. Match Drawn.
AUS: 318   (R. N. Harvey 122, G. B. Hole 66; A. V. Bedser 5 for 115)
&   35–8   (J. H. Wardle 4 for 7)
ENG: 276   (L. Hutton 66)
Fourth Test at Headingley, July 23–28. Match Drawn.
ENG: 167   (T. W. Graveney 55; R. R. Lindwall 5 for 54)
&   275   (W. J. Edrich 64, D. C. S. Compton 61; K. R. Miller 4 for 63)
AUS: 266   (R. N. Harvey 71, G. B. Hole 53; A. V. Bedser 6 for 95)
&   147–4
Fifth Test at The Oval, Aug. 15–19. Eng won by 8 wickets.
AUS: 275   (R. R. Lindwall 62, A. L. Hassett 53; F. S. Trueman 4 for 86)
&   162   (G. A. R. Lock 5 for 45, J. C. Laker 4 for 75)
ENG: 306   (L. Hutton 82, T. E. Bailey 64; R. R. Lindwall 4 for 70)
&   132–2 (W. J. Edrich 55*)

1953–54: South Africa v New Zealand (Played 5, SA won 4, NZ won 0, Drawn 1)
First Test at Durban, Dec. 11–15. SA won by an innings and 58 runs.
SA: 437–9 dec. (R. A. McLean 101, D. J. McGlew 84, C. B. van Ryneveld 68*)
NZ: 230   (G. O. Rabone 107; H. J. Tayfield 6 for 62)
&   149   (G. O. Rabone 68)
Second Test at Johannesburg, Dec. 24–29. SA won by 132 runs.
SA: 271   (W. R. Endean 93, C. B. van Ryneveld 65)
&   148   (J. R. Reid 4 for 34, A. R. MacGibbon 4 for 62)
NZ: 187   (B. Sutcliffe 80*; D. E. J. Ironside 5 for 51)
&   100   (N. A. T. Adcock 5 for 43)
Third Test at Cape Town, Jan. 1–5. Match Drawn.
NZ: 505   (J. R. Reid 135, J. E. F. Beck 99, M. E. Chapple 76, B. Sutcliffe 66,
               G. O. Rabone 56; D. E. J. Ironside 4 for 117)
SA: 326   (J. E. Cheetham 89, D. J. McGlew 86; G. O. Rabone 6 for 68, A. R.
               MacGibbon 4 for 71)
&   159–3 (R. J. Westcott 62)
Fourth Test at Johannesburg, Jan. 29–Feb. 2. SA won by 9 wickets.
SA: 243   (D. J. McGlew 61, J. H. B. Waite 52)
&   25–1
NZ: 79   (H. J. Tayfield 6 for 13)
&   188   (N. A. T. Adcock 5 for 45)
Fifth Test at Port Elizabeth, Feb. 5–9. SA won by 5 wickets.
NZ: 226   (J. C. Watkins 4 for 34, N. A. T. Adcock 4 for 86)
&   222   (J. R. Reid 73, B. Sutcliffe 52; C. B. van Ryneveld 4 for 67)
SA: 237   (J. R. Reid 4 for 51)
&   215–5 (W. R. Endean 87)

1953–54: West Indies v England (Played 5, WI won 2, Eng won 2, Drawn 1)
First Test at Kingston, Jan. 15–21. WI won by 140 runs.
WI: 417   (J. K. Holt 94, C. L. Walcott 65, J. B. Stollmeyer 60, E. D. Weekes
               55, C. A. McWatt 54; J. B. Statham 4 for 90)
&   209–6 dec. (E. D. Weekes 90*)

ENG: 170   (S. Ramadhin 4 for 65)
     &   316   (W. Watson 116, P. B. H. May 69, L. Hutton 56; E. S. M. Kentish 5 for 49)

Second Test at Bridgetown, Feb. 6–12. WI won by 181 runs.
WI: 383   (C. L. Walcott 220, B. H. Pairaudeau 71, D. S. Atkinson 53; J. C. Laker 4 for 81)
     &   292–2 dec. (J. K. Holt 166, F. M. M. Worrell 76*)
ENG: 181   (L. Hutton 72; S. Ramadhin 4 for 50)
     &   313   (D. C. S. Compton 93, L. Hutton 77, T. W. Graveney 64*, P. B. H. May 62)

Third Test at Georgetown, Feb. 24–Mar. 2. Eng won by 9 wickets.
ENG: 435   (L. Hutton 169, D. C. S. Compton 64; S. Ramadhin 6 for 113)
     &   75–1
WI: 251   (E. D. Weekes 94, C. A. McWatt 54; J. B. Statham 4 for 64)
     &   256   (J. K. Holt 64)

Fourth Test at Port of Spain, Mar. 17–23. Match Drawn.
WI: 681–8 dec. (E. D. Weekes 206, F. M. M. Worrell 167, C. L. Walcott 124, D. S. Atkinson 74)
     &   212–4 dec. (F. M. M. Worrell 56, D. S. Atkinson 53*, C. L. Walcott 51*)
ENG: 537   (P. B. H. May 135, D. C. S. Compton 133, T. W. Graveney 92)
     &   98–3

Fifth Test at Kingston, Mar. 30–April 3. Eng won by nine wickets.
WI: 139   (C. L. Walcott 50; T. E. Bailey 7 for 34)
     &   346   (C. L. Walcott 116, J. B. Stollmeyer 64; J. C. Laker 4 for 71)
ENG: 414   (L. Hutton 205, J. H. Wardle 66; G. S. Sobers 4 for 75)
     &   72–1

1954: England v Pakistan (Played 4, Eng won 1, Pak won 1, Drawn 2)
First Test at Lord's, June 10–15. Match Drawn.
PAK: 87   (J. B. Statham 4 for 18, J. H. Wardle 4 for 33)
     &   121–3 (Waqar Hassan 53)
ENG: 117–9 dec. (Khan Mohammad 5 for 61, Fazal Mahmood 4 for 54)

Second Test at Trent Bridge, July 1–5. Eng won by an innings and 129 runs.
PAK: 157   (R. Appleyard 5 for 51)
     &   272   (Maqsood Ahmed 69, Hanif Mohammad 51)
ENG: 558–6 dec. (D. C. S. Compton 278, R. T. Simpson 101, T. W. Graveney 84)

Third Test at Old Trafford, July 22–27. Match Drawn.
ENG: 359–8 dec. (D. C. S. Compton 93, T. W. Graveney 65, J. H. Wardle 54; Fazal Mahmood 4 for 107)
PAK: 90   (J. H. Wardle 4 for 19)
     &   25–4

Fourth Test at The Oval, Aug. 12–17. Pak won by 24 runs.
PAK: 133   (F. H. Tyson 4 for 35)
     &   164   (J. H. Wardle 7 for 56)
ENG: 130   (D. C. S. Compton 53; Fazal Mahmood 6 for 53, Mahmood Hussain 4 for 58)
     &   143   (P. B. H. May 53; Fazal Mahmood 6 for 46)

1954–55: Australia v England (Played 5, Eng won 3, Aus won 1, Drawn 1)
First Test at Brisbane, Nov. 26–Dec. 1. Aus won by an innings and 154 runs.
AUS: 601–8 dec. (R. N. Harvey 162, A. R. Morris 153, R. R. Lindwall 64*, G. B. Hole 57)
ENG: 190   (T. E. Bailey 88)
     &   257   (W. J. Edrich 88)

Second Test at Sydney, Dec. 17–22. Eng won by 38 runs.
ENG: 154
     &   296   (P. B. H. May 104, M. C. Cowdrey 54)
AUS: 228   (F. H. Tyson 4 for 45, T. E. Bailey 4 for 59)
     &   184   (R. N. Harvey 92*; F. H. Tyson 6 for 85)

Third Test at Melbourne, Dec. 31–Jan. 5. Eng won by 128 runs.
ENG: 191   (M. C. Cowdrey 102; R. G. Archer 4 for 33)
     &   279   (P. B. H. May 91; W. A. Johnston 5 for 85)
AUS: 231   (J. B. Statham 5 for 60)
     &   111   (F. H. Tyson 7 for 27)

Fourth Test at Adelaide, Jan. 28–Feb. 2. Eng won by 5 wickets.
    AUS: 323   (L. V. Maddocks 69)
      &   111
    ENG: 341   (L. Hutton 80, M. C. Cowdrey 79; R. Benaud 4 for 120)
      &   97–5
Fifth Test at Sydney, Feb. 25–Mar. 3. Match Drawn.
    ENG: 371–7 dec. (T. W. Graveney 111, D. C. S. Compton 84, P. B. H. May 79,
                   T. E. Bailey 72)
    AUS: 221   (C. C. McDonald 72; J. H. Wardle 5 for 79)
      &   118–6

1954–55: Pakistan v India (Played 5, Pak won 0, India won 0, Drawn 5)
First Test at Dacca, Jan. 1–4. Match Drawn.
    PAK: 257   (Imtiaz Ahmed 54, Waqar Hassan 52; Ghulam Ahmed 5 for 109)
      &   158   (Alim-ud-Din 51, Waqar Hassan 51; S. P. Gupte 5 for 18)
    IND: 148   (Mahmood Hussain 6 for 67, Khan Mohammad 4 for 42)
      &   147–2 (V. L. Manjrekar 74*, P. Roy 67*)
Second Test at Bahawalpur, Jan. 15–18. Match Drawn.
    IND: 235   (N. S. Tamhane 54*, G. S. Ramchand 53, V. L. Manjrekar 50;
                   Khan Mohammad 5 for 74, Fazal Mahmood 4 for 86)
      &   209–5 (P. Roy 77, V. L. Manjrekar 59)
    PAK: 312–9 dec. (Hanif Mohammad 142, Alim-ud-Din 64; P. R. Umrigar
                   6 for 74)
Third Test at Lahore, Jan. 29–Feb. 1. Match Drawn.
    PAK: 328   (Maqsood Ahmed 99, Wazir Mohammad 55, Imtiaz Ahmed 55;
                   S. P. Gupte 5 for 133)
      &   136–5 dec. (Alim-ud-Din 58)
    IND: 251   (P. R. Umrigar 78; Mahmood Hussain 4 for 70)
      &   74–2
Fourth Test at Peshawar, Feb. 13–16. Match Drawn.
    PAK: 188   (S. P. Gupte 5 for 63)
      &   182   (Imtiaz Ahmed 69; V. M. Mankad 5 for 64)
    IND: 245   (P. R. Umrigar 108; Khan Mohammad 4 for 79)
      &   23–1
Fifth Test at Karachi, Feb. 26–Mar. 1. Match Drawn.
    PAK: 162   (G. S. Ramchand 6 for 49)
      &   241–5 dec. (Alim-ud-Din 103*, A. H. Kardar 93)
    IND: 145   (Fazal Mahmood 5 for 49, Khan Mohammad 5 for 72)
      &   69–2

1954–55: New Zealand v England (Played 2, Eng won 2)
First Test at Dunedin, Mar 11–16. Eng won by 8 wickets.
    NZ: 125   (B. Sutcliffe 74; J. B. Statham 4 for 24)
      &   132   (F. H. Tyson 4 for 16)
    ENG: 209–8 dec. (J. R. Reid 4 for 36)
      &   49–2
Second Test at Auckland, Mar. 25–28. Eng won by an innings and 20 runs.
    NZ: 200   (J. R. Reid 73; J. B. Statham 4 for 28)
      &   26   (R. Appleyard 4 for 7)
    ENG: 246   (L. Hutton 53; A. M. Moir 5 for 62)

1954–55: West Indies v Australia (Played 5, Aus won 3, WI won 0, Drawn 2)
First Test at Kingston, Mar. 26–31. Aus won by 9 wickets.
    AUS: 515–9 dec. (K. R. Miller 147, R. N. Harvey 133, A. R. Morris 65, C. C.
                   McDonald 50)
      &   20–1
    WI: 259   (C. L. Walcott 108; R. R. Lindwall 4 for 61)
      &   275   (O. G. Smith 104, J. K. Holt 60)
Second Test at Port of Spain, April 11–16. Match Drawn.
    WI: 382   (E. D. Weekes 139, C. L. Walcott 126; R. R. Lindwall 6 for 95)
      &   273–4 (C. L. Walcott 110, E. D. Weekes 87*)
    AUS: 600–9 dec. (R. N. Harvey 133, A. R. Morris 111, C. C. McDonald 110,
                   R. G. Archer 84, I. W. Johnson 66)
Third Test at Georgetown, April 26–29. Aus won by 8 wickets.
    WI: 182   (E. D. Weekes 81; R. Benaud 4 for 15)

       & 207   (C. L. Walcott 73, F. M. M. Worrell 56; I. W. Johnson 7 for 44)
AUS: 257   (R. Benaud 68, C. C. McDonald 61)
       & 133–2

Fourth Test at Bridgetown, May 14–20. Match Drawn.
AUS: 668   (K. R. Miller 137, R. R. Lindwall 118, R. G. Archer 98, R. N. Harvey 74, L. E. Favell 72, G. R. Langley 53; D. T. Dewdney 4 for 125)
       & 249   (I. W. Johnson 57, L. E. Favell 53; D. S. Atkinson 5 for 56)
WI: 510   (D. S. Atkinson 219, C. C. Depeiaza 122)
       & 234–6 (C. L. Walcott 83)

Fifth Test at Kingston, June 11–17. Aus won by an innings and 82 runs.
WI: 357   (C. L. Walcott 155, F. M. M. Worrell 61, E. D. Weekes 56; K. R. Miller 6 for 107)
       & 319   (C. L. Walcott 110, G. S. Sobers 64)
AUS: 758–8 dec. (R. N. Harvey 204, R. G. Archer 128, C. C. McDonald 127, R. Benaud 121, K. R. Miller 109)

1955: England v South Africa (Played 5, Eng won 3, SA won 2)
First Test at Trent Bridge, June 9–13. Eng won by innings and 5 runs.
ENG: 334   (D. Kenyon 87, P. B. H. May 83)
SA: 181   (D. J. McGlew 68, J. E. Cheetham 54; J. H. Wardle 4 for 24)
      & 148   (D. J. McGlew 51; F. H. Tyson 6 for 28)

Second Test at Lord's, June 23–27. Eng won by 71 runs.
ENG: 133   (P. S. Heine 5 for 60, T. L. Goddard 4 for 59)
      & 353   (P. B. H. May 112, D. C. S. Compton 69, T. W. Graveney 60; H. J. Tayfield 5 for 80)
SA: 304   (R. A. McLean 142, H. J. Keith 57; J. H. Wardle 4 for 65)
      & 111   (J. B. Statham 7 for 39)

Third Test at Old Trafford, July 7–12. SA won by 3 wickets.
ENG: 284   (D. C. S. Compton 158)
      & 381   (P. B. H. May 117, D. C. S. Compton 71, M. C. Cowdrey 50; P. S. Heine 5 for 86)
SA: 521–8 dec. (J. H. B. Waite 113, P. L. Winslow 108, D. J. McGlew 104*, T. L. Goddard 62)
      & 145–7 (R. A. McLean 50)

Fourth Test at Headingley, July 21–26. SA won by 224 runs.
SA: 171   (P. J. Loader 4 for 52)
      & 500   (D. J. McGlew 133, W. R. Endean 116*, T. L. Goddard 74, H. J. Keith 73; J. H. Wardle 4 for 100)
ENG: 191   (D. C. S. Compton 61; P. S. Heine 4 for 70, H. J. Tayfield 4 for 70)
      & 256   (P. B. H. May 97; T. L. Goddard 5 for 69, H. J. Tayfield 5 for 94)

Fifth Test at The Oval. Aug. 13–17. Eng won by 92 runs.
ENG: 151   (T. L. Goddard 5 for 31)
      & 204   (P. B. H. May 89*; H. J. Tayfield 5 for 60)
SA: 112   (G. A. R. Lock 4 for 39)
      & 151   (J. H. B. Waite 60; J. C. Laker 5 for 56, G. A. R. Lock 4 for 62)

1955–56: Pakistan v New Zealand (Played 3, Pak won 2, NZ won 0, Drawn 1)
First Test at Karachi, Oct. 13–17. Pak won by an innings and 1 run.
NZ: 164   (Zulfiqar Ahmed 5 for 37)
      & 124   (Zulfiqar Ahmed 6 for 42)
PAK: 289   (Imtiaz Ahmed 64; A. R. MacGibbon 4 for 98)

Second Test at Lahore, Oct. 26–31. Pak won by 4 wickets.
NZ: 348   (S. N. McGregor 111, N. S. Harford 93, A. R. MacGibbon 61; Khan Mohammad 4 for 78)
      & 328   (J. R. Reid 86, N. S. Harford 64; Zulfiqar Ahmed 4 for 114)
PAK: 561   (Imtiaz Ahmed 209, Waqar Hassan 189; A. M. Moir 4 for 114)
      & 117–6 (J. R. Reid 4 for 38)

Third Test at Dacca, Nov. 7–12. Match Drawn.
NZ: 70   (Khan Mohammad 6 for 21)
      & 69–6
PAK: 195–6 dec. (Hanif Mohammad 103)

1955–56: India v New Zealand (Played 5, India won 2, NZ won 0, Drawn 3)
First Test at Hyderabad, Nov. 19–24. Match Drawn.

IND: 498–4 dec. (P. R. Umrigar 223, V. L. Manjrekar 118, A. G. Kripal Singh 100*)
NZ: 326   (J. W. Guy 102, A. R. MacGibbon 59, J. R. Reid 54; S. P. Gupte
                  7 for 128)
    &   212–2 (B. Sutcliffe 137*)
Second Test at Bombay, Dec. 2–7. India won by an innings and 27 runs.
IND: 421–8 dec. (V. M. Mankad 223, A. G. Kripal Singh 63)
NZ: 258   (B. Sutcliffe 73)
    &   136   (S. P. Gupte 5 for 45)
Third Test at New Delhi, Dec. 16–21. Match Drawn.
NZ: 450–2 dec. (B. Sutcliffe 230*, J. R. Reid 119*, J. W. Guy 52)
    &   112–1 (J. G. Leggat 50*)
IND: 531–7 dec. (V. L. Manjrekar 177, G. S. Ramchand 72, R. G. Nadkarni
                  63*, N. J. Contractor 62)
Fourth Test at Calcutta, Dec. 28–Jan. 2. Match Drawn.
IND: 132
    &   438–7 dcc. (G. S. Ramchand 106*, P. Roy 100, V. L. Manjrekar 90, N. J.
                 Contractor 61)
NZ: 336   (J. R. Reid 120, J. W. Guy 91; S. P. Gupte 6 for 90)
    &   75–6
Fifth Test at Madras, Jan. 6–11. India won by an innings and 109 runs.
IND: 537–3 dec. (V. M. Mankad 231, P. Roy 173, P. R. Umrigar 79*)
NZ: 209   (S. P. Gupte 5 for 72)
    &   219   (J. G. Leggat 61, J. R. Reid 63; V. M. Mankad 4 for 65, S. P. Gupte
                 4 for 73)

1955–56: New Zealand v West Indies (Played 4, WI won 3, NZ won 1)

First Test at Dunedin, Feb. 3–6. WI won by an innings and 71 runs.
NZ: 74   (S. Ramadhin 6 for 23)
    &   208   (J. E. F. Beck 66)
WI: 353   (E. D. Weekes 123, O. G. Smith 64; R. W. Blair 4 for 90)
Second Test at Christchurch, Feb. 18–21. WI won by an innings and 64 runs.
WI: 386   (E. D. Weekes 103, D. S. Atkinson 85, J. D. C. Goddard 83*)
NZ: 158   (S. Ramadhin 5 for 46)
    &   164   (A. L. Valentine 5 for 32, O. G. Smith 4 for 75)
Third Test at Wellington, Mar. 3–7. WI won by 9 wickets.
WI: 404   (E. D. Weekes 156, B. H. Pairaudeau 68, D. S. Atkinson 60)
    &   13–1
NZ: 208   (J. E. F. Bcck 55)
    &   208   (D. D. Taylor 77; D. S. Atkinson 5 for 66)
Fourth Test at Auckland, Mar. 9–13. NZ won by 190 runs.
NZ: 255   (J. R. Reid 84; D. T. Dewdney 5 for 21)
    &   157–9 dec. (D. S. Atkinson 7 for 53)
WI: 145   (H. A. Furlonge 64; H. B. Cave 4 for 22, A. R. MacGibbon 4 for 44)
    &   77   (H. B. Cave 4 for 21)

1956: England v Australia (Played 5, Eng won 2, Aus won 1, Drawn 2)

First Test at Trent Bridge, June 7–12. Match Drawn.
ENG: 217–8 dec. (P. E. Richardson 81, P. B. H. May 73; K. R. Miller 4 for 69)
    &   188–3 dec. (M. C. Cowdrey 81, P. E. Richardson 73)
AUS: 148   (R. N. Harvey 64; J. C. Laker 4 for 58)
    &   120–3 (J. W. Burke 58*)
Second Test at Lord's, June 21–26. Aus won by 185 runs.
AUS: 285   (C. C. McDonald 78, J. W. Burke 65)
    &   257   (R. Benaud 97; F. S. Trueman 5 for 90, T. E. Bailey 4 for 64)
ENG: 171   (P. B. H. May 63; K. R. Miller 5 for 72)
    &   186   (P. B. H. May 53; K. R. Miller 5 for 80, R. G. Archer 4 for 71)
Third Test at Headingley, July 12–17. Eng won by an innings and 42 runs.
ENG: 325   (P. B. H. May 101, C. Washbrook 98)
AUS: 143   (J. C. Laker 5 for 58, G. A. R. Lock 4 for 41)
    &   140   (R. N. Harvey 69; J. C. Laker 6 for 55)
Fourth Test at Old Trafford, July 26–31. Eng won by an innings and 170 runs.
ENG: 459   (Rev. D. S. Sheppard 113, P. E. Richardson 104, M. C. Cowdrey
                 80; I. W. Johnson 4 for 151)
AUS: 84   (J. C. Laker 9 for 37)

    &   205   (C. C. McDonald 89; J. C. Laker 10 for 53)

Fifth Test at The Oval, Aug. 23–28. Match Drawn.

    ENG: 247   (D. C. S. Compton 94, P. B. H. May 83*; R. G. Archer 5 for 53,
                      K. R. Miller 4 for 91)

    &   182–3 dec. (Rev. D. S. Sheppard 62)

    AUS: 202   (K. R. Miller 61; J. C. Laker 4 for 80)

    &   27–5

1956–57: Pakistan v Australia (Played 1, Pak won 1)

Test at Karachi, Oct. 11–17. Pak won by 9 wickets.

    AUS: 80   (Fazal Mahmood 6 for 34, Khan Mohammad 4 for 43)

    &   187   (R. Benaud 56; Fazal Mahmood 7 for 80)

    PAK: 199   (A. H. Kardar 69, Wazir Mohammad 67; I. W. Johnson 4 for 50)

    &   69–1

1956–57: India v Australia (Played 3, Aus won 2, India won 0, Drawn 1)

First Test at Madras, Oct. 19–23. Aus won by an innings and 5 runs.

    IND: 161   (R. Benaud 7 for 72)

    &   153   (R. R. Lindwall 7 for 43)

    AUS: 319   (I. W. Johnson 73; V. M. Mankad 4 for 90)

Second Test at Bombay, Oct. 26–31. Match Drawn.

    IND: 251   (G. S. Ramchaud 109, V. L. Manjrekar 55)

    &   250–5 (P. Roy 79, P. R. Umrigar 78)

    AUS: 523–7 dec. (J. W. Burke 161, R. N. Harvey 140, P. J. Burge 83)

Third Test at Calcutta, Nov. 2–6. Aus won by 94 runs.

    AUS: 177   (P. J. Burge 58; Ghulam Ahmed 7 for 49)

    &   189–9 dec. (R. N. Harvey 69; V. M. Mankad 4 for 49)

    IND: 136   (R. Benaud 6 for 52)

    &   136   (R. Benaud 5 for 53, J. W. Burke 4 for 37)

1956–57: South Africa v England (Played 5, SA won 2, Eng won 2, Drawn 1)

First Test at Johannesburg, Dec. 24–29. Eng won by 131 runs.

    ENG: 268   (P. E. Richardson 117, M. C. Cowdrey 59; N. A. T. Adcock
                      4 for 36)

    &   150

    SA: 215

    &   72   (T. E. Bailey 5 for 20)

Second Test at Cape Town, Jan. 1–5. Eng won by 312 runs.

    ENG: 369   (M. C. Cowdrey 101, T. G. Evans 62, D. C. S. Compton 58; H. J.
                      Tayfield 5 for 130)

    &   220–6 dec. (D. C. S. Compton 64, M. C. Cowdrey 61)

    SA: 205   (J. H. Wardle 5 for 53)

    &   72   (J. H. Wardle 7 for 36)

Third Test at Durban, Jan. 25–30. Match Drawn.

    ENG: 218   (T. E. Bailey 80, P. E. Richardson 68; N. A. T. Adcock 4 for 39)

    &   254   (D. J. Insole 110*; H. J. Tayfield 8 for 69)

    SA: 283   (R. A. McLean 100, T. L. Goddard 69; J. H. Wardle 5 for 61)

    &   142–6

Fourth Test at Johannesburg, Feb. 15–20. SA won by 17 runs.

    SA: 340   (R. A. McLean 93, T. L. Goddard 67, J. H. B. Waite 61)

    &   142

    ENG: 251   (P. B. H. May 61; H. J. Tayfield 4 for 79)

    &   214   (D. J. Insole 68, M. C. Cowdrey 55; H. J. Tayfield 9 for 113)

Fifth Test at Port Elizabeth, Mar. 1–5. SA won by 58 runs.

    SA: 164   (W. R. Endean 70)

    &   134   (F. H. Tyson 6 for 40)

    ENG: 110   (N. A. T. Adcock 4 for 20, P. S. Heine 4 for 22)

    &   130   (H. J. Tayfield 6 for 78)

1957: England v West Indies (Played 5, Eng won 3, WI won 0, Drawn 2)

First Test at Edgbaston, May 30–June 4. Match Drawn.

    ENG: 186   (S. Ramadhin 7 for 49)

    &   583–4 dec. (P. B. H. May 285*, M. C. Cowdrey 154)

    WI: 474   (O. G. Smith 161, C. L. Walcott 90, F. M. M. Worrell 81, G. S.
                      Sobers 53; J. C. Laker 4 for 119)

    &   72–7

Second Test at Lord's, June 20–22. Eng won by an innings and 36 runs.
WI: 127   (T. E. Bailey 7 for 44)
&   261   (E. D. Weekes 90, G. S. Sobers 66; T. E. Bailey 4 for 54)
ENG: 424   (M. C. Cowdrey 152, T. G. Evans 82, P. E. Richardson 76; R.
Gilchrist 4 for 115)
Third Test at Trent Bridge, July 4–9. Match Drawn.
ENG: 619–6 dec. (T. W. Graveney 258, P. E. Richardson 126, P. B. H. May 104,
M. C. Cowdrey 55)
&   64–1
WI: 372   (F. M. M. Worrell 191*; F. S. Trueman 5 for 63)
&   367   (O. G. Smith 168, J. D. C. Goddard 61; J. B. Statham 5 for 118,
F. S. Trueman 4 for 80)
Fourth Test at Headingley, July 25–27. Eng won by an innings and 5 runs.
WI: 142   (P. J. Loader 6 for 36)
&   132
ENG: 279   (P. B. H. May 69, M. C. Cowdrey 68, Rev. D. S. Sheppard 68;
F. M. M. Worrell 7 for 70)
Fifth Test at The Oval, Aug. 22–24. Eng won by an innings and 237 runs.
ENG: 412   (T. W. Graveney 164, P. E. Richardson 107; S. Ramadhin
4 for 107)
WI: 89   (G. A. R. Lock 5 for 28)
&   86   (G. A. R. Lock 6 for 20)

1957–58: South Africa v Australia (Played 5, Aus won 3, SA won 0, Drawn 2)
First Test at Johannesburg, Dec. 23–28. Match Drawn.
SA: 470–9 dec. (J. H. B. Waite 115, D. J. McGlew 108, T. L. Goddard 90,
W. R. Endean 50, R. A. McLean 50; I. W. Meckiff 5 for 125)
&   201   (W. R. Endean 77, J. H. B. Waite 59; A. K. Davidson 6 for 34)
AUS: 368   (R. Benaud 122, C. C. McDonald 75, R. B. Simpson 60; P. S. Heine
6 for 58)
&   162–3 (K. D. Mackay 65*)
Second Test at Cape Town, Dec. 31–Jan. 3. Aus won by an innings and 141 runs.
AUS: 449   (J. W. Burke 189, C. C. McDonald 99, K. D. Mackay 63; H. J.
Tayfield 5 for 120)
SA: 209   (R. Benaud 4 for 95)
&   99   (T. L. Goddard 56*; R. Benaud 5 for 49)
Third Test at Durban, Jan. 24–29. Match Drawn.
AUS: 163   (I. D. Craig 52; N. A. T. Adcock 6 for 43)
&   292–7 (J. W. Burke 83, R. N. Harvey 68, K. D. Mackay 52*)
SA: 384   (J. H. B. Waite 134, D. J. McGlew 105; R. Benaud 5 for 114)
Fourth Test at Johannesburg, Feb. 7–12. Aus won by 10 wickets.
AUS: 401   (R. Benaud 100, K. D. Mackay 83*, J. W. Burke 81, A. K. Davidson
62; P. S. Heine 6 for 96)
&   1–0
SA: 203   (K. J. Funston 70; R. Benaud 4 for 70)
&   198   (D. J. McGlew 70, K. J. Funston 64*; R. Benaud 5 for 84)
Fifth Test at Port Elizabeth, Feb. 28–Mar. 4. Aus won by 8 wickets.
SA: 214   (H. J. Tayfield 66; L. F. Kline 4 for 33, A. K. Davidson 4 for 44)
&   144   (A. K. Davidson 5 for 38, R. Benaud 5 for 82)
AUS: 291   (K. D. Mackay 77*, C. C. McDonald 58)
&   68–2

1957–58 West Indies v Pakistan (Played 5, WI won 3, Pak won 1, Drawn 1)
First Test at Bridgetown, Jan. 17–23. Match Drawn.
WI: 579–9 dec. (E. D. Weekes 197, C. C. Hunte 142, O. G. Smith 78, G. S.
Sobers 52; Mahmood Hussain 4 for 153)
&   28–0
PAK: 106   (R. Gilchrist 4 for 32)
&   657–8 dec. (Hanif Mohammad 337, Imtiaz Ahmed 91, Saeed Ahmed 65)
Second Test at Port of Spain, Feb. 5–11. WI won by 120 runs.
WI: 325   (R. Kanhai 96, E. D. Weekes 78, G. S. Sobers 52)
&   312   (G. S. Sobers 80, F. C. M. Alexander 57, O. G. Smith 51; Fazal
Mahmood 4 for 89)
PAK: 282   (Wallis Mathias 73, Fazal Mahmood 60; O. G. Smith 4 for 71)

        &   235   (Hanif Mohammad 81, Saeed Ahmed 64; R. Gilchrist 4 for 61)
Third Test at Kingston, Feb. 26–Mar. 4. WI won by an innings and 174 runs.
    PAK: 328   (Imtiaz Ahmed 122, Wallis Mathias 77, Saeed Ahmed 52; E. S.
                   Atkinson 5 for 42)
        &   288   (Wazir Mohammad 106, A. H. Kardar 57)
    WI: 790–3 dec. (G. S. Sobers 365*, C. C. Hunte 260, C. L. Walcott 88*)
Fourth Test at Georgetown, Mar. 13–19. WI won by 8 wickets.
    PAK: 408   (Saeed Ahmed 150, Hanif Mohammad 79; R. Gilchrist 4 for 102)
        &   318   (Wazir Mohammad 97*, A. H. Kardar 56; L. R. Gibbs 5 for 80)
    WI: 410   (C. L. Walcott 145, G. S. Sobers 125; Nasim-ul-Ghani 5 for 116)
        &   317–2 (C. C. Hunte 114, G. S. Sobers 109*, R. Kanhai 62)
Fifth Test at Port of Spain, Mar. 26–31. Pak won by an innings and 1 run.
    WI: 268   (O. G. Smith 86, E. D. Weekes 51; Fazal Mahmood 6 for 83)
        &   227   (C. L. Walcott 62; Nasim-ul-Ghani 6 for 67)
    PAK: 496   (Wazir Mohammad 189, Saeed Ahmed 97, Hanif Mohammad 54;
                   J. Taylor 5 for 109, L. R. Gibbs 4 for 108)

1958: England v New Zealand (Played 5, Eng won 4, NZ won 0, Drawn 1)
First Test at Edgbaston, June 5–9. Eng won by 205 runs.
    ENG: 221   (P. B. H. May 84, M. C. Cowdrey 81; A. R. MacGibbon 5 for 64,
                   J. C. Alabaster 4 for 46)
        &   215–6 dec. (P. E. Richardson 100, M. C. Cowdrey 70)
    NZ: 94   (F. S. Trueman 5 for 31)
        &   137
Second Test at Lord's, June 19–21. Eng won by an innings and 148 runs.
    ENG: 269   (M. C. Cowdrey 65; J. A. Hayes 4 for 36, A. R. MacGibbon
                   4 for 86)
    NZ: 47   (G. A. R. Lock 5 for 17, J. C. Laker 4 for 13)
        &   74   (G. A. R. Lock 4 for 12)
Third Test at Headingley, July 3–8. Eng won by an innings and 71 runs.
    NZ: 67   (J. C. Laker 5 for 17, G. A. R. Lock 4 for 14)
        &   129   (G. A. R. Lock 7 for 51)
    ENG: 267–2 dec. (P. B. H. May 113*, C. A. Milton 104*)
Fourth Test at Old Trafford, July 24–29. Eng won by an innings and 13 runs.
    NZ: 267   (A. R. MacGibbon 66, J. T. Sparling 50; J. B. Statham 4 for 71)
        &   85   (G. A. R. Lock 7 for 35)
    ENG: 365–9 dec. (P. B. H. May 101, P. E. Richardson 74, W. Watson 66, E. R.
                   Dexter 52)
Fifth Test at The Oval, Aug. 21–26. Match Drawn.
    NZ: 161
        &   91–3 (J. R. Reid 51*)
    ENG: 219–9 dec. (A. R. MacGibbon 4 for 65)

1958–59: India v West Indies (Played 5, WI won 3, India won 0, Drawn 2)
First Test at Bombay, Nov. 28–Dec. 3. Match Drawn.
    WI: 227   (R. Kanhai 66, O. G. Smith 63; S. P. Gupte 4 for 86)
        &   323–4 dec. (G. S. Sobers 142*, B. F. Butcher 64*, O. G. Smith 58)
    IND: 152   (P. R. Umrigar 55; R. Gilchrist 4 for 39)
        &   289–5 (P. Roy 90, G. S. Ramchand 67*)
Second Test at Kanpur, Dec. 12–17. WI won by 203 runs.
    WI: 222   (F. C. M. Alexander 70; S. P. Gupte 9 for 102)
        &   443–7 dec. (G. S. Sobers 198, J. S. Solomon 86, B. F. Butcher 60)
    IND: 222   (P. R. Umrigar 57; W. W. Hall 6 for 50)
        &   240   (N. J. Contractor 50; W. W. Hall 5 for 76)
Third Test at Calcutta, Dec. 31–Jan. 4. WI won by an innings and 336 runs.
    WI: 614–5 dec. (R. Kanhai 256, G. S. Sobers 106*, B. F. Butcher 103, J. S.
                   Solomon 69*)
    IND: 124
        &   154   (V. L. Manjrekar 58*; R. Gilchrist 6 for 55)
Fourth Test at Madras, Jan. 21–26. WI won by 295 runs.
    WI: 500   (B. F. Butcher 142, R. Kanhai 99, J. K. Holt 63; V. M. Mankad
                   4 for 95)
        &   168–5 dec. (J. K. Holt 81*; S. P. Gupte 4 for 78)
    IND: 222   (A. G. Kripal Singh 53; G. S. Sobers 4 for 26)

&   151   (C. G. Borde 56)
Fifth Test at New Delhi, Feb. 6–11. Match Drawn.
IND: 415   (C. G. Borde 109, N. J. Contractor 92, P. R. Umrigar 76, H. R.
Adhikari 63; W. W. Hall 4 for 66)
&   275   (C. G. Borde 96, P. Roy 58, D. K. Gaekwad 52; O. G. Smith
5 for 90)
WI: 644–8 dec. (J. K. Holt 123, O. G. Smith 100, J. S. Solomon 100*, C. C.
Hunte 92, B. F. Butcher 71; R. B. Desai 4 for 169)

1958–59: Australia v England (Played 5, Aus won 4, Eng won 0, Drawn 1)
First Test at Brisbane, Dec. 5–10. Aus won by 8 wickets.
ENG: 134
&   198   (T. E. Bailey 68; R. Benaud 4 for 66)
AUS: 186   (P. J. Loader 4 for 56)
&   147–2 (N. C. O'Neill 71*)
Second Test at Melbourne, Dec. 31–Jan. 5. Aus won by 8 wickets.
ENG: 259   (P. B. H. May 113; A. K. Davidson 6 for 64)
&   87   (I. W. Meckiff 6 for 38)
AUS: 308   (R. N. Harvey 167; J. B. Statham 7 for 57)
&   42–2
Third Test at Sydney, Jan. 9–15. Match Drawn.
ENG: 219   (R. Benaud 5 for 83)
&   287–7 dec. (M. C. Cowdrey 100*, P. B. H. May 92; R. Benaud 4 for 94)
AUS: 357   (N. C. O'Neill 77, A. K. Davidson 71, K. D. Mackay 57, L. E.
Favell 54; J. C. Laker 5 for 107, G. A. R. Lock 4 for 130)
&   54–2
Fourth Test at Adelaide, Jan. 30–Feb. 5. Aus won by 10 wickets.
AUS: 476   (C. C. McDonald 170, J. W. Burke 66, N. C. O'Neill 56; F. S.
Trueman 4 for 90)
&   36–0
ENG: 240   (M. C. Cowdrey 84; R. Benaud 5 for 91)
&   270   (P. B. H. May 59, T. W. Graveney 53*; R. Benaud 4 for 82)
Fifth Test at Melbourne, Feb. 13–18. Aus won by 9 wickets.
ENG: 205   (P. E. Richardson 68; R. Benaud 4 for 43)
&   214   (T. W. Graveney 54)
AUS: 351   (C. C. McDonald 133, A. T. W. Grout 74, R. Benaud 64; F. S.
Trueman 4 for 92, J. C. Laker 4 for 93)
&   69–1 (C. C. McDonald 51*)

1958–59: Pakistan v West Indies (Played 3, Pak won 2, WI won 1)
First Test at Karachi, Feb. 20–25. Pak won by 10 wickets.
WI: 146   (Fazal Mahmood 4 for 35, Nasim-ul-Ghani 4 for 35)
&   245   (J. S. Solomon 66, B. F. Butcher 61)
PAK: 304   (Hanif Mohammad 103, Saeed Ahmed 78)
&   88–0
Second Test at Dacca, Mar. 6–8. Pak won by 41 runs.
PAK: 145   (Wallis Mathias 64; W. W. Hall 4 for 28)
&   144   (E. S. Atkinson 4 for 42, W. W. Hall 4 for 49)
WI: 76   (Fazal Mahmood 6 for 34)
&   172   (Fazal Mahmood for 66, Mahmood Hussain 4 for 48)
Third Test at Lahore, Mar. 26–31. WI won by an innings and 156 runs.
WI: 469   (R. Kanhai 217, G. S. Sobers 72, J. S. Solomon 56)
PAK: 209   (W. W. Hall 5 for 87)
&   104   (S. Ramadhin 4 for 25)

1958–59: New Zealand v England (Played 2, Eng won 1, NZ won 0, Drawn 1)
First Test at Christchurch, Feb. 27–Mar. 2. Eng won by an innings and 99 runs.
ENG: 374   (E. R. Dexter 141, P. B. H. May 71)
NZ: 142   (G. A. R. Lock 5 for 31)
&   133   (J. W. Guy 56; G. A. R. Lock 6 for 53)
Second Test at Auckland, Mar. 14–18. Match Drawn.
NZ: 181   (B. Sutcliffe 61)
ENG: 311–7 (P. B. H. May 124*, P. E. Richardson 67)

1959: England v India (Played 5, Eng won 5)
First Test at Trent Bridge, June 4–8. Eng won by an innings and 59 runs.

ENG: 422   (P. B. H. May 106, T. G. Evans 73, M. J. Horton 58, K. F. Bar-
              rington 56; S. P. Gupte 4 for 102)
IND: 206   (P. Roy 54; F. S. Trueman 4 for 45)
&   157   (J. B. Statham 5 for 31)
Second Test at Lord's, June 18–20. Eng won by 8 wickets.
IND: 168   (N. J. Contractor 81; T. Greenhough 5 for 35)
&   165   (V. L. Manjrekar 61)
ENG: 226   (K. F. Barrington 80; R. B. Desai 5 for 89)
&   108–2 (M. C. Cowdrey 63*)
Third Test at Headingley, July 2–4. Eng won by an innings and 173 runs.
IND: 161   (H. J. Rhodes 4 for 50)
&   149   (D. B. Close 4 for 35)
ENG: 483–8 dec. (M. C. Cowdrey 160, K. F. Barrington 80, W. G. A. Parkhouse
              78, G. Pullar 75; S. P. Gupte 4 for 111)
Fourth Test at Old Trafford, July 23–28. Eng won by 171 runs.
ENG: 490   (G. Pullar 131, M. J. K. Smith 100, K. F. Barrington 87, M. C.
              Cowdrey 67; R. Surendranath 5 for 115)
&   265–8 dec. (S. P. Gupte 4 for 76)
IND: 208   (C. G. Borde 75)
&   376   (P. R. Umrigar 118, A. A. Baig 112, N. J. Contractor 56)
Fifth Test at The Oval, Aug. 20–24. Eng won by an innings and 27 runs.
IND: 140   (F. S. Trueman 4 for 24)
&   194   (R. G. Nadkarni 76)
ENG: 361   (M. J. K. Smith 98, R. Subba Row 94, R. Swetman 65, R. Illing-
              worth 50; R. Surendranath 5 for 75)

1959–60: Pakistan v Australia (Played 3, Aus won 2, Pak won 0, Drawn 1)
First Test at Dacca, Nov. 13–18. Aus won by 8 wickets.
PAK: 200   (Hanif Mohammad 66, D. Sharpe 56; A. K. Davidson 4 for 42, R.
              Benaud 4 for 69)
&   134   (K. D. Mackay 6 for 42, R. Benaud 4 for 42)
AUS: 225   (R. N. Harvey 96, A. T. W. Grout 66*; Fazal Mahmood 5 for 71)
&   112–2
Second Test at Lahore, Nov. 21–26. Aus won by 7 wickets.
PAK: 146   (A. K. Davidson 4 for 48)
&   366   (Saeed Ahmed 166, Imtiaz Ahmed 54; L. F. Kline 7 for 75)
AUS: 391–9 dec. (N. C. O'Neill 134)
&   123–3
Third Test at Karachi, Dec. 4–9. Match Drawn.
PAK: 287   (Saeed Ahmed 91, Ijaz Butt 58, Hanif Mohammad 51; R. Benaud
              5 for 93)
&   194–8 dec. (Hanif Mohammad 101*)
AUS: 257   (R. N. Harvey 54; Fazal Mahmood 5 for 74)
&   83–2

1959–60: India v Australia (Played 5, Aus won 2, India won 1, Drawn 2)
First Test at New Delhi, Dec. 12–16. Aus won by an innings and 127 runs.
IND: 135
&   206   (P. Roy 99; R. Benaud 5 for 76, L. F. Kline 4 for 42)
AUS: 468   (R. N. Harvey 114, K. D. Mackay 78; P. R. Umrigar 4 for 49)
Second Test at Kanpur, Dec. 19–24. India won by 119 runs.
IND: 152   (A. K. Davidson 5 for 31, R. Benaud 4 for 63)
&   291   (N. J. Contractor 74, R. B. Kenny 51; A. K. Davidson 7 for 93)
AUS: 219   (C. C. McDonald 53, R. N. Harvey 51; J. M. Patel 9 for 69)
&   105   (J. M. Patel 5 for 55, P. R. Umrigar 4 for 27)
Third Test at Bombay, Jan. 1–6. Match Drawn.
IND: 289   (N. J. Contractor 108, A. A. Baig 50; A. K. Davidson 4 for 62, I. W.
              Meckiff 4 for 79)
&   226–5 dec. (A. A. Baig 58, P. Roy 57, R. B. Kenny 55*)
AUS: 387–8 dec. (N. C. O'Neill 163, R. N. Harvey 102; R. G. Nadkarni
              6 for 105)
&   34–1
Fourth Test at Madras, Jan. 13–17. Aus won by an innings and 55 runs.
AUS: 342   (L. E. Favell 101, K. D. Mackay 89; R. B. Desai 4 for 93)

IND: 149   (B. K. Kunderan 71; R. Benaud 5 for 43)
            & 138
Fifth Test at Calcutta, Jan. 23–28. Match Drawn.
IND: 194
            & 339   (M. L. Jaisimha 74, R. B. Kenny 62, C. G. Borde 50; R. Benaud
                      4 for 103)
AUS: 331   (N. C. O'Neill 113, P. J. Burge 60, A. T. W. Grout 50; R. B. Desai
                      4 for 111)
            & 121–2 (L. E. Favell 62*)

1959–60: West Indies v England (Played 5, Eng won 1, WI won 0, Drawn 4)
First Test at Bridgetown, Jan. 6–12. Match Drawn.
ENG: 482   (K. F. Barrington 128, E. R. Dexter 136*, G. Pullar 65)
            & 71–0
WI: 563–8 dec. (G. S. Sobers 226, F. M. M. Worrell 197*; F. S. Trueman
                      4 for 93)
Second Test at Port of Spain, Jan. 28–Feb. 3. Eng won by 256 runs.
ENG: 382   (K. F. Barrington 121, M. J. K. Smith 108, E. R. Dexter 77)
            & 230–9 dec.
WI: 112   (F. S. Trueman 5 for 35)
            & 244   (R. Kanhai 110)
Third Test at Kingston, Feb. 17–23. Match Drawn.
ENG: 277   (M. C. Cowdrey 114; W. W. Hall 7 for 69)
            & 305   (M. C. Cowdrey 97, G. Pullar 66; C. Watson 4 for 62)
WI: 353   (G. S. Sobers 147, E. D. A. S. McMorris 73, S. M. Nurse 70)
            & 175–6 (R. Kanhai 57; F. S. Trueman 4 for 54)
Fourth Test at Georgetown, Mar. 9–15. Match Drawn.
ENG: 295   (M. C. Cowdrey 65, D. A. Allen 55; W. W. Hall 6 for 90)
            & 334–8 (E. R. Dexter 110, R. Subba Row 100; F. M. M. Worrell 4 for 49)
WI: 402–8 dec. (G. S. Sobers 145, R. Kanhai 55)
Fifth Test at Port of Spain, Mar. 25–31. Match Drawn.
ENG: 393   (M. C. Cowdrey 119, E. R. Dexter 76, K. F. Barrington 69; S.
                      Ramadhin 4 for 73)
            & 350–7 dec. (J. M. Parks 101*, M. J. K. Smith 96, G. Pullar 54)
WI: 338–8 dec. (G. S. Sobers 92, C. C. Hunte 72*, C. L. Walcott 53)
            & 209–5 (F. M. M. Worrell 61)

1960: England v South Africa (Played 5, Eng won 3, SA won 0, Drawn 2)
First Test at Edgbaston, June 9–14. Eng won by 100 runs.
ENG: 292   (R. Subba Row 56, M. J. K. Smith 54, E. R. Dexter 52; N. A. T.
                      Adcock 5 for 62)
            & 203   (H. J. Tayfield 4 for 62)
SA: 186   (J. H. B. Waite 58; F. S. Trueman 4 for 58)
            & 209   (R. A. McLean 68, J. H. B. Waite 56*)
Second Test at Lord's, June 23–27. Eng won by an innings and 73 runs.
ENG: 362–8 dec. (M. J. K. Smith 99, R. Subba Row 90, E. R. Dexter 56, P. M.
                      Walker 52; G. M. Griffin 4 for 87)
SA: 152   (J. B. Statham 6 for 63, A. E. Moss 4 for 35)
            & 137   (J. B. Statham 5 for 34)
Third Test at Trent Bridge, July 7–11. Eng won by 8 wickets.
ENG: 287   (K. F. Barrington 80, M. C. Cowdrey 67; T. L. Goddard 5 for 80)
            & 49–2
SA: 88   (F. S. Trueman 5 for 27)
            & 247   (S. O'Linn 98, J. H. B. Waite 60; F. S. Trueman 4 for 77)
Fourth Test at Old Trafford, July 21–26. Match Drawn.
ENG: 260   (K. F. Barrington 76; N. A. T. Adcock 4 for 66)
            & 153–7 dec.
SA: 229   (R. A. McLean 109; D. A. Allen 4 for 58)
            & 46–0
Fifth Test at The Oval, Aug. 18–23. Match Drawn.
ENG: 155   (G. Pullar 59; N. A. T. Adcock 6 for 65, J. E. Pothecary 4 for 58)
            & 479–9 dec. (G. Pullar 175, M. C. Cowdrey 155)
SA: 419   (T. L. Goddard 99, J. H. B. Waite 77, S. O'Linn 55)
            & 97–4

1960–61: India v Pakistan (Played 5, India won 0, Pak won 0, Drawn 5)
First Test at Bombay, Dec. 2–7. Match Drawn.
PAK: 350 (Hanif Mohammad 160, Saeed Ahmed 121; S. P. Gupte 4 for 43)
& 166–4 (Imtiaz Ahmed 69)
IND: 449–9 dec. (R. B. Desai 85, V. L. Manjrekar 73, N. J. Contractor 62, P. G.
Joshi 52*; Mahmood Hussain 5 for 129, Mohammad Farooq
4 for 139)
Second Test at Kanpur, Dec. 16–21. Match Drawn.
PAK: 335 (Javed Burki 79, Nasim-ul-Ghani 70*; P. R. Umrigar 4 for 71)
& 140–3
IND: 404 (P. R. Umrigar 115, M. L. Jaisimha 99, V. L. Manjrekar 52; Haseeb
Ahsan 5 for 121)
Third Test at Calcutta, Dec. 30–Jan. 4. Match Drawn.
PAK: 301 (Mushtaq Mohammad 61, Intikhab Alam 56, Hanif Mohammad 56;
C. G. Borde 4 for 21, R. Surendranath 4 for 93)
& 146–3 dec. (Hanif Mohammad 63*)
IND: 180 (Fazal Mahmood 5 for 26)
& 127–4
Fourth Test at Madras, Jan. 13–18. Match Drawn.
PAK: 448–8 dec. (Imtiaz Ahmed 135, Saeed Ahmed 103, Hanif Mohammad 62;
R. B. Desai 4 for 66)
& 59–0
IND: 539–9 dec. (C. G. Borde 177*, P. R. Umrigar 117, N. J. Contractor 81;
Haseeb Ahsan 6 for 202)
Fifth Test at New Delhi, Feb. 8–13. Match Drawn.
IND: 463 (P. R. Umrigar 112, N. J. Contractor 92, R. F. Surti 64)
& 16–0
PAK: 286 (Mushtaq Mohammad 101, Javed Burki 61; V. V. Kumar 5 for 64,
R. B. Desai 4 for 103)
& 250 (Imtiaz Ahmed 53; R. G. Nadkarni 4 for 43, R. B. Desai 4 for 88)
1960–61: Australia v West Indies (Played 5, Aus won 2, WI won 1, Tied 1, Drawn 1)
First Test at Brisbane, Dec. 9–14. Match Tied.
WI: 453 (G. S. Sobers 132, F. M. M. Worrell 65, J. S. Solomon 65, F. C. M.
Alexander 60, W. W. Hall 50; A. K. Davidson 5 for 135)
& 284 (F. M. M. Worrell 65, R. Kanhai 54; A. K. Davidson 6 for 87)
AUS: 505 (N. C. O'Neill 181, R. B. Simpson 92, C. C. McDonald 57; W. W.
Hall 4 for 140)
& 232 (A. K. Davidson 80, R. Benaud 52; W. W. Hall 5 for 63)
Second Test at Melbourne, Dec. 30–Jan. 3. Aus won by 7 wickets.
AUS: 348 (K. D. Mackay 74, J. W. Martin 55, L. E. Favell 51; W. W. Hall
4 for 51)
& 70–3
WI: 181 (R. Kanhai 84, S. M. Nurse 70; A. K. Davidson 6 for 53)
& 233 (C. C. Hunte 110, F. C. M. Alexander 72)
Third Test at Sydney, Jan. 13–18. WI won by 222 runs.
WI: 339 (G. S. Sobers 168; A. K. Davidson 5 for 80, R. Benaud 4 for 86)
& 326 (F. C. M. Alexander 108, F. M. M. Worrell 82, C. W. Smith 55;
R. Benaud 4 for 113)
AUS: 202 (N. C. O'Neill 71; A. L. Valentine 4 for 67)
& 241 (R. N. Harvey 85, N. C. O'Neill 70; L. R. Gibbs 5 for 66, A. L.
Valentine 4 for 86)
Fourth Test at Adelaide, Jan. 27–Feb. 1. Match Drawn.
WI: 393 (R. Kanhai 117, F. M. M. Worrell 71, F. C. M. Alexander 63*;
R. Benaud 5 for 96)
& 432–6 dec. (R. Kanhai 115, F. C. M. Alexander 87*, C. C. Hunte 79,
F. M. M. Worrell 53)
AUS: 366 (R. B. Simpson 85, R. Benaud 77, C. C. McDonald 71; L. R. Gibbs
5 for 97)
& 273–9 (N. C. O'Neill 65, K. D. Mackay 62*)
Fifth Test at Melbourne, Feb. 10–15. Aus won by 2 wickets.
WI: 292 (G. S. Sobers 64; F. M. Misson 4 for 58)
& 321 (F. C. M. Alexander 73, C. C. Hunte 52; A. K. Davidson 5 for 84)
AUS: 356 (C. C. McDonald 91, R. B. Simpson 75, P. J. Burge 68; G. S.

Sobers 5 for 120, L. R. Gibbs 4 for 74)
      & 258–8 (R. B. Simpson 92, P. J. Burge 53)

1961: England v Australia (Played 5, Aus won 2, Eng won 1, Drawn 2)
First Test at Edgbaston, June 8–13. Match Drawn.
ENG: 195   (R. Subba Row 59; K. D. Mackay 4 for 57)
     & 401–4 (E. R. Dexter 180, R. Subba Row 112)
AUS: 516–9 dec. (R. N. Harvey 114, N. C. O'Neill 82, R. B. Simpson 76, K. D. Mackay 64, W. M. Lawry 57)
Second Test at Lord's, June 22–26. Aus won by 5 wickets.
ENG: 206   (A. K. Davidson 5 for 42)
     & 202   (K. F. Barrington 66; G. D. McKenzie 5 for 37)
AUS: 340   (W. M. Lawry 130, K. D. Mackay 54; F. S. Trueman 4 for 118)
     & 71–5
Third Test at Headingley, July 6–8. Eng won by 8 wickets.
AUS: 237   (R. N. Harvey 73, C. C. McDonald 54; F. S. Trueman 5 for 58)
     & 120   (R. N. Harvey 53; F. S. Trueman 6 for 30)
ENG: 299   (M. C. Cowdrey 93, G. Pullar 53; A. K. Davidson 5 for 63)
     & 62–2
Fourth Test at Old Trafford, July 27–Aug. 1. Aus won by 54 runs.
AUS: 190   (W. M. Lawry 74; J. B. Statham 5 for 53)
     & 432   (W. M. Lawry 102, A. K. Davidson 77*, N. C. O'Neill 67, R. B. Simpson 51; D. A. Allen 4 for 58)
ENG: 367   (P. B. H. May 95, K. F. Barrington 78, G. Pullar 63; R. B. Simpson 4 for 23)
     & 201   (E. R. Dexter 76; R. Benaud 6 for 70)
Fifth Test at The Oval, Aug. 17–22. Match Drawn.
ENG: 256   (P. B. H. May 71, K. F. Barrington 53; A. K. Davidson 4 for 83)
     & 370–8 (R. Subba Row 137, K. F. Barrington 83; K. D. Mackay 5 for 121)
AUS: 494   (P. J. Burge 181, N. C. O'Neill 117, B. C. Booth 71; D. A. Allen 4 for 133)

1961–62: India v England (Played 5, India won 2, Eng won 0, Drawn 3)
First Test at Bombay, Nov. 11–16. Match Drawn.
ENG: 500–8 dec. (K. F. Barrington 151*, E. R. Dexter 85, G. Pullar 83, P. E. Richardson 71; V. B. Ranjane 4 for 76)
     & 184–5 dec. (K. F. Barrington 52*)
IND: 390   (S. A. Durani 71, C. G. Borde 69, V. L. Manjrekar 68, M. L. Jaisimha 56; G. A. R. Lock 4 for 74)
     & 180–5 (V. L. Manjrekar 84, M. L. Jaisimha 51)
Second Test at Kanpur, Dec. 1–6. Match Drawn.
IND: 467–8 dec. (P. R. Umrigar 147*, V. L. Manjrekar 96, M. L. Jaisimha 70)
ENG: 244   (R. W. Barber 69*; S. P. Gupte 5 for 90)
     & 497–5 (K. F. Barrington 172, E. R. Dexter 126*, G. Pullar 119)
Third Test at New Delhi, Dec. 13–18. Match Drawn.
IND: 466   (V. L. Manjrekar 189*, M. L. Jaisimha 127; D. A. Allen 4 for 87)
ENG: 256–3 (K. F. Barrington 113*, G. Pullar 89)
Fourth Test at Calcutta, Dec. 30–Jan. 4. India won by 187 runs.
IND: 380   (C. G. Borde 68, M. A. K. Pataudi 64, V. L. Mehra 62; D. A. Allen 5 for 67)
     & 252   (C. G. Borde 61; D. A. Allen 4 for 95, G. A. R. Lock 4 for 111)
ENG: 212   (P. E. Richardson 62, E. R. Dexter 57; S. A. Durani 5 for 47, C. G. Borde 4 for 65)
     & 233   (E. R. Dexter 62)
Fifth Test at Madras, Jan. 10–15. India won by 128 runs.
IND: 428   (M. A. K. Pataudi 103, N. J. Contractor 86, F. M. Engineer 65, R. G. Nadkarni 63)
     & 190   (V. L. Manjrekar 85; G. A. R. Lock 6 for 65)
ENG: 281   (M. J. K. Smith 73; S. A. Durani 6 for 105)
     & 209   (S. A. Durani 4 for 72)

1961–62: Pakistan v England (Played 3, Eng won 1, Pak won 0, Drawn 2)
First Test at Lahore, Oct. 21–26. Eng won by 5 wickets.
PAK: 387–9 dec. (Javed Burki 138, Mushtaq Mohammad 76, Saeed Ahmed 74)
     & 200

ENG: 380   (K. F. Barrington 139, M. J. K. Smith 99; Mohammad Munaf 4 for 42)
&   209–5   (E. R. Dexter 66*)
Second Test at Dacca, Jan. 19–24. Match Drawn.
PAK: 393–9 dec. (Javed Burki 140, Hanif Mohammad 111, Saeed Ahmed 69; G. A. R. Lock 4 for 155)
&   216   (Hanif Mohammad 104, Alim-ud-Din 50; D. A. Allen 5 for 30, G. A. R. Lock 4 for 70)
ENG: 439   (G. Pullar 165, R. W. Barber 86, K. F. Barrington 84; A. D'Souza 4 for 94)
&   38–0
Third Test at Karachi, Feb. 2–7. Match Drawn.
PAK: 253   (Alim-ud-Din 109, Hanif Mohammad 67; B. R. Knight 4 for 66)
&   404–8   (Hanif Mohammad 89, Imtiaz Ahmed 86, Alim-ud-Din 53)
ENG: 507   (E. R. Dexter 205, P. H. Parfitt 111, G. Pullar 60, M. J. K. Smith 56; A. D'Souza 5 for 112)

1961–62: South Africa v New Zealand (Played 5, SA won 2, NZ won 2, Drawn 1)
First Test at Durban, Dec. 8–12. SA won by 30 runs.
SA: 292   (D. J. McGlew 127*, R. A. McLean 63; J. C. Alabaster 4 for 59)
&   149   (J. H. B. Waite 63)
NZ: 245   (P. G. Z. Harris 74, P. T. Barton 54; K. A. Walter 4 for 63)
&   166   (S. N. McGregor 55; P. M. Pollock 6 for 38)
Second Test at Johannesburg, Dec. 26–29. Match Drawn.
SA: 322   (J. H. B. Waite 101, M. K. Elgie 56; F. J. Cameron 5 for 83)
&   178–6 dec. (R. C. Motz 4 for 68)
NZ: 223   (G. T. Dowling 74; G. B. Lawrence 8 for 53)
&   165–4 (J. R. Reid 75*, G. T. Dowling 58)
Third Test at Cape Town, Jan. 1–4. NZ won by 72 runs.
NZ: 385   (P. G. Z. Harris 101, J. R. Reid 92, M. E. Chapple 69, S. N. McGregor 68; S. F. Burke 6 for 128)
&   212–9 dec. (A. E. Dick 50*; S. F. Burke 5 for 68)
SA: 190   (E. J. Barlow 51; F. J. Cameron 5 for 48, J. C. Alabaster 4 for 61)
&   335   (R. A. McLean 113, D. J. McGlew 63; J. C. Alabaster 4 for 119)
Fourth Test at Johannesburg, Feb. 2–5. SA won by an innings and 51 runs.
NZ: 164   (J. R. Reid 60; G. B. Lawrence 5 for 52)
&   249   (J. R. Reid 142; G. B. Lawrence 4 for 57)
SA: 464   (D. J. McGlew 120, R. A. McLean 78, E. J. Barlow 67)
Fifth Test at Port Elizabeth, Feb. 16–20. NZ won by 40 runs.
NZ: 275   (P. T. Barton 109)
&   228   (G. T. Dowling 78, J. R. Reid 69; G. B. Lawrence 4 for 85)
SA: 190
&   273   (E. J. Barlow 59, P. M. Pollock 54*; J. R. Reid 4 for 44)

1961–62: West Indies v India (Played 5, WI won 5, India won 0)
First Test at Port of Spain, Feb. 16–20. WI won by 10 wickets.
IND: 203   (R. F. Surti 57, S. A. Durani 56)
&   98   (G. S. Sobers 4 for 22)
WI: 289   (J. L. Hendriks 64, C. C. Hunte 58; S. A. Durani 4 for 82)
&   15–0
Second Test at Kingston, Mar. 7–12. WI won by an innings and 18 runs.
IND: 395   (C. G. Borde 93, R. G. Nadkarni 78*, F. M. Engineer 53, P. R. Umrigar 50; G. S. Sobers 4 for 75)
&   218   (W. W. Hall 6 for 49)
WI: 631–8 dec. (G. S. Sobers 153, R. Kanhai 138, E. D. A. S. McMorris 125, I. Mendonca 78, F. M. M. Worrell 58)
Third Test at Bridgetown, Mar. 23–28. WI won by an innings and 30 runs.
IND: 258
&   187   (D. N. Sardesai 60, V. L. Manjrekar 51; L. R. Gibbs 8 for 38)
WI: 475   (J. S. Solomon 96, R. Kanhai 89, F. M. M. Worrell 77, C. C. Hunte 59)
Fourth Test at Port of Spain, April 4–9. WI won by 7 wickets.
WI: 444–9 dec. (R. Kanhai 139, F. M. M. Worrell 73*, E. D. A. S. McMorris 50, W. V. Rodriguez 50, W. W. Hall 50*; P. R. Umrigar 5 for 107)

        &   176–3   (E. D. A. S. McMorris 56)
IND: 197   (P. R. Umrigar 56; W. W. Hall 5 for 20)
        &   422   (P. R. Umrigar 172*, S. A. Durani 104, V. L. Mehra 62; L. R.
                      Gibbs 4 for 112)
Fifth Test at Kingston, April 13–18. WI won by 123 runs.
WI: 253   (G. S. Sobers 104; V. B. Ranjane 4 for 72)
        &   283   (F. M. M. Worrell 98*, G. S. Sobers 50)
IND: 178   (R. G. Nadkarni 61; L. A. King 5 for 46)
        &   235   (P. R. Umrigar 60; G. S. Sobers 5 for 63)

1962: England v Pakistan (Played 5, Eng won 4, Pak won 0, Drawn 1)
First Test at Edgbaston, May 31–June 4. Eng won by an innings and 24 runs.
ENG: 544–5 dec. (M. C. Cowdrey 159, P. H. Parfitt 101*, T. W. Graveney 97,
                      D. A. Allen 79*, E. R. Dexter 72)
PAK: 246   (Mushtaq Mohammad 63; J. B. Statham 4 for 54)
        &   274   (Saeed Ahmed 65)
Second Test at Lord's, June 21–23. Eng won by 9 wickets.
PAK: 100   (F. S. Trueman 6 for 31)
        &   355   (Javed Burki 101, Nasim-ul-Ghani 101; L. J. Coldwell 6 for 85)
ENG: 370   (T. W. Graveney 153, E. R. Dexter 65; Mohammad Farooq
                      4 for 70)
        &   86–1
Third Test at Headingley, July 5–7. Eng won by an innings and 117 runs.
ENG: 428   (P. H. Parfitt 119, M. J. Stewart 86, D. A. Allen 62; Munir Malik
                      5 for 128)
PAK: 131   (Alim-ud-Din 50; E. R. Dexter 4 for 10)
        &   180   (Alim-ud-Din 60, Saeed Ahmed 54; J. B. Statham 4 for 50)
Fourth Test at Trent Bridge, July 26–31. Match Drawn.
ENG: 428–5 dec. (T. W. Graveney 114, P. H. Parfitt 101*, E. R. Dexter 85, Rev.
                      D. S. Sheppard 83)
PAK: 219   (Mushtaq Mohammad 55; B. R. Knight 4 for 38, F. S. Trueman
                      4 for 71)
        &   216–6 (Mushtaq Mohammad 100*, Saeed Ahmed 64)
Fifth Test at The Oval, Aug. 16–20. Eng won by 10 wickets.
ENG: 480–5 dec. (M. C. Cowdrey 182, E. R. Dexter 172, Rev. D. S. Sheppard
                      57, K. F. Barrington 50*)
        &   27–0
PAK: 183   (J. D. F. Larter 5 for 57)
        &   323   (Imtiaz Ahmed 98, Mushtaq Mohammad 72; J. D. F. Larter
                      4 for 88)

1962–63: Australia v England (Played 5, Aus won 1, Eng won 1, Drawn 3)
First Test at Brisbane, Nov. 30–Dec. 5. Match Drawn.
AUS: 404   (B. C. Booth 112, K. D. Mackay 86*, R. Benaud 51, R. B. Simpson 50)
        &   362–4 dec. (W. M. Lawry 98, R. B. Simpson 71, R. N. Harvey 57, N. C.
                      O'Neill 56)
ENG: 389   (P. H. Parfitt 80, K. F. Barrington 78, E. R. Dexter 70; R. Benaud
                      6 for 115)
        &   278–6 (E. R. Dexter 99, G. Pullar 56, Rev. D. S. Sheppard 53)
Second Test at Melbourne, Dec. 29–Jan. 3. Eng won by 7 wickets.
AUS: 316   (W. M. Lawry 52; F. J. Titmus 4 for 43)
        &   248   (B. C. Booth 103, W. M. Lawry 57; F. S. Trueman 5 for 62)
ENG: 331   (M. C. Cowdrey 113, E. R. Dexter 93; A. K. Davidson 6 for 75)
        &   237–3 (Rev. D. S. Sheppard 113, M. C. Cowdrey 58*, E. R. Dexter 52)
Third Test at Sydney, Jan. 11–15. Aus won by 8 wickets.
ENG: 279   (M. C. Cowdrey 85, G. Pullar 53; R. B. Simpson 5 for 57, A. K.
                      Davidson 4 for 54)
        &   104   (A. K. Davidson 5 for 25)
AUS: 319   (R. B. Simpson 91, B. K. Shepherd 71*, R. N. Harvey 64; F. J.
                      Titmus 7 for 79)
        &   67–2
Fourth Test at Adelaide, Jan. 25–30. Match Drawn.
AUS: 393   (R. N. Harvey 154, N. C. O'Neill 100)
        &   293   (B. C. Booth 77, R. B. Simpson 71; F. S. Trueman 4 for 60)

ENG: 331   (K. F. Barrington 63, E. R. Dexter 61, F. J. Titmus 59*; G. D. McKenzie 5 for 89)
  &   223–4 (K. F. Barrington 132*)
Fifth Test at Sydney, Feb. 15–20. Match Drawn.
ENG: 321   (K. F. Barrington 101)
  &   268–8 dec. (K. F. Barrington 94, Rev. D. S. Sheppard 68, M. C. Cowdrey 53)
AUS: 349   (P. J. Burge 103, N. C. O'Neill 73, R. Benaud 57; F. J. Titmus 5 for 103)
  &   152–4 (P. J. Burge 52*)

1962–63: New Zealand v England (Played 3, Eng won 3, NZ won 0)
First Test at Auckland, Feb. 23–27. Eng won by an innings and 215 runs.
ENG: 562–7 dec. (P. H. Parfitt 131*, K. F. Barrington 126, B. R. Knight 125, M. C. Cowdrey 86; F. J. Cameron 4 for 118)
NZ: 258   (B. W. Yuile 64, R. C. Motz 60, J. R. Reid 59)
  &   89   (J. D. F. Larter 4 for 26, R. Illingworth 4 for 34)
Second Test at Wellington, Mar. 1–4. Eng won by an innings and 47 runs.
NZ: 194   (R. W. Blair 64*; F. S. Trueman 4 for 46)
  &   187   (W. R. Playle 65; F. J. Titmus 4 for 50)
ENG: 428–8 dec. (M. C. Cowdrey 128*, K. F. Barrington 76, A. C. Smith 69*)
Third Test at Christchurch, Mar. 15–19. Eng won by 7 wickets.
NZ: 266   (J. R. Reid 74; F. S. Trueman 7 for 75)
  &   159   (J. R. Reid 100; F. J. Titmus 4 for 46)
ENG: 253
  &   173–3

1963: England v West Indies (Played 5, WI won 3, Eng won 1, Drawn 1)
First Test at Old Trafford, June 6–10. WI won by 10 wickets.
WI: 501–6 dec. (C. C. Hunte 182, R. Kanhai 90, F. M. M. Worrell 74*, G. S. Sobers 64)
  &   1–0
ENG: 205   (E. R. Dexter 73; L. R. Gibbs 5 for 59)
  &   296   (M. J. Stewart 87; L. R. Gibbs 6 for 98)
Second Test at Lord's, June 20–25. Match Drawn.
WI: 301   (R. Kanhai 73, J. S. Solomon 56; F. S. Trueman 6 for 100)
  &   229   (B. F. Butcher 133; F. S. Trueman 5 for 52, D. Shackleton 4 for 72)
ENG: 297   (K. F. Barrington 80, E. R. Dexter 70, F. J. Titmus 52*; C. C. Griffith 5 for 91)
  &   228–9 (D. B. Close 70, K. F. Barrington 60; W. W. Hall 4 for 93)
Third Test at Edgbaston, July 4–9. Eng won by 217 runs.
ENG: 216   (D. B. Close 55; G. S. Sobers 5 for 60)
  &   278–9 dec. (P. J. Sharpe 85*, E. R. Dexter 57, G. A. R. Lock 56; L. R. Gibbs 4 for 49)
WI: 186   (F. S. Trueman 5 for 75, E. R. Dexter 4 for 38)
  &   91   (F. S. Trueman 7 for 44)
Fourth Test at Headingley, July 25–29. WI won by 221 runs.
WI: 397   (G. S. Sobers 102, R. Kanhai 92, J. S. Solomon 62; F. S. Trueman 4 for 117)
  &   229   (B. F. Butcher 78, G. S. Sobers 52; F. J. Titmus 4 for 44)
ENG: 174   (G. A. R. Lock 53; C. C. Griffith 6 for 36)
  &   231   (J. M. Parks 57, D. B. Close 56; L. R. Gibbs 4 for 76)
Fifth Test at The Oval, Aug. 22–26. WI won by 8 wickets.
ENG: 275   (P. J. Sharpe 63; C. C. Griffith 6 for 71)
  &   223   (P. J. Sharpe 83; W. W. Hall 4 for 39)
WI: 246   (C. C. Hunte 80, B. F. Butcher 53)
  &   255–2 (C. C. Hunte 108*, R. Kanhai 77)

1963–64: Australia v South Africa (Played 5, Aus won 1, SA won 1, Drawn 3)
First Test at Brisbane, Dec. 6–11. Match Drawn.
AUS: 435   (B. C. Booth 169, N. C. O'Neill 82; P. M. Pollock 6 for 95)
  &   144–1 dec. (W. M. Lawry 87*)
SA: 346   (E. J. Barlow 114, J. H. B. Waite 66, T. L. Goddard 52; R. Benaud 5 for 68)
  &   13–1

Second Test at Melbourne, Jan. 1–6. Aus won by 8 wickets.
SA: 274   (E. J. Barlow 109, K. C. Bland 50; G. D. McKenzie 4 for 82)
&   306   (J. H. B. Waite 77, A. J. Pithey 76, E. J. Barlow 54)
AUS: 447   (W. M. Lawry 157, I. R. Redpath 97, B. K. Shepherd 96; J. T. Partridge 4 for 108)
&   136–2 (R. B. Simpson 55*)
Third Test at Sydney, Jan. 10–15. Match Drawn.
AUS: 260   (B. C. Booth 75, R. B. Simpson 58; P. M. Pollock 5 for 83, J. T. Partridge 4 for 88)
&   450–9 dec. (R. Benaud 90, W. M. Lawry 89, N. C. O'Neill 88, G. D. McKenzie 76; J. T. Partridge 5 for 123)
SA: 302   (R. G. Pollock 122, T. L. Goddard 80, K. C. Bland 51)
&   326–5 (K. C. Bland 85, T. L. Goddard 84, A. J. Pithey 53*)
Fourth Test at Adelaide, Jan. 24–29. SA won by 10 wickets.
AUS: 345   (P. J. Burge 91, R. B. Simpson 78, B. K. Shepherd 70, B. C. Booth 58; T. L. Goddard 5 for 60)
&   331   (B. K. Shepherd 78, N. C. O'Neill 66)
SA: 595   (E. J. Barlow 201, R. G. Pollock 175; N. J. N. Hawke 6 for 139)
&   82–0
Fifth Test at Sydney, Feb. 7–12. Match Drawn.
AUS: 311   (B. C. Booth 102*, P. J. Burge 56; J. T. Partridge 7 for 91)
&   270   (B. C. Booth 87)
SA: 411   (K. C. Bland 126, T. L. Goddard 93, D. Lindsay 65; R. Benaud 4 for 118)
&   76–0

1963–64: India v England (Played 5, India won 0, Eng won 0, Drawn 5)
First Test at Madras, Jan. 10–15. Match Drawn.
IND: 457–7 dec. (B. K. Kunderan 192, V. L. Manjrekar 108, D. N. Sardesai 65, M. L. Jaisimha 51; F. J. Titmus 5 for 116)
&   152–9 dec. (F. J. Titmus 4 for 46)
ENG: 317   (J. B. Bolus 88, K. F. Barrington 80; C. G. Borde 5 for 88)
&   241–5 (J. B. Mortimore 73*, M. J. K. Smith 57)
Second Test at Bombay, Jan. 21–26. Match Drawn.
IND: 300   (S. A. Durani 90, C. G. Borde 84)
&   249–8 dec. (D. N. Sardesai 66, M. L. Jaisimha 66)
ENG: 233   (F. J. Titmus 84*; B. S. Chandrasekhar 4 for 67)
&   206–3 (J. B. Bolus 57, J. G. Binks 55)
Third Test at Calcutta, Jan. 29–Feb. 3. Match Drawn.
IND: 241   (D. N. Sardesai 54; J. S. E. Price 5 for 73)
&   300–7 dec. (M. L. Jaisimha 129)
ENG: 267   (M. C. Cowdrey 107; R. B. Desai 4 for 62)
&   145–2 (M. J. K. Smith 75*)
Fourth Test at New Delhi, Feb. 8–13. Match Drawn.
IND: 344   (Hanumant Singh 105)
&   463–4 (M. A. K. Pataudi 203*, B. K. Kunderan 100, C. G. Borde 67*, M. L. Jaisimha 50)
ENG: 451   (M. C. Cowdrey 151, P. H. Parfitt 67, J. B. Bolus 58)
Fifth Test at Kanpur, Feb. 15–20. Match Drawn.
ENG: 559–8 dec. (B. R. Knight 127, P. H. Parfitt 121, J. B. Bolus 67, J. M. Parks 51*)
IND: 266   (D. N. Sardesai 79, R. G. Nadkarni 52*; F. J. Titmus 6 for 73)
&   347–3 (R. G. Nadkarni 122*, D. N. Sardesai 87, S. A. Durani 61*, B. K. Kunderan 55)

1963–64: New Zealand v South Africa (Played 3, NZ won 0, SA won 0, Drawn 3)
First Test at Wellington, Feb. 21–25. Match Drawn.
SA: 302
&   218–2 dec. (E. J. Barlow 92)
NZ: 253   (M. E. Chapple 59; P. M. Pollock 6 for 47)
&   138–6 (S. G. Gedye 52)
Second Test at Dunedin, Feb. 28–Mar. 3. Match Drawn.
NZ: 149   (B. W. Sinclair 52; J. T. Partridge 4 for 51)
&   138   (D. B. Pithey 6 for 58)

SA: 223   (T. L. Goddard 63; J. R. Reid 6 for 60)
&   42–3
Third Test at Auckland, Mar. 13–17. Match Drawn.
SA: 371   (K. C. Bland 83, T. L. Goddard 73, E. J. Barlow 61; R. W. Blair 4 for 85)
&   200–5 dec. (E. J. Barlow 58)
NZ: 263   (B. W. Sinclair 138, S. N. McGregor 62; J. T. Partridge 6 for 86)
&   191–8   (S. G. Gedye 55; T. L. Goddard 4 for 18)

1964: England v Australia (Played 5, Aus won 1, Eng won 0, Drawn 4)
First Test at Trent Bridge, June 4–9. Match Drawn.
ENG: 216–8 dec.
&   193–9 dec. (E. R. Dexter 68; G. D. McKenzie 5 for 53)
AUS: 168   (R. B. Simpson 50)
&   40–2
Second Test at Lord's, June 18–23. Match Drawn.
AUS: 176   (T. R. Veivers 54; F. S. Trueman 5 for 48)
&   168–4 (P. J. Burge 59)
ENG: 246   (J. H. Edrich 120; G. E. Corling 4 for 60)
Third Test at Headingley, July 2–6. Aus won by 7 wickets.
ENG: 268   (J. M. Parks 68, E. R. Dexter 66; N. J. N. Hawke 5 for 75, G. D. McKenzie 4 for 74)
&   229   (K. F. Barrington 85)
AUS: 389   (P. J. Burge 160, W. M. Lawry 78; F. J. Titmus 4 for 69)
&   111–3 (I. R. Redpath 58*)
Fourth Test at Old Trafford, July 23–28. Match Drawn.
AUS: 656–8 dec. (R. B. Simpson 311, W. M. Lawry 106, B. C. Booth 98)
&   4–0
ENG: 611   (K. F. Barrington 256, E. R. Dexter 174, J. M. Parks 60, G. Boycott 58; G. D. McKenzie 7 for 153)
Fifth Test at The Oval, Aug. 13–18. Match Drawn.
ENG: 182   (N. J. N. Hawke 6 for 47)
&   381–4 (G. Boycott 113, M. C. Cowdrey 93*, F. J. Titmus 56, K. F. Barrington 54*)
AUS: 379   (W. M. Lawry 94, B. C. Booth 74, T. R. Veivers 67*; F. S. Trueman 4 for 87)

1964–65: India v Australia (Played 3, India won 1, Aus won 1, Drawn 1)
First Test at Madras, Oct. 2–6. Aus won by 139 runs.
AUS: 211   (W. M. Lawry 62; R. G. Nadkarni 5 for 31)
&   397   (R. B. Simpson 77, T. R. Veivers 74, P. J. Burge 60; R. G. Nadkarni 6 for 91)
IND: 276   (M. A. K. Pataudi 128*; G. D. McKenzie 6 for 58)
&   193   (Hanumant Singh 94; G. D. McKenzie 4 for 33)
Second Test at Bombay, Oct. 10–15. India won by 2 wickets.
AUS: 320   (P. J. Burge 80, B. N. Jarman 78, T. R. Veivers 67; B. S. Chandrasekhar 4 for 50)
&   274   (R. M. Cowper 81, B. C. Booth 74, W. M. Lawry 68; R. G. Nadkarni 4 for 33, B. S. Chandrasekhar 4 for 73)
IND: 341   (M. A. K. Pataudi 86, M. L. Jaisimha 66, V. L. Manjrekar 59; T. R. Veivers 4 for 68)
&   256–8 (D. N. Sardesai 56, M. A. K. Pataudi 53)
Third Test at Calcutta, Oct. 7–12. Match Drawn.
AUS: 174   (R. B. Simpson 67, W. M. Lawry 50; S. A. Durani 6 for 73)
&   143–1 (R. B. Simpson 71)
ENG: 235   (C. G. Borde 68*, M. L. Jaisimha 57; R. B. Simpson 4 for 45)

1964–65: Pakistan v Australia (Played 1, Drawn 1)
Test at Karachi, Oct. 24–29. Match Drawn.
PAK: 414   (Khalid Ibadulla 166, Abdul Kadir 95, Intikhab Alam 53; G. D. McKenzie 6 for 69)
&   279–8 dec. (Javed Burki 62)
AUS: 352   (R. B. Simpson 153, P. J. Burge 54)
&   227–2 (R. B. Simpson 115)

1964–65: Australia v Pakistan (Played 1, Drawn 1)
Test at Melbourne, Dec. 4–8. Match Drawn.
PAK: 287 (Hanif Mohammad 104, Saeed Ahmed 80)
& 326 (Hanif Mohammad 93, Intikhab Alam 61; N. J. N. Hawke 4 for 72,
G. D. McKenzie 4 for 74)
AUS: 448 (T. R. Veivers 88, R. M. Cowper 83, B. C. Booth 57, B. K. Shep-
herd 55; Arif Butt 6 for 89)
& 88–2

1964–65: South Africa v England (Played 5, Eng won 1, SA won 0, Drawn 4)
First Test at Durban, Dec. 4–8. Eng won by an innings and 104 runs.
ENG: 485–5 dec. (K. F. Barrington 148*, J. M. Parks 108*, R. W. Barber 74, G.
Boycott 73)
SA: 155 (D. A. Allen 5 for 41)
& 226 (K. C. Bland 68; F. J. Titmus 5 for 66)
Second Test at Johannesburg, Dec. 23–29. Match Drawn.
ENG: 531 (E. R. Dexter 172, K. F. Barrington 121, R. W. Barber 97, P. H.
Parfitt 52; P. M. Pollock 5 for 129)
SA: 317 (A. J. Pithey 85, E. J. Barlow 71; F. J. Titmus 4 for 73)
& 336–6 (K. C. Bland 144*, R. G. Pollock 55, T. L. Goddard 50; D. A.
Allen 4 for 07)
Third Test at Cape Town, Jan. 1–6. Match Drawn.
SA: 501–7 dec. (A. J. Pithey 154, E. J. Barlow 138, K. C. Bland 78)
& 346 (E. J. Barlow 78, R. G. Pollock 73, K. C. Bland 64, D. Lindsay 50)
ENG: 442 (M. J. K. Smith 121, E. R. Dexter 61, J. M. Parks 59, R. W.
Barber 58; H. D. Bromfield 5 for 88)
& 15–0
Fourth Test at Johannesburg, Jan. 22–27. Match Drawn.
SA: 390–6 dec. (E. J. Barlow 96, A. J. Pithey 95, J. H. B. Waite 64, T. L.
Goddard 60, K. C. Bland 55)
& 307–3 dec. (T. L. Goddard 112, R. G. Pollock 65*)
ENG: 384 (P. H. Parfitt 122*, K. F. Barrington 93, R. W. Barber 61; A. H.
McKinnon 4 for 128)
& 153–6 (G. Boycott 76*)
Fifth Test at Port Elizabeth, Feb. 12–17. Match Drawn.
SA: 502 (R. G. Pollock 137, E. J. Barlow 69, P. L. van der Merwe 66, T. L.
Goddard 61)
& 178–4 dec. (R. G. Pollock 77*)
ENG: 435 (G. Boycott 117, K. F. Barrington 72)
& 29–1

1964–65: New Zealand v Pakistan (Played 3, NZ won 0, Pak won 0, Drawn 3)
First Test at Wellington, Jan. 22–26. Match Drawn.
NZ: 266 (J. R. Reid 97, B. W. Sinclair 65; Asif Iqbal 5 for 48)
& 179–7 dec.
PAK: 187 (R. C. Motz 4 for 45)
& 140–7 (Asif Iqbal 52*)
Second Test at Auckland, Jan. 29–Feb. 2. Match Drawn.
PAK: 226 (Javed Burki 63; F. J. Cameron 4 for 36, B. W. Yuile 4 for 43)
& 207 (Abdul Kadir 58; F. J. Cameron 5 for 34)
NZ: 214 (R. W. Morgan 66, J. R. Reid 52; Asif Iqbal 5 for 52)
& 166–7 (G. T. Dowling 62; Pervez Sajjad 5 for 42)
Third Test at Christchurch, Feb. 12–16. Match Drawn.
PAK: 206 (Mohammad Ilyas 88)
& 309–8 dec. (Hanif Mohammad 100*, Saeed Ahmed 87)
NZ: 202 (Asif Iqbal 4 for 46)
& 223–5 (R. W. Morgan 97)

1964–65: India v New Zealand (Played 4, India won 1, NZ won 0, Drawn 3)
First Test at Madras, Feb. 27–Mar. 2. Match Drawn.
IND: 397 (F. M. Engineer 90, R. G. Nadkarni 75, C. G. Borde 68, M. L.
Jaisimha 51)
& 199–2 dec. (V. L. Manjrekar 102*)
NZ: 315 (B. Sutcliffe 56)
& 62–0

Second Test at Calcutta, Mar. 5–8. Match Drawn.
  NZ: 462–9 dec. (B. Sutcliffe 151*, B. R. Taylor 105, J. R. Reid 82; R. B. Desai
             4 for 128)
    &   191–9 dec.
  IND: 380   (M. A. K. Pataudi 153, C. G. Borde 62; B. R. Taylor 5 for 86)
    &   92–3
Third Test at Bombay, Mar. 12–15. Match Drawn.
  NZ: 297   (G. T. Dowling 129, R. W. Morgan 71; R. B. Desai 6 for 56)
    &   80–8
  IND: 88   (B. R. Taylor 5 for 26)
    &   463–5 dec. (D. N. Sardesai 200*, C. G. Borde 109, Hanumant Singh 75*)
Fourth Test at New Delhi, Mar. 19–22. India won by 7 wickets.
  NZ: 262   (R. W. Morgan 82; S. Venkataraghavan 8 for 72)
    &   272   (T. W. Jarvis 77, B. Sutcliffe 54, R. O. Collinge 54; S. Venkataragh-
             avan 4 for 80)
  IND: 465–8 dec. (M. A. K. Pataudi 113, D. N. Sardesai 106, C. G. Borde 87,
             Hanumant Singh 82; R. O. Collinge 4 for 89)
    &   73–3

1964–65: West Indies v Australia (Played 5, WI won 2, Aus won 1, Drawn 2)
First Test at Kingston, Mar. 3–8. WI won by 179 runs.
  WI: 239   (W. A. White 57*; L. C. Mayne 4 for 43)
    &   373   (C. C. Hunte 81, J. S. Solomon 76, B. F. Butcher 71; L. C. Mayne
             4 for 56, P. I. Philpott 4 for 109)
  AUS: 217   (W. W. Hall 5 for 60)
    &   216   (B. C. Booth 56; W. W. Hall 4 for 45)
Second Test at Port of Spain, Mar. 26–April 1. Match Drawn.
  WI: 429   (B. F. Butcher 117, C. C. Hunte 89, G. S. Sobers 69, B. A. Davis
             54; N. C. O'Neill 4 for 41)
    &   386   (B. A. Davis 58, C. C. Hunte 53, R. Kanhai 53; R. B. Simpson
             4 for 83)
  AUS: 516   (R. M. Cowper 143, B. C. Booth 117, G. Thomas 61)
Third Test at Georgetown, April 14–20. WI won by 212 runs.
  WI: 355   (R. Kanhai 89; N. J. N. Hawke 6 for 72)
    &   180   (N. J. N. Hawke 4 for 43, P. I. Philpott 4 for 49)
  AUS: 179
    &   144   (L. R. Gibbs 6 for 29)
Fourth Test at Bridgetown, May 5–11. Match Drawn.
  AUS: 650–6 dec. (W. M. Lawry 210, R. B. Simpson 201, R. M. Cowper 102,
             N. C. O'Neill 51)
    &   175–4 dec. (N. C. O'Neill 74*, W. M. Lawry retired hurt 58)
  WI: 573   (S. M. Nurse 201, R. Kanhai 129, C. C. Hunte 75, G. S. Sobers 55,
             C. C. Griffith 54; G. D. McKenzie 4 for 114)
    &   242–5 (C. C. Hunte 81, B. A. Davis 68)
Fifth Test at Port of Spain, May 14–17. Aus won by 10 wickets.
  WI: 224   (R. Kanhai 121)
    &   131   (C. C. Hunte 60*; G. D. McKenzie 5 for 33)
  AUS: 294   (R. B. Simpson 72, R. M. Cowper 69; C. C. Griffith 6 for 46)
    &   63–0

1964–65: Pakistan v New Zealand (Played 3, Pak won 2, NZ won 0, Drawn 1)
First Test at Rawalpindi, Mar. 27–30. Pak won by an innings and 64 runs.
  NZ: 175   (B. R. Taylor 76; Pervez Sajjad 4 for 42)
    &   79   (Pervez Sajjad 4 for 5)
  PAK: 318   (Saeed Ahmed 68, Mohammad Ilyas 56, Asif Iqbal 51)
Second Test at Lahore, April 2–7. Match Drawn.
  PAK: 385–7 dec. (Hanif Mohammad 203*, Majid Jahangir 80; F. J. Cameron
             4 for 90)
    &   194–8 dec.
  NZ: 482–6 dec. (B. W. Sinclair 130, J. R. Reid 88, G. T. Dowling 83, T. W.
             Jarvis 55, R. W. Morgan 50)
Third Test at Karachi, April 9–14. Pak won by 8 wickets.
  NZ: 285   (J. R. Reid 128)
    &   223   (J. R. Reid 76, B. E. Congdon 57; Intikhab Alam 4 for 39)

PAK: 307–8 dec. (Saeed Ahmed 172)
      & 202–2 (Mohammad Ilyas 126)

1965: England v New Zealand (Played 3, Eng won 3, NZ won 0)
First Test at Edgbaston, May 27–June 1. Eng won by 9 wickets.
ENG: 435   (K. F. Barrington 137, M. C. Cowdrey 85, E. R. Dexter 57; R. C.
               Motz 5 for 108)
    & 96–1   (R. W. Barber 51)
NZ: 116   (F. J. Titmus 4 for 18)
    & 413   (V. Pollard 81*, B. Sutcliffe 53; R. W. Barber 4 for 132)
Second Test at Lord's, June 17–22. Eng won by 7 wickets.
NZ: 175   (V. Pollard 55, B. R. Taylor 51; F. E. Rumsey 4 for 25)
    & 347   (B. W. Sinclair 72, G. T. Dowling 66, V. Pollard 55)
ENG: 307   (M. C. Cowdrey 119, E. R. Dexter 62; R. O. Collinge 4 for 85)
    & 218–3   (E. R. Dexter 80*, G. Boycott 76)
Third Test at Headingley, July 8–13. Eng won by an innings and 187 runs.
ENG: 546–4 dec. (J. H. Edrich 310*, K. F. Barrington 163)
NZ: 193   (J. R. Reid 54; R. Illingworth 4 for 42, J. D. F. Larter 4 for 66)
    & 166   (V. Pollard 53; F. J. Titmus 5 for 19)

1965: England v South Africa (Played 3, SA won 1, Eng won 0, Drawn 2)
First Test at Lord's, July 22–27. Match Drawn.
SA: 280   (R. G. Pollock 56)
    & 248   (K. C. Bland 70, E. J. Barlow 52)
ENG: 338   (K. F. Barrington 91, F. J. Titmus 59, R. W. Barber 56)
    & 145–7   (R. Dumbrill 4 for 30)
Second Test at Trent Bridge, Aug. 5–9. SA won by 94 runs.
SA: 269   (R. G. Pollock 125; T. W. Cartwright 6 for 94)
    & 289   (E. J. Barlow 76, A. Bacher 67, R. G. Pollock 59; J. D. F. Larter
               5 for 68)
ENG: 240   (M. C. Cowdrey 105; P. M. Pollock 5 for 53)
    & 224   (P. H. Parfitt 86; P. M. Pollock 5 for 34)
Third Test at The Oval, Aug. 26–31. Match Drawn.
SA: 208   (H. R. Lance 69; J. B. Statham 5 for 40, K. Higgs 4 for 47)
    & 392   (K. C. Bland 127, A. Bacher 70, H. R. Lance 53; K. Higgs 4 for 96)
ENG: 202   (M. C. Cowdrey 58; P. M. Pollock 5 for 43)
    & 308–4   (M. C. Cowdrey 78*, K. F. Barrington 73, W. E. Russell 70)

1965–66: Australia v England (Played 5, Aus won 1, Eng won 1, Drawn 3)
First Test at Brisbane, Dec. 10–15. Match Drawn.
AUS: 443–6 dec. (W. M. Lawry 166, K. D. Walters 155, T. R. Veivers 56*)
ENG: 280   (F. J. Titmus 60, K. F. Barrington 53, J. M. Parks 52; P. I. Philpott
               5 for 90)
    & 186–3   (G. Boycott 63*)
Second Test at Melbourne, Dec. 30–Jan. 4. Match Drawn.
AUS: 358   (R. M. Cowper 99, W. M. Lawry 88, R. B. Simpson 59; B. R.
               Knight 4 for 84)
    & 426   (P. J. Burge 120, K. D. Walters 115, W. M. Lawry 78, R. B.
               Simpson 67)
ENG: 558   (J. H. Edrich 109, M. C. Cowdrey 104, J. M. Parks 71, K. F.
               Barrington 63, F. J. Titmus 56*, G. Boycott 51; G. D. McKenzie
               5 for 134)
    & 5–0
Third Test at Sydney, Jan. 7–11. Eng won by an innings and 93 runs.
ENG: 488   (R. W. Barber 185, J. H. Edrich 103, G. Boycott 84, D. A. Allen
               50*; N. J. N. Hawke 7 for 105)
AUS: 221   (R. M. Cowper 60, G. Thomas 51; D. J. Brown 5 for 63)
    & 174   (F. J. Titmus 4 for 40, D. A. Allen 4 for 47)
Fourth Test at Adelaide, Jan. 28–Feb. 1. Aus won by an innings and 9 runs.
ENG: 241   (K. F. Barrington 60; G. D. McKenzie 6 for 48)
    & 266   (K. F. Barrington 102, F. J. Titmus 53; N. J. N. Hawke 5 for 54)
AUS: 516   (R. B. Simpson 225, W. M. Lawry 119, G. Thomas 52; I. J. Jones
               6 for 118)
Fifth Test at Melbourne, Feb. 11–16. Match Drawn.
ENG: 485–9 dec. (K. F. Barrington 115, J. M. Parks 89, J. H. Edrich 85, M. C.

Cowdrey 79; K. D. Walters 4 for 53)
  & 69–3
AUS: 543–8 dec. (R. M. Cowper 307, W. M. Lawry 108, K. D. Walters 60)

1965–66: New Zealand v England (Played 3, NZ won 0, Eng won 0, Drawn 3)
First Test at Christchurch, Feb. 25–Mar. 1. Match Drawn.
ENG: 342 (D. A. Allen 88, M. J. K. Smith 54, P. H. Parfitt 54)
  & 201–5 dec. (M. J. K. Smith 87)
NZ: 347 (B. E. Congdon 104, R. C. Motz 58, E. C. Petrie 55; I. J. Jones 4 for 71)
  & 48–8 (K. Higgs 4 for 5)
Second Test at Dunedin, Mar. 4–8. Match Drawn.
NZ: 192 (R. C. Motz 57)
  & 147–9 (D. A. Allen 4 for 46)
ENG: 254–8 dec. (M. C. Cowdrey 89*, J. T. Murray 50)
Third Test at Auckland, Mar. 11–15. Match Drawn.
NZ: 296 (B. W. Sinclair 114, B. E. Congdon 64; D. A. Allen 5 for 123)
  & 129
ENG: 222 (M. C. Cowdrey 59, W. E. Russell 56)
  & 159–4

1966: England v West Indies (Played 5, WI won 3, Eng won 1, Drawn 1)
First Test at Old Trafford, June 2–4. WI won by an innings and 40 runs.
WI: 484 (C. C. Hunte 135, G. S. Sobers 161; F. J. Titmus 5 for 83)
ENG: 167 (L. R. Gibbs 5 for 37)
  & 277 (C. Milburn 94, M. C. Cowdrey 69; L. R. Gibbs 5 for 69)
Second Test at Lord's, June 16–21. Match Drawn.
WI: 269 (S. M. Nurse 64; K. Higgs 6 for 91)
  & 369–5 dec. (G. S. Sobers 163*, D. A. J. Holford 105*)
ENG: 355 (T. W. Graveney 96, J. M. Parks 91, G. Boycott 60; W. W. Hall 4 for 106)
  & 197–4 (C. Milburn 126*)
Third Test at Trent Bridge, June 30–July 5. WI won by 139 runs.
WI: 235 (S. M. Nurse 93; K. Higgs 4 for 71, J. A. Snow 4 for 82)
  & 482–5 dec. (B. F. Butcher 209*, G. S. Sobers 94, R. Kanhai 63, S. M. Nurse 53)
ENG: 325 (T. W. Graveney 109, M. C. Cowdrey 96, B. L. d'Oliveira 76; G. S. Sobers 4 for 90, W. W. Hall 4 for 105)
  & 253 (G. Boycott 71, B. L. d'Oliveira 54; C. C. Griffith 4 for 34)
Fourth Test at Headingley, Aug. 4–8. WI won by an innings and 55 runs.
WI: 500–9 dec. (G. S. Sobers 174, S. M. Nurse 137; K. Higgs 4 for 94)
ENG: 240 (B. L. d'Oliveira 88; G. S. Sobers 5 for 41)
  & 205 (R. W. Barber 55; L. R. Gibbs 6 for 39)
Fifth Test at The Oval, Aug. 18–22. Eng won by an innings and 34 runs.
WI: 268 (R. Kanhai 104, G. S. Sobers 81)
  & 225 (S. M. Nurse 70, B. F. Butcher 60)
ENG: 527 (T. W. Graveney 165, J. T. Murray 112, K. Higgs 63, J. A. Snow 59*)

1966–67: India v West Indies (Played 3, WI won 2, India won 0, Drawn 1)
First Test at Bombay, Dec. 13–18. WI won by 6 wickets.
IND: 296 (C. G. Borde 121, S. A. Durani 55)
  & 316 (B. K. Kunderan 79, M. A. K. Pataudi 51; L. R. Gibbs 4 for 67)
WI: 421 (C. C. Hunte 101, C. H. Lloyd 82, D. A. J. Holford 80, G. S. Sobers 50; B. S. Chandrasekhar 7 for 157)
  & 192–4 (C. H. Lloyd 78*, G. S. Sobers 53*; B. S. Chandrasekhar 4 for 78)
Second Test at Calcutta, Dec. 31–Jan. 5. WI won by an innings and 45 runs.
WI: 390 (R. Kanhai 90, G. S. Sobers 70, S. M. Nurse 56)
IND: 167 (L. R. Gibbs 5 for 51)
  & 178 (G. S. Sobers 4 for 56)
Third Test at Madras, Jan. 13–18. Match Drawn.
IND: 404 (C. G. Borde 125, F. M. Engineer 109, R. F. Surti 50*)
  & 323 (A. L. Wadekar 67, V. Subramanya 61, Hanumant Singh 50; C. C. Griffith 4 for 61, L. R. Gibbs 4 for 96)
WI: 406 (G. S. Sobers 95, R. Kanhai 77; B. S. Chandrasekhar 4 for 130)
  & 270–7 (G. S. Sobers 74*; B. S. Bedi 4 for 81)

1966–67: South Africa v Australia (Played 5, SA won 3, Aus won 1, Drawn 1)
First Test at Johannesburg, Dec. 23–28. SA won by 233 runs.
  SA: 199 (D. Lindsay 69; G. D. McKenzie 5 for 46)
   & 620 (D. Lindsay 182, R. G. Pollock 90, P. L. van der Merwe 76, H. R.
       Lance 70, A. Bacher 63, E. J. Barlow 50)
  AUS: 325 (W. M. Lawry 98, R. B. Simpson 65)
   & 261 (T. R. Veivers 55; T. L. Goddard 6 for 53)
Second Test at Cape Town, Dec. 31–Jan. 5. Aus won by 6 wickets.
  AUS: 542 (R. B. Simpson 153, K. R. Stackpole 134, I. R. Redpath 54, G. D.
       Watson 50; E. J. Barlow 5 for 85)
   & 180–4 (I. R. Redpath 69*)
  SA: 353 (R. G. Pollock 209, P. L. van der Merwe 50; G. D. McKenzie
       5 for 65)
   & 367 (D. Lindsay 81, P. M. Pollock 75*, D. B. Pithey 55, H. R. Lance 53)
Third Test at Durban, Jan. 20–25. SA won by 8 wickets.
  SA: 300 (D. Lindsay 137)
   & 185–2 (R. G. Pollock 67*, A. Bacher 60*)
  AUS: 147
   & 334 (R. B. Simpson 94, I. R. Redpath 80; M. J. Procter 4 for 71)
Fourth Test at Johannesburg, Feb. 3–8. Match Drawn.
  AUS: 143 (M. J. Procter 4 for 32)
   & 148–8
  SA: 332–9 dec. (D. Lindsay 131; D. A. Renneberg 5 for 97)
Fifth Test at Port Elizabeth, Feb. 24–28. SA won by 7 wickets.
  AUS: 173 (R. M. Cowper 60)
   & 278 (R. M. Cowper 54)
  SA: 276 (R. G. Pollock 105, T. L. Goddard 74; G. D. McKenzie 5 for 65)
   & 179–3 (T. L. Goddard 59)

1967: England v India (Played 3, Eng won 3, India won 0)
First Test at Headingley, June 8–13. Eng won by 6 wickets.
  ENG: 550–4 dec. (G. Boycott 246*, B. L. d'Oliveira 109, K. F. Barrington 93,
       T. W. Graveney 59)
   & 126–4
  IND: 164 (M. A. K. Pataudi 64)
   & 510 (M. A. K. Pataudi 148, A. L. Wadekar 91, F. M. Engineer 87,
       Hanumant Singh 73; R. Illingworth 4 for 100)
Second Test at Lord's, June 22–26. Eng won by an innings and 124 runs.
  IND: 152 (A. L. Wadekar 57)
   & 110 (R. Illingworth 6 for 29)
  ENG: 386 (T. W. Graveney 151, K. F. Barrington 97; B. S. Chandrasekhar
       5 for 127)
Third Test at Edgbaston, July 13–15. Eng won by 132 runs.
  ENG: 298 (J. T. Murray 77, K. F. Barrington 75)
   & 203 (E. A. S. Prasanna 4 for 60)
  IND: 92
   & 277 (A. L. Wadekar 70; D. B. Close 4 for 68, R. Illingworth 4 for 92)

1967: England v Pakistan (Played 3, Eng won 2, Pak won 0, Drawn 1)
First Test at Lord's, July 27–Aug. 1. Match Drawn.
  ENG: 369 (K. F. Barrington 148, T. W. Graveney 81, B. L. d'Oliveira 59)
   & 241–9 dec. (B. L. d'Oliveira 81*)
  PAK: 354 (Hanif Mohammad 187*, Asif Iqbal 76)
   & 88–3
Second Test at Trent Bridge, Aug. 10–15. Eng won by 10 wickets.
  PAK: 140 (K. Higgs 4 for 35)
   & 114 (Saeed Ahmed 68; D. L. Underwood 5 for 52)
  ENG: 252–8 dec. (K. F. Barrington 109*)
   & 3–0
Third Test at The Oval, Aug. 24–28. Eng won by 8 wickets.
  PAK: 216 (Mushtaq Mohammad 66; G. G. Arnold 5 for 58)
   & 255 (Asif Iqbal 146, Intikhab Alam 51; K. Higgs 5 for 58)
  ENG: 440 (K. F. Barrington 142, T. W. Graveney 77, F. J. Titmus 65, G. G.
       Arnold 59; Mushtaq Mohammad 4 for 80)
   & 34–2

1967–68: Australia v India (Played 4, Aus won 4, India won 0)
First Test at Adelaide, Dec. 23–28. Aus won by 146 runs.

AUS: 335 (R. M. Cowper 92, A. P. Sheahan 81, R. B. Simpson 55; S. Abid
Ali 6 for 55)
& 369 (R. M. Cowper 108, R. B. Simpson 103; R. F. Surti 5 for 74)
IND: 307 (F. M. Engineer 89, R. F. Surti 70, C. G. Borde 69; A. N. Connolly
4 for 54)
& 251 (V. Subramanya 75, R. F. Surti 53; D. A. Renneberg 5 for 39)

Second Test at Melbourne, Dec. 30–Jan. 3. Aus won by an innings and 4 runs.

IND: 173 (M. A. K. Pataudi 75; G. D. McKenzie 7 for 66)
& 352 (A. L. Wadekar 99, M. A. K. Pataudi 85)
AUS: 529 (I. M. Chappell 151, R. B. Simpson 109, W. M. Lawry 100, B. N.
Jarman 65; E. A. S. Prasanna 6 for 141)

Third Test at Brisbane, Jan. 19–24. Aus won by 39 runs.

AUS: 379 (K. D. Walters 93, W. M. Lawry 64, A. P. Sheahan 58, R. M.
Cowper 51)
& 294 (I. R. Redpath 79, K. D. Walters 62*; E. A. S. Prasanna 6 for 104)
IND: 279 (M. A. K. Pataudi 74, M. L. Jaisimha 74, R. F. Surti 52)
& 355 (M. L. Jaisimha 101, R. F. Surti 64, C. G. Borde 63; R. M. Cowper
4 for 104)

Fourth Test at Sydney, Jan. 26–31. Aus won by 144 runs.

AUS: 317 (K. D. Walters 94*, A. P. Sheahan 72, W. M. Lawry 66)
& 292 (R. M. Cowper 165, W. M. Lawry 52; E. A. S. Prasanna 4 for 96)
IND: 268 (S. Abid Ali 78, M. A. K. Pataudi 51; E. W. Freeman 4 for 86)
& 197 (S. Abid Ali 81; R. B. Simpson 5 for 59, R. M. Cowper 4 for 49)

1967–68: West Indies v England (Played 5, Eng won 1, WI won 0, Drawn 4)
First Test at Port of Spain, Jan. 19–24. Match Drawn.

ENG: 568 (K. F. Barrington 143, T. W. Graveney 118, M. C. Cowdrey 72,
G. Boycott 68; C. C. Griffith 5 for 69)
WI: 363 (C. H. Lloyd 118, R. Kanhai 85)
& 243–8 (B. F. Butcher 52)

Second Test at Kingston, Feb. 8–14. Match Drawn.

ENG: 376 (M. C. Cowdrey 101, J. H. Edrich 96, K. F. Barrington 63; W. W.
Hall 4 for 63)
& 68–8
WI: 143 (J. A. Snow 7 for 49)
& 391–9 dec. (G. S. Sobers 113*, S. M. Nurse 73)

Third Test at Bridgetown, Feb. 29–Mar. 5. Match Drawn.

WI: 349 (B. F. Butcher 86, G. S. Sobers 68, G. S. Camacho 57; J. A. Snow
5 for 86)
& 284–6 (C. H. Lloyd 113*, B. F. Butcher 60)
ENG: 449 (J. H. Edrich 146, G. Boycott 90, T. W. Graveney 55, B. L.
d'Oliveira 51)

Fourth Test at Port of Spain, Mar. 14–19. Eng won by 7 wickets.

WI: 526–7 dec. (R. Kanhai 153, S. M. Nurse 136, G. S. Camacho 87)
& 92–2 dec.
ENG: 404 (M. C. Cowdrey 148, A. P. E. Knott 69*, G. Boycott 62; B. F.
Butcher 5 for 34)
& 215–3 (G. Boycott 80*, M. C. Cowdrey 71)

Fifth Test at Georgetown, Mar. 28–April 3. Match Drawn.

WI: 414 (R. Kanhai 150, G. S. Sobers 152; J. A. Snow 4 for 82)
& 264 (G. S. Sobers 95*; J. A. Snow 6 for 60)
ENG: 371 (G. Boycott 116, G. A. R. Lock 89, M. C. Cowdrey 59)
& 206–9 (M. C. Cowdrey 82, A. P. E. Knott 73*; L. R. Gibbs 6 for 60)

1967–68: New Zealand v India (Played 4, India won 3, NZ won 1)
First Test at Dunedin, Feb. 15–20. India won by 5 wickets.

NZ: 350 (G. T. Dowling 143, B. E. Congdon 58, M. G. Burgess 50; S. Abid
Ali 4 for 26)
& 208 (B. A. G. Murray 54; E. A. S. Prasanna 6 for 94)
IND: 359 (A. L. Wadekar 80, F. M. Engineer 63; R. C. Motz 5 for 86)
& 200–5 (A. L. Wadekar 71)

Second Test at Christchurch, Feb. 22–27. NZ won by 6 wickets.

NZ: 502   (G. T. Dowling 239, B. A. G. Murray 74, K. Thomson 69; B. S.
                Bedi 6 for 127)
&   88–4   (B. E. Congdon 61*)
IND: 288   (R. F. Surti 67, C. G. Borde 57, M. A. K. Pataudi 52; R. C. Motz
                6 for 63)
&   301   (F. M. Engineer 63; G. A. Bartlett 6 for 38)
Third Test at Wellington, Feb. 29–Mar. 4. India won by 8 wickets.
NZ: 186   (M. G. Burgess 66; E. A. S. Prasanna 5 for 32)
&   199   (M. G. Burgess 60, B. E. Congdon 51; R. G. Nadkarni 6 for 43)
IND: 327   (A. L. Wadekar 143)
&   59–2
Fourth Test at Auckland, Mar. 7–12. India won by 272 runs.
IND: 252   (M. A. K. Pataudi 51; R. C. Motz 4 for 51)
&   261–5 dec. (R. F. Surti 99, C. G. Borde 65*)
NZ: 140   (E. A. S. Prasanna 4 for 44)
&   101   (E. A. S. Prasanna 4 for 40)

1968: England v Australia (Played 5, Eng won 1, Aus won 1, Drawn 3)
First Test at Old Trafford, June 6–11. Aus won by 159 runs.
AUS: 357   (A. P. Sheahan 88, W. M. Lawry 81, K. D. Walters 81, I. M.
                Chappell 73; J. A. Snow 4 for 97)
&   220   (K. D. Walters 86; P. I. Pocock 6 for 79)
ENG: 165   (R. M. Cowper 4 for 48)
&   253   (B. L. d'Oliveira 87*)
Second Test at Lord's, June 20–25. Match Drawn.
ENG: 351–7 dec. (C. Milburn 83, K. F. Barrington 75)
AUS: 78   (D. J. Brown 5 for 42)
&   127–4   (I. R. Redpath 53)
Third Test at Edgbaston, July 11–16. Match Drawn.
ENG: 409   (M. C. Cowdrey 104, T. W. Graveney 96, J. H. Edrich 88; E. W.
                Freeman 4 for 78)
&   142–3 dec. (J. H. Edrich 64)
AUS: 222   (I. M. Chappell 71, R. M. Cowper 57)
&   68–1
Fourth Test at Headingley, July 25–30. Match Drawn.
AUS: 315   (I. R. Redpath 92, I. M. Chappell 65; D. L. Underwood 4 for 41)
&   312   (I. M. Chappell 81, K. D. Walters 56; R. Illingworth 6 for 87)
ENG: 302   (R. M. Prideaux 64, J. H. Edrich 62; A. N. Connolly 5 for 72)
&   230–4   (J. H. Edrich 65)
Fifth Test at The Oval, Aug. 22–27. Eng won by 226 runs.
ENG: 494   (J. H. Edrich 164, B. L. d'Oliveira 158, T. W. Graveney 63)
&   181   (A. N. Connolly 4 for 65)
AUS: 324   (W. M. Lawry 135, I. R. Redpath 67)
&   125   (R. J. Inverarity 56; D. L. Underwood 7 for 50)

1968–69: Australia v West Indies (Played 5, Aus won 3, WI won 1, Drawn 1)
First Test at Brisbane, Dec. 6–10. WI won by 125 runs.
WI: 296   (R. Kanhai 94, M. C. Carew 83; A. N. Connolly 4 for 60)
&   353   (C. H. Lloyd 129, M. C. Carew 71*; J. W. Gleeson 5 for 122)
AUS: 284   (I. M. Chappell 117, W. M. Lawry 105; L. R. Gibbs 5 for 88)
&   240   (I. M. Chappell 50; G. S. Sobers 6 for 73)
Second Test at Melbourne, Dec. 26–30. Aus won by an innings and 30 runs.
WI: 200   (R. C. Fredericks 76; G. D. McKenzie 8 for 71)
&   280   (S. M. Nurse 74, G. S. Sobers 67; J. W. Gleeson 5 for 61)
AUS: 510   (W. M. Lawry 205, I. M. Chappell 165, K. D. Walters 76; G. S.
                Sobers 4 for 97, L. R. Gibbs 4 for 139)
Third Test at Sydney, Jan. 3–8. Aus won by 10 wickets.
WI: 264   (C. H. Lloyd 50; G. D. McKenzie 4 for 85)
&   324   (B. F. Butcher 101, R. Kanhai 69; J. W. Gleeson 4 for 91)
AUS: 547   (K. D. Walters 118, I. R. Redpath 80, E. W. Freeman 76, K. R.
                Stackpole 58)
&   42–0
Fourth Test at Adelaide, Jan. 24–29. Match Drawn.
WI: 276   (G. S. Sobers 110, B. F. Butcher 52; E. W. Freeman 4 for 52)

        &   616   (B. F. Butcher 118, M. C. Carew 90, R. Kanhai 80, D. A. J. Holford 80, G. S. Sobers 52; A. N. Connolly 5 for 122)
AUS: 533   (K. D. Walters 110, I. M. Chappell 76, W. M. Lawry 62, K. R. Stackpole 62, G. D. McKenzie 59, A. P. Sheahan 51; L. R. Gibbs 4 for 145)
        & 339–9 (I. M. Chappell 96, W. M. Lawry 89, K. R. Stackpole 50, K. D. Walters 50)

Fifth Test at Sydney, Feb. 14–20. Aus won by 382 runs.
AUS: 619   (K. D. Walters 242, W. M. Lawry 151, E. W. Freeman 56)
        & 394–8 dec. (I. R. Redpath 132, K. D. Walters 103)
WI: 279   (M. C. Carew 64, C. H. Lloyd 53; A. N. Connolly 4 for 61)
        &   352   (S. M. Nurse 137, G. S. Sobers 113)

1968–69: Pakistan v England (Played 3, Eng won 0, Pak won 0, Drawn 3)
First Test at Lahore, Feb. 21–24. Match Drawn.
ENG: 306   (M. C. Cowdrey 100, J. H. Edrich 54, A. P. E. Knott 52; Saeed Ahmed 4 for 64, Intikhab Alam 4 for 117)
        & 225–9 dec. (K. W. R. Fletcher 83)
PAK: 209   (Asif Iqbal 70; R. M. H. Cottam 4 for 50)
        & 203–5 (Majid Jahangir 68)

Second Test at Dacca, Feb. 28–Mar. 3. Match Drawn.
PAK: 246   (Mushtaq Mohammad 52; J. A. Snow 4 for 70)
        & 195–6 dec. (D. L. Underwood 5 for 94)
ENG: 274   (B. L. d'Oliveira 114*; Pervez Sajjad 4 for 75)
        &   33–0

Third Test at Karachi, Mar. 6–8. Match Drawn.
ENG: 502–7 (C. Milburn 139, T. W. Graveney 105, A. P. E. Knott 96*)

1968–69: New Zealand v West Indies (Played 3, NZ won 1, WI won 1, Drawn 1)
First Test at Auckland, Feb. 27–Mar. 3. WI won by 5 wickets.
NZ: 323   (B. R. Taylor 124, B. E. Congdon 85)
        & 297–8 dec. (G. T. Dowling 71, V. Pollard 51*)
WI: 276   (M. C. Carew 109, S. M. Nurse 95)
        & 348–5 (S. M. Nurse 168, B. F. Butcher 78*)

Second Test at Wellington, Mar. 7–11. NZ won by 6 wickets.
WI: 297   (J. L. Hendriks 54*, B. F. Butcher 50; R. C. Motz 6 for 69)
        &   148   (B. F. Butcher 59)
NZ: 282   (G. M. Turner 74, B. E. Congdon 52; R. M. Edwards 5 for 84)
        & 166–4 (B. F. Hastings 62*)

Third Test at Christchurch, Mar. 13–17. Match Drawn.
WI: 417   (S. M. Nurse 258, M. C. Carew 91; R. C. Motz 5 for 113)
NZ: 217   (D. A. J. Holford 4 for 66)
        & 367–6 (B. F. Hastings 117*, G. T. Dowling 76)

1969: England v West Indies (Played 3, Eng won 2, WI won 0, Drawn 1)
First Test at Old Trafford, June 12–17. Eng won by 10 wickets.
ENG: 413   (G. Boycott 128, T. W. Graveney 75, J. H. Edrich 58, B. L. d'Oliveira 57; J. N. Shepherd 5 for 104)
        &   12–0
WI: 147   (D. J. Brown 4 for 39, J. A. Snow 4 for 54)
        &   275   (R. C. Fredericks 64)

Second Test at Lord's, June 26–July 1. Match Drawn.
WI: 380   (C. A. Davis 103, G. S. Camacho 67, R. C. Fredericks 63; J. A. Snow 5 for 114)
        & 295–9 dec. (C. H. Lloyd 70, R. C. Fredericks 60, G. S. Sobers 50*)
ENG: 344   (R. Illingworth 113, J. H. Hampshire 107, A. P. E. Knott 53)
        & 295–7 (G. Boycott 106, P. J. Sharpe 86)

Third Test at Headingley, July 10–15. Eng won by 30 runs.
ENG: 223   (J. H. Edrich 79; V. A. Holder 4 for 48)
        &   240   (G. S. Sobers 5 for 42)
WI: 161   (B. R. Knight 4 for 63)
        &   272   (B. F. Butcher 91, G. S. Camacho 71; D. L. Underwood 4 for 55)

1969: England v New Zealand (Played 3, Eng won 2, NZ won 0, Drawn 1)
First Test at Lord's, July 24–28. Eng won by 230 runs.

```
ENG:   190   (R. Illingworth 53)
  &    340   (J. H. Edrich 115)
 NZ:   169   (R. Illingworth 4 for 37, D. L. Underwood 4 for 38)
  &    131   (D. L. Underwood 7 for 32)
```
Second Test at Trent Bridge, Aug. 7–12. Match Drawn.
```
 NZ:   294   (B. F. Hastings 83, B. E. Congdon 66; A. Ward 4 for 61)
  &     66–1
ENG:   451–8 dec. (J. H. Edrich 155, P. J. Sharpe 111; D. R. Hadlee 4 for 88)
```
Third Test at The Oval, Aug. 21–26. Eng won by 8 wickets.
```
 NZ:   150   (G. M. Turner 53; D. L. Underwood 6 for 41)
  &    229   (B. F. Hastings 61; D. L. Underwood 6 for 60)
ENG:   242   (J. H. Edrich 68; B. R. Taylor 4 for 47)
  &    138–2 (M. H. Denness 55*)
```

1969–70: India v New Zealand (Played 3, India won 1, NZ won 1, Drawn 1)
First Test at Bombay, Sept. 25–30. India won by 60 runs.
```
IND:   156
  &    260   (M. A. K. Pataudi 67)
 NZ:   229   (B. E. Congdon 78; E. A. S. Prasanna 4 for 97)
  &    127   (B. S. Bedi 6 for 42, E. A. S. Prasanna 4 for 74)
```
Second Test at Nagpur, Oct. 3–8. NZ won by 167 runs.
```
 NZ:   319   (M. G. Burgess 89, G. T. Dowling 69, B. E. Congdon 64; B. S.
             Bedi 4 for 98)
  &    214   (G. M. Turner 57; S. Venkataraghavan 6 for 74)
IND:   257   (S. Abid Ali 63; H. J. Howarth 4 for 66)
  &    109   (H. J. Howarth 5 for 34)
```
Third Test at Hyderabad, Oct. 15–20. Match Drawn.
```
 NZ:   181   (B. A. G. Murray 80; E. A. S. Prasanna 5 for 51)
  &    175–8 dec. (G. T. Dowling 60)
IND:    89   (D. R. Hadlee 4 for 30)
  &     76–7
```

1969–70: Pakistan v New Zealand (Played 3, NZ won 1, Pak won 0, Drawn 2)
First Test at Karachi, Oct. 24–27. Match Drawn.
```
PAK:   220   (Sadiq Mohammad 69; H. J. Howarth 5 for 80)
  &    283–8 dec. (Younis Ahmed 62)
 NZ:   274   (D. R. Hadlee 56, B. A. G. Murray 50; Mohammad Nazir 7 for 99)
  &    112–5 (Pervez Sajjad 5 for 33)
```
Second Test at Lahore, Oct. 30–Nov. 2. NZ won by 5 wickets.
```
PAK:   114
  &    208   (Shafqat Rana 95)
 NZ:   241   (B. A. G. Murray 90, B. F. Hastings 80*; Pervez Sajjad 7 for 74)
  &     82–5
```
Third Test at Dacca, Nov. 8–11. Match Drawn.
```
 NZ:   273   (G. M. Turner 110, M. G. Burgess 59; Intikhab Alam 5 for 91)
  &    200   (M. G. Burgess 119*; Intikhab Alam 5 for 91, Pervez Sajjad
             4 for 60)
PAK:   290–7 dec. (Asif Iqbal 92, Shafqat Rana 65; H. J. Howarth 4 for 85)
  &     51–4 (R. S. Cunis 4 for 21)
```

1969–70: India v Australia (Played 5, Aus won 3, India won 1, Drawn 1)
First Test at Bombay, Nov. 4–9. Aus won by 8 wickets.
```
IND:   271   (M. A. K. Pataudi 95, A. V. Mankad 74; G. D. McKenzie 5 for 69)
  &    137   (J. W. Gleeson 4 for 56)
AUS:   345   (K. R. Stackpole 103, I. R. Redpath 77; E. A. S. Prasanna 5 for 121)
  &     67–2
```
Second Test at Kanpur, Nov. 15–20. Match Drawn.
```
IND:   320   (F. M. Engineer 77, A. V. Mankad 64; A. N. Connolly 4 for 91)
  &    312–7 dec. (G. R. Viswanath 137, A. V. Mankad 68)
AUS:   348   (A. P. Sheahan 114, I. R. Redpath 70, K. D. Walters 53)
  &     95–0 (W. M. Lawry 56*)
```
Third Test at New Delhi, Nov. 28–Dec. 2. India won by 7 wickets.
```
AUS:   296   (I. M. Chappell 138, K. R. Stackpole 61; B. S. Bedi 4 for 71, E. A. S.
             Prasanna 4 for 111)
  &    107   (B. S. Bedi 5 for 37, E. A. S. Prasanna 5 for 42)
```

IND: 223   (A. V. Mankad 97; A. A. Mallett 6 for 64)
&   181–3   (A. L. Wadekar 91*)
Fourth Test at Calcutta, Dec. 12–16. Aus won by 10 wickets.
IND: 212   (G. R. Viswanath 54; G. D. McKenzie 6 for 67)
&   161   (A. L. Wadekar 62; A. N. Connolly 4 for 31, E. W. Freeman
4 for 54)
AUS: 335   (I. M. Chappell 99, K. D. Walters 56; B. S. Bedi 7 for 98)
&   42–0
Fifth Test at Madras, Dec. 24–28. Aus won by 77 runs.
AUS: 258   (K. D. Walters 102; S. Venkataraghavan 4 for 71, E. A. S. Prasanna
4 for 100)
&   153   (I. R. Redpath 63; E. A. S. Prasanna 6 for 74)
IND: 163   (M. A. K. Pataudi 59; A. A. Mallett 5 for 91)
&   171   (G. R. Viswanath 59, A. L. Wadekar 55; A. A. Mallett 5 for 53)

1969–70: South Africa v Australia (Played 4, SA won 4, Aus won 0)
First Test at Cape Town, Jan. 22–27. SA won by 170 runs.
SA: 382   (E. J. Barlow 127, A. Bacher 57; A. A. Mallett 5 for 126)
&   232   (R. G. Pollock 50; A. N. Connolly 5 for 47, J. W. Gleeson 4 for 70)
AUS: 164   (K. D. Walters 73; P. M. Pollock 4 for 20)
&   280   (W. M. Lawry 83; M. J. Procter 4 for 47)
Second Test at Durban, Feb. 5–9. SA won by an innings and 129 runs.
SA: 622–9 dec. (R. G. Pollock 274, B. A. Richards 140, H. R. Lance 61)
AUS: 157   (A. P. Sheahan 62)
&   336   (I. R. Redpath 74*, K. D. Walters 74, K. R. Stackpole 71)
Third Test at Johannesburg, Feb. 19–24. SA won by 307 runs.
SA: 279   (B. L. Irvine 79, B. A. Richards 65, R. G. Pollock 52)
&   408   (E. J. Barlow 110, B. L. Irvine 73, R. G. Pollock 87; J. W. Gleeson
5 for 125)
AUS: 202   (K. D. Walters 64; P. M. Pollock 5 for 39)
&   178   (I. R. Redpath 66)
Fourth Test at Port Elizabeth, Mar. 5–10. SA won by 323 runs.
SA: 311   (B. A. Richards 81, E. J. Barlow 73; A. N. Connolly 6 for 47)
&   470–8 dec. (B. A. Richards 126, B. L. Irvine 102, A. Bacher 73, D. T.
Lindsay 60)
AUS: 212   (A. P. Sheahan 67, I. R. Redpath 55)
&   246   (M. J. Procter 6 for 73)

1970–71: Australia v England (Played 6, Eng won 2, Aus won 0, Drawn 4)
First Test at Brisbane, Nov. 27–Dec. 2. Match Drawn.
AUS: 433   (K. R. Stackpole 207, K. D. Walters 112, I. M. Chappell 59; J. A.
Snow 6 for 114)
&   214   (W. M. Lawry 84; K. Shuttleworth 5 for 47)
ENG: 464   (J. H. Edrich 79, B. W. Luckhurst 74, A. P. E. Knott 73, B. L.
d'Oliveira 57)
&   39–1
Second Test at Perth, Dec. 11–16. Match Drawn.
ENG: 397   (B. W. Luckhurst 131, G. Boycott 70; G. D. McKenzie 4 for 66)
&   287–6 dec. (J. H. Edrich 115*, G. Boycott 50)
AUS: 440   (I. R. Redpath 171, G. S. Chappell 108, I. M. Chappell 50; J. A.
Snow 4 for 143)
&   100–3
(Third Test at Melbourne: Abandoned – no play)
Fourth Test at Sydney, Jan. 9–14. Eng won by 299 runs.
ENG: 332   (G. Boycott 77, J. H. Edrich 55; A. A. Mallett 4 for 40, J. W.
Gleeson 4 for 83)
&   319–5 dec. (G. Boycott 142*, B. L. d'Oliveira 56, R. Illingworth 53)
AUS: 236   (I. R. Redpath 64, K. D. Walters 55; D. L. Underwood 4 for 66)
&   116   (W. M. Lawry 60*; J. A. Snow 7 for 40)
Fifth Test at Melbourne, Jan. 21–26. Match Drawn.
AUS: 493–9 dec. (I. M. Chappell 111, R. W. Marsh 92*, I. R. Redpath 72, W.M.
Lawry 56, K. D. Walters 55)
&   169–4 dec.
ENG: 392   (B. L. d'Oliveira 117, B. W. Luckhurst 109)

          &   161–0 (G. Boycott 76*, J. H. Edrich 74*)
Sixth Test at Adelaide, Jan. 29–Feb. 3. Match Drawn.
    ENG: 470   (J. H. Edrich 130, K. W. R. Fletcher 80, G. Boycott 58, J. H.
                     Hampshire 55; D. K. Lillee 5 for 84)
       &   233–4 dec. (G. Boycott 119*)
    AUS: 235   (K. R. Stackpole 87; P. Lever 4 for 49)
       &   328–3 (K. R. Stackpole 136, I. M. Chappell 104)
Seventh Test at Sydney, Feb. 12–17. Eng won by 62 runs.
    ENG: 184
       &   302   (B. W. Luckhurst 59, J. H. Edrich 57)
    AUS: 264   (G. S. Chappell 65, I. R. Redpath 59)
       &   160   (K. R. Stackpole 67)

1970–71: West Indies v India (Played 5, India won 1, WI won 0, Drawn 4)
First Test at Kingston, Feb. 18–23. Match Drawn.
    IND: 387   (D. N. Sardesai 212, E. D. Solkar 61; V. A. Holder 4 for 60)
    WI: 217   (R. Kanhai 56; E. A. S. Prasanna 4 for 65)
       &   385–5 (R. Kanhai 158*, G. S. Sobers 93, C. H. Lloyd 57)
Second Test at Port of Spain, Mar. 6–10. India won by 7 wickets.
    WI: 214   (C. A. Davis 71*; E. A. S. Prasanna 4 for 54)
       &   261   (R. C. Fredericks 80, C. A. Davis 74*; S. Venkataraghavan 5 for 95)
    IND: 352   (D. N. Sardesai 112, S. M. Gavaskar 65, E. D. Solkar 55; J. M.
                     Noreiga 9 for 95)
       &   125–3 (S. M. Gavaskar 67*)
Third Test at Georgetown, Mar. 19–24. Match Drawn.
    WI: 363   (D. M. Lewis 81*, C. H. Lloyd 60)
       &   307–3 dec. (C. A. Davis 125*, G. S. Sobers 108*)
    IND: 376   (S. M. Gavaskar 116, G. R. Viswanath 50, S. Abid Ali 50*)
       &   123–0 (S. M. Gavaskar 64*, A. V. Mankad 53*)
Fourth Test at Bridgetown, April 1–6. Match Drawn.
    WI: 501–5 dec. (G. S. Sobers 178*, D. M. Lewis 88, R. Kanhai 85, C. A.
                     Davis 79)
       &   180–6 dec.
    IND: 347   (D. N. Sardesai 150, E. D. Solkar 65; U. G. Dowe 4 for 69)
       &   221 5 (E. M. Gavaskar 117*)
Fifth Test at Port of Spain, April 13–19. Match Drawn.
    IND: 360   (S. M. Gavaskar 124, D. N. Sardesai 75, S. Venkataraghavan 51)
       &   427   (S. M. Gavaskar 220, A. L. Wadekar 54; J. M. Noreiga 5 for 129)
    WI: 526   (G. S. Sobers 132, C. A. Davis 105, M. L. C. Foster 99, D. M.
                     Lewis 72; S. Venkataraghavan 4 for 100)
       &   165–8 (C. H. Lloyd 64)

1970–71: New Zealand v England (Played 2, Eng won 1, NZ won 0, Drawn 1)
First Test at Christchurch, Feb. 25–Mar. 1. Eng won by 8 wickets.
    NZ: 65   (D. L. Underwood 6 for 12)
       &   254   (G. M. Turner 76, B. E. Congdon 55; D. L. Underwood 6 for 85)
    ENG: 231   (B. L. d'Oliveira 100; H. J. Howarth 4 for 46)
       &   89–2 (J. H. Hampshire 51*)
Second Test at Auckland, Mar. 5–8. Match Drawn.
    ENG: 321   (A. P. E. Knott 101, P. Lever 64, B. L. d'Oliveira 58, M. C.
                     Cowdrey 54; R. S. Cunis 6 for 76)
       &   237   (A. P. E. Knott 96; R. O. Collinge 4 for 41)
    NZ: 313–7 dec. (M. G. Burgess 104, G. M. Turner 65, G. T. Dowling 53;
                     D. L. Underwood 5 for 108)
       &   40–0

1971: England v Pakistan (Played 3, Eng won 1, Pak won 0. Drawn 2)
First Test at Edgbaston, June 3–8. Match Drawn.
    PAK: 608–7 dec. (Zaheer Abbas 274, Asif Iqbal 104*, Mushtaq Mohammad 100)
    ENG: 353   (A. P. E. Knott 116, B. L. d'Oliveira 73; Aisf Masood 5 for 111)
       &   229–5 (B. W. Luckhurst 108*; Asif Masood 4 for 49)
Second Test at Lord's, June 17–22. Match Drawn.
    ENG: 241–2 dec. (G. Boycott 121*)
       &   117–0 (R. A. Hutton 58*, B. W. Luckhurst 53*)
    PAK: 148

Third Test at Headingley, July 8–13. Eng won by 25 runs.
ENG: 316   (G. Boycott 112, B. L. d'Oliveira 74)
  &   264   (B. L. d'Oliveira 72, D. L. Amiss 56; Saleem Altaf 4 for 11)
PAK: 350   (Zaheer Abbas 72, Wasim Bari 63, Mushtaq Mohammad 57)
  &   205   (Sadiq Mohammad 91)

1971: England v India (Played 3, India won 1, Eng won 0, Drawn 2)
First Test at Lord's, July 22–27. Match Drawn.
ENG: 304   (J. A. Snow 73, A. P. E. Knott 67; B. S. Bedi 4 for 70)
  &   191   (J. H. Edrich 62; S. Venkataraghavan 4 for 52)
IND: 313   (A. L. Wadekar 85, G. R. Viswanath 68, E. D. Solkar 67; N. Gifford
            4 for 84)
  &   145–8 (S. M. Gavaskar 53; N. Gifford 4 for 43)
Second Test at Old Trafford, Aug. 5–10. Match Drawn.
ENG: 386   (R. Illingworth 107, P. Lever 88*, B. W. Luckhurst 78; S. Abid Ali
            4 for 64)
  &   245–3 dec. (B. W. Luckhurst 101, J. H. Edrich 59)
IND: 212   (S. M. Gavaskar 57, E. D. Solkar 50; P. Lever 5 for 70)
  &   65–3
Third Test at The Oval, Aug. 19–24. India won by 4 wickets.
ENG: 355   (A. P. E. Knott 90, J. A. Jameson 82, R. A. Hutton 81)
  &   101   (B. S. Chandrasekhar 6 for 38)
IND: 284   (F. M. Engineer 59, D. N. Sardesai 54; R. Illingworth 5 for 70)
  &   174–6

1971–72: West Indies v New Zealand (Played 5, WI won 0, NZ won 0, Drawn 5)
First Test at Kingston, Feb. 16–21. Match Drawn.
WI: 508–4 dec. (L. G. Rowe 214, R. C. Fredericks 163)
  &   218–3 dec. (L. G. Rowe 100*)
NZ: 386   (G. M. Turner 223*, K. J. Wadsworth 78)
  &   236–6 (M. G. Burgess 101; D. A. J. Holford 4 for 55)
Second Test at Port of Spain, Mar. 9–14. Match Drawn.
NZ: 348   (B. E. Congdon 166*, R. S. Cunis 51; V. A. Holder 4 for 60)
  &   288–3 dec. (G. M. Turner 95, B. E. Congdon 82, M. G. Burgess 62*)
WI: 341   (C. A. Davis 90, R. C. Fredericks 69; B. R. Taylor 4 for 41)
  &   121–5
Third Test at Bridgetown, Mar. 23–28. Match Drawn.
WI: 133   (B. R. Taylor 7 for 74)
  &   564–8 (C. A. Davis 183, G. S. Sobers 142, L. G. Rowe 51, D. A. J.
            Holford 50)
NZ: 422   (B. E. Congdon 126, B. F. Hastings 105; G. S. Sobers 4 for 64)
Fourth Test at Georgetown, April 6–11. Match Drawn.
WI: 365–7 dec. (A. I. Kallicharran 100*, G. A. Greenidge 50)
  &   86–0
NZ: 543–3 dec. (G. M. Turner 259, T. W. Jarvis 182, B. E. Congdon 61*)
Fifth Test at Port of Spain, April 20–26. Match Drawn.
WI: 368   (A. I. Kallicharran 101, R. C. Fredericks 60)
  &   194   (B. R. Taylor 5 for 41)
NZ: 162   (Inshan Ali 5 for 59)
  &   253–7 (B. E. Congdon 58, G. M. Turner 50; V. A. Holder 4 for 41)

1972: England v Australia (Played 5, Eng won 2, Aus won 2, Drawn 1)
First Test at Old Trafford, June 8–13. Eng won by 89 runs.
ENG: 249   (A. W. Greig 57)
  &   234   (A. W. Greig 62; D. K. Lillee 6 for 66)
AUS: 142   (K. R. Stackpole 53; J. A. Snow 4 for 41, G. G. Arnold 4 for 62)
  &   252   (R. W. Marsh 91, K. R. Stackpole 67; A. W. Greig 4 for 53, J. A.
            Snow 4 for 87)
Second Test at Lord's, June 22–26. Aus won by 8 wickets.
ENG: 272   (A. W. Greig 54; R. A. L. Massie 8 for 84)
  &   116   (R. A. L. Massie 8 for 53)
AUS: 308   (G. S. Chappell 131, I. M. Chappell 56, R. W. Marsh 50; J. A.
            Snow 5 for 57)
  &   81–2 (K. R. Stackpole 57*)
Third Test at Trent Bridge, July 13–18. Match Drawn.

AUS: 315   (K. R. Stackpole 114, D. J. Colley 54; J. A. Snow 5 for 92)
  & 324-4 dec. (R. Edwards 170*, G. S. Chappell 72, I. M. Chappell 50)
ENG: 189   (D. K. Lillee 4 for 35, R. A. L. Massie 4 for 43)
  & 290-4 (B. W. Luckhurst 96, B. L. d'Oliveira 50*)
Fourth Test at Headingley, July 27-29. Eng won by 9 wickets.
AUS: 146   (K. R. Stackpole 52; D. L. Underwood 4 for 37)
  & 136   (D. L. Underwood 6 for 45)
ENG: 263   (R. Illingworth 57; A. A. Mallett 5 for 114)
  &   21-1
Fifth Test at The Oval, Aug. 10-16. Aus won by 5 wickets.
ENG: 284   (A. P. E. Knott 92, P. H. Parfitt 51; D. K. Lillee 5 for 58)
  & 356   (B. Wood 90, A. P. E. Knott 63; D. K. Lillee 5 for 123)
AUS: 399   (I. M. Chappell 118, G. S. Chappell 113, R. Edwards 79; D. L.
           Underwood 4 for 90)
  & 242-5 (K. R. Stackpole 79)

1972-73: India v England (Played 5, India won 2, Eng won 1, Drawn 2)
First Test at New Delhi, Dec. 20-25. Eng won by 6 wickets.
IND: 173   (S. Abid Ali 58; G. G. Arnold 6 for 45)
  & 233   (E. D. Solkar 75, F. M. Engineer 63; D. L. Underwood 4 for 56)
ENG: 200   (A. W. Greig 68*; B. S. Chandrasekhar 8 for 79)
  & 208-4 (A. R. Lewis 70*)
Second Test at Calcutta, Dec. 30-Jan. 4. India won by 28 runs.
IND: 210   (F. M. Engineer 75)
  & 155   (S. A. Durani 53; A. W. Greig 5 for 24, C. M. Old 4 for 43)
ENG: 174   (B. S. Chandrasekhar 5 for 65)
  & 163   (A. W. Greig 67; B. S. Bedi 5 for 63, B. S. Chandrasekhar 4 for 42)
Third Test at Madras, Jan. 12-17. India won by 4 wickets.
ENG: 242   (K. W. R. Fletcher 97*; B. S. Chandrasekhar 6 for 90)
  & 159   (M. H. Denness 76; E. A. S. Prasanna 4 for 16, B. S. Bedi 4 for 38)
IND: 316   (M. A. K. Pataudi 73; P. I. Pocock 4 for 114)
  &   86-6 (P. I. Pocock 4 for 28)
Fourth Test at Kanpur, Jan. 25-30. Match Drawn.
IND: 357   (A. L. Wadekar 90, S. M. Gavaskar 69, M. A. K. Pataudi 54; C. M.
           Old 4 for 69)
  & 186-6 (G. R. Viswanath 75*)
ENG: 397   (A. R. Lewis 125, J. Birkenshaw 64, K. W. R. Fletcher 58; B. S.
           Chandrasekhar 4 for 86)
Fifth Test at Bombay, Feb. 6-11. Match Drawn.
IND: 448   (F. M. Engineer 121, G. R. Viswanath 113, A. L. Wadekar 87, S. A.
           Durani 73)
  & 244-5 dec. (S. M. Gavaskar 67, F. M. Engineer 66)
ENG: 480   (A. W. Greig 148, K. W. R. Fletcher 113, A. P. E. Knott 56; B. S.
           Chandrasekhar 5 for 135)
  &   67-2

1972-73: Australia v Pakistan (Played 3, Aus won 3, Pak won 0)
First Test at Adelaide, Dec. 22-27. Aus won by an innings and 114 runs.
PAK: 257   (Wasim Bari 72, Intikhab Alam 64; D. K. Lillee 4 for 49, R. A. L.
           Massie 4 for 70)
  & 214   (Sadiq Mohammad 81; A. A. Mallett 8 for 59)
AUS: 585   (I. M. Chappell 196, R. W. Marsh 118, R. Edwards 89)
Second Test at Melbourne, Dec. 29-Jan. 3. Aus won by 92 runs.
AUS: 441-5 dec. (I. R. Redpath 135, G. S. Chappell 116*, R. W. Marsh 74,
           I. M. Chappell 66)
  & 425   (J. Benaud 142, A. P. Sheahan 127, G. S. Chappell 62)
PAK: 574-8 dec. (Majid Khan 158, Sadiq Mohammad 137, Intikhab Alam 68,
           Mushtaq Mohammad 60, Zaheer Abbas 51, Saeed Ahmed 50)
  & 200
Third Test at Sydney, Jan. 6-11. Aus won by 52 runs.
AUS: 334   (I. R. Redpath 79, R. Edwards 69; Sarfraz Nawaz 4 for 53)
  & 184   (Sarfraz Nawaz 4 for 56, Saleem Altaf 4 for 60)
PAK: 360   (Mushtaq Mohammad 121, Asif Iqbal 65, Nasim-ul-Ghani 64;
           G. S. Chappell 5 for 61)

                    &   106   (M. H. N. Walker 6 for 15)

1972-73: New Zealand v Pakistan (Played 3, Pak won 1, NZ won 0, Drawn 2)
First Test at Wellington, Feb. 2-5. Match Drawn.
PAK: 357   (Sadiq Mohammad 166, Majid Khan 79; B. R. Taylor 4 for 110)
    &   290-6 dec. (Majid Khan 79, Sadiq Mohammad 68, Intikhab Alam 53*;
                H. J. Howarth 4 for 99)
NZ: 325   (M. G. Burgess 79, B. F. Hastings 72; Sarfraz Nawaz 4 for 126)
    &   78-3
Second Test at Dunedin, Feb. 7-10. Pak won by an innings and 166 runs.
PAK: 507-6 dec. (Mushtaq Mohammad 201, Asif Iqbal 175, Sadiq Mohammad
                61)
NZ: 156   (Intikhab Alam 7 for 52)
    &   185   (V. Pollard 61; Mushtaq Mohammad 5 for 49, Intikhab Alam
                4 for 78)
Third Test at Auckland, Feb. 16-19. Match Drawn.
PAK: 402   (Majid Khan 110, Mushtaq Mohammad 61, Saleem Altaf 53*;
                B. R. Taylor 4 for 86)
    &   271   (Mushtaq Mohammad 52)
NZ: 402   (B. F. Hastings 110, R. E. Redmond 107, R. O. Collinge 68*, G. M.
                Turner 58; Intikhab Alam 6 for 127)
    &   92-3 (R. E. Redmond 56)

1972-73: West Indies v Australia (Played 5, Aus won 2, WI won 0, Drawn 3)
First Test at Kingston, Feb. 16-21. Match Drawn.
AUS: 428-7 dec. (R. W. Marsh 97, K. D. Walters 72, R. Edwards 63; L. R.
                Gibbs 4 for 85)
    &   260-2 dec. (K. R. Stackpole 142, I. R. Redpath 60)
WI: 428   (M. L. C. Foster 125, R. Kanhai 84, L. G. Rowe 76, A. I.
                Kallicharran 50; M. H. N. Walker 6 for 114, J. R. Hammond
                4 for 79)
    &   67-3
Second Test at Bridgetown, Mar. 9-14. Match Drawn.
AUS: 324   (G. S. Chappell 106, R. W. Marsh 78, I. M. Chappell 72)
    &   300-2 dec. (I. M. Chappell 106*, K. D. Walters 102*, K. R. Stackpole 53)
WI: 391   (R. Kanhai 105, R. C. Fredericks 98, D. L. Murray 90; M. H. N.
                Walker 5 for 97)
    &   36-0
Third Test at Port of Spain, Mar. 23-28. Aus won by 44 runs.
AUS: 332   (K. D. Walters 112, I. R. Redpath 66, G. S. Chappell 56)
    &   281   (I. M. Chappell 97; L. R. Gibbs 5 for 102)
WI: 280   (R. Kanhai 56, A. I. Kallicharran 53; T. J. Jenner 4 for 98)
    &   289   (A. I. Kallicharran 91, R. C. Fredericks 76; K. J. O'Keeffe 4 for 57)
Fourth Test at Georgetown, April 6-11. Aus won by 10 wickets.
WI: 366   (C. H. Lloyd 178, R. Kanhai 57; K. D. Walters 5 for 66)
    &   109   (J. R. Hammond 4 for 38, M. H. N. Walker 4 for 45)
AUS: 341   (I. M. Chappell 109, K. D. Walters 81, G. S. Chappell 51)
    &   135-0 (K. R. Stackpole 76*, I. R. Redpath 57*)
Fifth Test at Port of Spain, April 21-26. Match Drawn.
AUS: 419-8 dec. (R. Edwards 74, K. D. Walters 70, I. M. Chappell 56, R. W.
                Marsh 56)
    &   218-7 dec. (L. R. Gibbs 4 for 66)
WI: 319   (R. C. Fredericks 73, C. H. Lloyd 59; M. H. N. Walker 5 for 75,
                T. J. Jenner 5 for 90)
    &   135-5

1972-73: Pakistan v England (Played 3, Pak won 0, Eng won 0, Drawn 3)
First Test at Lahore, Mar. 2-7. Match Drawn.
ENG: 355   (D. L. Amiss 112, K. W. R. Fletcher 55, M. H. Denness 50)
    &   306-7 dec. (A. R. Lewis 74, A. W. Greig 72, M. H. Denness 68; Intikhab
                Alam 4 for 80)
PAK: 422   (Sadiq Mohammad 119, Asif Iqbal 102, Mushtaq Mohammad 66;
                A. W. Greig 4 for 86)
    &   124-3 (Talaat Ali 57)

Second Test at Hyderabad, Mar. 16–21. Match Drawn.
ENG: 487   (D. L. Amiss 158, K. W. R. Fletcher 78, A. P. E. Knott 71;
                      Mushtaq Mohammad 4 for 93, Intikhab Alam 4 for 137)
            &   218–6 (A. W. Greig 64, A. P. E. Knott 63*)
PAK: 569–9 dec. (Mushtaq Mohammad 157, Intikhab Alam 138, Asif Iqbal 68;
                      P. I. Pocock 5 for 169)
Third Test at Karachi, Mar. 24–29. Match Drawn.
PAK: 445–6 dec. (Majid Khan 99, Mushtaq Mohammad 99, Sadiq Mohammad
                      89, Intikhab Alam 61)
            &   199   (N. Gifford 5 for 55, J. Birkenshaw 5 for 57)
ENG: 386   (D. L. Amiss 99, A. R. Lewis 88, K. W. R. Fletcher 54; Intikhab
                      Alam 4 for 105)
            &   30–1

1973: England v New Zealand (Played 3, Eng won 2, NZ won 0, Drawn 1)
First Test at Trent Bridge, June 7–12. Eng won by 38 runs.
ENG: 250   (G. Boycott 51; D. R. Hadlee 4 for 42, B. R. Taylor 4 for 53)
            &   325–8 dec. (A. W. Greig 139, D. L. Amiss 138*)
NZ: 97   (A. W. Greig 4 for 33)
            &   440   (B. E. Congdon 176, V. Pollard 116; G. G. Arnold 5 for 131)
Second Test at Lord's, June 21–26. Match Drawn.
ENG: 253   (A. W. Greig 63, G. Boycott 61, G. R. J. Roope 56)
            &   463–9 (K. W. R. Fletcher 178, G. Boycott 92, D. L. Amiss 53, G. R. J.
                      Roope 51; H. J. Howarth 4 for 144)
NZ: 551–9 dec. (B. E. Congdon 175, M. G. Burgess 105, V. Pollard 105*, B. F.
                      Hastings 86; C. M. Old 5 for 113)
Third Test at Headingley, July 5–10. Eng won by an innings and 1 run.
NZ: 276   (M. G. Burgess 87, V. Pollard 62; C. M. Old 4 for 71)
            &   142   (G. M. Turner 81; G. G. Arnold 5 for 27)
ENG: 419   (G. Boycott 115, K. W. R. Fletcher 81, R. Illingworth 65; R. O.
                      Collinge 5 for 74)

1973: England v West Indies (Played 3, WI won 2, Eng won 0, Drawn 1)
First Test at The Oval, July 26–31. WI won by 158 runs.
WI: 415   (C. H. Lloyd 132, A. I. Kallicharran 80, K. D. Boyce 72; G. G.
                      Arnold 5 for 113)
            &   255   (A. I. Kallicharran 80, G. S. Sobers 51)
ENG: 257   (G. Boycott 97; K. D. Boyce 5 for 70)
            &   255   (F. C. Hayes 106*; K. D. Boyce 6 for 77)
Second Test at Edgbaston, Aug. 9–14. Match Drawn.
WI: 327   (R. C. Fredericks 150, B. D. Julien 54)
            &   302   (C. H. Lloyd 94, G. S. Sobers 74, R. Kanhai 54; G. G. Arnold 4
                      for 43)
ENG: 305   (G. Boycott 56*, D. L. Amiss 56, K. W. R. Fletcher 52)
            &   182–2 (D. L. Amiss 86*)
Third Test at Lord's, Aug. 23–27. WI won by an innings and 226 runs.
WI: 652–8 dec. (R. Kanhai 157, G. S. Sobers 150*, B. D. Julien 121, C. H.
                      Lloyd 63, R. C. Fredericks 51; R. G. D. Willis 4 for 118)
ENG: 233   (K. W. R. Fletcher 68; K. D. Boyce 4 for 50, V. A. Holder 4 for 56)
            &   193   (K. W. R. Fletcher 86*; K. D. Boyce 4 for 49)

1973–74: Australia v New Zealand (Played 3, Aus won 2, NZ won 0, Drawn 1)
First Test at Melbourne, Dec. 29–Jan. 2. Aus won by an innings and 25 runs.
AUS: 462–8 dec. (K. R. Stackpole 122, K. D. Walters 79, G. S. Chappell 60,
                      I. M. Chappell 54, G. J. Gilmour 52; D. R. Hadlee 4 for 102)
NZ: 237   (K. J. Wadsworth 80; G. J. Gilmour 4 for 75)
            &   200   (A. A. Mallett 4 for 63)
Second Test at Sydney, Jan. 5–10. Match Drawn.
NZ: 312   (J. M. Parker 108, K. J. Wadsworth 54; K. D. Walters 4 for 39)
            &   305–9 dec. (J. F. M. Morrison 117, B. F. Hastings 83)
AUS: 162   (R. J. Hadlee 4 for 33)
            &   30–2
Third Test at Adelaide, Jan. 26–31. Aus won by an innings and 57 runs.
AUS: 477   (R. W. Marsh 132, K. D. Walters 94, K. J. O'Keeffe 85; D. R.
                      O'Sullivan 5 for 148)
NZ: 218

     &   202   (B. E. Congdon 71*; G. Dymock 5 for 58)

1973–74: West Indies v England (Played 5, WI won 1, Eng won 1, Drawn 3)
First Test at Port of Spain, Feb. 2–7. WI won by 7 wickets.
    ENG: 131   (K. D. Boyce 4 for 42)
        &   392   (D. L. Amiss 174, G. Boycott 93; L. R. Gibbs 6 for 108)
    WI: 392   (A. I. Kallicharran 158, B. D. Julien 86*; P. I. Pocock 5 for 110)
       &   132–3 (R. C. Fredericks 65*)
Second Test at Kingston, Feb. 16–21. Match Drawn.
    ENG: 353   (G. Boycott 68, M. H. Denness 67)
       &   432–9 (D. L. Amiss 262*)
    WI: 583–9 dec. (L. G. Rowe 120, R. C. Fredericks 94, A. I. Kallicharran 93,
                    B. D. Julien 66, G. S. Sobers 57)
Third Test at Bridgetown, Mar. 6–11. Match Drawn.
    ENG: 395   (A. W. Greig 148, A. P. E. Knott 87; B. D. Julien 5 for 57)
       &   277–7 (K. W. R. Fletcher 129*, A. P. E. Knott 67)
    WI: 596–8 dec. (L. G. Rowe 302, A. I. Kallicharran 119, D. L. Murray 53*;
                    A. W. Greig 6 for 164)
Fourth Test at Georgetown, Mar. 22–27. Match Drawn.
    ENG: 448   (A. W. Greig 121, D. L. Amiss 118, A. P. E. Knott 61)
    WI: 198–4 (R. C. Fredericks 98)
Fifth Test at Port of Spain, Mar. 30–April 5. Eng won by 26 runs.
    ENG: 267   (G. Boycott 99)
       &   263   (G. Boycott 112)
    WI: 305   (L. G. Rowe 123, R. C. Fredericks 67, C. H. Lloyd 52; A. W. Greig
                    8 for 86)
       &   199   (A. W. Greig 5 for 70)

1973–74: New Zealand v Australia (Played 3, NZ won 1, Aus won 1, Drawn 1)
First Test at Wellington, Mar. 1–6. Match Drawn.
    AUS: 511–6 dec. (G. S. Chappell 247*, I. M. Chappell 145)
       &   460–8 (G. S. Chappell 133, I. M. Chappell 121, I. R. Redpath 93)
    NZ: 484   (B. E. Congdon 132, B. F. Hastings 101, G. M. Turner 79, J. F. M.
                    Morrison 66)
Second Test at Christchurch, Mar. 8–13. NZ won by 5 wickets.
    AUS: 223   (I. R. Redpath 71)
       &   259   (K. D. Walters 65, I. R. Redpath 58, I. C. Davis 50; R. J. Hadlee
                    4 for 71, D. R. Hadlee 4 for 75)
    NZ: 255   (G. M. Turner 101; M. H. N. Walker 4 for 60)
       &   230–5 (G. M. Turner 110*)
Third Test at Auckland, Mar. 22–24. Aus won by 297 runs.
    AUS: 221   (K. D. Walters 104*; R. O. Collinge 5 for 82, B. E. Congdon
                    4 for 46)
       &   346   (I. R. Redpath 159*; R. O. Collinge 4 for 84)
    NZ: 112   (G. J. Gilmour 5 for 64, A. A. Mallett 4 for 22)
       &   158   (G. M. Turner 72; M. H. N. Walker 4 for 39)

1974: England v India (Played 3, Eng won 3, Ind won 0)
First Test at Old Trafford, June 6–11. Eng won by 113 runs.
    ENG: 328–9 dec. (K. W. R. Fletcher 123*, D. L. Amiss 56, A. W. Greig 53)
       &   213–3 dec. (J. H. Edrich 100*)
    IND: 246   (S. M. Gavaskar 101, S. Abid Ali 71; R. G. D. Willis 4 for 64)
       &   182   (S. M. Gavaskar 58, G. R. Viswanath 50; C. M. Old 4 for 20)
Second Test at Lord's, June 20–24. Eng won by an innings and 285 runs.
    ENG: 629   (D. L. Amiss 188, M. H. Denness 118, A. W. Greig 106, J. H.
                    Edrich 96; B. S. Bedi 6 for 226)
    IND: 302   (F. M. Engineer 86, G. R. Viswanath 52; C. M. Old 4 for 67)
       &   42   (C. M. Old 5 for 21, G. G. Arnold 4 for 19)
Third Test at Edgbaston, July 4–8. Eng won by an innings and 78 runs.
    IND: 165   (F. M. Engineer 64*; M. Hendrick 4 for 28)
       &   216   (S. S. Naik 77)
    ENG: 459–2 dec. (D. Lloyd 214*, M. H. Denness 100, D. L. Amiss 79, K. W. R.
                    Fletcher 51*)

1974: England v Pakistan (Played 3, Eng won 0, Pak won 0, Drawn 3)
First Test at Headingley, July 25–30. Match Drawn.

PAK: 285   (Majid Khan 75, Sarfraz Nawaz 53)
    & 179
ENG: 183
    & 238–6 (J. H. Edrich 70, K. W. R. Fletcher 67*; Sarfraz Nawaz 4 for 56)
Second Test at Lord's, Aug. 8–13. Match Drawn.
PAK: 130–9 dec. (D. L. Underwood 5 for 20)
    & 226 (Mushtaq Mohammad 76, Wasim Raja 53; D. L. Underwood
                8 for 51)
ENG: 270 (A. P. E. Knott 83)
    &   27–0
Third Test at The Oval, Aug. 22–27. Match Drawn.
PAK: 600–7 dec. (Zaheer Abbas 240, Majid Khan 98, Mushtaq Mohammad 76)
    &   94–4
ENG: 545 (D. L. Amiss 183, K. W. R. Fletcher 122, C. M. Old 65; Intikhab
                Alam 5 for 116)

1974–75: India v West Indies (Played 5, WI won 3, Ind won 2)
First Test at Bangalore, Nov. 22–27. WI won by 267 runs.
WI: 289 (A. I. Kallicharran 124, C. G. Greenidge 93; S. Venkataraghavan
                4 for 75, B. S. Chandrasekhar 4 for 112)
    & 356–6 dec. (C. H. Lloyd 163, C. G. Greenidge 107)
IND: 260 (H. S. Kanitkar 65)
    & 118
Second Test at New Delhi, Dec. 11–15. WI won by an innings and 17 runs.
IND: 220 (P. Sharma 54)
    & 256 (F. M. Engineer 75; L. R. Gibbs 6 for 76)
WI: 493 (I. V. A. Richards 192*, C. H. Lloyd 71, K. D. Boyce 68; E. A. S.
                Prasanna 4 for 147)
Third Test at Calcutta, Dec. 27–Jan. 1. India won by 85 runs.
IND: 233 (G. R. Viswanath 52; A. M. E. Roberts 5 for 50)
    & 316 (G. R. Viswanath 139, F. M. Engineer 61)
WI: 240 (R. C. Fredericks 100; S. Madan Lal 4 for 22)
    & 224 (A. I. Kallicharran 57; B. S. Bedi 4 for 52)
Fourth Test at Madras, Jan. 11–15. India won by 100 runs.
IND: 190 (G. R. Viswanath 97*; A. M. E. Roberts 7 for 64)
    & 256 (A. D. Gaekwad 80; A. M. E. Roberts 5 for 57)
WI: 192 (I. V. A. Richards 50; E. A. S. Prasanna 5 for 70)
    & 154 (A. I. Kallicharran 51; E. A. S. Prasanna 4 for 41)
Fifth Test at Bombay, Jan. 23–29. WI won by 201 runs.
WI: 604–6 dec. (C. H. Lloyd 242*, R. C. Fredericks 104, A. I. Kallicharran 98,
                D. L. Murray 91; K. Ghavri 4 for 140)
    & 205–3 dec. (C. G. Greenidge 54)
IND: 406 (E. D. Solkar 102, G. R. Viswanath 95, S. M. Gavaskar 86, A. D.
                Gaekwad 51; L. R. Gibbs 7 for 98)
    & 202 (B. P. Patel 73*; V. A. Holder 6 for 39)

1974–75: Australia v England (Played 6, Aus won 4, Eng won 1, Drawn 1)
First Test at Brisbane, Nov. 29–Dec. 4. Aus won by 166 runs.
AUS: 309 (I. M. Chappell 90, G. S. Chappell 58; R. G. D. Willis 4 for 56)
    & 288–5 dec. (G. S. Chappell 71, K. D. Walters 62*, R. Edwards 53)
ENG: 265 (A. W. Greig 110; M. H. N. Walker 4 for 73)
    & 166 (J. R. Thomson 6 for 46)
Second Test at Perth, Dec. 13–17. Aus won by 9 wickets.
ENG: 208 (A. P. E. Knott 51)
    & 293 (F. J. Titmus 61; J. R. Thomson 5 for 93)
AUS: 481 (R. Edwards 115, K. D. Walters 103, G. S. Chappell 62)
    &   23–1
Third Test at Melbourne, Dec. 26–31. Match Drawn.
ENG: 242 (A. P. E. Knott 52; J. R. Thomson 4 for 72)
    & 244 (D. L. Amiss 90, A. W. Greig 60; J. R. Thomson 4 for 71, A. A.
                Mallett 4 for 60)
AUS: 241 (I. R. Redpath 55; R. G. D. Willis 5 for 61)
    & 238–8 (G. S. Chappell 61; A. W. Greig 4 for 56)
Fourth Test at Sydney, Jan. 4–9. Aus won by 171 runs.
AUS: 405 (G. S. Chappell 84, R. B. McCosker 80, I. M. Chappell 53; G. G.

Arnold 5 for 86, A. W. Greig 4 for 104)
   & 289–4 dec. (G. S. Chappell 144, I. R. Redpath 105)
ENG: 295 (A. P. E. Knott 82, J. H. Edrich 50; J. R. Thomson 4 for 74)
   & 228 (A. W. Greig 54; A. A. Mallett 4 for 21)
Fifth Test at Adelaide, Jan. 25–30. Aus won by 163 runs.
AUS: 304 (T. J. Jenner 74, K. D. Walters 55; D. L. Underwood 7 for 113)
   & 272–5 dec. (K. D. Walters 71*, R. W. Marsh 55, I. R. Redpath 52; D. L. Underwood 4 for 102)
ENG: 172 (M. H. Denness 51; D. K. Lillee 4 for 49)
   & 241 (A. P. E. Knott 106*, K. W. R. Fletcher 63; D. K. Lillee 4 for 69)
Sixth Test at Melbourne, Feb. 8–13. Eng won by an innings and 4 runs.
AUS: 152 (I. M. Chappell 65; P. Lever 6 for 38)
   & 373 (G. S. Chappell 102, I. R. Redpath 83, R. B. McCosker 76, I. M. Chappell 50; A. W. Greig 4 for 88)
ENG: 529 (M. H. Denness 188, K. W. R. Fletcher 146, A. W. Greig 89, J. H. Edrich 70; M. H. N. Walker 8 for 143)

1974–75: Pakistan v West Indies (Played 2, Pak won 0, WI won 0, Drawn 2)
First Test at Lahore, Feb. 15–20. Match Drawn.
PAK: 199 (A. M. E. Roberts 5 for 66)
   & 373–7 dec. (Mushtaq Mohammad 123, Aftab Baloch 60*, Asif Iqbal 52; A. M. E. Roberts 4 for 121)
WI: 214 (A. I. Kallicharran 92*; Sarfraz Nawaz 6 for 89)
   & 258–4 (L. Baichan 105*, C. H. Lloyd 83)
Second Test at Karachi, Mar. 1–6. Match Drawn.
PAK: 406–8 dec. (Wasim Raja 107*, Majid Khan 100, Wasim Bari 58)
   & 256 (Sadiq Mohammad 98*, Asif Iqbal 77)
WI: 493 (A. I. Kallicharran 115, B. D. Julien 101, R. C. Fredericks 77, C. H. Lloyd 73)
   & 1–0

1974–75: New Zealand v England (Played 2, Eng won 1, NZ won 0, Drawn 1)
First Test at Auckland, Feb. 20–25. Eng won by an innings and 83 runs.
ENG: 593–6 dec. (K. W. R. Fletcher 216, M. H. Denness 181, J. H. Edrich 64, A. W. Greig 51)
NZ: 326 (J. M. Parker 121, J. F. M. Morrison 58, K. J. Wadsworth 58; A. W. Greig 5 for 98)
   & 184 (J. F. M. Morrison 58, G. P. Howarth 51*; A. W. Greig 5 for 51)
Second Test at Christchurch, Feb. 28–Mar. 5. Match Drawn.
NZ: 342 (G. M. Turner 98, K. J. Wadsworth 58)
ENG: 272–2 (D. L. Amiss 164*, M. H. Denness 59*)

1975: England v Australia (Played 4, Aus won 1, Eng won 0, Drawn 3)
First Test at Edgbaston, July 10–14. Aus won by an innings and 85 runs.
AUS: 359 (R. W. Marsh 61, R. B. McCosker 59, R. Edwards 56, I. M. Chappell 52)
ENG: 101 (D. K. Lillee 5 for 15; M. H. N. Walker 5 for 48)
   & 173 (K. W. R. Fletcher 51; J. R. Thomson 5 for 38)
Second Test at Lord's, July 31–Aug. 5. Match Drawn.
ENG: 315 (A. W. Greig 96, A. P. E. Knott 69, D. S. Steele 50; D. K. Lillee 4 for 84)
   & 436–7 dec. (J. H. Edrich 175, B. Wood 52)
AUS: 268 (R. Edwards 99, D. K. Lillee 73*; J. A. Snow 4 for 66)
   & 329–3 (I. M. Chappell 86, R. B. McCosker 79, G. S. Chappell 73*, R. Edwards 52*)
Third Test at Headingley, Aug. 14–19. Match Drawn.
ENG: 288 (D. S. Steele 73, J. H. Edrich 62, A. W. Greig 51; G. J. Gilmour 6 for 85)
   & 291 (D. S. Steele 92)
AUS: 135 (P. H. Edmonds 5 for 28)
   & 220–3 (R. B. McCosker 95*, I. M. Chappell 62)
Fourth Test at The Oval, Aug. 28–Sept. 3. Match Drawn.
AUS: 532–9 dec. (I. M. Chappell 192, R. B. McCosker 127, K. D. Walters 65)
   & 40–2
ENG: 191 (J. R. Thomson 4 for 50, M. H. N. Walker 4 for 63)

   &   538   (R. A. Woolmer 149, J. H. Edrich 96, G. R. J. Roope 77, D. S. Steele 66, A. P. E. Knott 64; K. D. Walters 4 for 34, D. K. Lillee 4 for 91)

1975-76: Australia v West Indies (Played 6, Aus won 5, WI won 1)

First Test at Brisbane, Nov. 28–Dec. 2. Aus won by 8 wickets.

WI: 214   (D. L. Murray 66; G. J. Gilmour 4 for 42)
  &   370   (L. G. Rowe 107, A. I. Kallicharran 101, D. L. Murray 55)
AUS: 366   (G. S. Chappell 123, A. Turner 81; L. R. Gibbs 5 for 102)
  &   219–2   (G. S. Chappell 109*, I. M. Chappell 74*)

Second Test at Perth, Dec. 12–16. WI won by an innings and 87 runs.

AUS: 329   (I. M. Chappell 156; M. A. Holding 4 for 88)
  &   169   (A. M. E. Roberts 7 for 54)
WI: 585   (R. C. Fredericks 169, C. H. Lloyd 149, D. L. Murray 63, A. I. Kallicharran 57)

Third Test at Melbourne, Dec. 26–30. Aus won by 8 wickets.

WI: 224   (R. C. Fredericks 59; J. R. Thomson 5 for 62, D. K. Lillee 4 for 56)
  &   312   (C. H. Lloyd 102)
AUS: 485   (G. J. Cosier 109, I. R. Redpath 102, R. W. Marsh 56, G. S. Chappell 52; A. M. E. Roberts 4 for 126)
  &   55–2

Fourth Test at Sydney, Jan. 3–7. Aus won by 7 wickets.

WI: 355   (L. G. Rowe 67, C. H. Lloyd 51; M. H. N. Walker 4 for 70)
  &   128   (D. L. Murray 50; J. R. Thomson 6 for 50)
AUS: 405   (G. S. Chappell 182*, A. Turner 53)
  &   82–3

Fifth Test at Adelaide, Jan. 23–28. Aus won by 190 runs.

AUS: 418   (I. R. Redpath 103, G. J. Gilmour 95; V. A. Holder 5 for 108)
  &   345–7 dec. (A. Turner 136, I. R. Redpath 65)
WI: 274   (K. D. Boyce 95*, A. I. Kallicharran 76; J. R. Thomson 4 for 68)
  &   299   (I. V. A. Richards 101, K. D. Boyce 69, A. I. Kallicharran 67)

Sixth Test at Melbourne, Jan. 31–Feb. 5. Aus won by 165 runs.

AUS: 351   (I. R. Redpath 101, G. S. Chappell 68, G. N. Yallop 57)
  &   300–3 dec. (R. B. McCosker 109*, I. R. Redpath 70, G. S. Chappell 54*)
WI: 160   (I. V. A. Richards 50; G. J. Gilmour 5 for 34, D. K. Lillee 5 for 63)
  &   326   (I. V. A. Richards 98, C. H. Lloyd 91*; J. R. Thomson 4 for 80)

1975-76: New Zealand v India (Played 3, NZ won 1, India won 1, Drawn 1)

First Test at Auckland, Jan. 24–28. India won by 8 wickets.

NZ: 266   (B. E. Congdon 54; B. S. Chandrasekhar 6 for 94)
  &   215   (J. M. Parker 70, B. E. Congdon 54; E. A. S. Prasanna 8 for 76)
IND: 414   (S. Amarnath 124, S. M. Gavaskar 116, M. Amarnath 64; B. E. Congdon 5 for 65)
  &   71–2

Second Test at Christchurch, Feb. 5–10. Match Drawn.

IND: 270   (G. R. Viswanath 83; R. O. Collinge 6 for 63)
  &   255–6   (G. R. Viswanath 79, S. M. Gavaskar 71)
NZ: 403   (G. M. Turner 117, B. E. Congdon 58; S. Madan Lal 5 for 134, M. Amarnath 4 for 63)

Third Test at Wellington, Feb. 13–17. NZ won by an innings and 33 runs.

IND: 220   (B. P. Patel 81; R. J. Hadlee 4 for 35)
  &   81   (R. J. Hadlee 7 for 23)
NZ: 334   (M. G. Burgess 95, G. M. Turner 64, B. E. Congdon 52)

1975-76: West Indies v India (Played 4, WI won 2, India won 1, Drawn 1)

First Test at Bridgetown, Mar. 10–13. WI won by an innings and 97 runs.

IND: 177   (D. A. J. Holford 5 for 23)
  &   214   (G. R. Viswanath 62, S. Madan Lal 55*)
WI: 488–9 dec. (I. V. A. Richards 142, C. H. Lloyd 102, A. I. Kallicharran 93, R. C. Fredericks 54; B. S. Chandrasekhar 4 for 163)

Second Test at Port of Spain, Mar. 24–29. Match Drawn.

WI: 241   (I. V. A. Richards 130; B. S. Bedi 5 for 82)
  &   215–8   (C. H. Lloyd 70)
IND: 402–5 dec. (S. M. Gavaskar 156, B. P. Patel 115*)

Third Test at Port of Spain, April 7–12. Ind won by 6 wickets.

WI: 359 (I. V. A. Richards 177, C. H. Lloyd 68; B. S. Chandrasekhar
6 for 120, B. S. Bedi 4 for 73)
& 271–6 dec. (A. I. Kallicharran 103*)
IND: 228 (M. A. Holding 6 for 65)
& 406–4 (G. R. Viswanath 112, S. M. Gavaskar 102, M. Amarnath 85)
Fourth Test at Kingston, April 21–25. WI won by 10 wickets.
IND: 306–6 dec. (A. D. Gaekwad 81, S. M. Gavaskar 66; M. A. Holding
4 for 82)
& 97 (M. Amarnath 60)
WI: 391 (R. C. Fredericks 82, D. L. Murray 71, I. V. A. Richards 64, M. A.
Holding 55; B. S. Chandrasekhar 5 for 153)
& 13–0

1976: England v West Indies (Played 5, WI won 3, Eng won 0, Drawn 2)
First Test at Trent Bridge, June 3–8. Match Drawn.
WI: 494 (I. V. A. Richards 232, A. I. Kallicharran 97; D. L. Underwood
4 for 82)
& 176–5 dec. (I. V. A. Richards 63; J. A. Snow 4 for 53)
ENG: 332 (D. S. Steele 106, R. A. Woolmer 82; W. W. Daniel 4 for 53)
& 156–2 (J. H. Edrich 76*)
Second Test at Lord's, June 17–22. Match Drawn.
ENG: 250 (D. B. Close 60; A. M. E. Roberts 5 for 60)
& 254 (D. S. Steele 64; A. M. E. Roberts 5 for 63)
WI: 182 (C. G. Greenidge 84, C. H. Lloyd 50; D. L. Underwood 5 for 39,
J. A. Snow 4 for 68)
& 241–6 (R. C. Fredericks 138)
Third Test at Old Trafford, July 8–13. WI won by 425 runs.
WI: 211 (C. G. Greenidge 134; M. W. W. Selvey 4 for 41)
& 411–5 dec. (I. V. A. Richards 135, C. G. Greenidge 101, R. C. Fredericks 50)
ENG: 71 (M. A. Holding 5 for 17)
& 126 (A. M. E. Roberts 6 for 37)
Fourth Test at Headingley, July 22–27. WI won by 55 runs.
WI: 450 (C. G. Greenidge 115, R. C. Fredericks 109, I. V. A. Richards 66,
L. G. Rowe 50; J. A. Snow 4 for 77)
& 196 (C. L. King 58; R. G. D. Willis 5 for 42)
ENG: 387 (A. W. Greig 116, A. P. E. Knott 116)
& 204 (A. W. Greig 76*)
Fifth Test at The Oval, Aug. 12–17. WI won by 231 runs.
WI: 687–8 dec. (I. V. A. Richards 291, C. H. Lloyd 84, R. C. Fredericks 71,
L. G. Rowe 70, C. L. King 63)
& 182–0 dec. (R. C. Fredericks 86*, C. G. Greenidge 85*)
ENG: 435 (D. L. Amiss 203, A. P. E. Knott 50; M. A. Holding 8 for 92)
& 203 (A. P. E. Knott 57; M. A. Holding 6 for 57)

1976–77: Pakistan v New Zealand (Played 3, Pak won 2, NZ won 0, Drawn 1)
First Test at Lahore, Oct. 9–13. Pak won by 6 wickets.
PAK: 417 (Asif Iqbal 166, Javed Miandad 163; R. J. Hadlee 5 for 121)
& 105–4
NZ: 157 (Intikhab Alam 4 for 35)
& 360 (M. G. Burgess 111, R. W. Anderson 92; Imran Khan 4 for 59)
Second Test at Hyderabad, Oct. 23–27. Pak won by 10 wickets.
PAK: 473–8 dec. (Sadiq Mohammad 103*, Mushtaq Mohammad 101, Majid
Khan 98, Asif Iqbal 73)
& 4–0
NZ: 219
& 254 (J. M. Parker 82; Intikhab Alam 4 for 44)
Third Test at Karachi, Oct. 30–Nov. 4. Match Drawn.
PAK: 565–9 dec. (Javed Miandad 206, Majid Khan 112, Mushtaq Mohammad
107, Imran Khan 59; R. J. Hadlee 4 for 138)
& 290–5 dec. (Javed Miandad 85, Mushtaq Mohammad 67*, Majid Khan
50)
NZ: 468 (W. K. Lees 152, R. J. Hadlee 87, B. L. Cairns 52*)
& 262–7

1976–77: India v New Zealand (Played 3, India won 2, NZ won 0, Drawn 1)
First Test at Bombay, Nov. 10–15. India won by 162 runs.
IND: 399   (S. M. Gavaskar 119, S. M. H. Kirmani 88; R. J. Hadlee 4 for 95)
      & 202–4 dec. (B. P. Patel 82)
NZ: 298   (J. M. Parker 104, G. M. Turner 65; B. S. Chandrasekhar 4 for 77)
      & 141   (B. S. Bedi 5 for 27)
Second Test at Kanpur, Nov. 18–23. Match Drawn.
IND: 524–9 dec. (M. Amarnath 70, G. R. Viswanath 68, S. M. H. Kirmani 64,
                S. M. Gavaskar 66, A. V. Mankad 50, B. S. Bedi 50*)
      & 208–2 dec. (G. R. Viswanath 103*, A. D. Gaekwad 77*)
NZ: 350   (G. M. Turner 113, A. D. G. Roberts 84*, M. G. Burgess 54)
      & 193–7
Third Test at Madras, Nov. 26–Dec. 2. India won by 216 runs.
IND: 298   (G. R. Viswanath 87, S. Venkataraghavan 64; B. L. Cairns 5 for 55)
      & 201–5 dec. (M. Amarnath 55)
NZ: 140   (B. S. Bedi 5 for 48)
      & 143   (B. S. Bedi 4 for 22)

1976–77: India v England (Played 5, Eng won 3, India won 1, Drawn 1)
First Test at New Delhi, Dec. 17–22. Eng won by an innings and 25 runs.
ENG: 381   (D. L. Amiss 179, A. P. E. Knott 75, J. K. Lever 53; B. S. Bedi
                4 for 92)
IND: 122   (J. K. Lever 7 for 46)
      & 234   (S. M. Gavaskar 71; D. L. Underwood 4 for 78)
Second Test at Calcutta, Jan. 1–6. Eng won by 10 wickets.
IND: 155   (R. G. D. Willis 5 for 27)
      & 181   (B. P. Patel 56)
ENG: 321   (A. W. Greig 103, R. W. Tolchard 67, C. M. Old 52; B. S. Bedi
                5 for 110, E. A. S. Prasanna 4 for 93)
      & 16–0
Third Test at Madras, Jan. 14–19. Eng won by 200 runs.
ENG: 262   (J. M. Brearley 59, A. W. Greig 54; B. S. Bedi 4 for 72)
      & 185–9 dec. (B. S. Chandrasekhar 5 for 50, E. A. S. Prasanna 4 for 55)
IND: 164   (J. K. Lever 5 for 59)
      & 83   (D. L. Underwood 4 for 28)
Fourth Test at Bangalore, Jan. 28–Feb. 2. India won by 140 runs.
IND: 253   (S. Amarnath 63, S. M. H. Kirmani 52; R. G. D. Willis 6 for 53)
      & 259–9 dec. (G. R. Viswanath 79*, S. M. Gavaskar 50; D. L. Underwood
                4 for 76)
ENG: 195   (D. L. Amiss 82; B. S. Chandrasekhar 6 for 76)
      & 177   (A. P. E. Knott 81*; B. S. Bedi 6 for 71)
Fifth Test at Bombay, Feb. 11–16. Match Drawn.
IND: 338   (S. M. Gavaskar 108, B. P. Patel 83; D. L. Underwood 4 for 89)
      & 192   (S. Amarnath 63; D. L. Underwood 5 for 84)
ENG: 317   (J. M. Brearley 91, A. W. Greig 76, D. L. Amiss 50; E. A. S.
                Prasanna 4 for 73, B. S. Bedi 4 for 109)
      & 152–7 (K. W. R. Fletcher 58*; K. Ghavri 5 for 33)

1976–77: Australia v Pakistan (Played 3, Aus won 1, Pak won 1, Drawn 1)
First Test at Adelaide, Dec. 24–29. Match Drawn.
PAK: 272   (Zaheer Abbas 85)
      & 466   (Asif Iqbal 152*, Zaheer Abbas 101, Javed Miandad 54; D. K.
                Lillee 5 for 163)
AUS: 454   (K. D. Walters 107, I. C. Davis 105, R. B. McCosker 65, G. S.
                Chappell 52; Mushtaq Mohammad 4 for 58)
      & 261–6 (G. S. Chappell 70, K. D. Walters 51; Iqbal Qasim 4 for 84)
Second Test at Melbourne, Jan. 1–6. Aus won by 348 runs.
AUS: 517–8 dec. (G. J. Cosier 168, G. S. Chappell 121, A. Turner 82, I. C.
                Davis 56; Iqbal Qasim 4 for 111)
      & 315–8 dec. (R. B. McCosker 105, I. C. Davis 88, G. S. Chappell 67; Imran
                Khan 5 for 122)
PAK: 333   (Sadiq Mohammad 105, Zaheer Abbas 90, Majid Khan 76; D. K.
                Lillee 6 for 82)
      & 151   (Zaheer Abbas 58; K. J. O'Keeffe 4 for 38, D. K. Lillee 4 for 53)

Third Test at Sydney, Jan. 14–18. Pak won by 8 wickets.
```
AUS:   211   (G. J. Cosier 50; Imran Khan 6 for 102)
  &    180   (Imran Khan 6 for 63)
PAK:   360   (Asif Iqbal 120, Javed Miandad 64, Haroon Rashid 57; M. H. N.
             Walker 4 for 112)
  &     32–2
```

1976–77: New Zealand v Australia (Played 2, Aus won 1, NZ won 0, Drawn 1)
First Test at Christchurch, Feb. 18–23. Match Drawn.
```
AUS:   552   (K. D. Walters 250, G. J. Gilmour 101)
  &    154–4 dec. (R. B. McCosker 77*)
NZ:    357   (M. G. Burgess 66, H. J. Howarth 61; K. J. O'Keeffe 5 for 101)
  &    293–8 (B. E. Congdon 107*; M. H. N. Walker 4 for 65)
```
Second Test at Auckland, Feb. 25–28. Aus won by 10 wickets.
```
NZ:    229   (G. P. Howarth 59, G. N. Edwards 51; D. K. Lillee 5 for 51)
  &    175   (R. J. Hadlee 81; D. K. Lillee 6 for 72)
AUS:   377   (R. B. McCosker 84, G. J. Gilmour 64, G. S. Chappell 58; E. J.
             Chatfield 4 for 100)
  &     28–0
```

1976–77: West Indies v Pakistan (Played 5, WI won 2, Pak won 1, Drawn 2)
First Test at Bridgetown, Feb. 18–23. Match Drawn.
```
PAK:   435   (Wasim Raja 117*, Majid Khan 88; J. Garner 4 for 130)
  &    291   (Wasim Raja 71, Wasim Bari 60*; C. E. H. Croft 4 for 47)
WI:    421   (C. H. Lloyd 157, D. L. Murray 52)
  &    251–9 (I. V. A. Richards 92, R. C. Fredericks 52; Sarfraz Nawaz 4 for 79)
```
Second Test at Port of Spain, Mar. 4–9. West Indies won by 6 wickets.
```
PAK:   180   (Wasim Raja 65; C. E. H. Croft 8 for 29)
  &    340   (Wasim Raja 84, Sadiq Mohammad 81, Majid Khan 54; A. M. E.
             Roberts 4 for 85)
WI:    316   (R. C. Fredericks 120; Mushtaq Mohammad 4 for 50)
  &    206–4 (C. G. Greenidge 70, R. C. Fredericks 57)
```
Third Test at Georgetown, Mar. 18–23. Match Drawn.
```
PAK:   194   (J. Garner 4 for 48)
  &    540   (Majid Khan 167, Zaheer Abbas 80, Haroon Rashid 60; J. Garner
             4 for 100)
WI:    448   (I. T. Shillingford 120, C. G. Greenidge 91, A. I. Kallicharran 72,
             I. V. A. Richards 50; Majid Khan 4 for 45)
  &    154–1 (C. G. Greenidge 96, R. C. Fredericks 52*)
```
Fourth Test at Port of Spain, April 1–6. Pak won by 266 runs.
```
PAK:   341   (Mushtaq Mohammad 121, Majid Khan 92)
  &    301–9 dec. (Wasim Raja 70, Mushtaq Mohammad 56, Sarfraz Nawaz 51)
WI:    154   (Mushtaq Mohammad 5 for 28, Imran Khan 4 for 64)
  &    222
```
Fifth Test at Kingston, April 15–20. WI won by 140 runs.
```
WI:    280   (C. G. Greenidge 100; Imran Khan 6 for 90)
  &    359   (R. C. Fredericks 83, C. G. Greenidge 82)
PAK:   198   (Haroon Rashid 72; C. E. H. Croft 4 for 49)
  &    301   (Asif Iqbal 135, Wasim Raja 64)
```

1976–77: Australia v England (Played 1, Aus won 1)
Test at Melbourne (Centenary Test), Mar. 12–17. Aus won by 45 runs.
```
AUS:   138
  &    419–9 dec. (R. W. Marsh 110*, I. C. Davis 68, K. D. Walters 66, D. W.
             Hookes 56; C. M. Old 4 for 104)
ENG:    95   (D. K. Lillee 6 for 26, M. H. N. Walker 4 for 54)
  &    417   (D. W. Randall 174, D. L. Amiss 64; D. K. Lillee 5 for 139)
```

1977: England v Australia (Played 5, Eng won 3, Aus won 0, Drawn 2)
First Test at Lord's (Jubilee Test), June 16–21. Match Drawn.
```
ENG:   216   (R. A. Woolmer 79, D. W. Randall 53; J. R. Thomson 4 for 41)
  &    305   (R. A. Woolmer 120, A. W. Greig 91; J. R. Thomson 4 for 86)
AUS:   296   (C. S. Serjeant 81, G. S. Chappell 66, K. D. Walters 53; R. G. D.
             Willis 7 for 78)
  &    114–6 (D. W. Hookes 50)
```

Second Test at Old Trafford, July 7-12. Eng won by 9 wickets.
```
AUS:   297   (K. D. Walters 88)
  &    218   (G. S. Chappell 112; D. L. Underwood 6 for 66)
ENG:   437   (R. A. Woolmer 137, D. W. Randall 79, A. W. Greig 76)
  &    82-1
```
Third Test at Trent Bridge, July 28-Aug. 2. Eng won by 7 wickets.
```
AUS:   243   (R. B. McCosker 51; I. T. Botham 5 for 74)
  &    309   (R. B. McCosker 107; R. G. D. Willis 5 for 88)
ENG:   364   (A. P. E. Knott 135, G. Boycott 107; L. S. Pascoe 4 for 80)
  &    189-3 (J. M. Brearley 81, G. Boycott 80*)
```
Fourth Test at Headingley, Aug. 11-15. Eng won by an innings and 85 runs.
```
ENG:   436   (G. Boycott 191, A. P. E. Knott 57; L. S. Pascoe 4 for 91, J. R.
             Thomson 4 for 113)
AUS:   103   (I. T. Botham 5 for 21, M. Hendrick 4 for 41)
  &    248   (R. W. Marsh 63; M. Hendrick 4 for 54)
```
Fifth Test at The Oval, Aug. 25-30. Match Drawn.
```
ENG:   214   (M. F. Malone 5 for 63, J. R. Thomson 4 for 87)
  &    57-2
AUS:   385   (D. W. Hookes 85, M. H. N. Walker 78*, R. W. Marsh 57; R. G. D.
             Willis 5 for 102)
```
1977-78: Australia v India (Played 5, Aus won 3, Ind won 2)
First Test at Brisbane, Dec. 2-6. Aus won by 16 runs.
```
AUS:   166   (P. M. Toohey 82; B. S. Bedi 5 for 55)
  &    327   (R. B. Simpson 89, P. M. Toohey 57; S. Madan Lal 5 for 72)
IND:   153   (W. M. Clark 4 for 46)
  &    324   (S. M. Gavaskar 113, S. M. H. Kirmani 55; J. R. Thomson 4 for 76,
             W. M. Clark 4 for 101)
```
Second Test at Perth, Dec. 16-21. Aus won by 2 wickets.
```
IND:   402   (M. Amarnath 90, C. P. Chauhan 88; J. R. Thomson 4 for 101)
  &    330-9 dec. (S. M. Gavaskar 127, M. Amarnath 100; J. B. Gannon 4 for 77)
AUS:   394   (R. B. Simpson 176, J. Dyson 53, S. J. Rixon 50; B. S. Bedi 5 for 89)
  &    342-8 (A. L. Mann 105, P. M. Toohey 83; B. S. Bedi 5 for 105)
```
Third Test at Melbourne, Dec. 30-Jan. 4. India won by 222 runs.
```
IND:   256   (M. Amarnath 72, G. R. Viswanath 59; W. M. Clark 4 for 73)
  &    343   (S. M. Gavaskar 118, G. R. Viswanath 54; W. M. Clark 4 for 96)
AUS:   213   (C. S. Serjeant 85, G. J. Cosier 67; B. S. Chandrasekhar 6 for 52)
  &    164   (B. S. Chandrasekhar 6 for 52, B. S. Bedi 4 for 58)
```
Fourth Test at Sydney, Jan. 7-12. India won by an innings and 2 runs.
```
AUS:   131   (B. S. Chandrasekhar 4 for 30)
  &    263   (P. M. Toohey 85, G. J. Cosier 68; E. A. S. Prasanna 4 for 51)
IND:   396-8 dec. (G. R. Viswanath 79, K. D. Ghavri 64; J. R. Thomson 4 for 83)
```
Fifth Test at Adelaide, Jan. 28-Feb. 3. Aus won by 47 runs.
```
AUS:   505   (G. N. Yallop 121, R. B. Simpson 100, W. M. Darling 65, P. M.
             Toohey 60; B. S. Chandrasekhar 5 for 136)
  &    256   (W. M. Darling 56, R. B. Simpson 51; K. D. Ghavri 4 for 45, B. S.
             Bedi 4 for 53)
IND:   269   (G. R. Viswanath 89; W. M. Clark 4 for 62)
  &    445   (M. Amarnath 86, D. B. Vengsarkar 78, G. R. Viswanath 73,
             S. M. H. Kirmani 51; B. Yardley 4 for 134)
```
1977-78: Pakistan v England (Played 3, Pak won 0, Eng won 0, Drawn 3)
First Test at Lahore, Dec. 14-19. Match Drawn.
```
PAK:   407-9 dec. (Haroon Rashid 122, Mudassar Nazar 114, Javed Miandad 71)
  &    106-3
ENG:   288   (G. Miller 98*, G. Boycott 63; Sarfraz Nawaz 4 for 68)
```
Second Test at Hyderabad, Jan. 2-7. Match Drawn.
```
PAK:   275   (Haroon Rashid 108, Javed Miandad 88*)
  &    259-4 dec. (Mudassar Nazar 66, Javed Miandad 61*)
ENG:   191   (G. Boycott 79; Abdul Qadir 6 for 44)
  &    186-1 (G. Boycott 100*, J. M. Brearley 74)
```
Third Test at Karachi, Jan. 18-23. Match Drawn.
```
ENG:   266   (G. R. J. Roope 56; Abdul Qadir 4 for 81)
  &    222-5 (G. Boycott 56, D. W. Randall 55)
PAK:   281   (Mudassar Nazar 76; P. H. Edmonds 7 for 66)
```

1977–78: New Zealand v England (Played 3, NZ won 1, Eng won 1, Drawn 1)
First Test at Wellington, Feb. 10–15. NZ won by 72 runs.
```
    NZ:   228    (J. G. Wright 55; C. M. Old 6 for 54)
      &   123    (R. G. D. Willis 5 for 32)
   ENG:   215    (G. Boycott 77; R. J. Hadlee 4 for 74)
      &    64    (R. J. Hadlee 6 for 26)
```
Second Test at Christchurch, Feb. 24–Mar. 1. Eng won by 174 runs.
```
   ENG:   418    (I. T. Botham 103, G. Miller 89, G. R. J. Roope 50, P. H. Edmonds
                  50; R. J. Hadlee 4 for 147)
      &  96–4 dec.
    NZ:   235    (R. W. Anderson 62, J. M. Parker 53*; I. T. Botham 5 for 73, P. H.
                  Edmonds 4 for 38)
      &   105    (R. G. D. Willis 4 for 14)
```
Third Test at Auckland, Mar. 4–10. Match Drawn.
```
    NZ:   315    (G. P. Howarth 122, G. N. Edwards 55, M. G. Burgess 50; I. T.
                  Botham 5 for 109)
      &  382–8   (G. P. Howarth 102, R. W. Anderson 55, G. N. Edwards 54)
   ENG:   429    (C. T. Radley 158, G. R. J. Roope 68, G. Boycott 54, I. T. Botham
                  53; S. L. Boock 5 for 67, R. O. Collinge 4 for 98)
```

1977–78: West Indies v Australia (Played 5, WI won 3, Aus won 1, Drawn 1)
First Test at Port of Spain, Mar. 3–5. WI won by an innings and 106 runs.
```
   AUS:    90    (C. E. H. Croft 4 for 15)
      &   209    (G. N. Yallop 81; A. M. E. Roberts 5 for 56)
    WI:   405    (A. I. Kallicharran 127, C. H. Lloyd 86, D. L. Haynes 61; J. D.
                  Higgs 4 for 91)
```
Second Test at Bridgetown, Mar. 17–19. WI won by 9 wickets.
```
   AUS:   250    (B. Yardley 74, G. M. Wood 69; C. E. H. Croft 4 for 47, J. Garner
                  4 for 65)
      &   178    (G. M. Wood 56; A. M. E. Roberts 4 for 50, J. Garner 4 for 56)
    WI:   288    (D. L. Haynes 66, D. L. Murray 60; J. R. Thomson 6 for 77)
      &  141–1   (C. G. Greenidge 80*, D. L. Haynes 55)
```
Third Test at Georgetown, Mar. 31–April 5. Aus won by 3 wickets.
```
    WI:   205    (A. T. Greenidge 56, S. Shivnarine 53; J. R. Thomson 4 for 56,
                  W. M. Clark 4 for 65)
      &   439    (H. A. Gomes 101, B. Williams 100, S. Shivnarine 63, D. R. Parry
                  51; W. M. Clark 4 for 124)
   AUS:   286    (R. B. Simpson 67, S. J. Rixon 54, G. M. Wood 50; N. Phillip
                  4 for 75)
      &  362–7   (G. M. Wood 126, C. S. Serjeant 124)
```
Fourth Test at Port of Spain, April 15–18. WI won by 198 runs.
```
    WI:   292    (A. I. Kallicharran 92, B. Williams 87)
      &   290    (A. T. Greenidge 69, D. R. Parry 65; B. Yardley 4 for 40)
   AUS:   290    (G. N. Yallop 75; V. A. Holder 6 for 28)
      &    94    (D. R. Parry 5 for 15)
```
Fifth Test at Kingston, April 28–May 3. Match Drawn.
```
   AUS:   343    (P. M. Toohey 122, G. N. Yallop 57; R. R. Jumadeen 4 for 72)
      &  305–3 dec. (P. M. Toohey 97, G. M. Wood 90)
    WI:   280    (H. A. Gomes 115, S. Shivnarine 53; T. J. Laughlin 5 for 101)
      &  258–9   (A. I. Kallicharran 126; B. Yardley 4 for 35)
```

1978: England v Pakistan (Played 3, Eng won 2, Pak won 0, Drawn 1)
First Test at Edgbaston, June 1–5. Eng won by an innings and 57 runs.
```
   PAK:   164    (C. M. Old 7 for 50)
      &   231    (Sadiq Mohammad 79; P. H. Edmonds 4 for 44)
   ENG:   452–8 dec. (C. T. Radley 106, I. T. Botham 100, D. I. Gower 58; Sikander
                  Bakht 4 for 132)
```
Second Test at Lord's, June 15–19. Eng won by an innings and 120 runs.
```
   ENG:   364    (I. T. Botham 108, G. R. J. Roope 69, D. I. Gower 56, G. A.
                  Gooch 54)
   PAK:   105    (R. G. D. Willis 5 for 47, P. H. Edmonds 4 for 6)
      &   139    (I. T. Botham 8 for 34)
```
Third Test at Headingley, June 29–July 4. Match Drawn.
```
   PAK:   201    (Sadiq Mohammad 97; C. M. Old 4 for 41, I. T. Botham 4 for 59)
   ENG:   119–7  (Sarfraz Nawaz 5 for 39)
```

1978: England v New Zealand (Played 3, Eng won 3, NZ won 0)
First Test at The Oval, July 27–Aug 1. Eng won by 7 wickets.
NZ: 234 (G. P. Howarth 94, J. G. Wright 62; R. G. D. Willis 5 for 42)
& 182 (P. H. Edmonds 4 for 20)
ENG: 279 (D. I. Gower 111)
& 138–3 (G. A. Gooch 91*)
Second Test at Trent Bridge, Aug 10–14. Eng won by an innings and 119 runs.
ENG: 429 (G. Boycott 131, C. T. Radley 59, G. A. Gooch 55, J. M. Brearley
50; R. J. Hadlee 4 for 94)
NZ: 120 (I. T. Botham 6 for 34)
& 190 (B. A. Edgar 60; P. H. Edmonds 4 for 44)
Third Test at Lord's, Aug. 24–28. Eng won by 7 wickets.
NZ: 339 (G. P. Howarth 123, M. G. Burgess 68; I. T. Botham 6 for 101)
& 67 (I. T. Botham 5 for 39, R. G. D. Willis 4 for 16)
ENG: 289 (C. T. Radley 77, D. I. Gower 71; R. J. Hadlee 5 for 84)
& 118–3

Table of Results for each Test Series

England v Australia

Season		M	Won by Eng	Won by Aus	Drawn	Eng captain(s)	Aus captain(s)
1876–77	A	2	1	1	–	James Lillywhite	D. W. Gregory
1878–79	A	1	–	1	–	Lord Harris	D. W. Gregory
1880	E	1	1	–	–	Lord Harris	W. L. Murdoch
1881–82	A	4	–	2	2	A. Shaw	W. L. Murdoch
1882	E	1	–	1	–	A. N. Hornby	W. L. Murdoch
1882–83	A	4	2	2	–	Hon. Ivo Bligh	W. L. Murdoch
1884	E	3	1	–	2	Lord Harris (2)	W. L. Murdoch
						A. N. Hornby (1)	
1884–85	A	5	3	2	–	A. Shrewsbury	T. P. Horan (2)
							W. L. Murdoch (1)
							H. H. Massie (1)
							J. M. Blackham (1)
1886	E	3	3	–	–	A. G. Steel	H. J. H. Scott
1886–87	A	2	2	–	–	A. Shrewsbury	P. S. McDonnell
1887–88	A	1	1	–	–	W. W. Read	P. S. McDonnell
1888	E	3	2	1	–	W. G. Grace (2)	P. S. McDonnell
						A. G. Steel (1)	
1890	E	2	2	–	–	W. G. Grace	W. L. Murdoch
1891–92	A	3	1	2	–	W. G. Grace	J. M. Blackham
1893	E	3	1	–	2	W. G. Grace (2)	J. M. Blackham
						A. E. Stoddart (1)	
1894–95	A	5	3	2	–	A. E. Stoddart	G. Giffen (4)
							J. M. Blackham (1)
1896	E	3	2	1	–	W. G. Grace	G. H. S. Trott
1897–98	A	5	1	4	–	A. C. MacLaren (3)	G. H. S. Trott
						A. E. Stoddart (2)	
1899	E	5	–	1	4	A. C. MacLaren (4)	J. Darling
						W. G. Grace (1)	
1901–02	A	5	1	4	–	A. C. MacLaren	J. Darling (3)
							H. Trumble (2)
1902	E	5	1	2	2	A. C. MacLaren	J. Darling
1903–04	A	5	3	2	–	P. F. Warner	M. A. Noble
1905	E	5	2	–	3	Hon. F. S. Jackson	J. Darling
1907–08	A	5	1	4	–	F. L. Fane (3)	M. A. Noble
						A. O. Jones (2)	
1909	E	5	1	2	2	A. C. MacLaren	M. A. Noble
1911–12	A	5	4	1	–	J. W. H. T. Douglas	C. Hill
1912	E	3	1	–	2	C. B. Fry	S. E. Gregory

Season	M		Won by Eng	Won by Aus	Drawn	Eng captain(s)	Aus captain(s)
1920–21	A	5	–	5	–	J. W. H. T. Douglas	W. W. Armstrong
1921	E	5	–	3	2	Hon. L. H. Tennyson (3)	W. W. Armstrong
						J. W. H. T. Douglas (2)	
1924–25	A	5	1	4	–	A. E. R. Gilligan	H. L. Collins
1926	E	5	1	–	4	A. W. Carr (4)	H. L. Collins (3)
						A. P. F. Chapman (1)	W. Bardsley (2)
1928–29	A	5	4	1	–	A. P. F. Chapman (4)	J. Ryder
						J. C. White (1)	
1930	E	5	1	2	2	A. P. F. Chapman (4)	W. M. Woodfull
						R. E. S. Wyatt (1)	
1932–33	A	5	4	1	–	D. R. Jardine	W. M. Woodfull
1934	E	5	1	2	2	R. E. S. Wyatt (4)	W. M. Woodfull
						C. F. Walters (1)	
1936–37	A	5	2	3	–	G. O. B. Allen	D. G. Bradman
1938	E	4	1	1	2	W. R. Hammond	D. G. Bradman
1946–47	A	5	–	3	2	W. R. Hammond (4)	D. G. Bradman
						N. W. D. Yardley (1)	
1948	E	5	–	4	1	N. W. D. Yardley	D. G. Bradman
1950–51	A	5	1	4	–	F. R. Brown	A. L. Hassett
1953	E	5	1	–	4	L. Hutton	A. L. Hassett
1954–55	A	5	3	1	1	L. Hutton	I. W. Johnson (4)
							A. R. Morris (1)
1956	E	5	2	1	2	P. B. H. May	I. W. Johnson
1958–59	A	5	–	4	1	P. B. H. May	R. Benaud
1961	E	5	1	2	2	P. B. H. May (3)	R. Benaud (4)
						M. C. Cowdrey (2)	R. N. Harvey (1)
1962–63	A	5	1	1	3	E. R. Dexter	R. Benaud
1964	E	5	–	1	4	E. R. Dexter	R. B. Simpson
1965–66	A	5	1	1	3	M. J. K. Smith	R. B. Simpson (3)
							B. C. Booth (2)
1968	E	5	1	1	3	M. C. Cowdrey (4)	W. M. Lawry (4)
						T. W. Graveney (1)	B. N. Jarman (1)
1970–71	A	6	2	–	4	R. Illingworth	W. M. Lawry (5)
							I. M. Chappell (1)
1972	E	5	2	2	1	R. Illingworth	I. M. Chappell
1974–75	A	6	1	4	1	M. H. Denness (5)	I. M. Chappell
						J. H. Edrich (1)	
1975	E	4	–	1	3	A. W. Greig (3)	I. M. Chappell
						M. H. Denness (1)	
1976–77	A	1	–	1	–	A. W. Greig	G. S. Chappell
1977	E	5	3	–	2	J. M. Brearley	G. S. Chappell
In Eng		110	31	28	51		
In Aus		120	43	60	17		
TOTALS		230	74	88	68		

Note: These records do not include the matches at Old Trafford in 1890 and 1938 and the Third Test at Melbourne in 1970–71 which were abandoned without a ball being bowled.

England v South Africa

Season	M		Won by Eng	Won by SA	Drawn	Eng captain(s)	SA captain(s)
1888–89	S	2	2	–	–	C. A. Smith (1)	O. R. Dunell (1)
						M. P. Bowden (1)	W. H. Milton (1)
1891–92	S	1	1	–	–	W. W. Read	W. H. Milton
1895–96	S	3	3	–	–	Lord Hawke (2)	E. A. Halliwell (2)
						Sir T. C. O'Brien (1)	A. Richards (1)
1898–99	S	2	2	–	–	Lord Hawke	M. Bisset

Season	M		Won by Eng	Won by SA	Drawn	Eng captain(s)	SA captain(s)
1905–06	S	5	1	4	–	P. F. Warner	P. W. Sherwell
1907	E	3	1	–	2	R. E. Foster	P. W. Sherwell
1909–10	S	5	2	3	–	H. D. G. Leveson-Gower (3) F. L. Fane (2)	S. J. Snooke
1912	E	3	3	–	–	C. B. Fry	L. J. Tancred (2) F. Mitchell (1)
1913–14	S	5	4	–	1	J. W. H. T. Douglas	H. W. Taylor
1922–23	S	5	2	1	2	F. T. Mann	H. W. Taylor
1924	E	5	3	–	2	A. E. R. Gilligan (4) J. W. H. T. Douglas (1)	H. W. Taylor
1927–28	S	5	2	2	1	R. T. Stanyforth (4) G. T. S. Stevens (1)	H. G. Deane
1929	E	5	2	–	3	J. C. White (3) A. W. Carr (2)	H. G. Deane
1930–31	S	5	–	1	4	A. P. F. Chapman	H. G. Deane (2) H. B. Cameron (2) E. P. Nupen (1)
1935	E	5	–	1	4	R. E. S. Wyatt	H. F. Wade
1938–39	S	5	1	–	4	W. R. Hammond	A. Melville
1947	E	5	3	–	2	N. W. D. Yardley	A. Melville
1948–49	S	5	2	–	3	F. G. Mann	A. D. Nourse
1951	E	5	3	1	1	F. R. Brown	A. D. Nourse
1955	E	5	3	2	–	P. B. H. May	J. E. Cheetham (3) D. J. McGlew (2)
1956–57	S	5	2	2	1	P. B. H. May	C. B. van Ryneveld (4) D. J. McGlew (1)
1960	E	5	3	–	2	M. C. Cowdrey	D. J. McGlew
1964–65	S	5	1	–	4	M. J. K. Smith	T. L. Goddard
1965	E	3	–	1	2	M. J. K. Smith	P. L. van der Merwe
In Eng	44		21	5	10		
In SA	58		25	13	20		
TOTALS	102		46	18	38		

England v West Indies

Season	M		Won by Eng	Won by WI	Drawn	Eng captain(s)	WI captain(s)
1928	E	3	3	–	–	A. P. F. Chapman	R. K. Nunes
1929–30	WI	4	1	1	2	Hon. F. S. Gough-Calthorpe	E. L. G. Hoad (1) N. Betancourt (1) M. P. Fernandes (1) R. K. Nunes (1)
1933	E	3	2	–	1	D. R. Jardine (2) R. E. S. Wyatt (1)	G. C. Grant
1934–35	WI	4	1	2	1	R. E. S. Wyatt	G. C. Grant
1939	E	3	1	–	2	W. R. Hammond	R. S. Grant
1947–48	WI	4	–	2	2	G. O. B. Allen (3) K. Cranston (1)	J. D. C. Goddard (2) G. A. Headley (1) G. E. Gomez (1)
1950	E	4	1	3	–	N. W. D. Yardley (3) F. R. Brown (1)	J. D. C. Goddard
1953–54	WI	5	2	2	1	L. Hutton	J. B. Stollmeyer
1957	E	5	3	–	2	P. B. H. May	J. D. C. Goddard
1959–60	WI	5	1	–	4	P. B. H. May (3) M. C. Cowdrey (2)	F. C. M. Alexander
1963	E	5	1	3	1	E. R. Dexter	F. M. M. Worrell
1966	E	5	1	3	1	M. C. Cowdrey (3) M. J. K. Smith (1) D. B. Close (1)	G. S. Sobers

Season	M	Won by Eng	Won by WI	Drawn	Eng captain(s)	WI captain(s)
1967–68	WI 5	1	–	4	M. C. Cowdrey	G. S. Sobers
1969	E 3	2	–	1	R. Illingworth	G. S. Sobers
1973	E 3	–	2	1	R. Illingworth	R. B. Kanhai
1973–74	WI 5	1	1	3	M. H. Denness	R. B. Kanhai
1976	E 5	–	3	2	A. W. Greig	C. H. Lloyd
In Eng	39	14	14	11		
In WI	32	7	8	17		
TOTALS	71	21	22	28		

England v New Zealand

Season	M	Won by Eng	Won by NZ	Drawn	Eng captain(s)	NZ captain(s)
1929–30	NZ 4	1	–	3	A. H. H. Gilligan	T. C. Lowry
1931	E 3	1	–	2	D. R. Jardine	T. C. Lowry
1932–33	NZ 2	–	–	2	D. R. Jardine (1) R. E. S. Wyatt (1)	M. L. Page
1937	E 3	1	–	2	R. W. V. Robins	M. L. Page
1946–47	NZ 1	–	–	1	W. R. Hammond	W. A. Hadlee
1949	E 4	–	–	4	F. G. Mann (2) F. R. Brown (2)	W. A. Hadlee
1950–51	NZ 2	1	–	1	F. R. Brown	W. A. Hadlee
1954–55	NZ 2	2	–	–	L. Hutton	G. O. Rabone
1958	E 5	4	–	1	P. B. H. May	J. R. Reid
1958–59	NZ 2	1	–	1	P. B. H. May	J. R. Reid
1962–63	NZ 3	3	–	–	E. R. Dexter	J. R. Reid
1965	E 3	3	–	–	M. J. K. Smith	J. R. Reid
1965–66	NZ 3	–	–	3	M. J. K. Smith	B. W. Sinclair (2) M. E. Chapple (1)
1969	E 3	2	–	1	R. Illingworth	G. T. Dowling
1970–71	NZ 2	1	–	1	R. Illingworth	G. T. Dowling
1973	E 3	2	–	1	R. Illingworth	B. E. Congdon
1974–75	NZ 2	1	–	1	M. H. Denness	B. E. Congdon
1977–78	NZ 3	1	1	1	G. Boycott	M. G. Burgess
1978	E 3	3	–	–	J. M. Brearley	M. G. Burgess
In Eng	27	16	–	11		
In NZ	26	11	1	14		
TOTALS	53	27	1	25		

England v India

Season	M	Won by Eng	Won by Ind	Drawn	Eng captain(s)	Ind captain(s)
1932	E 1	1	–	–	D. R. Jardine	C. K. Nayudu
1933–34	I 3	2	–	1	D. R. Jardine	C. K. Nayudu
1936	E 3	2	–	1	G. O. B. Allen	Maharaj of Vizianagram
1946	E 3	1	–	2	W. R. Hammond	Nawab of Pataudi sr.
1951–52	I 5	1	1	3	N. D. Howard (4) D. B. Carr (1)	V. S. Hazare
1952	E 4	3	–	1	L. Hutton	V. S. Hazare
1959	E 5	5	–	–	P. B. H. May (3) M. C. Cowdrey (2)	D. K. Gaekwad (4) P. Roy (1)
1961–62	I 5	–	2	3	E. R. Dexter	N. J. Contractor
1963–64	I 5	–	–	5	M. J. K. Smith	M. A. K. Pataudi
1967	E 3	3	–	–	D. B. Close	M. A. K. Pataudi

Season		M	Won by Eng	Won by Ind	Drawn	Eng captain(s)	Ind captain(s)
1971	E	3	–	1	2	R. Illingworth	A. L. Wadekar
1972–73	I	5	1	2	2	A. R. Lewis	A. L. Wadekar
1974	E	3	3	–	–	M. H. Denness	A. L. Wadekar
1976–77	I	5	3	1	1	A. W. Greig	B. S. Bedi
In Eng		25	18	1	6		
In Ind		28	7	6	15		
TOTALS		53	25	7	21		

England v Pakistan

Season		M	Won by Eng	Won by Pak	Drawn	Eng captain(s)	Pak captain(s)
1954	E	4	1	1	2	L. Hutton (2)	A. H. Kardar
						D. S. Sheppard (2)	
1961–62	P	3	1	–	2	E. R. Dexter	Imtiaz Ahmed
1962	E	5	4	–	1	E. R. Dexter (4)	Javed Burki
						M. C. Cowdrey (1)	
1967	E	3	2	–	1	D. B. Close	Hanif Mohammad
1968–69	P	3	–	–	3	M. C. Cowdrey	Saeed Ahmed
1971	E	3	1	–	2	R. Illingworth	Intikhab Alam
1972–73	P	3	–	–	3	A. R. Lewis	Majid J. Khan
1974	E	3	–	–	3	M. H. Denness	Intikhab Alam
1977–78	P	3	–	–	3	J. M. Brearley (2)	Wasim Bari
						G. Boycott (1)	
1978	E	3	2	–	1	J. M. Brearley	Wasim Bari
In Eng		21	10	1	10		
In Pak		12	1	–	11		
TOTALS		33	11	1	21		

Australia v South Africa

Season		M	Won by Aus	Won by SA	Drawn	Aus Captain(s)	SA captain(s)
1902–03	S	3	2	–	1	J. Darling	H. M. Taberer (1)
							J. H. Anderson (1)
							E. A. Halliwell (1)
1910–11	A	5	4	1	–	C. Hill	P. W. Sherwell
1912	E	3	2	–	1	S. E. Gregory	F. Mitchell (2)
							L. J. Tancred (1)
1921–22	S	3	1	–	2	H. L. Collins	H. W. Taylor
1931–32	A	5	5	–	–	W. M. Woodfull	H. B. Cameron
1935–36	S	5	4	–	1	V. Y. Richardson	H. F. Wade
1949–50	S	5	4	–	1	A. L. Hassett	A. D. Nourse
1952–53	A	5	2	2	1	A. L. Hassett	J. E. Cheetham
1957–58	S	5	3	–	2	I. D. Craig	C. B. van Ryneveld (4)
							D. J. McGlew (1)
1963–64	A	5	1	1	3	R. B. Simpson (4)	T. L. Goddard
						R. Benaud (1)	
1966–67	S	5	1	3	1	R. B. Simpson	P. L. van der Merwe
1969–70	S	4	–	4	–	W. M. Lawry	A. Bacher
In Aus		20	12	4	4		
In SA		30	15	7	8		
In Eng		3	2	–	1		
TOTALS		53	29	11	13		

Australia v West Indies

Season		M	Won by Aus	Won by WI	Drawn	Tied	Aus captain(s)	WI captain(s)
1930–31	A	5	4	1	–	–	W. M. Woodfull	G. C. Grant
1951–52	A	5	4	1	–	–	A. L. Hassett (4)	J. D. C. Goddard (4)
							A. R. Morris (1)	J. B. Stollmeyer (1)
1954–55	WI	5	3	–	2	–	I. W. Johnson	D. S. Atkinson (3) J. B. Stollmeyer (2)
1960–61	A	5	2	1	1	1	R. Benaud	F. M. M. Worrell
1964–65	WI	5	1	2	2	–	R. B. Simpson	G. S. Sobers
1968–69	A	5	3	1	1	–	W. M. Lawry	G. S. Sobers
1972–73	WI	5	2	–	3	–	I. M. Chappell	R. B. Kanhai
1975–76	A	6	5	1	–	–	G. S. Chappell	C. H. Lloyd
1977–78	WI	5	1	3	1	–	R. B. Simpson	A. I. Kallicharran (3) C. H. Lloyd (2)
In Aus		26	18	5	2	1		
In WI		20	7	5	8	–		
TOTALS		46	25	10	10	1		

Australia v New Zealand

Season		M	Won by Aus	Won by NZ	Drawn	Aus captain(s)	NZ captain(s)
1945–46	NZ	1	1	–	–	W. A. Brown	W. A. Hadlee
1973–74	A	3	2	–	1	I. M. Chappell	B. E. Congdon
1973–74	NZ	3	1	1	1	I. M. Chappell	B. E. Congdon
1976–77	NZ	2	1	–	1	G. S. Chappell	G. M. Turner
In Aus		3	2	–	1		
In NZ		6	3	1	2		
TOTALS		9	5	1	3		

Australia v India

Season		M	Won by Aus	Won by Ind	Drawn	Aus captain(s)	Ind captain (s)
1947–48	A	5	4	–	1	D. G. Bradman	L. Amarnath
1956–57	I	3	2	–	1	I. W. Johnson (2) R. R. Lindwall (1)	P. R. Umrigar
1959–60	I	5	2	1	2	R. Benaud	G. S. Ramchand
1964–65	I	3	1	1	1	R. B. Simpson	M. A. K. Pataudi
1967–68	A	4	4	–	–	R. B. Simpson (2) W. M. Lawry (2)	M. A. K. Pataudi (3) C. G. Borde (1)
1969–70	I	5	3	1	1	W. M. Lawry	M. A. K. Pataudi
1977–78	A	5	3	2	–	R. B. Simpson	B. S. Bedi
In Aus		14	11	2	1		
In Ind		16	8	3	5		
TOTALS		30	19	5	6		

Australia v Pakistan

Season		M	Won by Aus	Won by Pak	Drawn	Aus captain(s)	Pak captain(s)
1956–57	P	1	–	1	–	I. W. Johnson	A. H. Kardar
1959–60	P	3	2	–	1	R. Benaud	Fazal Mahmood (2) Imtiaz Ahmed (1)

Season		M	Won by Aus	Won by Pak	Drawn	Aus captain(s)	Pak captain(s)
1964–65	P	1	–	–	1	R. B. Simpson	Hanif Mohammad
1964–65	A	1	–	–	1	R. B. Simpson	Hanif Mohammad
1972–73	A	3	3	–	–	I. M. Chappell	Intikhab Alam
1976–77	A	3	1	1	1	G. S. Chappell	Mushtaq Mohammad
In Aus		7	4	1	2		
In Pak		5	2	1	2		
TOTALS		12	6	2	4		

South Africa v New Zealand

Season		M	Won by SA	Won by NZ	Drawn	SA captain(s)	NZ captain(s)
1931–32	NZ	2	2	–	–	H. B. Cameron	M. L. Page
1952–53	NZ	2	1	–	1	J. E. Cheetham	W. M. Wallace
1953–54	SA	5	4	–	1	J. E. Cheetham	G. O. Rabone (3)
							B. Sutcliffe (2)
1961–62	SA	5	2	2	1	D. J. McGlew	J. R. Reid
1963–64	NZ	3	–	–	3	T. L. Goddard	J. R. Reid
In SA		10	6	2	2		
In NZ		7	3	–	4		
TOTALS		17	9	2	6		

West Indies v India

Season		M	Won by WI	Won by Ind	Drawn	WI captain(s)	Ind captain(s)
1948–49	I	5	1	–	4	J. D. C. Goddard	L. Amarnath
1952–53	WI	5	1	–	4	J. B. Stollmeyer	V. S. Hazare
1958–59	I	5	3	–	2	F. C. M. Alexander	Ghulam Ahmed (2)
							V. M. Mankad (1)
							P. R. Umrigar (1)
							H. R. Adhikari (1)
1961–62	WI	5	5	–	–	F. M. M. Worrell	M. A. K. Pataudi (3)
							N. J. Contractor (2)
1966–67	I	3	2	–	1	G. S. Sobers	M. A. K. Pataudi
1970–71	WI	5	–	1	4	G. S. Sobers	A. L. Wadekar
1974–75	I	5	3	2	–	C. H. Lloyd	M. A. K. Pataudi (4)
							S. Venkataraghavan (1)
1975–76	WI	4	2	1	1	C. H. Lloyd	B. S. Bedi
In Ind		18	9	2	7		
In WI		19	8	2	9		
TOTALS		37	17	4	16		

West Indies v New Zealand

Season		M	Won by WI	Won by NZ	Drawn	WI captain(s)	NZ captain(s)
1951–52	NZ	2	1	–	1	J. D. C. Goddard	B. Sutcliffe
1955–56	NZ	4	3	1	–	D. S. Atkinson	J. R. Reid (3)
							H. B. Cave (1)
1968–69	NZ	3	1	1	1	G. S. Sobers	G. T. Dowling
1971–72	WI	5	–	–	5	G. S. Sobers	B. E. Congdon (3)
							G. T. Dowling (2)
In NZ		9	5	2	2		
In WI		5	–	–	5		
TOTALS		14	5	2	7		

India v Pakistan

Season		M	Won by Ind	Won by Pak	Drawn	Ind captain(s)	Pak captain(s)
1952–53	I	5	2	1	2	L. Amarnath	A. H. Kardar
1954–55	P	5	–	–	5	V. M. Mankad	A. H. Kardar
1960–61	I	5	–	–	5	N. J. Contractor	Fazal Mahmood
In Ind		10	2	1	7		
In Pak		5	–	–	5		
TOTALS		15	2	1	12		

Pakistan v New Zealand

Season		M	Won by Pak	Won by NZ	Drawn	Pak captain(s)	NZ captain(s)
1955–56	P	3	2	–	1	A. H. Kardar	H. B. Cave
1964–65	NZ	3	–	–	3	Hanif Mohammad	J. R. Reid
1964–65	P	3	2	–	1	Hanif Mohammad	J. R. Reid
1969–70	P	3	–	1	2	Intikhab Alam	G. T. Dowling
1972–73	NZ	3	1	–	2	Intikhab Alam	B. E. Congdon
1976–77	P	3	2	–	1	Mushtaq Mohammad	G. M. Turner (2)
							J. M. Parker (1)
In Pak		12	6	1	5		
In NZ		6	1	–	5		
TOTALS		18	7	1	10		

India v New Zealand

Season		M	Won by Ind	Won by NZ	Drawn	Ind captain(s)	NZ captain(s)
1955–56	I	5	2	–	3	P. R. Umrigar (4)	H. B. Cave
						Ghulam Ahmed (1)	
1964–65	I	4	1	–	3	M. A. K. Pataudi	J. R. Reid
1967–68	NZ	4	3	1	–	M. A. K. Pataudi	G. T. Dowling (3)
							B. W. Sinclair (1)
1969–70	I	3	1	1	1	M. A. K. Pataudi	G. T. Dowling
1975–76	NZ	3	1	1	1	B. S. Bedi (2)	G. M. Turner
						S. M. Gavaskar (1)	
1976–77	I	3	2	–	1	B. S. Bedi	G. M. Turner
In Ind		15	6	1	8		
In NZ		7	4	2	1		
TOTALS		22	10	3	9		

West Indies v Pakistan

Season		M	Won by WI	Won by Pak	Drawn	WI captain(s)	Pak captain(s)
1957–58	WI	5	3	1	1	F. C. M. Alexander	A. H. Kardar
1958–59	P	3	1	2	–	F. C. M. Alexander	Fazal Mahmood
1974–75	P	2	–	–	2	C. H. Lloyd	Intikhab Alam
1976–77	WI	5	2	1	2	C. H. Lloyd	Mushtaq Mohammad
In WI		10	5	2	3		
In Pak		5	1	2	2		
TOTALS		15	6	4	5		

Summary of All Tests

(To Sept. 1978)

	M	W	D	L	T	Runs	Wkts	Avge	% Wins	100s	100 ptshps	Plrs
England	542	204	201	137	–	253187	7905	32·02	37·63	449	523	480
Australia	380	172	104	103	1	186163	5854	31·80	45·26	339	362	296
South Africa	172	38	57	77	–	78397	2904	26·99	22·09	105	134	235
West Indies	183	60	66	56	1	97957	2833	34·57	32·78	202	211	171
New Zealand	133	10	60	63	–	54650	2223	24·58	7·51	66	72	143
India	157	28	64	65	–	72646	2561	28·36	17·83	102	121	140
Pakistan	93	15	52	26	–	43627	1467	29·73	16·12	71	74	79
TOTALS	830	527	302	527	1	786627	25747	30·55		1334	1497*	1544

* As 12 players have represented two countries the total number of players who have appeared in Test cricket is 1532.

Test Match Grounds

Test matches have been played at more than one ground in several cities around the world, e.g. Brisbane, Johannesburg, Bombay. The following summary indicates which matches have been played on each ground and in which year(s).

No attempt has been made within the main body of Test records to distinguish between different grounds at a particular centre: for this reference should be made to the list below.

Names of English cricket grounds, e.g. Old Trafford, Trent Bridge, have been used throughout the records. Names of Test match centres rather than grounds have been used for overseas Tests as the former are usually more familiar.

England

			Tests	Year of first and last Test
Birmingham		(Edgbaston)	18	1902 (v Aus) to date
Leeds		(Headingley)	41	1899 (v Aus) to date
Lord's, London		(Lord's Cricket Ground)	68	1884 (v Aus) to date
Oval, London		(Kennington Oval)	61	1880 (v Aus) to date
Manchester		(Old Trafford)	*49	1884 (v Aus) to date
Nottingham		(Trent Bridge)	31	1899 (v Aus) to date
Sheffield		(Bramall Lane)	1	1902 (v Aus)

**269

* The total of 49 Tests at Old Trafford does not include the matches of 1890 and 1938 where rain prevented a ball being bowled.
** These totals include the 3 Tests between Australia and South Africa played in England during the Triangular Tournament of 1912.

Australia

			Tests	Year of first and last Test
Adelaide		(Adelaide Oval)	36	1884–85 (v Eng) to date
Brisbane	1	(Exhibition Ground)	2	1928–29 (v Eng) to 1930–31 (v WI)
	2	(Woolloongabba)	20	1931–32 (v SA) to date
Melbourne		(Melbourne Cricket Ground)	*66	1876–77 (v Eng) to date
Perth		(W.A.C.A. Ground)	4	1970–71 (v Eng) to date
Sydney		(Sydney Cricket Ground)	62	1881–82 (v Eng) to date

190

* The total of Tests at Melbourne does not include the Third Test of 1970–71 which was abandoned without a ball being bowled.

South Africa

Cape Town		(Newlands)	24	1888–89 (v Eng) to date
Durban	1	(Lord's)	4	1909–10 (v Eng) to 1921–22 (v Aus)
	2	(Kingsmead)	19	1922–23 (v Eng) to date
Johannesburg	1	(Old Wanderers)	22	1895–96 (v Eng) to 1938–39 (v Eng)
	2	(Ellis Park)	6	1948–49 (v Eng) to 1953–54 (v NZ)
	3	(Wanderers Stadium)	11	1956–57 (v Eng) to date
Port Elizabeth		(St George's Park)	12	1888–89 (v Eng) to date

98

West Indies

Bridgetown	(Kensington Oval)	18	1929–30 (v Eng) to date
Georgetown	(Bourda Oval)	16	1929–30 (v Eng) to date
Kingston	(Sabina Park)	21	1929–30 (v Eng) to date
Port of Spain	(Queen's Park Oval)	31	1929–30 (v Eng) to date

86

New Zealand

Auckland	(Eden Park)	21	1929–30 (v Eng) to date
Christchurch	(Lancaster Park)	19	1929–30 (v Eng) to date
Dunedin	(Carisbrook Ground)	6	1954–55 (v Eng) to date
Wellington	(Basin Reserve)	15	1929–30 (v Eng) to date

61

India

Bangalore		(Karnataka C.A. Ground)	2	1974–75 (v WI) to date
Bombay	1	(Gymkhana Ground)	1	1933–34 (v Eng)
	2	(Brabourne Stadium)	17	1948–49 (v WI) to 1972–73 (v Eng)
	3	(Wankhede Stadium)	3	1974–75 (v WI) to date
Calcutta		(Eden Gardens)	18	1933–34 (v Eng) to date
Hyderabad	1	(Fateh Maidan)	1	1955–56 (v NZ)
(Deccan)	2	(Lal Bahadur Stadium)	1	1969–70 (v NZ)
Kanpur		(Green Park)	9	1951–52 (v Eng) to date
Lucknow		(University Ground)	1	1952–53 (v Pak)
Madras	1	(Chepauk Stadium)	10	1933–34 (v Eng) to 1952–53 (v Eng) 1966–67 (v WI) to date
	2	(Corporation (Nehru) Stadium)	9	1955–56 (v NZ) to 1964–65 (v NZ)
Nagpur		(Vidarbha C.A. Ground)	1	1969–70 (v NZ)
New Delhi		(Ferozsha Kotla Ground)	14	1948–49 (v WI) to date

87

Pakistan

Bahawalpur		(Dring Stadium)	1	1954–55 (v Ind)
Dacca		(Dacca Stadium)	7	1954–55 (v Ind) to 1969–70 (v NZ)
Hyderabad (Sind)		(Niaz Stadium)	3	1972–73 (v Eng) to date
Karachi		(National Stadium)	14	1954–55 (v Ind) to date
Lahore	1	(Lawrence Gardens (Bagh-i-Jinnah))	3	1954–55 (v Ind) to 1958–59 (v WI)
	2	(Lahore Stadium, renamed the Gaddafi Stadium)	9	1959–60 (v Aus) to date
Peshawar		(Gymkhana Ground)	1	1954–55 (v Ind)
Rawalpindi		(Club Ground)	1	1964–65 (v NZ)

39

Most wins and defeats

A side winning every match in a series

5 Tests	Aus v Eng	in Australia	1920–21

Aus v SA	in Australia	1931–32
Eng v Ind	in India	1959
WI v Ind	in West Indies	1961–62

(Note: Australia won 5 Tests and lost 1 in the 6-match series v West Indies in Australia, 1975–76).

Most consecutive wins

8	Australia	(Sydney 1920–21 to Headingley 1921)
7	England	(Melbourne 1884–85 to Sydney 1887–88)
7	England	(Lord's 1928 to Adelaide 1928–29)

Most consecutive defeats

8	South Africa	(Port Elizabeth 1888–89 to Cape Town 1898–99)
8	England	(Sydney 1920–21 to Headingley 1921)
7	Australia	(Melbourne 1884–85 to Sydney 1887–88)
7	England	(Lord's 1950 to Adelaide 1950–51)
7	India	(Headingley 1967 to Sydney 1967–68)

(Note: South Africa lost all their first 7 matches in Test cricket).

Most consecutive matches without defeat

26	England	(Lord's 1968 to Old Trafford 1971)
25	Australia	(Wellington 1945–46 to Adelaide 1950–51)

Most consecutive matches without a win

44	New Zealand	(Christchurch 1929–30 to Wellington 1955–56)
28	South Africa	(Headingley 1935 to Port Elizabeth 1949–50)
24	India	(Lord's 1932 to Kanpur 1951–52)

Most consecutive draws

10	West Indies	(Georgetown 1970–71 to Bridgetown 1972–73)
9	India	(Port of Spain 1952–53 to Hyderabad 1955–56)
9	India	(Calcutta 1959–60 to New Delhi 1961–62)

All 5 Tests of a series drawn

Pak v Ind	in Pakistan	1954–55
Ind v Pak	in India	1960–61
Ind v Eng	in India	1963–64
WI v NZ	in West Indies	1971–72

Captains in Test Cricket

Players captaining their country in 10 or more Tests

England	Tests as Capt	W	L	D	Toss Won	Times Captain v Aus	v SA	v WI	v NZ	v Ind	v Pak
P. B. H. May	41	20	10	11	26	13	10	8	7	3	–
R. Illingworth	31	12	5	14	15	11	–	6	8	3	3
E. R. Dexter	30	9	7	14	13	10	–	5	3	5	7
M. C. Cowdrey	27	8	4	15	17	6	5	10	–	2	4
M. J. K. Smith	25	5	3	17	10	5	8	1	6	5	–
L. Hutton	23	11	4	8	7	10	–	5	2	4	2
A. C. MacLaren	22	4	11	7	11	22	–	–	–	–	–
W. R. Hammond	20	4	3	13	12	8	5	3	1	3	–
M. H. Denness	19	6	5	8	9	6	–	5	2	3	3
J. W. H. T. Douglas	18	8	8	2	7	12	6	–	–	–	–
A. P. F. Chapman	17	9	2	6	9	9	5	3	–	–	–
R. E. S. Wyatt	16	3	5	8	12	5	5	5	1	–	–
F. R. Brown	15	5	6	4	3	5	5	1	4	–	–
D. R. Jardine	15	9	1	5	7	5	–	2	4	4	–
A. W. Greig	14	3	5	6	6	4	–	5	–	5	–
N. W. D. Yardley	14	4	7	3	9	6	5	3	–	–	–
J. M. Brearley	13	8	–	5	4	5	–	–	3	–	5
W. G. Grace	13	8	3	2	4	13	–	–	–	–	–

G. O. B. Allen	11	4	5	2	6	5	–	3	–	3	–
P. F. Warner	10	4	6	–	5	5	5	–	–	–	–

Note: In all 60 players have captained England.

Australia	Tests as Capt	W	L	D	Toss Won	vEng	vSA	vWI	vNZ	vInd	vPak
R. B. Simpson	39	12	12	15	19	8	9	10	–	10	2
I. M. Chappell	30	15	5	10	17	16	–	5	6	–	3
R. Benaud	28	12	4	11	11	14	1	5	–	5	3
W. M. Lawry	25	9	8	8	8	9	4	5	–	7	–
W. M. Woodfull	25	14	7	4	12	15	5	5	–	–	–
D. G. Bradman	24	15	3	6	10	19	–	–	–	5	–
A. L. Hassett	24	14	4	6	18	10	10	4	–	–	–
J. Darling	21	7	4	10	7	18	3	–	–	–	–
G. S. Chappell	17	8	5	4	10	6	–	6	2	–	3
I. W. Johnson	17	7	5	5	6	9	–	5	–	2	1
W. L. Murdoch	16	5	7	4	7	16	–	–	–	–	–
M. A. Noble	15	8	5	2	11	15	–	–	–	–	–
H. L. Collins	11	5	2	4	7	8	3	–	–	–	–
W. W. Armstrong	10	8	–	2	4	10	–	–	–	–	–
C. Hill	10	5	5	–	5	5	5	–	–	–	–

Note: In all 35 players have captained Australia.

South Africa	Tests as Capt	W	L	D	Toss Won	vEng	vAus	vNZ
H. W. Taylor	18	1	10	7	11	15	3	–
J. E. Cheetham	15	7	5	3	6	3	5	7
A. D. Nourse	15	1	9	5	7	10	5	–
D. J. McGlew	14	4	6	4	4	8	1	5
T. L. Goddard	13	1	2	10	4	5	5	3
P. W. Sherwell	13	5	6	2	5	8	5	–
H. G. Deane	12	2	4	6	9	12	–	–
A. Melville	10	–	4	6	4	10	–	–
H. F. Wade	10	1	4	5	5	5	5	–

Note: In all 24 players have captained South Africa.

West Indies	Tests as Capt	W	L	D	Toss Won	v Eng	vAus	vNZ	vInd	vPak
G. S. Sobers	39	9	10	20	27	13	10	8	8	–
C. H. Lloyd	29	13	9	7	14	5	8	–	9	7
J. D. C. Goddard	22	8	7	7	12	11	4	2	5	–
F. C. M. Alexander	18	7	4	7	9	5	–	–	5	8
F. M. M. Worrell	15	9	3	2	9	5	5	–	5	–
R. B. Kanhai	13	3	3	7	6	8	5	–	–	–
J. B. Stollmeyer	13	3	4	6	7	5	3	–	5	–
G. C. Grant	12	3	7	2	5	7	5	–	–	–

Note: In all 16 players have captained West Indies.

New Zealand	Tests as Capt	W	L	D	Toss Won	vEng	vAus	vSA	vWI	vInd	vPak
J. R. Reid	34	3	18	13	17	13	–	8	3	4	6
G. T. Dowling	19	4	7	8	10	5	–	–	5	6	3
B. E. Congdon	17	1	7	9	4	5	6	–	3	–	3
G. M. Turner	10	1	6	3	3	–	2	–	–	6	2

Note: In all 15 players have captained New Zealand.

India	Tests as Capt	W	L	D	Toss Won	vEng	vAus	vWI	vNZ	vPak
M. A. K. Pataudi	40	9	19	12	20	8	11	10	11	–
B. S. Bedi	19	6	9	4	12	5	5	4	5	–
A. L. Wadekar	16	4	4	8	7	11	–	5	–	–
L. Amarnath	15	2	6	7	4	–	5	5	–	5
V. S. Hazare	14	1	5	8	8	9	–	5	–	–
N. J. Contractor	12	2	2	8	7	5	–	2	–	5

Note: In all 18 players have captained India.

Pakistan	Tests as Capt	W	L	D	Toss Won	v Eng	v Aus	v WI	v NZ	v Ind
A. H. Kardar	23	6	6	11	10	4	1	5	3	10
Intikhab Alam	17	1	5	11	12	6	3	2	6	–
Hanif Mohammad	11	2	2	7	6	3	2	–	6	–
Mushtaq Mohammad	11	4	3	4	6	–	3	5	3	–
Fazal Mahmood	10	2	2	6	6	–	2	3	–	5

Note: In all 9 players have captained Pakistan.

Most consecutive Tests as captain

		Tests	
G. S. Sobers	(WI)	39	1964–65 to 1971–72
P. B. H. May	(Eng)	35	1955 to 1959
J. R. Reid	(NZ)	34	1955–56 to 1965
I. M. Chappell	(Aus)	30	1970–71 to 1975
C. H. Lloyd	(WI)	29	1974–75 to 1977–78
R. Illingworth	(Eng)	25	1969 to 1972
W. M. Woodfull	(Aus)	25	1930 to 1934
A. H. Kardar	(Pak)	23	1952–53 to 1957–58
M. A. K. Pataudi	(Ind)	21	1961–62 to 1967–68
W. M. Lawry	(Aus)	20	1968 to 1970–71
M. J. K. Smith	(Eng)	20	1964–65 to 1966

Note: The most for South Africa is 18, by H. W. Taylor from 1913–14 to 1924.

Captains winning all five tosses in a series

Hon. F. S. Jackson	Eng v Aus in England	1905
M. A. Noble	Aus v Eng in England	1909
H. G. Deane	SA v Eng in South Africa	1927–28
J. D. C. Goddard	WI v Ind in India	1948–49
A. L. Hassett	Aus v Eng in England	1953
M. C. Cowdrey	Eng v SA in England	1960
M. A. K. Pataudi	Ind v Eng in India	1963–64
G. S. Sobers	WI v Eng in England	1966
G. S. Sobers	WI v NZ in West Indies	1971–72

Notes: I. M. Chappell won the toss 5 times in the 6-Test series v England, 1974–75.
G. S. Chappell also won the toss 5 times in the 6-Test series v West Indies, 1975–76.
M. C. Cowdrey won the toss in nine consecutive Tests as England captain from 1959–60 to 1961.

Captains who put the opposition into bat

England (20 captains, 29 occasions)

A. E. Stoddart	v Aus	Sydney	1894–95	L	Inns & 147 runs
Lord Hawke	v SA	Cape Town	1895–96	W	Inns & 33 runs
A. C. MacLaren	v Aus	Melbourne	1901–02	L	229 runs
A. O. Jones	v Aus	Sydney	1907–08	L	49 runs
J. W. H. T. Douglas	v Aus	Melbourne	1911–12	W	Inns & 225 runs
A. W. Carr	v Aus	Headingley	1926	D	
A. P. F. Chapman	v SA	Johannesburg	1930–31	L	28 runs
A. P. F. Chapman	v SA	Durban	1930–31	D	
R. E. S. Wyatt	v WI	Bridgetown	1934–35	W	4 wkts
R. E. S. Wyatt	v WI	Port of Spain	1934–35	L	217 runs
R. E. S. Wyatt	v SA	The Oval	1935	D	
G. O. B. Allen	v Ind	Lord's	1936	W	9 wkts
W. R. Hammond	v NZ	Christchurch	1946–47	D	
F. R. Brown	v NZ	Old Trafford	1949	D	
L. Hutton	v Pak	Lord's	1954	D	
L. Hutton	v Aus	Brisbane	1954–55	L	Inns & 154 runs
L. Hutton	v NZ	Dunedin	1954–55	W	8 wkts
P. B. H. May	v Aus	Adelaide	1958–59	L	10 wkts
E. R. Dexter	v NZ	Wellington	1962–63	W	Inns & 47 runs
E. R. Dexter	v Aus	Lord's	1964	D	

M. J. K. Smith	v SA	Johannesburg	1964–65	D	
M. J. K. Smith	v SA	The Oval	1965	D	
D. B. Close	v Pak	The Oval	1967	W	8 wkts
R. Illingworth	v Aus	Trent Bridge	1972	D	
M. H. Denness	v Aus	Adelaide	1974–75	L	163 runs
M. H. Denness	v NZ	Christchurch	1974–75	D	
M. H. Denness	v Aus	Edgbaston	1975	L	Inns & 85 runs
A. W. Greig	v Aus	Melbourne	1976–77	L	45 runs
G. Boycott	v NZ	Wellington	1977–78	L	72 runs

Australia (11 captains, 26 occasions)

P. S. McDonnell	v Eng	Sydney	1886–87	L	13 runs
P. S. McDonnell	v Eng	Sydney	1887–88	L	126 runs
G. Giffen	v Eng	Melbourne	1894–95	L	94 runs
M. A. Noble	v Eng	Lord's	1909	W	9 wkts
A. L. Hassett	v WI	Sydney	1951–52	W	7 wkts
A. L. Hassett	v Eng	Headingley	1953	D	
A. R. Morris	v Eng	Sydney	1954–55	L	38 runs
I. W. Johnson	v Eng	Sydney	1954–55	D	
R. Benaud	v Eng	Melbourne	1958–59	W	9 wkts
R. Benaud	v Pak	Dacca	1959–60	W	8 wkts
R. Benaud	v WI	Melbourne	1960–61	W	2 wkts
R. B. Simpson	v SA	Melbourne	1963–64	W	8 wkts
R. B. Simpson	v Pak	Melbourne	1964–65	D	
R. B. Simpson	v WI	Port of Spain	1964–65	D	
R. B. Simpson	v SA	Durban	1966–67	L	8 wkts
W. M. Lawry	v WI	Melbourne	1968–69	W	Inns & 30 runs
W. M. Lawry	v Ind	Calcutta	1969–70	W	7 wkts
W. M. Lawry	v Eng	Perth	1970–71	D	
I. M. Chappell	v Eng	Sydney	1970–71	L	62 runs
I. M. Chappell	v NZ	Sydney	1973–74	D	
I. M. Chappell	v Eng	Perth	1974–75	W	9 wkts
I. M. Chappell	v Eng	Melbourne	1974–75	D	
G. S. Chappell	v WI	Melbourne	1975–76	W	8 wkts
G. S. Chappell	v WI	Sydney	1975–76	W	7 wkts
G. S. Chappell	v Eng	The Oval	1977	D	
R. B. Simpson	v WI	Port of Spain	1977–78	L	198 runs

South Africa (6 captains, 10 occasions)

E. A. Halliwell	v Eng	Port Elizabeth	1895–96	L	288 runs
P. W. Sherwell	v Aus	Melbourne	1910–11	L	530 runs
P. W. Sherwell	v Aus	Sydney	1910–11	L	7 wkts
H. W. Taylor	v Eng	Edgbaston	1924	L	Inns & 18 runs
H. G. Deane	v Eng	Cape Town	1927–28	L	87 runs
H. G. Deane	v Eng	Johannesburg	1927–28	W	4 wkts
H. G. Deane	v Eng	Durban	1927–28	W	8 wkts
H. G. Deane	v Eng	The Oval	1929	D	
T. L. Goddard	v Aus	Sydney	1963–64	D	
P. L. van der Merwe	v Aus	Port Elizabeth	1966–67	W	7 wkts

West Indies (6 captains, 15 occasions)

R. S. Grant	v Eng	Old Trafford	1939	D	
F. C. M. Alexander	v Pak	Dacca	1958–59	L	41 runs
F. M. M. Worrell	v Ind	Bridgetown	1961–62	W	Inns & 30 runs
G. S. Sobers	v Aus	Sydney	1968–69	L	382 runs
G. S. Sobers	v NZ	Auckland	1968–69	W	5 wkts
G. S. Sobers	v Ind	Kingston	1970–71	D	
G. S. Sobers	v NZ	Port of Spain	1971–72	D	
R. B. Kanhai	v Eng	Port of Spain	1973–74	W	7 wkts
R. B. Kanhai	v Eng	Bridgetown	1973–74	D	
C. H. Lloyd	v Pak	Lahore	1974–75	D	
C. H. Lloyd	v Ind	Kingston	1975–76	W	10 wkts
C. H. Lloyd	v Pak	Georgetown	1976–77	D	

C. H. Lloyd	v Pak	Port of Spain	1976–77	L	266 runs
C. H. Lloyd	v Aus	Port of Spain	1977–78	W	Inns & 106 runs
C. H. Lloyd	v Aus	Bridgetown	1977–78	W	9 wkts

New Zealand (6 captains, 13 occasions)

T. C. Lowry	v Eng	Auckland	1929–30	D	
T. C. Lowry	v Eng	Old Trafford	1931	D	
B. Sutcliffe	v WI	Auckland	1951–52	D	
B. Sutcliffe	v SA	Johannesburg	1953–54	L	9 wkts
J. R. Reid	v SA	Auckland	1963–64	D	
J. R. Reid	v Pak	Lahore	1964–65	D	
G. T. Dowling	v Ind	Auckland	1967–68	L	272 runs
G. T. Dowling	v WI	Wellington	1968–69	W	6 wkts
G. T. Dowling	v Eng	Auckland	1970–71	D	
B. E. Congdon	v Eng	Lord's	1973	D	
B. E. Congdon	v Aus	Christchurch	1973–74	W	5 wkts
B. E. Congdon	v Aus	Auckland	1973–74	L	297 runs
G. M. Turner	v Aus	Christchurch	1976–77	D	

India (6 captains, 11 occasions)

Nawab of Pataudi sr.	v Eng	Old Trafford	1946	D	
L. Amarnath	v Pak	Calcutta	1952–53	D	
P. R. Umrigar	v Aus	Calcutta	1956–57	L	94 runs
M. A. K. Pataudi	v Eng	Kanpur	1963–64	D	
M. A. K. Pataudi	v Aus	Calcutta	1964–65	D	
M. A. K. Pataudi	v Aus	Brisbane	1967–68	L	39 runs
M. A. K. Pataudi	v Aus	Sydney	1967–68	L	144 runs
M. A. K. Pataudi	v NZ	Christchurch	1967–68	L	6 wkts
A. L. Wadekar	v WI	Bridgetown	1970–71	D	
M. A. K. Pataudi	v WI	Bangalore	1974–75	L	267 runs
B. S. Bedi	v WI	Port of Spain	1975–76	D	

Pakistan (4 captains, 6 occasions)

Fazal Mahmood	v WI	Karachi	1958–59	W	10 wkts
Javed Burki	v Eng	Headingley	1962	L	Inns & 117 runs
Javed Burki	v Eng	Trent Bridge	1962	D	
Hanif Mohammad	v NZ	Wellington	1964–65	D	
Hanif Mohammad	v NZ	Rawalpindi	1964–65	W	Inns & 64 runs
Intikhab Alam	v Aus	Sydney	1972–73	L	52 runs

Highs and Lows

Highest innings totals (600 and over)

Number of centuries scored in the innings given in brackets.

903–7 dec	(3)	Eng v Aus	The Oval	1938
849	(2)	Eng v WI	Kingston	1929–30
790–3 dec	(2)	WI v Pak	Kingston	1957–58
758–8 dec	(5)	Aus v WI	Kingston	1954–55
729–6 dec	(2)	Aus v Eng	Lord's	1930
701	(2)	Aus v Eng	The Oval	1934
695	(2)	Aus v Eng	The Oval	1930
687–8 dec	(1)	WI v Eng	The Oval	1976
681–8 dec	(3)	WI v Eng	Port of Spain	1953–54
674	(3)	Aus v Ind	Adelaide	1947–48
668	(2)	Aus v WI	Bridgetown	1954–55
659–8 dec	(2)	Aus v Eng	Sydney	1946–47
658–8 dec	(4)	Eng v Aus	Trent Bridge	1938
657–8 dec	(1)	Pak v WI	Bridgetown	1957–58
656–8 dec	(2)	Aus v Eng	Old Trafford	1964
654–5	(3)	Eng v SA	Durban	1938–39

652–8 dec	(3)	WI v Eng	Lord's	1973
650–6 dec	(3)	Aus v WI	Bridgetown	1964–65
645	(2)	Aus v Eng	Brisbane	1946–47
644–8 dec	(3)	WI v Ind	New Delhi	1958–59
636	(1)	Eng v Aus	Sydney	1928–29
631–8 dec	(3)	WI v Ind	Kingston	1961–62
631	(4)	WI v Ind	New Delhi	1948–49
629–6 dec	(2)	WI v Ind	Bombay	1948–49
629	(3)	Eng v Ind	Lord's	1974
627–9 dec	(2)	Eng v Aus	Old Trafford	1934
622–9 dec	(2)	SA v Aus	Durban	1969–70
620	(1)	SA v Aus	Johannesburg	1966–67
619–6 dec	(3)	Eng v WI	Trent Bridge	1957
619	(2)	Aus v WI	Sydney	1968–69
616	(1)	WI v Aus	Adelaide	1968–69
614–5 dec	(3)	WI v Ind	Calcutta	1958–59
611	(2)	Eng v Aus	Old Trafford	1964
608	(3)	Eng v SA	Johannesburg	1948–49
608–7 dec	(3)	Pak v Eng	Edgbaston	1971
604	(3)	Aus v Eng	Melbourne	1936–37
604–6 dec	(2)	WI v Ind	Bombay	1974–75
601–8 dec	(2)	Aus v Eng	Brisbane	1954–55
600	(2)	Aus v Eng	Melbourne	1924–25
600–9 dec	(3)	Aus v WI	Port of Spain	1954–55
600–7 dec	(1)	Pak v Eng	The Oval	1974

Highest total for each country

England	903–7 dec	v	Aus	The Oval	1938
Australia	758–8 dec	v	WI	Kingston	1954–55
South Africa	622–9 dec	v	Aus	Durban	1969–70
West Indies	790–3 dec	v	Pak	Kingston	1957–58
New Zealand	551–9 dec	v	Eng	Lord's	1973
India	539–9 dec	v	Pak	Madras	1960–61
Pakistan	657–8 dec	v	WI	Bridgetown	1957–58

Most runs in both innings of a match

England	1121	(849 & 272–9 dec)	v	WI	Kingston	1929–30
Australia	1028	(701 & 327)	v	Eng	The Oval	1934
South Africa	1011	(530 & 481)	v	Eng	Durban	1938–39
West Indies	893	(681–8 dec & 212–4 dec)	v	Eng	Port of Spain	1953–54
New Zealand	730	(468 & 262–7)	v	Pak	Karachi	1976–77
India	807	(344 & 463–4)	v	Eng	New Delhi	1963–64
Pakistan	855	(565–9 dec & 290–5 dec)	v	NZ	Karachi	1976–77

Highest second innings totals

657–8 dec	Pak v WI	Bridgetown	1957–58
654–5	Eng v SA	Durban	1938–39
620	SA v Aus	Johannesburg	1966–67
616	WI v Aus	Adelaide	1968–69

Note: Pakistan's 657–8 dec is the highest total made by a side following on in a Test match.

Most centuries in a Test innings

Five (C. C. McDonald 127, R. N. Harvey 204, K. R. Miller 109, R. G. Archer 128, R. Benaud 121)

    758–8 dec   by Aus v WI   Kingston   1954–55

Four (L. Hutton 100, C. J. Barnett 126, E. Paynter 216*, D. C. S. Compton 102)

    658–8 dec   by Eng v Aus   Trent Bridge   1938

    (C. L. Walcott 152, G. E. Gomez 101, E. D. Weekes 128, R. J. Christiani 107)

    631   by WI v Ind   New Delhi   1948–49

Most fifties in a Test innings

Seven (C. F. Walters 52, H. Sutcliffe 63, E. H. Hendren 132, M. Leyland 153, L. E. G.
Ames 72, G. O. B. Allen 61, H. Verity 60*)
627–9 dec   by Eng v Aus   Old Trafford   1934

NOTES:
There have been 168 totals of 500 or more in Tests up to 1978, divided among the countries as follows:

England	50		New Zealand	4
Australia	55		India	5
West Indies	32		Pakistan	9
South Africa	13			

No country has made 500 or more in both innings of a Test. South Africa have come
closest with 530 and 481 v England at Durban, 1938–39.
Only once have both sides reached 600 in the same match:
Australia (656–8 dec) v England (611)   Old Trafford   1964
The following made over 500 batting second but were still behind on first innings:

Eng	(505)	v	SA	(538)	Headingley	1951
Eng	(537)	v	WI	(681–8 dec)	Port of Spain	1953–54
Eng	(611)	v	Aus	(656–8 dec)	Old Trafford	1964
WI	(573)	v	Aus	(650–6 dec)	Bridgetown	1964–65
Eng	(545)	v	Pak	(600–7 dec)	The Oval	1974

The highest number of runs made by a losing side in a Test match is 861 (496 & 365–8
dec) by England who lost by seven wickets to Australia (458 & 404–3), Headingley, 1948.

Lowest completed innings totals

(70 and under)

Total	Highest score			
26	11 – B. Sutcliffe	NZ v Eng	Auckland	1954–55
30	10 – R. M. Poore	SA v Eng	Port Elizabeth	1895–96
30	7 – H. W. Taylor	SA v Eng	Edgbaston	1924
35	11 – A. W. Powell	SA v Eng	Cape Town	1898–99
36	18 – V. T. Trumper	Aus v Eng	Edgbaston	1902
36	11 – H. B. Cameron	SA v Aus	Melbourne	1931–32
42	10 – T. W. Garrett	Aus v Eng	Sydney	1887–88
42	14 – V. J. Scott	NZ v Aus	Wellington	1945–46
†42	18*– E. D. Solkar	Ind v Eng	Lord's	1974
43	11 – F. W. Smith	SA v Eng	Cape Town	1888–89
44	16 – T. R. McKibbin	Aus v Eng	The Oval	1896
45	17 – G. A. Lohmann	Eng v Aus	Sydney	1886–87
45	16 – S. H. Curnow	SA v Aus	Melbourne	1931–32
47	26*– A. B. Tancred	SA v Eng	Cape Town	1888–89
52	30 – L. Hutton	Eng v Aus	The Oval	1948
53	17 – J. Briggs	Eng v Aus	Lord's	1888
53	22 – J. Darling	Aus v Eng	Lord's	1896
54	14 – W. M. Wallace	NZ v Aus	Wellington	1945–46
†58	26*– A. G. Chipperfield	Aus v Eng	Brisbane	1936–37
58	22 – L. Amarnath	Ind v Aus	Brisbane	1947–48
58	22 – V. L. Manjrekar	Ind v Eng	Old Trafford	1952
60	20*– J. J. Ferris	Aus v Eng	Lord's	1888
61	27 – G. L. Jessop	Eng v Aus	Melbourne	1901–02
61	18 – R. E. Foster	Eng v Aus	Melbourne	1903–04
62	24 – W. G. Grace	Eng v Aus	Lord's	1888
63	17 – J. M. Blackham	Aus v Eng	The Oval	1882
64	19 – I. T. Botham	Eng v NZ	Wellington	1977–78
†65	20*– J. T. Brown	Eng v Aus	Sydney	1894–95
65	30 – C. G. Macartney	Aus v Eng	The Oval	1912
65	18 – V. Pollard	NZ v Eng	Christchurch	1970–71

††66	30*–	W. M. Woodfull	Aus v Eng	Brisbane	1928–29
67	17 –	H. R. Adhikari	Ind v Aus	Melbourne	1947–48
67	26 –	L. S. M. Miller	NZ v Eng	Headingley	1958
67	14*–	G. P. Howarth	NZ v Eng	Lord's	1978
68	15 –	G. E. Palmer	Aus v Eng	The Oval	1886
70	29*–	A. R. MacGibbon	NZ v Pak	Dacca	1955–56

† one man absent hurt or ill   †† two men absent hurt

Lowest total for each country (home and away)

England	H	52	v	Aus	The Oval	1948
	A	45	v	Aus	Sydney	1886–87
Australia	H	42	v	Eng	Sydney	1887–88
	A	36	v	Eng	Edgbaston	1902
South Africa	H	30	v	Eng	Port Elizabeth	1895–96
	A	30	v	Eng	Edgbaston	1924
West Indies	H	102	v	Eng	Bridgetown	1934–35
	A	76	v	Pak	Dacca	1958–59
New Zealand	H	26	v	Eng	Auckland	1954–55
	A	47	v	Eng	Lord's	1958
India	H	88	v	NZ	Bombay	1964–65
	A	42	v	Eng	Lord's	1974
Pakistan	H	104	v	WI	Lahore	1958–59
	A	87	v	Eng	Lord's	1954

Highest and lowest total for each Test match centre

In England

Edgbaston	608–7 dec	Pak v Eng	1971	30	SA v Eng	1924
Headingley	584	Aus v Eng	1934	67	NZ v Eng	1958
Lord's	729–6 dec	Aus v Eng	1930	42	Ind v Eng	1974
Old Trafford	656–8 dec	Aus v Eng	1964	58	Ind v Eng	1952
The Oval	903–7 dec	Eng v Aus	1938	44	Aus v Eng	1896
Sheffield	289	Aus v Eng	1902	145	Eng v Aus	1902
Trent Bridge	658–8 dec	Eng v Aus	1938	88	SA v Eng	1960

In Australia

Adelaide	674	Aus v Ind	1947–48	82	Aus v WI	1951–52
Brisbane	645	Aus v Eng	1946–47	58	Aus v Eng	1936–37
				58	Ind v Aus	1947–48
Melbourne	604	Aus v Eng	1936–37	36	SA v Aus	1931–32
Perth	585	WI v Aus	1975–76	169	Aus v WI	1975–76
Sydney	659–8 dec	Aus v Eng	1946–47	42	Aus v Eng	1887–88

In South Africa

Cape Town	559–9 dec	Eng v SA	1938–39	35	SA v Eng	1898–99
Durban	654–5	Eng v SA	1938–39	75	Aus v SA	1949–50
Johannesburg	620	SA v Aus	1966–67	72	SA v Eng	1956–57
Port Elizabeth	549–7 dec	Aus v SA	1949–50	30	SA v Eng	1895–96

In West Indies

Bridgetown	668	Aus v WI	1954–55	102	WI v Eng	1934–35
Georgetown	543–3 dec	NZ v WI	1971–72	109	WI v Aus	1972–73
Kingston	849	Eng v WI	1929–30	97	Ind v WI	1975–76
Port of Spain	681–8 dec	WI v Eng	1953–54	90	Aus v WI	1977–78

In New Zealand

Auckland	593–6 dec	Eng v NZ	1974–75	26	NZ v Eng	1954–55
Christchurch	560–8 dec	Eng v NZ	1932–33	65	NZ v Eng	1970–71
Dunedin	507–6 dec	Pak v NZ	1972–73	74	NZ v WI	1955–56
Wellington	524–8 dec	SA v NZ	1952–53	42	NZ v Aus	1945–46

In India

Bangalore	356–6 dec	WI v Ind	1974–75	118	Ind v WI	1974–75
Bombay	629–6 dec	WI v Ind	1948–49	88	Ind v NZ	1964–65
Calcutta	614–5 dec	WI v Ind	1958–59	124	Ind v WI	1958–59

Hyderabad	498–4 dec	Ind v NZ	1955–56	89	Ind v NZ	1969–70
Kanpur	559–8 dec	Eng v Ind	1963–64	105	Aus v Ind	1959–60
Lucknow	331	Pak v Ind	1952–53	106	Ind v Pak	1952–53
Madras	582	WI v Ind	1948–49	83	Ind v Eng	1976–77
Nagpur	319	NZ v Ind	1969–70	109	Ind v NZ	1969–70
New Delhi	644–8 dec	WI v Ind	1958–59	107	Aus v Ind	1969–70

In Pakistan

Bahawalpur	312–9 dec	Pak v Ind	1954–55	235	Ind v Pak	1954–55
Dacca	439	Eng v Pak	1961–62	70	NZ v Pak	1955–56
Hyderabad	569–9 dec	Pak v Eng	1972–73	191	Eng v Pak	1977–78
Karachi	565–9 dec	Pak v NZ	1976–77	80	Aus v Pak	1956–57
Lahore	561	Pak v NZ	1955–56	104	Pak v WI	1958–59
Peshawar	245	Ind v Pak	1954–55	182	Pak v Ind	1954–55
Rawalpindi	318	Pak v NZ	1964–65	79	NZ v Pak	1964–65

Note: India's total of 97 at Kingston in 1975–76 included five players absent hurt. The next lowest total at Kingston is 103 by England v West Indies in 1934–35.

Highest match aggregates

Runs	Wkts			
1981	35	SA v Eng	Durban	1938–39
1815	34	WI v Eng	Kingston	1929–30
1764	39	Aus v WI	Adelaide	1968–69
1753	40	Aus v Eng	Adelaide	1920–21
1723	31	Eng v Aus	Headingley	1948
1661	36	WI v Aus	Bridgetown	1954–55
1646	40	Aus v SA	Adelaide	1910–11
1644	38	Aus v WI	Sydney	1968–69
1640	24	WI v Aus	Bridgetown	1964–65
1640	33	Aus v Pak	Melbourne	1972–73
1619	40	Aus v Eng	Melbourne	1924–25
1611	40	Aus v Eng	Sydney	1924–25
1601	29	Eng v Aus	Lord's	1930

Note: Highest match aggregates in Tests played in other countries are:

In New Zealand:	1455 – 24	NZ v Aus	Wellington	1973–74
In India:	1417 – 29	Ind v WI	Bombay	1974–75
In Pakistan:	1585 – 31	Pak v NZ	Karachi	1976–77

Matches dominated by batsmen

(60 runs or more per wicket taken)

Runs per wkt	Runs	Wkts			
109·30	1093	10	Ind v NZ	New Delhi	1955–56
99·40	994	10	WI v NZ	Georgetown	1971–72
70·61	1271	18	Eng v Aus	Old Trafford	1964
68·33	1640	24	WI v Aus	Bridgetown	1964–65
66·95	1406	21	WI v Pak	Kingston	1957–58
65·35	1307	20	Eng v Aus	Old Trafford	1934
65·00	1235	19	Ind v WI	Bombay	1948–49
64·75	1036	16	Ind v NZ	Hyderabad	1955–56
63·66	1528	24	WI v Eng	Port of Spain	1953–54
62·33	1496	24	Eng v Aus	Trent Bridge	1938
62·00	1116	18	WI v Eng	Bridgetown	1959–60
61·52	1046	17	Ind v Pak	Madras	1960–61
60·62	1455	24	NZ v Aus	Wellington	1973–74

Lowest match aggregates

(Completed Matches)

Runs	Wkts			
234	29	Aus v SA	Melbourne	1931–32
291	40	Eng v Aus	Lord's	1888

Runs	Wkts			
295	28	NZ v Aus	Wellington	1945–46
309	29	WI v Eng	Bridgetown	1934–35
323	30	Eng v Aus	Old Trafford	1888
363	40	Eng v Aus	The Oval	1882
374	40	Aus v Eng	Sydney	1887–88
378	30	Eng v SA	The Oval	1912
382	30	SA v Eng	Cape Town	1888–89
389	38	Eng v Aus	The Oval	1890
390	30	Eng v NZ	Lord's	1958
392	40	Eng v Aus	The Oval	1896

Most runs in consecutive innings by a side

645 & 659–8 dec	Aus v Eng	1946–47
584 & 701	Aus v Eng	1934
631 & 629–6 dec	WI v Ind	1948–49

Notes:
Australia scored four totals of over 500 v West Indies, 1954–55 and again v West Indies, 1968–69.

Australia had consecutive totals of 645, 659–8 dec, 365, 536, 487 and 215–1 v England in 1946–47.

West Indies scored 631. 629–6 dec, 366. 336–9 dec and 582 in successive innings v India, 1948–49.

India scored totals of 400 or more in all five Tests of the series v New Zealand, 1955–56.

Least runs in consecutive innings by a side

47, 74, 67	NZ v Eng	1958
60, 80, 100	Aus v Eng	1888

Notes:
New Zealand were dismissed for under 100 on five occasions in the series v England, 1958.

Australia's scores v England in the three-match series of 1888 were: 116, 60, 80, 100, 81 and 70. In 14 innings v England from 1886 to 1888 Australia were dismissed nine times for under 100. They failed to reach a total of 200 in 21 successive innings between 1886 and 1890.

South Africa failed to reach three figures in seven out of their first eight innings in Test Cricket, all v England, from 1888–89 to 1895–96.

Highest run aggregate in a 5-match series

England:	3757	v Aus	1928–29
Australia:	3630	v Eng	1924–25
South Africa:	3258	v Eng	1964–65
West Indies:	3256	v Pak	1957–58
New Zealand:	2638	v WI	1971–72
India:	3119	v Eng	1963–64
Pakistan:	3121	v WI	1976–77

Note:
To date none of the above aggregates have been exceeded in a 6-match rubber.

The series which has produced most runs by both sides is Australia v England in 1928–29, in which 6826 runs were scored.

Lowest run aggregate in a 5-match series

England:	1646	v Aus	1902
Australia:	1395	v Eng	1902
South Africa:	1769	v Eng	1956–57
West Indies:	1763	v Aus	1930–31
New Zealand:	1152	v Eng	1958
India:	1546	v Pak	1954–55
Pakistan:	1898	v Ind	1952–53

Note: Australia scored only 507 runs in six completed innings v England in 1888, in a 3-match rubber. In all the series produced only 1111 runs by both sides.

Extras in Test Cricket

Most extras in an innings

68   (29 byes, 11 leg byes, 28 no balls) in Pak's 291 v WI Bridgetown 1976–77

Most extras in a match

173   (38 byes, 30 leg byes, 2 wides, 103 no balls) WI v Pak Bridgetown 1976–77

Notes:
The records for the various extras are as follows:
Most byes in an innings: 38 in WI's 391–9 dec v Eng at Kingston 1967–68.
Most leg byes: 30 in WI's 411–5 dec v Eng at Old Trafford, 1976.
Most wides: 12 in Ind's 306–6 dec v WI at Kingston, 1975–76.
Most no balls (from which no runs were scored by batsmen): 35 in WI's 596–8 dec v Eng at Bridgetown, 1973–74.
The highest total with no extras is 328 by Pak v Ind at Lahore, 1954–55.
There was only 1 extra in Australia's total of 549–7 dec v SA at Port Elizabeth, 1949–50.
There were only 2 extras in the three completed innings of the match between England and New Zealand at Lord's, 1958.

Most centuries in a match (both sides)

7	England (4) v Australia (3)	Trent Bridge	1938
7	West Indies (2) v Australia (5)	Kingston	1954–55

Note: There were 17 scores of 50 or more (7 by WI and 10 by Aus) in the 4th Test at Adelaide, 1968–69.

Most centuries in a series (one side)

12	Aus v WI	1954–55
11	Eng v SA	1938–39
11	WI v Ind	1948–49
11	Aus v SA	1949–50

Note: The highest number of different players scoring a century for one side in a series is
7, by: Eng v Aus   1938
Aus v Eng   1946–47
Aus v WI   1954–55

Most centuries in a series (both sides)

21	WI (9)	v	Aus (12)	1954–55
17	Aus (9)	v	Eng (8)	1928–29
17	SA (6)	v	Eng (11)	1938–39
16	Ind (5)	v	WI (11)	1948–49
16	Aus (10)	v	WI (6)	1968–69
16	Aus (10)	v	WI (6)	1975–76

Unchanged team throughout a complete series

	Venue		No. of Tests
Eng v Aus	Australia	1881–82	4
Aus v Eng	England	1884	3
Eng v Aus	Australia	1884–85	5
Aus v Eng	England	1893	3
SA v Eng	South Africa	1905–06	5
Pak v NZ	Pakistan	1964–65	3
Ind v Eng	England	1971	3

Most players appearing for one side in a series

		Venue		No. of Tests
30	Eng v Aus	England	1921	5
28	WI v Eng	West Indies	1929–30	4

		Venue		No. of Tests
28	Aus v Eng	Australia	1884–85	5
25	Eng v Aus	England	1909	5
25	Eng v SA	England	1935	5
25	Eng v WI	England	1950	4
25	Eng v SA	England	1955	5

Biggest Victories in Test Cricket

By an innings margin

Innings & 579 runs	Eng v Aus	The Oval	1938
Innings & 336 runs	WI v Ind	Calcutta	1958–59
Innings & 332 runs	Aus v Eng	Brisbane	1946–47
Innings & 285 runs	Eng v Ind	Lord's	1974
Innings & 259 runs	Aus v SA	Port Elizabeth	1949–50
Innings & 237 runs	Eng v WI	The Oval	1957
Innings & 230 runs	Eng v Aus	Adelaide	1891–92
Innings & 226 runs	WI v Eng	Lord's	1973
Innings & 225 runs	Eng v Aus	Melbourne	1911–12
Innings & 217 runs	Eng v Aus	The Oval	1886
Innings & 217 runs	Aus v WI	Brisbane	1930–31
Innings & 215 runs	Eng v NZ	Auckland	1962–63
Innings & 207 runs	Eng v Ind	Old Trafford	1952
Innings & 202 runs	Eng v SA	Melbourne	1910–11
Innings & 200 runs	Aus v Eng	Melbourne	1936–37

Notes:
The biggest wins for the other countries are as follows:

South Africa	Innings & 180 runs	v NZ	Wellington	1952–53
India	Innings & 109 runs	v NZ	Madras	1955–56
Pakistan	Innings & 166 runs	v NZ	Dunedin	1972–73
New Zealand	Innings & 33 runs	v Ind	Wellington	1975–76

There have been 144 victories by an innings in Test Cricket up to September 1978, 68 by England, 41 by Australia, 18 by West Indies, 6 by South Africa, 5 by Pakistan, 5 by India and 1 by New Zealand. New Zealand did not record an innings victory till their 119th Test, at Wellington, 1975–76.

By a runs margin

675 runs	Eng v Aus	Brisbane	1928–29
562 runs	Aus v Eng	The Oval	1934
530 runs	Aus v SA	Melbourne	1910–11
425 runs	WI v Eng	Old Trafford	1976
409 runs	Aus v Eng	Lord's	1948
382 runs	Aus v Eng	Adelaide	1894–95
382 runs	Aus v WI	Sydney	1968–69
377 runs	Aus v Eng	Sydney	1920–21
365 runs	Aus v Eng	Melbourne	1936–37
348 runs	Aus v Pak	Melbourne	1976–77
338 runs	Eng v Aus	Adelaide	1932–33
326 runs	WI v Eng	Lord's	1950

Close Matches

A tie	Aus v WI	Brisbane	1960–61
Won by one wicket	Eng v Aus	The Oval	1902
	SA v Eng	Johannesburg	1905–06
	Eng v Aus	Melbourne	1907–08
	Eng v SA	Cape Town	1922–23

	Aus v WI	Melbourne	1951–52
Won by two wickets	Eng v Aus	The Oval	1890
	Aus v Eng	Sydney	1907–08
	Eng v SA	Durban	1948–49
	Aus v WI	Melbourne	1960–61
	Ind v Aus	Bombay	1964–65
	Aus v Ind	Perth	1977–78

Less than 20 runs	3 runs	Aus v Eng	Old Trafford	1902
	6 runs	Aus v Eng	Sydney	1884–85
	7 runs	Aus v Eng	The Oval	1882
	10 runs	Eng v Aus	Sydney	1894–95
	11 runs	Aus v Eng	Adelaide	1924–25
	12 runs	Eng v Aus	Adelaide	1928–29
	13 runs	Eng v Aus	Sydney	1886–87
	16 runs	Aus v Ind	Brisbane	1977–78
	17 runs	SA v Eng	Johannesburg	1956–57
	19 runs	SA v Eng	Johannesburg	1909–10

Close and exciting finishes

At Brisbane in 1960–61 Australia needed six runs to win off the last over to beat West Indies with three wickets left. The match ended in a tie, I. W. Meckiff being run out off he seventh ball when J. S. Solomon hit the stumps direct with a throw from square leg.

England beat South Africa off the last possible ball of the First Test at Durban in 1948–49, C. Gladwin scrambling a leg bye off L. Tuckett. Later in the same series England, set to make 172 in 95 minutes, won the Fifth Test with one minute to spare.

At Port of Spain in 1934–35 West Indies captured England's last wicket, that of M. Leyland lbw to L. N. Constantine, with the penultimate delivery of the match.

England beat Australia at The Oval in 1968 with only six minutes to spare, D. L. Underwood dismissing R. J. Inverarity lbw to take the final wicket.

At Bombay in 1948–49 India (355–8) needed only six runs to beat West Indies but the umpires called time with 1½ minutes remaining!

At Lord's in 1963 England (228–8) needed eight runs to win off the last over, bowled by W. W. Hall. The match was drawn with England finishing at 228–9.

England's last pair, S. F. Barnes and A. Fielder, put on 39 runs to give England victory over Australia at Melbourne in 1907–08. The match almost ended in a tie, G. R. Hazlitt's throw missing the stumps as the winning run was scored.

Highest fourth innings totals

To win the match

406–4		Ind v WI	Port of Spain	1975–76
404–3		Aus v Eng	Headingley	1948
362–7		Aus v WI	Georgetown	1977–78
348–5		WI v NZ	Auckland	1968–69
342–8		Aus v Ind	Perth	1977–78
336–5		Aus v SA	Durban	1949–50
332–7		Eng v Aus	Melbourne	1928–29
317–2		WI v Pak	Georgetown	1957–58
315–6		Aus v Eng	Adelaide	1901–02

To draw the match

654–5	(set 696)	Eng v SA	Durban	1938–39
423–7	(set 451)	SA v Eng	The Oval	1947
408–5	(set 836)	WI v Eng	Kingston	1929–30
355–8	(set 361)	Ind v WI	Bombay	1948–49
339–9	(set 360)	Aus v WI	Adelaide	1968–69
329–3	(set 484)	Aus v Eng	Lord's	1975
328–3	(set 469)	Aus v Eng	Adelaide	1970–71
326–5	(set 409)	SA v Aus	Sydney	1963–64
325–3	(set 431)	Ind v WI	Calcutta	1948–49

To lose the match

445	(lost by 47)	Ind v Aus	Adelaide	1977–78

440	(lost by 38)	NZ v Eng	Trent Bridge	1973
417	(lost by 45)	Eng v Aus	Melbourne	1976–77
411	(lost by 193)	Eng v Aus	Sydney	1924–25
376	(lost by 171)	Ind v Eng	Old Trafford	1959
370	(lost by 119)	Eng v Aus	Adelaide	1920–21
363	(lost by 11)	Eng v Aus	Adelaide	1924–25
355	(lost by 39)	Ind v Aus	Brisbane	1967–68
352	(lost by 382)	WI v Aus	Sydney	1968–69

Matches completed in two days

Eng	(101 & 77)	v	Aus	(63 & 122)	The Oval	1882
Eng	(53 & 62)	v	Aus	(116 & 60)	Lord's	1888
Eng	(317)	v	Aus	(80 & 100)	The Oval	1888
Eng	(172)	v	Aus	(81 & 70)	Old Trafford	1888
SA	(84 & 129)	v	Eng	(148 & 67–2)	Port Elizabeth	1888–89
SA	(47 & 43)	v	Eng	(292)	Cape Town	1888–89
Eng	(100 & 95–8)	v	Aus	(92 & 102)	The Oval	1890
SA	(93 & 30)	v	Eng	(185 & 226)	Port Elizabeth	1895–96
SA	(115 & 117)	v	Eng	(265)	Cape Town	1895–96
Eng	(176 & 14–0)	v	SA	(95 & 93)	The Oval	1912
Aus	(448)	v	SA	(265 & 95)	Old Trafford	1912
Eng	(112 & 147)	v	Aus	(232 & 30–0)	Trent Bridge	1921
Aus	(328–8 dec)	v	WI	(99 & 107)	Melbourne	1930–31
SA	(157 & 98)	v	Aus	(439)	Johannesburg	1935–36
NZ	(42 & 54)	v	Aus	(199–8 dec)	Wellington	1945–46

Longest matches

				Result
10 days	SA v Eng	Durban	1938–39	Match Drawn
9 days	WI v Eng	Kingston	1929–30	Match Drawn
8 days	Aus v Eng	Melbourne	1928–29	Aus won by 5 wickets
7 days	Aus v Eng	Sydney	1911–12	Eng won by 70 runs
7 days	Aus v Eng	Sydney	1924–25	Aus won by 193 runs
7 days	Aus v Eng	Melbourne	1924–25	Aus won by 81 runs
7 days	Aus v Eng	Adelaide	1924–25	Aus won by 11 runs
7 days	Aus v Eng	Melbourne	1928–29	Eng won by 3 wickets
7 days	Aus v Eng	Adelaide	1928–29	Eng won by 12 runs

Most wickets to fall in a day's play

27	Eng (18–3 to 53 & 62) v Aus (60)	2nd day	Lord's	1888
25	Aus (112 & 48–5) v Eng (61)	1st day	Melbourne	1901–02

Note: 18 wickets fell before lunch on the 2nd day at Old Trafford in 1888, Australia going from 32–2 to 81 then following on to be all out for 70. R. Peel took 9 of the wickets to fall.

No wickets falling in a full day's play

Eng	283–0	v Aus	3rd Day	Melbourne	1924–25
WI	187–6 to 494–6	v Aus	4th Day	Bridgetown	1954–55
Ind	234–0	v NZ	1st Day	Madras	1955–56
WI	147–1 to 504–1	v Pak	3rd Day	Kingston	1957–58
WI	114–3 to 279–3 } 279–3 to 486–3 }	v Eng	4th & 5th Days	Bridgetown	1959–60
Aus	263–0	v WI	1st Day	Bridgetown	1964–65
WI	310–7 to 365–7 dec }				
NZ	163–0 }		3rd Day	Georgetown	1971–72

Notes:
   G. S. Sobers and F. M. M. Worrell are the only pair of batsmen to have batted right through two consecutive days in Test cricket, v England at Bridgetown, 1959–60.
   The following other pairs of batsmen have batted right through one day's play:

J. B. Hobbs and H. Sutcliffe	1924–25
D. S. Atkinson and C. C. Depeiaza	1954–55

V. M. Mankad and P. Roy	1955–56
C. C. Hunte and G. S. Sobers	1957–58
W. M. Lawry and R. B. Simpson	1964–65

The following batsmen batted on all five days of a Test match:

M. L. Jaisimha (20* and 74)	Ind v Aus	Calcutta	1959–60
G. Boycott (107 and 80*)	Eng v Aus	Trent Bridge	1977

Best Batting Figures in Test Cricket

Highest individual innings in Test Cricket

(300 or more)

365*	G. S. Sobers	WI v Pak	Kingston	1957–58
364	L. Hutton	Eng v Aus	The Oval	1938
337	Hanif Mohammad	Pak v WI	Bridgetown	1957–58
336*	W. R. Hammond	Eng v NZ	Auckland	1932–33
334	D. G. Bradman	Aus v Eng	Headingley	1930
325	A. Sandham	Eng v WI	Kingston	1929–30
311	R. B. Simpson	Aus v Eng	Old Trafford	1964
310*	J. H. Edrich	Eng v NZ	Headingley	1965
307	R. M. Cowper	Aus v Eng	Melbourne	1965–66
304	D. G. Bradman	Aus v Eng	Headingley	1934
302	L. G. Rowe	WI v Eng	Bridgetown	1973–74

Highest innings for each country

England

364	L. Hutton	v Aus	The Oval	1938
336*	W. R. Hammond	v NZ	Auckland	1932–33
325	A. Sandham	v WI	Kingston	1929–30
310*	J. H. Edrich	v NZ	Headingley	1964
287	R. E. Foster	v Aus	Sydney	1903–04
285*	P. B. H. May	v WI	Edgbaston	1957
278	D. C. S. Compton	v Pak	Trent Bridge	1954
262*	D. L. Amiss	v WI	Kingston	1973–74
258	T. W. Graveney	v WI	Trent Bridge	1957
256	K. F. Barrington	v Aus	Old Trafford	1964
251	W. R. Hammond	v Aus	Sydney	1928–29
246*	G. Boycott	v Ind	Headingley	1967
243	E. Paynter	v SA	Durban	1938–39
240	W. R. Hammond	v Aus	Lord's	1938
231*	W. R. Hammond	v Aus	Sydney	1936–37
227	W. R. Hammond	v NZ	Christchurch	1932–33
219	W. J. Edrich	v SA	Durban	1938–39
217	W. R. Hammond	v Ind	The Oval	1936
216*	E. Paynter	v Aus	Trent Bridge	1938
216	K. W. R. Fletcher	v NZ	Auckland	1974–75
214*	D. Lloyd	v Ind	Edgbaston	1974
211	J. B. Hobbs	v SA	Lord's	1924
208	D. C. S. Compton	v SA	Lord's	1947
206	L. Hutton	v NZ	The Oval	1949
205*	E. H. Hendren	v WI	Port of Spain	1929–30
205*	J. Hardstaff jnr.	v Ind	Lord's	1946
205	L. Hutton	v WI	Kingston	1953–54
205	E. R. Dexter	v Pak	Karachi	1961–62
203	D. L. Amiss	v WI	The Oval	1976
202*	L. Hutton	v WI	The Oval	1950
200	W. R. Hammond	v Aus	Melbourne	1928–29

Australia

334	D. G. Bradman	v Eng	Headingley	1930
311	R. B. Simpson	v Eng	Old Trafford	1964
307	R. M. Cowper	v Eng	Melbourne	1965–66
304	D. G. Bradman	v Eng	Headingley	1934
299*	D. G. Bradman	v SA	Adelaide	1931–32
270	D. G. Bradman	v Eng	Melbourne	1936–37
266	W. H. Ponsford	v Eng	The Oval	1934
254	D. G. Bradman	v Eng	Lord's	1930
250	K. D. Walters	v NZ	Christchurch	1976–77
247*	G. S. Chappell	v NZ	Wellington	1973–74
244	D. G. Bradman	v Eng	The Oval	1934
242	K. D. Walters	v WI	Sydney	1968–69
234	S. G. Barnes	v Eng	Sydney	1946–47
234	D. G. Bradman	v Eng	Sydney	1946–47
232	D. G. Bradman	v Eng	The Oval	1930
232	S. J. McCabe	v Eng	Trent Bridge	1938
226	D. G. Bradman	v SA	Brisbane	1931–32
225	R. B. Simpson	v Eng	Adelaide	1965–66
223	D. G. Bradman	v WI	Brisbane	1930–31
214*	V. T. Trumper	v SA	Adelaide	1910–11
212	D. G. Bradman	v Eng	Adelaide	1936–37
211	W. L. Murdoch	v Eng	The Oval	1884
210	W. M. Lawry	v WI	Bridgetown	1964–65
207	K. R. Stackpole	v Eng	Brisbane	1970–71
206*	W. A. Brown	v Eng	Lord's	1938
206	A. R. Morris	v Eng	Adelaide	1950–51
205	R. N. Harvey	v SA	Melbourne	1952–53
205	W. M. Lawry	v WI	Melbourne	1968–69
204	R. N. Harvey	v WI	Kingston	1954–55
203	H. L. Collins	v SA	Johannesburg	1921–22
201	S. E. Gregory	v Eng	Sydney	1894–95
201*	J. Ryder	v Eng	Adelaide	1924–25
201	D. G. Bradman	v Ind	Adelaide	1947–48
201	R. B. Simpson	v WI	Bridgetown	1964–65

South Africa

274	R. G. Pollock	v Aus	Durban	1969–70
255*	D. J. McGlew	v NZ	Wellington	1952–53
236	E. A. B. Rowan	v Eng	Headingley	1951
231	A. D. Nourse	v Aus	Johannesburg	1935–36
209	R. G. Pollock	v Aus	Cape Town	1966–67
208	A. D. Nourse	v Eng	Trent Bridge	1951
204	G. A. Faulkner	v Aus	Melbourne	1910–11
201	E. J. Barlow	v Aus	Adelaide	1963–64

West Indies

365*	G. S. Sobers	v Pak	Kingston	1957–58
302	L. G. Rowe	v Eng	Bridgetown	1973–74
291	I. V. A. Richards	v Eng	The Oval	1976
270*	G. A. Headley	v Eng	Kingston	1934–35
261	F. M. M. Worrell	v Eng	Trent Bridge	1950
260	C. C. Hunte	v Pak	Kingston	1957–58
258	S. M. Nurse	v NZ	Christchurch	1968–69
256	R. B. Kanhai	v Ind	Calcutta	1958–59
242*	C. H. Lloyd	v Ind	Bombay	1974–75
237	F. M. M. Worrell	v Ind	Kingston	1952–53
232	I. V. A. Richards	v Eng	Trent Bridge	1976
226	G. S. Sobers	v Eng	Bridgetown	1959–60
223	G. A. Headley	v Eng	Kingston	1929–30
220	C. L. Walcott	v Eng	Bridgetown	1953–54
219	D. S. Atkinson	v Aus	Bridgetown	1954–55
217	R. B. Kanhai	v Pak	Lahore	1958–59
214	L. G. Rowe	v NZ	Kingston	1971–72

209	C. A. Roach	v Eng	Georgetown	1929–30
209*	B. F. Butcher	v Eng	Trent Bridge	1966
207	E. D. Weekes	v Ind	Port of Spain	1952–53
206	E. D. Weekes	v Eng	Port of Spain	1953–54
201	S. M. Nurse	v Aus	Bridgetown	1964–65

New Zealand

259	G. M. Turner	v WI	Georgetown	1971–72
239	G. T. Dowling	v Ind	Christchurch	1967–68
230*	B. Sutcliffe	v Ind	New Delhi	1955–56
223*	G. M. Turner	v WI	Kingston	1971–72
206	M. P. Donnelly	v Eng	Lord's	1949

India

231	V. M. Mankad	v NZ	Madras	1955–56
223	V. M. Mankad	v NZ	Bombay	1955–56
223	P. R. Umrigar	v NZ	Hyderabad	1955–56
220	S. M. Gavaskar	v WI	Port of Spain	1970–71
212	D. N. Sardesai	v WI	Kingston	1970–71
203*	M. A. K. Pataudi	v Eng	New Delhi	1963–64
200*	D. N. Sardesai	v NZ	Bombay	1964–65

Pakistan

337	Hanif Mohammad	v WI	Bridgetown	1957–58
274	Zaheer Abbas	v Eng	Edgbaston	1971
240	Zaheer Abbas	v Eng	The Oval	1974
209	Imtiaz Ahmed	v NZ	Lahore	1955–56
206	Javed Miandad	v NZ	Karachi	1976–77
203*	Hanif Mohammad	v NZ	Lahore	1964–65
201	Mushtaq Mohammad	v NZ	Dunedin	1972–73

Highest individual score at each Test centre

In England

Edgbaston	285*	P. B. H. May	Eng v WI	1957
Headingley	334	D. G. Bradman	Aus v Eng	1930
Lord's	254	D. G. Bradman	Aus v Eng	1930
Old Trafford	311	R. B. Simpson	Aus v Eng	1964
The Oval	364	L. Hutton	Eng v Aus	1938
Sheffield	119	C. Hill	Aus v Eng	1902
Trent Bridge	278	D. C. S. Compton	Eng v Pak	1954

In Australia

Adelaide	299*	D. G. Bradman	Aus v SA	1931–32
Brisbane	226	D. G. Bradman	Aus v SA	1931–32
Melbourne	307	R. M. Cowper	Aus v Eng	1965–66
Perth	176	R. B. Simpson	Aus v Ind	1977–78
Sydney	287	R. E. Foster	Eng v Aus	1903–04

In South Africa

Cape Town	209	R. G. Pollock	SA v Aus	1966–67
Durban	274	R. G. Pollock	SA v Aus	1969–70
Johannesburg	231	A. D. Nourse	SA v Aus	1935–36
Port Elizabeth	167	A. L. Hassett	Aus v SA	1949–50

In West Indies

Bridgetown	337	Hanif Mohammad	Pak v WI	1957–58
Georgetown	259	G. M. Turner	NZ v WI	1971–72
Kingston	365*	G. S. Sobers	WI v Pak	1957–58
Port of Spain	220	S. M. Gavaskar	Ind v WI	1970–71

In New Zealand

Auckland	336*	W. R. Hammond	Eng v NZ	1932–33
Christchurch	258	S. M. Nurse	WI v NZ	1968–69
Dunedin	201	Mushtaq Mohammad	Pak v NZ	1972–73
Wellington	255*	D. J. McGlew	SA v NZ	1952–53

In India

Bangalore	163	C. H. Lloyd	WI v Ind	1974–75
Bombay	242*	C. H. Lloyd	WI v Ind	1974–75
Calcutta	256	R. Kanhai	WI v Ind	1958–59
Hyderabad	223	P. R. Umrigar	Ind v NZ	1955–56
Kanpur	198	G. S. Sobers	WI v Ind	1958–59
Lucknow	124*	Nazar Mohammad	Pak v Ind	1952–53
Madras	231	V. M. Mankad	Ind v NZ	1955–56
New Delhi	230*	B. Sutcliffe	NZ v Ind	1955–56
Nagpur	89	M. G. Burgess	NZ v Ind	1969–70

In Pakistan

Bahawalpur	142	Hanif Mohammad	Pak v Ind	1954–55
Dacca	165	G. Pullar	Eng v Pak	1961–62
Hyderabad	158	D. L. Amiss	Eng v Pak	1972–73
Karachi	206	Javed Miandad	Pak v NZ	1976–77
Lahore	217	R. Kanhai	WI v Pak	1958–59
Peshawar	108	P. R. Umrigar	Ind v Pak	1954–55
Rawalpindi	76	B. R. Taylor	NZ v Pak	1964–65

Longest innings for each country

England	797 mins	364	L. Hutton (v Aus)	The Oval	1938
Australia	762 mins	311	R. B. Simpson (v Eng)	Old Trafford	1964
South Africa	575 mins	105	D. J. McGlew (v Aus)	Durban	1957–58
West Indies	682 mins	197*	F. M. M. Worrell (v Eng)	Bridgetown	1959–60
New Zealand	704 mins	259	G. M. Turner (v WI)	Georgetown	1971–72
India	587 mins	163*	M. L. Apte (v WI)	Port of Spain	1952–53
Pakistan	970 mins	337	Hanif Mohammad (v WI)	Bridgetown	1957–58

Most runs scored in boundaries in an innings

Total	6s	5s	4s					
238	5	–	52	310*	J. H. Edrich	Eng v NZ	Headingley	1965
196	10	–	34	336*	W. R. Hammond	Eng v NZ	Auckland	1932–33
184	–	–	46	334	D. G. Bradman	Aus v Eng	Headingley	1930
184	2	–	43	304	D. G. Bradman	Aus v Eng	Headingley	1934
177	–	1	43	274	R. G. Pollock	SA v Aus	Durban	1969–70
168	–	–	42	256	R. B. Kanhai	WI v Ind	Calcutta	1958–59
166	1	–	40	262*	D. L. Amiss	Eng v WI	Kingston	1973–74
157	–	1	38	365*	G. S. Sobers	WI v Pak	Kingston	1957–58
152	2	–	35	261	F. M. M. Worrell	WI v Eng	Trent Bridge	1950
152	–	–	38	274	Zaheer Abbas	Pak v Eng	Edgbaston	1971
152	–	–	38	291	I. V. A. Richards	WI v Eng	The Oval	1976

Note: The most runs scored in boundaries for India is 124 (31–4s) by B. K. Kunderan (192) v England at Madras, 1963–64. This is also the record for most boundaries in a Test innings for India.

Most sixes in an innings

10 – W. R. Hammond (336*)	Eng v NZ	Auckland	1932–33
7 – B. Sutcliffe (80*)	NZ v SA	Johannesburg	1953–54
6 – J. H. Sinclair (104)	SA v Aus	Cape Town	1902–03
– I. V. A. Richards (192*)	WI v Ind	New Delhi	1974–75
– Haroon Rashid (108)	Pak v Eng	Hyderabad	1977–78

Notes:
Eight of Hammond's ten sixes were hit over extra cover or mid off.
Sutcliffe's display was remarkable in that he made all his runs after retiring hurt, having been struck on the ear by a ball from N. A. T. Adcock.

Most runs scored off one over

Eight-ball over
25 (66061600) B. Sutcliffe & R. W. Blair, off H. J. Tayfield, NZ v SA Johannesburg
1953–54

Six-ball over
22 (116626)	M. W. Tate & W. Voce, off A. E. Hall,	Eng v SA	Johannesburg	1930–31
22 (660046)	R. C. Motz, off D. A. Allen	NZ v Eng	Dunedin	1965–66

Most sixes off consecutive balls

3 – W. R. Hammond (336*) off J. Newman	Eng v NZ	Auckland	1932–33

Most fours off consecutive balls

5 – D. T. Lindsay (60) off J. W. Gleeson	SA v Aus	Port Elizabeth	1969–70
– R. E. Redmond (107) off Majid Khan	NZ v Pak	Auckland	1972–73

Highest totals without a century

				Highest score
524–9 dec	India v New Zealand	Kanpur	1976–77	M. Amarnath 70
476	Australia v England	Adelaide	1911–12	C. Hill 98
475	West Indies v India	Bridgetown	1961–62	J. S. Solomon 96
464–8 dec	South Africa v England	Durban	1927–28	J. F. W. Nicolson 78
464	England v Australia	Brisbane	1970–71	J. H. Edrich 79
454	South Africa v Australia	Johannesburg	1902–03	L. J. Tancred 97
450–9 dec	Australia v South Africa	Sydney	1963–64	R. Benaud 90

Highest totals without a half century

				Highest score
302	South Africa v New Zealand	Wellington	1963–64	P. L. van der Merwe 44
265–8 dec	England v India	Old Trafford	1959	W. G. A. Parkhouse 49
262–7	New Zealand v Pakistan	Karachi	1976–77	W. K. Lees 46

Highest proportion of runs by a batsman

In an innings (completed totals only)

%	Score	Total			
67·3	165*	245	C. Bannerman (Aus v Eng)	Melbourne	1876–77
63·5	134	211	C. G. Greenidge (WI v Eng)	Old Trafford	1976
62·9	100	159	J. R. Reid (NZ v Eng)	Christchurch	1962–63
61·9	258	417	S. M. Nurse (WI v NZ)	Christchurch	1968–69
60·7	74	122	V. T. Trumper (Aus v Eng)	Melbourne	1903–04
60·2	62	103	J. T. Tyldesley (Eng v Aus)	Melbourne	1903–04
59·9	106	177	J. H. Sinclair (SA v Eng)	Cape Town	1898–99
59·9	109	182	H. W. Taylor (SA v Eng)	Durban	1913–14
59·6	68	114	Saeed Ahmed (Pak v Eng)	Trent Bridge	1967
59·5	119*	200	M. G. Burgess (NZ v Pak)	Dacca	1969–70
59·2	74	125	B. Sutcliffe (NZ v Eng)	Dunedin	1954–55
59·2	209	353	R. G. Pollock (SA v Aus)	Cape Town	1966–67
59·0	334	566	D. G. Bradman (Aus v Eng)	Headingley	1930
58·7	202*	344	L. Hutton (Eng v WI)	The Oval	1950
58·3	299*	513	D. G. Bradman (Aus v SA)	Adelaide	1931–32
58·2	188	323	C. Hill (Aus v Eng)	Melbourne	1897–98
58·1	133	229	B. F. Butcher (WI v Eng)	Lord's	1963

In a match (completed totals only)

%	Scores	Totals			
51·9	106 / 4	177 / 35	J. H. Sinclair (SA v Eng)	Cape Town	1898–99
48·9	60 / 142	164 / 249	J. R. Reid (NZ v SA)	Johannesburg	1961–62
48·4	165* / 4	245 / 104	C. Bannerman (Aus v Eng)	Melbourne	1876–77
48·1	140 / 111	281 / 241	C. A. G. Russell (Eng v SA)	Durban	1922–23
47·7	124 / 83	243 / 191	P. S. McDonnell (Aus v Eng)	Adelaide	1884–85

%	Scores	Totals			
46·8	74	122	V. T. Trumper (Aus v Eng)	Melbourne	1903–04
	35	111			
46·3	39	89	G. S. Sobers (WI v Eng)	The Oval	1957
	42	86			

In a series (4 or more matches)

%	Runs	Side's Total			
33·7	974	2886	D. G. Bradman (Aus v Eng)		1930
33·4	806	2410	D. G. Bradman (Aus v SA)		1931–32
31·1	485	1558	G. A. Headley (WI v Eng)		1934–35
30·3	418	1378	E. D. Weekes (WI v NZ)		1955–56
29·9	715	2387	D. G. Bradman (Aus v Ind)		1947–48
29·6	709	2396	G. S. Sobers (WI v Eng)		1959–60
29·1	810	2785	D. G. Bradman (Aus v Eng)		1936–37
28·6	533	1865	L. Hutton (Eng v Aus)		1950–51
28·5	774	2718	S. M. Gavaskar (Ind v WI)		1970–71
28·1	556	1978	I. V. A. Richards (WI v Ind)		1975–76

A century in each innings of a Test match

136	and 130	W. Bardsley	Aus v Eng	The Oval	1909
140	and 111	C. A. G. Russell	Eng v SA	Durban	1922–23
176	and 127	H. Sutcliffe	Eng v Aus	Melbourne	1924–25
119*	and 177*	W. R. Hammond	Eng v Aus	Adelaide	1928–29
104	and 109*	H. Sutcliffe	Eng v SA	The Oval	1929
114	and 112	G. A. Headley	WI v Eng	Georgetown	1929–30
117	and 100	E. Paynter	Eng v SA	Johannesburg	1938–39
106	and 107	G. A. Headley	WI v Eng	Lord's	1939
147	and 103*	D. C. S. Compton	Eng v Aus	Adelaide	1946–47
122	and 124*	A. R. Morris	Aus v Eng	Adelaide	1946–47
189	and 104*	A. Melville	SA v Eng	Trent Bridge	1947
120	and 189*	B. Mitchell	SA v Eng	The Oval	1947
132	and 127*	D. G. Bradman	Aus v Ind	Melbourne	1947–48
145	and 116	V. S. Hazare	Ind v Aus	Adelaide	1947–48
162	and 101	E. D. Weekes	WI v Ind	Calcutta	1948–49
118	and 101*	J. R. Moroney	Aus v SA	Johannesburg	1949–50
126	and 110	C. L. Walcott	WI v Aus	Port of Spain	1954–55
155	and 110	C. L. Walcott	WI v Aus	Kingston	1954–55
125	and 109*	G. S. Sobers	WI v Pak	Georgetown	1957–58
117	and 115	R. B. Kanhai	WI v Aus	Adelaide	1960–61
111	and 104	Hanif Mohammad	Pak v Eng	Dacca	1961–62
153	and 115	R. B. Simpson	Aus v Pak	Karachi	1964–65
242	and 103	K. D. Walters	Aus v WI	Sydney	1968–69
124	and 220	S. M. Gavaskar	Ind v WI	Port of Spain	1970–71
214	and 100*	L. G. Rowe	WI v NZ	Kingston	1971–72
145	and 121	I. M. Chappell	Aus v NZ	Wellington	1973–74
247*	and 133	G. S. Chappell	Aus v NZ	Wellington	1973–74
101	and 110*	G. M. Turner	NZ v Aus	Christchurch	1973–74
123	and 109*	G. S. Chappell	Aus v WI	Brisbane	1975–76
134	and 101	C. G. Greenidge	WI v Eng	Old Trafford	1976
122	and 102	G. P. Howarth	NZ v Eng	Auckland	1977–78

TWICE: H. Sutcliffe (Eng), G. A. Headley (WI), G. S. Chappell (Aus)
TWICE IN SAME SERIES: C. L. Walcott (WI)

A century and ninety in same Test match

93	and 106	P. A. Gibb	Eng v SA	Johannesburg	1938–39
125	and 97	P. G. V. van der Bijl	SA v Eng	Durban	1938–39
109	and 96	C. G. Borde	Ind v WI	New Delhi	1958–59
114	and 97	M. C. Cowdrey	Eng v WI	Kingston	1959–60
101	and 94	K. F. Barrington	Eng v Aus	Sydney	1962–63
104	and 93	Hanif Mohammad	Pak v Aus	Melbourne	1964–65
152	and 95*	G. S. Sobers	WI v Eng	Georgetown	1967–68

92	and	108	R. M. Cowper	Aus v Ind	Adelaide	1967–68
95	and	168	S. M. Nurse	WI v NZ	Auckland	1968–69
101	and	96	A. P. E. Knott	Eng v NZ	Auckland	1970–71
99	and	112	G. Boycott	Eng v WI	Port of Spain	1973–74
93	and	107	C. G. Greenidge	WI v Ind	Bangalore	1974–75
90	and	100	M. Amarnath	Ind v Aus	Perth	1977–78
122	and	97	P. M. Toohey	Aus v WI	Kingston	1977–78

Most runs by a batsman in one match

380 (247* and 133)	G. S. Chappell	Aus v NZ	Wellington	1973–74
375 (325 and 50)	A. Sandham	Eng v WI	Kingston	1929–30

A century in first Test match

England

152	W. G. Grace	v Aus	The Oval	1880
154*	K. S. Ranjitsinhji	v Aus	Old Trafford	1896
132*	P. F. Warner	v SA	Johannesburg	1898–99
287	R. E. Foster	v Aus	Sydney	1903–04
119	G. Gunn	v Aus	Sydney	1907–08
102	Nawab of Pataudi	v Aus	Sydney	1932–33
136	B. H. Valentine	v Ind	Bombay	1933–34
106	P. A. Gibb	v SA	Johannesburg	1938–39
140	S. C. Griffith	v WI	Port of Spain	1947–48
138	P. B. H. May	v SA	Headingley	1951
104*	C. A. Milton	v NZ	Headingley	1958
107	J. H. Hampshire	v WI	Lord's	1969
106*	F. C. Hayes	v WI	The Oval	1973

Australia

165*	C. Bannerman	v Eng	Melbourne	1876–77
107	H. Graham	v Eng	Lord's	1893
104	R. A. Duff	v Eng	Melbourne	1901–02
116	R. J. Hartigan	v Eng	Adelaide	1907–08
104	H. L. Collins	v Eng	Sydney	1920–21
110	W. H. Ponsford	v Eng	Sydney	1924–25
164	A. Jackson	v Eng	Adelaide	1928–29
101*	J. W. Burke	v Eng	Adelaide	1950–51
155	K. D. Walters	v Eng	Brisbane	1965–66
108	G. S. Chappell	v Eng	Perth	1970–71
109	G. J. Cosier	v WI	Melbourne	1975–76

West Indies

176	G. A. Headley	v Eng	Bridgetown	1929–30
112	A. G. Ganteaume	v Eng	Port of Spain	1947–48
115	B. H. Pairaudeau	v Ind	Port of Spain	1952–53
104	O. G. Smith	v Aus	Kingston	1954–55
142	C. C. Hunte	v Pak	Bridgetown	1957–58
214 } 100* }	L. G. Rowe	v NZ	Kingston	1971–72
100*	A. I. Kallicharran	v NZ	Georgetown	1971–72
107	C. G. Greenidge	v Ind	Bangalore	1974–75
105*	L. Baichan	v Pak	Lahore	1974–75
100	A. B. Williams	v Aus	Georgetown	1977–78

New Zealand

117	J. E. Mills	v Eng	Wellington	1929–30
107	R. E. Redmond	v Pak	Auckland	1972–73

India

118	L. Amarnath	v Eng	Bombay	1933–34
110	R. H. Shodhan	v Pak	Calcutta	1952–53
100*	A. G. Kripal Singh	v NZ	Hyderabad	1955–56

112	A. A. Baig	v Eng	Old Trafford	1959
105	Hanumant Singh	v Eng	New Delhi	1963–64
137	G. R. Viswanath	v Aus	Kanpur	1969–70
124	S. Amarnath	v NZ	Auckland	1975–76

Pakistan

166	K. Ibadulla	v Aus	Karachi	1964–65
163	Javed Miandad	v NZ	Lahore	1976–77

South Africa
No instance. Highest score by a player in his first Test is 97 by L. J. Tancred v Aus at Johannesburg, 1902–03.

A century and a 'duck' in the same match

England

L. C. Braund	(102 and 0)	v Aus	Sydney	1903–04
J. T. Tyldesley	(0 and 100)	v Aus	Headingley	1905
G. Gunn	(122* and 0)	v Aus	Sydney	1907–08
F. E. Woolley	(0 and 123)	v Aus	Sydney	1924–25
G. B. Legge	(196 and 0)	v NZ	Auckland	1929–30
D. C. S. Compton	(145* and 0)	v Aus	Old Trafford	1948
L. Hutton	(101 and 0)	v NZ	Headingley	1949
P. B. H. May	(0 and 112)	v SA	Lord's	1955
M. C. Cowdrey	(119 and 0)	v WI	Port of Spain	1959–60
Rev. D. S. Sheppard	(0 and 113)	v Aus	Melbourne	1962–63
M. C. Cowdrey	(101 and 0)	v WI	Kingston	1967–68
D. L. Amiss	(158 and 0)	v Pak	Hyderabad	1972–73

Australia

W. L. Murdoch	(0 and 153*)	v Eng	The Oval	1880
G. H. S. Trott	(0 and 143)	v Eng	Lord's	1896
C. Hill	(188 and 0)	v Eng	Melbourne	1897–98
D. G. Bradman	(0 and 103*)	v Eng	Melbourne	1932–33
J. H. Fingleton	(100 and 0)	v Eng	Brisbane	1936–37
D. G. Bradman	(138 and 0)	v Eng	Trent Bridge	1948
S. G. Barnes	(0 and 141)	v Eng	Lord's	1948
R. N. Harvey	(122 and 0)	v Eng	Old Trafford	1953
I. R. Redpath	(0 and 132)	v WI	Sydney	1968–69
I. M. Chappell	(138 and 0)	v Ind	New Delhi	1969–70
I. C. Davis	(105 and 0)	v Pak	Adelaide	1976–77
R. B. McCosker	(0 and 105)	v Pak	Melbourne	1976–77
C. S. Serjeant	(0 and 124)	v WI	Georgetown	1977–78

South Africa

J. H. Sinclair	(0 and 104)	v Aus	Cape Town	1902–03
G. A. Faulkner	(122* and 0)	v Aus	Old Trafford	1912
R. H. Catterall	(0 and 120)	v Eng	Edgbaston	1924
A. D. Nourse	(0 and 231)	v Aus	Johannesburg	1935–36
E. J. Barlow	(114 and 0)	v Aus	Brisbane	1963–64

West Indies

I. Barrow	(105 and 0)	v Eng	Old Trafford	1933
F. C. M. Alexander	(0 and 108)	v Aus	Sydney	1960–61
S. M. Nurse	(201 and 0)	v Aus	Bridgetown	1964–65
G. S. Sobers	(0 and 113*)	v Eng	Kingston	1967–68
C. A. Davis	(103 and 0)	v Eng	Lord's	1969
G. S. Sobers	(132 and 0)	v Ind	Port of Spain	1970–71
A. I. Kallicharran	(0 and 103*)	v Ind	Port of Spain	1975–76
R. C. Fredericks	(0 and 138)	v Eng	Lord's	1976

New Zealand

G. T. Dowling	(129 and 0)	v Ind	Bombay	1964–65
B. F. Hastings	(0 and 117*)	v WI	Christchurch	1968–69

India

V. M. Mankad	(111 and 0)	v Aus	Melbourne	1947–48
P. Roy	(140 and 0)	v Eng	Bombay	1951–52
V. L. Manjrekar	(133 and 0)	v Eng	Headingley	1952
M. L. Apte	(0 and 163*)	v WI	Port of Spain	1952–53
V. L. Manjrekar	(108 and 0)	v Eng	Madras	1963–64
G. R. Viswanath	(0 and 137)	v Aus	Kanpur	1969–70
S. M. Gavaskar	(0 and 118)	v Ind	Melbourne	1977–78

Pakistan

Imtiaz Ahmed	(209 and 0)	v NZ	Lahore	1955–56
Imtiaz Ahmed	(122 and 0)	v WI	Kingston	1957–58
Hanif Mohammad	(160 and 0)	v Ind	Bombay	1960–61
J. Burki	(140 and 0)	v Eng	Dacca	1961–62
Asif Iqbal	(0 and 152*)	v Aus	Adelaide	1976–77
Sadiq Mohammad	(105 and 0)	v Aus	Melbourne	1976–77

Records involving ducks

Most successive noughts

4	R. Peel	Eng v Aus	1894–95	(including two 'pairs')
4	R. J. Crisp	SA v Aus	1935–36	(including two 'pairs')
4	P. Roy	Ind v Eng	1952	
4	L. S. M. Miller	NZ v SA	1953–54	
4	W. M. Clark	Aus v WI	1977–78	(including two 'pairs')

Most noughts in a series

| 5 | P. Roy | Ind v Eng | 1952 |
| 5 | W. M. Clark | Aus v WI | 1977–78 |

(Roy had seven innings in all in this series: 19, 0, 35, 0, 0, 0 and 0)

Most noughts in a Test career

0s	Inns			Runs	HS	Avge
21	72	B. S. Chandrasekhar	Ind	162	22	4·37
19	91	B. S. Bedi	Ind	621	50*	9·55
17	133	T. G. Evans	Eng	2439	104	20·49
17	71	J. A. Snow	Eng	772	73	13·54
15	109	L. R. Gibbs	WI	488	25	6·97
15	89	G. D. McKenzie	Aus	945	76	12·27
15	100	D. L. Underwood	Eng	824	45*	11·94
14	58	S. Ramadhin	WI	361	44	8·20
14	79	P. Roy	Ind	2441	173	32·54

Note: R. W. Blair (NZ) achieved 12 noughts in only 34 Test innings.

Other notes on ducks

C. L. Walcott (WI) was only once out for 0 in 74 Test innings.

H. Sutcliffe (Eng) had only 2 ducks in 84 Test innings, while C. C. McDonald (Aus) had two in 83 innings. W. R. Hammond (Eng) had only 4 ducks in 140 Test innings. C. H. Lloyd (WI) scored a run in each of his first 58 innings in Tests. B. F. Butcher (also WI) had 46 innings in Tests before his first duck.

R. N. Harvey and W. H. Ponsford (both Aus) had 41 and 40 innings respectively in Tests before their first duck. This was Ponsford's only duck in his 48 innings but Harvey achieved six more.

K. F. Barrington (Eng) played 78 successive Test innings without a duck, between Lord's 1962 and Georgetown 1967–68. He had only 5 noughts in 131 innings.

Batsmen dismissed for a 'pair'

Four times:	B. S. Chandrasekhar	Ind	(1975–76; 1976–77; 1977–78 twice)
Three times:	R. Peel	Eng	(1894–95 twice; 1896)
	R. W. Blair	NZ	(1955–56; 1962–63; 1963–64)
	D. L. Underwood	Eng	(1966; 1974–75; 1976)
	B. S. Bedi	Ind	(1974; 1974–75; 1976–77)

Twice:

D. L. Amiss	Eng	(1968; 1974–75)
A. V. Bedser	Eng	(1948; 1950)
W. M. Clark	Aus	(1977–78)
R. J. Crisp	SA	(1935–36)
J. W. Gleeson	Aus	(1969–70; 1970–71)
K. D. Mackay	Aus	(1956; 1959–60)
Q. McMillan	SA	(1931–32)
G. D. McKenzie	Aus	(1963–64; 1968)
C. A. Roach	WI	(1929–30; 1933)
L. J. Tancred	SA	(1907; 1912)
†A. L. Valentine	WI	(1950; 1953–54)

† indicates out for a 'pair' on Test debut.

Notes:
C. Wesley and T. A. Ward (both SA) achieved a 'king pair', being out first ball in both innings. Ward was the third victim of a hat-trick in both innings by the same bowler, T. J. Matthews of Australia, at Old Trafford in 1912.

R. Peel (Sydney, 1894–95), T. A. Ward (Old Trafford, 1912) and P. Roy (Old Trafford, 1952) each had two ducks in one day.

Three players – M. B. Poore, I. A. Colqhoun and J. A. Hayes – registered a 'pair' in the match between New Zealand and England at Auckland in 1954–55 when New Zealand were dismissed for 26 in their second innings.

Most ducks in an innings

5	Aus	(80)	v Eng	The Oval	1888
5	Aus	(70)	v Eng	Old Trafford	1888
5	Aus	(53)	v Eng	Lord's	1896
5	SA	(45)	v Aus	Melbourne	1931–32
5	Ind	(165)	v Eng	Headingley	1952
5	NZ	(79)	v SA	Johannesburg	1953–54
5	NZ	(74)	v WI	Dunedin	1955–56
5	WI	(146)	v Pak	Karachi	1958–59
5	WI	(76)	v Pak	Dacca	1958–59
5	NZ	(79)	v Pak	Rawalpindi	1964–65
5	Eng	(204)	v WI	Headingley	1976
5	NZ	(105)	v Eng	Christchurch	1977–78

Most ducks in a match

11	Eng	(3)	v Aus	(8)	Old Trafford	1888
11	Aus	(4)	v Eng	(7)	Melbourne	1903–04
11	Ind	(6)	v Aus	(5)	Madras	1964–65

Most ducks in a series

34	Aus	(16)	v Eng	(18)	in 5 Tests	1903–04

Note: There were 27 ducks, 9 by England and 18 by Australia in the 3-match series of 1888.

Centuries in Test cricket—summary

	Total	200+	v Eng	v Aus	v SA	v WI	v NZ	v Ind	v Pak
England	449	31	–	162	87	70	55	42	33
Australia	339	34	176	–	55	55	10	29	14
South Africa	105	8	58	36	–	–	11	–	–
West Indies	202	22	74	44	–	–	16	52	16
New Zealand	66	5	21	7	7	9	–	13	9
India	102	7	31	14	–	29	20	–	8
Pakistan	71	7	21	11	–	13	18	8	–
Totals	1334	114	381	274	149	176	130	144	80

Frequency of centuries

	Tests	100s	Avge per Test
England	542	449	0·82
Australia	380	339	0·89

	Tests	100s	Avge per Test
South Africa	172	105	0·61
West Indies	183	202	1·10
New Zealand	133	66	0·49
India	157	102	0·64
Pakistan	93	71	0·76
Totals	830	1334	1·60

Most runs in Tests

(4000 or over)

		M	I	Runs	Avge	v Eng	v Aus	v SA	v WI	v NZ	v Ind	v Pak
G. S. Sobers	(WI)	93	160	8032	57·78	3214	1510	–	–	404	1920	984
M. C. Cowdrey	(Eng)	114	188	7624	44·06	–	2433	1021	1751	1133	653	633
W. R. Hammond	(Eng)	85	140	7249	58·45	–	2852	2188	639	1015	555	–
D. G. Bradman	(Aus)	52	80	6996	99·94	5028	–	806	447	–	715	–
L. Hutton	(Eng)	79	138	6971	56·67	–	2428	1564	1661	777	522	19
K. F. Barrington	(Eng)	82	131	6806	58·67	–	2111	989	1042	594	1355	715
R. B. Kanhai	(WI)	79	137	6227	47·53	2267	1694	–	–	–	1693	573
R. N. Harvey	(Aus)	79	137	6149	48·41	2416	–	1625	1054	–	775	279
D. C. S. Compton	(Eng)	78	131	5807	50·06	–	1842	2205	592	510	205	453
G. Boycott	(Eng)	74	128	5675	51·12	–	1924	373	1542	916	320	591
J. B. Hobbs	(Eng)	61	102	5410	56·94	–	3636	1562	212	–	–	–
W. M. Lawry	(Aus)	67	123	5234	47·15	2233	–	985	1035	–	892	89
I. M. Chappell	(Aus)	72	130	5187	42·86	1986	–	288	1539	486	536	352
J. H. Edrich	(Eng)	77	127	5138	43·54	–	2644	7	792	840	494	361
K. D. Walters	(Aus)	68	116	4960	47·69	1981	–	258	1196	720	540	265
T. W. Graveney	(Eng)	79	123	4882	44·38	–	1075	234	1532	293	805	943
R. B. Simpson	(Aus)	62	111	4869	46·81	1405	–	980	1043	–	1125	316
I. R. Redpath	(Aus)	66	120	4737	43·45	1512	–	791	1247	413	475	299
C. H. Lloyd	(WI)	65	113	4594	40·73	1313	1209	–	–	131	1441	500
H. Sutcliffe	(Eng)	54	84	4555	60·73	–	2741	1336	206	250	22	–
P. B. H. May	(Eng)	66	106	4537	46·77	–	1566	906	986	603	356	120
E. R. Dexter	(Eng)	62	102	4502	47·89	–	1358	585	866	477	467	749
E. D. Weekes	(WI)	48	81	4455	58·61	1313	714	–	–	478	1495	455
R. C. Fredericks	(WI)	59	109	4334	42·49	1369	1069	–	–	537	767	592
A. P. E. Knott	(Eng)	89	138	4175	33·66	–	1504	–	958	352	685	676
G. S. Chappell	(Aus)	51	90	4097	53·20	1807	–	–	1044	661	–	585

Note:
Most runs for the other countries are as follows:

		M	I	Runs	Avge	v Eng	v Aus	v SA	v WI	v NZ	v Ind	v Pak
Hanif Mohammad	(Pak)	55	97	3915	43·98	1039	548	–	736	622	970	–
P. R. Umrigar	(Ind)	59	94	3631	42·22	770	227	–	1372	351	–	911
B. Mitchell	(SA)	42	80	3471	48·88	2732	573	–	–	166	–	–
B. E. Congdon	(NZ)	61	114	3448	32·22	1143	456	–	764	–	713	372

Most centuries in Tests

(10 or more)

		100s	Inns	Inns per 100	v Eng	v Aus	v SA	v WI	v NZ	v Ind	v Pak
D. G. Bradman	(Aus)	29	80	2·75	19	–	4	2	–	4	–
G. S. Sobers	(WI)	26	160	6·15	10	4	–	–	1	8	3
M. C. Cowdrey	(Eng)	22	188	8·54	–	5	3	6	2	3	3
W. R. Hammond	(Eng)	22	140	6·36	–	9	6	1	4	2	–
R. N. Harvey	(Aus)	21	137	6·52	6	–	8	3	–	4	–

		100s	Inns	Inns per 100	v Eng	v Aus	v SA	v WI	v NZ	v Ind	v Pak
K. F. Barrington	(Eng)	20	131	6·55	–	5	2	3	3	3	4
L. Hutton	(Eng)	19	138	7·26	–	5	4	5	3	2	–
D. C. S. Compton	(Eng)	17	131	7·70	–	5	7	2	2	–	1
G. Boycott	(Eng)	16	128	8·00	–	5	1	4	2	1	3
H. Sutcliffe	(Eng)	16	84	5·25	–	8	6	–	2	–	–
J. B. Hobbs	(Eng)	15	102	6·80	–	12	2	1	–	–	–
R. B. Kanhai	(WI)	15	137	9·13	5	5	–	–	–	4	1
C. L. Walcott	(WI)	15	74	4·93	4	5	–	–	1	4	1
E. D. Weekes	(WI)	15	81	5·40	3	1	–	–	3	7	1
G. S. Chappell	(Aus)	14	90	6·42	6	–	–	4	2	–	2
I. M. Chappell	(Aus)	14	130	9·28	4	–	–	5	2	2	1
K. D. Walters	(Aus)	14	116	8·28	4	–	–	6	2	1	1
S. M. Gavaskar	(Ind)	13	71	5·46	2	3	–	6	2	–	–
W. M. Lawry	(Aus)	13	123	9·46	7	–	1	4	–	1	–
P. B. H. May	(Eng)	13	106	8·15	–	3	3	3	3	1	–
J. H. Edrich	(Eng)	12	127	10·58	–	7	–	1	3	1	–
Hanif Mohammad	(Pak)	12	97	8·08	3	2	–	2	3	2	–
A. R. Morris	(Aus)	12	79	6·58	8	–	2	1	–	1	–
P. R. Umrigar	(Ind)	12	94	7·83	3	–	–	3	1	–	5
D. L. Amiss	(Eng)	11	88	8·00	–	–	–	4	2	2	3
T. W. Graveney	(Eng)	11	123	11·18	–	1	–	5	–	2	3
C. H. Lloyd	(WI)	11	113	10·27	3	4	–	–	–	3	1
A. L. Hassett	(Aus)	10	69	6·90	4	–	3	2	–	1	–
G. A. Headley	(WI)	10	40	4·00	8	2	–	–	–	–	–
A I. Kallicharran	(WI)	10	76	7·60	2	3	–	–	2	2	1
Mushtaq Mohammad	(Pak)	10	88	8·80	3	1	–	2	3	1	–
R. B. Simpson	(Aus)	10	111	11·10	2	–	1	1	–	4	2

Notes: No batsman has scored 10 or more centuries for South Africa or New Zealand. The best for these countries is as follows:

		100s	Inns	Inns per 100	v Eng	v Aus	v SA	v WI	v NZ	v Ind	v Pak
A. D. Nourse	(SA)	9	62	6·88	7	2	–	–	–	–	–
B. E. Congdon	(NZ)	7	114	16·28	3	2	–	2	–	–	–
G. M. Turner	(NZ)	7	70	10·00	–	2	–	2	–	2	1

I. V. A. Richards (WI) has scored 8 centuries in 47 Test innings to date, an average of one century every 5·87 innings.

The following batsmen have scored at least one century against every Test-playing country but their own: K. F. Barrington (1955–64), G. Boycott (1964–73), M. C. Cowdrey (1954–63) and E. R. Dexter (1958–64), all for England.

Batsmen scoring most fifties in Tests

		50s	v Eng	v Aus	v SA	v WI	v NZ	v Ind	v Pak
M. C. Cowdrey	(Eng)	60	–	16	10	16	10	5	3
G. S. Sobers	(WI)	56	23	10	–	–	1	15	7
K. F. Barrington	(Eng)	55	–	18	8	7	4	12	6
L. Hutton	(Eng)	52	–	19	11	11	7	4	–

Best batting averages

(Qualification: 1000 runs)

		M	I	NO	Runs	HS	Avge	100	50
D. G. Bradman	(Aus)	52	80	10	6996	334	99·94	29	13
S. G. Barnes	(Aus)	13	19	2	1072	234	63·05	3	5
R. G. Pollock	(SA)	23	41	4	2256	274	60·97	7	11
G. A. Headley	(WI)	22	40	4	2190	270*	60·83	10	5
H. Sutcliffe	(Eng)	54	84	9	4555	194	60·73	16	23
E. Paynter	(Eng)	20	31	5	1540	243	59·23	4	7

		M	I	NO	Runs	HS	Avge	100	50
K. F. Barrington	(Eng)	82	131	15	6806	256	58·67	20	35
E. D. Weekes	(WI)	48	81	5	4455	207	58·61	15	19
W. R. Hammond	(Eng)	85	140	16	7249	336*	58·45	22	24
G. S. Sobers	(WI)	93	160	21	8032	365*	57·78	26	30
J. B. Hobbs	(Eng)	61	102	7	5410	211	56·94	15	28
C. L. Walcott	(WI)	44	74	7	3798	220	56·68	15	14
L. Hutton	(Eng)	79	138	15	6971	364	56·67	19	33
I. V. A. Richards	(WI)	28	47	2	2500	291	55·55	8	8
C. A. Davis	(WI)	15	29	5	1301	183	54·20	4	4
A. D. Nourse	(SA)	34	62	7	2960	231	53·81	9	14
G. S. Chappell	(Aus)	51	90	13	4097	247*	53·20	14	20
J. Ryder	(Aus)	20	32	5	1394	201*	51·62	3	9
G. Boycott	(Eng)	74	128	17	5675	246*	51·12	16	32
D. C. S. Compton	(Eng)	78	131	15	5807	278	50·06	17	28

Centuries in most consecutive innings

Five

E. D. Weekes	141	WI v Eng	Kingston	1947–48
	128	WI v Ind	New Delhi	1948–49
	194	WI v Ind	Bombay	1948–49
	162 } 101	WI v Ind	Calcutta	1948–49

Note: Weekes scored 90 run out in his next Test innings, v India at Madras in 1948–49.

Four

J. H. W. Fingleton	112	Aus v SA	Cape Town	1935–36
	108	Aus v SA	Johannesburg	1935–36
	118	Aus v SA	Durban	1935–36
	100	Aus v Eng	Brisbane	1936–37
A. Melville	103	SA v Eng	Durban	1938–39
	189 } 104*	SA v Eng	Trent Bridge	1947
	117	SA v Eng	Lord's	1947

Three

W. Bardsley	136 } 130	Aus v Eng	The Oval	1909
	132	Aus v SA	Sydney	1910–11
G. Boycott	119*	Eng v Aus	Adelaide	1970–71
	121*	Eng v Pak	Lord's	1971
	112	Eng v Pak	Headingley	1971
D. G. Bradman	132 } 127*	Aus v Ind	Melbourne	1947–48
	201	Aus v Ind	Adelaide	1947–48
D. C. S. Compton	163	Eng v SA	Trent Bridge	1947
	208	Eng v SA	Lord's	1947
	115	Eng v SA	Old Trafford	1947
S. M. Gavaskar	117*	Ind v WI	Bridgetown	1970–71
	124 } 220	Ind v WI	Port of Spain	1970–71
C. G. Greenidge	134 } 101	WI v Eng	Old Trafford	1976
	115	WI v Eng	Headingley	1976
V. S. Hazare	122	Ind v WI	Bombay	1948–49
	164*	Ind v Eng	New Delhi	1951–52
	155	Ind v Eng	Bombay	1951–52
G. A. Headley	270*	WI v Eng	Kingston	1934–35
	106 } 107	WI v Eng	Lord's	1939
C. G. Macartney	133*	Aus v Eng	Lord's	1926
	151	Aus v Eng	Headingley	1926
	109	Aus v Eng	Old Trafford	1926

A. R. Morris	155	Aus v Eng	Melbourne	1946–47
	122 ⎫ 124* ⎭	Aus v Eng	Adelaide	1946–47
G. S. Sobers	365*	WI v Pak	Kingston	1957–58
	125 ⎫ 109* ⎭	WI v Pak	Georgetown	1957–58
H. Sutcliffe	115	Eng v Aus	Sydney	1924–25
	176 ⎫ 127 ⎭	Eng v Aus	Melbourne	1924–25
P. R. Umrigar	117	Ind v Pak	Madras	1960–61
	112	Ind v Pak	New Delhi	1960–61
	147*	Ind v Eng	Kanpur	1961–62
E. D. Weekes	123	WI v NZ	Dunedin	1955–56
	103	WI v NZ	Christchurch	1955–56
	156	WI v NZ	Wellington	1955–56

Note: A. P. E. Knott had consecutive innings of 101, 96 and 116 v NZ and v Pak 1970–71

Fifties in most consecutive innings

Seven
E. D. Weekes (WI) 141 (v Eng 1947–48)
  128, 194, 162, 101, 90, 56 (v Ind 1948–49)

Six
K. F. Barrington (Eng) 63, 132*, 101, 94 (v Aus 1962–63)
  126, 76 (v NZ 1962–63)
G. S. Chappell (Aus) 68, 54* (v WI 1975–76)
  52, 70, 121, 67 (v Pak 1976–77)
E. R. Dexter (Eng) 85, 172 (v Pak 1962)
  70, 99, 93, 52 (v Aus 1962–63)
G. A. Headley (WI) 93, 53, 270* (v Eng 1934–35)
  106, 107, 51 (v Eng 1939)
E. H. Hendren (Eng) 77, 205*, 56, 123, 61, 55 (v WI 1929–30)
A. Melville (SA) 67, 78, 103 (v Eng 1938–39)
  189, 104*, 117 (v Eng 1947)
J. Ryder (Aus) 78*, 58, 56, 142 (v SA 1921–22)
  201*, 88 (v Eng 1924–25)
G. S. Sobers (WI) 52, 52, 80, 365*, 125, 109* (v Pak 1957–58)
K. D. Walters (Aus) 76, 118, 110, 50, 242, 103 (v WI 1968–69)

Centuries in most consecutive Tests

Six
D. G. Bradman (Aus) 270, 212, 169 (v Eng 1936–37)
  144*, 102*, 103 (v Eng 1938)

Note: Due to injury Bradman did not bat in his next Test, v England at The Oval in 1938. In his next two matches, v England in 1946–47, he scored 187 and 234. Thus he scored centuries in eight consecutive Tests in which he batted.

Batsmen scoring fifty or more in both innings most times

		Times	50 & 50	50 & 100	100 & 100	200 & 100
G. Boycott	Eng	8	3	5	–	–
G. S. Chappell	Aus	8	3	3	1	1
G. S. Sobers	WI	8	3	5	1	–
M. C. Cowdrey	Eng	7	3	4	–	–
R. B. Simpson	Aus	7	4	2	1	–
H. Sutcliffe	Eng	7	1	4	2	–
K. F. Barrington	Eng	6	2	4	–	–
I. M. Chappell	Aus	6	3	2	1	–
D. C. S. Compton	Eng	6	2	3	1	–
L. Hutton	Eng	6	5	1	–	–
W. M. Lawry	Aus	6	4	2	–	–

Most runs in a rubber for each country

England

			M	I	NO	Runs	HS	Avge	100	50
W. R. Hammond	v Aus	1928–29	5	9	1	905	251	113·12	4	–
D. C. S. Compton	v SA	1947	5	8	0	753	208	94·12	4	2
H. Sutcliffe	v Aus	1924–25	5	9	0	734	176	81·55	4	2
E. Hendren	v WI	1929–30	4	8	2	693	205*	115·50	2	5
L. Hutton	v WI	1953–54	5	8	1	677	205	96·71	2	3
D. L. Amiss	v WI	1973–74	5	9	1	663	262*	82·88	3	–
J. B. Hobbs	v Aus	1911–12	5	9	1	662	187	82·75	3	1
G. Boycott	v Aus	1970–71	5	10	3	657	142*	93·85	2	5
E. Paynter	v SA	1938–39	5	8	0	653	243	81·62	3	2
J. H. Edrich	v Aus	1970–71	6	11	2	648	130	72·00	2	4
W. R. Hammond	v SA	1938–39	5	8	1	609	181	87·00	3	2
K. F. Barrington	v Ind	1961–62	5	9	3	594	172	99·00	3	1
A. Sandham	v WI	1929–30	4	8	0	592	325	74·00	2	2
P. B. H. May	v SA	1955	5	9	1	582	117	72·75	2	3
K. F. Barrington	v Aus	1962–63	5	10	2	582	132*	72·75	2	3
L. Hutton	v SA	1948–49	5	9	0	577	158	64·11	2	2
W. R. Hammond	v NZ	1932–33	2	2	1	563	336*	563·00	2	–
D. C. S. Compton	v Aus	1948	5	10	1	562	184	62·44	2	2
J. H. Edrich	v Aus	1968	5	9	0	554	164	61·55	1	4
W. J. Edrich	v SA	1947	4	6	1	552	191	110·40	2	2
C. Washbrook	v SA	1948–49	5	9	0	542	195	60·22	1	2
J. B. Hobbs	v SA	1909–10	5	9	1	539	187	67·37	1	4
M. C. Cowdrey	v WI	1967–68	5	8	0	534	148	66·75	2	4
L. Hutton	v Aus	1950–51	5	10	4	533	156*	88·83	1	4
K. F. Barrington	v Aus	1964	5	8	1	531	256	75·85	1	2
E. R. Dexter	v WI	1959–60	5	9	1	526	136*	65·75	2	2
G. E. Tyldesley	v SA	1927–28	5	9	1	520	122	65·00	2	3
W. R. Hammond	v SA	1930–31	5	9	1	517	136*	64·62	1	4
H. Sutcliffe	v SA	1929	5	9	1	513	114	64·12	4	–
K. F. Barrington	v SA	1964–65	5	7	2	508	148*	101·60	2	2
J. B. Hobbs	v Aus	1920–21	5	10	0	505	123	50·50	2	1

Australia

			M	I	NO	Runs	HS	Avge	100	50
D. G. Bradman	v Eng	1930	5	7	0	974	334	139·14	4	–
R. N. Harvey	v SA	1952–53	5	9	0	834	205	92·66	4	3
D. G. Bradman	v Eng	1936–37	5	9	0	810	270	90·00	3	1
D. G. Bradman	v SA	1931–32	5	5	1	806	299*	201·50	4	–
D. G. Bradman	v Eng	1934	5	8	0	758	304	94·75	2	1
D. G. Bradman	v Ind	1947–48	5	6	2	715	201	178·75	4	1
G. S. Chappell	v WI	1975–76	6	11	5	702	182*	117·00	3	3
K. D. Walters	v WI	1968–69	4	6	0	699	242	116·50	4	2
A. R. Morris	v Eng	1948	5	9	1	696	196	87·00	3	3
D. G. Bradman	v Eng	1946–47	5	8	1	680	234	97·14	2	3
W. M. Lawry	v WI	1968–69	5	8	0	667	205	83·37	3	2
V. T. Trumper	v SA	1910–11	5	9	2	661	214*	94·42	2	2
R. N. Harvey	v SA	1949–50	5	8	3	660	178	132·00	4	1
R. N. Harvey	v WI	1954–55	5	7	1	650	204	108·33	3	1
K. R. Stackpole	v Eng	1970–71	6	12	0	627	207	52·25	2	2
G. S. Chappell	v Eng	1974–75	6	11	0	608	144	55·27	2	5
W. M. Lawry	v Eng	1965–66	5	7	0	592	166	84·57	3	2
I. R. Redpath	v WI	1975–76	6	11	0	575	103	52·27	3	2
V. T. Trumper	v Eng	1903–04	5	10	1	574	185*	63·77	2	3
W. Bardsley	v SA	1910–11	5	9	0	573	132	63·66	1	5
W. H. Ponsford	v Eng	1934	4	7	1	569	266	94·83	2	1
H. L. Collins	v Eng	1920–21	5	9	0	557	162	61·88	2	3
I. M. Chappell	v WI	1968–69	5	8	0	548	165	68·50	2	3
I. M. Chappell	v WI	1972–73	5	9	2	542	109	77·42	2	3
J. M. Taylor	v Eng	1924–25	5	10	0	541	108	54·10	1	4
R. B. Simpson	v Ind	1977–78	5	10	0	539	176	53·90	2	2
J. Darling	v Eng	1897–98	5	8	0	537	178	67·12	3	–
B. C. Booth	v SA	1963–64	4	7	1	531	169	88·50	2	3

			M	I	NO	Run.	HS	Avge	100	50
N. C. O'Neill	v WI	1960–61	5	10	0	522	181	52·20	1	3
C. Hill	v Eng	1901–02	5	10	0	521	99	52·10	–	4
C. C. McDonald	v Eng	1958–59	5	9	1	519	170	64·87	2	1
W. A. Brown	v Eng	1938	4	8	1	512	206*	73·14	2	1
D. G. Bradman	v Eng	1948	5	9	2	508	173*	72·57	2	1
A. R. Morris	v Eng	1946–47	5	8	1	503	155	71·85	3	1

South Africa

			M	I	NO	Run.	HS	Avge	100	50
G. A. Faulkner	v Aus	1910–11	5	10	0	732	204	73·20	2	5
A. D. Nourse	v Eng	1947	5	9	0	621	149	69·00	2	5
D. T. Lindsay	v Aus	1966–67	5	7	0	606	182	86·57	3	2
E. J. Barlow	v Aus	1963–64	5	10	2	603	201	75·37	3	1
B. Mitchell	v Eng	1947	5	10	1	597	189*	66·33	2	3
H. W. Taylor	v Eng	1922–23	5	9	0	582	176	64·66	3	2
K. C. Bland	v Eng	1964–65	5	10	2	572	144*	71·50	1	4
A. Melville	v Eng	1947	5	10	1	569	189	63·22	3	1
E. J. Barlow	v Eng	1964–65	5	10	0	558	138	55·80	1	4
G. A. Faulkner	v Eng	1909–10	5	10	1	545	123	60·55	1	3
R. G. Pollock	v Aus	1966–67	5	9	2	537	209	76·71	2	2
A. D. Nourse	v Eng	1948–49	5	10	3	536	129*	76·57	2	2
A. D. Nourse	v Aus	1935–36	5	10	1	518	231	57·55	1	2
R. G. Pollock	v Aus	1969–70	4	7	0	517	274	73·85	1	3
E. A. B. Rowan	v Eng	1951	5	10	1	515	236	57·22	1	3
H. W. Taylor	v Eng	1913–14	5	10	0	508	109	50·80	1	3
B. A. Richards	v Aus	1969–70	4	7	0	508	140	72·57	2	2

West Indies

			M	I	NO	Run.	HS	Avge	100	50
I. V. A. Richards	v Eng	1976	4	7	0	829	291	118·42	3	2
C. L. Walcott	v Aus	1954–55	5	10	0	827	155	82·70	5	2
G. S. Sobers	v Pak	1957–58	5	8	2	824	365*	137·33	3	3
E. D. Weekes	v Ind	1948–49	5	7	0	779	194	111·28	4	2
G. S. Sobers	v Eng	1966	5	8	1	722	174	103·14	3	2
E. D. Weekes	v Ind	1952–53	5	8	1	716	207	102·28	3	2
G. S. Sobers	v Eng	1959–60	5	8	1	709	226	101·28	3	1
G. A. Headley	v Eng	1929–30	4	8	0	703	223	87·87	4	–
C. L. Walcott	v Eng	1953–54	5	10	2	698	220	87·25	3	3
C. H. Lloyd	v Ind	1974–75	5	9	1	636	242*	79·50	2	1
C. C. Hunte	v Pak	1957–58	5	9	1	622	260	77·75	3	–
L. G. Rowe	v Eng	1973–74	5	7	0	616	302	88·00	3	–
G. S. Sobers	v Ind	1970–71	5	10	2	597	178*	74·62	3	1
C. G. Greenidge	v Eng	1976	5	10	1	592	134	65·77	3	2
S. M. Nurse	v NZ	1968–69	3	5	0	558	258	111·60	2	1
G. S. Sobers	v Ind	1958–59	5	8	2	557	198	92·83	3	–
I. V. A. Richards	v Ind	1975–76	4	6	0	556	177	92·66	3	1
C. C. Hunte	v Aus	1964–65	5	10	1	550	89	61·11	–	6
G. S. Sobers	v Eng	1967–68	5	9	3	545	152	90·83	2	2
F. M. M. Worrell	v Eng	1950	4	6	0	539	261	89·83	2	1
R. B. Kanhai	v Ind	1958–59	5	8	0	538	256	67·25	1	2
C. G. Greenidge	v Pak	1976–77	5	10	0	536	100	53·60	1	4
R. B. Kanhai	v Eng	1967–68	5	10	1	535	153	59·44	2	1
C. A. Davis	v Ind	1970–71	4	8	4	529	125*	132·25	2	3
R. C. Fredericks	v Eng	1976	5	10	1	517	138	57·44	2	3
R. B. Kanhai	v Aus	1960–61	5	10	0	503	117	50·30	2	2
S. M. Nurse	v Eng	1966	5	8	0	501	137	62·62	1	4

New Zealand

			M	I	NO	Run.	HS	Avge	100	50
G. M. Turner	v WI	1971–72	5	8	1	672	259	96·00	2	2
B. Sutcliffe	v Ind	1955–56	5	9	2	611	230*	87·28	2	1
J. R. Reid	v SA	1961–62	5	10	1	546	142	60·66	1	4
B. E. Congdon	v WI	1971–72	5	8	2	531	166*	88·50	2	3

India

			M	I	NO	Run.	HS	Avge	100	50
S. M. Gavaskar	v WI	1970–71	4	8	3	774	220	154·80	4	3
D. N. Sardesai	v WI	1970–71	5	8	0	642	212	80·25	3	1

			M	I	NO	Runs	HS	Avge	100	50
V. L. Manjrekar	v Eng	1961–62	5	8	1	586	189*	83·71	1	4
G. R. Viswanath	v WI	1974–75	5	10	1	568	139	63·11	1	3
R. S. Modi	v WI	1948–49	5	10	0	560	112	56·00	1	5
P. R. Umrigar	v WI	1952–53	5	10	1	560	130	62·22	2	4
V. S. Hazare	v WI	1948–49	5	10	2	543	134*	67·87	2	3
V. M. Mankad	v NZ	1955–56	4	5	0	526	231	105·20	2	–
B. K. Kunderan	v Eng	1963–64	5	10	0	525	192	52·50	2	1

Pakistan
Hanif Mohammad	v WI	1957–58	5	9	0	628	337	69·77	1	3
Majid J. Khan	v WI	1976–77	5	10	0	530	167	53·00	1	3
Wasim Raja	v WI	1976–77	5	10	1	517	117*	57·44	1	5
Saeed Ahmed	v WI	1957–58	5	9	0	508	150	56·44	1	4
Javed Miandad	v NZ	1976–77	3	5	1	504	206	126·00	2	1

Fast scoring in Test cricket

Fast fifties

28 mins	J. T. Brown (140)	Eng v Aus	Melbourne	1894–95
29 mins	S. A. Durani (61*)	Ind v Eng	Kanpur	1963–64
30 mins	E. A. V. Williams (72)	WI v Eng	Bridgetown	1947–48
30 mins	B. R. Taylor (124)	NZ v WI	Auckland	1968–69
33 mins	C. A. Roach (56)	WI v Eng	The Oval	1933
34 mins	C. R. Browne (70*)	WI v Eng	Georgetown	1929–30
35 mins	J. H. Sinclair (104)	SA v Aus	Cape Town	1902–03
35 mins	C. G. Macartney (56)	Aus v SA	Sydney	1910–11
35 mins	J. W. Hitch (51*)	Eng v Aus	The Oval	1921
35 mins	J. M. Gregory (119)	Aus v SA	Johannesburg	1921–22
36 mins	J. J. Lyons (55)	Aus v Eng	Lord's	1890
36 mins	J. Ryder (79)	Aus v Eng	Sydney	1928–29
38 mins	R. Benaud (121)	Aus v WI	Kingston	1954–55

Note:
R. C. Fredericks (169) reached fifty (51*) off only 33 balls (45 minutes) for West Indies v Australia at Perth, 1975–76. Details of the number of balls needed to reach fifty are not available for the other batsmen above apart from B. R. Taylor, whose half-century took 36 balls.

Fast centuries

70 mins	J. M. Gregory (119)	Aus v SA	Johannesburg	1921–22
75 mins	G. L. Jessop (104)	Eng v Aus	The Oval	1902
78 mins	R. Benaud (121)	Aus v WI	Kingston	1954–55
80 mins	J. H. Sinclair (104)	SA v Aus	Cape Town	1902–03
86 mins	B. R. Taylor (124)	NZ v WI	Auckland	1968–69
91 mins	J. Darling (160)	Aus v Eng	Sydney	1897–98
91 mins	S. J. McCabe (189*)	Aus v SA	Johannesburg	1935–36
94 mins	V. T. Trumper (185*)	Aus v Eng	Sydney	1903–04
95 mins	J. T. Brown (140)	Eng v Aus	Melbourne	1894–95
95 mins	P. W. Sherwell (115)	SA v Eng	Lord's	1907
97 mins	C. G. Macartney (116)	Aus v SA	Durban	1921–22
98 mins	D. Denton (104)	Eng v SA	Johannesburg	1909–10
98 mins	C. Hill (191)	Aus v SA	Sydney	1910–11
98 mins	D. G. Bradman (167)	Aus v SA	Melbourne	1931–32
99 mins	D. G. Bradman (334)	Aus v Eng	Headingley	1930

Note:
Details of the number of balls received are not available in most of the above cases but G. L. Jessop took 75 balls to reach his hundred and B. R. Taylor 86. The fastest century in terms of balls received is probably R. C. Fredericks' 169 for West Indies v Australia at Perth, 1975–76: he reached three figures off only 71 balls (116 minutes).

Fast double centuries

214 mins	D. G. Bradman (334)	Aus v Eng	Headingley	1930
223 mins	S. J. McCabe (232)	Aus v Eng	Trent Bridge	1938
226 mins	V. T. Trumper (214*)	Aus v SA	Adelaide	1910–11

234 mins	D. G. Bradman (254)	Aus v Eng	Lord's	1930
241 mins	S. E. Gregory (201)	Aus v Eng	Sydney	1894–95
241 mins	W. R. Hammond (336*)	Eng v NZ	Auckland	1932–33
245 mins	D. C. S. Compton (278)	Eng v Pak	Trent Bridge	1954
251 mins	D. G. Bradman (223)	Aus v WI	Brisbane	1930–31
253 mins	D. G. Bradman (226)	Aus v SA	Brisbane	1931–32
265 mins	H. L. Collins (203)	Aus v SA	Johannesburg	1921–22

Fast triple centuries

288 mins	W. R. Hammond (336*)	Eng v NZ	Auckland	1932–33
336 mins	D. G. Bradman (334)	Aus v Eng	Headingley	1930

Note:
W. R. Hammond's third hundred v New Zealand took only 47 minutes: a record for all Test Cricket.
　　D. G. Bradman's first hundred took 99 minutes, his second 115 minutes and his third 122 minutes. He scored 309 of his runs in one day: 105 before lunch, 115 between lunch and tea and 89 between tea and stumps.

Fast innings

35	in	14 mins	W. P. Howell	Aus v Eng	Sydney	1901–02
49*	in	24 mins	F. G. Mann	Eng v NZ	Headingley	1949
42*	in	25 mins	A. P. F. Chapman	Eng v Aus	Headingley	1926
47	in	29 mins	T. G. Evans	Eng v Aus	Old Trafford	1956
61*	in	34 mins	S. A. Durani	Ind v Eng	Kanpur	1963–64
56	in	40 mins	C. G. Macartney	Aus v SA	Sydney	1910–11
63	in	50 mins	V. T. Trumper	Aus v SA	Johannesburg	1902–03
62	in	50 mins	V. T. Trumper	Aus v Eng	Sheffield	1902
72	in	63 mins	E. A. V. Williams	WI v Eng	Bridgetown	1947–48
104	in	77 mins	G. L. Jessop	Eng v Aus	The Oval	1902
104	in	80 mins	J. H. Sinclair	SA v Aus	Cape Town	1902–03
119	in	97 mins	J. M. Gregory	Aus v SA	Johannesburg	1921–22
115	in 105 mins	P. W. Sherwell	SA v Eng	Lord's	1907
124	in 110 mins	B. R. Taylor	NZ v WI	Auckland	1968–69
128	in 115 mins	G. J. Bonnor	Aus v Eng	Sydney	1884–85
137	in 135 mins	K. H. Weekes	WI v Eng	The Oval	1939
189*	in 165 mins	S. J. McCabe	Aus v SA	Johannesburg	1935–36
191	in 202 mins	C. Hill	Aus v SA	Sydney	1910–11
232	in 235 mins	S. J. McCabe	Aus v Eng	Trent Bridge	1938
278	in 290 mins	D. C. S. Compton	Eng v Pak	Trent Bridge	1954
336*	in 318 mins	W. R. Hammond	Eng v NZ	Auckland	1932–33

Fast partnerships

Runs	Wkt	Mins				
42*	9th	16	F. W. Freer (28*) & G. E. Tribe (25*)　A v E　Sydney			1946–47
63*	5th	25	C. J. Barnett (83*) & R. W. V. Robins (38*)　E v NZ　Lord's			1937
66*	5th	24	C. Washbrook (103*) & F. G. Mann (49*)　E v NZ　Headingley 1949			
77	10th	28	S. J. McCabe (232) & L. O'B. Fleetwood-Smith (5*)　A v E			
			Trent Bridge			1938
62	7th	29	Rev D. S. Sheppard (113) & T. G. Evans (47)　E v A			
			Old Trafford			1956
63	7th	30	L. E. G. Ames (65) & R. W. V. Robins (21)　E v I　Lord's			1932
77*	4th	34	R. G. Nadkarni (122*) & S. A. Durani (61*)　I v E　Kanpur 1963–64			
71	7th	35	D. P. B. Morkel (81) & H. G. Owen-Smith (26)　SA v E			
			The Oval			1929
80	7th	41	B. W. Yuile (20) & B. R. Taylor (124)　NZ v WI　Auckland 1968–69			
86	3rd	44	I. M. Chappell (121) & G. S. Chappell (133)　A v NZ			
			Wellington			1973–74
108	7th	45	F. R. Brown (74) & W. Voce (66)　E v NZ　Christchurch			1932–33
85	8th	46	W. A. Brown (206*) & W. J. O'Reilly (42)　A v E　Lord's			1938
121*	3rd	55	F. E. Woolley (134*) & E. H. Hendren (50*)　E v SA　Lord's			1924
144	3rd	64	C. Hill (191) & D. R. A. Gehrs (67)　A v SA　Sydney			1910–11
130	10th	66	R. E. Foster (287) & W. Rhodes (40*)　E v A　Sydney			1903–04
138	8th	70	R. W. V. Robins (76) & H. Verity (66*)　E v I　Old Trafford			1936

Fast partnerships

Runs	Wkt	Mins		
137	9th	70	E. L. Dalton (117) & A. B. C. Langton (73*) SA v E	
			The Oval	1935
154	9th	73	S. E. Gregory (201) & J. M. Blackham (74) A v E Sydney	1894–95
145	6th	75	L. C. Braund (104) & G. L. Jessop (93) E v SA Lord's	1907
154	8th	88	D. Tallon (92) & R. R. Lindwall (100) A v E Melbourne	1946–47
154	4th	89	D. C. S. Compton (278) & T. W. Graveney (84) E v P	
			Trent Bridge	1954
158	6th	90	J. T. Tyldesley (112*) & R. H. Spooner (79) E v A	
			The Oval	1905
209	3rd	97	H. L. Collins (203) & J. M. Gregory (119) A v SA	
			Johannesburg	1921–22
192	5th	108	D. C. S. Compton (278) & T. E. Bailey (36*) E v P	
			Trent Bridge	1954
224	2nd	115	W. Bardsley (132) & C. Hill (191) A v SA Sydney	1910–11
202	3rd	130	C. Kelleway (114) & W. Bardsley (121) A v SA Old	
			Trafford	1912
248	4th	140	L. Hutton (196) & D. C. S. Compton (120) E v WI Lord's	1939
242	5th	145	W. R. Hammond (227) & L. E. G. Ames (103) E v NZ	
			Christchurch	1932–33
231	2nd	154	W. M. Woodfull (155) & D. G. Bradman (254) A v E Lord's	1930
249	3rd	163	D. G. Bradman (169) & S. J. McCabe (112) A v E	
			Melbourne	1936–37
245	3rd	165	R. E. S. Wyatt (113) & F. E. Woolley (154) E v SA Old	
			Trafford	1929
246	8th	165	L. E. G. Ames (137) & G. O. B. Allen (122) E v NZ Lord's	1931
264	3rd	180	L. Hutton (165*) & W. R. Hammond (138) E v WI The Oval	1939
301	2nd	217	A. R. Morris (182) & D. G. Bradman (173*) A v E Headingley	1948
350	4th	274	Mushtaq Mohammad (201) & Asif Iqbal (175) P v NZ	
			Dunedin	1972–73
319	3rd	240	A. Melville (189) & A. D. Nourse (149) SA v E Trent Bridge	1947
341	3rd	283	E. J. Barlow (201) & R. G. Pollock (175) SA v A Adelaide	1963–64
388	4th	341	W. H. Ponsford (181) & D. G. Bradman (304) A v E Headingley	1934
451	2nd	316	W. H. Ponsford (266) & D. G. Bradman (244) A v E	
			The Oval	1934

A century before lunch

On first day

103*	V. T. Trumper (104)	Aus v Eng	Old Trafford	1902
112*	C. G. Macartney (151)	Aus v Eng	Headingley	1926
105*	D. G. Bradman (334)	Aus v Eng	Headingley	1930
108*	Majid Khan (112)	Pak v NZ	Karachi	1976–77

On other days

					Day
113 (41* to 154*)	K. S. Ranjitsinhji (154*)	Eng v Aus	Old Trafford	1896	3rd
116 (22* to 138*)	C. Hill (142)	Aus v SA	Johannesburg	1902–03	3rd
118 (32* to 150*)	W. Bardsley (164)	Aus v SA	Lord's	1912	2nd
109 (19* to 128*)	C. P. Mead (182*)	Eng v Aus	The Oval	1921	2nd
102 (12* to 114*)	J. B. Hobbs (211)	Eng v Aus	Lord's	1924	2nd
102 (27* to 129)	H. G. Owen-Smith (129)	SA v Eng	Headingley	1929	3rd
111 (41* to 152*)	W. R. Hammond (336*)	Eng v NZ	Auckland	1932–33	2nd
123 (25* to 148*)	L. E. G. Ames (148*)	Eng v SA	The Oval	1935	3rd
100 (59* to 159*)	S. J. McCabe (189*)	Aus v SA	Johannesburg	1935–36	4th

Note:

Five players have scored 98 before lunch in Test Cricket, as follows:

130* to 228*	D. G. Bradman (232)	Aus v Eng	The Oval	1930	(4th day)
0 to 98*	C. J. Barnett (126)	Eng v Aus	Trent Bridge	1938	(1st day)
0 to 98*	T. G. Evans (104)	Eng v Ind	Lord's	1952	(3rd day)
42* to 140*	C. H. Lloyd (149)	WI v Aus	Perth	1975–76	(3rd day)
0 to 98*	G. O. B. Allen (122)	Eng v NZ	Lord's	1931	(2nd day)

Most runs scored in a day's play

By one side

503	(28–0 to 531–2 dec)	Eng v SA	2nd day	Lord's	1924
494	(494–6)	Aus v SA	1st day	Sydney	1910–11
475	(475–2)	Aus v Eng	1st day	The Oval	1934
471	(471–8 dec)	Eng v Ind	1st day	The Oval	1936
458	(458–3)	Aus v Eng	1st day	Headingley	1930
455	(39–3 to 494–4)	Aus v Eng	2nd day	Headingley	1934
450	(450 all out)	Aus v SA	1st day	Johannesburg	1921–22

Notes:
Most runs in a day by the other Test-playing countries are as follows:

South Africa:	428–7	v Aus	1st day	Johannesburg	1902–03
West Indies:	437–9	v Eng	1st day	Headingley	1976
New Zealand:	364	v SA	1st day	Wellington	1931–32
India:	340–3	v NZ	2nd day	New Delhi	1964–65
Pakistan:	400–4 (107–2 to 507–6 dec)				
		v NZ	2nd day	Dunedin	1972–73

England scored 437 runs for the loss of four wickets in only 290 minutes (121–2 to 558–6 dec) on the second day v Pakistan at Trent Bridge, 1954.

England's 503 runs on the second day v South Africa at Lord's in 1924 were scored in only 315 minutes. J. B. Hobbs and H. Sutcliffe scored exactly 200 runs in the pre-lunch session (2¼ hours).

By both sides

588–6	Eng	(398–6)	v Ind	(190–0)	2nd day	Old Trafford	1936
522–2	Eng	(503–2)	v SA	(19–0)	2nd day	Lord's	1924
508–8	Eng	(221–2)	v SA	(287–6)	3rd day	The Oval	1935
496–4	Eng	(437–4)	v Pak	(59–0)	2nd day	Trent Bridge	1954
491–7	NZ	(29–1 & 195–2)	v Eng	(267–4 dec)	3rd day	Headingley	1949
473–4	SA	(209–3)	v Eng	(264–1)	3rd day	The Oval	1929
469–7	WI	(103–4)	v Eng	(366–3)	3rd day	The Oval	1939
464–11	Aus	(448)	v SA	(16–1)	1st day	Old Trafford	1912

By a batsman (210 runs or more)

	Out of				
309	456	D. G. Bradman (334)	Aus v Eng	Headingley	1930
295	421	W. R. Hammond (336*)	Eng v NZ	Auckland	1932–33
273	310	D. C. S. Compton (278)	Eng v Pak	Trent Bridge	1954
271	455	D. G. Bradman (304)	Aus v Eng	Headingley	1934
244	451	D. G. Bradman (244)	Aus v Eng	The Oval	1934
239	384	F. M. M. Worrell (261)	WI v Eng	Trent Bridge	1950
223	418	W. R. Hammond (227)	Eng v NZ	Christchurch	1932–33
223	427	D. G. Bradman (223)	Aus v WI	Brisbane	1930–31
217	403	W. R. Hammond (217)	Eng v Ind	The Oval	1936
214	334	R. E. Foster (287)	Eng v Aus	Sydney	1903–04
213	273	S. J. McCabe (232)	Aus v Eng	Trent Bridge	1938
210	389	W. R. Hammond (240)	Eng v Aus	Lord's	1938

Note:
The figure in the second column refers to the number of runs scored while each batsman was at the wicket during the day's play.

Slow scoring in Test cricket

Slowest fifties

357 mins	T. E. Bailey (68)	Eng v Aus	Brisbane	1958–59
313 mins	D. J. McGlew (70)	SA v Aus	Johannesburg	1957–58
302 mins	D. N. Sardesai (60)	Ind v WI	Bridgetown	1961–62
300 mins	G. S. Camacho (57)	WI v Eng	Bridgetown	1967–68
290 mins	G. Boycott (63)	Eng v Pak	Lahore	1977–78
282 mins	E. D. A. S. McMorris (73)	WI v Eng	Kingston	1959–60
280 mins	P. E. Richardson (117)	Eng v SA	Johannesburg	1956–57

Slowest centuries

557 mins	Mudassar Nazar (114)	Pak v Eng	Lahore	1977–78
545 mins	D. J. McGlew (105)	SA v Aus	Durban	1957–58
487 mins	C. T. Radley (158)	Eng v NZ	Auckland	1977–78
488 mins	P. E. Richardson (117)	Eng v SA	Johannesburg	1956–57
468 mins	Hanif Mohammad (142)	Pak v Ind	Bahawalpur	1954–55
460 mins	Hanif Mohammad (111)	Pak v Eng	Dacca	1961–62
458 mins	K. W. R. Fletcher (122)	Eng v Pak	The Oval	1974
435 mins	J. W. Guy (102)	NZ v Ind	Hyderabad	1955–56
434 mins	M. C. Cowdrey (154)	Eng v WI	Edgbaston	1957
414 mins	J. H. B. Waite (134)	SA v Aus	Durban	1957–58
414 mins	A. W. Greig (103)	Eng v Ind	Calcutta	1976–77

Slowest double centuries

608 mins	R. B. Simpson (311)	Aus v Eng	Old Trafford	1964
595 mins	G. S. Sobers (226)	WI v Eng	Bridgetown	1959–60
584 mins	Hanif Mohammad (337)	Pak v WI	Bridgetown	1957–58
570 mins	S. G. Barnes (234)	Aus v Eng	Sydney	1946–47

Slowest triple centuries

858 mins	Hanif Mohammad (337)	Pak v WI	Bridgetown	1957–58
753 mins	R. B. Simpson (311)	Aus v Eng	Old Trafford	1964

Slow innings

3* in 100 mins	J. T. Murray	Eng v Aus	Sydney	1962–63
5 in 102 mins	M. A. K. Pataudi	Ind v Eng	Bombay	1972–73
8 in 125 mins	T. E. Bailey	Eng v SA	Headingley	1955
10* in 133 mins	T. G. Evans	Eng v Aus	Adelaide	1946–47
18 in 194 mins	W. R. Playle	NZ v Eng	Headingley	1958
21 in 210 mins	P. G. Z. Harris	NZ v Pak	Karachi	1955–56
28* in 250 mins	J. W. Burke	Aus v Eng	Brisbane	1958–59
31 in 264 mins	K. D. Mackay	Aus v Eng	Lord's	1956
45 in 318 mins	Shuja-ud-Din	Pak v Aus	Lahore	1959–60
58 in 367 mins	Ijaz Butt	Pak v Aus	Karachi	1959–60
60 in 390 mins	D. N. Sardesai	Ind v WI	Bridgetown	1961–62
77 in 442 mins	G. Boycott	Eng v NZ	Wellington	1977–78
68 in 458 mins	T. E. Bailey	Eng v Aus	Brisbane	1958–59
99 in 505 mins	M. L. Jaisimha	Ind v Pak	Kanpur	1960–61
105 in 575 mins	D. J. McGlew	SA v Aus	Durban	1957–58
158 in 648 mins	C. T. Radley	Eng v NZ	Auckland	1977–78
197* in 682 mins	F. M. M. Worrell	WI v Eng	Bridgetown	1959–60
259 in 705 mins	G. M. Turner	NZ v WI	Georgetown	1971–72
337 in 970 mins	Hanif Mohammad	Pak v WI	Bridgetown	1957–58

Note:
J. T. Murray batted with the handicap of a sprained shoulder, injured while taking a catch earlier in the match. He scored from only two of the 100 balls he received.

Fewest boundaries

84	(0 fours)	W. M. Lawry	Aus v Eng	Brisbane	1970–71
67	(0 fours)	E. A. B. Rowan	SA v Eng	Durban	1938–39
120	(2 fours)	P. A. Gibb	Eng v SA	Durban	1938–39
94	(2 fours)	K. F. Barrington	Eng v Aus	Sydney	1962–63
102	(3 fours)	W. M. Woodfull	Aus v Eng	Melbourne	1928–29
161	(5 fours)	W. M. Woodfull	Aus v SA	Melbourne	1931–32

An hour before scoring first run
Mins

97	T. G. Evans (10*)	Eng v Aus	Adelaide	1946–47
82	P. I. Pocock (13)	Eng v WI	Georgetown	1967–68
74	J. T. Murray (3*)	Eng v Aus	Sydney	1962–63
70	W. L. Murdoch (17)	Aus v Eng	Sydney	1882–83
65	Shuja-ud-Din (45)	Pak v Aus	Lahore	1959–60

An hour without scoring a run
Mins

90	B. Mitchell (58)	SA v Aus	Brisbane	1931–32

79	T. E. Bailey (8)	Eng v SA	Headingley	1955
77	D. B. Close (20)	Eng v WI	Old Trafford	1976
67	W. H. Scotton (34)	Eng v Aus	The Oval	1886
65	M. A. K. Pataudi (5)	Ind v Eng	Bombay	1972–73
63	W. R. Endean (18)	SA v Eng	Johannesburg	1956–57
63	D. R. Jardine (24)	Eng v Aus	Brisbane	1932–33
63	W. R. Playle (18)	NZ v Eng	Headingley	1958
62	K. F. Barrington (137)	Eng v NZ	Edgbaston	1965
60	B. Mitchell (73)	SA v Eng	Johannesburg	1938–39
60	T. E. Bailey (80)	Eng v SA	Durban	1956–57

Fewest runs in a day (complete or near complete)

By one batsman

49	(5* to 54*)	M. L. Jaisimha (99)	Ind v Pak	Kanpur	1960–61
52	(52*)	Mudassar Nazar (114)	Pak v Eng	Lahore	1977–78
55	(55*)	J. G. Wright (55)	NZ v Eng	Wellington	1977–78
56	(1* to 57*)	D. J. McGlew (70)	SA v Aus	Johannesburg	1957–58
59	(0* to 59*)	M. L. Jaisimha (74)	Ind v Aus	Calcutta	1959–60

By a side or both sides

95	Aus (80) v Pak (15–2)		Karachi	1956–57
104	Pak (0–0 to 104–5) v Aus		Karachi	1959–60
106	Eng (92–2 to 198) v Aus		Brisbane	1958–59
112	Aus (138–6 to 187) v Pak (63–1)		Karachi	1956–57
117	Ind (117–5) v Aus		Madras	1956–57
119	SA (7–0 to 126–2) v Aus		Johannesburg	1957–58
120	Ind (15–0 to 135–8) v Aus		Calcutta	1956–57
122	Eng (110–9 to 110) v SA (122–7)		Port Elizabeth	1956–57
122	Aus (156–6 to 186) v Eng (92–2)		Brisbane	1958–59
122	Aus (282–6 to 308 & 9–1) v Eng (87)		Melbourne	1958–59
124	Pak (74–4 to 134) v Aus (64–1)		Dacca	1959–60
124	Ind (226–6 to 291) v Aus (59–2)		Kanpur	1959–60
125	NZ (125) v Eng		Dunedin	1954–55

Note: The fewest runs scored in a full day's play in a Test in England is **151** (England 175–2 to 289; New Zealand 37–7) on the third day at Lord's in 1978.

England made only 142–7 in 335 minutes (25 minutes lost because of rain) on the first day v Australia at Headingley in 1953.

G. S. Sobers (226) & F. M. M. Worrell (197*) added 399 for the fourth wicket in 579 minutes – the longest partnership in Test cricket – for West Indies v England at Bridgetown, 1959–60.

Best Bowling Figures in Test Cricket

Eight or more wickets in an innings

England

10–53	J. C. Laker	Eng v Aus	Old Trafford	1956
9–28	G. A. Lohmann	v SA	Johannesburg	1895–96
9–37	J. C. Laker	v Aus	Old Trafford	1956
9–103	S. F. Barnes	v SA	Johannesburg	1913–14
8–7	G. A. Lohmann	v SA	Port Elizabeth	1895–96
8–11	J. Briggs	v SA	Cape Town	1888–89
8–29	S. F. Barnes	v SA	The Oval	1912
8–31	F. S. Trueman	v Ind	Old Trafford	1952
8–34	I. T. Botham	v Pak	Lord's	1978
8–35	G. A. Lohmann	v Aus	Sydney	1886–87
8–43	H. Verity	v Aus	Lord's	1934
8–51	D. L. Underwood	v Pak	Lord's	1974
8–56	S. F. Barnes	v SA	Johannesburg	1913–14
8–58	G. A. Lohmann	v Aus	Sydney	1891–92
8–59	C. Blythe	v SA	Headingley	1907
8–68	W. Rhodes	v Aus	Melbourne	1903–04
8–81	L. C. Braund	v Aus	Melbourne	1903–04
8–86	A. W. Greig	v WI	Port of Spain	1973–74
8–94	T. Richardson	v Aus	Sydney	1897–98

| 8–107 | B. J. T. Bosanquet | | v Aus | Trent Bridge | 1905 |
| 8–126 | J. C. White | | v Aus | Adelaide | 1928–29 |

Australia

9–121	A. A. Mailey	Aus	v Eng	Melbourne	1920–21
8–31	F. Laver		v Eng	Old Trafford	1909
8–43	A. E. Trott		v Eng	Adelaide	1894–95
8–59	A. A. Mallett		v Pak	Adelaide	1972–73
8–65	H. Trumble		v Eng	The Oval	1902
8–53	R. A. L. Massie		v Eng	Lord's	1972
8–71	G. D. McKenzie		v WI	Melbourne	1968–69
8–84	R. A. L. Massie		v Eng	Lord's	1972
8–143	M. H. N. Walker		v Eng	Melbourne	1974–75

South Africa

9–113	H. J. Tayfield	SA	v Eng	Johannesburg	1956–57
8–53	G. B. Lawrence		v NZ	Johannesburg	1961–62
8–69	H. J. Tayfield		v Eng	Durban	1956–57
8–70	S. J. Snooke		v Eng	Johannesburg	1905–06

West Indies

9–95	J. M. Noreiga	WI	v Ind	Port of Spain	1970–71
8–29	C. E. H. Croft		v Pak	Port of Spain	1976–77
8–38	L. R. Gibbs		v Ind	Bridgetown	1961–62
8–92	M. A. Holding		v Eng	The Oval	1976
8–104	A. L. Valentine		v Eng	Old Trafford	1950

India

9–69	J. M. Patel	Ind	v Aus	Kanpur	1959–60
9–102	S. P. Gupte		v WI	Kanpur	1958–59
8–52	V. M. Mankad		v Pak	New Delhi	1952–53
8–55	V. M. Mankad		v Eng	Madras	1951–52
8–72	S. Venkataraghavan		v NZ	New Delhi	1964–65
8–76	E. A. S. Prasanna		v NZ	Auckland	1975–76
8–79	B. S. Chandrasekhar		v Eng	New Delhi	1972–73

Note: The best performance for the other countries is:

| 7–23 | R. J. Hadlee | NZ | v Ind | Wellington | 1975–76 |
| 7–42 | Fazal Mahmood | Pak | v Ind | Lucknow | 1952–53 |

Eleven or more wickets in a match

England

19–90	(9–37 & 10–53)	J. C. Laker	v Aus	Old Trafford	1956
17–159	(8–56 & 9–103)	S. F. Barnes	v SA	Johannesburg	1913–14
15–28	(7–17 & 8–11)	J. Briggs	v SA	Cape Town	1888–89
15–45	(7–38 & 8–7)	G. A. Lohmann	v SA	Port Elizabeth	1895–96
15–99	(8–59 & 7–40)	C. Blythe	v SA	Headingley	1907
15–104	(7–61 & 8–43)	H. Verity	v Aus	Lord's	1934
15–124	(7–56 & 8–68)	W. Rhodes	v Aus	Melbourne	1903–04
14–99	(7–55 & 7–44)	A. V. Bedser	v Aus	Trent Bridge	1953
14–102	(7–28 & 7–74)	W. Bates	v Aus	Melbourne	1882–83
14–144	(7–56 & 7–88)	S. F. Barnes	v SA	Durban	1913–14
13–57	(5–28 & 8–29)	S. F. Barnes	v SA	The Oval	1912
13–71	(5–20 & 8–51)	D. L. Underwood	v Pak	Lord's	1974
13–91	(6–54 & 7–37)	J. J. Ferris	v SA	Cape Town	1891–92
13–156	(8–86 & 5–70)	A. W. Greig	v WI	Port of Spain	1973–74
13–163	(6–42 & 7–121)	S. F. Barnes	v Aus	Melbourne	1901–02
13–244	(7–168 & 6–76)	T. Richardson	v Aus	Old Trafford	1896
13–256	(5–130 & 8–126)	J. C. White	v Aus	Adelaide	1928–29
12–71	(9–28 & 3–43)	G. A. Lohmann	v SA	Johannesburg	1895–96
12–89	(5–53 & 7–36)	J. H. Wardle	v SA	Cape Town	1956–57
12–97	(6–12 & 6–85)	D. L. Underwood	v NZ	Christchurch	1970–71
12–101	(7–52 & 5–49)	R. Tattersall	v SA	Lord's	1951
12–101	(6–41 & 6–60)	D. L. Underwood	v NZ	The Oval	1969
12–102	(6–50 & 6–52)	F. Martin	v Aus	The Oval	1890
12–104	(7–36 & 5–68)	G. A. Lohmann	v Aus	The Oval	1886
12–112	(7–58 & 5–54)	A. V. Bedser	v SA	Old Trafford	1951
12–119	(5–75 & 7–44)	F. S. Trueman	v WI	Edgbaston	1963

12–130	(7–70 & 5–60)	G. Geary	v SA	Johannesburg	1927–28
12–136	(6–49 & 6–87)	J. Briggs	v Aus	Adelaide	1891–92
12–171	(7–71 & 5–100)	A. P. Freeman	v SA	Old Trafford	1929
11–48	(5–28 & 6–20)	G. A. R. Lock	v WI	The Oval	1957
11–65	(4–14 & 7–51)	G. A. R. Lock	v NZ	Headingley	1958
11–68	(7–31 & 4–37)	R. Peel	v Aus	Old Trafford	1888
11–70	(4–38 & 7–32)	D. L. Underwood	v NZ	Lord's	1969
11–74	(5–29 & 6–45)	J. Briggs	v Aus	Lord's	1886
11–76	(6–48 & 5–28)	W. H. Lockwood	v Aus	Old Trafford	1902
11–84	(5–31 & 6–53)	G. A. R. Lock	v NZ	Christchurch	1958–59
11–88	(5–58 & 6–30)	F. S. Trueman	v Aus	Headingley	1961
11–90	(6–7 & 5–83)	A. E. R. Gilligan	v SA	Edgbaston	1924
11–93	(4–41 & 7–52)	A. V. Bedser	v Ind	Old Trafford	1946
11–96	(5–37 & 6–59)	C. S. Marriott	v WI	The Oval	1933
11–97	(6–63 & 5–34)	J. B. Statham	v SA	Lord's	1960
11–98	(7–44 & 4–54)	T. E. Bailey	v WI	Lord's	1957
11–102	(6–44 & 5–58)	C. Blythe	v Aus	Edgbaston	1909
11–110	(5–25 & 6–85)	S. F. Barnes	v SA	Lord's	1912
11–113	(5–58 & 6–55)	J. C. Laker	v Aus	Headingley	1956
11–118	(6–68 & 5–50)	C. Blythe	v SA	Cape Town	1905–06
11–140	(6–101 & 5–39)	I. T. Botham	v NZ	Lord's	1978
11–145	(7–49 & 4–96)	A. V. Bedser	v Ind	Lord's	1946
11–149	(4–79 & 7–70)	W. Voce	v WI	Port of Spain	1929–30
11–152	(6–100 & 5–52)	F. S. Trueman	v WI	Lord's	1963
11–153	(7–49 & 4–104)	H. Verity	v Ind	Madras	1933–34
11–173	(6–39 & 5–134)	T. Richardson	v Aus	Lord's	1896
11–215	(7–113 & 4–102)	D. L. Underwood	v Aus	Adelaide	1974–75
11–228	(6–130 & 5–98)	M. W. Tate	v Aus	Sydney	1924–25

Australia

16–137	(8–84 & 8–53)	R. A. L. Massie	v Eng	Lord's	1972
14–90	(7–46 & 7–44)	F. R. Spofforth	v Eng	The Oval	1882
14–199	(7–116 & 7–83)	C. V. Grimmett	v SA	Adelaide	1931–32
13–77	(7–17 & 6–60)	M. A. Noble	v Eng	Melbourne	1901–02
13–110	(6–48 & 7–62)	F. R. Spofforth	v Eng	Melbourne	1878–79
13–173	(7–100 & 6–73)	C. V. Grimmett	v SA	Durban	1935–36
13–236	(4–115 & 9–121)	A. A. Mailey	v Eng	Melbourne	1920–21
12–87	(5–44 & 7–43)	C. T. B. Turner	v Eng	Sydney	1887–88
12–89	(6–59 & 6–30)	H. Trumble	v Eng	The Oval	1896
12–124	(5–31 & 7–93)	A. K. Davidson	v Ind	Kanpur	1959–60
12–173	(8–65 & 4–108)	H. Trumble	v Eng	The Oval	1902
12–175	(5–85 & 7–90)	H. V. Hordern	v Eng	Sydney	1911–12
11–24	(5–6 & 6–18)	H. Ironmonger	v SA	Melbourne	1931–32
11–31	(5–2 & 6–29)	E. R. H. Toshack	v Ind	Brisbane	1947–48
11–79	(7–23 & 4–56)	H. Ironmonger	v WI	Melbourne	1930–31
11–82	(5–45 & 6–37)	C. V. Grimmett	v Eng	Sydney	1924–25
11–85	(7–58 & 4–27)	C. G. Macartney	v Eng	Headingley	1909
11–103	(5–51 & 6–52)	M. A. Noble	v Eng	Sheffield	1902
11–105	(6–52 & 5–53)	R. Benaud	v Ind	Calcutta	1956–57
11–117	(4–73 & 7–44)	F. R. Spofforth	v Eng	Sydney	1882–83
11–123	(5–51 & 6–72)	D. K. Lillee	v NZ	Auckland	1976–77
11–129	(4–75 & 7–54)	W. J. O'Reilly	v Eng	Trent Bridge	1934
11–165	(7–68 & 4–97)	G. E. Palmer	v Eng	Sydney	1881–82
11–165	(6–26 & 5–139)	D. K. Lillee	v Eng	Melbourne	1976–77
11–183	(7–87 & 4–96)	C. V. Grimmett	v WI	Adelaide	1930–31
11–222	(5–135 & 6–87)	A. K. Davidson	v WI	Brisbane	1960–61

South Africa

13–165	(6–84 & 7–81)	H. J. Tayfield	v Aus	Melbourne	1952–53
13–192	(4–79 & 9–113)	H. J. Tayfield	v Eng	Johannesburg	1956–57
12–127	(4–57 & 8–70)	S. J. Snooke	v Eng	Johannesburg	1905–06
12–181	(5–87 & 7–94)	A. E. E. Vogler	v Eng	Johannesburg	1909–10
11–112	(4–49 & 7–63)	A. E. Hall	v Eng	Cape Town	1922–23
11–150	(5–63 & 6–87)	E. P. Nupen	v Eng	Johannesburg	1930–31
11–196	(6–128 & 5–68)	S. F. Burke	v NZ	Cape Town	1961–62

West Indies

14–149 (8–92 & 6–57)	M. A. Holding	v Eng	The Oval	1976
12–121 (7–64 & 5–57)	A. M. E. Roberts	v Ind	Madras	1974–75
11–126 (6–50 & 5–76)	W. W. Hall	v Ind	Kanpur	1958–59
11–147 (5–70 & 6–77)	K. D. Boyce	v Eng	The Oval	1973
11–152 (5–66 & 6–86)	S. Ramadhin	v Eng	Lord's	1950
11–157 (5–59 & 6–98)	L. R. Gibbs	v Eng	Old Trafford	1963
11–204 (8–104 & 3–100)	A. L. Valentine	v Eng	Old Trafford	1950
11–229 (5–137 & 6–92)	W. Ferguson	v Eng	Port of Spain	1947–48

New Zealand

11–58 (4–35 & 7–23)	R. J. Hadlee	v Ind	Wellington	1975–76

India

14–124 (9–69 & 5–55)	J. M. Patel	v Aus	Kanpur	1959–60
13–131 (8–52 & 5–79)	V. M. Mankad	v Pak	New Delhi	1952–53
12–104 (6–52 & 6–52)	B. S. Chandrasekhar	v Aus	Melbourne	1977–78
12–108 (8–55 & 4–53)	V. M. Mankad	v Eng	Madras	1951–52
12–152 (8–72 & 4–80)	S. Venkataraghavan	v NZ	New Delhi	1964–65
11–122 (5–31 & 6–91)	R. G. Nadkarni	v Aus	Madras	1964–65
11–140 (3–64 & 8–76)	E. A. S. Prasanna	v NZ	Auckland	1975–76
11–235 (7–157 & 4–78)	B. S. Chandrasekhar	v WI	Bombay	1966–67

Pakistan

13–114 (6–34 & 7–80)	Fazal Mahmood	v Aus	Karachi	1956–57
12–94 (5–52 & 7–42)	Fazal Mahmood	v Ind	Lucknow	1952–53
12–99 (6–53 & 6–46)	Fazal Mahmood	v Eng	The Oval	1954
12–100 (6–34 & 6–66)	Fazal Mahmood	v WI	Dacca	1958–59
12–165 (6–102 & 6–63)	Imran Khan	v Aus	Sydney	1976–77
11–79 (5–37 & 6–42)	Zulfiqar Ahmed	v NZ	Karachi	1955–56
11–130 (7–52 & 4–78)	Intikhab Alam	v NZ	Dunedin	1972–73

Best innings bowling performance for each Test match centre

In England

Lord's	8–34	I. T. Botham	Eng v Pak	1978
The Oval	0–29	S. F. Barnes	Eng v SA	1912
Trent Bridge	8–107	B. T. J. Bosanquet	Eng v Aus	1905
Old Trafford	10–53	J. C. Laker	Eng v Aus	1956
Headingley	8–59	C. Blythe	Eng v SA	1907
Edgbaston	7–17	W. Rhodes	Eng v Aus	1902
Sheffield	6–49	S. F. Barnes	Eng v Aus	1902

In Australia

Sydney	8–35	G. A. Lohmann	Eng v Aus	1886–87
Melbourne	9–121	A. A. Mailey	Aus v Eng	1920–21
Adelaide	8–43	A. E. Trott	Aus v Eng	1894–95
Brisbane	7–60	K. R. Miller	Aus v Eng	1946–47
Perth	7–54	A. M. E. Roberts	WI v Aus	1975–76

In South Africa

Cape Town	8–11	J. Briggs	Eng v SA	1888–89
Durban	8–69	H. J. Tayfield	SA v Eng	1956–57
Johannesburg	9–28	G. A. Lohmann	Eng v SA	1895–96
Port Elizabeth	8–7	G. A. Lohmann	Eng v SA	1895–96

In West Indies

Bridgetown	8–38	L. R. Gibbs	WI v Ind	1961–62
Georgetown	7–44	I. W. Johnson	Aus v WI	1954–55
Kingston	7–34	T. E. Bailey	Eng v WI	1953–54
Port of Spain	9–95	J. Noreiga	WI v Ind	1970–71

In New Zealand

Auckland	8–76	E. A. S. Prasanna	Ind v NZ	1975–76
Christchurch	7–75	F. S. Trueman	Eng v NZ	1962–63
Dunedin	7–52	Intikhab Alam	Pak v NZ	1972–73
Wellington	7–23	R. J. Hadlee	NZ v Ind	1975–76

In India

Bombay	7–98	L. R. Gibbs	WI v Ind	1974–75
Calcutta	7–49	Ghulam Ahmed	Ind v Aus	1956–57
Hyderabad	7–128	S. P. Gupte	Ind v NZ	1955–56
Lucknow	7–42	Fazal Mahmood	Pak v Ind	1952–53
Kanpur	9–69	J. M. Patel	Ind v Aus	1959–60
Madras	8–55	V. M. Mankad	Ind v Eng	1951–52
New Delhi	8–52	V. M. Mankad	Ind v Pak	1952–53
Nagpur	6–74	S. Venkataraghavan	Ind v NZ	1969–70
Bangalore	6–53	R. G. D. Willis	Eng v Ind	1976–77

In Pakistan

Bahawalpur	6–74	P. R. Umrigar	Ind v Pak	1954–55
Dacca	6–21	Khan Mohammad	Pak v NZ	1955–56
Hyderabad	6–44	Abdul Qadir	Pak v Eng	1977–78
Karachi	7–66	P. H. Edmonds	Eng v Pak	1977–78
Lahore	7–74	Pervez Sajjad	Pak v NZ	1969–70
Peshawar	5–63	S. P Gupte	Ind v Pak	1954–55
Rawalpindi	4–5	Pervez Sajjad	Pak v NZ	1964–65

Outstanding bowling analyses

In a Test innings

O	M	R	W				
51·2	23	53	10	J. C. Laker	Eng v Aus	Old Trafford	1956
14·2	6	28	9	G. A. Lohmann	Eng v SA	Johannesburg	1895–96
16·4	4	37	9	J. C. Laker	Eng v Aus	Old Trafford	1956
9·4	5	7	8	G. A. Lohmann	Eng v SA	Port Elizabeth	1895–96
14·2	5	11	8	J. Briggs	Eng v SA	Cape Town	1888–89
19·1	11	17	7	J. Briggs	Eng v SA	Cape Town	1888–89
7·4	2	17	7	M. A. Noble	Aus v Eng	Melbourne	1901–02
11	3	17	7	W. Rhodes	Eng v Aus	Edgbaston	1902
6·3	4	7	6	A. E. R. Gilligan	Eng v SA	Edgbaston	1924
11·4	6	11	6	S. Haigh	Eng v SA	Cape Town	1898–99
12	7	12	6	D. L. Underwood	Eng v NZ	Christchurch	1970–71
14	7	13	6	H. J. Tayfield	SA v NZ	Johannesburg	1953–54
18	11	15	6	C. T. B. Turner	Aus v Eng	Sydney	1886–87
16	8	15	6	M. H. N. Walker	Aus v Pak	Sydney	1972–73
11	4	17	6	G. A. Faulkner	SA v Eng	Headingley	1907
16	7	17	6	W. J. Whitty	Aus v SA	Melbourne	1910–11
2·3	1	2	5	E. R. H. Toshack	Aus v Ind	Brisbane	1947–48
7·2	5	6	5	H. Ironmonger	Aus v SA	Melbourne	1931–32
15·1	7	14	5	T. W. Wall	Aus v SA	Brisbane	1931–32
12	5	14	5	W. J. O'Reilly	Aus v NZ	Wellington	1945–46
15	8	15	5	D. K. Lillee	Aus v Eng	Edgbaston	1975
10·4	4	15	5	D. R. Parry	WI v Aus	Port of Spain	1977–78
12	8	5	4	Pervez Sajjad	Pak v NZ	Rawalpindi	1964–65
9	7	5	4	K. Higgs	Eng v NZ	Christchurch	1965–66
8	6	6	4	P. H. Edmonds	Eng v Pak	Lord's	1978
6·3	2	7	4	J. C. White	Eng v Aus	Brisbane	1928–29
5	2	7	4	J. H. Wardle	Eng v Aus	Old Trafford	1953
6	3	7	4	R. Appleyard	Eng v NZ	Auckland	1954–55
8	4	8	4	A. J. L. Hill	Eng v SA	Cape Town	1895–96
10	6	9	4	M. G. Melle	SA v Eng	The Oval	1951
3·4	3	0	3	R. Benaud	Aus v Ind	New Delhi	1959–60
5	2	3	3	V. Pollard	NZ v Eng	Auckland	1965–66
13	10	4	3	R. E. S. Wyatt	Eng v SA	Durban	1927–28
7	5	4	3	Nasim-ul-Ghani	Pak v WI	Dacca	1958–59
3·1	1	4	3	K. F. Barrington	Eng v SA	Cape Town	1964–65

In a Test match

19–90 (9–37 & 10–53)	J. C. Laker	Eng v Aus	Old Trafford	1956
15–28 (7–17 & 8–11)	J. Briggs	Eng v SA	Cape Town	1888–89
15–45 (7–38 & 8–7)	G. A. Lohmann	Eng v SA	Port Elizabeth	1895–96
13–57 (5–29 & 8–28)	S. F. Barnes	Eng v SA	The Oval	1912

11–24 (5–6 & 5–18)	H. Ironmonger	Aus v SA	Melbourne	1931–32
11–31 (5–2 & 6–29)	E. R. H. Toshack	Aus v Ind	Brisbane	1947–48
11–48 (5–28 & 6–20)	G. A. R. Lock	Eng v WI	The Oval	1957
10–49 (5–29 & 5–20)	F. E. Woolley	Eng v Aus	The Oval	1912

Hat–tricks in Test Cricket

(Final innings analysis in brackets)

F. R. Spofforth	(6–48)	Aus v Eng	Melbourne	1878–79
W. Bates	(7–28)	Eng v Aus	Melbourne	1882–83
J. Briggs	(4–69)	Eng v Aus	Sydney	1891–92
G. A. Lohmann	(8–7)	Eng v SA	Port Elizabeth	1895–96
J. T. Hearne	(4–50)	Eng v Aus	Headingley	1899
H. Trumble	(4–49)	Aus v Eng	Melbourne	1901–02
H. Trumble	(7–28)	Aus v Eng	Melbourne	1903–04
T. J. Matthews	(3–16)	Aus v SA	Old Trafford	1912
T. J. Matthews	(3–38)	Aus v SA	Old Trafford	1912
M. J. C. Allom	(5–38)	Eng v NZ	Christchurch	1929–30
T. W. J. Goddard	(3–54)	Eng v SA	Johannesburg	1938–39
P. J. Loader	(6–36)	Eng v WI	Headingley	1957
L. F. Kline	(3–18)	Aus v SA	Cape Town	1957–58
W. W. Hall	(5–87)	WI v Pak	Lahore	1958–59
G. M. Griffin	(4–87)	SA v Eng	Lord's	1960
L. R. Gibbs	(5–97)	WI v Aus	Adelaide	1960–61
P. J. Petherick	(3–105)	NZ v Pak	Lahore	1976–77

Notes:

T. J. Matthews is the only bowler to achieve the hat-trick in each innings of a Test. He also performed both hat-tricks on the same day.

   M. J. C. Allom and P. J. Petherick are the only bowlers to do the hat-trick in their first Test match.

   J. Briggs and L. F. Kline are the only left arm bowlers to perform a Test hat-trick.

   Both of T. J. Matthews' hat-tricks were accomplished without the aid of another fielder: for the first he clean bowled R. Beaumont and had S. J. Pegler and T. A. Ward lbw and the second he bowled H. W. Taylor and had R. O. Schwarz and Ward caught and bowled.

   G. M. Griffin and H. Trumble both did the hat-trick in their last Test matches.

Four wickets in five balls

M. J. C. Allom	(5–38)	Eng v NZ	Christchurch	1929–30
C. M. Old	(7–50)	Eng v Pak	Edgbaston	1978

Three wickets with four consecutive balls

F. R. Spofforth	(7–44)	Aus v Eng	The Oval	1882
F. R. Spofforth	(4–54)	Aus v Eng	Sydney	1884–85
J. Briggs	(7–17)	Eng v SA	Cape Town	1888–89
W. P. Howell	(4–18)	Aus v SA	Cape Town	1902–03
E. P. Nupen	(6–46)	SA v Eng	Johannesburg	1930–31
W. J. O'Reilly	(7–189)	Aus v Eng	Old Trafford	1934
W. Voce	(4–10)	Eng v Aus	Sydney	1936–37
R. R. Lindwall	(4–52)	Aus v Eng	Adelaide	1946–47
K. Cranston	(4–12)	Eng v SA	Headingley	1947
R. Appleyard	(1–7)	Eng v NZ	Auckland	1954–55
R. Benaud	(4–15)	Aus v WI	Georgetown	1954–55
Fazal Mahmood	(7–80)	Pak v Aus	Karachi	1956–57
J. W. Martin	(3–56)	Aus v WI	Melbourne	1960–61
L. R. Gibbs	(3–46)	WI v Aus	Sydney	1960–61
K. D. Mackay	(4–57)	Aus v Eng	Edgbaston	1961
W. W. Hall	(3–11)	WI v Ind	Port of Spain	1961–62
G. D. McKenzie	(5–33)	Aus v WI	Port of Spain	1964–65
F. J. Titmus	(5–19)	Eng v NZ	Headingley	1965
G. S. Sobers	(5–41)	WI v Eng	Headingley	1966

P. Lever	(3–10)	Eng v Pak	Headingley	1971
D. K. Lillee	(6–66)	Aus v Eng	Old Trafford	1972
D. K. Lillee	(5–58)	Aus v Eng	The Oval	1972
C. M. Old	(7–50)	Eng v Pak	Edgbaston	1978

Notes:
K. Cranston, F. J. Titmus and C. M. Old all took four wickets in one over without achieving a hat-trick.

Old's performance did not include the hat-trick due to a no-ball, his sequence being w w nb w w l.

Successful bowling on debut in Test Cricket

A wicket with first ball

A. Coningham (dismissing A. C. MacLaren)	Aus v Eng	Melbourne	1894–95
E. G. Arnold (dismissing V. T. Trumper)	Eng v Aus	Sydney	1903–04
G. G. Macaulay (dismissing G. A. L. Hearne)	Eng v SA	Cape Town	1922–23
M. W. Tate (dismissing M. J. Susskind)	Eng v SA	Edgbaston	1924
H. D. Smith (dismissing E. Paynter)	NZ v Eng	Christchurch	1932–33
T. F. Johnson (dismissing W. W. Keeton)	WI v Eng	The Oval	1939
R. Howorth (dismissing D. V. Dyer)	Eng v SA	The Oval	1947
Intikhab Alam (dismissing C. C. McDonald)	Pak v Aus	Karachi	1959–60

Six or more wickets in an innings

7–55	T. Kendall	Aus v Eng	Melbourne	1876–77
6–120	W. H. Cooper	Aus v Eng	Melbourne	1881–82
6–15	C. T. B. Turner	Aus v Eng	Sydney	1886–87
7–95	W. H. Ashley	SA v Eng	Cape Town	1888–89
6–50 & 6–52	F. Martin	Eng v Aus	The Oval	1890
6–101	W. H. Lockwood	Eng v Aus	Lord's	1893
8–43	A. E. Trott	Aus v Eng	Adelaide	1894–95
6–49	M. A. Noble	Aus v Eng	Melbourne	1897–98
6–43	G. H. Simpson-Hayward	Eng v SA	Johannesburg	1909–10
7–63	A. E. Hall	SA v Eng	Cape Town	1922–23
6–152	G. M. Parker	SA v Eng	Edgbaston	1924
6–37	C. V. Grimmett	Aus v Eng	Sydney	1924–25
6–99	A. J. Bell	SA v Eng	Lord's	1929
7–56	James Langridge	Eng v WI	Old Trafford	1933
6–59	C. S. Marriott	Eng v WI	The Oval	1933
6–102	F. A. Ward	Aus v Eng	Brisbane	1936–37
7–49	A. V. Bedser	Eng v Ind	Lord's	1946
7–103	J. C. Laker	Eng v WI	Bridgetown	1947–48
6–43	C. N. McCarthy	SA v Eng	Durban	1948–49
6–118	T. E. Bailey	Eng v NZ	Headingley	1949
8–104	A. L. Valentine	WI v Eng	Old Trafford	1950
6–155	A. M. Moir	NZ v Eng	Christchurch	1950–51
6–38	P. M. Pollock	SA v NZ	Durban	1961–62
6–128	S. F. Burke	SA v NZ	Cape Town	1961–62
6–85	L. J. Coldwell	Eng v Pak	Lord's	1962
6–89	Arif Butt	Pak v Aus	Melbourne	1964–65
6–55	S. Abid Ali	Ind v Aus	Adelaide	1967–68
7–99	Mohammad Nazir	Pak v NZ	Karachi	1969–70
8–84 & 8–53	R. A. L. Massie	Aus v Eng	Lord's	1972
7–46	J. K. Lever	Eng v Ind	New Delhi	1976–77

Ten or more wickets in a match

16–137	R. A. L. Massie	Aus v Eng	Lord's	1972
12–102	F. Martin	Eng v Aus	The Oval	1890
11–82	C. V. Grimmett	Aus v Eng	Sydney	1924–25
11–96	C. S. Marriott	Eng v WI	The Oval	1933
11–112	A. E. Hall	SA v Eng	Cape Town	1922–23
11–145	A. V. Bedser	Eng v Ind	Lord's	1946
11–196	S. F. Burke	SA v NZ	Cape Town	1961–62
11–204	A. L. Valentine	WI v Eng	Old Trafford	1950
10–70	J. K. Lever	Eng v Ind	New Delhi	1976–77

10–96	H. H. H. Johnson	WI v Eng	Kingston	1947–48
10–156	T. Richardson	Eng v Aus	Old Trafford	1893
10–179	K. Farnes	Eng v Aus	Trent Bridge	1934

Hat-trick

| M. J. C. Allom | | Eng v NZ | Christchurch | 1929–30 |

(Allom took 4 wickets in 5 balls, his 8th over in Test Cricket reading .W.WWW)

| P. J. Petherick | | NZ v Pak | Lahore | 1976–77 |

Economical bowling

N. B. F. Mann (South Africa) began his Test career with eight successive maiden overs and conceded only 10 runs in 20 overs, with 13 maidens, v England at Trent Bridge, 1947.

25 wickets in a Test rubber

England			M	Overs	Mdns	Runs	Wkts	Avge	5wI	10wM
S. F. Barnes	v SA	1913–14	4	226	56	536	49	10·93	7	3
J. C. Laker	v Aus	1956	5	283·5	127	442	46	9·60	4	2
A. V. Bedser	v Aus	1953	5	265·1	58	682	39	17·48	5	1
M. W. Tate	v Aus	1924–25	5	*316	62	881	38	23·18	5	1
G. A. Lohmann	v SA	1895–96	3	†104	38	203	35	5·80	4	2
S. F. Barnes	v Aus	1911–12	5	297	64	778	34	22·88	3	–
S. F. Barnes	v SA	1912	3	128	38	282	34	8·29	5	3
G. A. R. Lock	v NZ	1958	5	176	93	254	34	7·47	3	1
F. S. Trueman	v WI	1963	5	236·4	53	594	34	17·47	4	2
H. Larwood	v Aus	1932–33	5	220·2	42	644	33	19·51	2	1
T. Richardson	v Aus	1894–95	5	291·1	63	849	32	26·53	4	–
F. R. Foster	v Aus	1911–12	5	276·4	58	692	32	21·62	3	–
W. Rhodes	v Aus	1903–04	5	172	36	488	31	15·74	3	1
A. S. Kennedy	v SA	1922–23	5	280·3	91	599	31	19·32	2	–
J. A. Snow	v Aus	1970–71	6	*225·5	47	708	31	22·83	2	–
J. N. Crawford	v Aus	1907–08	5	237·4	36	742	30	24·73	3	–
A. V. Bedser	v Aus	1950–51	5	*195	34	482	30	16·06	2	1
A. V. Bedser	v SA	1951	5	275·5	84	517	30	17·23	3	1
F. S. Trueman	v Ind	1952	4	119·4	25	386	29	13·31	2	–
D. L. Underwood	v Ind	1976–77	5	252·5	95	509	29	17·55	1	–
F. H. Tyson	v Aus	1954–55	5	*151	16	583	28	20·82	2	1
R. Peel	v Aus	1894–95	5	305·1	77	721	27	26·70	1	–
M. W. Tate	v SA	1924	5	221·2	68	424	27	15·70	1	–
J. B. Statham	v SA	1960	5	203	54	491	27	18·18	2	1
F. J. Titmus	v Ind	1963–64	5	398·5	156	747	27	27·66	2	–
J. A. Snow	v WI	1967–68	4	165	29	504	27	18·66	3	1
R. G. D. Willis	v Aus	1977	5	166·4	36	534	27	19·77	3	–
W. S. Lees	v SA	1905–06	5	209·2	69	467	26	17·96	2	–
C. Blythe	v SA	1907	3	100·3	26	270	26	10·38	3	1
W. Voce	v Aus	1936–37	5	*162·1	20	560	26	21·53	1	1
J. H. Wardle	v SA	1956–57	4	*139·6	37	359	26	13·80	3	1
J. K. Lever	v Ind	1976–77	5	149·4	29	380	26	14·61	2	1
A. Fielder	v Aus	1907–08	4	216·3	31	627	25	25·08	1	–
J. C. White	v Aus	1928–29	5	406·4	134	760	25	30·40	3	1
F. S. Trueman	v SA	1960	5	180·3	31	508	25	20·32	1	–
Australia										
C. V. Grimmett	v SA	1935–36	5	346·1	140	642	44	14·59	5	3
W. J. Whitty	v SA	1910–11	5	232·3	55	632	37	17·08	2	–
A. A. Mailey	v Eng	1920–21	5	244·1	27	946	36	26·27	4	2
G. Giffen	v Eng	1894–95	5	343·2	111	820	34	24·11	3	–
C. V. Grimmett	v WI	1930–31	5	238·5	60	593	33	17·96	2	1
C. V. Grimmett	v SA	1931–32	5	306	108	557	33	16·87	3	1
A. K. Davidson	v WI	1960–61	4	*173·7	25	612	33	18·54	5	1
J. R. Thomson	v Eng	1974–75	5	*175·1	34	592	33	17·93	2	–
M. A. Noble	v Eng	1901–02	5	230	68	608	32	19·00	4	1
H. V. Hordern	v Eng	1911–12	5	277·3	43	780	32	24·37	4	2
J. V. Saunders	v Eng	1907–08	5	267·1	52	716	31	23·09	3	–
H. Ironmonger	v SA	1931–32	4	221·5	112	296	31	9·54	3	1

			M	Overs	Mdns	Runs	Wkts	Avge	5wI	10wM
R. Benaud	v Eng	1958–59	5	*233·2	65	584	31	18·83	2	–
D. K. Lillee	v Eng	1972	5	249·5	83	548	31	17·67	3	1
R. Benaud	v SA	1957–58	5	*242·1	56	658	30	21·93	4	–
G. D. McKenzie	v WI	1968–69	5	*206·1	27	758	30	25·26	1	1
C. V. Grimmett	v Eng	1930	5	349·4	78	925	29	31·89	4	1
A. K. Davidson	v Ind	1959–60	5	244·5	85	431	29	14·86	2	1
R. Benaud	v Ind	1959–60	5	322·2	146	568	29	19·58	2	–
G. D. McKenzie	v Eng	1964	5	256	61	654	29	22·55	2	–
J. R. Thomson	v WI	1975–76	6	*150·5	15	831	29	28·65	2	–
H. Trumble	v Eng	1901–02	5	267·2	93	561	28	20·03	2	–
W. J. O'Reilly	v Eng	1934	5	333·4	128	698	28	24·92	2	1
A. A. Mallett	v Ind	1969–70	5	298·4	129	535	28	19·10	3	1
W. M. Clark	v Ind	1977–78	5	*198·1	27	701	28	25·03	–	–
E. A. McDonald	v Eng	1921	5	205·5	32	668	27	24·74	2	–
W. J. O'Reilly	v Eng	1932–33	5	383·4	144	724	27	26·81	2	1
W. J. O'Reilly	v SA	1935–36	5	250·2	112	460	27	17·03	2	–
R. R. Lindwall	v Eng	1948	5	222·5	57	530	27	19·62	2	–
W. A. Johnston	v Eng	1948	5	309·2	91	630	27	23·33	1	–
D. K. Lillee	v WI	1975–76	5	*129·3	7	712	27	26·37	1	–
E. Jones	v Eng	1899	5	†255·1	73	657	26	25·26	2	1
H. Trumble	v Eng	1902	3	172·4	55	371	26	14·26	2	2
R. R. Lindwall	v Eng	1953	5	240·4	62	490	26	18·84	3	–
J. W. Gleeson	v WI	1968–69	5	*250·6	57	844	26	32·46	2	–
M. H. N. Walker	v WI	1972–73	5	271·1	83	539	26	20·73	3	–
C. V. Grimmett	v Eng	1934	5	396·3	148	668	25	26·72	2	–
W. J. O'Reilly	v Eng	1936–37	5	*247·6	89	555	25	22·20	2	–
A. K. Davidson	v SA	1957–58	5	*201·5	47	425	25	17·00	2	–
D. K. Lillee	v Eng	1974–75	6	*182·6	36	596	25	23·84	–	–

South Africa

H. J. Tayfield	v Eng	1956–57	5	*285	105	636	37	17·18	4	1
A. E. E. Vogler	v Eng	1909–10	5	224·5	33	783	36	21·75	4	1
H. J. Tayfield	v Aus	1952–53	5	*278·4	58	843	30	28·10	2	1
G. A. Faulkner	v Eng	1909–10	5	209·1	45	635	29	21·89	2	–
G. B. Lawrence	v NZ	1961–62	5	222·2	62	512	28	18·28	1	–
A. E. Hall	v Eng	1922–23	4	250·5	82	501	27	18·55	2	1
H. J. Tayfield	v Eng	1955	5	313·3	124	568	26	21·84	3	–
N. A. T. Adcock	v Eng	1960	5	263	69	587	26	22·57	2	–
T. L. Goddard	v Aus	1966–67	5	255·3	101	422	26	16·23	1	–
M. J. Procter	v Aus	1969–70	4	143	50	353	26	13·57	1	–
C. B. Llewellyn	v Aus	1902–03	3	132·4	23	448	25	17·92	4	1
R. O. Schwarz	v Aus	1910–11	5	167·4	19	651	25	26·04	2	–
J. M. Blanckenberg	v Eng	1922–23	5	251·4	60	613	25	24·52	2	–
G. F. Bissett	v Eng	1927–28	4	164·5	28	469	25	18·76	2	–
T. L. Goddard	v Eng	1955	5	315·4	148	528	25	21·12	2	–
J. T. Partridge	v Aus	1963–64	5	*247·4	33	833	25	33·32	2	–
P. M. Pollock	v Aus	1963–64	5	*159·3	11	710	25	28·40	2	–

West Indies

A. L. Valentine	v Eng	1950	4	422·3	197	674	33	20·42	2	2
C. E. H. Croft	v Pak	1976–77	5	217·5	45	676	33	20·48	1	–
C. C. Griffith	v Eng	1963	5	223·5	54	519	32	16·21	3	–
A. M. E. Roberts	v Ind	1974–75	5	208·4	53	585	32	18·28	3	1
W. W. Hall	v Ind	1958–59	5	221·4	65	530	30	17·66	2	1
A. L. Valentine	v Ind	1952–53	5	430	179	828	28	29·57	2	–
M. A. Holding	v Eng	1976	4	159·3	54	356	28	12·71	3	1
A. M. E. Roberts	v Eng	1976	5	221·4	69	537	28	19·17	3	1
W. W. Hall	v Ind	1961–62	5	167·4	37	425	27	15·74	2	–
S. Ramadhin	v Eng	1950	4	377·5	170	604	26	23·23	3	1
R. Gilchrist	v Ind	1958–59	4	198·1	73	419	26	16·11	1	–
L. R. Gibbs	v Eng	1963	5	249·3	74	554	26	21·30	2	–
L. R. Gibbs	v Aus	1972–73	5	325	108	696	26	26·76	1	–
J. Garner	v Pak	1976–77	5	219·3	41	688	25	27·52	–	–

New Zealand			M	Overs	Mdns	Runs	Wkts	Avge	5wI	10wM
B. R. Taylor	v WI	1971–72	4	172·2	39	478	27	17·70	2	–
India										
B. S. Chandrasekhar	v Eng	1972–73	5	291·1	83	662	35	18·91	4	–
V. M. Mankad	v Eng	1951–52	5	370·4	151	571	34	16·79	1	1
S. P. Gupte	v NZ	1955–56	5	356·4	152	669	34	19·67	4	–
B. S. Bedi	v Aus	1977–78	5	*219·7	39	740	31	23·87	3	1
B. S. Chandrasekhar	v Aus	1977–78	5	*197·3	25	704	28	25·14	3	1
S. P. Gupte	v WI	1952–53	5	329·3	87	789	27	29·22	3	–
E. A. S. Prasanna	v Aus	1969–70	5	295	107	672	26	25·84	3	1
V. M. Mankad	v Pak	1952–53	4	265·2	100	514	25	20·56	3	1
E. A. S. Prasanna	v Aus	1967–68	4	*197·5	34	686	25	27·44	2	–
B. S. Bedi	v Eng	1972–73	5	372·5	134	632	25	25·28	1	–
B. S. Bedi	v Eng	1976–77	5	298	106	574	25	22·96	2	–
Pakistan										
Imran Khan	v WI	1976–77	5	236·1	52	790	25	31·60	1	–

*8-ball overs   †5-ball overs

Most wickets in Tests (150 or over)

		Wkts	M	Avge	v Eng	v Aus	v SA	v WI	v NZ	v Ind	v Pak
L. R. Gibbs	(WI)	309	79	29·09	100	103	–	–	11	63	22
F. S. Trueman	(Eng)	307	67	21·57	–	79	27	86	40	53	22
D. L. Underwood	(Eng)	265	74	24·90	–	92	–	37	48	52	36
J. B. Statham	(Eng)	252	70	24·84	–	69	69	42	20	25	27
R. Benaud	(Aus)	248	63	27·03	83	–	52	42	–	52	19
G. D. McKenzie	(Aus)	246	60	29·78	96	–	41	47	–	47	15
B. S. Bedi	(Ind)	246	58	26·89	78	56	–	55	57	–	–
A. V. Bedser	(Eng)	236	51	24·89	–	104	54	11	13	44	10
G. S. Sobers	(WI)	235	93	34·03	102	51	–	–	19	59	4
R. R. Lindwall	(Aus)	228	61	23·03	114	–	31	41	2	36	4
B. S. Chandrasekhar	(Ind)	222	50	28·24	95	38	–	53	36	–	–
C. V. Grimmett	(Aus)	216	37	24·21	106	–	77	33	–	–	–
J. A. Snow	(Eng)	202	49	26·66	–	83	4	72	20	16	7
J. C. Laker	(Eng)	193	46	21·24	–	79	32	51	21	8	2
W. W. Hall	(WI)	192	48	26·38	65	45	–	–	1	65	16
S. F. Barnes	(Eng)	189	27	16·43	–	106	83	–	–	–	–
E. A. S. Prasanna	(Ind)	187	47	29·36	41	57	–	34	55	–	–
A. K. Davidson	(Aus)	186	44	20·53	84	–	25	33	–	30	14
G. A. R. Lock	(Eng)	174	49	25·58	–	31	15	39	47	26	16
D. K. Lillee	(Aus)	171	32	23·49	96	–	–	27	15	–	33
K. R. Miller	(Aus)	170	55	22·97	87	–	30	40	2	9	2
H. J. Tayfield	(SA)	170	37	25·91	75	64	–	–	31	–	–
V. M. Mankad	(Ind)	162	44	32·32	54	23	–	36	12	–	37
W. A. Johnston	(Aus)	160	40	23·91	75	–	44	25	–	16	–
S. Ramadhin	(WI)	158	43	28·98	80	22	–	–	32	15	9
M. W. Tate	(Eng)	155	39	26·16	–	83	53	13	6	–	–
F. J. Titmus	(Eng)	153	53	32·22	–	47	27	15	28	27	9
R. G. D. Willis	(Eng)	151	41	24·19	–	58	–	18	28	25	22

Note: The most wickets for the other countries is as follows:

R. O. Collinge	(NZ)	116	35	29·25	48	17	–	–	–	23	28
Fazal Mahmood	(Pak)	139	34	24·70	25	24	–	41	5	44	–

Best bowling averages
(Qualification: 25 wickets)

		M	Balls	Mdns	Runs	Wkts	Avge
G. A. Lohmann	(Eng)	18	3821	364	1205	112	10·75
J. J. Ferris	(Aus & Eng)	9	2302	251	775	61	12·70
A. E. Trott	(Aus & Eng)	5	948	54	390	26	15·00
M. J. Procter	(SA)	7	1514	80	616	41	15·02

		M	Balls	Mdns	Runs	Wkts	Avge
W. Barnes	(Eng)	21	2285	271	793	51	15·54
W. Bates	(Eng)	15	2364	282	821	50	16·42
S. F. Barnes	(Eng)	27	7873	356	3106	189	16·43
C. T. B. Turner	(Aus)	17	5195	457	1670	101	16·53
I. T. Botham	(Eng)	11	2554	94	1059	64	16·54
R. Peel	(Eng)	20	5216	444	1715	102	16·81
J. Briggs	(Eng)	33	5332	389	2094	118	17·74
R. Appleyard	(Eng)	9	1596	70	554	31	17·87
W. S. Lees	(Eng)	5	1256	69	467	26	17·96
H. Ironmonger	(Aus)	14	4695	328	1330	74	17·97

Most frequent wicket-takers
(Qualification: 25 wickets)

		Balls per wkt	M	Balls	Wkts	Avge
G. A. Lohmann	(Eng)	34·11	18	3821	112	10·75
A. E. Trott	(Aus & Eng)	36·46	5	948	26	15·00
M. J. Procter	(SA)	36·92	7	1514	41	15·02
J. J. Ferris	(Aus & Eng)	37·73	9	2302	61	12·70
C. E. H. Croft	(WI)	39·00	7	1638	42	20·14
G. F. Bissett	(SA)	39·56	4	989	25	18·76
B. J. T. Bosanquet	(Eng)	39·56	7	989	25	24·16
I. T. Botham	(Eng)	39·90	11	2554	64	16·54
S. F. Barnes	(Eng)	41·65	27	7873	189	16·43
E. A. Martindale	(WI)	43·37	10	1605	37	21·72

Most wickets per Test
(Qualification: 50 wickets)

		Wkts	Tests	Av per Test
S. F. Barnes	(Eng)	189	27	7·00
J. J. Ferris	(Aus & Eng)	61	9	6·77
T. Richardson	(Eng)	88	14	6·28
G. A. Lohmann	(Eng)	112	18	6·22
C. T. B. Turner	(Aus)	101	17	5·94
I. T. Botham	(Eng)	64	11	5·81
J. V. Saunders	(Aus)	79	14	5·64
A. P. Freeman	(Eng)	66	12	5·50
D. K. Lillee	(Aus)	171	32	5·34
W. J. O'Reilly	(Aus)	144	27	5·33
H. Ironmonger	(Aus)	74	14	5·28
C. Blythe	(Eng)	100	19	5·26
F. R. Spofforth	(Aus)	94	18	5·22
R. Peel	(Eng)	102	20	5·10

Most economical bowlers
(Fewest runs conceded per 100 balls. Qualification: 2000 balls)

		Runs/100 b	M	Balls	Mdns	Runs	Wkts	Avge
W. Attewell	(Eng)	21·96	10	2850	326	626	27	23·18
C. Gladwin	(Eng)	26·82	8	2129	89	571	15	38·06
T. L. Goddard	(SA)	27·49	41	11735	706	3226	123	26·22
R. G. Nadkarni	(Ind)	27·88	41	9175	666	2558	88	29·06
H. Ironmonger	(Aus)	28·32	14	4695	328	1330	74	17·97
J. C. Watkins	(SA)	29·09	15	2805	134	816	29	28·13
K. D. Mackay	(Aus)	29·71	37	5792	267	1721	50	34·42
A. R. A. Murray	(SA)	29·90	10	2374	111	710	18	39·44
P. H. Edmonds	(Eng)	29·90	13	3013	138	901	43	20·95
G. E. Gomez	(WI)	30·36	29	5236	288	1590	58	27·41
R. Kilner	(Eng)	30·99	9	2368	79	734	24	30·58
P. R. Umrigar	(Ind)	31·13	59	4737	258	1475	35	42·14
R. G. Barlow	(Eng)	31·22	17	2456	315	767	35	21·91
E. R. H. Toshack	(Aus)	31·47	12	3142	155	989	47	21·04

		Runs/100 b	M	Balls	Mdns	Runs	Wkts	Avge
H. Verity	(Eng)	31·49	40	11173	604	3510	144	24·37
J. H. Wardle	(Eng)	31·52	28	6597	404	2080	102	20·39
G. A. Lohmann	(Eng)	31·53	18	3821	364	1205	112	10·75
D. S. Atkinson	(WI)	31·66	22	5201	312	1647	47	35·04
R. Illingworth	(Eng)	31·90	61	11934	715	3807	122	31·20
J. A. Young	(Eng)	31·96	8	2368	119	757	17	44·52

Most wickets by one bowler in a day

15	(for 28)	J. Briggs	Eng v SA	Cape Town	1888–89
14	(for 80)	H. Verity	Eng v Aus	Lord's	1934

Bowlers unchanged in a completed innings

England

		Total		
F. Morley (2–34) & R. G. Barlow (7–40)	v Aus	83	Sydney	1882–83
G. A. Lohmann (7–36) & J. Briggs (3–28)	v Aus	68	The Oval	1886
G. A. Lohmann (5–17) & R. Peel (5–18)	v Aus	42	Sydney	1887–88
J. Briggs (8–11) & A. J. Fothergill (1–30)	v SA	43	Cape Town	1888–89
J. J. Ferris (7–37) & F. Martin (2–39)	v SA	83	Cape Town	1891–92
J. Briggs (6–49) & G. A. Lohmann (3–46)	v Aus	100	Adelaide	1891–92
T. Richardson (6–39) & G. A. Lohmann (3–13)	v Aus	53	Lord's	1896
S. Haigh (6–11) & A. E. Trott (4–19)	v SA	35	Cape Town	1898–99
S. F. Barnes (6–42) & C. Blythe (4–64)	v Aus	112	Melbourne	1901–02
G. H. Hirst (4–28) & C. Blythe (6–44)	v Aus	74	Edgbaston	1909
F. R. Foster (5–16) & S. F. Barnes (5–25)	v SA	58	Lord's	1912
A. E. R. Gilligan (6–7) & M. W. Tate (4–12)	v SA	30	Edgbaston	1924
G. O. B. Allen (5–36) & W. Voce (4–16)	v Aus	58	Brisbane	1936–37

Australia

G. E. Palmer (7–68) & E. Evans (3–64)	v Eng	133	Sydney	1881–82
F. R. Spofforth (5–30) & G. E. Palmer (4–32)	v Eng	77	Sydney	1884–85
C. T. B. Turner (6–15) & J. J. Ferris (4–27)	v Eng	45	Sydney	1886–87
C. T. B. Turner (5–36) & J. J. Ferris (5–26)	v Eng	62	Lord's	1888
G. Giffen (5–26) & C. T. B. Turner (4–33)	v Eng	72	Sydney	1894–95
H. Trumble (3–38) & M. A. Noble (7–17)	v Eng	61	Melbourne	1901–02
M. A. Noble (5–54) & J. V. Saunders (5–43)	v Eng	99	Sydney	1901–02

Pakistan

Fazal Mahmood (6–34) & Khan Mohammad (4–43) v Aus		80	Karachi	1956–57

Note: The above feat has now become extremely rare in Test cricket though in India's total of 42 v England at Lord's in 1974 two bowlers (G. G. Arnold and C. M. Old) bowled all but one over.

Only four bowlers in a long innings (300 or over)
(Bowling side given first)

Total				
349	Eng v Aus	The Oval	1893	
403–8 dec	Aus v Eng	The Oval	1921	
421–8	SA v Eng	The Oval	1924	
342–8 dec	Aus v Eng	Brisbane	1928–29	
372	NZ v Eng	Headingley	1949	
482	NZ v Eng	The Oval	1949	
426	Eng v Aus	Sydney	1950–51	(2 bowlers injured)
318	Eng v Aus	Old Trafford	1953	
325 / 312	Pak v WI	Port of Spain	1957–58	
361	Ind v Eng	The Oval	1959	
371	NZ v SA	Auckland	1963–64	
307–3 dec	Eng v SA	Johannesburg	1964–65	
315	Aus v Eng	Lord's	1975	
357	Aus v NZ	Christchurch	1976–77	
301–9 dec	WI v Pak	Port of Spain	1976–77	

Eleven bowlers in an innings

England v Australia   (551)   The Oval   1884

Most players bowling in a match

20   SA v Eng   Cape Town   1964–65
(Every player bowled except the two wicket-keepers, J. M. Parks and D. T. Lindsay).

Expensive bowling in Test cricket

Most runs conceded in an innings

O	M	R	W				
87	11	298	1	L. O'B. Fleetwood-Smith	Aus v Eng	The Oval	1938
80·2	13	266	5	O. C. Scott	WI v Eng	Kingston	1929–30
54	5	259	0	Khan Mohammad	Pak v WI	Kingston	1957–58
85·2	20	247	2	Fazal Mahmood	Pak v WI	Kingston	1957–58
82	17	228	5	V. M. Mankad	Ind v WI	Kingston	1952–53
64·2	8	226	6	B. S. Bedi	Ind v Eng	Lord's	1974
71	8	204	6	I. A. R. Peebles	Eng v Aus	The Oval	1930
75	16	202	3	V. M. Mankad	Ind v WI	Bombay	1948–49
84	19	202	6	Haseeb Ahsan	Pak v Ind	Madras	1960–61

In a match

O	M	R	W				
105·2	13	374	9	O. C. Scott	WI v Eng	Kingston	1929–30
63	2	308	7	A. A. Mailey	Aus v Eng	Sydney	1924–25
61·3	6	302	10	A. A. Mailey	Aus v Eng	Adelaide	1920–21
84·1	11	298	9	C. V. Grimmett	Aus v Eng	Brisbane	1928–29
87	11	298	1	L. O'B. Fleetwood-Smith	Aus v Eng	The Oval	1938
94·2	19	290	9	R. O. Jenkins	Eng v WI	Lord's	1950

In a series

O	M	R	W	Avge			
398·2	96	1024	23	44·52	C. V. Grimmett	Aus v Eng	1928–29
244	20	999	24	41·62	A. A. Mailey	Aus v Eng	1924–25
240·2	23	990	23	43·04	D. V. P. Wright	Eng v Aus	1946–47

Most balls delivered by one bowler

In an innings

O	M	R	W	Balls			
98	35	179	2	588	S. Ramadhin	WI v Eng	Edgbaston	1957
95·1	36	155	3	571	T. R. Veivers	Aus v Eng	Old Trafford	1964
92	49	140	3	552	A. L. Valentine	WI v Eng	Trent Bridge	1950
87	11	298	1	522	L. O'B. Fleetwood-Smith	Aus v Eng	The Oval	1938
85·2	20	247	2	512	Fazal Mahmood	Pak v WI	Kingston	1957–58
85	26	178	3	510	W. J. O'Reilly	Aus v Eng	The Oval	1938
84	19	202	6	504	Haseeb Ahsan	Pak v Ind	Madras	1960–61

In a match

O	M	R	W	Balls			
129	51	228	9	774	S. Ramadhin	WI v Eng	Edgbaston	1957
95·6	23	184	4	766	H. Verity	Eng v SA	Durban	1938–39
124·5	37	256	13	749	J. C. White	Eng v Aus	Adelaide	1928–29
92·2	17	256	1	738	N. Gordon	SA v Eng	Durban	1938–39
91	24	203	4	728	A. B. C. Langton	SA v Eng	Durban	1938–39
89	19	228	11	712	M. W. Tate	Eng v Aus	Sydney	1924–25
118	42	239	8	708	G. Giffen	Aus v Eng	Sydney	1894–95

In a series

O	M	R	W	Balls			
430	179	828	28	2580	A. L. Valentine	WI v Ind	1952–53
422·3	197	674	33	2535	A. L. Valentine	WI v Eng	1950
316	62	881	38	2528	M. W. Tate	Eng v Aus	1924–25
406·4	134	760	25	2440	J. C. White	Eng v Aus	1928–29
398·5	156	747	27	2393	F. J. Titmus	Eng v Ind	1963–64
398·2	96	1024	23	2390	C. V. Grimmett	Aus v Eng	1928–29
396·3	148	668	25	2379	C. V. Grimmett	Aus v Eng	1934

O	M	R	W	Balls			
292·2	52	923	24	2338	L. R. Gibbs	WI v Aus	1968–69
383·4	144	724	27	2302	W. J. O'Reilly	Aus v Eng	1932–33

Wicket-keeping Records

Most dismissals in a Test career

(75 or over)

		M	Total	Ct	St	Avge per Test
A. P. E. Knott	(Eng)	89	252	233	19	2·83
T. G. Evans	(Eng)	91	219	173	46	2·40
R. W. Marsh	(Aus)	52	198	190	8	3·80
A. T. W. Grout	(Aus)	51	187	163	24	3·66
D. L. Murray	(WI)	51	158	150	8	3·09
J. H. B. Waite	(SA)	50	141	124	17	2·82
W. A. S. Oldfield	(Aus)	54	130	78	52	2·40
J. M. Parks	(Eng)	46	114	103	11	2·47
Wasim Bari	(Pak)	42	109	94	15	2·59
G. R. A. Langley	(Aus)	26	98	83	15	3·76
L. E. G. Ames	(Eng)	47	97	74	23	2·06
K. J. Wadsworth	(NZ)	33	96	92	4	2·90
Imtiaz Ahmed	(Pak)	41	93	77	16	2·26
A. F. A. Lilley	(Eng)	35	92	70	22	2·62
F. C. M. Alexander	(WI)	25	90	85	5	3·60
F. M. Engineer	(Ind)	46	82	66	16	1·78

Note: The above totals include catches taken when not keeping wicket by the following players: J. M. Parks 2, L. E. G. Ames 2, Imtiaz Ahmed 3, F. C. M. Alexander 3.

Most dismissals in a Test innings

	Total	Ct	St			
A. T. W. Grout	6	6	–	Aus v SA	Johannesburg	1957–58
D. T. Lindsay	6	6	–	SA v Aus	Johannesburg	1966–67
J. T. Murray	6	6	–	Eng v Ind	Lord's	1967
S. M. H. Kirmani	6	5	1	Ind v NZ	Christchurch	1975–76
W. A. S. Oldfield	5	1	4	Aus v Eng	Melbourne	1924–25
G. R. A. Langley	5	2	3	Aus v WI	Georgetown	1954–55
G. R. A. Langley	5	5	–	Aus v WI	Kingston	1954–55
G. R. A. Langley	5	5	–	Aus v Eng	Lord's	1956
A. T. W. Grout	5	4	1	Aus v SA	Durban	1957–58
A. T. W. Grout	5	5	–	Aus v Pak	Lahore	1959–60
Imtiaz Ahmed	5	4	1	Pak v Aus	Lahore	1959–60
F. C. M. Alexander	5	5	–	WI v Eng	Bridgetown	1959–60
A. T. W. Grout	5	4	1	Aus v WI	Brisbane	1960–61
A. T. W. Grout	5	5	–	Aus v Eng	Lord's	1961
B. K. Kunderan	5	3	2	Ind v Eng	Bombay	1961–62
J. G. Binks	5	5	–	Eng v Ind	Calcutta	1963–64
B. N. Jarman	5	4	1	Aus v Pak	Melbourne	1964–65
A. T. W. Grout	5	5	–	Aus v Eng	Sydney	1965–66
J. M. Parks	5	3	2	Eng v Aus	Sydney	1965–66
J. M. Parks	5	5	–	Eng v NZ	Christchurch	1965–66
H. B. Taber	5	5	–	Aus v SA	Johannesburg	1966–67
R. I. Harford	5	5	–	NZ v Ind	Wellington	1967–68
H. B. Taber	5	5	–	Aus v WI	Sydney	1968–69
H. B. Taber	5	5	–	Aus v SA	Port Elizabeth	1969–70
Wasim Bari	5	5	–	Pak v Eng	Headingley	1971
R. W. Marsh	5	5	–	Aus v Eng	Old Trafford	1972
R. W. Marsh	5	5	–	Aus v Eng	Trent Bridge	1972
K. J. Wadsworth	5	5	–	NZ v Pak	Auckland	1972–73
R. W. Marsh	5	5	–	Aus v NZ	Sydney	1973–74
R. W. Marsh	5	5	–	Aus v NZ	Christchurch	1973–74

	Total	Ct	St			
A. P. E. Knott	5	4	1	Eng v Ind	Old Trafford	1974
R. W. Marsh	5	5	–	Aus v WI	Melbourne	1975–76
D. L. Murray	5	5	–	WI v Eng	Headingley	1976
R. W. Marsh	5	5	–	Aus v NZ	Christchurch	1976–77
D. L. Murray	5	5	–	WI v Pak	Georgetown	1976–77
R. W. Taylor	5	5	–	Eng v NZ	Trent Bridge	1978

Most dismissals in a Test match

	Total	Ct	St			
G. R. A. Langley	9	8	1	Aus v Eng	Lord's	1956
J. J. Kelly	8	8	–	Aus v Eng	Sydney	1901–02
L. E. G. Ames	8	6	2	Eng v WI	The Oval	1933
G. R. A. Langley	8	8	–	Aus v WI	Kingston	1954–55
A. T. W. Grout	8	6	2	Aus v Pak	Lahore	1959–60
A. T. W. Grout	8	8	–	Aus v Eng	Lord's	1961
J. M. Parks	8	8	–	Eng v NZ	Christchurch	1965–66
D. T. Lindsay	8	8	–	SA v Aus	Johannesburg	1966–67
H. B. Taber	8	7	1	Aus v SA	Johannesburg	1966–67
Wasim Bari	8	8	–	Pak v Eng	Headingley	1971
R. W. Marsh	8	8	–	Aus v WI	Melbourne	1975–76
R. W. Marsh	8	8	–	Aus v NZ	Christchurch	1976–77

Most dismissals in a Test series

	Total	Ct	St	Tests			
J. H. B. Waite	26	23	3	5	SA v NZ		1961–62
R. W. Marsh	26	26	–	6	Aus v WI		1975–76
D. L. Murray	24	22	2	5	WI v Eng		1963
D. T. Lindsay	24	24	–	5	SA v Aus		1966–67
A. P. E. Knott	24	21	3	6	Eng v Aus		1970–71
J. H. B. Waite	23	16	7	5	SA v NZ		1953–54
F. C. M. Alexander	23	22	1	5	WI v Eng		1959–60
A. T. W. Grout	23	20	3	5	Aus v WI		1960–61
A. E. Dick	23	21	2	5	NZ v SA		1961–62
R. W. Marsh	23	21	2	5	Aus v Eng		1972
A. P. E. Knott	23	22	1	6	Eng v Aus		1974–75
S. J. Rixon	22	22	–	5	Aus v Ind		1977–78
H. Strudwick	21	15	6	5	Eng v SA		1913–14
R. A. Saggers	21	13	8	5	Aus v SA		1949–50
G. R. A. Langley	21	16	5	5	Aus v WI		1951–52
A. T. W. Grout	21	20	1	5	Aus v Eng		1961
D. Tallon	20	16	4	5	Aus v Eng		1946–47
G. R. A. Langley	20	16	4	4	Aus v WI		1954–55
T. G. Evans	20	18	2	5	Eng v SA		1956–57
A. T. W. Grout	20	17	3	5	Aus v Eng		1958–59
H. B. Taber	20	19	1	5	Aus v SA		1966–67

No byes conceded in large total (500 or over)

551	J. J. Kelly	Aus v Eng	Sydney	1897–98
521	W. A. S. Oldfield	Aus v Eng	Brisbane	1928–29
559–9 dec	W. W. Wade	SA v Eng	Cape Town	1938–39
659–8 dec	T. G. Evans	Eng v Aus	Sydney	1946–47
520	J. H. B. Waite	SA v Aus	Melbourne	1952–53
544–5 dec	Imtiaz Ahmed	Pak v Eng	Edgbaston	1962
531	D. T. Lindsay	SA v Eng	Johannesburg	1964–65
526–7 dec	A. P. E. Knott	Eng v WI	Port of Spain	1967–68
510	J. L. Hendriks	WI v Aus	Melbourne	1968–69
619	J. L. Hendriks	WI v Aus	Sydney	1968–69
543–3 dec	T. M. Findlay	WI v NZ	Georgetown	1971–72
507–6 dec	K. J. Wadsworth	NZ v Pak	Dunedin	1972–73
551–9 dec	A. P. E. Knott	Eng v NZ	Lord's	1973
532–9 dec	A. P. E. Knott	Eng v Aus	The Oval	1975

Most byes conceded in a Test innings
38   J. M. Parks   Eng v WI (391–9 dec)   Kingston   1967–68

Players deputising for wicket-keeper
There have been several instances of players deputising successfully for an injured wicket-keeper in Test cricket:

    Hanif Mohammad (Pak) took 4 catches in an innings and 5 in the match v Australia at Melbourne, 1964–65.

    Majid J. Khan (Pak) also took 4 catches in an innings deputising as wicket-keeper v West Indies at Kingston, 1976–77. The regular 'keeper, Wasim Bari, later returned to take three catches himself, making this the only innings in Test cricket where seven batsmen have been caught by the wicket-keeper.

    L. Amarnath held 5 catches (3 in the first innings and 2 in the second) as deputy wicket-keeper v West Indies at Bombay, 1948–49.

All-Rounders' Records

A century and 5 wickets in a match

J. H. Sinclair	106	& 6–26	SA v Eng	Cape Town	1898–99
G. A. Faulkner	123	& 5–120	SA v Eng	Johannesburg	1909–10
C. Kelleway	114	& 5 33	Aus v SA	Old Trafford	1912
J. M. Gregory	100	& 7–69	Aus v Eng	Melbourne	1920–21
V. M. Mankad	184	& 5–196	Ind v Eng	Lord's	1952
D. S. Atkinson	219	& 5–56	WI v Aus	Bridgetown	1954–55
K. R. Miller	109	& 6–107	Aus v WI	Kingston	1954–55
R. Benaud	100	& 5–84	Aus v SA	Johannesburg	1957–58
O. G. Smith	100	& 5–90	WI v Ind	New Delhi	1958–59
P. R. Umrigar	172*	& 5–107	Ind v WI	Port of Spain	1961–62
G. S. Sobers	104	& 5–63	WI v Ind	Kingston	1961–62
B. R. Taylor (debut)	105	& 5–86	NZ v Ind	Calcutta	1964–65
G. S. Sobers	174	& 5–41	WI v Eng	Headingley	1966
Mushtaq Mohammad	201	& 5–49	Pak v NZ	Dunedin	1972–73
A. W. Greig	148	& 6–164	Eng v WI	Bridgetown	1973–74
Mushtaq Mohammad	121	& 5–28	Pak v WI	Port of Spain	1976–77
I. T. Botham	103	& 5 73	Eng v NZ	Christchurch	1977–78
I. T. Botham	108	& 8–34	Eng v Pak	Lord's	1978

100 runs and 10 wickets in the same Test

A. K. Davidson	44	5–135	Aus v WI	Brisbane	1960–61
	80	6–87			

100 runs and 8 wickets in a match

G. Giffen	161	4–75	Aus v Eng	Sydney	1894–95
	41	4–164			
A. E. Trott (debut)	38*	0–9	Aus v Eng	Adelaide	1894–95
	72*	8–43			
J. H. Sinclair	106	6–26	SA v Eng	Cape Town	1898–99
	4	3–63			
G. A. Faulkner	78	5–120	SA v Eng	Johannesburg	1909–10
	123	3–40			
J. M. Gregory	100	7–69	Aus v Eng	Melbourne	1920–21
		1–32			
H. Larwood	70	6–32	Eng v Aus	Brisbane	1928–29
	37	2–30			
G. O. B. Allen	35	3–71	Eng v Aus	Brisbane	1936–37
	68	5–36			
W. J. Edrich	191	4–95	Eng v SA	Old Trafford	1947
	22*	4–77			
K. R. Miller	109	6–107	Aus v WI	Kingston	1954–55
		2–58			
R. Benaud	100	4–70	Aus v SA	Johannesburg	1957–58
		5–84			
O. G. Smith	100	3–94	WI v Ind	New Delhi	1958–59
		5–90			

G. S. Sobers	174	5–41		WI v Eng	Headingley	1966
		3–39				
Mushtaq Mohammad	121	5–28		Pak v WI	Port of Spain	1976–77
	56	3–69				
I. T. Botham	103	5–73		Eng v NZ	Christchurch	1977–78
	30*	3–38				
I. T. Botham	108	0–17		Eng v Pak	Lord's	1978
		8–34				

A half-century and 10 wickets in a match

W. Bates	55 & 14–102	Eng v Aus	Melbourne	1882–83
H. Trumble	64* & 12–173	Aus v Eng	The Oval	1902
F. E. Woolley	62 & 10–49	Eng v Aus	The Oval	1912
A. K. Davidson	80 & 11–222	Aus v WI	Brisbane	1960–61
K. D. Boyce	72 & 11–147	WI v Eng	The Oval	1973
A. W. Greig	51 & 10–149	Eng v NZ	Auckland	1974–75
J. K. Lever	53 & 10–70	Eng v Ind	New Delhi	1976–77

Wicket-keepers: a half-century and 8 dismissals in a match

D. T. Lindsay	69 & 182	8 ct	SA v Aus	Johannesburg	1966–67
Wasim Bari	63 & 10	8 ct	Pak v Eng	Headingley	1971
R. W. Marsh	56	8 ct	Aus v WI	Melbourne	1975–76

Best all-round records in a Test rubber

300 runs & 30 wickets

	Runs	HS	Avge	100	50	Wkts	Avge	5wI		
G. Giffen	475	161	52·77	1	3	34	24·11	3	Aus v Eng	1894–95
R. Benaud	329	122	54·83	2	–	30	21·93	4	Aus v SA	1957–58

300 runs & 20 wickets

	Runs	HS	Avge	100	50	Wkts	Avge	5wI		
G. A. Faulkner	545	123	60·55	1	3	29	21·89	2	SA v Eng	1909–10
J. M. Gregory	442	100	73·66	1	4	23	24·17	1	Aus v Eng	1920–21
K. R. Miller	362	129	40·22	1	1	20	19·90	2	Aus v WI	1951–52
K. R. Miller	439	147	73·16	3	–	20	32·00	1	Aus v WI	1954–55
G. S. Sobers	424	153	70·66	2	1	23	20·56	1	WI v Ind	1961–62
G. S. Sobers	322	102	40·25	1	2	20	28·55	1	WI v Eng	1963
G. S. Sobers	722	174	103·14	3	2	20	27·25	1	WI v Eng	1966
A. W. Greig	430	148	47·77	2	–	24	22·63	3	Eng v WI	1973–74

200 runs & 30 wickets

	Runs	HS	Avge	100	50	Wkts	Avge	5wI		
F. R. Foster	226	71	32·28	–	3	32	21·62	3	Eng v Aus	1911–12
V. M. Mankad	223	71*	31·85	–	2	34	16·79	1	Ind v Eng	1951–52
A. K. Davidson	212	80	30·28	–	1	33	18·54	5	Aus v WI	1960–61

200 runs & 20 wickets

	Runs	HS	Avge	100	50	Wkts	Avge	5wI		
L. C. Braund	256	103	36·57	1	1	21	35·14	2	Eng v Aus	1901–02
G. J. Thompson	267	63	33·37	–	2	23	26·91	–	Eng v SA	1909–10
J. M. Gregory	224	45	24·88	–	–	22	37·09	1	Aus v Eng	1924–25
R. R. Lindwall	211	61	26·37	–	1	21	23·04	1	Aus v WI	1951–52
T. L. Goddard	235	74	23·50	–	2	25	21·12	2	SA v Eng	1955
K. R. Miller	203	61	22·55	–	1	21	22·23	2	Aus v Eng	1956
T. L. Goddard	294	74	32·66	–	2	26	16·23	1	SA v Aus	1966–67
M. J. Procter	209	48	34·83	–	–	26	13·57	1	SA v Aus	1969–70
M. H. N. Walker	221	41*	44·20	–	–	23	29·73	1	Aus v Eng	1974–75
Imran Khan	215	47	21·50	–	–	25	31·60	1	Pak v WI	1976–77

Wicket-keepers: 200 runs & 20 dismissals

	Runs	HS	Avge	100	50	Ct	St	Total		
J. H. B. Waite	263	101	29·22	1	1	23	3	26	SA v NZ	1961–62
D. T. Lindsay	606	182	86·57	3	2	24	–	24	SA v Aus	1966–67
A. P. E. Knott	222	73	31·71	–	1	21	3	24	Eng v Aus	1970–71
R. W. Marsh	242	91	34·57	–	2	21	2	23	Aus v Eng	1972
A. P. E. Knott	364	106*	36·40	1	3	22	1	23	Eng v Aus	1974–75
R. W. Marsh	236	56	29·50	–	1	26	–	26	Aus v WI	1975–76

Best all-round records in a Test career

1000 runs & 100 wickets

		M	Runs	HS	Avge	100	Wkts	Avge	No of Tests to Double
T. E. Bailey	(Eng)	61	2290	134*	29·74	1	132	29·21	47
R. Benaud	(Aus)	63	2201	122	24·45	3	248	27·03	32
A. K. Davidson	(Aus)	44	1328	80	24·59	–	186	20·53	34
G. Giffen	(Aus)	31	1238	161	23·35	1	103	27·09	30
T. L. Goddard	(SA)	41	2516	112	34·46	1	123	26·22	36
A. W. Greig	(Eng)	58	3599	148	40·43	8	141	32·20	37
R. Illingworth	Eng)	61	1836	113	23·24	2	122	31·20	47
Intikhab Alam	(Pak)	47	1493	138	22·28	1	125	35·95	41
I. W. Johnson	(Aus)	45	1000	77	18·51	–	109	29·19	45
R. R. Lindwall	(Aus)	61	1502	118	21·15	2	228	23·03	38
V. M. Mankad	(Ind)	44	2109	231	31·47	5	162	32·32	23
K. R. Miller	(Aus)	55	2958	147	36·97	7	170	22·97	33
M. A. Noble	(Aus)	42	1997	133	30·25	1	121	25·00	27
W. Rhodes	(Eng)	58	2325	179	30·19	2	127	26·96	44
G. S. Sobers	(WI)	93	8032	365*	57·78	26	235	34·03	48
M. W. Tate	(Eng)	39	1198	100*	25·48	1	155	26·16	33
F. J. Titmus	(Eng)	53	1449	84*	22·29	–	153	32·22	40

Wicket-keepers: 1000 runs & 100 dismissals

		M	Runs	HS	Avge	100	Ct	St	Total	No of Tests to Double
T. G. Evans	(Eng)	91	2439	104	20·49	2	173	46	219	42
A. P. E. Knott	(Eng)	89	4175	135	33·66	5	233	19	252	90
R. W. Marsh	(Aus)	52	2396	132	32·82	3	190	8	198	25
D. L. Murray	(WI)	51	1705	91	23·68	–	150	8	158	33
J. M. Parks	(Eng)	46	1962	108*	32·16	2	103	11	114	41
W. A. S. Oldfield	(Aus)	54	1427	65*	22·65	–	78	52	130	41
J. H. B. Waite	(SA)	50	2405	134	30·44	4	124	17	141	36

1000 runs, 50 wickets & 50 catches

		M	Runs	HS	Avge	100	Wkts	Avge	Ct
R. Benaud	(Aus)	63	2201	122	24·45	3	248	27·03	65
A. W. Greig	(Eng)	58	3599	148	40·43	8	141	32·20	87
W. R. Hammond	(Eng)	85	7249	336*	58·45	22	83	37·83	110
W. Rhodes	(Eng)	58	2325	179	30·19	2	127	26·96	60
R. B. Simpson	(Aus)	62	4869	311	46·81	10	71	42·26	110
G. S. Sobers	(WI)	93	8032	365*	57·78	26	235	34·03	109
F. E. Woolley	(Eng)	64	3283	154	36·07	5	83	33·91	64

Fielding Statistics

Most catches in an innings

5	V. Y. Richardson	Aus v SA	Durban	1935–36
5	Yajurvindra Singh	Ind v Eng	Bangalore	1976–77

Notes:
Yajurvindra Singh achieved the above feat in his first Test match and Richardson in his last.

Instances of four catches in an innings by a fieldsman are too numerous to include but G. S. Sobers (WI) achieved the feat on three occasions. L. C. Braund (Eng), R. B. Simpson (Aus) and A. L. Wadekar (Ind) did it twice.

Most catches in a match

7	G. S. Chappell	Aus v Eng	Perth	1974–75
7	Yajurvindra Singh	Ind v Eng	Bangalore	1976–77
6	A. Shrewsbury	Eng v Aus	Sydney	1887–88

6	A. E. E. Vogler	SA v Eng	Durban	1909–10
6	F. E. Woolley	Eng v Aus	Sydney	1911–12
6	J. M. Gregory	Aus v Eng	Sydney	1920–21
6	B. Mitchell	SA v Aus	Melbourne	1931–32
6	V. Y. Richardson	Aus v SA	Durban	1935–36
6	R. N. Harvey	Aus v Eng	Sydney	1962–63
6	M. C. Cowdrey	Eng v WI	Lord's	1963
6	E. D. Solkar	Ind v WI	Port of Spain	1970–71
6	G. S. Sobers	WI v Eng	Lord's	1973
6	I. M. Chappell	Aus v NZ	Adelaide	1973–74
6	A. W. Greig	Eng v Pak	Headingley	1974

Most catches in a series

15	J. M. Gregory	Aus v Eng	1920–21	
14	G. S. Chappell	Aus v Eng	1974–75	(6 Tests)
13	R. B. Simpson	Aus v SA	1957–58	
13	R. B. Simpson	Aus v WI	1960–61	
12	L. C. Braund	Eng v Aus	1901–02	
12	A. E. E. Vogler	SA v Eng	1909–10	
12	B. Mitchell	SA v Eng	1930–31	
12	W. R. Hammond	Eng v Aus	1934	
12	J. T. Ikin	Eng v SA	1951	(3 Tests)
12	T. L. Goddard	SA v Eng	1956–57	
12	G. S. Sobers	WI v Aus	1960–61	
12	E. D. Solkar	Ind v Eng	1972–73	
12	A. W. Greig	Eng v Aus	1974–75	(6 Tests)

Most catches in a career

		Ct	Tests	Avge per Test
M. C. Cowdrey	(Eng)	120	114	1·05
R. B. Simpson	(Aus)	110	62	1·77
W. R. Hammond	(Eng)	110	85	1·29
G. S. Sobers	(WI)	109	93	1·17
I. M. Chappell	(Aus)	103	72	1·43
A. W. Greig	(Eng)	87	58	1·50
I. R. Redpath	(Aus)	83	66	1·25
T. W. Graveney	(Eng)	80	79	1·01
G. S. Chappell	(Aus)	73	51	1·43
R. Benaud	(Aus)	65	63	1·03
F. S. Trueman	(Eng)	64	67	0·95
F. E. Woolley	(Eng)	64	64	1·00
R. N. Harvey	(Aus)	64	79	0·81
R. C. Fredericks	(WI)	62	59	1·05
W. Rhodes	(Eng)	60	58	1·03
G. A. R. Lock	(Eng)	59	49	1·20
K. F. Barrington	(Eng)	58	82	0·70
L. Hutton	(Eng)	57	79	0·72
B. Mitchell	(SA)	56	42	1·33
M. J. K. Smith	(Eng)	53	50	1·06
E. D. Solkar	(Ind)	53	27	1·96
L. R. Gibbs	(WI)	52	79	0·65
R. B. Kanhai	(WI)	50	79	0·63

Notes: Most catches for the other countries are as follows:

New Zealand: B. E. Congdon   Ct 44 in 61 Tests   (Avge 0·72)

Pakistan: Majid Khan   Ct 47 in 37 Tests   (Avge 1·27)

Of the above, R. B. Kanhai took 9 of his catches while keeping wicket, Majid J. Khan 4, J. R. Reid 3 and F. E. Woolley and K. F. Barrington 1 each.

C. L. Walcott (West Indies) took 54 catches in his 44 Tests but exactly half his catches were taken as a wicket-keeper.

Partnership Records

Number of century partnerships for each country

	v Eng	v Aus	v SA	v WI	v NZ	v Ind	v Pak	Total
England	–	213	88	74	56	56	36	523
Australia	192	–	59	53	9	34	15	362
South Africa	75	43	–	–	16	–	–	134
West Indies	82	45	–	–	14	53	17	211
New Zealand	22	6	6	9	–	18	11	72
India	33	24	–	34	22	–	8	121
Pakistan	22	10	–	20	14	8	–	74
TOTALS	426	341	153	190	131	169	87	1497

Number of century partnerships for each wicket

	1st	2nd	3rd	4th	5th	6th	7th	8th	9th	10th	Total
England	103	103	86	79	55	57	22	9	7	2	523
Australia	49	83	69	65	44	20	14	11	5	2	362
South Africa	28	19	26	22	11	10	11	5	1	1	134
West Indies	27	34	40	41	27	28	11	1	2	–	211
New Zealand	14	8	12	12	12	5	5	3	–	1	72
India	15	21	26	21	14	13	5	2	3	1	121
Pakistan	12	13	14	13	7	8	3	1	1	2	74
TOTALS	248	281	273	253	170	141	71	32	19	9	1497

Note:
Partnerships involving three batsmen are included where 100 runs or more were added for each wicket.

Players sharing in most century partnerships

		Total	1st	2nd	3rd	4th	5th	6th	7th	8th	9th	10th
G. S. Sobers	WI	43	–	3	4	12	12	10	2	–	–	–
M. C. Cowdrey	Eng	41	5	8	6	13	4	3	1	–	1	–
L. Hutton	Eng	41	17	13	7	1	–	2	1	–	–	–
D. G. Bradman	Aus	36	–	15	11	3	6	1	–	–	–	–
K. F. Barrington	Eng	35	–	6	10	14	4	1	–	–	–	–
R. B. Kanhai	WI	34	2	9	11	7	3	2	–	–	–	–
G. Boycott	Eng	34	16	7	4	5	–	2	–	–	–	–
W. R. Hammond	Eng	33	1	6	12	11	2	1	–	–	–	–
R. N. Harvey	Aus	33	–	7	13	9	3	1	–	–	–	–
J. H. Edrich	Eng	32	9	10	7	5	1	–	–	–	–	–
J. B. Hobbs	Eng	32	24	6	1	–	–	–	1	–	–	–
H. Sutcliffe	Eng	32	21	10	1	–	–	1	–	–	–	–
D. C. S. Compton	Eng	30	–	–	14	7	7	1	–	1	–	–
I. M. Chappell	Aus	29	–	17	8	1	1	2	–	–	–	–
T. W. Graveney	Eng	26	–	7	6	7	4	1	–	1	–	–
G. S. Chappell	Aus	25	–	2	9	7	5	2	–	–	–	–
W. M. Lawry	Aus	25	12	6	4	2	1	–	–	–	–	–

Notes:
The most for the other countries is:

South Africa	24	B. Mitchell
New Zealand	13	G. M. Turner
India	16	C. G. Borde
Pakistan	18	Mushtaq Mohammad

Progressive wicket partnerships for each country

England
1st wkt

122 – R. G. Barlow (62) & G. Ulyett (67) v Aus	Sydney	1881–82
170 – W. G. Grace (170) & W. H. Scotton (34) v Aus	The Oval	1886
185 – F. S. Jackson (118) & T. Hayward (137) v Aus	The Oval	1899
221 – J. B. Hobbs (187) & W. Rhodes (77) v SA	Cape Town	1909–10

323 – J. B. Hobbs (178) & W. Rhodes (179) v Aus	Melbourne	1911–12
359 – L. Hutton (158) & C. Washbrook (195) v SA	Johannesburg	1948–49

2nd wkt

120 – W. G. Grace (152) & A. P. Lucas (55) v Aus	The Oval	1880
137 – G. Ulyett (87) & J. Selby (55) v Aus	Melbourne	1881–82
152 – A. Shrewsbury (81) & W. Gunn (77) v Aus	Lord's	1893
230 – H. Sutcliffe (102) & E. Tyldesley (122) v SA	Johannesburg	1927–28
382 – L. Hutton (364) & M. Leyland (187) v Aus	The Oval	1938

3rd wkt

175 – W. H. Scotton (82) & W. Barnes (134) v Aus	Adelaide	1884–85
210 – A. Ward (93) & J. T. Brown (140) v Aus	Melbourne	1894–95
262 – W. R. Hammond (177) & D. R. Jardine (98) v Aus	Adelaide	1928–29
264 – L. Hutton (165*) & W. R. Hammond (138) v WI	The Oval	1939
370 – W. J. Edrich (189) & D. C. S. Compton (208) v SA	Lord's	1947

4th wkt

122 – T. W. Hayward (122) & A. J. L. Hill (65) v SA	Johannesburg	1895–96
151 – C. B. Fry (144) & F. S. Jackson (76) v Aus	The Oval	1905
237 – E. H. Hendren (205*) & L. E. G. Ames (105) v WI	Port of Spain	1929–30
249 – A. Sandham (325) & L. E. G. Ames (149) v WI	Kingston	1929–30
266 – W. R. Hammond (217) & T. S. Worthington (128) v Ind	The Oval	1936
411 – P. B. H. May (285*) & M. C. Cowdrey (154) v WI	Edgbaston	1957

5th wkt

161 – A. Shrewsbury (164) & W. Barnes (58) v Aus	Lord's	1886
162 – A. C. MacLaren (120) & R. Peel (73) v Aus	Melbourne	1894–95
192 – R. E. Foster (287) & L. C. Braund (102) v Aus	Sydney	1903–04
242 – W. R. Hammond (227) & L. E. G. Ames (103) v NZ	Christchurch	1932–33
254 – K. W. R. Fletcher (113) & A. W. Greig (148) v Ind	Bombay	1972–73

6th wkt

115 – W. W. Read (66) & E. F. S. Tylecote (66) v Aus	Sydney	1882–83
131 – W. W. Read (52) & F. S. Jackson (103) v Aus	The Oval	1893
141 – F. S. Jackson (128) & L. C. Braund (65) v Aus	Old Trafford	1902
158 – J. T. Tyldesley (112*) & R. H. Spooner (79) v Aus	The Oval	1905
170 – H. Sutcliffe (161) & R. E. S. Wyatt (64) v Aus	The Oval	1930
186 – W. R. Hammond (240) & L. E. G. Ames (83) v Aus	Lord's	1938
215 – L. Hutton (364) & J. Hardstaff jr (169*) v Aus	The Oval	1938
240 – P. H. Parfitt (131*) & B. R. Knight (125) v NZ	Auckland	1962–63

7th wkt

102 – W. Flowers (56) & J. M. Read (56) v Aus	Sydney	1884–85
113 – T. W. Hayward (130) & A. F. A. Lilley (58) v Aus	Old Trafford	1899
124 – A. F. A. Lilley (84) & L. C. Braund (58) v Aus	Sydney	1901–02
142 – J. Sharp (105) & K. L. Hutchings (59) v Aus	The Oval	1909
143 – F. E. Woolley (133*) & J. Vine (36) v Aus	Sydney	1911–12
174 – M. C. Cowdrey (152) & T. G. Evans (82) v WI	Lord's	1957
197 – M. J. K. Smith (96) & J. M. Parks (101*) v WI	Port of Spain	1959–60

8th wkt

90 – W. W. Read (94) & J. Briggs (53) v Aus	The Oval	1886
154 – C. W. Wright (71) & H. R. Bromley-Davenport (84) v SA	Johannesburg	1895–96
246 – L. E. G. Ames (137) & G. O. B. Allen (122) v NZ	Lord's	1931

9th wkt

151 – W. H. Scotton (90) & W. W. Read (117) v Aus	The Oval	1884
163*– M. C. Cowdrey (128*) & A. C. Smith (69*) v NZ	Wellington	1962–63

10th wkt

98 – J. Briggs (121) & J. Hunter (39*) v Aus	Melbourne	1884–85
130 – R. E. Foster (287) & W. Rhodes (40*) v Aus	Sydney	1903–04

Australia
1st wkt

110 – A. C. Bannerman (37) & W. L. Murdoch (85) v Eng	Melbourne	1881–82
116 – C. E. McLeod (77) & J. Worrall (75) v Eng	The Oval	1899

135 – V. T. Trumper (104) & R. A. Duff (54) v Eng   Old Trafford   1902
180 – W. Bardsley (130) & S. E. Gregory (74) v Eng   The Oval   1909
233 – W. A. Brown (121) & J. H. Fingleton (112) v SA   Cape Town   1935–36
382 – W. M. Lawry (210) & R. B. Simpson (201) v WI   Bridgetown   1964–65

2nd wkt
143 – P. S. McDonnell (103) & W. L. Murdoch (211) v Eng   The Oval   1884
174 – A. C. Bannerman (91) & J. J. Lyons (134) v Eng   Sydney   1891–92
224 – W. Bardsley (132) & C. Hill (191) v SA   Sydney   1910–11
235 – W. M. Woodfull (141) & C. G. Macartney (151) v Eng   Headingley   1926
274 – W. M. Woodfull (161) & D. G. Bradman (167) v SA   Melbourne   1931–32
451 – W. H. Ponsford (266) & D. G. Bradman (244) v Eng   The Oval   1934

3rd wkt
207 – W. L. Murdoch (211) & H. J. H. Scott (102) v Eng   The Oval   1884
242 – W. Bardsley (164) & C. Kelleway (102) v SA   Lord's   1912
249 – D. G. Bradman (169) & S. J. McCabe (112) v Eng   Melbourne   1936–37
276 – D. G. Bradman (187) & A. L. Hassett (128) v Eng   Brisbane   1946–47
295 – C. C. McDonald (127) & R. N. Harvey (204) v WI   Kingston   1954–55

4th wkt
191 – A. C. Bannerman (70) & P. S. McDonnell (147) v Eng   Sydney   1881–82
221 – G. H. S. Trott (143) & S. E. Gregory (103) v Eng   Lord's   1896
243 – D. G. Bradman (232) & A. Jackson (73) v Eng   The Oval   1930
388 – W. H. Ponsford (181) & D. G. Bradman (304) v Eng   Headingley   1934

5th wkt
107 – T. P. Horan (124) & G. Giffen (30) v Eng   Melbourne   1881–82
139 – G. Giffen (161) & S. E. Gregory (201) v Eng   Sydney   1894–95
142 – S. E. Gregory (70) & J. Darling (74) v Eng   Melbourne   1894–95
143 – W. W. Armstrong (132) & V. T. Trumper (87) v SA   Melbourne   1910–11
183 – D. G. Bradman (123) & A. G. Fairfax (65) v Eng   Melbourne   1928–29
405 – S. G. Barnes (234) & D. G. Bradman (234) v Eng   Sydney   1946–47

6th wkt
142 – S. E. Gregory (57) & H. Graham (107) v Eng   Lord's   1893
187 – C. Kelleway (78) & W. W. Armstrong (158) v Eng   Sydney   1920–21
346 – J. H. Fingleton (136) & D. G. Bradman (270) v Eng   Melbourne   1936–37

7th wkt
79 – T. P. Horan (124) & G. E. Palmer (34) v Eng   Melbourne   1881–82
165 – C. Hill (188) & H. Trumble (46) v Eng   Melbourne   1897–98
168 – R. W. Marsh (132) & K. J. O'Keeffe (85) v NZ   Adelaide   1973–74
217 – K. D. Walters (250) & G. J. Gilmour (101) v NZ   Christchurch   1976–77

8th wkt
73 – A. H. Jarvis (82) & J. Worrall (34) v Eng   Melbourne   1884–85
154 – G. J. Bonnor (128) & S. P. Jones (40) v Eng   Sydney   1884–85
243 – C. Hill (160) & R. J. Hartigan (116) v Eng   Adelaide   1907–08

9th wkt
52 – W. L. Murdoch (153*) & G. Alexander (33) v Eng   The Oval   1880
154 – S. E. Gregory (201) & J. M. Blackham (74) v Eng   Sydney   1894–95

10th wkt
88 – W. L. Murdoch (153*) & W. H. Moule (34) v Eng   The Oval   1880
120 – R. A. Duff (104) & W. W. Armstrong (45*) v Eng   Melbourne   1901–02
127 – J. M. Taylor (108) & A. A. Mailey (46*) v Eng   Sydney   1924–25

South Africa
1st wkt
153 – H. W. Taylor (70) & J. W. Zulch (82) v Eng   Johannesburg   1913–14
171 – B. Mitchell (61*) & R. H. Catterall (98) v Eng   Edgbaston   1929
260 – B. Mitchell (123) & I. J. Siedle (141) v Eng   Cape Town   1930–31

2nd wkt
173 – L. J. Tancred (97) & C. B. Llewellyn (90) v Aus   Johannesburg   1902–03
198 – E. A. B. Rowan (236) & C. B. van Ryneveld (83) v Eng   Headingley   1951

3rd wkt

120 – G. C. White (147) & A. W. Nourse (55) v Eng	Johannesburg	1905–06
143 – J. W. Zulch (150) & G. A. Faulkner (92) v Aus	Sydney	1910–11
319 – A. Melville (189) & A. D. Nourse (149) v Eng	Trent Bridge	1947
341 – E. J. Barlow (201) & R. G. Pollock (175) v Aus	Adelaide	1963–64

4th wkt

98 – A. W. Nourse (62) & G. A. Faulkner (44) v Eng	Lord's	1907
143 – A. W. Nourse (69) & G. C. White (118) v Eng	Durban	1909–10
206 – C. N. Frank (152) & A. W. Nourse (111) v Aus	Johannesburg	1921–22
214 – H. W. Taylor (121) & H. G. Deane (93) v Eng	The Oval	1929

5th wkt

109 – G. A. Faulkner (115) & C. B. Llewellyn (80) v Aus	Adelaide	1910–11
114 – R. H. Catterall (120) & J. M. Blanckenberg (56) v Eng	Edgbaston	1924
135 – R. H. Catterall (119) & H. B. Cameron (53) v Eng	Durban	1927–28
157 – A. J. Pithey (95) & J. H. B. Waite (64) v Eng	Johannesburg	1964–65

6th wkt

99 – G. A. Faulkner (123) & S. J. Snooke (47) v Eng	Johannesburg	1909–10
106 – A. D. Nourse (231) & F. Nicholson (29) v Aus	Johannesburg	1935–36
109 – R. A. McLean (142) & H. J. Keith (57) v Eng	Lord's	1955
171 – J. H. B. Waite (113) & P. L. Winslow (108) v Eng	Old Trafford	1955
200 – R. G. Pollock (274) & H. R. Lance (61) v Aus	Durban	1969–70

7th wkt

121 – G. C. White (81) & A. W. Nourse (93*) v Eng	Johannesburg	1905–06
123 – H. G. Deane (73) & E. P. Nupen (69) v Eng	Durban	1927–28
246 – D. J. McGlew (255*) & A. R. A. Murray (109) v NZ	Wellington	1952–53

8th wkt

124 – A. W. Nourse (72) & E. A. Halliwell (57) v Aus	Johannesburg	1902–03

9th wkt

59 – A. E. E. Vogler (65) & S. J. Pegler (11*) v Eng	Johannesburg	1909–10
63 – L. E. Tapscott (50*) & E. P. Nupen (12) v Eng	Johannesburg	1922–23
80 – S. K. Coen (41*) & C. L. Vincent (53) v Eng	Johannesburg	1927–28
137 – E. L. Dalton (117) & A. B. C. Langton (73*) v Eng	The Oval	1935

10th wkt

94 – P. W. Sherwell (30) & A. E. E. Vogler (62*) v Eng	Cape Town	1905–06
103 – H. G. Owen-Smith (129) & A. J. Bell (26) v Eng	Headingley	1929

West Indies

1st wkt

144 – C. A. Roach (209) & E. A. C. Hunte (53) v Eng	Georgetown	1929–30
173 – G. M. Carew (107) & A. G. Ganteaume (112) v Eng	Port of Spain	1947–48
239 – J. B. Stollmeyer (160) & A. F. Rae (109) v Ind	Madras	1948–49

2nd wkt

156 – C. A. Roach (77) & G. A. Headley (176) v Eng	Bridgetown	1929–30
192 – C. A. Roach (209) & G. A. Headley (114) v Eng	Georgetown	1929–30
228 – R. K. Nunes (92) & G. A. Headley (223) v Eng	Kingston	1929–30
446 – C. C. Hunte (260) & G. S. Sobers (365*) v Pak	Kingston	1957–58

3rd wkt

142 – G. A. Headley (176) & F. I. de Caires (70) v Eng	Bridgetown	1929–30
202 – G. A. Headley (270*) & J. E. D. Sealy (91) v Eng	Kingston	1934–35
338 – E. D. Weekes (206) & F. M. M. Worrell (167) v Eng	Port of Spain	1953–54

4th wkt

124 – F. I. de Caires (80) & J. E. D. Sealy (58) v Eng	Bridgetown	1929–30
267 – C. L. Walcott (152) & G. E. Gomez (101) v Ind	New Delhi	1948–49
283 – F. M. M. Worrell (261) & E. D. Weekes (129) v Eng	Trent Bridge	1950
399 – G. S. Sobers (226) & F. M. M. Worrell (197*) v Eng	Bridgetown	1959–60

5th wkt

163 – V. H. Stollmeyer (96) & K. H. Weekes (137) v Eng	The Oval	1939
170 – E. D. Weekes (194) & R. J. Christiani (74) v Ind	Bombay	1948-49

189 – F. M. M. Worrell (100) & C. L. Walcott (115) v NZ   Auckland   1951–52
219 – E. D. Weekes (207) & B. H. Pairaudeau (115) v Ind   Port of Spain   1952–53
265 – S. M. Nurse (137) & G. S. Sobers (174) v Eng   Headingley   1966

6th wkt
114 – G. C. Grant (53*) & E. L. Bartlett (84) v Aus   Adelaide   1930–31
211 – C. L. Walcott (168*) & G. E. Gomez (70) v Eng   Lord's   1950
274*– G. S. Sobers (163*) & D. A. J. Holford (105*) v Eng   Lord's   1966

7th wkt
147 – G. A. Headley (270*) & R. S. Grant (77) v Eng   Kingston   1934–35
347 – D. S. Atkinson (219) & C. C. Depeiaza (122) v Aus   Bridgetown   1954–55

8th wkt
71 – L. N. Constantine (52) & N. Betancourt (39) v Eng   Port of Spain   1929–30
87 – C. L. Walcott (45) & W. F. Ferguson (75) v Eng   Kingston   1947–48
99 – C. A. McWatt (54) & J. K. Holt (48) v Eng   Georgetown   1953–54
124 – I. V. A. Richards (192*) & K. D. Boyce (68) v Ind   New Delhi   1974–75

9th wkt
106 – R. J. Christiani (107) & D. S. Atkinson (45) v Ind   New Delhi   1948–49
122 – D. A. J. Holford (80) & J. L. Hendriks (37*) v Aus   Adelaide   1968–69

10th wkt
55 – F. M. M. Worrell (191*) & S. Ramadhin (19) v Eng   Trent Bridge   1957
98*– F. M. M. Worrell (73*) & W. W. Hall (50*) v Ind   Port of Spain   1961–62

New Zealand
1st wkt
276 – C. S. Dempster (136) & J. W. E. Mills (117) v Eng   Wellington   1929–30
387 – G. M. Turner (259) & T. W. Jarvis (182) v WI   Georgetown   1971–72

2nd wkt
99 – C. S. Dempster (120) & G. L. Weir (40) v Eng   Lord's   1931
131 – B. Sutcliffe (116) & J. R. Reid (50) v Eng   Christchurch   1950–51
155 – G. T. Dowling (143) & B. E. Congdon (58) v Ind   Dunedin   1967–68

3rd wkt
118 – C. S. Dempster (120) & M. L. Page (104) v Eng   Lord's   1931
222*– B. Sutcliffe (230*) & J. R. Reid (119*) v Ind   New Delhi   1955–56

4th wkt
142 – M. L. Page (104) & R. C. Blunt (96) v Eng   Lord's   1931
171 – B. W. Sinclair (138) & S. N. McGregor (62) v SA   Auckland   1963–64
175 – B. E. Congdon (126) & B. F. Hastings (105) v WI   Bridgetown   1971–72
229 – B. E. Congdon (132) & B. F. Hastings (101) v Aus   Wellington   1973–74

5th wkt
120 – M. P. Donnelly (64) & F. B. Smith (96) v Eng   Headingley   1949
174 – J. R. Reid (135) & J. E. F. Beck (99) v SA   Cape Town   1953–54
177 – B. E. Congdon (176) & V. Pollard (116) v Eng   Trent Bridge   1973
183 – M. G. Burgess (111) & R. W. Anderson (92) v Pak   Lahore   1976–77

6th wkt
100 – H. G. Vivian (100) & F. T. Badcock (53) v SA   Wellington   1931–32
220 – G. M. Turner (223*) & K. J. Wadsworth (78) v WI   Kingston   1971–72

7th wkt
100 – T. C. Lowry (80) & H. M. McGirr (51) v Eng   Auckland   1929–30
163 – B. Sutcliffe (151*) & B. R. Taylor (105) v Ind   Calcutta   1964–65
186 – W. K. Lees (152) & R. J. Hadlee (87) v Pak   Karachi   1976–77

8th wkt
104 – D. A. R. Moloney (64) & A. W. Roberts (66*) v Eng   Lord's   1937
136 – B. E. Congdon (166*) & R. S. Cunis (51) v WI   Port of Spain   1971–72

9th wkt
69 – C. F. W. Allcott (26) & I. B. Cromb (51*) v SA   Wellington   1931–32
96 – M. G. Burgess (119*) & R. S. Cunis (23) v Pak   Dacca   1969–70

10th wkt
57 – F. L. H. Mooney (46) & J. Cowie (26*) v Eng	Headingley	1949
63 – B. E. Congdon (57) & F. J. Cameron (10*) v Pak	Karachi	1964–65
151 – B. F. Hastings (110) & R. O. Collinge (68*) v Pak	Auckland	1972–73

India
1st wkt
203 – V. M. Merchant (114) & S. Mushtaq Ali (112) v Eng	Old Trafford	1936
413 – V. Mankad (231) & P. Roy (173) v NZ	Madras	1955–56

2nd wkt
124 – V. M. Mankad (111) & H. R. Adhikari (38) v Aus	Melbourne	1947–48
237 – P. Roy (150) & V. L. Manjrekar (118) v WI	Kingston	1952–53

3rd wkt
186 – L. Amarnath (118) & C. K. Nayudu (67) v Eng	Bombay	1933–34
211 – V. M. Merchant (154) & V. S. Hazare (164*) v Eng	New Delhi	1951–52
211 – V. M. Mankad (184) & V. S. Hazare (49) v Eng	Lord's	1952
238 – P. R. Umrigar (223) & V. L. Manjrekar (118) v NZ	Hyderabad	1955–56

4th wkt
144*– V. S. Hazare (134*) & L. Amarnath (58*) v WI	Bombay	1948–49
222 – V. S. Hazare (89) & V. L. Manjrekar (133) v Eng	Headingley	1952

5th wkt
131 – P. R. Umrigar (69) & D. G. Phadkar (65) v WI	Port of Spain	1952–53
177 – P. R. Umrigar (117) & C. G. Borde (177*) v Pak	Madras	1960–61
190*– M. A. K. Pataudi (203*) & C. G. Borde (67*) v Eng	New Delhi	1963–64
204 – S. M. Gavaskar (156) & B. P. Patel (115*) v WI	Port of Spain	1975–76

6th wkt
188 – V. S. Hazare (116) & D. G. Phadkar (123) v Aus	Adelaide	1947–48
193*– D. N. Sardesai (200*) & Hanumant Singh (75*) v NZ	Bombay	1964–65

7th wkt
132 – V. S. Hazare (145) & H. R. Adhikari (51) v Aus	Adelaide	1947–48
153 – M. L. Apte (163*) & V. M. Mankad (96) v WI	Port of Spain	1952–53
153 – C. G. Borde (84) & S. A. Durani (90) v Eng	Bombay	1963–64
186 – D. N. Sardesai (150) & E. D. Solkar (65) v WI	Bridgetown	1970–71

8th wkt
74 – Lall Singh (29) & L. Amar Singh (51) v Eng	Lord's	1932
82 – G. S. Ramchand (53) & N. S. Tamhane (54*) v Pak	Bahawalpur	1954–55
101 – R. G. Nadkarni (63) & F. M. Engineer (65) v Eng	Madras	1961–62
143 – R. G. Nadkarni (75) & F. M. Engineer (90) v NZ	Madras	1964–65

9th wkt
54 – G. S. Ramchand (42) & S. G. Shinde (14) v Eng	Lord's	1952
54 – J. M. Ghorpade (35) & S. P. Gupte (17*) v WI	Port of Spain	1952–53
149 – P. G. Joshi (52*) & R. B. Desai (85) v Pak	Bombay	1960–61

10th wkt
43 – R. S. Modi (57*) & S. G. Shinde (10) v Eng	Lord's	1946
109 – H. R. Adhikari (81*) & Ghulam Ahmed (50) v Pak	New Delhi	1952–53

Pakistan
1st wkt
127 – Hanif Mohammad (142) & Alim-ud-Din (64) v Ind	Bahawalpur	1954–55
152 – Hanif Mohammad (137) & Imtiaz Ahmed (91) v WI	Bridgetown	1957–58
162 – Hanif Mohammad (62) & Imtiaz Ahmed (135) v Ind	Madras	1960–61
249 – K. Ibadulla (166) & Abdul Kadir (95) v Aus	Karachi	1964–65

2nd wkt
165 – Hanif Mohammad (96) & Waqar Hassan (65) v Ind	Bombay	1952–53
178 – Hanif Mohammad (103) & Saeed Ahmed (78) v WI	Karachi	1958–59
246 – Hanif Mohammad (160) & Saeed Ahmed (121) v Ind	Bombay	1960–61
291 – Zaheer Abbas (274) & Mushtaq Mohammad (100) v Eng	Edgbaston	1971

3rd wkt
154 – Hanif Mohammad (337) & Saeed Ahmed (65) v WI	Bridgetown	1957–58
169 – Saeed Ahmed (97) & Wazir Mohammad (189) v WI	Port of Spain	1957–58

169 – Saeed Ahmed (166) & Shuja-ud-Din (45) v Aus — Lahore — 1959–60
171 – Sadiq Mohammad (166) & Majid Khan (79) v NZ — Wellington — 1972–73
172 – Zaheer Abbas (240) & Mushtaq Mohammad (76) v Eng — The Oval — 1974
180 – Mudassar Nazar (114) & Haroon Rashid (122) v Eng — Lahore — 1977–78

4th wkt
136 – Maqsood Ahmed (99) & A. H. Kardar (44) v Ind — Lahore — 1954–55
154 – Wazir Mohammad (189) & Hanif Mohammad (54) v WI — Port of Spain — 1957–58
350 – Mushtaq Mohammad (201) & Asif Iqbal (175) v NZ — Dunedin — 1972–73

5th wkt
155 – Alim-ud-Din (103*) & A. H. Kardar (93) v Ind — Karachi — 1954–55
197 – J. Burki (101) & Nasim-ul-Ghani (101) v Eng — Lord's — 1962
281 – Javed Miandad (163) & Asif Iqbal (166) v NZ — Lahore — 1976–77

6th wkt
104 – Wazir Mohammad (67) & A. H. Kardar (69) v Aus — Karachi — 1956–57
166 – Wazir Mohammad (106) & A. H. Kardar (57) v WI — Kingston — 1957–58
217 – Hanif Mohammad (203*) & Majid Khan (80) v NZ — Lahore — 1964–65

7th wkt
308 – Waqar Hassan (189) & Imtiaz Ahmed (209) v NZ — Lahore — 1955–56

8th wkt
63 – Nazar Mohammad (124*) & Zulfiqar Ahmed (34) v Ind — Lucknow — 1952–53
63 – Imtiaz Ahmed (209) & Maqsood Ahmed (33) v NZ — Lahore — 1955–56
130 – Hanif Mohammad (187*) & Asif Iqbal (76) v Eng — Lord's — 1967

9th wkt
71 – Wallis Mathias (73) & Fazal Mahmood (60) v WI — Port of Spain — 1957–58
190 – Asif Iqbal (146) & Intikhab Alam (51) v Eng — The Oval — 1967

10th wkt
104 – Zulfiqar Ahmed (63*) & Amir Elahi (47) v Ind — Madras — 1952–53
133 – Wasim Raja (71) & Wasim Bari (60*) v WI — Bridgetown — 1976–77

Highest partnership for each wicket in all Test Cricket

1st – 413 V. M. Mankad (231) & P. Roy (173) — I v NZ — Madras — 1955–56
2nd – 451 W. H. Ponsford (266) & D. G. Bradman (244) — A v E — The Oval — 1934
3rd – 370 W. J. Edrich (189) & D. C. S. Compton (208) — E v SA — Lord's — 1947
4th – 411 P. B. H. May (285*) & M. C. Cowdrey (154) — E v WI — Edgbaston — 1957
5th – 405 S. G. Barnes (234) & D. G. Bradman (234) — A v E — Sydney — 1946–47
6th – 346 J. H. W. Fingleton (136) & D. G. Bradman (270) — A v E — Melbourne — 1936–37
7th – 347 D. S. Atkinson (219) & C. C. Depeiaza (122) — WI v A — Bridgetown — 1954–55
8th – 246 L. E. G. Ames (137) & G. O. B. Allen (122) — E v NZ — Lord's — 1931
9th – 190 Asif Iqbal (146) & Intikhab Alam (51) — P v E — The Oval — 1967
10th – 151 B. F. Hastings (110) & R. O. Collinge (68*) — NZ v P — Auckland — 1972–73

Wicket partnerships of 300 and over

1st wkt
413 V. M. Mankad (231) & P. Roy (173), Ind v NZ — Madras — 1955–56
387 G. M. Turner (259) & T. W. Jarvis (182), NZ v WI — Georgetown — 1971–72
382 R. B. Simpson (201) & W. M. Lawry (210), Aus v WI — Bridgetown — 1964–65
359 L. Hutton (158) & C. Washbrook (195), Eng v SA — Johannesburg — 1948–49
323 J. B. Hobbs (178) & W. Rhodes (179), Eng v Aus — Melbourne — 1911–12

2nd wkt
451 W. H. Ponsford (266) & D. G. Bradman (244), Aus v Eng — The Oval — 1934
446 C. C. Hunte (260) & G. S. Sobers (365*), WI v Pak — Kingston — 1957–58
382 L. Hutton (364) & M. Leyland (187), Eng v Aus — The Oval — 1938
369 J. H. Edrich (310*) & K. F. Barrington (163), Eng v NZ — Headingley — 1965
301 A. R. Morris (182) & D. G. Bradman (173*), Aus v Eng — Headingley — 1948

3rd wkt
370 W. J. Edrich (189) & D. C. S. Compton (208), Eng v SA — Lord's — 1947
341 E. J. Barlow (201) & R. G. Pollock (175), SA v Aus — Adelaide — 1963–64
338 E. D. Weekes (206) & F. M. M. Worrell (167), WI v Eng — Port of Spain — 1953–54

319	A. Melville (189) & A. D. Nourse (149), SA v Eng	Trent Bridge	1947
303	I. V. A. Richards (232) & A. I. Kallicharran (97), WI v Eng	Trent Bridge	1976

4th wkt

411	P. B. H. May (285*) & M. C. Cowdrey (154), Eng v WI	Edgbaston	1957
399	G. S. Sobers (226) & F. M. M. Worrell (197*), WI v Eng	Bridgetown	1959–60
388	W. H. Ponsford (181) & D. G. Bradman (304), Aus v Eng	Headingley	1934
350	Mushtaq Mohammad (201) & Asif Iqbal (175), Pak v NZ	Dunedin	1972–73
336	W. M. Lawry (151) & K. D. Walters (242), Aus v WI	Sydney	1968–69

5th wkt

405	S. G. Barnes (234) & D. G. Bradman (234), Aus v Eng	Sydney	1946–47

6th wkt

346	J. H. W. Fingleton (136) & D. G. Bradman (270), Aus v Eng	Melbourne	1936–37

7th wkt

347	D. S. Atkinson (219) & C. C. Depeiaza (122), WI v Aus	Bridgetown	1954–55
308	Waqar Hassan (189) & Imtiaz Ahmed (209), Pak v NZ	Lahore	1955–56

Most century partnerships in one innings

Four

Eng (382–2nd, 135–3rd, 215–6th, 106–7th)	v Aus	The Oval	1938
WI (267–4th, 101–6th, 118–7th, 106–9th)	v Ind	New Delhi	1948–49
Pak (152–1st, 112–2nd, 154–3rd, 121–4th)	v WI	Bridgetown	1957–58

(The only instance of the first four wickets each producing a century partnership in a Test innings.)

Three

Eng (151–1st, 103–4th, 131–6th)	v Aus	The Oval	1893
Aus (171–4th, 139–5th, 154–9th)	v Eng	Sydney	1894–95
Eng (119–3rd, 122–4th, 154–8th)	v SA	Johannesburg	1895–96
Eng (185–1st, 131–2nd, 110–4th)	v Aus	The Oval	1899
Eng (192–5th, 115–9th, 130–10th)	v Aus	Sydney	1903–04
Aus (123–1st, 111–2nd, 187–6th)	v Eng	Sydney	1920–21
Eng (268–1st, 142–2nd, 121*–3rd)	v SA	Lord's	1924
Aus (161–4th, 123–6th, 100–9th)	v Eng	Melbourne	1924–25
Eng (126–1st, 106–2nd, 133–7th)	v Aus	Melbourne	1924–25
Eng (182–1st, 140–3rd, 116*–4th)	v Aus	Lord's	1926
Eng (173–1st, 148–2nd, 249–4th)	v WI	Kingston	1929–30
Aus (162–1st, 231–2nd, 192–3rd)	v Eng	Lord's	1930
Eng (112–1st, 188–2nd, 123–3rd)	v Aus	Sydney	1932–33
Eng (134–2nd, 127–3rd, 138–8th)	v Ind	Old Trafford	1936
Aus (276–3rd, 106–4th, 131–6th)	v Eng	Brisbane	1946–47
Aus (236–2nd, 105–3rd, 142–4th)	v Ind	Adelaide	1947–48
Eng (168–1st, 100–2nd, 155–3rd)	v Aus	Headingley	1948
WI (197–1st, 115–3rd, 189–5th)	v NZ	Auckland	1951–52
Aus (122–1st, 103–3rd, 148–4th)	v SA	Melbourne	1952–53
Aus (108–1st, 100–3rd, 206–6th)	v WI	Bridgetown	1954–55
Aus (295–3rd, 220–5th, 137–8th)	v WI	Kingston	1954–55
WI (108–3rd, 217–4th, 160*–6th)	v Ind	Calcutta	1958–59
WI (255–2nd, 110–6th, 127–7th)	v Ind	Kingston	1961–62
Eng (166–2nd, 107–3rd, 153*–6th)	v Pak	Edgbaston	1962
Eng (111–2nd, 246–3rd, 143–5th)	v Aus	Old Trafford	1964
WI (110–3rd, 107–4th, 173–5th)	v Eng	Trent Bridge	1966
Eng (139–2nd, 107–3rd, 252–4th)	v Ind	Headingley	1967
NZ (126–1st, 103–4th, 119–5th)	v Ind	Christchurch	1967–68
WI (166–2nd, 167–4th, 107*–6th)	v Ind	Bridgetown	1970–71
Aus (100–2nd, 172–4th, 120–7th)	v Pak	Adelaide	1972–73
WI (206–1st, 112–3rd, 112–6th)	v Eng	Kingston	1973–74
Eng (116–1st, 221–2nd, 202–5th)	v Ind	Lord's	1974
Eng (129–2nd, 139–5th, 130–7th)	v Pak	The Oval	1974
WI (113–2nd, 104–3rd, 250–6th)	v Ind	Bombay	1974–75
Eng (149–3rd, 192–4th, 148–5th)	v Aus	Melbourne	1974–75
Eng (125–2nd, 122–4th, 151–6th)	v Aus	The Oval	1975
WI (116–1st, 108–2nd, 132–3rd)	v Eng	Old Trafford	1976
WI (154–2nd, 191–3rd, 174–4th)	v Eng	The Oval	1976

Aus (134–1st, 171–5th, 117–8th)   v Pak   Melbourne   1976–77
Note: Hanif Mohammad (Pakistan) is the only batsman to have participated in four
  century partnerships in the same innings v West Indies at Bridgetown, 1957–58.

Dismissals in Test Cricket

All 10 batsmen caught in an innings

Australia (1 c & b) v England	Melbourne	1903–04
South Africa (1 c & b) v Australia	Melbourne	1931–32
England v South Africa	Durban	1948–49
New Zealand v England	Headingley	1949
England v Pakistan	The Oval	1954
West Indies (1 c & b) v Australia	Sydney	1960–61
New Zealand v India	Wellington	1967–68
New Zealand (1 c & b) v West Indies	Auckland	1968–69
New Zealand (1 c & b) v India	Bombay	1969–70
India v West Indies	Port of Spain	1970–71
India v England	Lord's	1971
Australia v England	Trent Bridge	1972
England v India	Madras	1972–73
England v West Indies	Lord's	1973

Most batsmen caught in a match

32	England v Pakistan	Headingley	1971
31	India v New Zealand	Bombay	1969–70
31	New Zealand v Australia	Auckland	1973–74
31	West Indies v Pakistan	Kingston	1976–77

Most batsmen clean bowled in an innings

9	South Africa v England	Cape Town	1888–89
8	Australia v England	The Oval	1890
8	South Africa v England	Port Elizabeth	1895–96
8	South Africa v England	Edgbaston	1929
8	South Africa v Australia	Adelaide	1931–32
8	England v New Zealand	Wellington	1950–51

Most batsmen clean bowled in a match

23	South Africa v England	Port Elizabeth	1895–96

Most batsmen lbw in an innings

6	England v South Africa	Headingley	1955
6	England v West Indies	Port of Spain	1959–60
6	England v Pakistan	Karachi	1977–78
5	South Africa v England	The Oval	1965
5	West Indies v Pakistan	Lahore	1974–75
5	England v Australia	Lord's	1975

Most batsmen lbw in a match

11	Australia v South Africa	Brisbane	1952–53
11	West Indies v England	Port of Spain	1959–60
11	West Indies v India	Kingston	1961–62
11	England v Australia	Lord's	1975

Most batsmen run out in an innings

6	England v Pakistan	Karachi	1977–78
4	India v Pakistan	Peshawar	1954–55
4	Australia v West Indies	Adelaide	1968–69

Most batsmen run out in a match

7	Australia v Pakistan	Melbourne	1972–73
6	Australia v England	Sydney	1920–21
6	India v West Indies	Georgetown	1970–71

Most batsmen stumped in an innings

4	(by W. A. S. Oldfield) England v Australia	Melbourne	1924–25
4	(by P. Sen) England v India	Madras	1951–52

Most batsmen stumped in a match

6	Australia v England	Sydney	1894–95
6	India v England	Madras	1951–52

Most batsmen c & b in an innings

4	England v Australia	Lord's	1890

Most batsmen c & b in a match

| 6 | England v Australia | Lord's | 1890 |

Most batsmen hit wicket in an innings

2	South Africa v Australia	Johannesburg	1921–22
2	Australia v India	Brisbane	1947–48
2	India v West Indies	New Delhi	1958–59

Most batsmen hit wicket in a match

| 3 | Australia v England | Sydney | 1886–87 |
| 3 | Pakistan v Australia | Karachi | 1964–65 |

Miscellaneous

Of the 47 England wickets which fell to New Zealand in 1949 34 were caught and only 7 clean bowled.

J. H. Wardle took 7–56 and caught two batsmen off other bowlers for England v Pakistan at The Oval, 1954. The only other wicket in Pakistan's 2nd Innings was run out.

J. S. Solomon was out, hit wicket in successive Tests v Australia, 1960–61.

No catches were taken in Australia's first innings v India at Adelaide, 1947–48, 6 batsmen being clean bowled and 4 lbw.

H. Strudwick took 3 catches fielding substitute for England in Australia's first innings at Melbourne, 1903–04.

Five catches were taken by substitute fielders in the Second Test between West Indies v England, Port of Spain, 1929–30.

D. L. Underwood took three wickets c & b in New Zealand's innings of 313–7 dec at Auckland, 1970–71.

J. A. Jameson (England) was run out in three consecutive innings v India, 1971.

There are several instances of both opening batsmen being run out in a side's innings in Test cricket, namely:

S. G. Barnes and A. R. Morris	Australia v India	Melbourne	1947–48
V. Mankad and K. C. Ibrahim	India v West Indies	Bombay	1948–49
C. C. Hunte and M. R. Bynoe	West Indies v India	Calcutta	1966–67

W. E. Bowes took 6–34 v New Zealand at Auckland, 1932–33 – all clean bowled.

Mohammad Nazir clean bowled six batsmen while taking 7–99 for Pakistan v New Zealand at Karachi, 1969–70.

J. Briggs (England) clean bowled no less than 8 South African batsmen in his 8–11 at Cape Town 1888–89. He took 15 wickets for 28 in the match – 14 bowled and one lbw.

G. A. Lohmann (England) took 7–38 (all clean bowled) in South Africa's first innings at Port Elizabeth, 1895–96. Twelve of his 15 wickets in the match were clean bowled.

All twelve of Imran Khan's victims for Pakistan v Australia at Sydney, 1976–77, were out caught, one caught and bowled.

In India's second innings of 97 v West Indies at Kingston, 1975–76, no fewer than five men were absent hurt.

Two batsmen have been stumped by a substitute in Test cricket. At Durban in the 1909–10 series S. J. Snooke of South Africa was stumped by N. C. Tufnell, substituting for H. Strudwick of England, while at Lahore in 1964–65 Pervez Sajjad of Pakistan was stumped by B. E. Congdon, keeping wicket in place of A. E. Dick of New Zealand.

Three batsmen – B. D. Julien, C. H. Lloyd and M. A. Holding – retired hurt in West Indies' first innings of 355 v Australia at Sydney, 1975–76. All three batsmen returned later to resume their innings.

There are only two instances in Test cricket of a bowler dismissing all eleven members of the opposing team in the same match:

| J. C. Laker | 19–90 | Eng v Aus | Old Trafford | 1956 |
| S. Venkataraghavan | 12–152 | Ind v NZ | New Delhi | 1964–65 |

W. R. Endean (South Africa) was given out "handled ball" v England at Cape Town in 1956–57. He brushed away a ball from J. C. Laker which threatened to fall on to the stumps.

L. Hutton (England) was given out "obstructing the field" v South Africa at The Oval in 1951. A ball from A. M. B. Rowan struck him on his glove and when the batsmen fended at it with his bat the umpire ruled that he had prevented the wicket-keeper, W. R. Endean, from making a catch.

There are three instances of a bowler running out a batsman backing up prior to the ball being delivered in a Test:

V. M. Mankad (India) ran out W. A. Brown (18) of Australia at Sydney	1947–48
C. C. Griffith (West Indies) ran out I. R. Redpath (9) of Australia, at Adelaide	1968–69
E. J. Chatfield (NZ) ran out D. W. Randall (13) of England, at Christchurch	1977–78

Number of balls per over in Test series
(All dates are inclusive)

In England

1880 (v Aus) to 1888 (v Aus)	–	4 balls per over
1890 (v Aus) to 1899 (v Aus)	–	5 balls per over
1902 (v Aus) to 1938 (v Aus)	–	6 balls per over
1939 (v WI)	–	8 balls per over
1946 (v Ind) to date	–	6 balls per over

In Australia

1876–77 (v Eng) to 1887–88 (v Eng)	–	4 balls per over
1891–92 (v Eng) to 1920–21 (v Eng)	–	6 balls per over
1924–25 (v Eng)	–	8 balls per over
1928–29 (v Eng) to 1932–33 (v Eng)	–	6 balls per over
1936–37 (v Eng) to date	–	8 balls per over

In South Africa

1888–89 (v Eng)	–	4 balls per over
1891–92 (v Eng) to 1898–99 (v Eng)	–	5 balls per over
1902–03 (v Aus) to 1935–36 (v Aus)	–	6 balls per over
1938–39 (v Eng) to 1957–58 (v Aus)	–	8 balls per over
1961–62 (v NZ) to date	–	6 balls per over

In West Indies

1929–30 (v Eng) to date	–	6 balls per over

In New Zealand

1929–30 (v Eng) to 1967–68 (v Ind)	–	6 balls per over
1968–69 (v WI) to date	–	8 balls per over

In India

1933–34 (v Eng) to date	–	6 balls per over

In Pakistan

1954–55 (v Ind) to 1972–73 (v Eng)	–	6 balls per over
1974–75 (v WI) to date	–	8 balls per over

Most Test Appearances for Each Country

England

M. C. Cowdrey	114
T. G. Evans	91
A. P. E. Knott	89
W. R. Hammond	85
K. F. Barrington	82
T. W. Graveney	79
L. Hutton	79
D. C. S. Compton	78
J. H. Edrich	77
G. Boycott	74
D. L. Underwood	74
J. B. Statham	70
F. S. Trueman	67
P. B. H. May	66
F. E. Woolley	64
E. R. Dexter	62
T. E. Bailey	61
J. B. Hobbs	61
R. Illingworth	61

New Zealand

B. E. Congdon	61
J. R. Reid	58
M. G. Burgess	44
B. Sutcliffe	42
G. T. Dowling	39
G. M. Turner	39

Australia

R. N. Harvey	79
I. M. Chappell	72
K. D. Walters	68
W. M. Lawry	67
I. R. Redpath	66
R. Benaud	63
R. B. Simpson	62
R. R. Lindwall	61
G. D. McKenzie	60
S. E. Gregory	58
K. R. Miller	55
W. A. S. Oldfield	54
D. G. Bradman	52
R. W. Marsh	52

West Indies

G. S. Sobers	93
L. R. Gibbs	79
R. B. Kanhai	79
C. H. Lloyd	65
R. C. Fredericks	59
D. L. Murray	51
F. M. M. Worrell	51
W. W. Hall	48
E. D. Weekes	48
A. I. Kallicharran	45

South Africa

J. H. B. Waite	50
A. W. Nourse	45
B. Mitchell	42
H. W. Taylor	42
T. L. Goddard	41
R. A. McLean	40
H. J. Tayfield	37

India

P. R. Umrigar	59
B. S. Bedi	58
C. G. Borde	55
V. L. Manjrekar	55
B. S. Chandrasekhar	50
E. A. S. Prasanna	47
F. M. Engineer	46
M. A. K. Pataudi	46
V. M. Mankad	44

Pakistan

Hanif Mohammad	55
Mushtaq Mohammad	49
Intikhab Alam	47
Asif Iqbal	45
Wasim Bari	42
Imtiaz Ahmed	41
Saeed Ahmed	41

Most consecutive Test appearances

G. S. Sobers	WI	85	1954–55 to 1971–72
I. M. Chappell	Aus	71	1965–66 to 1975–76
A. P. E. Knott	Eng	65	1970–71 to 1977
R. B. Kanhai	WI	61	1957 to 1968–69
A. W. Greig	Eng	*58	1972 to 1977
J. R. Reid	NZ	*58	1949 to 1965
R. W. Marsh	Aus	*52	1970–71 to 1977
P. B. H. May	Eng	52	1953 to 1959
F. E. Woolley	Eng	52	1909 to 1926
G. S. Chappell	Aus	*51	1970–71 to 1977
C. G. Borde	Ind	49	1959 to 1967–68
V. T. Trumper	Aus	*48	1899 to 1911–12
B. E. Congdon	NZ	47	1964–65 to 1975–76
W. M. Lawry	Aus	47	1961 to 1968
R. N. Harvey	Aus	46	1948 to 1956–57
Asif Iqbal	Pak	*45	1964–65 to 1976–77
R. C. Fredericks	WI	45	1971–72 to 1976–77
A. W. Nourse	SA	*45	1902–03 to 1924
W. W. Hall	WI	44	1958–59 to 1967–68
E. R. Dexter	Eng	43	1959 to 1963
L. R. Gibbs	WI	42	1960–61 to 1969
C. C. McDonald	Aus	42	1954–55 to 1961
B. Mitchell	SA	*42	1929 to 1948–49
M. A. Noble	Aus	*42	1897–98 to 1909
P. R. Umrigar	Ind	41	1951–52 to 1959
D. L. Murray	WI	41	1972–73 to 1977–78
C. H. Lloyd	WI	40	1972–73 to 1977–78
J. H. B. Waite	SA	40	1952–53 to 1963–64

* indicates whole length of Test career

Players who have appeared for two countries

	Tests	
Amir Elahi	6	India (1) 1947–48 and Pakistan (5) 1952–53
J. J. Ferris	9	Australia (8) 1886–87 to 1890 and England (1) 1891–92
S. C. Guillen	8	West Indies (5) 1951–52 and New Zealand (3) 1955–56
Gul Mahomed	9	India (8) 1946 to 1952–53 and Pakistan (1) 1956–57
F. Hearne	6	England (2) 1888–89 and South Africa (4) 1891–92 to 1895–96
A. H. Kardar	26	India (3) as Abdul Hafeez 1946 and Pakistan (23) 1952–53 to 1957–58
W. E. Midwinter	12	Australia (8) 1876–77 to 1886–87 and England (4) 1881–82
F. Mitchell	5	England (2) 1898–99 and South Africa (3) 1912
W. L. Murdoch	19	Australia (18) 1876–77 to 1890 and England (1) 1891–92
Nawab of Pataudi, Snr	6	England (3) 1932–33 to 1934 and India (3) 1946
A. E. Trott	5	Australia (3) 1894–95 and England (2) 1898–99
S. M. J. Woods	6	Australia (3) 1888 and England (3) 1895–96

Youngest Test players

Years	Days				
15	124	Mushtaq Mohammad	Pak v WI	Lahore	1958–59
16	191	Aftab Baloch	Pak v NZ	Dacca	1969–70
16	248	Nasim-ul-Ghani	Pak v WI	Bridgetown	1957–58
16	352	Khalid Hassan	Pak v Eng	Trent Bridge	1954
17	122	J. E. D. Sealy	WI v Eng	Bridgetown	1929–30
17	239	I. D. Craig	Aus v SA	Melbourne	1952–53
17	245	G. S. Sobers	WI v Eng	Kingston	1953–54
17	265	V. L. Mehra	Ind v NZ	Bombay	1955–56
17	300	Hanif Mohammad	Pak v Ind	New Delhi	1952–53
17	341	Intikhab Alam	Pak v Aus	Karachi	1959–60

Note: The youngest players to represent the other countries are:

England	D. B. Close	18 yrs 149 days v NZ	Old Trafford	1949
South Africa	A. E. Ochse	19 yrs 1 day v Eng	Port Elizabeth	1888–89
New Zealand	D. L. Freeman	18 yrs 197 days v Eng	Christchurch	1932–33

Oldest Test players

Years	Days				
52	165	W. Rhodes	Eng v WI	Kingston	1929–30
50	320	W. G. Grace	Eng v Aus	Trent Bridge	1899
50	303	G. Gunn	Eng v WI	Kingston	1929–30
49	327	H. Ironmonger	Aus v Eng	Sydney	1932–33
49	139	J. Southerton	Eng v Aus	Melbourne	1876–77
47	302	Miran Bux	Pak v Ind	Peshawar	1954–55
47	249	J. B. Hobbs	Eng v Aus	The Oval	1930
47	87	F. E. Woolley	Eng v Aus	The Oval	1934

Oldest players to make their Test debut

Years	Days				
49	119	J. Southerton	Eng v Aus	Melbourne	1876–77
47	284	Miran Bux	Pak v Ind	Lahore	1954–55
46	253	D. D. J. Blackie	Aus v Eng	Sydney	1928–29
45	237	H. Ironmonger	Aus v Eng	Brisbane	1928–29
41	337	E. R. Wilson	Eng v Aus	Sydney	1920–21
41	27	R. J. D. Jamshedji	Ind v Eng	Bombay	1933–34
40	345	C. A. Wiles	WI v Eng	Old Trafford	1933

Note: The oldest players to make their Test debut for the other countries are:

South Africa	G. W. A. Chubb	40 yrs 56 days v Eng	Trent Bridge	1951
New Zealand	H. M. McGirr	38 yrs 101 days v Eng	Auckland	1929–30

Youngest Test captains

Years	Days				
21	77	M. A. K. Pataudi	Ind v WI	Bridgetown	1961–62
22	194	I. D. Craig	Aus v SA	Johannesburg	1957–58
22	306	M. Bisset	SA v Eng	Johannesburg	1898–99
23	144	M. P. Bowden	Eng v SA	Cape Town	1888–89
23	217	G. C. Grant	WI v Aus	Adelaide	1930–31
23	292	Hon Ivo Bligh	Eng v Aus	Melbourne	1882–83

Oldest Test captains

Years	Days				
50	320	W. G. Grace	Eng v Aus	Trent Bridge	1899
45	245	G. O. B. Allen	Eng v WI	Kingston	1947–48

Youngest players to score a Test century

Years	Days					
17	78	Mushtaq Mohammad	101	Pak v Ind	New Delhi	1960–61
18	251	Mushtaq Mohammad	100*	Pak v Eng	Trent Bridge	1962
19	26	Mohammad Ilyas	126	Pak v NZ	Karachi	1964–65
19	119	Javed Miandad	163	Pak v NZ	Lahore	1976–77
19	121	H. G. Vivian	100	NZ v SA	Wellington	1931–32
19	127	R. N. Harvey	153	Aus v Ind	Melbourne	1947–48
19	141	Javed Miandad	206	Pak v NZ	Karachi	1976–77
19	152	A. Jackson	164	Aus v Eng	Adelaide	1928–29
19	294	R. N. Harvey	112	Aus v Eng	Headingley	1948
19	318	R. G. Pollock	122	SA v Aus	Sydney	1963–64
19	332	R. G. Pollock	175	SA v Aus	Adelaide	1963–64
19	357	K. D. Walters	155	Aus v Eng	Brisbane	1965–66

Note: The youngest players to score a century for the other countries are:

England	D. C. S. Compton	20 yrs 19 days v Aus	Trent Bridge	1938
West Indies	G. A. Headley	20 yrs 230 days v Eng	Bridgetown	1929–30
India	A. A. Baig	20 yrs 131 days v Eng	Old Trafford	1959

Oldest players to score a Test century

Years Days

46	82	J. B. Hobbs	142	Eng v Aus	Melbourne	1928–29
45	240	J. B. Hobbs	159	Eng v WI	The Oval	1928
45	151	E. H. Hendren	132	Eng v Aus	Old Trafford	1934

Longest Test careers
(From first day of first Test to final day of last)

Years Days

30	315	W. Rhodes	Eng	from Trent Bridge 1899 to Kingston 1929–30
26	355	D. B. Close	Eng	from Old Trafford 1949 to Old Trafford 1976
25	13	F. E. Woolley	Eng	from The Oval 1909 to The Oval 1934
24	10	G. A. Headley	WI	from Bridgetown 1929–30 to Kingston 1953–54
22	233	J. B. Hobbs	Eng	from Melbourne 1907–08 to The Oval 1930
22	120	G. Gunn	Eng	from Sydney 1907–08 to Kingston 1929–30
22	18	S. E. Gregory	Aus	from Lord's 1890 to The Oval 1912

Longest intervals between Test appearances

Years Days

17	316	G. Gunn	Eng	from Sydney 1911–12 to Bridgetown 1929–30
14	28	D. C. Cleverley	NZ	from Christchurch 1931–32 to Wellington 1945–46
13	53	F. Mitchell	Eng & SA	from Cape Town 1898–99 to Old Trafford 1912
13	32	G. M. Carew	WI	from Bridgetown 1934–35 to Port of Spain 1947–48
12	160	L. Amarnath	Ind	from Madras 1933–34 to Lord's 1946
12	81	W. E. Hollies	Eng	from Kingston 1934–35 to Trent Bridge 1947
12	14	Nawab of Pataudi	Eng & Ind	from Trent Bridge 1934 to Lord's 1946

Complete Test Career Records of all Players

(Up to September 1, 1978)

England (480 players)
Batting and Fielding

		M	I	NO	Runs	HS	Avge	100	50	Ct	St
R. Abel	1888–1902	13	22	2	744	132*	37·20	2	2	13	–
C. A. Absolom	1878–1879	1	2	0	58	52	29·00	–	1	–	–
D. A. Allen	1959–1966	39	51	15	918	88	25·50	–	5	10	–
G. O. B. Allen	1930–1948	25	33	2	750	122	24·19	1	3	20	–
M. J. C. Allom	1929–1930	5	3	2	14	8*	14·00	–	–	–	–
L. E. G. Ames	1929–1939	47	72	12	2434	149	40·56	8	7	74	23
D. L. Amiss	1966–1977	50	88	10	3612	262*	46·30	11	11	24	–
K. V. Andrew	1954–1963	2	4	1	29	15	9·66	–	–	1	–
R. Appleyard	1954–1956	9	9	6	51	19*	17·00	–	–	4	–
A. G. Archer	1898–1899	1	2	1	31	24*	31·00	–	–	–	–
T. Armitage	1876–1877	2	3	0	33	21	11·00	–	–	–	–
E. G. Arnold	1903–1907	10	15	3	160	40	13·33	–	–	8	–
G. G. Arnold	1967–1975	34	46	11	421	59	12·02	–	1	9	–
J. Arnold	1931	1	2	0	34	34	17·00	–	–	–	–
W. E. Astill	1927–1930	9	15	0	190	40	12·66	–	–	7	–
W. Attewell	1884–1892	10	15	6	150	43*	16·66	–	–	9	–
T. E. Bailey	1949–1959	61	91	14	2290	134*	29·74	1	10	32	–
A. H. Bakewell	1931–1935	6	9	0	409	107	45·44	1	3	3	–
J. C. Balderstone	1976	2	4	0	39	35	9·75	–	–	1	–
R. W. Barber	1960–1968	28	45	3	1495	185	35·59	1	9	20	–
W. Barber	1935	2	4	0	83	44	20·75	–	–	1	–
G. D. Barlow	1976–1977	3	5	1	17	7*	4·25	–	–	–	–
R. G. Barlow	1881–1887	17	30	4	591	62	22·73	–	2	14	–
S. F. Barnes	1901–1914	27	39	9	242	38*	8·06	–	–	12	–
W. Barnes	1880–1890	21	33	2	725	134	23·38	1	5	19	–
C. J. Barnett	1933–1948	20	35	4	1098	129	35·41	2	5	14	–

		M	I	NO	Runs	HS	Avge	100	50	Ct	St
F. Barratt	1929–1930	5	4	1	28	17	9·33	–	–	2	–
K. F. Barrington	1955–1968	82	131	15	6806	256	58·67	20	35	58	–
V. A. Barton	1891–1892	1	1	0	23	23	23·00	–	–	–	–
W. Bates	1881–1887	15	26	2	656	64	27·33	–	5	9	–
G. Bean	1891–1892	3	5	0	92	50	18·40	–	1	4	–
A. V. Bedser	1946–1955	51	71	15	714	79	12·75	–	1	26	–
R. Berry	1950	2	4	2	6	4*	3·00	–	–	2	–
J. G. Binks	1963–1964	2	4	0	91	55	22·75	–	1	8	–
M. C. Bird	1909–1914	10	16	1	280	61	18·66	–	2	5	–
J. Birkenshaw	1972–1974	5	7	0	148	64	21·14	–	1	3	–
Hon I. F. W. Bligh	1882–1883	4	7	1	62	19	10·33	–	–	7	–
C. Blythe	1901–1910	19	31	12	183	27	9·63	–	–	6	–
J. H. Board	1898–1906	6	12	2	108	29	10·80	–	–	8	3
J. B. Bolus	1963–1964	7	12	0	496	88	41·33	–	4	2	–
M. W. Booth	1913–1914	2	2	0	46	32	23·00	–	–	–	–
B. J. T. Bosanquet	1903–1905	7	14	3	147	27	13·36	–	–	9	–
I. T. Botham	1977–1978	11	13	1	500	108	41·66	3	1	12	–
M. P. Bowden	1888–1889	2	2	0	25	25	12·50	–	–	1	–
W. E. Bowes	1932–1946	15	11	5	28	10*	4·66	–	–	2	–
E. H. Bowley	1929–1930	5	7	0	252	109	36·00	1	–	2	–
G. Boycott	1964–1978	74	128	17	5675	246*	51·12	16	32	22	–
W. M. Bradley	1899	2	2	1	23	23*	23·00	–	–	–	–
L. C. Braund	1901–1908	23	41	3	987	104	25·97	3	2	39	–
J. M. Brearley	1976–1978	21	34	1	845	91	25·60	–	5	32	–
W. Brearley	1905–1912	4	5	2	21	11*	7·00	–	–	–	–
D. Brennan	1951	2	2	0	16	16	8·00	–	–	–	1
J. Briggs	1884–1899	33	50	5	815	121	18·11	1	2	12	–
W. Brockwell	1893–1899	7	12	0	202	49	16·83	–	–	6	–
H. R. Bromley-Davenport	1895–1899	4	6	0	128	84	21·33	–	1	1	–
D. Brookes	1947–1948	1	2	0	17	10	8·50	–	–	1	–
A. Brown	1961–1962	2	1	1	3	3*	–	–	–	1	–
D. J. Brown	1965–1969	26	34	5	342	44*	11·79	–	–	7	–
F. R. Brown	1931–1953	22	30	1	734	79	25·31	–	5	22	–
G. Brown	1921–1923	7	12	2	299	84	29·90	–	2	9	3
J. T. Brown	1894–1899	8	16	3	470	140	36·15	1	1	7	–
C. P. Buckenham	1909–1910	4	7	0	43	17	6·14	–	–	2	–
H. J. Butler	1947–1948	2	2	1	15	15*	15·00	–	–	1	–
H. R. Butt	1895–1896	3	4	1	22	13	7·33	–	–	1	1
A. W. Carr	1922–1929	11	13	1	237	63	19·75	–	1	3	–
D. B. Carr	1951–1952	2	4	0	135	76	33·75	–	1	–	–
D. W. Carr	1909	1	1	0	0	0	0·00	–	–	–	–
T. W. Cartwright	1964–1965	5	7	2	26	9	5·20	–	–	2	–
A. P. F. Chapman	1924–1931	26	36	4	925	121	28·90	1	5	32	–
H. R. J. Charlwood	1876–1877	2	4	0	63	36	15·75	–	–	–	–
W. Chatterton	1891–1892	1	1	0	48	48	48·00	–	–	–	–
S. Christopherson	1884	1	1	0	17	17	17·00	–	–	–	–
E. W. Clark	1929–1934	8	9	5	36	10	9·00	–	–	–	–
J. C. Clay	1935	1	–	–	–	–	–	–	–	1	–
D. B. Close	1949–1976	22	37	2	887	70	25·34	–	4	24	–
L. J. Coldwell	1962–1964	7	7	5	9	6*	4·50	–	–	1	–
D. C. S. Compton	1937–1957	78	131	15	5807	278	50·06	17	28	49	–
C. Cook	1947	1	2	0	4	4	2·00	–	–	–	–
G. A. Cope	1977–1978	3	3	0	40	22	13·33	–	–	1	–
W. H. Copson	1939–1947	3	1	0	6	6	6·00	–	–	1	–
W. L. Cornford	1929–1930	4	4	0	36	18	9·00	–	–	5	3
R. M. H. Cottam	1968–1973	4	5	1	27	13	6·75	–	–	2	–
Hon C. J. Coventry	1888–1889	2	2	1	13	12	13·00	–	–	–	–
M. C. Cowdrey	1954–1975	114	188	15	7624	182	44·06	22	38	120	–
A. Coxon	1948	1	2	0	19	19	9·50	–	–	–	–
J. Cranston	1890	1	2	0	31	16	15·50	–	–	1	–
K. Cranston	1947–1948	8	14	0	209	45	14·92	–	–	3	–

		M	I	NO	Runs	HS	Avge	100	50	Ct	St
J. F. Crapp	1948–1949	7	13	2	319	56	29·00	–	3	7	–
J. N. Crawford	1905–1908	12	23	2	469	74	22·33	–	2	13	–
W. R. Cuttell	1898–1899	2	4	0	65	21	16·25	–	–	2	–
E. W. Dawson	1927–1930	5	9	0	175	55	19·44	–	1	–	–
H. Dean	1912	3	4	2	10	8	5·00	–	–	2	–
M. H. Denness	1969–1975	28	45	3	1667	188	39·69	4	7	28	–
D. Denton	1905–1910	11	22	1	424	104	20·19	1	1	8	–
J. G. Dewes	1948–1951	5	10	0	121	67	12·10	–	1	–	–
E. R. Dexter	1958–1968	62	102	8	4502	205	47·89	9	27	29	–
A. E. Dipper	1921	1	2	0	51	40	25·50	–	–	–	–
G. H. G. Doggart	1950	2	4	0	76	29	19·00	–	–	3	–
B. L. d'Oliveira	1966–1972	44	70	8	2484	158	40·06	5	15	29	–
H. E. Dollery	1947–1950	4	7	0	72	37	10·28	–	–	1	–
A. Dolphin	1920–1921	1	2	0	1	1	0·50	–	–	1	–
J. W. H. T. Douglas	1911–1925	23	35	2	962	119	29·15	1	6	9	–
N. F. Druce	1897–1898	5	9	0	252	64	28·00	–	1	5	–
A. Ducat	1921	1	2	0	5	3	2·50	–	–	1	–
G. Duckworth	1924–1936	24	28	12	234	39*	14·62	–	–	45	15
K. S. Duleepsinhji	1929–1931	12	19	2	995	173	58·52	3	5	10	–
F. J. Durston	1921	1	2	1	8	6*	8·00	–	–	–	–
P. H. Edmonds	1975–1978	13	16	4	195	50	16·25	–	1	19	–
J. H. Edrich	1963–1976	77	127	9	5138	310*	43·54	12	24	43	–
W. J. Edrich	1938–1955	39	63	2	2440	219	40·00	6	13	39	–
H. Elliott	1927–1934	4	5	1	61	37*	15·25	–	–	8	3
J. E. Emburey	1978	1	1	0	2	2	2·00	–	–	2	–
G. M. Emmett	1948	1	2	0	10	10	5·00	–	–	–	–
T. Emmett	1876–1882	7	13	1	160	48	13·33	–	–	9	–
A. J. Evans	1921	1	2	0	18	14	9·00	–	–	–	–
T. G. Evans	1946–1959	91	133	14	2439	104	20·49	2	8	173	46
A. E. Fagg	1936–1939	5	8	0	150	39	18·75	–	–	5	–
F. L. Fane	1905–1910	14	27	1	682	143	26·23	1	3	6	–
K. Farnes	1934–1939	15	17	5	58	20	4·83	–	–	1	–
W. Farrimond	1930–1935	4	7	0	116	35	16·57	–	–	6	2
P. G. H. Fender	1920–1929	13	21	1	380	60	19·00	–	2	14	–
J. J. Ferris	1891–1892	1	1	0	16	16	16·00	–	–	–	–
A. Fielder	1903–1908	6	12	5	78	20	11·14	–	–	4	–
L. B. Fishlock	1936–1947	4	5	1	47	19*	11·75	–	–	1	–
J. A. Flavell	1961–1964	4	6	2	31	14	7·75	–	–	–	–
K. W. R. Fletcher	1968–1977	52	85	11	2975	216	40·20	7	16	46	–
W. Flowers	1884–1893	8	14	0	254	56	18·14	–	1	3	–
F. G. J. Ford	1894–1895	5	9	0	168	48	18·66	–	–	5	–
F. R. Foster	1911–1912	11	15	1	330	71	23·57	–	3	11	–
R. E. Foster	1903–1907	8	14	1	602	287	46·30	1	1	13	–
A. J. Fothergill	1888–1889	2	2	0	33	32	16·50	–	–	–	–
A. P. Freeman	1924–1929	12	16	5	154	50*	14·00	–	1	4	–
C. B. Fry	1895–1912	26	41	3	1223	144	32·18	2	7	17	–
M. W. Gatting	1977–1978	2	3	0	11	6	3·66	–	–	3	–
L. H. Gay	1894–1895	1	2	0	37	33	18·50	–	–	3	1
G. Geary	1924–1934	14	20	4	249	66	15·56	–	2	13	–
P. A. Gibb	1938–1947	8	13	0	581	120	44·69	2	3	3	1
N. Gifford	1964–1973	15	20	9	179	25*	16·27	–	–	8	–
A. E. R. Gilligan	1922–1925	11	16	3	209	39*	16·07	–	–	3	–
A. H. H. Gilligan	1929–1930	4	4	0	71	32	17·75	–	–	–	–
H. Gimblett	1936–1939	3	5	1	129	67*	32·25	–	1	1	–
C. Gladwin	1947–1949	8	11	5	170	51*	28·33	–	1	2	–
T. W. J. Goddard	1930–1939	8	5	3	13	8	6·50	–	–	3	–
G. A. Gooch	1975–1978	7	11	2	301	91*	33·44	–	3	5	–
F. S. Gough-Calthorpe	1929–1930	4	7	0	129	49	18·42	–	–	3	–
A. R. Gover	1936–1946	4	1	1	2	2*	–	–	–	1	–
D. I. Gower	1978	6	8	0	438	111	54·75	1	3	–	–
E. M. Grace	1880	1	2	0	36	36	18·00	–	–	1	–
G. F. Grace	1880	1	2	0	0	0	0·00	–	–	2	–

		M	I	NO	Runs	HS	Avge	100	50	Ct	St
W. G. Grace	1880–1899	22	36	2	1098	170	32·29	2	5	39	–
T. W. Graveney	1951–1969	79	123	13	4882	258	44·38	11	20	80	–
T. Greenhough	1959–1960	4	4	1	4	2	1·33	–	–	1	–
A. Greenwood	1876–1877	2	4	0	77	49	19·25	–	–	2	–
A. W. Greig	1972–1977	58	93	4	3599	148	40·43	8	20	87	–
B. A. F. Grieve	1888–1889	2	3	2	40	14*	40·00	–	–	–	–
S. C. Griffith	1947–1949	3	5	0	157	140	31·40	1	–	5	–
G. Gunn	1907–1930	15	29	1	1120	122*	40·00	2	7	15	–
J. R. Gunn	1901–1905	6	10	2	85	24	10·62	–	–	3	–
W. Gunn	1886–1899	11	20	2	392	102*	21·77	1	1	5	–
N. E. Haig	1921–1930	5	9	0	126	47	14·00	–	–	4	–
S. Haigh	1898–1912	11	18	3	113	25	7·53	–	–	8	–
C. Hallows	1921–1928	2	2	1	42	26	42·00	–	–	–	–
W. R. Hammond	1927–1947	85	140	16	7249	336*	58·45	22	24	110	–
J. H. Hampshire	1969–1975	8	16	1	403	107	26·86	1	2	9	–
H. T. W. Hardinge	1921	1	2	0	30	25	15·00	–	–	–	–
J. Hardstaff snr	1907–1908	5	10	0	311	72	31·10	–	3	1	–
J. Hardstaff jnr	1935–1948	23	38	3	1636	205*	46·74	4	10	9	–
Lord Harris	1878–1884	4	6	1	145	52	29·00	–	1	2	–
J. C. Hartley	1905–1906	2	4	0	15	9	3·75	–	–	2	–
Lord Hawke	1895–1899	5	8	1	55	30	7·85	–	–	3	–
E. G. Hayes	1905–1912	5	9	1	86	35	10·75	–	–	2	–
F. C. Hayes	1973–1976	9	17	1	244	106*	15·25	1	–	7	–
T. W. Hayward	1895–1909	35	60	2	1999	137	34·45	3	12	19	–
A. Hearne	1891–1892	1	1	0	9	9	9·00	–	–	1	–
F. Hearne	1888–1889	2	2	0	47	27	23·50	–	–	1	–
G. G. Hearne	1891–1892	1	1	0	0	0	0·00	–	–	–	–
J. T. Hearne	1891–1899	12	18	4	126	40	9·00	–	–	4	–
J. W. Hearne	1911–1926	24	36	5	806	114	26·00	1	2	13	–
E. H. Hendren	1920–1935	51	83	9	3525	205*	47·63	7	21	33	–
M. Hendrick	1974–1978	16	17	5	64	15	5·33	–	–	19	–
C. Heseltine	1895–1896	2	2	0	18	18	9·00	–	–	3	–
K. Higgs	1965–1968	15	19	3	185	63	11·56	–	1	4	–
A. Hill	1876–1877	2	4	2	101	49	50·50	–	–	1	–
A. J. L. Hill	1895–1896	3	4	0	251	124	62·75	1	1	1	–
M. J. Hilton	1950–1952	4	6	1	37	15	7·40	–	–	1	–
G. H. Hirst	1897–1909	24	38	3	790	85	22·57	–	5	18	–
J. W. Hitch	1911–1921	7	10	3	103	51*	14·71	–	1	4	–
J. B. Hobbs	1907–1930	61	102	7	5410	211	56·94	15	28	17	–
R. N. S. Hobbs	1967–1971	7	8	3	34	15*	6·80	–	–	8	–
W. E. Hollies	1934–1950	13	15	8	37	18*	3·28	–	–	2	–
E. R. T. Holmes	1934–1935	5	9	2	114	85*	16·28	–	1	3	–
P. Holmes	1921–1932	7	14	1	357	88	27·46	–	4	3	–
L. Hone	1878–1879	1	2	0	13	7	6·50	–	–	2	–
J. L. Hopwood	1934	2	3	1	12	8	6·00	–	–	–	–
A. N. Hornby	1878–1884	3	6	0	21	9	3·50	–	–	–	–
M. J. Horton	1959	2	2	0	60	58	30·00	–	1	2	–
N. D. Howard	1951–1952	4	6	1	86	23	17·20	–	–	4	–
H. Howell	1920–1924	5	8	6	15	5	7·50	–	–	–	–
R. Howorth	1947–1948	5	10	2	145	45*	18·12	–	–	2	–
J. Humphries	1907–1908	3	6	1	44	16	8·80	–	–	7	–
J. Hunter	1884–1885	5	7	2	93	39*	18·60	–	–	8	3
K. L. Hutchings	1907–1909	7	12	0	341	126	28·41	1	1	9	–
L. Hutton	1937–1955	79	138	15	6971	364	56·67	19	33	57	–
R. A. Hutton	1971	5	8	2	219	81	36·50	–	2	9	–
J. Iddon	1934–1935	5	7	1	170	73	28·33	–	2	–	–
J. T. Ikin	1946–1955	18	31	2	606	60	20·89	–	3	31	–
R. Illingworth	1958–1973	61	90	11	1836	113	23·24	2	5	45	–
D. J. Insole	1950–1957	9	17	2	408	110*	27·20	1	1	8	–
Hon F. S. Jackson	1893–1905	20	33	4	1415	144*	48·79	5	6	10	–
H. L. Jackson	1949–1961	2	2	1	15	8	15·00	–	–	1	–
J. A. Jameson	1971–1974	4	8	0	214	82	26·75	–	1	–	–

		M	I	NO	Runs	HS	Avge	100	50	Ct	St
D. R. Jardine	1928–1934	22	33	6	1296	127	48·00	1	10	26	–
R. O. Jenkins	1948–1952	9	12	1	198	39	18·00	–	–	4	–
G. L. Jessop	1899–1912	18	26	0	569	104	21·88	1	3	11	–
A. O. Jones	1899–1909	12	21	0	291	34	13·85	–	–	15	–
I. J. Jones	1963–1968	15	17	9	38	16	4·75	–	–	4	–
H. Jupp	1876–1877	2	4	0	68	63	17·00	–	1	2	–
V. W. C. Jupp	1921–1928	8	13	1	208	38	17·33	–	–	5	–
W. W. Keeton	1934–1939	2	4	0	57	25	14·25	–	–	–	–
A. S. Kennedy	1922–1923	5	8	2	93	41*	15·50	–	–	5	–
D. Kenyon	1951–1955	8	15	0	192	87	12·80	–	1	5	–
E. T. Killick	1929	2	4	0	81	31	20·25	–	–	2	–
R. Kilner	1924–1926	9	8	1	233	74	33·28	–	2	6	–
J. H. King	1909	1	2	0	64	60	32·00	–	1	–	–
S. Kinneir	1911–1912	1	2	0	52	30	26·00	–	–	–	–
A. E. Knight	1903–1904	3	6	1	81	70*	16·20	–	1	1	–
B. R. Knight	1961–1969	29	38	7	812	127	26·19	2	–	14	–
D. J. Knight	1921	2	4	0	54	38	13·50	–	–	1	–
A. P. E. Knott	1967–1977	89	138	14	4175	135	33·66	5	28	233	19
N. A. Knox	1907	2	4	1	24	8*	8·00	–	–	–	–
J. C. Laker	1947–1959	46	63	15	676	63	14·08	–	2	12	–
James Langridge	1933–1947	8	9	0	242	70	26·88	–	1	6	–
J. D. F. Larter	1962–1965	10	7	2	16	10	3·20	–	–	5	–
H. Larwood	1926–1933	21	28	3	485	98	19·40	–	2	15	–
E. Leadbeater	1951–1952	2	2	0	40	38	20·00	–	–	3	–
H. W. Lee	1930–1931	1	2	0	19	18	9·50	–	–	–	–
W. S. Lees	1905–1906	5	9	3	66	25*	11·00	–	–	2	–
G. B. Legge	1927–1930	5	7	1	299	196	49·83	1	–	1	–
C. F. H. Leslie	1882–1883	4	7	0	106	54	15·14	–	1	1	–
J. K. Lever	1976–1978	13	19	3	199	53	12·43	–	1	8	–
P. Lever	1970–1975	17	18	2	350	88*	21·87	–	2	11	–
H. D. G. Leveson-Gower	1909–1910	3	6	2	95	31	23·75	–	–	1	–
W. H. V. Levett	1933–1934	1	2	1	7	5	7·00	–	–	3	–
A. R. Lewis	1972–1973	9	16	2	457	125	32·64	1	3	–	–
M. Leyland	1928–1938	41	65	5	2764	187	46·06	9	10	13	–
A. F. A. Lilley	1896–1909	35	52	8	903	84	20·52	–	4	70	22
James Lillywhite jnr	1876–1877	2	3	1	16	10	8·00	–	–	1	–
D. Lloyd	1974–1975	9	15	2	552	214*	42·46	1	–	11	–
P. J. Loader	1954–1959	13	19	6	76	17	5·84	–	–	2	–
G. A. R. Lock	1952–1968	49	63	9	742	89	13·74	–	3	59	–
W. H. Lockwood	1893–1902	12	16	3	231	52*	17·76	–	1	4	–
G. A. Lohmann	1886–1896	18	26	2	213	62*	8·87	–	1	28	–
F. A. Lowson	1951–1955	7	13	0	245	68	18·84	–	2	5	–
A. P. Lucas	1878–1884	5	9	1	157	55	19·62	–	1	1	–
B. W. Luckhurst	1970–1975	21	41	5	1298	131	36·05	4	5	14	–
Hon A. Lyttelton	1880–1884	4	7	1	94	31	15·66	–	–	2	–
G. G. Macaulay	1922–1933	8	10	4	112	76	18·66	–	1	5	–
J. C. W. MacBryan	1924	1	–	–	–	–	–	–	–	–	–
J. McConnon	1954	2	3	1	18	11	9·00	–	–	4	–
C. P. McGahey	1901–1902	2	4	0	38	18	9·50	–	–	1	–
G. MacGregor	1890–1893	8	11	3	96	31	12·00	–	–	14	3
A. J. W. McIntyre	1950–1955	3	6	0	19	7	3·16	–	–	8	–
F. A. MacKinnon	1878–1879	1	2	0	5	5	2·50	–	–	–	–
A. C. MacLaren	1894–1909	35	61	4	1931	140	33·87	5	8	29	–
J. E. P. McMaster	1888–1889	1	1	0	0	0	0·00	–	–	–	–
J. W. H. Makepeace	1920–1921	4	8	0	279	117	34·87	1	2	–	–
F. G. Mann	1948–1949	7	12	2	376	136*	37·60	1	–	3	–
F. T. Mann	1922–1923	5	9	1	281	84	35·12	–	2	4	–
C. S. Marriott	1933	1	1	0	0	0	0·00	–	–	1	–
F. Martin	1890–1892	2	2	0	14	13	7·00	–	–	2	–
J. W. Martin	1947	1	2	0	26	26	13·00	–	–	–	–
J. R. Mason	1897–1898	5	10	0	129	32	12·90	–	–	3	–

		M	I	NO	Runs	HS	Avge	100	50	Ct	St
A. D. G. Matthews	1937	1	1	1	2	2*	–	–	–	1	–
P. B. H. May	1951–1961	66	106	9	4537	285*	46·77	13	22	42	–
C. P. Mead	1911–1929	17	26	2	1185	182*	49·37	4	3	4	–
W. Mead	1899	1	2	0	7	7	3·50	–	–	1	–
W. E. Midwinter	1881–1882	4	7	0	95	36	13·57	–	–	5	–
C. Milburn	1966–1969	9	16	2	654	139	46·71	2	2	7	–
A. M. Miller	1895–1896	1	2	2	24	20*	–	–	–	–	–
G. Miller	1976–1978	14	17	2	398	98*	26·53	–	2	7	–
F. W. Milligan	1898–1899	2	4	0	58	38	14·50	–	–	1	–
G. Millman	1961–1962	6	7	2	60	32*	12·00	–	–	13	2
C. A. Milton	1958–1959	6	9	1	204	104*	25·50	1	–	5	–
A. Mitchell	1933–1936	6	10	0	298	72	29·80	–	2	9	–
F. Mitchell	1898–1899	2	4	0	88	41	22·00	–	–	2	–
T. B. Mitchell	1932–1935	5	6	2	20	9	5·00	–	–	1	–
N. S. Mitchell-Innes	1935	1	1	0	5	5	5·00	–	–	–	–
A. W. Mold	1893	3	3	1	0	0*	0·00	–	–	1	–
L. J. Moon	1905–1906	4	8	0	182	36	22·75	–	–	4	–
F. Morley	1880–1883	4	6	2	6	2*	1·50	–	–	4	–
J. B. Mortimore	1958–1964	9	12	2	243	73*	24·30	–	1	3	–
A. E. Moss	1953–1960	9	7	1	61	26	10·16	–	–	1	–
W. L. Murdoch	1891–1892	1	1	0	12	12	12·00	–	–	–	1
J. T. Murray	1961–1967	21	28	5	506	112	22·00	1	2	52	3
W. Newham	1887–1888	1	2	0	26	17	13·00	–	–	–	–
M. S. Nichols	1929–1939	14	19	7	355	78*	29·58	–	2	12	–
A. S. M. Oakman	1956	2	2	0	14	10	7·00	–	–	7	–
T. C. O'Brien	1884–1896	5	8	0	59	20	7·37	–	–	4	–
J. O'Connor	1929–1930	4	7	0	153	51	21·85	–	1	2	–
C. M. Old	1972–1978	40	57	6	722	65	14·15	–	2	22	–
N. Oldfield	1939	1	2	0	99	80	49·50	–	1	–	–
D. E. V. Padgett	1960	2	4	0	51	31	12·75	–	–	–	–
G. A. E. Paine	1934–1935	4	7	1	97	49	16·16	–	–	6	–
L. C. H. Palairet	1902	2	4	0	49	20	12·25	–	–	2	–
C. H. Palmer	1953–1954	1	2	0	22	22	11·00	–	–	–	–
K. E. Palmer	1964–1965	1	1	0	10	10	10·00	–	–	–	–
P. H. Parfitt	1961–1972	37	52	6	1882	131*	40·91	7	6	42	–
C. W. L. Parker	1921	1	1	1	3	3*	–	–	–	–	–
W. G. A. Parkhouse	1950–1959	7	13	0	373	78	28·69	–	2	3	–
C. H. Parkin	1920–1924	10	16	3	160	36	12·30	–	–	3	–
J. H. Parks	1937	1	2	0	29	22	14·50	–	–	–	–
J. M. Parks	1954–1968	46	68	7	1962	108*	32·16	2	9	103	11
Nawab of Pataudi	1932–1934	3	5	0	144	102	28·80	1	–	–	–
E. Paynter	1931–1939	20	31	5	1540	243	59·23	4	7	7	–
E. Peate	1881–1886	9	14	8	70	13	11·66	–	–	2	–
I. A. R. Peebles	1927–1931	13	17	8	98	26	10·88	–	–	5	–
R. Peel	1884–1896	20	33	4	427	83	14·72	–	3	17	–
F. Penn	1880	1	2	1	50	27*	50·00	–	–	–	–
R. T. D. Perks	1938–1939	2	2	2	3	2*	–	–	–	1	–
H. Philipson	1891–1895	5	8	1	63	30	9·00	–	–	8	3
R. Pilling	1881–1888	8	13	1	91	23	7·58	–	–	10	4
W. Place	1947–1948	3	6	1	144	107	28·80	1	–	–	–
P. I. Pocock	1967–1976	17	27	2	165	33	6·60	–	–	13	–
R. Pollard	1946–1948	4	3	2	13	10*	13·00	–	–	3	–
C. J. Poole	1951–1952	3	5	1	161	69*	40·25	–	2	1	–
G. H. Pope	1947	1	1	1	8	8*	–	–	–	–	–
A. D. Pougher	1891–1892	1	1	0	17	17	17·00	–	–	2	–
J. S. E. Price	1963–1972	15	15	6	66	32	7·33	–	–	7	–
W. F. F. Price	1938	1	2	0	6	6	3·00	–	–	2	–
R. M. Prideaux	1968–1969	3	6	1	102	64	20·40	–	1	–	–
G. Pullar	1959–1963	28	49	4	1974	175	43·86	4	12	2	–
W. Quaife	1899–1902	7	13	1	228	68	19·00	–	1	4	–
C. T. Radley	1977–1978	8	10	0	481	158	48·10	2	2	4	–
D. W. Randall	1976–1978	16	26	2	631	174	26·29	1	3	9	–

		M	I	NO	Runs	HS	Avge	100	50	Ct	St
K. S. Ranjitsinhji	1896–1902	15	26	4	989	175	44·95	2	6	13	–
H. D. Read	1935	1	–	–	–	–	–	–	–	–	–
J. M. Read	1882–1893	17	29	2	463	57	17·14	–	2	8	–
W. W. Read	1882–1893	18	27	1	720	117	27·69	1	5	16	–
A. E. Relf	1903–1914	13	21	3	416	63	23·11	–	1	14	–
H. J. Rhodes	1959	2	1	1	0	0*	–	–	–	–	–
W. Rhodes	1899–1930	58	98	21	2325	179	30·19	2	11	60	–
D. W. Richardson	1957	1	1	0	33	33	33·00	–	–	1	–
P. E. Richardson	1956–1963	34	56	1	2061	126	37·47	5	9	6	–
T. Richardson	1893–1898	14	24	8	177	25*	11·06	–	–	5	–
T. L. Richmond	1921	1	2	0	6	4	3·00	–	–	–	–
F. Ridgway	1951–1952	5	6	0	49	24	8·16	–	–	3	–
J. D. B. Robertson	1947–1952	11	21	2	881	133	46·36	2	6	6	–
R. W. V. Robins	1929–1937	19	27	4	612	108	26·60	1	4	12	–
G. R. J. Roope	1972–1978	21	32	4	860	77	30·71	–	7	35	–
C. F. Root	1926	3	–	–	–	–	–	–	–	1	–
V. P. F. A. Royle	1878–1879	1	2	0	21	18	10·50	–	–	2	–
B. C. Rose	1977–1978	5	8	1	100	27	14·28	–	–	2	–
F. E. Rumsey	1964–1965	5	5	3	30	21*	15·00	–	–	–	–
C. A. G. Russell	1920–1923	10	18	2	911	140	56·93	5	2	8	–
W. E. Russell	1961–1967	10	18	1	362	70	21·29	–	2	5	–
A. Sandham	1921–1930	14	23	0	878	325	38·17	2	3	4	–
S. S. Schultz	1878–1879	1	2	1	20	20	20·00	–	–	–	–
W. H. Scotton	1881–1887	15	25	2	510	90	22·27	–	3	4	–
J. Selby	1876–1882	6	12	1	256	70	23·27	–	2	1	–
M. W. W. Selvey	1976–1977	3	5	3	15	5*	7·50	–	–	1	–
D. Shackleton	1950–1963	7	13	7	112	42	18·66	–	–	1	–
J. Sharp	1909	3	6	2	188	105	47·00	1	1	1	–
J. W. Sharpe	1890–1892	3	6	4	44	26	22·00	–	–	2	–
P. J. Sharpe	1963–1969	12	21	4	786	111	46·23	1	4	17	–
A. Shaw	1876–1882	7	12	1	111	40	10·09	–	–	4	–
Rev D. S. Sheppard	1950–1963	22	33	2	1172	119	37·80	3	6	12	–
M. Sherwin	1886–1888	3	6	4	30	21*	15·00	–	–	5	2
A. Shrewsbury	1881–1893	23	40	4	1277	164	35·47	3	4	29	–
J. Shuter	1888	1	1	0	28	28	28·00	–	–	–	–
K. Shuttleworth	1970–1971	5	6	0	46	21	7·66	–	–	1	–
R. T. Simpson	1948–1955	27	45	3	1401	156*	33·35	4	6	5	–
G. H. T. Simpson-Hayward	1909–1910	5	8	1	105	29*	15·00	–	–	1	–
J. M. Sims	1935–1937	4	4	0	16	12	4·00	–	–	6	–
R. A. Sinfield	1938	1	1	0	6	6	6·00	–	–	–	–
T. F. Smailes	1946	1	1	0	25	25	25·00	–	–	–	–
A. C. Smith	1962–1963	6	7	3	118	69*	29·50	–	1	20	–
C. A. Smith	1888–1889	1	1	0	3	3	3·00	–	–	–	–
C. I. J. Smith	1934–1937	5	10	0	102	27	10·20	–	–	1	–
D. Smith	1935	2	4	0	128	57	32·00	–	1	1	–
D. R. Smith	1961–1962	5	5	1	38	34	9·50	–	–	2	–
D. V. Smith	1957	3	4	1	25	16*	8·33	–	–	–	–
E. J. Smith	1911–1914	11	14	1	113	22	8·69	–	–	17	3
H. Smith	1928	1	1	0	7	7	7·00	–	–	1	–
M. J. K. Smith	1958–1972	50	78	6	2278	121	31·63	3	11	53	–
T. P. B. Smith	1946–1947	4	5	0	33	24	6·60	–	–	1	–
G. A. Smithson	1947–1948	2	3	0	70	35	23·33	–	–	–	–
J. A. Snow	1965–1976	49	71	14	772	73	13·54	–	2	16	–
J. Southerton	1876–1877	2	3	1	7	6	3·50	–	–	2	–
R. H. Spooner	1905–1912	10	15	0	481	119	32·06	1	4	4	–
R. T. Spooner	1951–1955	7	14	1	354	92	27·23	–	3	10	2
R. T. Stanyforth	1927–1928	4	6	1	13	6*	2·60	–	–	7	2
S. J. Staples	1927–1928	3	5	0	65	39	13·00	–	–	–	–
J. B. Statham	1950–1965	70	87	28	675	38	11·44	–	–	28	–
A. G. Steel	1880–1888	13	20	3	600	148	35·29	2	–	5	–
D. S. Steele	1975–1976	8	16	0	673	106	42·06	1	5	7	–

		M	I	NO	Runs	HS	Avge	100	50	Ct	St
G. T. S. Stevens	1922–1930	10	17	0	263	69	15·47	–	1	9	–
M. J. Stewart	1962–1964	8	12	1	385	87	35·00	–	2	6	–
A. E. Stoddart	1887–1898	16	30	2	996	173	35·57	2	3	6	–
W. Storer	1897–1899	6	11	0	215	51	19·54	–	1	11	–
G. B. Street	1922–1923	1	2	1	11	7*	11·00	–	–	–	1
H. Strudwick	1909–1926	28	42	13	230	24	7·93	–	–	60	12
C. T. Studd	1882–1883	5	9	1	160	48	20·00	–	–	5	–
G. B. Studd	1882–1883	4	7	0	31	9	4·42	–	–	8	–
R. Subba Row	1958–1961	13	22	1	984	137	46·85	3	4	5	–
F. H. Sugg	1888	2	2	0	55	31	27·50	–	–	–	–
H. Sutcliffe	1924–1935	54	84	9	4555	194	60·73	16	23	23	–
R. Swetman	1958–1960	11	17	2	254	65	16·93	–	1	24	2
F. W. Tate	1902	1	2	1	9	5*	9·00	–	–	2	–
M. W. Tate	1924–1935	39	52	5	1198	100*	25·48	1	5	11	–
R. Tattersall	1950–1954	16	17	7	50	10*	5·00	–	–	8	–
K. Taylor	1959–1964	3	5	0	57	24	11·40	–	–	1	–
R. W. Taylor	1970–1978	13	14	1	202	45	15·53	–	–	36	3
Hon L. H. Tennyson	1913–1921	9	12	1	345	74*	31·36	–	4	6	–
G. J. Thompson	1909–1910	6	10	1	273	63	30·33	–	2	5	–
N. I. Thomson	1964–1965	5	4	1	69	39	23·00	–	–	3	–
F. J. Titmus	1955–1975	53	76	11	1449	84*	22·29	–	10	35	–
R. W. Tolchard	1976–1977	4	7	2	129	67	25·80	–	1	5	–
C. L. Townsend	1899	2	3	0	51	38	17·00	–	–	–	–
D. C. H. Townsend	1934–1935	3	6	0	77	36	12·83	–	–	1	–
L. F. Townsend	1929–1934	4	6	0	97	40	16·16	–	–	2	–
M. F. Tremlett	1947–1948	3	5	2	20	18*	6·66	–	–	–	–
A. E. Trott	1898–1899	2	4	0	23	16	5·75	–	–	–	–
F. S. Trueman	1952–1965	67	85	14	981	39*	13·81	–	–	64	–
N. C. Tufnell	1909–1910	1	1	0	14	14	14·00	–	–	–	1
M. J. L. Turnbull	1929–1936	9	13	2	224	61	20·36	–	1	1	–
G. E. Tyldesley	1921–1929	14	20	2	990	122	55·00	3	6	2	–
J. T. Tyldesley	1898–1909	31	55	1	1661	138	30·75	4	9	16	–
R. K. Tyldesley	1924–1930	7	7	1	47	29	7·83	–	–	1	–
E. F. S. Tylecote	1882–1886	6	9	1	152	66	19·00	–	1	5	5
E. J. Tyler	1895–1896	1	1	0	0	0	0·00	–	–	–	–
F. H. Tyson	1954–1959	17	24	3	230	37*	10·95	–	–	4	–
G. Ulyett	1876–1890	25	39	0	949	149	24·33	1	7	19	–
D. L. Underwood	1966–1977	74	100	31	824	45*	11·94	–	–	39	–
B. H. Valentine	1933–1939	7	9	2	454	136	64·85	2	1	2	–
H. Verity	1931–1939	40	44	12	669	66*	20·90	–	3	30	–
G. F. Vernon	1882–1883	1	2	1	14	11*	14·00	–	–	–	–
J. Vine	1911–1912	2	3	2	46	36	46·00	–	–	–	–
W. Voce	1930–1947	27	38	15	308	66	13·39	–	1	15	–
A. Waddington	1920–1921	2	4	0	16	7	4·00	–	–	1	–
E. Wainwright	1893–1898	5	9	0	132	49	14·66	–	–	2	–
P. M. Walker	1960	3	4	0	128	52	32·00	–	1	5	–
C. F. Walters	1933–1934	11	18	3	784	102	52·26	1	7	6	–
Alan Ward	1969–1976	5	6	1	40	21	8·00	–	–	3	–
Albert Ward	1893–1895	7	13	0	487	117	37·46	1	3	1	–
J. H. Wardle	1947–1957	28	41	8	653	66	19·78	–	2	12	–
P. F. Warner	1898–1912	15	28	2	622	132*	23·92	1	3	3	–
J. J. Warr	1950–1951	2	4	0	4	4	1·00	–	–	–	–
A. Warren	1905	1	1	0	7	7	7·00	–	–	1	–
C. Washbrook	1937–1956	37	66	6	2569	195	42·81	6	12	12	–
A. J. Watkins	1948–1952	15	24	4	811	138*	40·55	2	4	17	–
W. Watson	1951–1959	23	37	3	879	116	25·85	2	3	8	–
A. J. Webbe	1878–1879	1	2	0	4	4	2·00	–	–	2	–
A. W. Wellard	1937–1938	2	4	0	47	38	11·75	–	–	2	–
A. Wharton	1949	1	2	0	20	13	10·00	–	–	–	–
J. C. White	1921–1931	15	22	9	239	29	18·38	–	–	6	–
D. W. White	1961–1962	2	2	0	0	0	0·00	–	–	–	–
W. W. Whysall	1924–1930	4	7	0	209	76	29·85	–	2	7	–

		M	I	NO	Runs	HS	Avge	100	50	Ct	St
L. L. Wilkinson	1938–1939	3	2	1	3	2	3·00	–	–	–	–
P. Willey	1976	2	4	0	115	45	28·75	–	–	–	–
R. G. D. Willis	1970–1978	41	56	31	328	24*	13·12	–	–	19	–
C. E. M. Wilson	1898–1899	2	4	1	42	18	14·00	–	–	–	–
D. Wilson	1963–1971	6	7	1	75	42	12·50	–	–	1	–
E. R. Wilson	1920–1921	1	2	0	10	5	5·00	–	–	–	–
A. Wood	1938–1939	4	5	1	80	53	20·00	–	1	10	1
B. Wood	1972–1978	12	21	0	454	90	21·61	–	2	6	–
G. E. C. Wood	1924	3	2	0	7	6	3·50	–	–	5	1
H. Wood	1888–1892	4	4	1	204	134*	68·00	1	1	2	1
R. Wood	1886–1887	1	2	0	6	6	3·00	–	–	–	–
S. M. J. Woods	1895–1896	3	4	0	122	53	30·50	–	1	4	–
F. E. Woolley	1909–1934	64	98	7	3283	154	36·07	5	23	64	–
R. A. Woolmer	1975–1977	15	26	1	920	149	36·80	3	2	8	–
T. S. Worthington	1929–1937	9	11	0	321	128	29·18	1	1	8	–
C. W. Wright	1895–1896	3	4	0	125	71	31·25	–	1	–	–
D. V. P. Wright	1938–1951	34	39	13	289	45	11·11	–	–	10	–
R. E. S. Wyatt	1927–1937	40	64	6	1839	149	31·70	2	12	16	–
E. G. Wynyard	1896–1906	3	6	0	72	30	12·00	–	–	–	–
N. W. D. Yardley	1938–1950	20	34	2	812	99	25·37	–	4	14	–
H. I. Young	1899	2	2	0	43	43	21·50	–	–	1	–
J. A. Young	1947–1949	8	10	5	28	10*	5·60	–	–	5	–
R. A. Young	1907–1908	2	4	0	27	13	6·75	–	–	6	–
							Substitutes			59	1

Bowling

	M	Balls	Mdns	Runs	Wkts	Avge	5wI	10wM	Best
D. A. Allen	39	11297	679	3778	122	30·96	4	–	5–30
G. O. B. Allen	25	4390	116	2379	81	29·37	5	1	7–80
M. J. C. Allom	5	817	28	265	14	18·92	1	–	5–38
R. Appleyard	9	1596	70	554	31	17·87	1	–	5–51
T. Armitage	2	12	0	15	0	–	–	–	–
E. G. Arnold	10	1677	64	788	31	25·41	1	–	5–37
G. G. Arnold	34	7650	284	3254	115	28·29	6	–	6–45
W. E. Astill	9	2181	98	856	25	34·24	–	–	4–58
W. Attewell	10	2850	326	626	27	23·18	–	–	4–42
T. E. Bailey	61	9712	379	3856	132	29·21	5	1	7–34
A. H. Bakewell	6	18	0	8	0	–	–	–	–
J. C. Balderstone	2	96	0	80	1	80·00	–	–	1–80
R. W. Barber	28	3426	101	1806	42	43·00	–	–	4–132
W. Barber	2	2	0	0	1	0·00	–	–	1–0
R. G. Barlow	17	2456	315	767	35	21·91	3	–	7–40
S. F. Barnes	27	7873	356	3106	189	16·43	24	7	9–103
W. Barnes	21	2285	271	793	51	15·54	3	–	6–28
C. J. Barnett	20	256	11	93	0	–	–	–	–
F. Barratt	5	750	33	235	5	47·00	–	–	1–8
K. F. Barrington	82	2715	102	1300	29	44·82	–	–	3–4
W. Bates	15	2364	282	821	50	16·42	4	1	7–28
A. V. Bedser	51	15918	574	5876	236	24·89	15	5	7–44
R. Berry	2	653	47	228	9	25·33	1	–	5–63
M. C. Bird	10	264	12	120	8	15·00	–	–	3–11
J. Birkenshaw	5	1017	33	469	13	36·07	1	–	5–57
C. Blythe	19	4438	231	1863	100	18·63	9	4	8–59
J. B. Bolus	7	18	0	16	0	–	–	–	–
M. W. Booth	2	312	8	130	7	18·57	–	–	4–49
B. J. T. Bosanquet	7	989	10	604	25	24·16	2	–	8–107
I. T. Botham	11	2554	94	1059	64	16·54	8	1	8–34
W. E. Bowes	15	3655	131	1519	68	22·33	6	–	6–33
E. H. Bowley	5	252	7	116	0	–	–	–	–
G. Boycott	74	816	36	350	7	50·00	–	–	3–47
W. M. Bradley	2	625	49	233	6	38·83	1	–	5–67
L. C. Braund	23	3693	144	1810	47	38·51	3	–	8–81

	M	Balls	Mdns	Runs	Wkts	Avge	5wI	10wM	Best
W. Brearley	4	705	25	359	17	21·11	1	–	5–110
J. Briggs	33	5332	389	2094	118	17·74	9	4	8–11
W. Brockwell	7	582	31	309	5	61·80	–	–	3–33
H. R. Bromley-Davenport	4	155	6	98	4	24·50	–	–	2–46
A. Brown	2	323	9	148	3	49·33	–	–	3–25
D. J. Brown	26	5098	183	2237	79	28·31	2	–	5–42
F. R. Brown	22	3260	117	1398	45	31·06	1	–	5–49
J. T. Brown	8	35	0	22	0	–	–	–	–
C. P. Buckenham	4	1182	25	593	21	28·23	1	–	5–115
H. J. Butler	2	552	30	215	12	17·91	–	–	4–34
D. B. Carr	2	210	6	140	2	70·00	–	–	2–84
D. W. Carr	1	414	3	282	7	40·28	1	–	5–146
T. W. Cartwright	5	1611	97	544	15	36·26	1	–	6–94
A. P. F. Chapman	26	40	1	20	0	–	–	–	–
S. Christopherson	1	136	13	69	1	69·00	–	–	1–52
E. W. Clark	8	1931	70	899	32	28·09	1	–	5–98
J. C. Clay	1	192	7	75	0	–	–	–	–
D. B. Close	22	1212	56	532	18	29·55	–	–	4–35
L. J. Coldwell	7	1662	60	610	22	27·72	1	–	6–85
D. C. S. Compton	78	2722	70	1410	25	56·40	1	–	5–70
C. Cook	1	180	4	127	0	–	–	–	–
G. A. Cope	3	864	29	277	8	34·62	–	–	3–102
W. H. Copson	3	762	31	297	15	19·80	1	–	5–85
R. M. H. Cottam	4	903	41	327	14	23·35	–	–	4–50
M. C. Cowdrey	114	119	0	104	0	–	–	–	–
A. Coxon	1	378	13	172	3	57·33	–	–	2–90
K. Cranston	8	1010	37	461	18	25·61	–	–	4–12
J. N. Crawford	12	2203	61	1150	39	29·48	3	–	5–48
W. R. Cuttell	2	285	32	73	6	12·16	–	–	3–17
H. Dean	3	447	23	153	11	13·90	–	–	4–19
E. R. Dexter	62	5317	186	2306	66	34·93	–	–	4–10
B. L. d'Oliveira	44	5706	318	1859	47	39·55	–	–	3–46
J. W. H. T. Douglas	23	2812	66	1486	45	33·02	1	–	5–46
K. S. Duleepsinhji	12	6	0	7	0	–	–	–	–
F. J. Durston	1	202	2	136	5	27·20	–	–	4–102
P. H. Edmonds	13	3013	138	901	43	20·95	2	–	7–66
J. H. Edrich	77	30	1	23	0	–	–	–	–
W. J. Edrich	39	3226	79	1693	41	41·29	–	–	4–68
J. E. Emburey	1	175	14	40	2	20·00	–	–	2–39
T. Emmett	7	728	92	284	9	31·55	1	–	7–68
K. Farnes	15	3932	103	1719	60	28·65	3	1	6–96
P. G. H. Fender	13	2178	67	1185	29	40·86	2	–	5–90
J. J. Ferris	1	272	27	91	13	7·00	2	1	7–37
A. Fielder	6	1491	42	711	26	27·34	1	–	6–82
J. A. Flavell	4	792	25	367	7	52·42	–	–	2–65
K. W. R. Fletcher	52	249	4	173	1	173·00	–	–	1–48
W. Flowers	8	858	92	296	14	21·14	1	–	5–46
F. G. J. Ford	5	210	6	129	1	129·00	–	–	1–47
F. R. Foster	11	2447	108	926	45	20·57	4	–	6–91
A. J. Fothergill	2	321	42	90	8	11·25	–	–	4–19
A. P. Freeman	12	3732	142	1707	66	25·86	5	3	7–71
C. B. Fry	26	10	1	3	0	–	–	–	–
M. W. Gatting	2	8	0	1	0	–	–	–	–
G. Geary	14	3810	181	1353	46	29·41	4	1	7–70
N. Gifford	15	3084	173	1026	33	31·09	1	–	5–55
A. E. R. Gilligan	11	2405	74	1046	36	29·05	2	1	6–7
C. Gladwin	8	2129	89	571	15	38·06	–	–	3–21
T. W. J. Goddard	8	1563	62	588	22	26·72	1	–	6–29
G. A. Gooch	7	60	0	29	0	–	–	–	–
F. S. Gough-Calthorpe	4	204	8	91	1	91·00	–	–	1–38
A. R. Gover	4	816	26	359	8	44·87	–	–	3–85
W. G. Grace	22	663	65	236	9	26·22	–	–	2–12

	M	Balls	Mdns	Runs	Wkts	Avge	5wI	10wM	Best
T. W. Graveney	79	260	6	167	1	167·00	–	–	1–34
T. Greenhough	4	1129	66	357	16	22·31	1	–	5–35
A. W. Greig	58	9802	339	4541	141	32·20	6	2	8–86
G. Gunn	15	12	0	8	0	–	–	–	
J. R. Gunn	6	903	54	387	18	21·50	1	–	5–76
N. E. Haig	5	1026	54	448	13	34·46	–	–	3–73
S. Haigh	11	1294	61	622	24	25·91	1	–	6–11
W. R. Hammond	85	7969	300	3138	83	37·80	2	–	5–36
Lord Harris	4	32	1	29	0	–	–	–	
J. C. Hartley	2	192	2	115	1	115·00	–	–	1–62
E. G. Hayes	5	90	1	52	1	52·00	–	–	1–28
T. W. Hayward	35	869	42	514	14	36·71	–	–	4–22
J. T. Hearne	12	2976	211	1082	49	22·08	4	1	6–41
J. W. Hearne	24	2926	56	1462	30	48·73	1	–	5–49
E. H. Hendren	51	47	0	31	1	31·00	–	–	1–27
M. Hendrick	16	3136	119	1249	47	26·57	–	–	4–28
C. Heseltine	2	157	3	84	5	16·80	1	–	5–38
K. Higgs	15	4112	193	1473	71	20·74	2	–	6–91
A. Hill	2	340	37	130	6	21·66	–	–	4–27
A. J. L. Hill	3	40	4	8	4	2·00	–	–	4–8
M. J. Hilton	4	1238	69	471	14	33·64	1	–	5–61
G. H. Hirst	24	3979	146	1770	59	30·00	3	–	5–48
J. W. Hitch	7	462	5	325	7	46·42	–	–	2–31
J. B. Hobbs	61	376	15	165	1	165·00	–	–	1–19
R. N. S. Hobbs	7	1291	67	481	12	40·08	–	–	3–25
W. E. Hollies	13	3554	176	1332	44	30·27	5	–	7–50
E. R. T. Holmes	5	108	4	76	2	38·00	–	–	1–10
J. L. Hopwood	2	462	32	155	0	–	–	–	
A. N. Hornby	3	28	7	0	1	0·00	–	–	1–0
M. J. Horton	2	238	18	59	2	29·50	–	–	2–24
H. Howell	5	918	23	559	7	79·85	–	–	4–115
R. Howorth	5	1535	61	635	19	33·42	1	–	6–124
K. L. Hutchings	7	90	1	81	1	81·00	–	–	1–5
L. Hutton	79	260	4	232	3	77·33	–	–	1–2
R. A. Hutton	5	738	27	257	9	28·55	–	–	3–72
J. Iddon	5	66	3	27	0	–	–	–	
J. T. Ikin	18	572	12	354	3	118·00	–	–	1–38
R. Illingworth	61	11934	715	3807	122	31·20	3	–	6–29
Hon F. S. Jackson	20	1587	77	799	24	33·29	1	–	5–52
H. L. Jackson	2	498	30	155	7	22·14	–	–	2–26
J. A. Jameson	4	42	2	17	1	17·00	–	–	1–17
D. R. Jardine	22	6	0	10	0	–	–	–	
R. O. Jenkins	9	2118	51	1098	32	34·31	1	–	5–116
G. L. Jessop	18	672	28	354	10	35·40	–	–	4–68
A. O. Jones	12	228	14	133	3	44·33	–	–	3–73
I. J. Jones	15	3545	98	1769	44	37·63	1	–	6–118
V. W. C. Jupp	8	1301	55	616	28	22·00	–	–	4–37
A. S. Kennedy	5	1683	91	599	31	19·32	2	–	5–76
R. Kilner	9	2368	79	734	24	30·58	–	–	4–51
J. H. King	1	162	5	99	1	99·00	–	–	1–99
B. R. Knight	29	5384	204	2223	70	31·75	–	–	4–38
N. A. Knox	2	132	2	105	3	35·00	–	–	2–39
J. C. Laker	46	12027	674	4101	193	21·24	9	3	10–53
James Langridge	8	1074	51	413	19	21·73	2	–	7–56
J. D. F. Larter	10	2172	88	941	37	25·43	2	–	5–57
H. Larwood	21	4969	167	2216	78	28·41	4	1	6–32
E. Leadbeater	2	289	9	218	2	109·00	–	–	1–38
W. S. Lees	5	1256	69	467	26	17·96	2	–	6–78
G. B. Legge	5	30	0	34	0	–	–	–	
C. F. H. Leslie	4	96	10	44	4	11·00	–	–	3–31
J. K. Lever	13	2562	76	1058	44	24·04	2	1	7–46
P. Lever	17	3571	92	1509	41	36·80	2	–	6–38

	M	Balls	Mdns	Runs	Wkts	Avge	5wI	10wM	Best
M. Leyland	41	1103	35	585	6	97·50	–	–	3–91
A. F. A. Lilley	35	25	1	23	1	23·00	–	–	1–23
James Lillywhite jnr	2	340	37	126	8	15·75	–	–	4–70
D. Lloyd	9	24	0	17	0		–	–	
P. J. Loader	13	2662	117	878	39	22·51	1	–	6–36
G. A. R. Lock	49	13147	819	4451	174	25·58	9	3	7–35
W. H. Lockwood	12	1970	100	884	43	20·55	5	1	7–71
G. A. Lohmann	18	3821	364	1205	112	10·75	9	5	9–28
A. P. Lucas	5	120	13	54	0		–	–	
B. W. Luckhurst	21	57	2	32	1	32·00	–	–	1–9
Hon A. Lyttelton	4	48	5	19	4	4·75	–	–	4–19
G. G. Macaulay	8	1701	79	662	24	27·58	1	–	5–64
J. McConnon	2	216	12	74	4	18·50	–	–	3–19
C. S. Marriott	1	247	8	96	11	8·72	2	1	6–59
F. Martin	2	410	30	141	14	10·07	2	1	6–50
J. W. Martin	1	270	6	129	1	129·00	–	–	1–111
J. R. Mason	5	324	13	149	2	74·50	–	–	1–8
A. D. G. Matthews	1	180	8	65	2	32·50	–	–	1–13
W. Mead	1	265	24	91	1	91·00	–	–	1–91
W. E. Midwinter	4	776	79	272	10	27·20	–	–	4–81
G. Miller	14	1736	79	654	17	38·47	–	–	3–99
F. W. Milligan	2	45	2	29	0		–	–	
C. A. Milton	6	24	2	12	0		–	–	
A. Mitchell	6	6	0	4	0		–	–	
T. B. Mitchell	5	894	21	498	8	62·25	–	–	2–49
A. W. Mold	3	491	32	234	7	33·42	–	–	3–44
F. Morley	4	972	124	296	16	18·50	1	–	5–56
J. B. Mortimore	9	2162	133	733	13	56·38	–	–	3–36
A. E. Moss	9	1657	79	626	21	29·80	–	–	4–35
M. S. Nichols	14	2565	98	1152	41	28·09	2	–	6–35
A. S. M. Oakman	2	48	3	21	0		–	–	
J. O'Connor	4	162	6	72	1	72·00	–	–	1–31
C. M. Old	40	7540	254	3510	125	28·08	4	–	7–50
D. E. V. Padgett	2	12	0	8	0		–	–	
G. A. E. Paine	4	1044	39	467	17	27·47	1	–	5–168
C. H. Palmer	1	30	1	15	0		–	–	
K. E. Palmer	1	378	7	189	1	189·00	–	–	1–113
P. H. Parfitt	37	1308	68	574	12	47·83	–	–	2–5
C. W. L. Parker	1	168	16	32	2	16·00	–	–	2–32
C. H. Parkin	10	2095	55	1128	32	35·25	2	–	5–38
J. H. Parks	1	126	9	36	3	12·00	–	–	2–26
J. M. Parks	46	54	1	51	1	51·00	–	–	1–43
E. Peate	9	2096	260	682	31	22·00	2	–	6–85
I. A. R. Peebles	13	2882	78	1391	45	30·91	3	–	6–63
R. Peel	20	5216	444	1715	102	16·81	6	2	7–31
F. Penn	1	12	1	2	0		–	–	
R. T. D. Perks	2	829	17	355	11	32·27	2	–	5–100
P. I. Pocock	17	4482	184	2023	47	43·04	3	–	6–79
R. Pollard	4	1102	63	378	15	25·20	1	–	5–24
C. J. Poole	3	30	1	9	0		–	–	
G. H. Pope	1	218	12	85	1	85·00	–	–	1–49
A. D. Pougher	1	105	8	26	3	8·66	–	–	3–26
J. S. E. Price	15	2724	90	1401	40	35·02	1	–	5–73
R. M. Prideaux	3	12	2	0	0		–	–	
G. Pullar	28	66	3	37	1	37·00	–	–	1–1
W. Quaife	7	15	1	6	0		–	–	
D. W. Randall	16	16	0	3	0		–	–	
K. S. Ranjitsinhji	15	97	6	39	1	39·00	–	–	1–23
H. D. Read	1	270	14	200	6	33·33	–	–	4–136
W. W. Read	18	60	2	63	0		–	–	
A. E. Relf	13	1764	91	624	25	24·96	1	–	5–85
H. J. Rhodes	2	449	10	244	9	27·11	–	–	4–50

	M	Balls	Mdns	Runs	Wkts	Avge	5wI	10wM	Best
W. Rhodes	58	8220	368	3425	127	26·96	6	1	8–68
P. E. Richardson	34	120	9	48	3	16·00	–	–	2–10
T. Richardson	14	4497	191	2220	88	25·22	11	4	8–94
T. L. Richmond	1	114	3	86	2	43·00	–	–	2–69
F. Ridgway	5	793	23	379	7	54·14	–	–	4–83
J. D. B. Robertson	11	138	4	58	2	29·00	–	–	2–17
R. W. V. Robins	19	3318	77	1758	64	27·46	1	–	6–32
G. R. J. Roope	21	172	5	76	0	–	–	–	
C. F. Root	3	642	47	194	8	24·25	–	–	4–84
V. P. F. A. Royle	1	16	1	6	0	–	–	–	
F. E. Rumsey	5	1145	53	461	17	27·11	–	–	4–25
W. E. Russell	10	144	9	44	0	–	–	–	
S. S. Schultz	1	34	3	26	1	26·00	–	–	1–16
W. H. Scotton	15	20	1	20	0	–	–	–	
M. W. W. Selvey	3	492	9	343	6	57·16	–	–	4–41
D. Shackleton	7	2078	96	768	18	42·66	–	–	4–72
J. Sharp	3	183	3	111	3	37·00	–	–	3–67
J. W. Sharpe	3	975	61	305	11	27·72	1	–	6–84
A. Shaw	7	1099	155	285	12	23·75	1	–	5–38
A. Shrewsbury	23	12	2	2	0	–	–	–	
K. Shuttleworth	5	1071	20	427	12	35·58	1	–	5–47
R. T. Simpson	27	45	2	22	2	11·00	–	–	2–4
G. H. T. Simpson-Hayward	5	898	18	420	23	18·26	2	–	6–43
J. M. Sims	4	887	21	480	11	43·63	1	–	5–73
R. A. Sinfield	1	378	16	123	2	61·50	–	–	1–51
T. F. Smailes	1	120	3	62	3	20·66	–	–	3–44
C. A. Smith	1	154	16	61	7	8·71	1	–	5–19
C. I. J. Smith	5	930	40	393	15	26·20	1	–	5–16
D. R. Smith	5	972	47	359	6	59·83	–	–	2–60
D. V. Smith	3	270	13	97	1	97·00	–	–	1–12
M. J. K. Smith	50	214	4	128	1	128·00	–	–	1–10
T. P. B. Smith	4	538	5	319	3	106·33	–	–	2–172
J. A. Snow	49	12021	415	5387	202	26·66	8	1	7–40
J. Southerton	2	263	24	107	7	15·28	–	–	4–46
S. J. Staples	3	1149	50	435	15	29·00	–	–	3–50
J. B. Statham	70	16056	595	6261	252	24·84	9	1	7–39
A. G. Steel	13	1364	108	605	29	20·86	–	–	3–27
D. S. Steele	8	88	5	39	2	19·50	–	–	1–1
G. T. S. Stevens	10	1186	24	648	20	32·40	1	1	5–90
A. E. Stoddart	16	162	7	94	2	47·00	–	–	1–10
W. Storer	6	168	5	108	2	54·00	–	–	1–24
C. T. Studd	5	384	60	98	3	32·66	–	–	2–35
R. Subba Row	13	6	0	2	0	–	–	–	
F. W. Tate	1	96	4	51	2	25·50	–	–	2–7
M. W. Tate	39	12523	581	4055	155	26·16	7	1	6–42
R. Tattersall	16	4240	208	1519	58	26·18	4	1	7–52
K. Taylor	3	12	0	6	0	–	–	–	
Hon L. H. Tennyson	9	6	0	1	0	–	–	–	
G. J. Thompson	6	1367	66	638	23	27·73	–	–	4–50
N. I. Thomson	5	1488	68	568	9	63·11	–	–	2–55
F. J. Titmus	53	15118	777	4931	153	32·22	7	–	7–79
C. L. Townsend	2	140	5	75	3	25·00	–	–	3–50
D. C. H. Townsend	3	6	0	9	0	–	–	–	
L. F. Townsend	4	399	22	205	6	34·16	–	–	2–22
M. F. Tremlett	3	492	13	226	4	56·50	–	–	2–98
A. E. Trott	2	474	37	198	17	11·64	1	–	5–49
F. S. Trueman	67	15178	522	6625	307	21·57	17	3	8–31
G. E. Tyldesley	14	3	0	2	0	–	–	–	
R. K. Tyldesley	7	1615	76	619	19	32·57	–	–	3–50
E. J. Tyler	1	145	6	65	4	16·25	–	–	3–49
F. H. Tyson	17	3452	97	1411	76	18·56	4	1	7–27
G. Ulyett	25	2627	299	1020	51	20·00	1	–	7–36

		M	Balls	Mdns	Runs	Wkts	Avge	5wI	10wM	Best
D. L. Underwood		74	18979	1063	6600	265	24·90	16	6	8–51
H. Verity		40	11173	604	3510	144	24·37	5	2	8–43
W. Voce		27	6360	210	2733	98	27·88	3	2	7–70
A. Waddington		2	276	7	119	1	119·00	–	–	1–35
E. Wainwright		5	127	6	73	0	–	–	–	
P. M. Walker		3	78	3	34	0	–	–	–	
Alan Ward		5	761	20	453	14	32·35	–	–	4–61
J. H. Wardle		28	6597	404	2080	102	20·39	5	1	7–36
J. J. Warr		2	584	6	281	1	281·00	–	–	1–76
A. Warren		1	236	9	113	6	18·83	1	–	5–57
C. Washbrook		37	36	0	33	1	33·00	–	–	1–25
A. J. Watkins		15	1364	45	554	11	50·36	–	–	3–20
A. W. Wellard		2	456	9	237	7	33·85	–	–	4–81
D. W. White		2	220	5	119	4	29·75	–	–	3–65
J. C. White		15	4819	253	1581	49	32·26	3	1	8–126
W. W. Whysall		4	16	0	9	0	–	–	–	
L. L. Wilkinson		3	573	9	271	7	38·71	–	–	2–12
P. Willey		2	24	0	15	0	–	–	–	
R. G. D. Willis		41	7887	220	3653	151	24·19	10	–	7–78
D. Wilson		6	1472	92	466	11	42·36	–	–	2–17
E. R. Wilson		1	123	5	36	3	12·00	–	–	2–28
B. Wood		12	98	4	50	0	–	–	–	
S. M. J. Woods		3	195	8	129	5	25·80	–	–	3–28
F. E. Woolley		64	6495	251	2815	83	33·91	4	1	7–76
R. A. Woolmer		15	546	16	299	4	74·75	–	–	1–8
T. S. Worthington		9	633	18	316	8	39·50	–	–	2–19
D. V. P. Wright		34	8141	177	4224	108	39·11	6	1	7–105
R. E. S. Wyatt		40	1397	67	642	18	35·66	–	–	3–4
E. G. Wynyard		3	24	0	17	0	–	–	–	
N. W. D. Yardley		20	1662	41	707	21	33·66	–	–	3–67
H. I. Young		2	556	38	262	12	21·83	–	–	4–30
J. A. Young		8	2368	119	757	17	44·52	–	–	3–65

Australia (296 players)

Batting and Fielding

		M	I	NO	Runs	HS	Avge	100	50	Ct	St
E. L. a'Beckett	1928–1932	4	7	0	143	41	20·42	–	–	4	–
G. Alexander	1880–1885	2	4	0	52	33	13·00	–	–	2	–
H. H. Alexander	1932–1933	1	2	1	17	17*	17·00	–	–	–	–
F. E. Allan	1878–1879	1	1	0	5	5	5·00	–	–	–	–
P. J. Allan	1965–1966	1	–	–	–	–	–	–	–	–	–
R. C. Allen	1886–1887	1	2	0	44	30	22·00	–	–	2	–
T. J. E. Andrews	1921–1926	16	23	1	592	94	26·90	–	4	12	–
K. A. Archer	1950–1952	5	9	0	234	48	26·00	–	–	–	–
R. G. Archer	1952–1957	19	30	1	713	128	24·58	1	2	20	–
W. W. Armstrong	1901–1921	50	84	10	2863	159*	38·68	6	8	44	–
C. L. Badcock	1936–1938	7	12	1	160	118	14·54	1	–	3	–
A. C. Bannerman	1878–1893	28	50	2	1108	94	23·08	–	8	21	–
C. Bannerman	1876–1879	3	6	2	239	165*	59·75	1	–	–	–
W. Bardsley	1909–1926	41	66	5	2469	193*	40·47	6	14	12	–
S. G. Barnes	1938–1948	13	19	2	1072	234	63·05	3	5	14	–
B. A. Barnett	1938	4	8	1	195	57	27·85	–	1	3	2
J. E. Barrett	1890	2	4	1	80	67*	26·66	–	1	1	–
J. Benaud	1972–1973	3	5	0	223	142	44·60	1	–	–	–
R. Benaud	1951–1964	63	97	7	2201	122	24·45	3	9	65	–
J. M. Blackham	1876–1895	35	62	11	800	74	15·68	–	4	36	24
D. D. Blackie	1928–1929	3	6	3	24	11*	8·00	–	–	2	–
G. J. Bonnor	1880–1888	17	30	0	512	128	17·06	1	2	16	–
B. C. Booth	1961–1966	29	48	6	1773	169	42·21	5	10	17	–
H. F. Boyle	1878–1885	12	16	4	153	36*	12·75	–	–	10	–
D. G. Bradman	1928–1948	52	80	10	6996	334	99·94	29	13	32	–
R. J. Bright	1976–1977	3	5	1	42	16	10·50	–	–	2	–

		M	I	NO	Runs	HS	Avge	100	50	Ct	St
E. H. Bromley	1932–1934	2	4	0	38	26	9·50	–	–	2	–
W. A. Brown	1934–1948	22	35	1	1592	206*	46·82	4	9	14	–
W. Bruce	1884–1895	14	26	2	702	80	29·25	–	5	12	–
P. J. Burge	1954–1966	42	68	8	2290	181	38·16	4	12	23	–
J. W. Burke	1950–1959	24	44	7	1280	189	34·59	3	5	19	–
K. E. Burn	1890	2	4	0	41	19	10·25	–	–	–	–
F. J. Burton	1886–1888	2	4	2	4	2*	2·00	–	–	1	1
S. T. Callaway	1891–1895	3	6	1	87	41	17·40	–	–	–	–
I. W. Callen	1977–1978	1	2	2	26	22*	–	–	–	1	–
W. Carkeek	1912	6	5	2	16	6*	5·33	–	–	6	–
H. Carter	1907–1922	28	47	9	873	72	22·97	–	4	44	21
G. S. Chappell	1970–1977	51	90	13	4097	247*	53·20	14	20	73	–
I. M. Chappell	1964–1976	72	130	9	5187	196	42·86	14	25	103	–
P. C. Charlton	1890	2	4	0	29	11	7·25	–	–	–	–
A. G. Chipperfield	1934–1938	14	20	3	552	109	32·47	1	2	15	–
W. M. Clark	1977–1978	9	17	2	89	33	5·93	–	–	5	–
D. J. Colley	1972	3	4	0	84	54	21·00	–	1	1	–
H. L. Collins	1920–1926	19	31	1	1352	203	45·06	4	6	13	–
A. Coningham	1894–1895	1	2	0	13	10	6·50	–	–	–	–
A. N. Connolly	1963–1971	29	45	20	260	37	10·40	–	–	17	–
B. B. Cooper	1876–1877	1	2	0	18	15	9·00	–	–	2	–
W. H. Cooper	1881–1885	2	3	1	13	7	6·50	–	–	1	–
G. E. Corling	1964	5	4	1	5	3	1·66	–	–	–	–
G. J. Cosier	1975–1978	16	28	1	845	168	31·29	2	3	12	–
J. T. Cottam	1886–1887	1	2	0	4	3	2·00	–	–	1	–
A. Cotter	1903–1912	21	37	2	457	45	13·05	–	–	8	–
G. Coulthard	1881–1882	1	1	1	6	6*	–	–	–	–	–
R. M. Cowper	1964–1968	27	46	2	2061	307	46·84	5	10	21	–
I. D. Craig	1952–1958	11	18	0	358	53	19·88	–	2	2	–
P. Crawford	1956–1957	4	5	2	53	34	17·66	–	–	1	–
J. Darling	1894–1905	34	60	2	1657	178	28·56	3	8	27	–
L. S. Darling	1932–1937	12	18	1	474	85	27·88	–	3	8	–
W. M. Darling	1977–1978	4	8	0	164	65	20·50	–	2	1	–
A. K. Davidson	1953–1963	44	61	7	1328	80	24·59	–	5	42	–
I. C. Davis	1973–1977	15	27	1	692	105	26·61	1	4	9	–
J. H. de Courcy	1953	3	6	1	81	41	16·20	–	–	3	–
A. R. Dell	1970–1974	2	2	2	6	3*	–	–	–	–	–
H. Donnan	1891–1896	5	10	1	75	15	8·33	–	–	1	–
B. Dooland	1946–1948	3	5	1	76	29	19·00	–	–	3	–
R. A. Duff	1901–1905	22	40	3	1317	146	35·59	2	6	14	–
J. R. F. Duncan	1970–1971	1	1	0	3	3	3·00	–	–	–	–
G. Dymock	1973–1975	4	5	1	13	13	3·25	–	–	–	–
J. Dyson	1977–1978	3	6	0	101	53	16·83	–	1	–	–
C. J. Eady	1896–1902	2	4	1	20	10*	6·66	–	–	2	–
K. H. Eastwood	1970–1971	1	2	0	5	5	2·50	–	–	–	–
H. I. Ebeling	1934	1	2	0	43	41	21·50	–	–	–	–
J. D. Edwards	1888	3	6	1	48	26	9·60	–	–	1	–
R. Edwards	1972–1975	20	32	3	1171	170*	40·37	2	9	7	–
W. J. Edwards	1974–1975	3	6	0	68	30	11·33	–	–	–	–
S. H. Emery	1912	4	2	0	6	5	3·00	–	–	2	–
E. Evans	1881–1886	6	10	2	82	33	10·25	–	–	5	–
A. G. Fairfax	1928–1931	10	12	4	410	65	51·25	–	4	15	–
L. E. Favell	1954–1961	19	31	3	757	101	27·03	1	5	9	–
J. J. Ferris	1886–1890	8	16	4	98	20*	8·16	–	–	4	–
J. H. W. Fingleton	1931–1938	18	29	1	1189	136	42·46	5	3	13	–
L. O'B. Fleetwood-Smith	1935–1938	10	11	5	54	16*	9·00	–	–	–	–
B. C. Francis	1972	3	5	0	52	27	10·40	–	–	1	–
E. W. Freeman	1967–1970	11	18	0	345	76	19·16	–	2	5	–
F. W. Freer	1946–1947	1	1	1	28	28*	–	–	–	–	–
J. B. Gannon	1977–1978	3	5	4	3	3*	3·00	–	–	3	–
T. W. Garrett	1876–1888	19	33	6	339	51*	12·55	–	1	7	–

		M	I	NO	Runs	HS	Avge	100	50	Ct	St
R. A. Gaunt	1957–1964	3	4	2	6	3	3·00	–	–	1	–
D. R. A. Gehrs	1903–1911	6	11	0	221	67	20·09	–	2	6	–
G. Giffen	1881–1896	31	53	0	1238	161	23·35	1	6	24	–
W. F. Giffen	1886–1892	3	6	0	11	3	1·83	–	–	1	–
G. J. Gilmour	1973–1977	15	22	1	483	101	23·00	1	3	8	–
J. W. Gleeson	1967–1972	29	46	8	395	45	10·39	–	–	17	–
H. Graham	1893–1896	6	10	0	301	107	30·10	2	–	3	–
D. W. Gregory	1876–1879	3	5	2	60	43	20·00	–	–	–	–
E. J. Gregory	1876–1877	1	2	0	11	11	5·50	–	–	1	–
J. M. Gregory	1920–1929	24	34	3	1146	119	36·96	2	7	37	–
R. G. Gregory	1936–1937	2	3	0	153	80	51·00	–	2	1	–
S. E. Gregory	1890–1912	58	100	7	2282	201	24·53	4	8	25	–
C. V. Grimmett	1924–1936	37	50	10	557	50	13·92	–	1	17	–
T. U. Groube	1880	1	2	0	11	11	5·50	–	–	–	–
A. T. W. Grout	1957–1966	51	67	8	890	74	15·08	–	3	163	24
C. E. J. Guest	1962–1963	1	1	0	11	11	11·00	–	–	–	–
R. A. Hamence	1946–1948	3	4	1	81	30*	27·00	–	–	1	–
J. R. Hammond	1972–1973	5	5	2	28	19	9·33	–	–	2	–
J. Harry	1894–1895	1	2	0	8	6	4·00	–	–	1	–
R. J. Hartigan	1907–1908	2	4	0	170	116	42·50	1	–	1	–
A. E. V. Hartkopf	1924–1925	1	2	0	80	80	40·00	–	1	–	–
M. R. Harvey	1946–1947	1	2	0	43	31	21·50	–	–	–	–
R. N. Harvey	1947–1963	79	137	10	6149	205	48·41	21	24	64	–
A. L. Hassett	1938–1953	43	69	3	3073	198*	46·56	10	11	30	–
N. J. N. Hawke	1962–1968	27	37	15	365	45*	16·59	–	–	9	–
G. R. Hazlitt	1907–1912	9	12	4	89	34*	11·12	–	–	4	–
H. S. T. L. Hendry	1921–1929	11	18	2	335	112	20·93	1	–	10	–
P. A. Hibbert	1977–1978	1	2	0	15	13	7·50	–	–	1	–
J. D. Higgs	1977–1978	4	7	4	10	4*	3·33	–	–	–	–
C. Hill	1896–1912	49	89	2	3412	191	39·21	7	19	33	–
J. C. Hill	1953–1955	3	6	3	21	8*	7·00	–	–	2	–
D. E. Hoare	1960–1961	1	2	0	35	35	17·50	–	–	2	–
J. H. Hodges	1876–1877	2	4	1	10	8	3·33	–	–	–	–
G. B. Hole	1950–1955	18	33	2	789	66	25·45	–	6	21	–
D. W. Hookes	1976–1977	6	11	0	356	85	32·36	–	3	2	–
A. J. Y. Hopkins	1901–1909	20	33	2	509	43	16·42	–	–	11	–
T. P. Horan	1876–1885	15	27	2	471	124	18·84	1	1	6	–
H. V. Hordern	1910–1912	7	13	2	254	50	23·09	–	1	6	–
P. M. Hornibrook	1928–1930	6	7	1	60	26	10·00	–	–	7	–
W. P. Howell	1897–1904	18	27	6	158	35	7·52	–	–	12	–
K. J. Hughes	1977–1978	3	5	0	65	28	13·00	–	–	2	–
W. A. Hunt	1931–1932	1	1	0	0	0	0·00	–	–	1	–
A. G. Hurst	1973–1978	2	3	1	42	26	21·00	–	–	1	–
A. Hurwood	1930–1931	2	2	0	5	5	2·50	–	–	2	–
R. J. Inverarity	1968–1972	6	11	1	174	56	17·40	–	1	4	–
F. A. Iredale	1894–1899	14	23	1	807	140	36·68	2	4	16	–
H. Ironmonger	1928–1933	14	21	5	42	12	2·62	–	–	3	–
J. B. Iverson	1950–1951	5	7	3	3	1*	0·75	–	–	2	–
A. Jackson	1928–1931	8	11	1	474	164	47·40	1	2	7	–
B. N. Jarman	1959–1969	19	30	3	400	78	14·81	–	2	50	4
A. H. Jarvis	1884–1895	11	21	3	303	82	16·83	–	1	9	8
T. J. Jenner	1970–1976	9	14	5	208	74	23·11	–	1	5	–
C. B. Jennings	1912	6	8	2	107	32	17·83	–	–	5	–
I. W. Johnson	1945–1957	45	66	12	1000	77	18·51	–	6	30	–
L. J. Johnson	1947–1948	1	1	1	25	25*	–	–	–	2	–
W. A. Johnston	1947–1955	40	49	25	273	29	11·37	–	–	16	–
E. Jones	1894–1903	19	26	1	126	20	5·04	–	–	21	–
S. P. Jones	1881–1888	12	24	4	432	87	21·60	–	1	12	–
L. R. Joslin	1967–1968	1	2	0	9	7	4·50	–	–	–	–
C. Kelleway	1910–1929	26	42	4	1422	147	37·42	3	6	24	–
J. J. Kelly	1896–1905	36	56	17	664	46*	17·02	–	–	43	20
T. J. D. Kelly	1876–1879	2	3	0	64	35	21·33	–	–	1	–

		M	I	NO	Runs	HS	Avge	100	50	Ct	St
T. Kendall	1876–1877	2	4	1	39	17*	13·00	–	–	2	–
A. F. Kippax	1924–1934	22	34	1	1192	146	36·12	2	8	13	–
L. F. Kline	1957–1961	13	16	9	58	15*	8·28	–	–	9	–
G. R. A. Langley	1951–1957	26	37	12	374	53	14·96	–	1	83	15
F. Laver	1899–1909	15	23	6	196	45	11·52	–	–	8	–
T. J. Laughlin	1977–1978	2	3	0	80	35	26·66	–	–	1	–
W. M. Lawry	1961–1971	67	123	12	5234	210	47·15	13	27	30	–
P. K. Lee	1931–1933	2	3	0	57	42	19·00	–	–	1	–
D. K. Lillee	1970–1977	32	40	14	448	73*	17·23	–	1	9	–
R. R. Lindwall	1945–1960	61	84	13	1502	118	21·15	2	5	26	–
H. S. B. Love	1932–1933	1	2	0	8	5	4·00	–	–	3	–
S. J. E. Loxton	1947–1951	12	15	0	554	101	36·93	1	3	7	–
J. J. Lyons	1886–1898	14	27	0	731	134	27·07	1	3	3	–
P. A. McAlister	1903–1909	8	16	1	252	41	16·80	–	–	10	–
C. G. Macartney	1907–1926	35	55	4	2131	170	41·78	7	9	17	–
S. J. McCabe	1930–1938	39	62	5	2748	232	48·21	6	13	42	–
C. L. McCool	1945–1950	14	17	4	459	104*	35·30	1	1	14	–
E. L. McCormick	1935–1938	12	14	5	54	17*	6·00	–	–	8	–
R. B. McCosker	1974–1977	22	40	5	1498	127	42·80	4	9	18	–
C. C. McDonald	1951–1961	47	83	4	3107	170	39·32	5	17	13	–
E. A. McDonald	1920–1922	11	12	5	116	36	16·57	–	–	3	–
P. S. McDonnell	1880–1888	19	34	1	950	147	28·78	3	2	6	–
J. McIlwraith	1886	1	2	0	9	7	4·50	–	–	1	–
K. D. Mackay	1956–1963	37	52	7	1507	89	33·48	–	13	16	–
G. D. McKenzie	1961–1971	60	89	12	945	76	12·27	–	2	34	–
T. R. McKibbin	1894–1898	5	8	2	88	28	14·66	–	–	4	–
J. W. McLaren	1911–1912	1	2	2	0	0*	–	–	–	–	–
C. E. McLeod	1894–1905	17	29	5	573	112	23·87	1	4	9	–
R. W. McLeod	1891–1893	6	11	0	146	31	13·27	–	–	3	–
P. G. McShane	1884–1888	3	6	1	26	12*	5·20	–	–	2	–
L. V. Maddocks	1954–1957	7	12	2	177	69	17·70	–	1	18	1
A. A. Mallett	1968–1976	35	47	13	393	43*	11·55	–	–	29	–
A. A. Mailey	1920–1926	21	29	9	222	46*	11·10	–	–	14	–
M. F. Malone	1977	1	1	0	46	46	46·00	–	–	–	–
A. L. Mann	1977–1978	4	8	0	189	105	23·62	1	–	2	–
A. P. Marr	1884–1885	1	2	0	5	5	2·50	–	–	–	–
R. W. Marsh	1970–1977	52	82	9	2396	132	32·82	3	12	190	8
J. W. Martin	1960–1967	8	13	1	214	55	17·83	–	1	5	–
H. H. Massie	1881–1885	9	16	0	249	55	15·56	–	1	5	–
R. A. L. Massie	1972–1973	6	8	1	78	42	11·14	–	–	1	–
T. J. Matthews	1911–1912	8	10	1	153	53	17·00	–	1	7	–
E. R. Mayne	1912–1922	4	4	1	64	25*	21·33	–	–	2	–
L. C. Mayne	1964–1970	6	11	3	75	13	9·37	–	–	3	–
I. Meckiff	1957–1964	18	20	7	154	45*	11·84	–	–	9	–
K. D. Meuleman	1945–1946	1	1	0	0	0	0·00	–	–	1	–
W. E. Midwinter	1876–1886	8	14	1	174	37	13·38	–	–	5	–
K. R. Miller	1945–1957	55	87	7	2958	147	36·97	7	13	38	–
R. B. Minnett	1911–1912	9	15	0	391	90	26·06	–	3	–	–
F. M. Misson	1960–1961	5	5	3	38	25*	19·00	–	–	6	–
J. R. Moroney	1949–1952	7	12	1	383	118	34·81	2	1	–	–
A. R. Morris	1946–1955	46	79	3	3533	206	46·48	12	12	15	–
S. Morris	1884–1885	1	2	1	14	10*	14·00	–	–	–	–
H. Moses	1886–1895	6	10	0	198	33	19·80	–	–	1	–
W. H. Moule	1880	1	2	0	40	34	20·00	–	–	1	–
W. L. Murdoch	1876–1890	18	33	5	896	211	32·00	2	1	13	1
H. Musgrove	1884–1885	1	2	0	13	9	6·50	–	–	–	–
L. E. Nagel	1932–1933	1	2	1	21	21*	21·00	–	–	–	–
L. J. Nash	1931–1937	2	2	0	30	17	15·00	–	–	6	–
H. C. Nitschke	1931–1932	2	2	0	53	47	26·50	–	–	3	–
M. A. Noble	1897–1909	42	73	7	1997	133	30·25	1	16	26	–
G. Noblet	1949–1953	3	4	1	22	13*	7·33	–	–	1	–
O. E. Nothling	1928–1929	1	2	0	52	44	26·00	–	–	–	–

		M	I	NO	Runs	HS	Avge	100	50	Ct	St
L. P. J. O'Brien	1932–1937	5	8	0	211	61	26·37	–	2	3	–
J. D. A. O'Connor	1907–1909	4	8	1	86	20	12·28	–	–	3	–
A. D. Ogilvie	1977–1978	5	10	0	178	47	17·80	–	–	5	–
K. J. O'Keeffe	1970–1977	24	34	9	644	85	25·76	–	1	15	–
W. A. S. Oldfield	1920–1937	54	80	17	1427	65*	22·65	–	4	78	52
N. C. O'Neill	1958–1965	42	69	8	2779	181	45·55	6	15	21	–
W. J. O'Reilly	1931–1946	27	39	7	410	56*	12·81	–	1	7	–
R. K. Oxenham	1928–1932	7	10	0	151	48	15·10	–	–	4	–
G. E. Palmer	1880–1886	17	25	4	296	48	14·09	–	–	13	–
R. L. Park	1920–1921	1	1	0	0	0	0·00	–	–	–	–
L. S. Pascoe	1977	3	5	2	23	20	7·66	–	–	–	–
C. E. Pellew	1920–1922	10	14	1	484	116	37·23	2	1	4	–
P. I. Philpott	1964–1966	8	10	1	93	22	10·33	–	–	5	–
W. H. Ponsford	1924–1934	29	48	4	2122	266	48·22	7	6	21	–
R. J. Pope	1884–1885	1	2	0	3	3	1·50	–	–	–	–
V. S. Ransford	1907–1912	20	38	6	1211	143*	37·84	1	7	10	–
I. R. Redpath	1963–1976	66	120	11	4737	171	43·45	8	31	83	–
J. C. Reedman	1894–1895	1	2	0	21	17	10·50	–	–	1	–
D. A. Renneberg	1966–1968	8	13	7	22	9	3·66	–	–	2	–
A. J. Richardson	1924–1926	9	13	0	403	100	31·00	1	2	1	–
V. Y. Richardson	1924–1936	19	30	0	706	138	23·53	1	1	24	–
K. E. Rigg	1930–1937	8	12	0	401	127	33·41	1	1	5	–
D. T. Ring	1947–1953	13	21	2	426	67	22·42	–	4	5	–
S. J. Rixon	1977–1978	10	19	3	341	54	21·31	–	2	31	4
W. R. Robertson	1884–1885	1	2	0	2	2	1·00	–	–	–	–
R. D. Robinson	1977	3	6	0	100	34	16·66	–	–	4	–
R. H. Robinson	1936–1937	1	2	0	5	3	2·50	–	–	1	–
G. F. Rorke	1958–1960	4	4	2	9	7	4·50	–	–	1	–
J. Rutherford	1956–1957	1	1	0	30	30	30·00	–	–	–	–
J. Ryder	1920–1929	20	32	5	1394	201*	51·62	3	9	17	–
R. A. Saggers	1948–1950	6	5	2	30	14	10·00	–	–	16	8
J. V. Saunders	1901–1908	14	23	6	39	11*	2·29	–	–	5	–
H. J. H. Scott	1884–1886	8	14	1	359	102	27·61	1	1	8	–
R. H. D. Sellers	1964–1965	1	1	0	0	0	0·00	–	–	1	–
C. S. Serjeant	1977–1978	12	23	1	522	124	23·72	1	2	13	–
A. P. Sheahan	1967–1974	31	53	6	1594	127	33·91	2	7	17	–
B. K. Shepherd	1962–1965	9	14	2	502	96	41·83	–	5	2	–
M. W. Sievers	1936–1937	3	6	1	67	25*	13·40	–	–	4	–
R. B. Simpson	1957–1978	62	111	7	4869	311	46·81	10	27	110	–
D. J. Sincock	1964–1966	3	4	1	80	29	26·66	–	–	2	–
K. N. Slater	1958–1959	1	1	1	1	1*	–	–	–	–	–
J. Slight	1880	1	2	0	11	11	5·50	–	–	–	–
D. B. M. Smith	1912	2	3	1	30	24*	15·00	–	–	–	–
F. R. Spofforth	1876–1887	18	29	6	217	50	9·43	–	1	11	–
K. R. Stackpole	1965–1974	43	80	5	2807	207	37·42	7	14	47	–
G. B. Stevens	1959–1960	4	7	0	112	28	16·00	–	–	2	–
H. B. Taber	1966–1970	16	27	5	353	48	16·04	–	–	56	4
D. Tallon	1945–1953	21	26	3	394	92	17·13	–	2	50	8
J. M. Taylor	1920–1926	20	28	0	997	108	35·60	1	8	11	–
G. Thomas	1964–1966	8	12	1	325	61	29·54	–	3	3	–
N. Thompson	1876–1877	2	4	0	67	41	16·75	–	–	3	–
G. R. Thoms	1951–1952	1	2	0	44	28	22·00	–	–	–	–
A. L. Thomson	1970–1971	4	5	4	22	12*	22·00	–	–	–	–
J. R. Thomson	1972–1978	32	43	7	424	49	11·77	–	–	13	–
H. M. Thurlow	1931–1932	1	1	0	0	0	0·00	–	–	–	–
P. M. Toohey	1977–1978	8	15	0	705	122	47·00	1	6	2	–
E. R. H. Toshack	1945–1948	12	11	6	73	20*	14·60	–	–	4	–
J. P. F. Travers	1901–1902	1	2	0	10	9	5·00	–	–	1	–
G. E. Tribe	1946–1947	3	3	1	35	25*	17·50	–	–	–	–
A. E. Trott	1894–1895	3	5	3	205	85*	102·50	–	2	4	–
G. H. S. Trott	1888–1898	24	42	0	921	143	21·92	1	4	21	–

		M	I	NO	Runs	HS	Avge	100	50	Ct	St
H. Trumble	1890–1904	32	57	14	851	70	19·79	–	4	45	–
J. W. Trumble	1884–1886	7	13	1	243	59	20·25	–	1	3	–
V. T. Trumper	1899–1912	48	89	8	3163	214*	39·04	8	13	31	–
A. Turner	1975–1977	14	27	1	768	136	29·53	1	3	15	–
C. T. B. Turner	1886–1895	17	32	4	323	29	11·53	–	–	8	–
T. R. Veivers	1963–1967	21	30	4	813	88	31·26	–	7	7	–
M. G. Waite	1938	2	3	0	11	8	3·66	–	–	1	–
M. H. N. Walker	1972–1977	34	43	13	586	78*	19·53	–	1	12	–
T. W. Wall	1928–1934	18	24	5	121	20	6·36	–	–	11	–
F. H. Walters	1884–1885	1	2	0	12	7	6·00	–	–	2	–
K. D. Walters	1965–1977	68	116	12	4960	250	47·69	14	30	38	–
F. A. Ward	1936–1938	4	8	2	36	18	6·00	–	–	1	–
J. R. Watkins	1972–1973	1	2	1	39	36	39·00	–	–	1	–
G. D. Watson	1966–1972	5	9	0	97	50	10·77	–	1	1	–
W. Watson	1954–1955	4	7	1	106	30	17·66	–	–	2	–
W. J. Whitty	1909–1912	14	19	7	161	39*	13·41	–	–	4	–
J. W. Wilson	1956–1957	1	–	–	–	–	–	–	–	–	–
G. M. Wood	1977–1978	6	12	0	521	126	43·41	1	4	7	–
A. J. Woodcock	1973–1974	1	1	0	27	27	27·00	–	–	1	–
W. M. Woodfull	1926–1934	35	54	4	2300	161	46·00	7	13	7	–
S. M. J. Woods	1888	3	6	0	32	18	5·33	–	–	1	–
J. Worrall	1884–1899	11	22	3	478	76	25·15	–	5	13	–
G. N. Yallop	1975–1978	8	15	2	641	121	49·30	1	4	5	–
B. Yardley	1977–1978	6	11	2	254	74	28·22	–	1	5	–
								Substitutes		43	–

Bowling

	M	Balls	Mdns	Runs	Wkts	Avge	5wI	10wM	Best
E. L. a'Beckett	4	1062	47	317	3	105·66	–	–	1–41
G. Alexander	2	168	13	93	2	46·50	–	–	2–69
H. H. Alexander	1	276	3	154	1	154·00	–	–	1–129
F. E. Allan	1	180	15	80	4	20·00	–	–	2–30
P. J. Allan	1	192	6	83	2	41·50	–	–	2–58
T. J. E. Andrews	16	156	5	116	1	116·00	–	–	1–23
R. G. Archer	19	3571	160	1313	48	27·35	1	–	5–53
W. W. Armstrong	50	8052	403	2923	87	33·59	3	–	6–35
A. C. Bannerman	28	292	17	163	4	40·75	–	–	3–111
S. G. Barnes	13	594	11	218	4	54·50	–	–	2–25
J. Benaud	3	24	1	12	2	6·00	–	–	2–12
R. Benaud	63	19108	805	6704	248	27·03	16	1	7–72
D. D. Blackie	3	1260	51	444	14	31·71	1	–	6–94
G. J. Bonnor	17	164	16	84	2	42·00	–	–	1–5
B. C. Booth	29	436	27	146	3	48·66	–	–	2–33
H. F. Boyle	12	1744	175	641	32	20·03	1	–	6–42
D. G. Bradman	52	164	4	72	2	36·00	–	–	1–8
R. J. Bright	3	433	27	147	5	29·40	–	–	3–69
E. H. Bromley	2	60	4	19	0	–	–	–	–
W. Bruce	14	954	71	440	12	36·66	–	–	3–88
J. W. Burke	24	814	40	230	8	28·75	–	–	4–37
S. T. Callaway	3	471	33	142	6	23·66	1	–	5–37
I. W. Callen	1	440	5	191	6	31·83	–	–	3–83
G. S. Chappell	51	3752	125	1399	32	43·71	1	–	5–61
I. M. Chappell	72	2873	87	1316	20	65·80	–	–	2–21
P. C. Charlton	2	45	1	24	3	8·00	–	–	3–18
A. G. Chipperfield	14	926	28	437	5	87·40	–	–	3–91
W. M. Clark	9	2489	53	1162	43	27·02	–	–	4–46
D. J. Colley	3	729	20	312	6	52·00	–	–	3–83
H. L. Collins	19	654	31	252	4	63·00	–	–	2–47
A. Coningham	1	186	9	76	2	38·00	–	–	2–17
A. N. Connolly	29	7818	289	2981	102	29·22	4	–	6–47
W. H. Cooper	2	466	31	226	9	25·11	1	–	6–120

	M	Balls	Mdns	Runs	Wkts	Avge	5wI	10wM	Best
G. E. Corling	5	1159	50	447	12	37·25	–	–	4–60
G. J. Cosier	16	803	27	306	5	61·20	–	–	2–26
A. Cotter	21	4633	86	2549	89	28·64	7	–	7–148
R. M. Cowper	27	3005	138	1139	36	31·63	–	–	4–48
P. Crawford	4	437	27	107	7	15·28	–	–	3–28
L. S. Darling	12	162	7	65	0	–	–	–	
A. K. Davidson	44	11587	431	3819	186	20·53	14	2	7–93
A. R. Dell	2	559	18	160	6	26·66	–	–	3–65
H. Donnan	5	54	2	22	0	–	–	–	
B. Dooland	3	880	9	419	9	46·55	–	–	4–69
R. A. Duff	22	180	8	85	4	21·25	–	–	2–43
J. R. F. Duncan	1	112	4	30	0	–	–	–	
G. Dymock	4	1352	36	452	14	32·28	1	–	5–58
C. J. Eady	2	223	14	112	7	16·00	–	–	3–30
K. H. Eastwood	1	40	0	21	1	21·00	–	–	1–21
H. I. Ebeling	1	186	9	89	3	29·66	–	–	3–74
R. Edwards	20	12	0	20	0	–	–	–	
S. H. Emery	4	462	13	249	5	49·80	–	–	2–46
E. Evans	6	1247	166	332	7	47·42	–	–	3–64
A. G. Fairfax	10	1520	54	645	21	30·71	–	–	4–31
J. J. Ferris	8	2030	224	684	48	14·25	4	–	5–26
L. O'B. Fleetwood-Smith	10	3093	78	1570	42	37·38	2	1	6–110
E. W. Freeman	11	2183	58	1128	34	33·17	–	–	4–52
F. W. Freer	1	160	3	74	3	24·66	–	–	2–49
J. B. Gannon	3	726	13	361	11	32·81	–	–	4–77
T. W. Garrett	19	2708	297	970	36	26·94	2	–	6–78
R. A. Gaunt	3	716	14	310	7	44·28	–	–	3–53
D. R. A. Gehrs	6	6	0	4	0	–	–	–	
G. Giffen	31	6325	434	2791	103	27·09	7	1	7–117
G. J. Gilmour	15	2661	51	1406	54	26·03	3	–	6–85
J. W. Gleeson	29	8857	378	3367	93	36·20	3	–	5–61
D. W. Gregory	3	20	1	9	0	–	–	–	
J. M. Gregory	24	5581	138	2648	85	31·15	4	–	7–60
R. G. Gregory	2	24	0	14	0	–	–	–	
S. E. Gregory	58	30	0	33	0	–	–	–	
C. V. Grimmett	37	14513	735	5231	216	24·21	21	7	7–40
C. E. J. Guest	1	144	0	59	0	–	–	–	
J. R. Hammond	5	1031	47	488	15	32·53	–	–	4–38
R. J. Hartigan	2	12	0	7	0	–	–	–	
A. E. V. Hartkopf	1	240	2	134	1	134·00	–	–	1–120
R. N. Harvey	79	414	23	120	3	40·00	–	–	1–8
A. L. Hassett	43	111	2	78	0	–	–	–	
N. J. N. Hawke	27	6974	238	2677	91	29·41	6	1	7–105
G. R. Hazlitt	9	1563	74	623	23	27·08	1	–	7–25
H. S. T. L. Hendry	11	1706	73	640	16	40·00	–	–	3–36
J. D. Higgs	4	836	33	384	15	25·60	–	–	4–91
J. C. Hill	3	606	29	273	8	34·12	–	–	3–35
D. E. Hoare	1	232	0	156	2	78·00	–	–	2–68
J. H. Hodges	2	136	9	84	6	14·00	–	–	2–7
G. B. Hole	18	398	14	126	3	42·00	–	–	1–9
A. J. Y. Hopkins	20	1327	49	696	26	26·76	–	–	4–81
T. P. Horan	15	373	45	143	11	13·00	1	–	6–40
H. V. Hordern	7	2148	50	1075	46	23·36	5	2	7–90
P. M. Hornibrook	6	1579	63	664	17	39·05	1	–	7–92
W. P. Howell	18	3892	245	1407	49	28·71	1	–	5–81
W. A. Hunt	1	96	2	39	0	–	–	–	
A. G. Hurst	2	408	8	154	3	51·33	–	–	2–50
A. Hurwood	2	517	28	170	11	15·45	–	–	4–22
R. J. Inverarity	6	372	26	93	4	23·25	–	–	3–26
F. A. Iredale	14	12	0	3	0	–	–	–	
H. Ironmonger	14	4695	328	1330	74	17·97	4	2	7–23
J. D. Iverson	5	1108	29	320	21	15·23	1	–	6–27

	M	Balls	Mdns	Runs	Wkts	Avge	5wI	10wM	Best
T. J. Jenner	9	1881	62	749	24	31·20	1	–	5–90
I. W. Johnson	45	8773	328	3182	109	29·19	3	–	7–44
L. J. Johnson	1	282	10	74	6	12·33	–	–	3–8
W. A. Johnston	40	11048	372	3826	160	23·91	7	–	6–44
E. Jones	19	3748	160	1857	64	29·01	3	1	7–88
S. P. Jones	12	262	26	112	6	18·66	–	–	4–47
C. Kelleway	26	4363	146	1683	52	32·36	1	–	5–33
T. Kendall	2	563	56	215	14	15·35	1	–	7–55
A. F. Kippax	22	72	5	19	0	–	–	–	
L. F. Kline	13	2373	113	776	34	22·82	1	–	7–75
F. Laver	15	2367	122	964	37	26·05	2	–	8–31
T. J. Laughlin	2	316	10	202	6	33·66	1	–	5–101
W. M. Lawry	67	14	1	6	0	–	–	–	
P. K. Lee	2	436	19	212	5	42·40	–	–	4–111
D. K. Lillee	32	8783	264	4017	171	23·49	12	4	6–26
R. R. Lindwall	61	13650	419	5251	228	23·03	12	–	7–38
S. J. E. Loxton	12	906	20	349	8	43·62	–	–	3–55
J. J. Lyons	14	316	17	149	6	24·83	1	–	5–30
C. G. Macartney	35	3615	175	1240	45	27·55	2	1	7–58
S. J. McCabe	39	3746	127	1543	36	42·86	–	–	4–13
C. L. McCool	14	2512	45	958	36	26·61	3	–	5–41
E. L. McCormick	12	2107	50	1079	36	29·97	–	–	4–101
C. C. McDonald	47	8	0	3	0	–	–	–	
E. A. McDonald	11	2885	90	1431	43	33·27	2	–	5–32
P. S. McDonnell	19	52	1	53	0	–	–	–	
K. D. Mackay	37	5792	267	1721	50	34·42	2	–	6–42
G. D. McKenzie	60	17681	547	7328	246	29·78	16	3	8–71
T. R. McKibbin	5	1032	41	496	17	29·17	–	–	3–35
J. W. McLaren	1	144	3	70	1	70·00	–	–	1–23
C. E. McLeod	17	3374	171	1325	33	40·15	2	–	5–65
R. W. McLeod	6	1089	67	384	12	32·00	1	–	5–55
P. G. McShane	3	108	9	48	1	48·00	–	–	1–39
A. A. Mailey	21	6119	113	3358	99	33·91	6	2	9–121
A. A. Mallett	35	9136	392	3494	125	27·95	6	1	8–59
M. F. Malone	1	342	24	77	6	12·83	1	–	5–63
A. L. Mann	4	552	4	316	4	79·00	–	–	3–12
A. P. Marr	1	48	6	14	0	–	–	–	
J. W. Martin	8	1834	57	832	17	48·94	–	–	3–56
R. A. L. Massie	6	1739	74	647	31	20·87	2	1	8–53
T. J. Matthews	8	1111	46	419	16	26·18	–	–	4–29
E. R. Mayne	4	6	0	1	0	–	–	–	
L. C. Mayne	6	1251	37	628	19	33·05	–	–	4–43
I. Meckiff	18	3734	118	1423	45	31·62	2	–	6–38
W. E. Midwinter	8	949	102	333	14	23·78	1	–	5–78
K. R. Miller	55	10461	337	3906	170	22·97	7	1	7–60
R. B. Minnett	9	589	26	290	11	26·36	–	–	4–34
F. M. Misson	5	1197	30	616	16	38·50	–	–	4–58
A. R. Morris	46	111	1	50	2	25·00	–	–	1–5
S. Morris	1	136	14	73	2	36·50	–	–	2–73
W. H. Moule	1	51	4	23	3	7·66	–	–	3–23
L. E. Nagel	1	262	9	110	2	55·00	–	–	2–110
L. J. Nash	2	311	12	126	10	12·60	–	–	4–18
M. A. Noble	42	7109	361	3025	121	25·00	9	2	7–17
G. Noblet	3	774	25	183	7	26·14	–	–	3–21
O. E. Nothling	1	276	15	72	0	–	–	–	
J. D. A. O'Connor	4	692	24	340	13	26·15	1	–	5–40
K. J. O'Keeffe	24	5384	190	2018	53	38·07	1	–	5–101
N. C. O'Neill	42	1391	48	667	17	39·23	–	–	4–41
W. J. O'Reilly	27	10024	585	3254	144	22·59	11	3	7–54
R. K. Oxenham	7	1802	112	522	14	37·28	–	–	4–39
G. E. Palmer	17	4517	452	1678	78	21·51	6	2	7–65
R. L. Park	1	6	0	9	0	–	–	–	

	M	Balls	Mdns	Runs	Wkts	Avge	5wI	10wM	Best
L. S. Pascoe	3	826	35	363	13	27·92	–	–	4–80
C. E. Pellew	10	78	3	34	0	–	–	–	
P. I. Philpott	8	2268	67	1000	26	38·46	1	–	5–90
V. S. Ransford	20	43	3	28	1	28·00	–	–	1–9
I. R. Redpath	66	64	2	41	0	–	–	–	
J. C. Reedman	1	57	2	24	1	24·00	–	–	1–12
D. A. Renneberg	8	1598	42	830	23	36·08	2	–	5–39
A. J. Richardson	9	1812	91	521	12	43·41	–	–	2–20
D. T. Ring	13	3024	69	1305	35	37·28	2	–	6–72
W. R. Robertson	1	44	3	24	0	–	–	–	
G. F. Rorke	4	703	26	203	10	20·30	–	–	3–23
J. Rutherford	1	36	2	15	1	15·00	–	–	1–11
J. Ryder	20	1897	73	743	17	43·70	–	–	2–20
J. V. Saunders	14	3565	116	1796	79	22·73	6	–	7–34
H. J. H. Scott	8	28	1	26	0	–	–	–	
R. H. D. Sellers	1	30	1	17	0	–	–	–	
B. K. Shepherd	9	26	1	9	0	–	–	–	
M. W. Sievers	3	602	25	161	9	17·88	1	–	5–21
R. B. Simpson	62	6881	253	3001	71	42·26	2	–	5–57
D. J. Sincock	3	724	7	410	8	51·25	–	–	3–67
K. N. Slater	1	256	9	101	2	50·50	–	–	2–40
F. R. Spofforth	18	4185	416	1731	94	18·41	7	4	7–44
K. R. Stackpole	43	2321	86	1001	15	66·73	–	–	2–33
J. M. Taylor	20	114	5	45	1	45·00	–	–	1–25
N. Thompson	2	112	16	31	1	31·00	–	–	1–14
A. L. Thomson	4	1519	33	654	12	54·50	–	–	3–79
J. R. Thomson	32	7158	198	3699	145	25·51	5	–	6–46
H. M. Thurlow	1	234	7	86	0	–	–	–	
E. R. H. Toshack	12	3142	155	989	47	21·04	4	1	6–29
J. P. F. Travers	1	48	2	14	1	14·00	–	–	1–14
G. E. Tribe	3	760	9	330	2	165·00	–	–	2–48
A. E. Trott	3	474	17	192	9	21·33	1	–	8–43
G. H. S. Trott	24	1890	48	1019	29	35·13	–	–	4–71
H. Trumble	32	8099	452	3072	141	21·78	9	3	8–65
J. W. Trumble	7	600	59	222	10	22·20	–	–	3–29
V. T. Trumper	48	546	20	317	8	39·62	–	–	3–60
C. T. B. Turner	17	5195	457	1670	101	16·53	11	2	7–43
T. R. Veivers	21	4191	196	1375	33	41·66	–	–	4–68
M. G. Waite	2	552	23	190	1	190·00	–	–	1–150
M. H. N. Walker	34	10094	380	3792	138	27·47	6	–	8–143
T. W. Wall	18	4812	154	2010	56	35·89	3	–	5–14
K. D. Walters	68	3211	75	1378	49	28·12	1	–	5–66
F. A. Ward	4	1268	30	574	11	52·18	1	–	6–102
J. R. Watkins	1	48	1	21	0	–	–	–	
G. D. Watson	5	552	23	254	6	42·33	–	–	2–67
W. Watson	4	6	0	5	0	–	–	–	
W. J. Whitty	14	3357	163	1373	65	21·12	3	–	6–17
J. Wilson	1	216	17	64	1	64·00	–	–	1–25
S. M. J. Woods	3	217	18	121	5	24·20	–	–	2–35
J. Worrall	11	255	29	127	1	127·00	–	–	1–97
G. N. Yallop	8	18	1	8	0	–	–	–	
B. Yardley	6	1447	62	573	19	30·15	–	–	4–35

South Africa (235 players)

Batting and Fielding

		M	I	NO	Runs	HS	Avge	100	50	Ct	St
N. A. T. Adcock	1953–1962	26	39	12	146	24	5·40	–	–	4	–
J. H. Anderson	1902–1903	1	2	0	43	32	21·50	–	–	1	–
W. H. Ashley	1888–1889	1	2	0	1	1	0·50	–	–	–	–
A. Bacher	1965–1970	12	22	1	679	73	32·33	–	6	10	–
X. C. Balaskas	1930–1939	9	13	1	174	122*	14·50	1	–	5	–

		M	I	NO	Runs	HS	Avge	100	50	Ct	St
E. J. Barlow	1961–1970	30	57	2	2516	201	45·74	6	15	35	–
H. V. Baumgartner	1913–1914	1	2	0	19	16	9·50	–	–	1	–
R. Beaumont	1912–1914	5	9	0	70	31	7·77	–	–	2	–
D. W. Begbie	1948–1950	5	7	0	138	48	19·71	–	–	2	–
A. J. Bell	1929–1936	16	23	12	69	26*	6·27	–	–	6	–
M. Bisset	1898–1910	3	6	2	103	35	25·75	–	–	2	1
G. F. Bissett	1927–1928	4	4	2	38	23	19·00	–	–	–	–
J. M. Blanckenberg	1913–1924	18	30	7	455	59	19·78	–	2	9	–
K. C. Bland	1961–1967	21	39	5	1669	144*	49·08	3	9	10	–
E. G. Bock	1935–1936	1	2	2	11	9*	–	–	–	–	–
G. E. Bond	1938–1939	1	1	0	0	0	0·00	–	–	–	–
J. T. Botten	1965	3	6	0	65	33	10·83	–	–	1	–
W. H. Brann	1922–1923	3	5	0	71	50	14·20	–	1	2	–
A. W. Briscoe	1935–1939	2	3	0	33	16	11·00	–	–	1	–
H. D. Bromfield	1961–1965	9	12	7	59	21	11·80	–	–	13	–
L. S. Brown	1931–1932	2	3	0	17	8	5·66	–	–	–	–
C. G. de V. Burger	1957–1958	2	4	1	62	37*	20·66	–	–	1	–
S. F. Burke	1961–1965	2	4	1	42	20	14·00	–	–	–	–
I. D. Buys	1922–1923	1	2	1	4	4*	4·00	–	–	–	–
H. B. Cameron	1927–1935	26	45	4	1239	90	30·21	–	10	39	12
T. Campbell	1909–1912	5	9	3	90	48	15·00	–	–	7	1
P. R. Carlstein	1957–1964	8	14	1	190	42	14·61	–	–	3	–
C. P. Carter	1912–1924	10	15	5	181	45	18·10	–	–	2	–
R. H. Catterall	1922–1931	24	43	2	1555	120	37·92	3	11	12	–
H. W. Chapman	1913–1922	2	4	1	39	17	13·00	–	–	1	–
J. E. Cheetham	1948–1955	24	43	6	883	89	23·86	–	5	13	–
G. A. Chevalier	1969–1970	1	2	1	0	0*	–	–	–	1	–
J. A. J. Christy	1929–1932	10	18	0	618	103	34·33	1	5	3	–
G. W. A. Chubb	1951	5	9	3	63	15*	10·50	–	–	–	–
J. A. K. Cochran	1930–1931	1	1	0	4	4	4·00	–	–	–	–
S. K. Coen	1927–1928	2	4	2	101	41*	50·50	–	–	1	–
J. M. M. Commaille	1909–1928	12	22	1	355	47	16·90	–	–	1	–
D. P. Conyngham	1922–1923	1	2	2	6	3*	–	–	–	1	–
F. J. Cook	1895–1896	1	2	0	7	7	3·50	–	–	–	–
A. H. C. Cooper	1913–1914	1	2	0	6	6	3·00	–	–	1	–
J. L. Cox	1913–1914	3	6	1	17	12*	3·40	–	–	1	–
G. Cripps	1891–1892	1	2	0	21	18	10·50	–	–	–	–
R. J. Crisp	1935–1936	9	13	1	123	35	10·25	–	–	3	–
S. H. Curnow	1930–1932	7	14	0	168	47	12·00	–	–	5	–
E. L. Dalton	1929–1939	15	24	2	698	117	31·72	2	3	5	–
E. Q. Davies	1935–1939	5	8	3	9	3	1·80	–	–	–	–
O. C. Dawson	1947–1949	9	15	1	293	55	20·92	–	1	10	–
H. G. Deane	1924–1931	17	27	2	628	93	25·12	–	3	8	–
C. D. Dixon	1913–1914	1	2	0	0	0	0·00	–	–	1	–
R. R. Dower	1898–1899	1	2	0	9	9	4·50	–	–	2	–
R. G. Draper	1949–1950	2	3	0	25	15	8·33	–	–	–	–
C. A. R. Duckworth	1956–1957	2	4	0	28	13	7·00	–	–	3	–
R. Dumbrill	1965–1967	5	10	0	153	36	15·30	–	–	3	–
J. P. Duminy	1927–1929	3	6	0	30	12	5·00	–	–	2	–
O. R. Dunell	1888–1889	2	4	1	42	26*	14·00	–	–	1	–
J. H. du Preez	1966–1967	2	2	0	0	0	0·00	–	–	2	–
J. F. du Toit	1891–1892	1	2	2	2	2*	–	–	–	1	–
D. V. Dyer	1947	3	6	0	96	62	16·00	–	1	–	–
M. K. Elgie	1961–1962	3	6	0	75	56	12·50	–	1	4	–
W. R. Endean	1951–1958	28	52	4	1630	162*	33·95	3	8	41	–
W. S. Farrer	1961–1964	6	10	2	221	40	27·62	–	–	2	–
G. A. Faulkner	1905–1924	25	47	4	1754	204	40·79	4	8	20	–
J. P. Fellows-Smith	1960	4	8	2	166	35	27·66	–	–	2	–
C. G. Fichardt	1891–1896	2	4	0	15	10	3·75	–	–	2	–
C. E. Finlason	1888–1889	1	2	0	6	6	3·00	–	–	–	–
C. E. Floquet	1909–1910	1	2	1	12	11*	12·00	–	–	–	–
H. H. Francis	1898–1899	2	4	0	39	29	9·75	–	–	1	–

		M	I	NO	Runs	HS	Avge	100	50	Ct	St
C. M. Francois	1922–1923	5	9	1	252	72	31·50	–	1	5	–
C. N. Frank	1921–1922	3	6	0	236	152	39·33	1	–	–	–
W. H. B. Frank	1895–1896	1	2	0	7	5	3·50	–	–	–	–
E. R. H. Fuller	1952–1958	7	9	1	64	17	8·00	–	–	3	–
G. M. Fullerton	1947–1951	7	13	0	325	88	25·00	–	3	10	2
K. J. Funston	1952–1958	18	33	1	824	92	25·75	–	5	7	–
D. Gamsy	1969–1970	2	3	1	39	30*	19·50	–	–	5	–
R. A. Gleeson	1895–1896	1	2	1	4	3	4·00	–	–	2	–
G. K. Glover	1895–1896	1	2	1	21	18*	21·00	–	–	–	–
T. L. Goddard	1955–1970	41	78	5	2516	112	34·46	1	18	48	–
N. Gordon	1938–1939	5	6	2	8	7*	2·00	–	–	1	–
R. Graham	1898–1899	2	4	0	6	4	1·50	–	–	2	–
R. E. Grieveson	1938–1939	2	2	0	114	75	57·00	–	1	8	2
G. M. Griffin	1960	2	4	0	25	14	6·25	–	–	–	–
A. E. Hall	1922–1931	7	8	2	11	5	1·83	–	–	4	–
G. G. Hall	1964–1965	1	1	0	0	0	0·00	–	–	–	–
E. A. Halliwell	1891–1903	8	15	0	188	57	12·53	–	1	9	2
C. G. Halse	1963–1964	3	3	3	30	19*	–	–	–	1	–
P. A. M. Hands	1913–1924	7	12	0	300	83	25·00	–	2	3	–
R. H. M. Hands	1913–1914	1	2	0	7	7	3·50	–	–	–	–
M. A. Hanley	1948–1949	1	1	0	0	0	0·00	–	–	–	–
T. A. Harris	1947–1949	3	5	1	100	60	25·00	–	1	1	–
G. P. D. Hartigan	1912–1914	5	10	0	114	51	11·40	–	1	–	–
R. L. Harvey	1935–1936	2	4	0	51	28	12·75	–	–	–	–
C. M. H. Hathorn	1902–1911	12	20	1	325	102	17·10	1	–	5	–
F. Hearne	1891–1896	4	8	0	121	30	15·12	–	–	2	–
G. A. L. Hearne	1922–1924	3	5	0	59	28	11·80	–	–	3	–
P. S. Heine	1955–1962	14	24	3	209	31	9·95	–	–	8	–
C. F. W. Hime	1895–1896	1	2	0	8	8	4·00	–	–	–	–
P. Hutchinson	1888–1889	2	4	0	14	11	3·50	–	–	3	–
A. R. Innes	1888–1889	2	4	0	14	13	3·50	–	–	2	–
D. E. J. Ironside	1953–1954	3	4	2	37	13	18·50	–	–	1	–
B. L. Irvine	1969–1970	4	7	0	353	102	50·42	1	2	2	–
C. L. Johnson	1895–1896	1	2	0	10	7	5·00	–	–	1	–
P. S. T. Jones	1902–1903	1	2	0	0	0	0·00	–	–	–	–
H. J. Keith	1952–1957	8	16	1	318	73	21·20	–	2	9	–
G. A. Kempis	1888–1889	1	2	1	0	0*	0·00	–	–	–	–
J. J. Kotze	1902–1907	3	3	0	2	2	0·40	–	–	3	–
F. Kuys	1898–1899	1	2	0	26	26	13·00	–	–	–	–
H. R. Lance	1961–1970	13	22	1	591	70	28·14	–	5	7	–
A. B. C. Langton	1935–1939	15	23	4	298	73*	15·68	–	2	8	–
G. B. Lawrence	1961–1962	5	8	0	141	43	17·62	–	–	2	–
F. L. Le Roux	1913–1914	1	2	0	1	1	0·50	–	–	–	–
P. T. Lewis	1913–1914	1	2	0	0	0	0·00	–	–	–	–
D. T. Lindsay	1963–1970	19	31	1	1130	182	37·66	3	5	57	2
J. D. Lindsay	1947	3	5	2	21	9*	7·00	–	–	4	1
N. V. Lindsay	1921–1922	1	2	0	35	29	17·50	–	–	1	–
W. V. S. Ling	1921–1923	6	10	0	168	38	16·80	–	–	1	–
C. B. Llewellyn	1895–1912	15	28	1	544	90	20·14	–	4	7	–
E. B. Lundie	1913–1914	1	2	1	1	1	1·00	–	–	–	–
M. J. Macaulay	1964–1965	1	2	0	33	21	16·50	–	–	–	–
C. N. McCarthy	1948–1951	15	24	15	28	5	3·11	–	–	6	–
D. J. McGlew	1951–1962	34	64	6	2440	255*	42·06	7	10	18	–
A. H. McKinnon	1960 1967	8	13	7	107	27	17·83	–	–	1	–
R. A. McLean	1951–1965	40	73	3	2120	142	30·28	5	10	23	–
Q. McMillan	1929–1932	13	21	4	306	50*	18·00	–	1	8	–
N. B. F. Mann	1947–1951	19	31	1	400	52	13·33	–	1	3	–
P. N. F. Mansell	1951–1955	13	22	2	355	90	17·75	–	2	15	–
L. A. Markham	1948–1949	1	1	0	20	20	20·00	–	–	–	–
W. F. E. Marx	1921–1922	3	6	0	125	36	20·83	–	–	3	–
D. J. Meintjies	1922–1923	2	3	0	43	21	14·33	–	–	3	–
M. G. Melle	1949–1953	7	12	4	68	17	8·50	–	–	4	–

		M	I	NO	Runs	HS	Avge	100	50	Ct	St
A. Melville	1938–1949	11	19	2	894	189	52·58	4	3	8	–
J. Middleton	1895–1903	6	12	5	52	22	7·42	–	–	1	–
C. Mills	1891–1892	1	2	0	25	21	12·50	–	–	2	–
W. H. Milton	1888–1892	3	6	0	68	21	11·33	–	–	1	–
B. Mitchell	1929–1949	42	80	9	3471	189*	48·88	8	21	56	–
F. Mitchell	1912	3	6	0	28	12	4·66	–	–	–	–
D. P. B. Morkel	1927–1932	16	28	1	663	88	24·55	–	4	13	–
A. R. A. Murray	1952–1954	10	14	1	289	109	22·23	1	1	3	–
J. D. Nel	1949–1958	6	11	0	150	38	13·63	–	–	1	–
C. Newberry	1913–1914	4	8	0	62	16	7·75	–	–	3	–
E. S. Newson	1930–1939	3	5	1	30	16	7·50	–	–	3	–
F. Nicholson	1935–1936	4	8	1	76	29	10·85	–	–	3	–
J. F. W. Nicolson	1927–1928	3	5	0	179	78	35·80	–	1	–	–
N. O. Norton	1909–1910	1	2	0	9	7	4·50	–	–	–	–
A. D. Nourse	1935–1951	34	62	7	2960	231	53·81	9	14	12	–
A. W. Nourse	1902–1924	45	83	8	2234	111	29·78	1	15	43	–
E. P. Nupen	1921–1936	17	31	7	348	69	14·50	–	2	9	–
A. E. Ochse	1888–1889	2	4	0	16	8	4·00	–	–	–	–
A. L. Ochse	1927–1929	3	4	1	11	4*	3·66	–	–	1	–
S. O'Linn	1960–1962	7	12	1	297	98	27·00	–	2	4	–
H. G. Owen-Smith	1929	5	8	2	252	129	42·00	1	1	4	–
A. W. Palm	1927–1928	1	2	0	15	13	7·50	–	–	1	–
G. M. Parker	1924	2	4	2	3	2*	1·50	–	–	–	–
D. C. Parkin	1891–1892	1	2	0	6	6	3·00	–	–	1	–
J. T. Partridge	1963–1965	11	12	5	73	13*	10·42	–	–	6	–
C. O. C. Pearse	1910–1911	3	6	0	55	31	9·16	–	–	1	–
S. J. Pegler	1909–1924	16	28	5	356	35*	15·47	–	–	5	–
A. J. Pithey	1956–1965	17	27	1	819	154	31·50	1	4	3	–
D. B. Pithey	1963–1967	8	12	1	138	55	12·54	–	1	6	–
J. B. Plimsoll	1947	1	2	1	16	8*	16·00	–	–	–	–
P. M. Pollock	1961–1970	28	41	13	607	75*	21·67	–	2	9	–
R. G. Pollock	1963–1970	23	41	4	2256	274	60·97	7	11	17	–
R. M. Poore	1895–1896	3	6	0	76	20	12·66	–	–	3	–
J. E. Pothecary	1960	3	4	0	26	12	6·50	–	–	2	–
A. W. Powell	1898–1899	1	2	0	16	11	8·00	–	–	2	–
C. F. H. Prince	1898–1899	1	2	0	6	5	3·00	–	–	–	–
M. J. Procter	1966–1970	7	10	1	226	48	25·11	–	–	4	–
H. L. E. Promnitz	1927–1928	2	4	0	14	5	3·50	–	–	2	–
N. A. Quinn	1929–1932	12	18	3	90	28	6·00	–	–	1	–
N. Reid	1921–1922	1	2	0	17	11	8·50	–	–	–	–
A. R. Richards	1895–1896	1	2	0	6	6	3·00	–	–	–	–
B. A. Richards	1969–1970	4	7	0	508	140	72·57	2	2	3	–
W. H. M. Richards	1888–1889	1	2	0	4	4	2·00	–	–	–	–
J. B. Robertson	1935–1936	3	6	1	51	17	10·20	–	–	2	–
T. W. Routledge	1891–1896	4	8	0	72	24	9·00	–	–	2	–
A. M. B. Rowan	1947–1951	15	23	6	290	41	17·05	–	–	7	–
E. A. B. Rowan	1935–1951	26	50	5	1965	236	42·66	3	12	14	–
G. A. Rowe	1895–1903	5	9	3	26	13*	4·33	–	–	4	–
S. V. Samuelson	1909–1910	1	2	0	22	15	11·00	–	–	1	–
R. O. Schwarz	1905–1912	20	35	8	374	61	13·85	–	1	18	–
A. W. Seccull	1895–1896	1	2	1	23	17*	23·00	–	–	1	–
M. A. Seymour	1963–1970	7	10	3	84	36	12·00	–	–	2	–
W. A. Shalders	1898–1907	12	23	1	355	42	16·13	–	–	3	–
G. H. Shepstone	1895–1899	2	4	0	38	21	9·50	–	–	2	–
P. W. Sherwell	1905–1911	13	22	4	427	115	23·72	1	1	20	16
I. J. Siedle	1927–1936	18	34	0	977	141	28·73	1	5	7	–
J. H. Sinclair	1895–1911	25	47	1	1069	106	23·23	3	3	9	–
C. J. E. Smith	1902–1903	3	6	1	106	45	21·20	–	–	2	–
F. W. Smith	1888–1896	3	6	1	45	12	9·00	–	–	2	–
V. I. Smith	1947–1958	9	16	6	39	11*	3·90	–	–	3	–
S. D. Snooke	1907	1	1	0	0	0	0·00	–	–	2	–
S. J. Snooke	1905–1923	26	46	1	1008	103	22·40	1	5	24	–

		M	I	NO	Runs	HS	Avge	100	50	Ct	St
W. R. T. Solomon	1898–1899	1	2	0	4	2	2·00	–	–	1	–
R. B. Stewart	1888–1889	1	2	0	13	9	6·50	–	–	2	–
L. A. Stricker	1909–1912	13	24	0	342	48	14·25	–	–	3	–
M. J. Susskind	1924	5	8	0	268	65	33·50	–	4	1	–
H. M. Taberer	1902–1903	1	1	0	2	2	2·00	–	–	–	–
A. B. Tancred	1888–1889	2	4	1	87	29	29·00	–	–	2	–
L. J. Tancred	1905–1914	14	26	1	530	97	21·20	–	2	3	–
V. M. Tancred	1898–1899	1	2	0	25	18	12·50	–	–	–	–
G. L. Tapscott	1913–1914	1	2	0	5	4	2·50	–	–	1	–
L. E. Tapscott	1922–1923	2	3	1	58	50*	29·00	–	1	–	–
H. J. Tayfield	1949–1960	37	60	9	862	75	16·90	–	2	26	–
A. I. Taylor	1956–1957	1	2	0	18	12	9·00	–	–	–	–
D. Taylor	1913–1914	2	4	0	85	36	21·25	–	–	–	–
H. W. Taylor	1912–1932	42	76	4	2936	176	40·77	7	17	19	–
N. H. Theunissen	1888–1889	1	2	1	2	2*	2·00	–	–	–	–
P. G. Thornton	1902–1903	1	1	1	1	1*	–	–	–	1	–
D. S. Tomlinson	1935	1	1	0	9	9	9·00	–	–	–	–
A. J. Traicos	1969–1970	3	4	2	8	5*	4·00	–	–	4	–
P. H. J. Trimborn	1966–1970	4	4	2	13	11*	6·50	–	–	7	–
L. Tuckett	1947–1949	9	14	3	131	40*	11·90	–	–	9	–
L. R. Tuckett	1913–1914	1	2	1	0	0*	0·00	–	–	2	–
P. G. V. van der Bijl	1938–1939	5	9	0	460	125	51·11	1	2	1	–
E. A. van der Merwe	1929–1936	2	4	1	27	19	9·00	–	–	3	–
P. L. van der Merwe	1963–1967	15	23	2	533	76	25·38	–	3	11	–
C. B. van Ryneveld	1951–1958	19	33	6	724	83	26·81	–	3	14	–
G. D. Varnals	1964–1965	3	6	0	97	23	16·16	–	–	–	–
K. G. Viljoen	1930–1949	27	50	2	1365	124	28·43	2	9	5	–
C. L. Vincent	1927–1935	25	38	12	526	60	20·23	–	2	27	–
C. H. Vintcent	1888–1892	3	6	0	26	9	4·33	–	–	1	–
A. E. E. Vogler	1905–1911	15	26	6	340	65	17·00	–	2	20	–
H. F. Wade	1935–1936	10	18	2	327	40*	20·43	–	–	4	–
W. W. Wade	1938–1950	11	19	1	511	125	28·38	1	3	13	4
J. H. B. Waite	1951–1965	50	86	7	2405	134	30·44	4	16	124	17
K. A. Walter	1961–1962	2	3	0	11	10	3·66	–	–	3	–
T. A. Ward	1912–1924	23	42	9	459	64	13·90	–	2	19	12
J. C. Watkins	1949–1957	15	27	1	612	92	23·53	–	3	12	–
C. Wesley	1960	3	5	0	49	35	9·80	–	–	1	–
R. J. Westcott	1953–1958	5	9	0	166	62	18·44	–	1	–	–
G. C. White	1905–1912	17	31	2	872	147	30·06	2	4	10	–
J. T. Willoughby	1895–1896	2	4	0	8	5	2·00	–	–	–	–
C. S. Wimble	1891–1892	1	2	0	0	0	0·00	–	–	–	–
P. L. Winslow	1949–1955	5	9	0	186	108	20·66	1	–	1	–
O. E. Wynne	1948–1950	6	12	0	219	50	18·25	–	1	3	–
J. W. Zulch	1909–1922	16	32	2	985	150	32·83	2	4	4	–
							Substitutes		20		–

Bowling

	M	Balls	Mdns	Runs	Wkts	Avge	5wI	10wM	Best
N. A. T. Adcock	26	6391	218	2195	104	21·10	5	–	6–43
W. H. Ashley	1	173	18	95	7	13·57	1	–	7–95
X. C. Balaskas	9	1584	28	806	22	36·63	1	–	5–49
E. J. Barlow	30	3021	115	1362	40	34·05	1	–	5–85
H. V. Baumgartner	1	166	3	99	2	49·50	–	–	2–99
R. Beaumont	5	6	1	0	0	–	–	–	
D. W. Begbie	5	160	0	130	1	130·00	–	–	1–38
A. J. Bell	16	3342	89	1567	48	32·64	4	–	6–99
G. F. Bissett	4	989	28	469	25	18·76	2	–	7–29
J. M. Blanckenberg	18	3888	132	1817	60	30·28	4	–	6–76
K. C. Bland	21	400	19	125	2	62·50	–	–	2–16
E. G. Bock	1	138	2	91	0	–	–	–	
G. E. Bond	1	16	0	16	0	–	–	–	
J. T. Botten	3	828	37	337	8	42·12	–	–	2–56

	M	Balls	Mdns	Runs	Wkts	Avge	5wI	10wM	Best
H. D. Bromfield	9	1810	101	599	17	35·23	1	–	5–88
L. S. Brown	2	318	7	189	3	63·00	–	–	1–30
S. F. Burke	2	660	37	257	11	23·36	2	1	6–128
I. D. Buys	1	144	4	52	0	–	–	–	
C. P. Carter	10	1475	47	694	28	24·78	2	–	6–50
R. H. Catterall	24	342	7	162	7	23·14	–	–	3–15
H. W. Chapman	1	126	1	104	1	104·00	–	–	1–51
J. E. Cheetham	24	6	0	2	0	–	–	–	
G. A. Chevalier	1	253	11	100	5	20·00	–	–	3–68
J. A. J. Christy	10	138	4	92	2	46·00	–	–	1–15
G. W. A. Chubb	5	1424	63	577	21	27·47	2	–	6–51
J. A. K. Cochran	1	138	5	47	0	–	–	–	
S. K. Coen	2	12	0	7	0	–	–	–	
D. P. Conyngham	1	366	22	103	2	51·50	–	–	1–40
J. L. Cox	3	576	24	245	4	61·25	–	–	2–74
G. Cripps	1	15	0	23	0	–	–	–	
R. J. Crisp	9	1428	30	747	20	37·35	1	–	5–99
E. L. Dalton	15	864	7	490	12	40·83	–	–	4–59
E. Q. Davies	5	768	7	481	7	68·71	–	–	4–75
O. C. Dawson	9	1294	41	578	10	57·80	–	–	2–57
C. D. Dixon	1	240	6	118	3	39·33	–	–	2–62
R. Dumbrill	5	816	40	336	9	37·33	–	–	4–30
J. P. Duminy	3	60	0	39	1	39·00	–	–	1–17
J. H. du Preez	2	144	12	51	3	17·00	–	–	2–22
J. F. du Toit	1	85	5	47	1	47·00	–	–	1–47
M. K. Elgie	3	66	2	46	0	–	–	–	
G. A. Faulkner	25	4231	124	2180	82	26·58	4	–	7–84
J. P. Fellows-Smith	4	114	1	61	0	–	–	–	
C. E. Finlason	1	12	0	7	0	–	–	–	
C. E. Floquet	1	48	2	24	0	–	–	–	
C. M. Francois	5	684	36	225	6	37·50	–	–	3–23
W. H. B. Frank	1	58	3	52	1	52·00	–	–	1–52
E. R. H. Fuller	7	1898	61	668	22	30·36	1	–	5–66
G. K. Glover	1	65	4	28	1	28·00	–	–	1–28
T. L. Goddard	41	11735	706	3226	123	26·22	5	–	6–53
N. Gordon	5	1966	28	807	20	40·35	2	–	5–103
R. Graham	2	240	13	127	3	42·33	–	–	2–22
G. M. Griffin	2	432	14	192	8	24·00	–	–	4–87
A. E. Hall	7	2361	107	886	40	22·15	3	1	7–63
G. G. Hall	1	186	7	94	1	94·00	–	–	1–94
C. G. Halse	3	587	7	260	6	43·33	–	–	3–50
P. A. M. Hands	7	37	0	18	0	–	–	–	
M. A. Hanley	1	232	7	88	1	88·00	–	–	1–57
G. P. D. Hartigan	5	252	7	141	1	141·00	–	–	1–72
F. Hearne	4	62	0	40	2	20·00	–	–	2–40
P. S. Heine	14	3890	106	1455	58	25·08	4	–	6–58
C. F. W. Hime	1	55	4	31	1	31·00	–	–	1–20
A. R. Innes	2	128	8	89	5	17·80	1	–	5–43
D. E. J. Ironside	3	986	41	275	15	18·33	1	–	5–51
C. L. Johnson	1	140	12	57	0	–	–	–	
H. J. Keith	8	108	1	63	0	–	–	–	
G. A. Kempis	1	168	17	76	4	19·00	–	–	3–53
J. J. Kotze	3	413	8	243	6	40·50	–	–	3–64
F. Kuys	1	60	4	31	2	15·50	–	–	2–31
H. R. Lance	13	948	38	479	12	39·91	–	–	3–30
A. B. C. Langton	15	4199	104	1827	40	45·67	1	–	5–58
G. B. Lawrence	5	1334	62	512	28	18·28	2	–	8–53
F. L. Le Roux	1	54	3	24	0	–	–	–	
W. V. S. Ling	6	18	0	20	0	–	–	–	
C. B. Llewellyn	15	2292	55	1421	48	29·60	4	–	6–92
E. B. Lundie	1	286	9	107	4	26·75	–	–	4–101

	M	Balls	Mdns	Runs	Wkts	Avge	5wI	10wM	Best
M. J. Macaulay	1	276	17	73	2	36·50	–	–	1–10
C. N. McCarthy	15	3499	63	1510	36	41·94	2	–	6–43
D. J. McGlew	34	32	0	23	0	–	–	–	
A. H. McKinnon	8	2546	153	925	26	35·57	–	–	4–128
R. A. McLean	40	4	0	1	0	–	–	–	
Q. McMillan	13	2021	38	1243	36	34·52	2	–	5–66
N. B. F. Mann	19	5796	260	1920	58	33·10	1	–	6–59
P. N. F. Mansell	13	1506	31	736	11	66·90	–	–	3–58
L. A. Markham	1	104	1	72	1	72·00	–	–	1–34
W. F. E. Marx	3	228	1	144	4	36·00	–	–	3–85
D. J. Meintjies	2	246	7	115	6	19·16	–	–	3–38
M. G. Melle	7	1667	20	851	26	32·73	2	–	6–71
J. Middleton	6	1064	61	442	24	18·41	2	–	5–51
C. Mills	1	140	7	83	2	41·50	–	–	2–83
W. H. Milton	3	79	5	48	2	24·00	–	–	1–5
B. Mitchell	42	2519	26	1380	27	51·11	1	–	5–87
D. P. B. Morkel	16	1704	55	821	18	45·61	–	–	4–93
A. R. A. Murray	10	2374	111	710	18	39·44	–	–	4–169
C. Newberry	4	558	15	268	11	24·36	–	–	4–72
E. S. Newson	3	874	18	265	4	66·25	–	–	2–58
J. F. W. Nicolson	3	24	0	17	0	–	–	–	
N. O. Norton	1	90	4	47	4	11·75	–	–	4–47
A. D. Nourse	34	20	1	9	0	–	–	–	
A. W. Nourse	45	3234	120	1553	41	37·87	–	–	4–25
E. P. Nupen	17	4159	133	1788	50	35·76	5	1	6–46
A. L. Ochse	3	649	10	362	10	36·20	–	–	4–79
H. G. Owen-Smith	5	156	0	113	0	–	–	–	
G. M. Parker	2	366	2	273	8	34·12	1	–	6–152
D. C. Parkin	1	130	4	82	3	27·33	–	–	3–82
J. T. Partridge	11	3684	135	1373	44	31·20	3	–	7–91
C. O. C. Pearse	3	144	3	106	3	35·33	–	–	3–56
S. J. Pegler	16	2989	84	1572	47	33·44	2	–	7–65
A. J. Pithey	17	12	0	5	0	–	–	–	
D. B. Pithey	8	1424	67	577	12	48·08	1	–	6–58
J. B. Plimsoll	1	237	9	143	3	47·66	–	–	3–128
P. M. Pollock	28	6522	269	2806	116	24·18	9	1	6–38
R. G. Pollock	23	414	16	204	4	51·00	–	–	2–50
R. M. Poore	3	9	0	4	1	4·00	–	–	1–4
J. E. Pothecary	3	828	32	354	9	39·33	–	–	4–58
A. W. Powell	1	20	1	10	1	10·00	–	–	1–10
M. J. Procter	7	1514	80	616	41	15·02	1	–	6–73
H. L. E. Promnitz	2	528	30	161	8	20·12	1	–	5–58
N. A. Quinn	12	2922	103	1145	35	32·71	1	–	6–92
N. Reid	1	126	3	63	2	31·50	–	–	2–63
B. A. Richards	4	72	3	26	1	26·00	–	–	1–12
J. B. Robertson	3	738	26	321	6	53·50	–	–	3–143
A. M. B. Rowan	15	5193	136	2084	54	38·59	4	–	5–68
E. A. B. Rowan	26	19	1	7	0	–	–	–	
G. A. Rowe	5	998	50	456	15	30·40	1	–	5–115
S. V. Samuelson	1	108	2	64	0	–	–	–	
R. O. Schwarz	20	2639	66	1417	55	25·76	2	–	6–47
A. W. Seccull	1	60	2	37	2	18·50	–	–	2–37
M. A. Seymour	7	1452	35	588	9	65·33	–	–	3–80
W. A. Shalders	12	48	3	6	1	6·00	–	–	1–6
G. H. Shepstone	2	115	9	47	0	–	–	–	
I. J. Siedle	18	19	1	7	1	7·00	–	–	1–7
J. H. Sinclair	25	3598	110	1996	63	31·68	1	–	6–26
V. I. Smith	9	1655	55	769	12	64·08	–	–	4–143
S. J. Snooke	26	1620	62	702	35	20·05	1	1	8–70
L. A. Stricker	13	174	3	105	1	105·00	–	–	1–36
H. M. Taberer	1	60	2	48	1	48·00	–	–	1–25
L. E. Tapscott	2	12	1	2	0	–	–	–	

	M	Balls	Mdns	Runs	Wkts	Avge	5wI	10wM	Best
H. J. Tayfield	37	13568	602	4405	170	25·91	14	2	9–113
H. W. Taylor	30	342	18	156	5	31·20	–	–	3–15
N. H. Theunissen	1	80	5	51	0	–	–	–	–
P. G. Thornton	1	24	0	20	1	20·00	–	–	–
D. S. Tomlinson	1	60	0	38	0	–	–	–	–
A. J. Traicos	3	470	24	207	4	51·75	–	–	2–70
P. H. J. Trimborn	4	747	31	257	11	23·36	–	–	3–12
L. Tuckett	9	2104	46	980	19	51·57	2	–	5–68
L. R. Tuckett	1	120	4	69	0	–	–	–	–
P. L. van der Merwe	15	79	7	22	1	22·00	–	–	1–6
C. B. van Ryneveld	19	1554	27	671	17	39·47	–	–	4–67
G. D. Varnals	3	12	1	2	0	–	–	–	–
K. G. Viljoen	27	48	1	23	0	–	–	–	–
C. L. Vincent	25	5863	194	2631	84	31·32	3	–	6–51
C. H. Vintcent	3	369	23	193	4	48·25	–	–	3–88
A. E. E. Vogler	15	2764	96	1455	64	22·73	5	1	7–94
K. A. Walter	2	495	20	197	6	32·83	–	–	4–63
J. C. Watkins	15	2805	134	816	29	28·13	–	–	4–22
R. J. Westcott	5	32	0	22	0	–	–	–	–
G. C. White	17	498	14	301	9	33·44	–	–	4–47
J. T. Willoughby	2	275	12	159	6	26·50	–	–	2–37
J. W. Zulch	16	24	0	28	0	–	–	–	–

West Indies (171 players)

Batting and Fielding

		M	I	NO	Runs	HS	Avge	100	50	Ct	St
E. E. Achong	1929–1935	6	11	1	81	22	8·10	–	–	6	–
F. C. M. Alexander	1957–1961	25	38	6	961	108	30·03	1	7	85	5
D. W. Allan	1961–1966	5	7	1	75	40*	12·50	–	–	15	3
N. R. Asgarali	1957	2	4	0	62	29	15·50	–	–	–	–
D. S. Atkinson	1948–1958	22	35	6	922	219	31·79	1	5	11	–
E. S. Atkinson	1957–1959	8	9	1	126	37	15·75	–	–	2	–
R. A. Austin	1977–1978	2	2	0	22	20	11·00	–	–	2	–
S. F. A. Bacchus	1977–1978	2	4	0	42	21	10·50	–	–	3	–
L. Baichan	1974–1976	3	6	2	184	105*	46·00	1	–	2	–
A. G. Barrett	1970–1975	6	7	1	40	19	6·66	–	–	–	–
I. Barrow	1929–1939	11	19	2	276	105	16·23	1	–	17	5
E. L. Bartlett	1928–1931	5	8	1	131	84	18·71	–	1	2	–
N. Betancourt	1929–1930	1	2	0	52	39	26·00	–	–	–	–
A. P. Binns	1952–1956	5	8	1	64	27	9·14	–	–	14	3
L. S. Birkett	1930–1931	4	8	0	136	64	17·00	–	1	4	–
K. D. Boyce	1970–1976	21	30	3	657	95*	24·33	–	4	5	–
C. R. Browne	1928–1930	4	8	1	176	70*	25·14	–	1	1	–
B. F. Butcher	1958–1969	44	78	6	3104	209*	43·11	7	16	15	–
L. S. Butler	1954–1955	1	1	0	16	16	16·00	–	–	–	–
M. R. Bynoe	1958–1967	4	6	0	111	48	18·50	–	–	4	–
G. S. Camacho	1967–1971	11	22	0	640	87	29·09	–	4	4	–
F. J. Cameron	1948–1949	5	7	1	151	75*	25·16	–	1	–	–
J. H. Cameron	1939	2	3	0	6	5	2·00	–	–	–	–
G. M. Carew	1934–1949	4	7	1	170	107	28·33	1	–	1	–
M. C. Carew	1963–1972	19	36	3	1127	109	34·15	1	5	13	–
G. Challenor	1928	3	6	0	101	46	16·83	–	–	–	–
C. M. Christiani	1934–1935	4	7	2	98	32*	19·60	–	–	6	1
R. J. Christiani	1947–1954	22	37	3	896	107	26·35	1	4	19	2
C. B. Clarke	1939	3	4	1	3	2	1·00	–	–	–	–
S. Clarke	1977–1978	1	2	1	11	6	11·00	–	–	–	–
L. N. Constantine	1928–1939	18	33	0	635	90	19·24	–	4	28	–
C. E. H. Croft	1976–1978	7	10	8	60	23*	30·00	–	–	7	–
O. C. da Costa	1929–1935	5	9	1	153	39	19·12	–	–	5	–
W. W. Daniel	1975–1976	5	5	2	29	11	9·66	–	–	2	–
B. A. Davis	1964–1965	4	8	0	245	68	30·62	–	3	1	–

		M	I	NO	Runs	HS	Avge	100	50	Ct	St
C. A. Davis	1968–1973	15	29	5	1301	183	54·20	4	4	4	–
F. I. de Caires	1929–1930	3	6	0	232	80	38·66	–	2	1	–
C. C. Depeiaza	1954–1956	5	8	2	187	122	31·16	1	–	7	4
D. T. Dewdney	1954–1958	9	12	5	17	5*	2·42	–	–	–	–
U. G. Dowe	1970–1973	4	3	2	8	5*	8·00	–	–	3	–
R. M. Edwards	1968–1969	5	8	1	65	22	9·28	–	–	–	–
W. Ferguson	1947–1954	8	10	3	200	75	28·57	–	2	11	–
M. P. Fernandes	1928–1930	2	4	0	49	22	12·25	–	–	–	–
T. M. Findlay	1969–1973	10	16	3	212	44*	16·30	–	–	19	2
M. L. C. Foster	1969–1978	14	24	5	580	125	30·52	1	1	3	–
G. N. Francis	1928–1933	10	18	4	81	19*	5·78	–	–	7	–
M. Frederick	1953–1954	1	2	0	30	30	15·00	–	–	–	–
R. C. Fredericks	1968–1977	59	109	7	4334	169	42·49	8	26	62	–
R. L. Fuller	1934–1935	1	1	0	1	1	1·00	–	–	–	–
H. A. Furlonge	1954–1956	3	5	0	99	64	19·80	–	1	–	–
A. G. Ganteaume	1947–1948	1	1	0	112	112	112·00	1	–	–	–
J. Garner	1976–1978	7	10	1	97	43	10·77	–	–	6	–
B. B. M. Gaskin	1947–1948	2	3	0	17	10	5·66	–	–	1	–
G. L. Gibbs	1954–1955	1	2	0	12	12	6·00	–	–	1	–
L. R. Gibbs	1957–1976	79	109	39	488	25	6·97	–	–	52	–
R. Gilchrist	1957–1959	13	14	3	60	12	5·45	–	–	4	–
G. Gladstone	1929–1930	1	1	1	12	12*	–	–	–	–	–
J. D. C. Goddard	1947–1957	27	39	11	859	83*	30·67	–	4	22	–
H. A. Gomes	1976–1978	5	9	0	276	115	30·66	2	–	1	–
G. E. Gomez	1939–1954	29	46	5	1243	101	30·31	1	8	18	–
G. C. Grant	1930–1935	12	21	5	413	71*	25·81	–	3	10	–
R. S. Grant	1934–1939	7	11	1	220	77	22·00	–	1	13	–
A. T. Greenidge	1977–1978	2	4	0	142	69	35·50	–	2	2	–
C. G. Greenidge	1974–1978	19	36	2	1641	134	48·26	5	9	22	–
G. A. Greenidge	1971–1973	5	9	2	209	50	29·85	–	1	3	–
M. G. Grell	1929–1930	1	2	0	34	21	17·00	–	–	1	–
C. C. Griffith	1959–1969	28	42	10	530	54	16·56	–	1	16	–
H. C. Griffith	1928–1933	13	23	5	91	18	5·05	–	–	4	–
S. C. Guillen	1951–1952	5	6	2	104	54	26·00	–	1	9	2
W. W. Hall	1958–1969	48	66	14	818	50*	15·73	–	2	11	–
D. L. Haynes	1977–1978	2	3	0	182	66	60·66	–	3	1	–
G. A. Headley	1929–1954	22	40	4	2190	270*	60·83	10	5	14	–
R. G. A. Headley	1973	2	4	0	62	42	15·50	–	–	2	–
J. L. Hendriks	1961–1969	20	32	8	447	64	18·62	–	2	42	5
E. L. G. Hoad	1928–1933	4	8	0	98	36	12·25	–	–	1	–
V. A. Holder	1969–1978	34	51	9	603	42	14·35	–	–	15	–
M. A. Holding	1975–1976	13	20	1	213	55	11·21	–	1	3	–
D. A. J. Holford	1966–1977	24	39	5	768	105*	22·58	1	3	18	–
J. K. Holt	1953–1959	17	31	2	1066	166	36·75	2	5	8	–
A. B. Howard	1970–1971	1	–	–	–	–	–	–	–	–	–
C. C. Hunte	1957–1967	44	78	6	3245	260	45·06	8	13	17	–
E. A. C. Hunte	1929–1930	3	6	1	166	58	33·20	–	2	5	–
L. G. Hylton	1934–1939	6	8	2	70	19	11·66	–	–	1	–
Imtiaz Ali	1975–1976	1	1	1	1	1*	–	–	–	–	–
Inshan Ali	1970–1977	12	18	2	172	25	10·75	–	–	7	–
H. H. H. Johnson	1947–1950	3	4	0	38	22	9·50	–	–	–	–
T. F. Johnson	1939	1	1	1	9	9*	–	–	–	1	–
C. M. Jones	1929–1934	4	7	0	63	19	9·00	–	–	3	–
P. E. Jones	1947–1952	9	11	2	47	10*	5·22	–	–	4	–
B. D. Julien	1973–1977	24	34	6	866	121	30·92	2	3	14	–
R. R. Jumadeen	1971–1978	10	12	9	26	11*	8·66	–	–	4	–
A. I. Kallicharran	1971–1978	45	76	7	3331	158	48·27	10	17	35	–
R. B. Kanhai	1957–1974	79	137	6	6227	256	47·53	15	28	50	–
E. S. M. Kentish	1947–1954	2	2	1	1	1*	1·00	–	–	1	–
C. L. King	1976–1977	4	7	1	211	63	35·16	–	2	3	–
F. M. King	1952–1956	14	17	3	116	21	8·28	–	–	5	–
L. A. King	1961–1968	2	4	0	41	20	10·25	–	–	2	–

		M	I	NO	Runs	HS	Avge	100	50	Ct	St
P. D. Lashley	1960–1966	4	7	0	159	49	22·71	–	–	4	–
R. A. Legall	1952–1953	4	5	0	50	23	10·00	–	–	8	1
D. M. Lewis	1970–1971	3	5	2	259	88	86·33	–	3	8	–
C. H. Lloyd	1966–1978	65	113	8	4594	242*	43·75	11	22	43	–
E. D. A. S. McMorris	1957–1966	13	21	0	564	125	26·85	1	3	5	–
C. A. McWatt	1953–1955	6	9	2	202	54	28·85	–	2	9	1
I. S. Madray	1957–1958	2	3	0	3	2	1·00	–	–	1	–
N. E. Marshall	1954–1955	1	2	0	8	8	4·00	–	–	–	–
R. E. Marshall	1951–1952	4	7	0	143	30	20·42	–	–	1	–
F. R. Martin	1928–1931	9	18	1	486	123*	28·58	1	–	2	–
E. A. Martindale	1933–1939	10	14	3	58	22	5·27	–	–	4	–
I. L. Mendonca	1961–1962	2	2	0	81	78	40·50	–	1	8	2
C. A. Merry	1933	2	4	0	34	13	8·50	–	–	1	–
R. C. Miller	1952–1953	1	1	0	23	23	23·00	–	–	–	–
G. H. Moodie	1934–1935	1	1	0	5	5	5·00	–	–	–	–
D. A. Murray	1977–1978	3	6	0	67	21	11·16	–	–	6	3
D. L. Murray	1963–1978	51	80	8	1705	91	23·68	–	10	150	8
J. M. Neblett	1934–1935	1	2	1	16	11*	16·00	–	–	–	–
J. M. Noreiga	1970–1971	4	5	2	11	9	3·66	–	–	2	–
R. K. Nunes	1928–1930	4	8	0	245	92	30·62	–	2	2	–
S. M. Nurse	1959–1969	29	54	1	2523	258	47·60	6	10	21	–
A. L. Padmore	1975–1976	2	2	1	8	8*	8·00	–	–	–	–
B. H. Pairaudeau	1952–1957	13	21	0	454	115	21·61	1	3	6	–
D. R. Parry	1977–1978	5	9	2	193	65	27·57	–	2	3	–
C. C. Passailaigue	1929–1930	1	2	1	46	44	46·00	–	–	3	–
N. Phillip	1977–1978	3	6	1	120	46	24·00	–	–	2	–
L. R. Pierre	1947–1948	1	–	–	–	–	–	–	–	–	–
A. F. Rae	1948–1953	15	24	2	1016	109	46·18	4	4	9	–
S. Ramadhin	1950–1961	43	58	14	361	44	8·20	–	–	9	–
I. V. A. Richards	1974–1978	28	47	2	2500	291	55·55	8	8	26	–
K. R. Rickards	1947–1952	2	3	0	104	67	34·66	–	1	–	–
C. A. Roach	1928–1935	16	32	1	952	209	30·70	2	6	5	–
A. M. E. Roberts	1973–1978	27	36	5	229	35	7·38	–	–	5	–
A. T. Roberts	1955–1956	1	2	0	28	28	14·00	–	–	–	–
W. V. Rodriguez	1961–1968	5	7	0	96	50	13·71	–	1	3	–
L. G. Rowe	1971–1976	24	38	2	1706	302	47·38	6	5	13	–
E. L. St Hill	1929–1930	2	4	0	18	12	4·50	–	–	–	–
W. H. St Hill	1928–1930	3	6	0	117	38	19·50	–	–	1	–
R. Scarlett	1959–1960	3	4	1	54	29*	18·00	–	–	2	–
A. P. H. Scott	1952–1953	1	1	0	5	5	5·00	–	–	–	–
O. C. Scott	1928–1931	8	13	3	171	35	17·10	–	–	–	–
B. J. Sealey	1933	1	2	0	41	29	20·50	–	–	–	–
J. E. D. Sealy	1929–1939	11	19	2	478	92	28·11	–	3	6	1
J. N. Shepherd	1969–1971	5	8	0	77	32	9·62	–	–	4	–
G. C. Shillingford	1969–1972	7	8	1	57	25	8·14	–	–	2	–
I. T. Shillingford	1976–1978	4	7	0	218	120	31·14	1	–	1	–
S. Shivnarine	1977–1978	3	6	0	217	63	36·16	–	3	1	–
C. K. Singh	1959–1960	2	3	0	11	11	3·66	–	–	2	–
J. A. Small	1928–1930	3	6	0	79	52	13·16	–	1	3	–
C. W. Smith	1960–1962	5	10	1	222	55	24·66	–	1	4	1
O. G. Smith	1954–1959	26	42	0	1331	168	31·69	4	6	9	–
G. S. Sobers	1953–1974	93	160	21	8032	365*	57·78	26	30	109	–
J. S. Solomon	1958–1965	27	46	7	1326	100*	34·00	1	9	13	–
S. C. Stayers	1961–1962	4	4	1	58	35*	19·33	–	–	–	–
J. B. Stollmeyer	1939–1955	32	56	5	2159	160	42·33	4	12	20	–
V. H. Stollmeyer	1939	1	1	0	96	96	96·00	–	1	–	–
J. O. Taylor	1957–1959	3	5	3	4	4*	2·00	–	–	–	–
J. Trim	1947–1952	4	5	1	21	12	5·25	–	–	2	–
A. L. Valentine	1950–1962	36	51	21	141	14	4·70	–	–	13	–
V. A. Valentine	1933	2	4	1	35	19*	11·66	–	–	–	–
C. L. Walcott	1947–1960	44	74	7	3798	220	56·68	15	14	54	11
L. A. Walcott	1929–1930	1	2	1	40	24	40·00	–	–	–	–

		M	I	NO	Runs	HS	Avge	100	50	Ct	St
C. D. Watson	1959–1962	7	6	1	12	5	2·40	–	–	1	–
E. D. Weekes	1947–1958	48	81	5	4455	207	58·61	15	19	49	–
K. H. Weekes	1939	2	3	0	173	137	57·66	1	–	–	–
W. A. White	1964–1965	2	4	1	71	57*	23·66	–	1	1	–
C. V. Wight	1928–1930	2	4	1	67	23	22·33	–	–	–	–
G. L. Wight	1952–1953	1	1	0	21	21	21·00	–	–	–	–
C. A. Wiles	1933	1	2	0	2	2	1·00	–	–	–	–
A. B. Williams	1977–1978	3	6	0	257	100	42·83	1	1	4	–
E. A. V. Williams	1939–1948	4	6	0	113	72	18·83	–	1	2	–
E. T. Willett	1972–1975	5	8	3	74	26	14·80	–	–	–	–
K. L. Wishart	1934–1935	1	2	0	52	52	26·00	–	1	–	–
F. M. M. Worrell	1947–1963	51	87	9	3860	261	49·48	9	22	43	–
							Substitutes		42	–

Bowling

	M	Balls	Mdns	Runs	Wkts	Avge	5wI	10wM	Best
E. E. Achong	6	918	34	378	8	47·25	–	–	2–64
D. S. Atkinson	22	5201	312	1647	47	35·04	3	–	7–53
E. S. Atkinson	8	1634	77	589	25	23·56	1	–	5–42
R. A. Austin	2	6	0	5	0	–	–	–	
A. G. Barrett	6	1612	83	603	13	46·38	–	–	3–43
L. S. Birkett	4	126	1	71	1	71·00	–	–	1–16
K. D. Boyce	21	3501	99	1801	60	30·01	2	1	6–77
C. R. Browne	4	840	38	288	6	48·00	–	–	2–72
B. F. Butcher	44	256	15	90	5	18·00	1	–	5–34
L. S. Butler	1	240	7	151	2	75·50	–	–	2–151
M. R. Bynoe	4	30	4	5	1	5·00	–	–	1–5
G. S. Camacho	11	18	1	12	0	–	–	–	
F. J. Cameron	5	786	34	278	3	92·66	–	–	2–74
J. H. Cameron	2	232	6	88	3	29·33	–	–	3–66
G. M. Carew	4	18	2	2	0	–	–	–	
M. C. Carew	19	1174	46	437	8	54·62	–	–	1–11
R. J. Christiani	22	234	1	108	3	36·00	–	–	3–52
C. B. Clarke	3	430	2	261	6	43·50	–	–	3–59
S. Clarke	1	294	8	141	6	23·50	–	–	3–58
L. N. Constantine	18	3583	125	1746	58	30·10	2	–	5–75
C. E. H. Croft	7	1638	58	846	42	20·14	1	–	8–29
O. C. da Costa	5	372	13	175	3	58·33	–	–	1–14
W. W. Daniel	5	788	35	381	15	25·40	–	–	4–53
C. A. Davis	15	894	32	330	2	165·00	–	–	1–27
F. I. de Caires	3	12	0	9	0	–	–	–	
C. C. Depeiaza	5	30	0	15	0	–	–	–	
D. T. Dewdney	9	1641	67	807	21	38·42	1	–	5–21
U. G. Dowe	4	1008	30	533	12	44·41	–	–	4–69
R. M. Edwards	5	1311	25	626	18	34·77	1	–	5–84
W. Ferguson	8	2556	90	1165	34	34·26	3	1	6–92
M. L. C. Foster	14	1776	106	600	9	66·66	–	–	2–41
G. N. Francis	10	1619	54	763	23	33·17	–	–	4–40
R. C. Fredericks	59	1187	41	548	7	78·28	–	–	1–12
R. L. Fuller	1	48	2	12	0	–	–	–	
J. Garner	7	1690	57	883	38	23·23	–	–	4–48
B. B. M. Gaskin	2	474	24	158	2	79·00	–	–	1–15
G. L. Gibbs	1	24	1	7	0	–	–	–	
L. R. Gibbs	79	27115	1313	8989	309	29·09	18	2	8–38
R. Gilchrist	13	3227	124	1521	57	26·68	1	–	6–55
G. Gladstone	1	300	5	189	1	189·00	–	–	1–139
J. D. C. Goddard	27	2931	148	1050	33	31·81	1	–	5–31
H. A. Gomes	5	96	2	34	0	–	–	–	
G. E. Gomez	29	5236	288	1590	58	27·41	1	1	7–55
G. C. Grant	12	24	0	18	0	–	–	–	
R. S. Grant	7	986	32	353	11	32·09	–	–	3–68
C. G. Greenidge	19	8	1	0	0	–	–	–	

	M	Balls	Mdns	Runs	Wkts	Avge	5wI	10wM	Best
G. A. Greenidge	5	156	4	75	0	–	–	–	
M. G. Grell	1	30	1	17	0	–	–	–	
C. C. Griffith	28	5631	177	2683	94	28·54	5	–	6–36
H. C. Griffith	13	2663	89	1243	44	28·25	2	–	6–103
W. W. Hall	48	10421	312	5066	192	26·38	9	1	7–69
G. A. Headley	22	398	7	230	0	–	–	–	
V. A. Holder	34	7877	332	3079	101	30·48	3	–	6–28
M. A. Holding	13	2910	104	1348	57	23·64	4	1	8–92
D. A. J. Holford	24	4816	163	2009	51	39·39	1	–	5–23
J. K. Holt	17	30	2	20	1	20·00	–	–	1–20
A. B. Howard	1	372	16	140	2	70·00	–	–	2–140
C. C. Hunte	44	270	11	110	2	55·00	–	–	1–17
L. G. Hylton	6	965	32	418	16	26·12	–	–	4–27
Imtiaz Ali	1	204	10	89	2	44·50	–	–	2–37
Inshan Ali	12	3718	137	1621	34	47·67	1	–	5–59
H. H. H. Johnson	3	789	37	238	13	18·30	2	1	5–41
T. F. Johnson	1	240	3	129	3	43·00	–	–	2–53
C. M. Jones	4	102	11	11	0	–	–	–	
P. E. Jones	9	1842	64	751	25	30·04	1	–	5–85
B. D. Julien	24	4542	191	1868	50	37·36	1	–	5–57
R. R. Jumadeen	10	2638	123	933	26	35·88	–	–	4–72
A. I. Kallicharran	45	151	6	73	1	73·00	–	–	1–7
R. B. Kanhai	79	183	7	85	0	–	–	–	
E. S. M. Kentish	2	540	31	178	8	22·25	1	–	5–49
C. L. King	4	276	13	113	2	56·50	–	–	1–30
F. M. King	14	2869	140	1159	29	39·96	1	–	5–74
L. A. King	2	476	19	154	9	17·11	1	–	5–46
P. D. Lashley	4	18	2	1	1	1·00	–	–	1–1
C. H. Lloyd	65	1710	75	621	10	62·10	–	–	2–13
C. A. McWatt	6	24	1	16	1	16·00	–	–	1–16
I. S. Madray	2	210	6	108	0	–	–	–	
N. E. Marshall	1	279	21	63	1	31·50	–	–	1–22
R. E. Marshall	4	52	2	15	0	–	–	–	
F. R. Martin	9	1346	27	619	8	77·37	–	–	3–91
E. A. Martindale	10	1605	40	804	37	21·72	3	–	5–22
R. C. Miller	1	96	8	28	0	–	–	–	
G. H. Moodie	1	174	12	40	3	13·33	–	–	2–23
J. M. Neblett	1	216	11	75	1	75·00	–	–	1–44
J. M. Noreiga	4	1322	47	493	17	29·00	2	–	9–95
S. M. Nurse	29	42	4	7	0	–	–	–	
A. L. Padmore	2	474	23	135	1	135·00	–	–	1–36
B. H. Pairaudeau	13	6	0	3	0	–	–	–	
D. R. Parry	5	748	20	360	12	30·00	1	–	5–15
C. C. Passailaigue	1	12	0	15	0	–	–	–	
N. Phillip	3	660	8	391	9	43·44	–	–	4–75
L. R. Pierre	1	42	0	28	0	–	–	–	
S. Ramadhin	43	13939	813	4579	158	28·98	10	1	7–49
I. V. A. Richards	28	644	27	235	4	58·75	–	–	2–34
C. A. Roach	16	222	5	103	2	51·50	–	–	1–18
A. M. E. Roberts	27	6858	222	3298	134	24·61	9	2	7–54
W. V. Rodriguez	5	573	10	374	7	53·42	–	–	3–51
L. G. Rowe	24	56	1	40	0	–	–	–	
E. L. St Hill	2	558	29	221	3	73·66	–	–	2–110
W. H. St Hill	3	12	0	9	0	–	–	–	
R. Scarlett	3	804	53	209	2	104·50	–	–	1–46
A. P. H. Scott	1	264	9	140	0	–	–	–	
O. C. Scott	8	1405	17	925	22	42·04	1	–	5–266
B. J. Sealey	1	30	1	10	1	10·00	–	–	1–10
J. E. D. Sealy	11	156	4	94	3	31·33	–	–	2–7
J. N. Shepherd	5	1445	70	479	19	25·21	1	–	5–104
G. C. Shillingford	7	1181	38	537	15	35·80	–	–	3–63
S. Shivnarine	3	264	6	139	1	139·00	–	–	1–13

	M	Balls	Mdns	Runs	Wkts	Avge	5wI	10wM	Best
C. K. Singh	2	506	35	165	5	33·00	–	–	2–28
J. A. Small	3	366	11	184	3	61·33	–	–	2–67
O. G. Smith	26	4431	229	1625	48	33·85	1	–	5–90
G. S. Sobers	93	21599	974	7999	235	34·03	6	–	6–73
J. S. Solomon	27	702	39	268	4	67·00	–	–	1–20
S. C. Stayers	4	636	20	364	9	40·44	–	–	3–65
J. B. Stollmeyer	32	978	30	507	13	39·00	–	–	3–32
J. O. Taylor	3	672	33	273	10	27·30	1	–	5–109
J. Trim	4	794	28	291	18	16·16	1	–	5–34
A. L. Valentine	36	12961	789	4215	139	30·32	8	2	8–104
V. A. Valentine	2	288	14	104	1	104·00	–	–	1–55
C. L. Walcott	44	1194	72	408	11	37·09	–	–	3–50
L. A. Walcott	1	48	1	32	1	32·00	–	–	1–17
C. D. Watson	7	1458	47	724	19	38·10	–	–	4–62
E. D. Weekes	48	128	3	77	1	77·00	–	–	1–8
W. A. White	2	491	26	152	3	50·66	–	–	2–34
C. V. Wight	2	30	1	6	0	–	–	–	–
E. A. V. Williams	4	796	46	241	9	26·77	–	–	3–51
E. T. Willett	5	1326	78	482	11	43·81	–	–	3–33
F. M. M. Worrell	51	7147	276	2673	69	38·73	2	–	7–70

New Zealand (143 players)

Batting and Fielding

		M	I	NO	Runs	HS	Avge	100	50	Ct	St
J. C. Alabaster	1955–1972	21	34	6	272	34	9·71	–	–	7	–
C. F. W. Allcott	1929–1932	6	7	2	113	33	22·60	–	–	3	–
R. W. Anderson	1976–1978	9	18	0	423	92	23·50	–	3	1	–
W. M. Anderson	1945–1946	1	2	0	5	4	2·50	–	–	1	–
B. Andrews	1973–1974	2	3	2	22	17	22·00	–	–	1	–
F. T. Badcock	1929–1933	7	9	2	137	64	19·57	–	2	1	–
R. T. Barber	1955–1956	1	2	0	17	12	8·50	–	–	1	–
G. A. Bartlett	1961–1968	10	18	1	263	40	15·47	–	–	8	–
P. T. Barton	1961–1963	7	14	0	285	109	20·35	1	1	4	–
D. D. Beard	1951–1956	4	7	2	101	31	20·20	–	–	2	–
J. E. F. Beck	1953–1956	8	15	0	394	99	26·26	–	3	–	–
W. Bell	1953–1954	2	3	3	21	21*	–	–	–	1	–
G. P. Bilby	1965–1966	2	4	0	55	28	13·75	–	–	3	–
R. W. Blair	1952–1964	19	34	6	189	64*	6·75	–	1	5	–
R. C. Blunt	1929–1932	9	13	1	330	96	27·50	–	1	5	–
B. A. Bolton	1958–1959	2	3	0	59	33	19·66	–	–	1	–
S. L. Boock	1977–1978	6	11	4	24	8	3·42	–	–	3	–
B. P. Bracewell	1978	3	6	1	4	4	0·80	–	–	1	–
W. P. Bradburn	1963–1964	2	4	0	62	32	15·50	–	–	2	–
M. G. Burgess	1967–1978	44	81	5	2426	119*	31·92	5	13	33	–
C. Burke	1945–1946	1	2	0	4	3	2·00	–	–	–	–
T. B. Burtt	1945–1953	10	15	3	252	42	21·00	–	–	2	–
L. A. Butterfield	1945–1946	1	2	0	0	0	0·00	–	–	–	–
B. L. Cairns	1973–1978	11	20	4	279	52*	17·43	–	1	4	–
F. J. Cameron	1961–1965	19	30	20	116	27*	11·60	–	–	2	–
H. B. Cave	1949–1958	19	31	5	229	22*	8·80	–	–	8	–
M. E. Chapple	1952–1966	14	27	1	497	76	19·11	–	3	10	–
E. J. Chatfield	1974–1978	4	7	3	31	13*	7·75	–	–	–	–
D. C. Cleverley	1931–1946	2	4	3	19	10*	19·00	–	–	–	–
R. O. Collinge	1964–1978	35	50	13	533	68*	14·40	–	2	10	–
I. A. Colquhoun	1954–1955	2	4	2	1	1*	0·50	–	–	4	–
J. V. Coney	1973–1974	4	7	0	123	45	17·57	–	–	6	–
B. E. Congdon	1964–1978	61	114	7	3448	176	32·22	7	19	44	–
J. Cowie	1937–1949	9	13	4	90	45	10·00	–	–	3	–
G. F. Cresswell	1949–1951	3	5	3	14	12*	7·00	–	–	–	–
I. B. Cromb	1931–1932	5	8	2	123	51*	20·50	–	1	1	–
R. S. Cunis	1963–1972	20	31	8	295	51	12·82	–	1	1	–

		M	I	NO	Runs	HS	Avge	100	50	Ct	St
J. W. D'Arcy	1958	5	10	0	136	33	13·60	–	–	–	–
C. S. Dempster	1929–1933	10	15	4	723	136	65·72	2	5	2	–
E. W. Dempster	1952–1954	5	8	2	106	47	17·66	–	–	1	–
A. E. Dick	1961–1965	17	30	4	370	50*	14·23	–	1	47	4
G. R. Dickinson	1929–1932	3	5	0	31	11	6·20	–	–	3	–
M. P. Donnelly	1937–1949	7	12	1	582	206	52·90	1	4	7	–
G. T. Dowling	1961–1972	39	77	3	2306	239	31·16	3	11	23	–
J. A. Dunning	1932–1937	4	6	1	38	19	7·60	–	–	2	–
B. A. Edgar	1978	3	6	0	147	60	24·50	–	1	3	–
G. N. Edwards	1976–1978	5	10	0	244	55	24·40	–	3	7	–
R. W. G. Emery	1951–1952	2	4	0	46	28	11·50	–	–	–	–
F. E. Fisher	1952–1953	1	2	0	23	14	11·50	–	–	–	–
H. Foley	1929–1930	1	2	0	4	2	2·00	–	–	–	–
D. L. Freeman	1932–1933	2	2	0	2	1	1·00	–	–	–	–
N. Gallichan	1937	1	2	0	32	30	16·00	–	–	1	–
S. G. Gedye	1963–1965	4	8	0	193	55	24·12	–	2	–	–
S. C. Guillen	1955–1956	3	6	0	98	41	16·33	–	–	4	1
J. W. Guy	1955–1962	12	23	2	440	102	20·95	1	3	2	–
D. R. Hadlee	1969–1978	26	42	5	530	56	14·32	–	1	8	–
R. J. Hadlee	1972–1978	23	42	4	729	87	19·18	–	2	13	–
W. A. Hadlee	1937–1951	11	19	1	543	116	30·16	1	2	6	–
N. S. Harford	1955–1958	8	15	0	229	93	15·26	–	2	–	–
R. I. Harford	1967–1968	3	5	2	7	6	2·33	–	–	11	–
P. G. Z. Harris	1955–1965	9	18	1	378	101	22·23	1	1	6	–
R. M. Harris	1958–1959	2	3	0	31	13	10·33	–	–	–	–
B. F. Hastings	1968–1976	31	56	6	1510	117*	30·20	4	7	23	–
J. A. Hayes	1950–1958	15	22	7	73	19	4·86	–	–	3	–
M. Henderson	1929–1930	1	2	1	8	6	8·00	–	–	1	–
K. W. Hough	1958–1959	2	3	2	62	31*	62·00	–	–	1	–
G. P. Howarth	1974–1978	14	27	3	864	123	36·00	3	3	6	–
H. J. Howarth	1969–1977	30	42	18	291	61	12·12	–	1	33	–
K. C. James	1929–1933	11	13	2	52	14	4·72	–	–	11	5
T. W. Jarvis	1964–1973	13	22	1	625	182	29·76	1	2	3	–
J. L. Kerr	1931–1937	7	12	1	212	59	19·27	–	1	4	–
W. K. Lees	1976–1978	9	18	1	452	152	26·58	1	–	15	7
I. B. Leggat	1953–1954	1	1	0	0	0	0·00	–	–	2	–
J. G. Leggat	1951–1956	9	18	2	351	61	21·93	–	2	–	–
A. F. Lissette	1955–1956	2	4	2	2	1*	1·00	–	–	1	–
T. C. Lowry	1929–1931	7	8	0	223	80	27·87	–	2	8	–
A. R. MacGibbon	1950–1958	26	46	5	814	66	19·85	–	3	13	–
H. M. McGirr	1929–1930	2	1	0	51	51	51·00	–	1	–	–
S. N. McGregor	1954–1965	25	47	2	892	111	19·82	1	3	9	–
E. G. McLeod	1929–1930	1	2	1	18	16	18·00	–	–	–	–
T. G. McMahon	1955–1956	5	7	4	7	4*	2·33	–	–	7	1
D. A. N. McRae	1945–1946	1	2	0	8	8	4·00	–	–	–	–
A. M. Matheson	1929–1931	2	1	0	7	7	7·00	–	–	2	–
T. Meale	1958	2	4	0	21	10	5·25	–	–	–	–
W. E. Merritt	1929–1931	6	8	1	73	19	10·42	–	–	2	–
E. M. Meuli	1952–1953	1	2	0	38	23	19·00	–	–	–	–
B. D. Milburn	1968–1969	3	3	2	8	4*	8·00	–	–	6	2
L. S. M. Miller	1952–1958	13	25	0	346	47	13·84	–	–	1	–
J. E. Mills	1929–1933	7	10	1	241	117	26·77	1	–	1	–
A. M. Moir	1950–1959	17	30	8	327	41*	14·86	–	–	2	–
D. A. R. Moloney	1937	3	6	0	156	64	26·00	–	1	3	–
F. L. H. Mooney	1949–1954	14	22	2	343	46	17·15	–	–	22	8
R. W. Morgan	1964–1972	20	34	1	734	97	22·24	–	5	12	–
B. D. Morrison	1962–1963	1	2	0	10	10	5·00	–	–	1	–
J. F. M. Morrison	1973–1977	14	24	0	610	117	25·41	1	3	9	–
R. C. Motz	1961–1969	32	56	3	612	60	11·54	–	3	9	–
B. A. G. Murray	1967–1971	13	26	1	598	90	23·92	–	5	21	–
J. Newman	1931–1933	3	4	0	33	19	8·25	–	–	–	–
D. R. O'Sullivan	1972–1977	11	21	4	158	23*	9·29	–	–	2	–

		M	I	NO	Runs	HS	Avge	100	50	Ct	St
G. W. F. Overton	1953–1954	3	6	1	8	3*	1·60	–	–	1	–
M. L. Page	1929–1937	14	20	0	492	104	24·60	1	2	6	–
J. M. Parker	1972–1978	28	49	2	1278	121	27·19	3	3	24	–
N. M. Parker	1976–1977	3	6	0	89	40	14·83	–	–	2	–
P. J. Petherick	1976–1977	6	11	4	34	13	4·85	–	–	4	–
E. C. Petrie	1955–1966	14	25	5	258	55	12·90	–	1	25	–
W. R. Playle	1958–1963	8	15	0	151	65	10·06	–	1	4	–
V. Pollard	1964–1973	32	59	7	1266	116	24·34	2	7	19	–
M. B. Poore	1952–1956	14	24	1	355	45	15·43	–	–	1	–
N. Puna	1965–1966	3	5	3	31	18*	15·50	–	–	1	–
G. O. Rabone	1949–1955	12	20	2	562	107	31·22	1	2	5	–
R. E. Redmond	1972–1973	1	2	0	163	107	81·50	1	1	–	–
J. R. Reid	1949–1965	58	108	5	3428	142	33·28	6	22	43	1
A. D. G. Roberts	1975–1977	7	12	1	254	84*	23·09	–	1	4	–
A. W. Roberts	1929–1937	5	10	1	248	66*	27·55	–	3	4	–
C. G. Rowe	1945–1946	1	2	0	0	0	0·00	–	–	1	–
R. H. Scott	1946–1947	1	1	0	18	18	18·00	–	–	–	–
V. J. Scott	1945–1952	10	17	1	458	84	28·62	–	3	7	–
M. J. F. Shrimpton	1962–1974	10	19	0	265	46	13·94	–	–	2	–
B. W. Sinclair	1962–1968	21	40	1	1148	138	29·43	3	3	8	–
I. M. Sinclair	1955–1956	2	4	1	25	18*	8·33	–	–	1	–
F. B. Smith	1946–1952	4	6	1	237	96	47·40	–	2	1	–
H. D. Smith	1932–1933	1	1	0	4	4	4·00	–	–	–	–
C. A. Snedden	1946–1947	1	–	–	–	–	–	–	–	–	–
J. T. Sparling	1958–1964	11	20	2	229	50	12·72	–	1	3	–
B. Sutcliffe	1946–1965	42	76	8	2727	230*	40·10	5	15	20	–
B. R. Taylor	1964–1973	30	50	6	898	124	20·40	2	2	10	–
D. D. Taylor	1946–1956	3	5	0	159	77	31·80	–	1	2	–
K. Thomson	1967–1968	2	4	1	94	69	31·33	–	1	–	–
E. W. T. Tindill	1937–1947	5	9	1	73	37*	9·12	–	–	6	1
G. B. Troup	1976–1977	1	1	0	0	0	0·00	–	–	1	–
P. B. Truscott	1964–1965	1	2	0	29	26	14·50	–	–	1	–
G. M. Turner	1968–1977	39	70	6	2920	259	45·62	7	14	40	–
G. E. Vivian	1964–1972	5	6	0	110	43	18·33	–	–	3	–
H. G. Vivian	1931–1937	7	10	0	421	100	42·10	1	5	4	–
K. J. Wadsworth	1969–1976	33	51	4	1010	80	21·48	–	5	92	4
W. M. Wallace	1937–1953	13	21	0	439	66	20·90	–	5	5	–
J. T. Ward	1963–1968	8	12	6	75	35*	12·50	–	–	16	1
L. Watt	1954–1955	1	2	0	2	2	1·00	–	–	–	–
M. G. Webb	1970–1974	3	2	0	12	12	6·00	–	–	–	–
G. L. Weir	1929–1937	11	16	2	416	74*	29·71	–	3	3	–
P. E. Whitelaw	1932–1933	2	4	2	64	30	32·00	–	–	–	–
J. G. Wright	1977–1978	5	10	0	223	62	22·30	–	2	2	–
B. W. Yuile	1962–1970	17	33	6	481	64	17·81	–	1	12	–
							Substitutes			21	1

Bowling

	M	Balls	Mdns	Runs	Wkts	Avge	5wI	10wM	Best
J. C. Alabaster	21	3992	178	1863	49	38·02	–	–	4–46
C. F. W. Allcott	6	1206	41	541	6	90·16	–	–	2–102
B. Andrews	2	256	3	154	2	77·00	–	–	2–40
F. T. Badcock	7	1608	66	610	16	38·12	–	–	4–80
G. A. Bartlett	10	1768	64	792	24	33·00	1	–	6–38
D. D. Beard	4	812	38	302	9	33·55	–	–	3–22
W. Bell	2	491	13	235	2	117·50	–	–	1–54
R. W. Blair	19	3525	114	1515	43	35·23	–	–	4–85
R. C. Blunt	9	936	34	472	12	39·33	–	–	3–17
S. L. Boock	6	1153	73	318	13	24·46	1	–	5–67
B. P. Bracewell	3	536	14	282	9	31·33	–	–	3–110
M. G. Burgess	44	498	27	212	6	35·33	–	–	3–23
C. Burke	1	66	2	30	2	15·00	–	–	2–30
T. B. Burtt	10	2593	119	1170	33	35·45	3	–	6–162

	M	Balls	Mdns	Runs	Wkts	Avge	5wI	10wM	Best
L. A. Butterfield	1	78	6	24	0	–	–	–	
B. L. Cairns	11	2400	81	909	20	45·45	1	–	5–55
F. J. Cameron	19	4570	220	1849	61	30·31	3	–	5–34
H. B. Cave	19	4074	242	1467	34	43·14	–	–	4–21
M. E. Chapple	14	248	17	84	1	84·00	–	–	1–24
E. J. Chatfield	4	1054	18	485	8	60·62	–	–	4–100
D. C. Cleverley	2	222	3	130	0	–	–	–	
R. O. Collinge	35	7689	228	3393	116	29·25	3	–	6–63
J. V. Coney	4	16	0	13	0	–	–	–	
B. E. Congdon	61	5620	197	2154	59	36·50	1	–	5–65
J. Cowie	9	2028	65	969	45	21·53	4	1	6–40
G. F. Cresswell	3	650	30	292	13	22·46	1	–	6–168
I. B. Cromb	5	960	27	442	8	55·25	–	–	3–113
R. S. Cunis	20	4250	140	1887	51	37·00	1	–	6–76
C. S. Dempster	10	5	0	10	0	–	–	–	
E. W. Dempster	5	544	17	219	2	109·50	–	–	1–24
G. R. Dickinson	3	451	13	245	8	30·62	–	–	3–66
M. P. Donnelly	7	30	0	20	0	–	–	–	
G. T. Dowling	39	36	2	19	1	19·00	–	–	1–19
J. A. Dunning	4	830	20	493	5	98·60	–	–	2–35
R. W. G. Emery	2	46	0	52	2	26·00	–	–	2–52
F. E. Fisher	1	204	6	78	1	78·00	–	–	1–78
D. L. Freeman	2	240	3	169	1	169·00	–	–	1–91
N. Gallichan	1	264	11	113	3	37·66	–	–	3–99
D. R. Hadlee	26	4883	114	2389	71	33·64	–	–	4–30
R. J. Hadlee	23	5434	112	2811	89	31·58	4	2	7–23
P. G. Z. Harris	9	42	2	14	0	–	–	–	
B. F. Hastings	31	22	0	9	0	–	–	–	
J. A. Hayes	15	2681	87	1217	30	40·56	–	–	4–36
M. Henderson	1	90	3	64	2	32·00	–	–	2–38
K. W. Hough	2	462	23	175	6	29·16	–	–	3–79
G. P. Howarth	14	240	2	109	2	54·50	–	–	1–13
H. J. Howarth	30	8833	393	3178	86	36·95	2	–	5–34
T. W. Jarvis	13	12	1	3	0	–	–	–	
W. K. Lees	9	5	0	4	0	–	–	–	
I. B. Leggat	1	24	0	6	0	–	–	–	
A. F. Lissette	2	288	16	124	3	41·33	–	–	2–73
T. C. Lowry	7	12	1	5	0	–	–	–	
A. R. MacGibbon	26	5659	228	2160	70	30·85	1	–	5–64
H. M. McGirr	2	180	5	115	1	115·00	–	–	1–65
E. G. McLeod	1	12	0	5	0	–	–	–	
D. A. N. McRae	1	84	3	44	0	–	–	–	
A. M. Matheson	2	282	9	136	2	68·00	–	–	2–7
W. E. Merritt	6	936	10	617	12	51·41	–	–	4–104
L. S. M. Miller	13	2	0	1	0	–	–	–	
A. M. Moir	17	2650	82	1418	28	50·64	2	–	6–155
D. A. R. Moloney	3	12	1	9	0	–	–	–	
F. L. H. Mooney	14	8	1	0	0	–	–	–	
R. W. Morgan	20	1114	38	609	5	121·80	–	–	1–16
B. D. Morrison	1	186	5	129	2	64·50	–	–	2–129
J. F. M. Morrison	14	24	0	9	0	–	–	–	
R. C. Motz	32	7034	279	3148	100	31·48	5	–	6–63
B. A. G. Murray	13	6	1	0	1	0·00	–	–	1–0
J. Newman	3	425	11	254	2	127·00	–	–	2–76
D. R. O'Sullivan	11	2744	75	1221	18	67·83	1	–	5–148
G. W. F. Overton	3	729	23	258	9	28·66	–	–	3–65
M. L. Page	14	379	11	231	5	46·20	–	–	2–21
J. M. Parker	28	40	2	24	1	24·00	–	–	1–24
P. J. Petherick	6	1305	37	685	16	42·81	–	–	3–90
V. Pollard	32	4433	206	1853	40	46·32	–	–	3–3
M. B. Poore	14	788	24	367	9	40·77	–	–	2–28
N. Puna	3	480	20	240	4	60·00	–	–	2–40

	M	Balls	Mdns	Runs	Wkts	Avge	5wI	10wM	Best
G. O. Rabone	12	1385	48	635	16	39·68	1	–	6–68
J. R. Reid	58	7725	444	2835	85	33·35	1	–	6–60
A. D. G. Roberts	7	440	15	182	4	45·50	–	–	1–12
A. W. Roberts	5	459	19	209	7	29·85	–	–	4–101
R. H. Scott	1	138	3	74	1	74·00	–	–	1–74
V. J. Scott	10	18	0	14	0	–	–	–	–
M. J. F. Shrimpton	10	257	1	158	5	31·60	–	–	3–35
B. W. Sinclair	21	60	3	32	2	16·00	–	–	2–32
I. M. Sinclair	2	233	9	120	1	120·00	–	–	1–79
H. D. Smith	1	120	0	113	1	113·00	–	–	1–113
C. A. Snedden	1	96	5	46	0	–	–	–	–
J. T. Sparling	11	708	33	327	5	65·40	–	–	1–9
B. Sutcliffe	42	538	10	344	4	86·00	–	–	2–38
B. R. Taylor	30	6334	206	2953	111	26·60	4	–	7–74
K. Thomson	2	21	1	9	1	9·00	–	–	1–9
G. B. Troup	1	180	3	116	1	116·00	–	–	1–69
G. M. Turner	39	12	1	5	0	–	–	–	–
G. E. Vivian	5	198	7	107	1	107·00	–	–	1–14
H. G. Vivian	7	1311	44	633	17	37·23	–	–	4–58
W. M. Wallace	13	6	0	5	0	–	–	–	–
M. G. Webb	3	732	6	471	4	117·75	–	–	2–114
G. L. Weir	11	342	7	209	7	29·85	–	–	3–38
B. W. Yuile	17	2897	168	1213	34	35·67	–	–	4–43

India (140 players)
Batting and Fielding

		M	I	NO	Runs	HS	Avge	100	50	Ct	St
S. Abid Ali	1967–1975	29	53	3	1018	81	20·36	–	6	33	–
H. R. Adhikari	1947–1959	21	36	8	872	114*	31·14	1	4	8	–
L. Amarnath	1933–1953	24	40	4	878	118	24·38	1	4	13	–
M. Amarnath	1969–1978	18	33	1	1183	100	36·96	1	8	20	–
S. Amarnath	1975–1977	7	13	0	403	124	31·00	1	2	4	–
L. Amar Singh	1932–1936	7	14	1	292	51	22·46	–	1	3	–
Amir Elahi	1947–1948	1	2	0	17	13	8·50	–	–	–	–
A. L. Apte	1959	1	2	0	15	8	7·50	–	–	–	–
M. L. Apte	1952–1953	7	13	2	542	163*	49·27	1	3	2	–
A. A. Baig	1959–1967	10	18	0	428	112	23·77	1	2	6	–
S. A. Banerjee	1948–1949	1	1	0	0	0	0·00	–	–	3	–
S. N. Banerjee	1948–1949	1	2	0	13	8	6·50	–	–	–	–
M. Baqa Jilani	1936	1	2	1	16	12	16·00	–	–	–	–
B. S. Bedi	1966–1978	58	91	26	621	50*	9·55	–	1	24	–
P. Bhandari	1954–1957	3	4	0	77	39	19·25	–	–	1	–
C. G. Borde	1958–1970	55	97	11	3061	177*	35·59	5	18	38	–
B. S. Chandrasekhar	1963–1978	50	72	35	162	22	4·37	–	–	23	–
C. P. Chauhan	1969–1978	9	17	0	368	88	21·64	–	1	12	–
N. R. Chowdhury	1948–1952	2	2	1	3	3*	3·00	–	–	–	–
S. H. M. Colah	1932–1934	2	4	0	69	31	17·25	–	–	2	–
N. J. Contractor	1955–1962	31	52	1	1611	108	31·58	1	11	18	–
H. T. Dani	1952–1953	1	–	–	–	–	–	–	–	1	–
R. B. Desai	1958–1968	28	44	13	418	85	13·48	–	1	9	–
R. V. Divecha	1951–1953	5	5	0	60	26	12·00	–	–	5	–
S. A. Durani	1959–1973	29	50	2	1202	104	25·04	1	7	14	–
Dilawar Hussain	1933–1936	3	6	0	254	59	42·33	–	3	6	1
F. M. Engineer	1961–1975	46	87	3	2611	121	31·08	2	16	66	16
C. V. Gadkari	1952–1955	6	10	4	133	50*	22·16	–	1	6	–
A. D. Gaekwad	1974–1978	14	26	2	742	81*	30·91	–	4	5	–
D. K. Gaekwad	1951–1961	11	20	1	350	52	18·42	–	1	5	–
H. G. Gaekwad	1952–1953	1	2	0	22	14	11·00	–	–	–	–
A. Gandotra	1969–1970	2	4	0	54	18	13·50	–	–	1	–
S. M. Gavaskar	1970–1978	37	71	5	3226	220	48·87	13	14	35	–
K. D. Ghavri	1974–1978	11	19	3	333	64	20·81	–	1	8	–

		M	I	NO	Runs	HS	Avge	100	50	Ct	St
J. M. Ghorpade	1952–1959	8	15	0	229	41	15·26	–	–	4	–
Ghulam Ahmed	1948–1959	22	31	9	192	50	8·72	–	1	11	–
M. J. Gopalan	1933–1934	1	2	1	18	11*	18·00	–	–	3	–
C. D. Gopinath	1951–1960	8	12	1	242	50*	22·00	–	1	2	–
G. M. Guard	1958–1960	2	2	0	11	7	5·50	–	–	2	–
S. Guha	1967–1970	4	7	2	17	6	3·40	–	–	2	–
Gul Mahomed	1946–1953	8	15	0	166	34	11·06	–	–	3	–
B. P. Gupte	1960–1965	3	3	2	28	17*	28·00	–	–	–	–
S. P. Gupte	1951–1962	36	42	13	183	21	6·31	–	–	14	–
Abdul Hafeez (Kardar)	1946	3	5	0	80	43	16·00	–	–	1	–
Hanumant Singh	1963–1970	14	24	2	686	105	31·18	1	5	11	–
M. S. Hardikar	1958–1959	2	4	1	56	32*	18·66	–	–	3	–
V. S. Hazare	1946–1953	30	52	6	2192	164*	47·65	7	9	11	–
D. D. Hindlekar	1936–1946	4	7	2	71	26	14·20	–	–	3	–
K. C. Ibrahim	1948–1949	4	8	0	169	85	21·12	–	1	–	–
K. S. Indrajitsinhji	1964–1970	4	7	1	51	23	8·50	–	–	6	3
J. K. Irani	1947–1948	2	3	2	3	2*	3·00	–	–	2	1
M. Jahangir Khan	1932–1936	4	7	0	39	13	5·57	–	–	4	–
L. P. Jai	1933–1934	1	2	0	19	19	9·50	–	–	–	–
M. L. Jaisimha	1959–1971	39	71	4	2056	129	30·68	3	12	17	–
R. J. D. Jamshedji	1933–1934	1	2	2	5	4*	–	–	–	2	–
K. Jayantilal	1970–1971	1	1	0	5	5	5·00	–	–	–	–
P. G. Joshi	1951–1961	12	20	1	207	52*	10·89	–	1	18	9
H. S. Kanitkar	1974–1975	2	4	0	111	65	27·75	–	1	–	–
R. B. Kenny	1958–1960	5	10	1	245	62	27·22	–	3	1	–
S. M. H. Kirmani	1975–1978	20	32	4	795	88	28·39	–	5	35	15
G. Kishenchand	1947–1953	5	10	0	89	44	8·90	–	–	1	–
A. G. Kripal Singh	1955–1965	14	20	5	422	100*	28·13	1	2	4	–
P. Krishnamurthy	1970–1971	5	6	0	33	20	5·50	–	–	7	1
U. N. Kulkarni	1967–1968	4	8	5	13	7	4·33	–	–	–	–
V. V. Kumar	1960–1962	2	2	0	6	6	3·00	–	–	2	–
B. K. Kunderan	1959–1967	18	34	4	981	192	32·70	2	3	22	8
Lall Singh	1932	1	2	0	44	29	22·00	–	–	1	–
S. Madan Lal	1974–1978	16	30	6	428	55*	17·83	–	1	8	–
E. S. Maka	1952–1953	2	1	1	2	2*	–	–	–	2	1
V. L. Manjrekar	1951–1965	55	92	10	3208	189*	39·12	7	15	19	2
A. V. Mankad	1969–1978	22	42	3	991	97	25·41	–	6	12	–
V. M. Mankad	1946–1959	44	72	5	2109	231	31·47	5	6	33	–
Mansur Ali Khan, see M. A. K. Pataudi											
M. K. Mantri	1951–1955	4	8	1	67	39	9·57	–	–	8	1
K. R. Meherhomji	1936	1	1	1	0	0*	–	–	–	1	–
V. L. Mehra	1955–1964	8	14	1	329	62	25·30	–	2	1	–
V. M. Merchant	1933–1952	10	18	0	859	154	47·72	3	3	7	–
A. G. Milkha Singh	1959–1962	4	6	0	92	35	15·33	–	–	2	–
R. S. Modi	1946–1953	10	17	1	736	112	46·00	1	6	3	–
V. M. Muddiah	1959–1961	2	3	1	11	11	5·50	–	–	–	–
S. Mushtaq Ali	1933–1952	11	20	1	612	112	32·21	2	3	7	–
R. G. Nadkarni	1955–1968	41	67	12	1414	122*	25·70	1	7	22	–
S. S. Naik	1974–1975	3	6	0	141	77	23·50	–	1	–	–
M. Naoomal Jeoomal	1932–1934	3	5	1	108	43	27·00	–	–	–	–
J. G. Navle	1932–1934	2	4	0	42	13	10·50	–	–	1	–
C. K. Nayudu	1932–1936	7	14	0	350	81	25·00	–	2	4	–
C. S. Nayudu	1933–1952	11	19	3	147	36	9·18	–	–	3	–
S. Nazir Ali	1932–1934	2	4	0	30	13	7·50	–	–	–	–
M. Nissar	1932–1936	6	11	3	55	14	6·87	–	–	2	–
S. Nyalchand	1952–1953	1	2	1	7	6*	7·00	–	–	–	–
A. M. Pai	1969–1970	1	2	0	10	9	5·00	–	–	–	–
P. E. Palia	1932–1936	2	4	1	29	16	9·66	–	–	–	–
R. D. Parkar	1972–1973	2	4	0	80	35	20·00	–	–	–	–
C. T. Patankar	1955–1956	1	2	1	14	13	14·00	–	–	3	1
Nawab of Pataudi	1946	3	5	0	55	22	11·00	–	–	–	–
M. A. K. Pataudi	1961–1975	46	83	3	2792	203*	34·90	6	16	27	–

		M	I	NO	Runs	HS	Avge	100	50	Ct	St
B. P. Patel	1974–1978	21	38	5	972	115*	29·45	1	5	17	–
J. M. Patel	1954–1960	7	10	1	25	12	2·77	–	–	2	–
Yuvraj of Patiala	1933–1934	1	2	0	84	60	42·00	–	1	2	–
S. R. Patil	1955–1956	1	1	1	14	14*	–	–	–	1	–
D. G. Phadkar	1947–1959	31	45	7	1229	123	32·34	2	8	21	–
E. A. S. Prasanna	1961–1978	47	81	18	720	37	11·42	–	–	18	–
P. H. Punjabi	1954–1955	5	10	0	164	33	16·40	–	–	5	–
K. Rai Singh	1947–1948	1	2	0	26	24	13·00	–	–	–	–
V. Rajindernath	1952–1953	1	–	–	–	–	–	–	–	1	3
Rajinder Pal	1963–1964	1	2	1	6	3*	6·00	–	–	–	–
C. Ramaswami	1936	2	4	1	170	60	56·66	–	1	–	–
G. S. Ramchand	1952–1960	33	53	5	1180	109	24·58	2	5	20	–
L. Ramji	1933–1934	1	2	0	1	1	0·50	–	–	1	–
C. R. Rangachari	1947–1949	4	6	3	8	8*	2·66	–	–	–	–
K. M. Rangnekar	1947–1948	3	6	0	33	18	5·50	–	–	1	–
V. B. Ranjane	1958–1965	7	9	3	40	16	6·66	–	–	1	–
M. R. Rege	1948–1949	1	2	0	15	15	7·50	–	–	1	–
A. Roy	1969–1970	4	7	0	91	48	13·00	–	–	–	–
P. Roy	1951–1961	43	79	4	2441	173	32·54	5	9	16	–
D. N. Sardesai	1961–1973	30	55	4	2001	212	39·23	5	9	4	–
C. T. Sarwate	1946–1952	9	17	1	208	37	13·00	–	–	–	–
R. C. Saxena	1967	1	2	0	25	16	12·50	–	–	–	–
P. Sen	1947–1953	14	18	4	165	25	11·78	–	–	20	11
A. K. Sengupta	1958–1959	1	2	0	9	8	4·50	–	–	–	–
P. Sharma	1974–1977	5	10	0	187	54	18·70	–	1	1	–
S. G. Shinde	1946–1952	7	11	5	85	14	14·16	–	–	–	–
R. H. Shodhan	1952–1953	3	4	1	181	110	60·33	1	–	1	–
S. W. Sohoni	1946–1952	4	7	2	83	29*	16·60	–	–	2	–
E. D. Solkar	1969–1977	27	48	6	1068	102	25·42	1	6	53	–
M. M. Sood	1959–1960	1	2	0	3	3	1·50	–	–	–	–
V. Subramanya	1964–1968	9	15	1	263	75	18·78	–	2	9	–
G. R. Sunderram	1955–1956	2	1	1	3	3*	–	–	–	–	–
R. Surendranath	1958–1961	11	20	7	136	27	10·46	–	–	4	–
R. F. Surti	1960–1970	26	48	4	1263	99	28·70	–	9	25	–
V. N. Swamy	1955–1956	1	–	–	–	–	–	–	–	–	–
N. S. Tamhane	1954–1961	21	27	5	222	54*	10·09	–	1	35	16
K. K. Tarapore	1948–1949	1	1	0	2	2	2·00	–	–	–	–
P. R. Umrigar	1948–1962	59	94	8	3631	223	42·22	12	14	33	–
D. B. Vengsarkar	1975–1978	11	20	1	472	78	24·84	–	1	11	–
S. Venkataraghavan	1964–1978	37	55	8	660	64	14·04	–	2	32	–
G. R. Viswanath	1969–1978	43	82	7	3154	139	42·05	5	21	33	–
Maharaj Sir Vijaya of Vizianagram	1936	3	6	2	33	19*	8·25	–	–	1	–
A. L. Wadekar	1966–1974	37	71	3	2113	143	31·07	1	14	46	–
S. Wazir Ali	1932–1936	7	14	0	237	42	16·92	–	–	1	–
Yajurvindra Singh	1976–1977	2	4	0	50	21	12·50	–	–	8	–
							Substitutes			46	–

Bowling

	M	Balls	Mdns	Runs	Wkts	Avge	5wI	10wM	Best
S. Abid Ali	29	4164	119	1980	47	42·12	1	–	6–55
H. R. Adhikari	21	170	2	82	3	27·33	–	–	3–68
L. Amarnath	24	4241	195	1481	45	32·91	2	–	5–96
M. Amarnath	18	1803	56	726	17	42·70	–	–	4–63
L. Amar Singh	7	2182	95	858	28	30·64	2	–	7–86
M. L. Apte	7	6	0	3	0	–	–	–	–
A. A. Baig	10	18	0	15	0	–	–	–	–
S. A. Banerjee	1	306	3	181	5	36·20	–	–	4–120
S. N. Banerjee	1	273	8	127	5	25·40	–	–	4–54
M. Baqa Jilani	1	90	4	55	0	–	–	–	–
B. S. Bedi	58	19135	1009	6615	246	26·89	14	1	7–98
P. Bhandari	3	78	2	39	0	–	–	–	–

	M	Balls	Mdns	Runs	Wkts	Avge	5wI	10wM	Best
C. G. Borde	55	5695	236	2417	52	46·48	1	–	5–88
B. S. Chandrasekhar	50	14253	538	6270	222	28·24	15	2	8–79
N. R. Chowdhury	2	516	21	205	1	205·00	–	–	1–130
N. J. Contractor	31	186	6	80	1	80·00	–	–	1–9
H. T. Dani	1	60	5	19	1	19·00	–	–	1–9
R. B. Desai	28	5597	177	2762	74	37·32	2	–	6–56
R. V. Divecha	5	1044	44	361	11	32·81	–	–	3–102
S. A. Durani	29	6446	316	2657	75	35·42	3	1	6–73
C. V. Gadkari	6	102	4	45	0		–	–	
A. D. Gaekwad	14	76	0	53	0		–	–	
D. K. Gaekwad	11	12	0	12	0		–	–	
H. G. Gaekwad	1	222	21	47	0		–	–	
A. Gandotra	2	6	0	5	0		–	–	
S. M. Gavaskar	37	172	8	72	0		–	–	
K. D. Ghavri	11	1550	45	833	30	27·76	1	–	5–33
J. M. Ghorpade	8	150	1	131	0		–	–	
Ghulam Ahmed	22	5650	253	2052	68	30·17	4	1	7–49
M. J. Gopalan	1	114	7	39	1	39·00	–	–	1–39
C. D. Gopinath	8	48	2	11	1	11·00	–	–	1–11
G. M. Guard	2	396	16	182	3	60·66	–	–	2–69
S. Guha	4	674	23	311	3	103·66	–	–	2–55
Gul Mahomed	8	77	4	24	2	12·00	–	–	2–21
B. P. Gupte	3	678	28	349	3	116·33	–	–	1–54
S. P. Gupte	36	11284	598	4402	149	29·54	12	1	9–102
Hanumant Singh	14	66	0	51	0		–	–	
M. S. Hardikar	2	108	7	55	1	55·00	–	–	1–9
V. S. Hazare	30	2840	97	1220	20	61·00	–	–	4–29
M. Jahangir Khan	4	606	28	255	4	63·75	–	–	4–60
M. L. Jaisimha	39	2097	109	829	9	92·11	–	–	2–54
R. J. D. Jamshedji	1	210	4	137	3	45·66	–	–	3–137
A. G. Kripal Singh	14	1518	75	584	10	58·40	–	–	3–43
U. N. Kulkarni	4	448	5	238	5	47·60	–	–	2–37
V. V. Kumar	2	598	46	202	7	28·85	1	–	5–64
B. K. Kunderan	18	24	0	13	0		–	–	
S. Madan Lal	16	2457	71	977	29	33·68	2	–	5–72
V. L. Manjrekar	55	204	17	44	1	44·00	–	–	1–16
A. V. Mankad	22	41	1	43	0		–	–	
V. M. Mankad	44	14685	777	5236	162	32·32	8	2	8–52
V. L. Mehra	8	36	1	6	0		–	–	
V. M. Merchant	10	54	0	40	0		–	–	
A. G. Milkha Singh	4	6	0	2	0		–	–	
R. S. Modi	10	30	1	14	0		–	–	
V. M. Muddiah	2	318	17	134	3	44·66	–	–	2–40
S. Mushtaq Ali	11	378	9	202	3	67·33	–	–	1–45
R. G. Nadkarni	41	9175	666	2558	88	29·06	4	1	6–43
M. Naoomal Jeoomal	3	108	0	68	2	34·00	–	–	1–4
C. K. Nayudu	7	858	24	386	9	42·88	–	–	3–40
C. S. Nayudu	11	522	6	359	2	179·50	–	–	1–19
S. Nazir Ali	2	138	1	83	4	20·75	–	–	4–83
M. Nissar	6	1211	34	707	25	28·28	3	–	5–90
S. Nyalchand	1	384	33	97	3	32·33	–	–	3–97
A. M. Pai	1	114	5	31	2	15·50	–	–	2–29
P. E. Palia	2	42	3	13	0		–	–	
M. A. K. Pataudi	46	132	6	88	1	88·00	–	–	1–10
J. M. Patel	7	1665	94	636	29	21·93	2	1	9–69
S. R. Patil	1	138	7	51	2	25·50	–	–	1–15
D. G. Phadkar	31	5975	275	2284	62	36·83	3	–	7–159
E. A. S. Prasanna	47	13867	585	5491	187	29·36	10	2	8–76
Rajinder Pal	1	78	4	22	0		–	–	
G. S. Ramchand	33	4976	255	1899	41	46·31	1	–	6–49
L. Ramji	1	138	5	64	0		–	–	
C. R. Rangachari	4	846	11	493	9	54·77	1	–	5–107

	M	Balls	Mdns	Runs	Wkts	Avge	5wI	10wM	Best
V. B. Ranjane	7	1265	33	649	19	34·15	-	-	4-72
P. Roy	43	104	4	66	1	66·00	-	-	1-6
D. N. Sardesai	30	59	2	45	0	-	-	-	-
C. T. Sarwate	9	658	5	374	3	124·66	-	-	1-16
R. C. Saxena	1	12	0	11	0	-	-	-	-
P. Sharma	5	24	0	8	0	-	-	-	-
S. G. Shinde	7	1515	60	717	12	59·75	1	-	6-91
R. H. Shodhan	3	60	3	26	0	-	-	-	-
S. W. Sohoni	4	532	20	202	2	101·00	-	-	1-16
E. D. Solkar	27	2265	82	1070	18	59·44	-	-	3-28
V. Subramanya	9	444	17	201	3	67·00	-	-	2-32
G. R. Sunderram	2	396	12	166	3	55·33	-	-	2-46
R. Surendranath	11	2602	145	1053	26	40·50	2	-	5-75
R. F. Surti	26	3870	115	1962	42	46·71	1	-	5-74
V. N. Swamy	1	108	5	45	0	-	-	-	-
K. K. Tarapore	1	114	2	72	0	-	-	-	-
P. R. Umrigar	59	4737	258	1475	35	42·14	2	-	6-74
D. B. Vengsarkar	11	5	0	7	0	-	-	-	-
S. Venkataraghavan	37	10301	496	3796	113	33·59	3	1	8-72
G. R. Viswanath	43	24	0	18	0	-	-	-	-
A. L. Wadekar	37	61	1	55	0	-	-	-	-
S. Wazir Ali	7	30	1	25	0	-	-	-	-
Yajurvindra Singh	2	6	0	2	0	-	-	-	-

Pakistan (79 players)
Batting and Fielding

		M	I	NO	Runs	HS	Avge	100	50	Ct	St
Abdul Kadir	1964-1965	4	8	0	272	95	34·00	-	2	-	1
Abdul Qadir	1977-1978	3	3	0	36	21	12·00	-	-	2	-
Afaq Hussain	1961-1965	2	4	4	64	33*	-	-	-	2	-
Aftab Baloch	1969-1975	2	3	1	97	60*	48·50	-	1	-	-
Aftab Gul	1968-1971	6	8	0	182	33	22·75	-	-	3	-
Agha Saadat Ali	1955-1956	1	1	1	8	8*	-	-	-	3	-
Agha Zahid	1974-1975	1	2	0	15	14	7·50	-	-	-	-
Alim-ud-Din	1954-1962	25	45	2	1091	109	25·37	2	7	7	-
Amir Elahi	1952-1953	5	7	1	65	47	10·83	-	-	-	-
Anwar Hussain	1952-1953	4	6	0	42	17	7·00	-	-	-	-
Arif Butt	1964-1965	3	5	0	59	20	11·80	-	-	-	-
Asif Iqbal	1964-1977	45	77	4	2748	175	37·64	8	10	29	-
Asif Masood	1968-1977	16	19	10	93	30*	10·33	-	-	5	-
Javed Burki	1960-1970	25	48	4	1341	140	30·47	3	4	7	-
Antao D'Souza	1958-1962	6	10	8	76	23*	38·00	-	-	3	-
Farooq Hamid	1964-1965	1	2	0	3	3	1·50	-	-	-	-
Farrukh Zaman	1976-1977	1	-	-	-	-	-	-	-	-	-
Fazal Mahmood	1952-1962	34	50	6	620	60	14·09	-	1	11	-
M. E. Z. Ghazali	1954	2	4	0	32	18	8·00	-	-	-	-
Ghulam Abbas	1967	1	2	0	12	12	6·00	-	-	-	-
Gul Mahomed	1956-1957	1	2	1	39	27*	39·00	-	-	-	-
Hanif Mohammad	1952-1970	55	97	8	3915	337	43·98	12	15	40	-
Haroon Rashid	1976-1978	12	21	1	727	122	36·35	2	3	6	-
Haseeb Ahsan	1957-1962	12	16	7	61	14	6·77	-	-	1	-
K. Ibadulla	1964-1967	4	8	0	253	166	31·62	1	-	3	-
Ijaz Butt	1958-1962	8	16	2	279	58	19·92	-	1	5	-
Imran Khan	1971-1977	15	26	2	503	59	20·95	-	1	8	-
Imtiaz Ahmed	1952-1962	41	72	1	2079	209	29·28	3	11	77	16
Intikhab Alam	1959-1977	47	77	10	1493	138	22·28	1	8	20	-
Iqbal Qasim	1976-1978	11	16	5	34	8*	3·09	-	-	8	-
Israr Ali	1952-1960	4	8	1	33	10	4·71	-	-	1	-
Javed Akhtar	1962	1	2	1	4	2*	4·00	-	-	-	-
Javed Miandad	1976-1978	13	22	4	994	206	55·22	2	6	10	-
A. H. Kardar	1952-1958	23	37	3	847	93	24·91	-	5	15	-
Khalid Hassan	1954	1	2	1	17	10	17·00	-	-	-	-

		M	I	NO	Runs	HS	Avge	100	50	Ct	St
Khalid Wazir	1954	2	3	1	14	9*	7·00	–	–	–	–
Majid Jahangir Khan	1964–1977	37	64	2	2651	167	42·75	5	13	47	–
Khan Mohammad	1952–1959	13	17	7	100	26*	10·00	–	–	4	–
Liaquat Ali	1974–1978	5	7	3	28	12	7·00	–	–	1	–
Mahmood Hussain	1952–1962	27	39	6	336	35	10·18	–	–	5	–
Maqsood Ahmed	1952–1956	16	27	1	507	99	19·50	–	2	13	–
Wallis Mathias	1955–1962	21	36	3	783	77	23·72	–	3	22	–
Miran Bux	1954–1955	2	3	2	1	1*	1·00	–	–	–	–
Mohammad Aslam	1954	1	2	0	34	18	17·00	–	–	–	–
Mohammad Farooq	1960–1965	7	9	4	85	47	17·00	–	–	1	–
Mohammad Ilyas	1964–1969	10	19	0	441	126	23·21	1	2	6	–
Mohammad Munaf	1959–1962	4	7	2	63	19	12·60	–	–	–	–
Mohammad Nazir	1969–1973	4	5	4	84	29*	84·00	–	–	1	–
Mohsin Khan	1977–1978	4	6	0	235	46	39·16	–	–	3	–
Mudassar Nazar	1976–1978	7	12	0	430	114	35·83	1	2	4	–
Mufasir-ul-Haq	1964–1965	1	1	1	8	8*	–	–	–	1	–
Mushtaq Mohammad	1958–1977	49	88	7	3283	201	40·53	10	17	33	–
Munir Malik	1959–1962	3	4	1	7	4	2·33	–	–	1	–
Nasim-ul-Ghani	1957–1973	29	50	5	747	101	16·60	1	2	11	–
Naushad Ali	1964–1965	6	11	0	156	39	14·18	–	–	9	–
Nazar Mohammad	1952–1953	5	8	1	277	124*	39·57	1	1	7	–
Niaz Ahmed	1967–1969	2	3	3	17	16*	–	–	–	1	–
Pervez Sajjad	1964–1973	19	20	11	123	24	13·66	–	–	9	–
S. F. Rahman	1957–1958	1	2	0	10	8	5·00	–	–	1	–
Sadiq Mohammad	1969–1978	34	62	2	2330	166	38·83	5	10	24	–
Saeed Ahmed	1957–1973	41	78	4	2991	172	40·41	5	16	13	–
Salah-ud-Din	1964–1970	5	8	2	117	34*	19·50	–	–	3	–
Salim Altaf	1967–1977	20	31	12	276	53*	14·52	–	1	3	–
Sarfraz Nawaz	1968–1978	26	37	7	443	53	14·76	–	2	15	–
Shafiq Ahmed	1974–1978	4	7	1	82	27*	13·66	–	–	–	–
Shafqat Rana	1964–1970	5	7	0	221	95	31·57	–	2	5	–
Shahid Israr	1976–1977	1	1	1	7	7*	–	–	–	2	–
Shahid Mahmood	1962	1	2	0	25	16	12·50	–	–	–	–
D. Sharpe	1959–1960	3	6	0	134	56	22·33	–	1	2	–
Shuja-ud-Din	1954–1962	19	32	6	395	47	15·19	–	–	9	–
Sikander Bakht	1976–1978	7	9	3	22	7*	3·66	–	–	1	–
Talaat Ali	1972–1978	7	12	1	243	57	22·09	–	1	3	–
Waqar Hassan	1952–1960	21	35	1	1071	189	31·50	1	6	10	–
Wasim Bari	1967–1978	42	64	16	748	72	15·58	–	4	94	15
Wasim Raja	1972–1978	20	35	5	1096	117*	36·53	2	6	4	–
Wazir Mohammad	1952–1960	20	33	4	801	189	27·62	2	3	5	–
Younis Ahmed	1969–1970	2	4	0	89	62	22·25	–	1	–	–
Zaheer Abbas	1969–1977	26	47	1	1583	274	34·41	3	6	18	–
Zulfiqar Ahmed	1952–1957	9	10	4	200	63*	33·33	–	1	5	–
								Substitutes		13	–

Bowling

	M	Balls	Mdns	Runs	Wkts	Avge	5wI	10wM	Best
Abdul Qadir	3	1056	31	305	12	25·41	1	–	6–44
Afaq Hussain	2	240	7	106	1	106·00	–	–	1–40
Aftab Baloch	2	44	0	17	0	–	–	–	–
Aftab Gul	6	6	0	4	0	–	–	–	–
Alim-ud-Din	25	84	1	75	1	75·00	–	–	1–17
Amir Elahi	5	400	5	248	7	35·42	–	–	4–134
Anwar Hussain	4	36	1	29	1	29·00	–	–	1–25
Arif Butt	3	666	26	288	14	20·57	1	–	6–89
Asif Iqbal	45	3574	165	1401	50	28·02	2	–	5–48
Asif Masood	16	3038	79	1568	38	41·26	1	–	5–111
Javed Burki	25	42	2	23	0	–	–	–	–
Antao D'Souza	6	1587	56	745	17	43·82	1	–	5–112
Farooq Hamid	1	184	1	107	1	107·00	–	–	1–82
Farrukh Zaman	1	80	2	15	0	–	–	–	–

	M	Balls	Mdns	Runs	Wkts	Avge	5wI	10wM	Best
Fazal Mahmood	34	9834	563	3434	139	24·70	13	4	7–42
M. E. Z. Ghazali	2	48	1	18	0	–	–	–	
Hanif Mohammad	55	206	9	94	1	94·00	–	–	1–1
Haroon Rashid	12	8	0	3	0	–	–	–	
Haseeb Ahsan	12	2847	100	1330	27	49·25	2	–	6–202
K. Ibadulla	4	336	21	99	1	99·00	–	–	1–42
Imran Khan	15	4128	115	2043	62	32·95	4	1	6–63
Imtiaz Ahmed	41	6	1	0	0	–	–	–	
Intikhab Alam	47	10474	383	4494	125	35·95	5	2	7–52
Iqbal Qasim	11	2710	112	934	27	34·59	–	–	4–84
Israr Ali	4	318	12	165	6	27·50	–	–	2–29
Javed Akhtar	1	96	5	52	0	–	–	–	
Javed Miandad	13	1162	27	510	15	34·00	–	–	3–74
A. H. Kardar	23	2712	141	954	21	45·42	–	–	3–35
Khalid Hassan	1	126	1	116	2	58·00	–	–	2–116
Majid Jahangir Khan	37	2668	87	1066	24	44·41	–	–	4–45
Khan Mohammad	13	3169	153	1291	54	23·90	4	–	6–21
Liaquat Ali	5	808	23	359	6	59·83	–	–	3–80
Mahmood Hussain	27	5976	228	2628	68	38·64	2	–	6–67
Maqsood Ahmed	16	462	21	191	3	63·66	–	–	2–12
Wallis Mathias	21	24	0	20	0	–	–	–	
Miran Bux	2	348	22	115	2	57·50	–	–	2–82
Mohammad Farooq	7	1422	49	682	21	32·47	–	–	4–70
Mohammad Ilyas	10	84	1	63	0	–	–	–	
Mohammad Munaf	4	769	31	341	11	31·00	–	–	4–42
Mohammad Nazir	4	1066	56	353	10	35·30	1	–	7–99
Mohsin Khan	4	8	0	3	0	–	–	–	
Mudassar Nazar	7	226	9	88	2	44·00	–	–	1–16
Mufasir-ul-Haq	1	222	12	84	3	28·00	–	–	2–50
Mushtaq Mohammad	49	4063	149	1769	62	28·53	2	–	5–28
Munir Malik	3	684	21	358	9	39·77	1	–	5–128
Nasim-ul-Ghani	29	4400	204	1959	52	37·67	2	–	6–67
Nazar Mohammad	5	12	1	4	0	–	–	–	
Niaz Ahmed	2	294	14	94	3	31·33	–	–	2–72
Pervez Sajjad	19	4145	217	1410	59	23·89	3	–	7–74
S. F. Rahman	1	204	3	99	1	99·00	–	–	1–43
Sadiq Mohammad	34	170	5	78	0	–	–	–	
Saeed Ahmed	41	1980	89	802	22	36·45	–	–	4–64
Salah-ud-Din	5	546	27	187	7	26·71	–	–	2–36
Salim Altaf	20	3827	115	1640	45	36·44	–	–	4–11
Sarfraz Nawaz	26	6194	202	2626	82	32·02	2	–	6–89
Shafiq Ahmed	4	8	0	1	0	–	–	–	
Shafqat Rana	5	36	1	9	1	9·00	–	–	1–2
Shahid Mahmood	1	36	1	23	0	–	–	–	
Shuja-ud-Din	20	2319	121	801	20	40·05	–	–	3–18
Sikander Bakht	7	1346	43	641	18	35·61	–	–	4–132
Talaat Ali	7	20	1	7	0	–	–	–	
Waqar Hassan	21	6	0	10	0	–	–	–	
Wasim Bari	42	8	0	2	0	–	–	–	
Wasim Raja	20	1316	39	598	17	35·17	–	–	3–22
Wazir Mohammad	20	24	0	15	0	–	–	–	
Zaheer Abbas	26	20	1	2	0	–	–	–	
Zulfiqar Ahmed	9	1285	78	366	20	18·30	2	1	6–42

Combined records of players who represented two countries

Batting and fielding

		M	I	NO	Runs	HS	Avge	100	50	Ct	St
Amir Elahi	Ind & Pak	6	9	1	82	47	10·25	–	–	–	–
J. J. Ferris	Aus & Eng	9	17	4	114	20*	8·76	–	–	4	–
S. C. Guillen	WI and NZ	8	12	2	202	54	20·20	–	1	13	3
Gul Mahomed	Ind & Pak	9	17	1	205	34	12·81	–	–	3	–
F. Hearne	Eng & SA	6	10	0	168	30	16·80	–	–	3	–

		M	I	NO	Runs	HS	Avge	100	50	Ct	St
A. H. Kardar	Ind & Pak	26	42	3	927	93	23·76	–	5	16	–
W. E. Midwinter	Aus & Eng	12	21	1	269	37	13·45	–	–	10	–
F. Mitchell	Eng & SA	5	10	0	116	41	11·60	–	–	2	–
W. L. Murdoch	Aus & Eng	19	34	5	908	211	31·31	2	1	13	2
Nawab of Pataudi	Eng & Ind	6	10	0	199	102	19·90	1	–	–	–
A. E. Trott	Aus & Eng	5	9	3	228	85*	38·00	–	2	4	–
S. M. J. Woods	Aus & Eng	6	10	0	154	53	15·40	–	1	5	–

Bowling	M	Balls	Mdns	Runs	Wkts	Avge	5wI	10wM	Best
Amir Elahi	6	400	5	248	7	35·42	–	–	4–134
J. J. Ferris	9	2302	251	775	61	12·70	6	1	7–37
Gul Mahomed	9	77	4	24	2	12·00	–	–	2–21
F. Hearne	6	62	0	40	2	20·00	–	–	2–40
A. H. Kardar	26	2712	141	954	21	45·42	–	–	3–35
W. E. Midwinter	12	1725	181	605	24	25·20	1	–	5–78
A. E. Trott	5	948	54	390	26	15·00	2	–	8–43
S. M. J. Woods	6	412	26	250	10	25·00	–	–	3–28

Test match umpires – most appearances

	Tests		Venue
F. Chester	48	1924 to 1955	England
C. S. Elliott	42	1957 to 1974	England (41) New Zealand (1)
J. S. Buller	33	1956 to 1969	England
R. W. Crockett	32	1901–02 to 1924–25	Australia
C. J. Egar	29	1960–61 to 1968–69	Australia
F. S. Lee	29	1949 to 1962	England
J. Phillips	29	1884–85 to 1905–06	England (11) Australia (13) South Africa (5)
D. Sang Hue	28	1961–62 to 1977–78	West Indies
R. Gosein	25	1964–65 to 1977–78	West Indies
L. P. Rowan	25	1962–63 to 1970–71	Australia

Notes:
None of the above appeared as players in Test matches but several umpires have also been Test players. Of these A. E. Fagg (England) umpired in most Tests – 18, from 1967 to 1975.
The Australian pair of C. J. Egar and L. P. Rowan umpired together in 19 Tests.

Supplement 1978-79

Three Test series completed in 1978–79 are included: Pakistan v India (3), India v West Indies (6), Australia v England (6); but not New Zealand v Pakistan (3) or Australia v Pakistan (2). Lack of space prevents the inclusion of new material for all tables on pp. 85–162. The Test Career Records for England and India are complete prior to the start of the first Test at Edgbaston on 12 July 1979.

Abbreviated scores of all Test Matches (Contd from p. 85)
1978–79: Pakistan v India (Played 3, Pak won 2, Ind won 0, Drawn 1)
First Test at Faisalabad, Oct. 16–21. Match Drawn.
    PAK: 503–8 dec. (Zaheer Abbas 176, Javed Miandad 154*; B. S. Chandrasekhar 4 for 130)
       &   264–4 dec. (Asif Iqbal 104, Zaheer Abbas 96)
    IND: 462–9 dec. (G. R. Viswanath 145, S. M. Gavaskar 89, D. B. Vengsarkar 83; Mushtaq Mohammad 4 for 55)
       &   43–0
Second Test at Lahore, Oct. 27–Nov. 1. Pak won by eight wickets.
    IND: 199   (D. B. Vengsarkar 76; Sarfraz Nawaz 4 for 46, Imran Khan 4 for 54)
       &   465   (S. M. Gavaskar 97, C. P. Chauhan 93, G. R. Viswanath 83, S. Amarnath 60)

PAK: 539–6 dec. (Zaheer Abbas 235*, Wasim Bari 85, Mushtaq Mohammad 67)
    & 128–2
Third Test at Karachi, Nov. 14–19. Pak won by eight wickets.
    IND: 344   (S. M. Gavaskar 111, Kapil Dev 59; Sarfraz Nawaz 4 for 89)
      & 300   (S. M. Gavaskar 137, M. Amarnath 53; Sarfraz Nawaz 5 for 70)
    PAK: 481–9 dec. (Javed Miandad 100, Mushtaq Mohammad 78, Mudassar
                Nazar 57)
      & 164–2 (Javed Miandad 62*)

1978–79: India v West Indies (Played 6, Ind won 1, WI won 0, Drawn 5)
First Test at Bombay, Dec. 1–6. Match Drawn.
    IND: 424   (S. M. Gavaskar 205, C. P. Chauhan 52, G. R. Viswanath 52;
                V. A. Holder 4 for 94, S. T. Clarke 4 for 98)
      & 224–2 (C. P. Chauhan 84, S. M. Gavaskar 73)
    WI: 493   (A. I. Kallicharran 187, D. A. Murray 84, H. A. Gomes 63, D. R.
                Parry 55; B. S. Chandrasekhar 5 for 116)
Second Test at Bangalore, Dec. 15–20. Match Drawn.
    WI: 437   (S. F. A. Bacchus 96, A. I. Kallicharran 71, S. Shivnarine 62, H. A.
                Gomes 51)
      & 200–8 (H. A. Gomes 82; K. D. Ghavri 5 for 51)
    IND: 371   (A. D. Gaekwad 87, D. B. Vengsarkar 73, G. R. Viswanath 70;
                S. T. Clarke 5 for 126)
Third Test at Calcutta, Dec. 29–Jan. 3. Match Drawn.
    IND: 300   (S. M. Gavaskar 107, Kapil Dev 61; N. Phillip 4 for 64)
      & 361–1 dec. (S. M. Gavaskar 182*, D. B. Vengsarkar 157*)
    WI: 327   (A. B. Williams 111, A. I. Kallicharran 55; S. Venkataraghavan 4
                for 55)
      & 197–9 (D. A. Murray 66; K. D. Ghavri 4 for 46)
Fourth Test at Madras, Jan. 12–16. Ind won by three wickets.
    WI: 228   (A. I. Kallicharran 98; Kapil Dev 4 for 38)
      & 151   (H. A. Gomes 91; S. Venkataraghavan 4 for 43)
    IND: 255   (G. R. Viswanath 124; N. Phillip 4 for 48, S. T. Clarke 4 for 75)
      & 125–7
Fifth Test at New Delhi, Jan. 24–29. Match Drawn.
    IND.   566–8 dec. (Kapil Dev 126*, S. M. Gavaskar 120, D. B. Vengsarkar 109,
                C. P. Chauhan 60)
    WI: 172
      & 179–3 (S. F. A. Bacchus 61)
Sixth Test at Kanpur, Feb. 2–8. Match Drawn.
    IND: 644–7 dec. (G. R. Viswanath 179, A. D. Gaekwad 102, M. Amarnath 101*,
                C. P. Chauhan 79, Kapil Dev 62)
    WI: 452–8 (S. F. A. Bacchus 250, R. R. Jumadeen 56; K. D. Ghavri 4 for 118)

1978–79: Australia v England (Played 6, Eng won 5, Aus won 1)
First Test at Brisbane, Dec. 1–6. Eng won by seven wickets.
    AUS: 116   (R. G. D. Willis 4 for 44)
      & 339   (K. J. Hughes 129, G. N. Yallop 102)
    ENG: 286   (D. W. Randall 75; R. M. Hogg 6 for 74, A. G. Hurst 4 for 93)
      & 170–3 (D. W. Randall 74*)
Second Test at Perth, Dec. 15–20. Eng won by 166 runs.
    ENG: 309   (D. I. Gower 102, G. Boycott 77; R. M. Hogg 5 for 65)
      & 208   (R. M. Hogg 5 for 57)
    AUS: 190   (P. M. Toohey 81*; R. G. D. Willis 5 for 44)
      & 161   (G. M. Wood 64; J. K. Lever 4 for 28)
Third Test at Melbourne, Dec. 29–Jan. 3. Aus won by 103 runs.
    AUS: 258   (G. M. Wood 100)
      & 167
    ENG: 143   (R. M. Hogg 5 for 30)
      & 179   (R. M. Hogg 5 for 36)
Fourth Test at Sydney, Jan. 6–11. Eng won by 93 runs.
    ENG: 152   (I. T. Botham 59; A. G. Hurst 5 for 28)
      & 346   (D. W. Randall 150, J. M. Brearley 53; J. D. Higgs 5 for 148,
                R. M. Hogg 4 for 67)

AUS: 294   (W. M. Darling 91, A. R. Border 60*)
    & 111   (J. E. Emburey 4 for 46)
Fifth Test at Adelaide, Jan. 27–Feb. 1. Eng won by 205 runs.
ENG: 169   (I. T. Botham 74; R. M. Hogg 4 for 26)
    & 360   (R. W. Taylor 97, G. Miller 64; A. G. Hurst 4 for 97)
AUS: 164   (I. T. Botham 4 for 42)
    & 160
Sixth Test at Sydney, Feb. 10–14. Eng won by nine wickets.
AUS: 198   (G. N. Yallop 121; I. T. Botham 4 for 57)
    & 143   (B. Yardley 61*; G. Miller 5 for 44, J. E. Emburey 4 for 52)
ENG: 308   (G. A. Gooch 74, D. I. Gower 65; J. D. Higgs 4 for 69)
    &   35–1

Complete Test Career Records of all Players (Contd from p. 205)

(Up to February 15, 1979)

England (480 players)

Batting and Fielding

		M	I	NO	Runs	HS	Avge	100	50	Ct	St
I. T. Botham	1977–1979	17	23	1	791	108	35·95	3	3	23	–
G. Boycott	1964–1979	80	140	17	5938	246*	48·27	16	33	24	–
J. M. Brearley	1976–1979	27	46	2	1029	91	23·38	–	6	37	–
P. H. Edmonds	1975–1979	14	17	4	196	50	15·07	–	1	20	–
J. E. Emburey	1978–1979	5	8	1	69	42	9·85	–	–	8	–
G. A. Gooch	1975–1979	13	22	2	547	91*	27·35	–	4	14	–
D. I. Gower	1978–1979	12	19	1	858	111	47·66	2	4	4	–
M. Hendrick	1974–1979	21	26	9	98	15	5·76	–	–	22	–
J. K. Lever	1976–1979	14	21	3	223	53	12·38	–	1	8	–
G. Miller	1976–1979	20	27	2	632	98*	25·28	–	3	8	–
C. M. Old	1972–1979	41	58	7	751	65	14·72	–	2	22	–
D. W. Randall	1976–1979	22	38	4	1016	174	29·88	2	5	13	–
R. W. Taylor	1970–1979	19	24	3	410	97	19·52	–	1	54	5
R. G. D. Willis	1970–1979	47	66	33	416	24*	12·60	–	–	22	–
Substitutes										60	1

Bowling

	M	Balls	Mdns	Runs	Wkts	Avge	5wI	10wM	Best
I. T. Botham	17	3822	119	1626	87	18·68	8	1	8–34
G. Boycott	80	824	36	356	7	50·85	–	–	3–47
P. H. Edmonds	14	3117	140	928	43	21·58	2	–	7–66
J. E. Emburey	5	1331	63	346	18	19·22	–	–	4–46
G. A. Gooch	13	108	1	44	0	–	–	–	–
M. Hendrick	21	4296	149	1548	66	23·45	–	–	4–28
J. K. Lever	14	2683	78	1106	49	22·57	2	1	7–46
G. Miller	20	3153	133	1000	40	25·00	1	–	5–44
C. M. Old	41	7755	256	3594	129	27·86	4	–	7–50
D. W. Randall	22	16	0	3	0	–	–	–	–
R. G. D. Willis	47	9010	243	4114	171	24·05	11	–	7–78

Australia (302 players)

Batting and Fielding

		M	I	NO	Runs	HS	Avge	100	50	Ct	St
A. R. Border	1978–1979	3	6	2	146	60*	36·50	–	1	3	–
P. H. Carlson	1978–1979	2	4	0	23	21	5·75	–	–	2	–
G. J. Cosier	1975–1979	18	32	1	897	168	28·93	2	3	14	–
W. M. Darling	1977–1979	8	16	0	385	91	24·06	–	3	5	–
G. Dymock	1973–1979	7	11	2	41	13	4·55	–	–	–	–
J. D. Higgs	1977–1979	9	17	8	56	16	6·22	–	–	–	–
A. M. Hilditch	1978–1979	1	2	0	4	3	2·00	–	–	2	–
R. M. Hogg	1978–1979	6	12	0	95	36	7·91	–	–	–	–
K. J. Hughes	1977–1979	9	17	0	410	129	24·11	1	–	7	–
A. G. Hurst	1973–1979	8	15	3	86	26	7·16	–	–	2	–
T. J. Laughlin	1977–1979	3	5	0	87	35	17·40	–	–	3	–

		M	I	NO	Runs	HS	Avge	100	50	Ct	St
J. A. Maclean	1978–1979	4	8	1	79	33*	11·28	–	–	18	–
P. M. Toohey	1977–1979	13	25	1	854	122	35·58	1	7	7	–
G. M. Wood	1977–1979	12	24	0	865	126	36·04	2	5	13	–
K. J. Wright	1978–1979	2	4	0	37	29	9·25	–	–	7	1
G. N. Yallop	1975–1979	14	27	2	1032	124	41·28	3	4	8	–
B. Yardley	1977–1979	10	19	3	402	74	25·12	–	2	9	–
							Substitutes			43	–

Bowling

	M	Balls	Mdns	Runs	Wkts	Avge	5wI	10wM	Best
A. R. Border	3	248	13	50	1	50·00	–	–	1–31
P. H. Carlson	2	368	10	99	2	49·50	–	–	2–41
G. J. Cosier	18	899	30	341	5	68·20	–	–	2–26
G. Dymock	7	2265	55	721	21	34·33	1	–	5–58
J. D. Higgs	9	2410	80	852	34	25·05	1	–	5–148
R. M. Hogg	6	1740	60	527	41	12·85	5	2	6–74
A. G. Hurst	8	2042	52	731	28	26·10	1	–	5–28
T. J. Laughlin	3	516	16	262	6	43·66	1	–	5–101
G. N. Yallop	14	18	1	8	0	–	–	–	
B. Yardley	10	2353	74	962	26	37·00	–	–	4–35

West Indies (173 players)
Batting and Fielding

		M	I	NO	Runs	HS	Avge	100	50	Ct	St
S. F. A. Bacchus	1977–1979	8	14	0	514	250	36·71	1	2	10	–
H. S. Chang	1978–1979	1	2	0	8	6	4·00	–	–	–	–
S. T. Clarke	1977–1979	6	9	3	50	15	8·33	–	–	1	–
H. A. Gomes	1976–1979	11	19	0	681	115	35·84	2	4	2	–
A. T. Greenidge	1977–1979	6	10	0	222	69	22·20	–	2	5	–
V. A. Holder	1969–1979	40	59	11	682	42	14·20	–	–	16	–
R. R. Jumadeen	1971–1979	12	14	10	84	56	21·00	–	1	4	–
A. I. Kallicharran	1978–1979	51	86	8	3869	187	49·60	11	20	38	–
M. D. Marshall	1978–1979	3	3	1	8	5	2·00	–	–	1	–
D. A. Murray	1977–1979	9	16	1	328	84	21·86	–	2	23	4
D. R. Parry	1977–1979	11	18	3	363	65	24·20	–	3	5	–
N. Phillip	1977–1979	9	15	5	297	47	29·70	–	–	5	–
S. Shivnarine	1977–1979	8	14	1	379	63	29·15	–	4	6	–
A. B. Williams	1977–1979	7	12	0	469	111	39·08	2	1	5	–
							Substitutes			43	–

Bowling

	M	Balls	Mdns	Runs	Wkts	Avge	5wI	10wM	Best
S. T. Clarke	6	1696	45	852	27	31·55	1	–	5–126
H. A. Gomes	11	192	5	99	1	99·00	–	–	1–54
V. A. Holder	40	9095	367	3627	109	33·27	3	–	6–28
R. R. Jumadeen	12	3140	140	1141	29	39·34	–	–	4–72
A. I. Kallicharran	51	186	8	82	1	82·00	–	–	1–7
M. D. Marshall	3	462	11	265	3	88·33	–	–	1–44
D. R. Parry	11	1777	61	873	21	41·57	1	–	5–15
N. Phillip	9	1820	46	1041	28	37·17	–	–	4–48
S. Shivnarine	8	336	10	167	1	167·00	–	–	1–13

India (143 players)
Batting and Fielding

		M	I	NO	Runs	HS	Avge	100	50	Ct	St
M. Amarnath	1969–1979	23	41	3	1423	101*	37·44	2	9	21	–
S. Amarnath	1975–1979	10	18	0	550	124	30·55	1	3	4	–
B. S. Bedi	1966–1979	64	99	28	655	50*	9·22	–	1	26	–
B. S. Chandrasekhar	1963–1979	57	78	37	167	22	4·07	–	–	25	–
C. P. Chauhan	1969–1979	18	31	1	911	93	30·36	–	6	22	–
A. D. Gaekwad	1974–1979	19	33	2	1035	102	33·38	1	5	5	–
S. M. Gavaskar	1970–1979	46	86	7	4405	220	55·75	19	17	42	–

		M	I	NO	Runs	HS	Avge	100	50	Ct	St
K. D. Ghavri	1974–1979	18	28	5	502	64	21·82	–	1	10	–
Kapil Dev	1978–1979	9	12	2	488	126*	48·80	1	3	3	–
S. M. H. Kirmani	1975–1979	29	44	6	966	88	25·42	–	5	47	18
M. V. Narasimha Rao	1978–1979	2	3	0	11	6	3·66	–	–	5	–
D. D. Parsana	1978–1979	2	2	0	1	1	0·50	–	–	–	–
E. A. S. Prasanna	1961–1979	49	84	20	735	37	11·48	–	–	18	–
D. B. Vengsarkar	1975–1979	20	34	3	1077	157*	34·74	2	4	20	–
S. Venkataraghavan	1964–1979	43	60	10	686	64	13·72	–	2	35	–
G. R. Viswanath	1969–1979	52	94	7	3900	179	44·82	8	24	36	–
									Substitutes	53	–

Bowling

	M	Balls	Mdns	Runs	Wkts	Avge	5wI	10wM	Best
M. Amarnath	23	2390	61	1049	21	49·95	–	–	4–63
S. Amarnath	10	13	0	5	1	5·00	–	–	1–5
B. S. Bedi	64	21019	1073	7388	259	28·52	14	1	7–98
B. S. Chandrasekhar	57	15981	583	7086	242	29·28	16	2	8–79
C. P. Chauhan	18	54	0	31	0	–	–	–	
A. D. Gaekwad	19	88	0	68	0	–	–	–	
S. M. Gavaskar	46	244	9	116	1	116·00	–	–	1–34
K. D. Ghavri	18	3020	92	1569	59	26·59	2	–	5–33
Kapil Dev	9	1870	38	987	24	41·12	–	–	4–38
M. V. Narasimha Rao	2	229	7	107	1	107·00	–	–	1–43
D. D. Parsana	2	120	6	50	1	50·00	–	–	1–32
E. A. S. Prasanna	49	14515	602	5742	189	30·38	10	2	8–76
D. B. Vengsarkar	20	11	0	10	0	–	–	–	
S. Venkataraghavan	43	11876	595	4291	133	32·26	3	1	8–72
G. R. Viswanath	52	28	0	25	0	–	–	–	

Pakistan (79 players)
Batting and Fielding

		M	I	NO	Runs	HS	Avge	100	50	Ct	St
Asif Iqbal	1964–1979	48	83	5	2947	175	37·78	9	10	30	–
Imran Khan	1971–1979	18	30	4	607	59	23·34	–	1	8	–
Iqbal Qasim	1976–1979	14	17	6	63	29*	5·72	–	–	11	–
Javed Miandad	1976–1979	16	27	7	1352	206	67·60	4	7	11	–
Majid J. Khan	1964–1979	40	70	2	2873	167	42·25	5	13	52	–
Mudassar Nazar	1976–1979	9	15	0	528	114	35·20	1	3	6	–
Mushtaq Mohammad	1958–1979	52	91	7	3433	201	40·86	10	19	37	–
Sadiq Mohammad	1969–1979	35	64	2	2387	166	38·50	5	10	25	–
Salim Altaf	1967–1979	21	31	12	276	53*	14·52	–	1	3	–
Sarfraz Nawaz	1968–1979	29	39	7	489	53	15·28	–	2	17	–
Sikander Bakht	1976–1979	9	11	5	60	22*	10·00	–	–	1	–
Wasim Bari	1967–1979	45	67	16	839	85	16·45	–	5	104	15
Zaheer Abbas	1969–1979	29	52	3	2166	274	44·20	5	7	18	–
									Substitutes	14	–

Bowling

	M	Balls	Mdns	Runs	Wkts	Avge	5wI	10wM	Best
Asif Iqbal	48	3574	165	1401	50	28·02	2	–	5–48
Imran Khan	18	5422	159	2484	76	32·68	4	1	6–63
Iqbal Qasim	14	3406	138	1161	29	40·03	–	–	4–84
Javed Miandad	16	1242	29	536	16	33·50	–	–	3–74
Majid J. Khan	40	2684	89	1071	24	44·62	–	–	4–45
Mudassar Nazar	9	330	14	115	5	23·00	–	–	2–4
Mushtaq Mohammad	52	4663	166	2004	68	29·47	2	–	5–28
Sadiq Mohammad	35	202	5	94	0	–	–	–	
Salim Altaf	21	4059	124	1710	46	37·17	–	–	4–11
Sarfraz Nawaz	29	7380	228	3051	99	30·81	3	–	6–89
Sikander Bakht	9	1794	52	845	21	40·23	–	–	4–132
Wasim Bari	45	8	0	2	0	–	–	–	
Zaheer Abbas	29	20	1	2	0	–	–	–	